T0321928

Research Anthology on Big Data Analytics, Architectures, and Applications

Information Resources Management Association
USA

Volume IV

Published in the United States of America by
IGI Global
Engineering Science Reference (an imprint of IGI Global)
701 E. Chocolate Avenue
Hershey PA, USA 17033
Tel: 717-533-8845
Fax: 717-533-8661
E-mail: cust@igi-global.com
Web site: http://www.igi-global.com

Library of Congress Cataloging-in-Publication Data

Names: Information Resources Management Association, editor.
Title: Research anthology on big data analytics, architectures, and
  applications / Information Resources Management Association, editor.
Description: Hershey, PA : Engineering Science Reference, an imprint of IGI
  Global, [2022] | Includes bibliographical references and index. |
  Contents: Overview of big data and its visualization / Richard S.
  Segall, Arkansas State University, USA, Gao Niu, Bryant University, USA
  -- Big data analytics and visualization of performance of stock exchange
  companies based on balanced scorecard indicators / Iman Raeesi Vanani,
  Allameh Tabataba'i University, Iran, Maziar Shiraj Kheiri, Allameh
  Tabataba'i University, Iran. | Summary: "This complete reference source
  on big data analytics that offers the latest, innovative architectures
  and frameworks, as well as explores a variety of applications within
  various industries offering an international perspective on a variety of
  topics such as advertising curricula, driven supply chain, and smart
  cities"-- Provided by publisher.
Identifiers: LCCN 2021039213 (print) | LCCN 2021039214 (ebook) | ISBN
  9781668436622 (h/c) | ISBN 9781668436639 (eisbn)
Subjects: LCSH: Big data. | Quantitative research.
Classification: LCC QA76.9.B45 .R437 2022 (print) | LCC QA76.9.B45
  (ebook) | DDC 005.7--dc23/eng/20211019
LC record available at https://lccn.loc.gov/2021039213
LC ebook record available at https://lccn.loc.gov/2021039214

British Cataloguing in Publication Data
A Cataloguing in Publication record for this book is available from the British Library.

The views expressed in this book are those of the authors, but not necessarily of the publisher.

For electronic access to this publication, please contact: eresources@igi-global.com.

List of Contributors

Table of Contents

Section 2
Development and Design Methodologies

Volume II

Section 3
Tools and Technologies

Section 4
Utilization and Applications

Volume IV

Section 5
Organizational and Social Implications

Section 6
Managerial Impact

Section 7
Critical Issues and Challenges

Preface

Society is now completely driven by data with many industries relying on data to conduct business or basic functions within the organization. With the efficiencies that big data bring to all institutions, data are continuously being collected and analyzed. However, data sets may be too complex for traditional data processing, and therefore, different strategies must evolve to solve the issue. For managers, data management can be particularly overwhelming as businesses sift through information and determine how to utilize it. Thus, investigating the current architectures and applications of data analytics is integral for achieving efficient and productive processes. The field of big data works as a valuable tool for many different industries.

Staying informed of the most up-to-date research trends and findings is of the utmost importance. That is why IGI Global is pleased to offer this four-volume reference collection of reprinted IGI Global book chapters and journal articles that have been handpicked by senior editorial staff. This collection will shed light on critical issues related to the trends, techniques, and uses of various applications by providing both broad and detailed perspectives on cutting-edge theories and developments. This collection is designed to act as a single reference source on conceptual, methodological, technical, and managerial issues, as well as to provide insight into emerging trends and future opportunities within the field.

The *Research Anthology on Big Data Analytics, Architectures, and Applications* is organized into seven distinct sections that provide comprehensive coverage of important topics. The sections are:

1. Fundamental Concepts and Theories;
2. Development and Design Methodologies;
3. Tools and Technologies;
4. Utilization and Applications;
5. Organizational and Social Implications;
6. Managerial Impact; and
7. Critical Issues and Challenges.

The following paragraphs provide a summary of what to expect from this invaluable reference tool.

Section 1, "Fundamental Concepts and Theories," serves as a foundation for this extensive reference tool by addressing crucial theories essential to understanding the concepts and uses of big data in multidisciplinary settings. Opening this reference book is the chapter "Understanding Big Data" by Profs. Naciye Güliz Uğur and Aykut Hamit Turan of Sakarya University, Turkey, which defines big data basically and provides an overview of big data in terms of status, organizational effects (technology, healthcare, education, etc.), implementation challenges, and big data projects. This first section ends with the chapter "A Brief Survey on Big Data in Healthcare" by Prof. Ebru Aydindag Bayrak of Istanbul University-Cerrahpaşa, Turkey and Prof. Pinar Kirci of Bursa Uludağ University, Turkey, which presents a brief introduction to big data and big data analytics and their roles in the healthcare system.

Section 2, "Development and Design Methodologies," presents in-depth coverage of the design and development of big data architectures for their use in different applications. This section starts with "Big Data Analytics and Models" by Prof. Ferdi Sönmez of Istanbul Arel University, Turkey; Prof. Ziya Nazım Perdahçı of Mimar Sinan Fine Arts University, Turkey; and Prof. Mehmet Nafiz Aydın of Kadir Has University, Turkey, which explores big data analytics as a comprehensive technique for processing large amounts of data to uncover insights. This section ends with the chapter "Big Data Analytics and Visualization for Food Health Status Determination Using Bigmart Data" by Profs. Sumit Arun Hirve and Pradeep Reddy C. H. of VIT-AP University, India, which elaborates on pre-processing a commercial market dataset using the R tool and its packages for information and visual analytics.

Section 3, "Tools and Technologies," explores the various tools and technologies used in the implementation of big data analytics for various uses. This section begins with "Big Data and Advance Analytics: Architecture, Techniques, Applications, and Challenges" by Prof. Surabhi Verma of National Institute of Industrial Engineering, Mumbai, India, which investigates the characteristics of big data, processes of data management, advance analytic techniques, applications across sectors, and issues that are related to their effective implementation and management within broader context of big data analytics. This section ends with the chapter "Big Data for Satellite Image Processing: Analytics, Tools, Modeling, and Challenges" by Prof. P. Swarnalatha of Vellore Institute of Technology, Vellore, India and Prof. Prabu Sevugan of VIT University, India, which presents an introduction to the basics in big data including architecture, modeling, and the tools used.

Section 4, "Utilization and Applications," describes how big data is used and applied in diverse industries for various technologies and applications. The opening chapter in this section, "An Analysis of Big Data Analytics," by Profs. Vijander Singh, Amit Kumar Bairwa and Deepak Sinwar of Manipal University Jaipur, India, explains that the immense measure of organized, unstructured, and semi-organized information is produced each second around the cyber world, which should be managed efficiently. This section ends with the chapter "Computational and Data Mining Perspectives on HIV/AIDS in Big Data Era: Opportunities, Challenges, and Future Directions" by Prof. Ali Al Mazari of Alfaisal University, Saudi Arabia, which provides a review on the computational and data mining perspectives on HIV/AIDS in big data era.

Section 5, "Organizational and Social Implications," includes chapters discussing the ways in which big data impacts society and shows the ways in which big data is used in different industries and how this impacts business. The chapter "Big Data and IoT Applications in Real Life Environment" by Prof. Anjali Chaudhary of Noida International University, India and Pradeep Tomar of Gautam Buddha University, India, discusses various applications of big data and IoT in detail and discusses how both the technologies are affecting our daily life and how it can make things better. This section ends with the chapter "Cloud Computing Big Data Adoption Impacts on Teaching and Learning in Higher Education: A Systematic Review" by Prof Fahad Nasser Alhazmi of King Abdulaziz University, Saudi Arabia, which evaluates and assesses the impact of big data and cloud computing in higher education.

Section 6, "Managerial Impact," presents coverage of academic and research perspectives on the way big data analytics affects management in the workplace. Starting this section is "Big Data Technologies and Management" by Profs. Jayashree K. and Abirami R. of Rajalakshmi Engineering College, India, which discusses the background of big data. It also discusses the various application of big data in detail. This section ends with the chapter "Exploring Big Data Analytic Approaches to Cancer Blog Text Analysis" by Prof. Viju Raghupathi of Koppelman School of Business, Brooklyn College of the City University of New York, Brooklyn, USA and Profs. Yilu Zhou and Wullianallur Raghupathi of Gabelli School of Business, Fordham University, New York, USA, which establishes an exploratory approach to involving big data analytics methods in developing text analytics applications for the analysis of cancer blogs.

Section 7, "Critical Issues and Challenges," highlights current problems within the field and offers solutions for future improvement. Opening this final section is the chapter "A Survey on Comparison of Performance Analysis on a Cloud-Based Big Data Framework" by Profs. Krishan Tuli and Amanpreet Kaur of Chandigarh University, India and Prof. Meenakshi Sharma of Galgotias University, India, which discusses the survey on the performance of the big data framework based on a cloud from various endeavors which assists ventures to pick a suitable framework for their work and get a desired outcome. This section ends with the chapter "How Big Data Transforms Manufacturing Industry: A Review Paper" by Profs. Victor I. C. Chang and Wanxuan Lin of Xi'an Jiaotong-Liverpool University, Suzhou, China, which defines what big data means for the manufacturing industry. It explains four advantages about big data analytics and their benefits to manufacturing.

Although the primary organization of the contents in this multi-volume work is based on its seven sections, offering a progression of coverage of the important concepts, methodologies, technologies, applications, social issues, and emerging trends, the reader can also identify specific contents by utilizing the extensive indexing system listed at the end of each volume. As a comprehensive collection of research on the latest findings related to big data, the *Research Anthology on Big Data Analytics, Architectures, and Applications* provides data scientists, data analysts, computer engineers, software engineers, technologists, government officials, managers, CEOs, professors, graduate students, researchers, and academicians with a complete understanding of the application and impact of big data. Given the vast number of issues concerning usage, failure, success, strategies, and applications of big data in modern technologies and processes, the *Research Anthology on Big Data Analytics, Architectures, and Applications* encompasses the most pertinent research on its uses and impact on global institutions.

Chapter 72
Computational and Data Mining Perspectives on HIV/AIDS in Big Data Era:
Opportunities, Challenges, and Future Directions

Ali Al Mazari

Alfaisal University, Saudi Arabia

ABSTRACT

HIV/AIDS big data analytics evolved as a potential initiative enabling the connection between three major scientific disciplines: (1) the HIV biology emergence and evolution; (2) the clinical and medical complex problems and practices associated with the infections and diseases; and (3) the computational methods for the mining of HIV/AIDS biological, medical, and clinical big data. This chapter provides a review on the computational and data mining perspectives on HIV/AIDS in big data era. The chapter focuses on the research opportunities in this domain, identifies the challenges facing the development of big data analytics in HIV/AIDS domain, and then highlights the future research directions of big data in the healthcare sector.

INTRODUCTION

Recent quick raise within digital data's generation as well as the quick development concerns computational science permit us extracting recent insights from the massive sets of data, recognized as huge data, within a variety of disciplines, involving internet finance and business (Lee & Yoon, 2017; Lane et al., 2014).In the area of healthcare, discovering recent actionable insights has not been recognized widespread, even though many success achievement stories are mostly published in the academic journals and media (Edmunds et al., 2014). This postponed development of the big data technology in the sector of healthcare is unusual, taken into account a previous prediction, which is the big data technology's

DOI: 10.4018/978-1-6684-3662-2.ch072

application that was predictable. In addition, the sector of health care could be one of the most important sectors predicted to be profited the most from the technology of big data (Murdoch & Detsky, 2013).

The growing gap among outcomes and healthcare costs is recognized as one of the most significant issues and there are many efforts under way in order to fill this gap within several developed countries (Savel & Foldy, 2012). It is demonstrated that the gap among outcomes and healthcare costs was analyzed in order to consider the poor management's result of insights from the research. The poor use of obtainable evidence, in addition to the poor imprison of care experience, each of which contributes to lead to wasted resources, missed chances in addition to possible harm to the patients (Curry, 2005). It has been proposed that the gap could be defeated through the improvement of a "continuous learning healthcare system" since an honorable cycle is shaped among the research as well as the healthcare's arms, and data could be utilized successfully (Rumsfeld, Joynt & Maddox, 2016). Consequently, an imperative demand to enhance patient outcomes and healthcare quality, developing the availability of data in addition to improving analytic capabilities are the big data era's drivers of healthcare (Rumsfeld, Joynt & Maddox, 2016; Groves et al., 2016). There are several challenges to defeat before the technology of big data has the ability to considerably enhance healthcare outcomes, quality and healthcare.

THE ERA OF BIG DATA IN THE DOMAIN OF HEALTHCARE AND MEDICINE

The Concept of Big Data

The "Big Data" term was first initiated into the computing world through Roger Magoulas from the publication of O'Reilly in 2005 to identify a huge amount of data, which the techniques of conventional data management cannot process and process because of the size and complexity of this data (Ularu et al., 2012; Chaorasiya & Shrivastava, 2015). A conducted study on the development of Big Data as a Scientific Topic and Research indicates that the "Big Data" term was offered in the starting of research with1970s; however, has been encompassed within the publications in 2008 (Halevi & Moed, 2012; Sharma, Joshi &Manisha, 2015).

Each day, we generate 2.5 quintillion bytes of data — so much that ninety percent of the data within the world nowadays has been generated in the most recent two years only. This data arrives from each place: sensors utilized to collect climate information, place to the site of social media, videos and digital pictures, phone GPS signals in order to name a few and purchase transaction records (Mukherjee & Shaw, 2016; Jewell et al., 2014). Such massive amount of data which is being formed incessantly is what has the ability to coin as Big Data (Mukherjee & Shaw, 2016).

The decodes of Big Data formerly undamaged data in order to obtain recent insight that is incorporated into the operations of business. Nonetheless, because the amounts of data develop exponential, the recent methods are becoming outdated. Dealing with Big Data entails widespread skills of coding, statistics and domain knowledge. In spite of being Herculean within nature, the applications of Big Data are approximately ubiquitous- from the research of marketing into the scientific research to the interests of customer and so on. We have the ability to witness Big Data within action approximately every place these days (Sabia & Kalra, 2014; Kaisler et al., 2013).

In excess of a year ago, the World Bank prepared the first Innovation Challenge of WBG Big Data that promote many distinctive ideas concerning Big Data like big data in order to expect poverty as well as for climate smart agriculture and for user concentrated Identification of Road Infrastructure Condition in addition to safety and so on (Big Data Solutions, 2017). Big Data has the ability to be merely identified through the volume of 3V, variety and velocity that are considered the driving dimensions of the quantification of Big Data. Gartner analyst, Doug Laney set up the famous concept of 3 V in his 2001 Metagroup publication, Controlling the management of 3D data Controlling Velocity, Variety and Data Volume (Mukherjee & Shaw, 2016).

Figure 1. Schematic representation of the 3V's of Big Data
Mukherjee & Shaw, 2016.

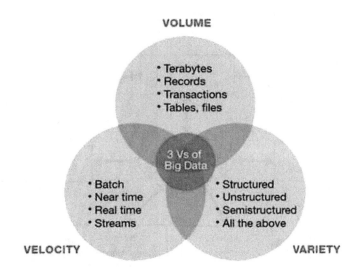

The following is demonstration for the 3V's of Big Data (Mukherjee & Shaw, 2016):

1. **Volume:** This fundamentally distresses huge quantities of data, which is created constantly. Originally, such data was considered problematic due to the high costs of storage. Nonetheless, with the developing costs of storage, this challenge has been reserved to some extent at bay as of now. Nevertheless, this is just a momentary solution, as well as better technology requires to be improved. Social networking websites, E-Commerce and Smartphones are recognized as examples wherever huge amounts of data are being created. This data has the ability to be effortlessly made differences between semi-structured data, unstructured data and structured data.

2. **Velocity:** In what recently appear like the pre-historic times, data was mostly procedure within the batches. nevertheless, this method is just possible while the rate of incoming data is slower comparing with the rate of batch processing as well as the postponed is much of an obstruction. at current days, at current days, the speed at which such massive amounts of data are being created is incredibly high. Take Facebook for instance- it creates2.7 billion like actions for every day as well as three hundreds photos among the others approximately amounting to 2.5 million pieces of content for each day at the same time as Google Now procedures over 1.2 trillion searches for every year around all over the world

3. **Variety:** Databases' Documents to excel tables to pictures and videos and audios in several formats, recently data are strongly losing structure. Structure does not have the ability to be compulsory like

before data analysis. The generated data has the ability to be one of any kind- unstructured, semi-structured and structures. The traditional shape of data is known as structured data. for instance, text that is Unstructured data has the ability to be created from satellites, sensors and social networking sites.

Big Data has the ability to be depicted utilizing the model of 5Vs, which is demonstrated in the Figure 2 (Lomotey & Deters, 2014).

Figure 2. The model of 5V that presently identifies Big Data
Lomotey & Deters, 2014.

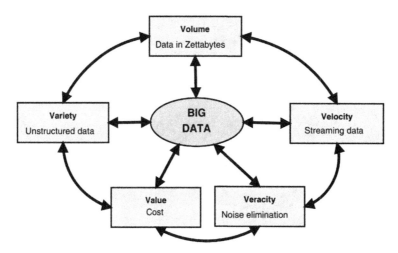

This model is an extension of the previously defined 3V model in (Laney, 2001), and involves:

1. Volume (the size's era) with the collection and generation of data masses, the scale of data becomes progressively big. The data fashioned these days is for zetta bytes order, as well as it is increasing around forty- percent for each year (Fan & Bifet, 2013).
2. Velocity (the streaming data era) indicates to the timeliness of Big Data, particularly, data analysis and collection and has to be timely and rapidly carried out, so to increase the usage of the commercial value concerns Big Data.
3. Variety (the unstructured data era) demonstrates the different kinds of data that involve unstructured and semi-structured data like text, webpage, video and audio in addition to the conventional structured data.
4. Value (the cost associated with data era) whilst the data are greatly being analyzed, collected and generated from various quarters, it is significant to demonstrate that the data of today have a number of costs. The data itself has the ability to be a "commodity" that has the ability to be sold to the third parties for proceeds. In addition, being familiar with the value or cost of the data has the ability to help in the processes of decision making concerns budget at evaluating the data storage cost.

5.   Veracity (the era of data pollution, which requires cleansing) there is a great demand to ensure data's accuracy through eradicating the noise depending on the methodologies like data sanitization and pedigree. This is to make sure about the quality of data, consequently that the decisions, which are made from the gathered data, are effective and accurate.

Implementing Big Data is recognized as an enormous task granted to large variety, velocity and volume. Big Data is known as a term surrounding the usage of method to visualize, analyze, process and process potentially huge datasets within a sensible timeframe not available to the standard technologies of IT. By expansion, the software, tools and platform utilized for this purpose are the platform, tools and software used for this purpose are cooperatively called —— the technologies of Big Data (Erdman, Keefe & Schiestl, 2013). Presently, the most normally implemented technology is Hadoop. Hadoop is defined as the conclusion of many other technologies such as the systems of Hadoop Distribution File, HBase, Pig, Hive, Etc. Nonetheless, even Hadoop as well as other methods will be extremely unable to deal with the difficulties of Big Data in the future (Lin & Ryaboy, 2013; Zicari, 2014).

Big Data Analytics' Concept

Today, the world is constructed on the base of data. The lives of these days are influenced through the ability of corporations to manage, interrogate and dispose data. The development of the infrastructure of technology for the purpose of help to create data, consequently, each of the provided service has the ability to be enhanced as they are utilized (Mitchell & Wilson, 2012). As an instance, internet these days became an enormous information-collecting platform because of online services and social media. At any time they could add data. Data explosion could not be measured in gigabytes; because data is superior; they are utilized Yottabytes (YB), Zettabytes (ZB), Exabytes (EB) and Petabytes (PB). For managing stored unstructured data's giant volume, it has been emerged the phenomena of "Big Data" (Forsyth, 2012; Stone, 2014).

It relates to the reason that the Big-Data of commercial sector had been adopted quickly in the industries of data driven such as telecommunications and financial service that could be discussed, have been experiencing a more speedy development in the volumes of data comparing to the sectors of other market, falling profitability and tighter regulatory requirements. Firstly, "Big Data" was recognized as a method to reduce and manage data management' costs. At the present, the corporations concentrate on the creation potential of value. To get benefit from further insight gained, there is a demand to evaluate execution and analytical capabilities of "Big Data" (Ventura et al., 2015; Ularu et al., 2012).

Up till the mid of 2009, the landscape of data management was simple: the systems of Online transaction processing (OLTP) (particularly databases) hold up the business processes of the company; operational data stores (ODSs) gathered the transactions of business to hold up operational reporting, as well as company data warehouses (EDWs) gathered and transformed the transactions of business in order to support both strategic and operational decision making. The Management of Big Data is mostly depended on organizing and capturing related data. Data analytics presume to be familiar that occurred, why and expect what will occur. A deeper analytics indicates recent analytical means for deeper insights (Forsyth, 2012).

The Apache Hadoop open source project and big data analytics are speedily appearing as the favored resolution to the trends of technology and business, which are unsettling the conventional processing landscape and data management. Companies have the ability to get a competitive advantage through being untimely adopters for the analytics of big data. Although big data analytics have the ability to be theoretically transforming, companies are not supposed to postpone implementation. Since mature and business intelligence (BI) tool and the Hadoop projects, the complexity of big data analytics implementation will greatly reduce; nevertheless, the untimely adopter competitive advantage will wane. The risk of Technology implementation has the ability to be lessened through adapting the existing architectural patterns and principles to the changing requirements and new technology more willingly than rejecting those (Brown et al., 2011).

Big data analytics have the ability to be distinguished from the conventional architectures of data processing through several dimensions and they are as the following (Forsyth, 2012; Russom, 2011):

- Decision making's Speed being very significant for the makers of decision
- The complexity of Processing since it makes the process of decision making very easy
- The volumes of Transactional data that are very huge
- Data structure has the ability to be unstructured and structured
- Flexibility of analysis /processing involved within the amount of analysis, which has the ability to be be performed on it
- Concurrency

The initiative of big data analytics are supposed to be combined project contains business and IT. IT is supposed to be accountable in order to deploy the right analysis tools for big data as well as implementing the management practices of sound data. Each group is supposed to that success will be evaluated through the added value by the improvements of business, which appears through the initiative (Nitrd, 2016).

"Big Data" is recognized as an Analytics market and Data Management opportunity driven by the requirements of recent market. Within -Database Analytics – Data Mining, there are Big Data Connectors used in order to join the data of DBMS and Hadoop. Moreover, there is a great demand to reuse the skills of SQL for applying the techniques of deeper data mining, or to re-use skills for the purpose of statistical analysis. The whole subject is about "Big Data" instead of the data of RAM-scale. This indicates to analytical learning of relationships among business events and knowledge concepts (Chen et al., 2015).

Big-Data represents an important chance for generating recent value from massive data. It is significant to specify suitable procedures for governance to manage implementations and development over the data and technology life. Not a success to believe the longer-term implications of improvement will guide to cost escalations and productivity issues (Fan, Han & Liu, 2014; Ularu et al., 2012).

The cost of actually storing great amount of data is radically lessen through the ease by which data has the ability to be loaded into the cluster of Big-Data since it is indicated that there is no longer needed a multifaceted layer of ETL seen in any more solutions of conventional Data Warehouse. Moreover, the cluster itself is characteristically constructed through the usage of commodity hardware with low cost and analysts are free for writing code in approximately any modern language through the API streaming obtainable in Hadoop (Agrawal, Joshi & Velez, 2017).

The Importance of Big Data Era in Healthcare

Health data volume mostly is predicted to raise noticeably in the future (Cottle et al., 2013). Moreover, the models of healthcare reimbursement are transforming; significant pay and usage to the performance are promising as decisive recent factors in the healthcare environment of these days. even though proceeds are not supposed to be the a main motivator, it is crucially significant for the organizations of healthcare in order to obtain available techniques, infrastructure and tools to influence big data efficiently or other risks losing many millions in profits and revenue (LaValle et al., 2011).

A report transported to the U.S. Congress in August 2012 identified big data as great volumes of high variable, complex and velocity data, which need advanced technologies and techniques in order to enable the analysis, management, distribution, storage and capture of the information (Cottle et al., 2013). Big data includes such features as velocity, variety and with respect especially to veracity, healthcare (Unit, 2012; Connolly, Wooledge & Aster, 2013; Courtney, 2012; Sagiroglu & Sinanc, 2013). Obtainable analytical methods have the ability to be applied to the enormous amount of existing (but presently unanalyzed) medical data and patient-related health in order attain outcomes' deeper understanding, which after that have the ability to be applied at the care's point. Preferably, population and individual data would notify every physician as well as her patient throughout the process of decision-making in addition to aid specifies the most suitable treatment choice for that specific patient (Raghupathi & Raghupathi, 2014).

Through using, combining and effectively digitizing big data, the organization of healthcare ranging from multi-provider groups and the offices of single-physician to great hospital networks as well as the organizations of accountable care tends to recognize important benefits (Burghard, 2012).

Possible benefits involve distinguishing diseases at earlier stages, while they have the ability to be treated more effectively and easily. Managing particular population and individual health in addition to identify health care fraud more are efficiently and quickly. Many questions have the ability to be addressed with the analytics of big data. Particular outcomes and developments may be expected or/and evaluated depended on great amounts of the historical data; for instance, length of stay (LOS); patients who will selective surgery; complications; patients who probable will not get benefit from the surgery, patients at the risk of medical complications, patients at risk for sepsis; illness/disease progression; other hospital-acquired illness; patients at risk for progression in the states of disease causal factors of disease/ illness development and probable co-morbid conditions (EMC Consulting). McKinsey evaluated that big data analytics have the ability to enable in excess of $300 billion in saving for each year in the healthcare of the United States, two thirds of this amount is through the reductions of mostly8% in the national expenditures of healthcare. R & D and Clinical operations are recognized as two of the greatest areas for possible savings with $165 billion as well as108 billion in waste correspondingly (Brown et al., 2011; Manyika et al., 2011).

Bigdata may aid decrease waste and incompetence in the subsequent three areas (Manyika et al., 2011):

1. **Clinical Processes:** Comparative research of effectiveness in order to specify more clinically cost-effective and relevant methods to treat and diagnose patients.
2. **Research & Development:** That involves:
    a. Prognostic modeling for inferior attrition as well as create a targeted, faster and leaner, R & D pipeline in the devices and drugs
    b. Statistical algorithms and tools in order to enhance clinical trial design as well as patient employment for enhanced competition treatments to patients, consequently speeding recent treatments for the market and lessening trial failures
    c. Analyzing and patient records and clinical trials in order to define the indications of follow-on as well as find out adverse influences before the products arrive at the market.

3. **Public Health:**
   a. Analyzing the patterns of disease in addition to tracking disease transmission and outbreaks in order to enhance speed response and the surveillance of public health;
   b. Earlier improvement of more precisely besieged vaccines; for instance, selecting the yearly influenza strains; and,
   c. Rotating huge amounts of data to actionable information, which has the ability to be utilized to provide services, identify needs, prevent and predict crises, particularly for the populations 'benefit

Furthermore, big data analytics in healthcare have the ability to contribute to the following (Raghupathi & Raghupathi, 2014):

1. **Evidence-Depended on Medicine:** Analyze and Combine a diversity of unstructured and structured data-EMRs, genomic data, clinical data, forecast patients at risk for readmission or disease as well as offer more well-organized care.
2. **Genomic Analytics:** Carry out gene sequencing more professionally as well as cost efficiently in addition to make genomic analysis a part of the regular processes of the medical care decision as well as the growing medical record of patient.
3. **The Analysis of Pre-Adjudication Fraud:** Quickly analyze great numbers of claim requests in order to lessen fraud, abuse and waste
4. **Remote/Device Monitoring:** Analyze and Capture in real-time great volumes of speedy-moving data from the devices of in-home and in-hospital, for safety adverse and monitoring the prediction of event.
5. **Patient Profile Analytics:** Pertain superior analytics to the profiles of patient (for example, predictive and segmentation modeling) in order to recognize persons who would get benefit from lifestyle changes or practical care, for instance, the patients at risk of improving a particular disease (e.g., diabetes) who would get benefit from defensive care

The Applications of Big Data Analytical in Medicine and Healthcare

An extensive usage of big data within the sector of health has the ability to aid help doctors make the correct choices quickly depending on the information gathered by other medical staff. Patients have the ability to benefit from more appropriate and timely treatments as well as be superior informed about the providers of health care. Moreover, a developed usage of data analysis within the sector of health sector could lead to massive cost savings throughout a more accurate recognition of needless duplication or procedures of the tests. It is demonstrated that the analysis of great clinical datasets has the ability to significantly contribute in the optimization of the cost and clinical effectiveness of recent treatments and drugs (Raghupathi & Raghupathi, 2014).

The performance analysis of many mining classification techniques of data was examined based on three major various machine learning methods and tools over the datasets of healthcare. Various data mining categorization methods have been examined depending on four diverse datasets of healthcare. The utilized standards are considered percentage of error and accuracy and rate of each applied categorization method (Gupta, Kumar & Sharma, 2011). A wide spread confusion framework, called kernelized locality sensitive hashing is used to deal with this problem in order to increase time series resemblance search by means of a series of characterized resemblance metrics. The results of Experiments indicates to the efficiency of the suggested approach (Kale et al., 2014).

Practical applications and data mining perception in healthcare was considered a way further than its stable development in the field of academic research, that raises a hypothesis, which comparatively considered a little percentage of the efforts of the academic research results in practical applications of DM in healthcare out of which they was finish that the recent interdisciplinary approach does not consider competent enough (Niakšu & Kurasova, 2012).Statistical methods for evaluating complex structure of correlation from large datasets of pharmaco-genomics. They selectively viewed many famous statistical methods and means in order to evaluate great covariance matrix for being familiar with the structure of correlation, opposite covariance matrix for the modeling of network, simultaneous tests of large-scale for choosing considerably in a different way expressed proteins and genes as well as genetic markers for multifaceted diseases in addition to elevated dimensional changeable collection for recognized significant molecules for being familiar with molecule mechanisms within pharma-cogenomics (Fan & Liu, 2013). The technique of data mining is used for diseases' prediction and develops the diagnostic accurateness. Moreover, reduced the constraint of time and cost in terms of expertise and human resources (Durairaj & Ranjani, 2013).

Medical data are frequently noisy as well as gathered in elevated dimensional format. The usage of fuzzy system aids to hold the complexity and noisiness of medical data. In addition, SAM aids to lessen the superior dimensional data (Nguyen et al., 2015). In addition, there is an intensive data incorporated framework to help with the control and prevention of silicosis (HATS), TB and HIV/AIDS in the mining industry. The purpose behind suggested big data framework is to address the requirements of prognostic epidemiology that is significant in disease control and forecasting in the mining industry (Jokonya, 2014).

Moreover, there is an approach and recent statistical model learning, which have been utilized in the statistical relationship of learning from big data in the behavioural science and medicine, which characteristically involve environmental, genomic and clinical variable. This model is very appropriate for analyzing the sets of big data that is involved with the diverse kinds of large data form environmental, genomic and clinical data (Yoo, Ramirez &Liuzzi, 2014).

This section shows instances of health-related Big Data projects, among an importance of the quantified-self movement and data from the social media (Table 1). About the big data the research related to genetic data, EMRs, omics sources and digital enterprise, readers can consult the subsequent reviews in addition to the perspectives conducted lately (Bourne, 2014; Kum et al., 2014; Shivade et al., 2013; Shoenbill et al., 2013; Tenenbaum, Sansone & Haendel, 2013).

ANALYTICAL PERSPECTIVES OF BIG DATA

Computational Perspectives

Fascinatingly, the statisticians and the computer scientists - the two researchers' communities, which are may be most frankly influenced by the phenomenon of big data-have, intended for cultural reasons, adopted separate early examples in response to it. The main interest of the computer scientists, who have to design file structures andwell-organized data is to accumulate enormous datasets as well as put into practice algorithms on them-stems from computational difficulty. It interests the needed number of the steps of computing in order to resolve an agreed problem whose difficulty is recognized in terms of input data's length as presented through a rational encoding instruments (binary string) (Pyne, Rao & Rao, 2016).

Table 1. Some examples about the health-related Big Data projects associated to social media in addition to the quantified-self movement

Data Type	How Has It Been Used in Health?	Examples
Quantified-self data (via devices, self-reporting, or sensors)	• Permits data collection being potentially longer follow-up stages than is presently possible by standard questionnaires (Swan, 2013) • Provides richer as well as more exhaustive data on probable risk factors (behavioral, biological, environmental or physical) (Swan, 2013) • Engaged during the self-tracking of behaviors and/or signs as n=1 in groups or individual, where there is frequently a proactive position to acting on the information (Swan, 2013)	• Grin triggered electro-myogram (EMG) muscle to make unexpected joy moments in human interaction (Tasse, 2012) • Food consumption (Yau,2017) • Coffee consumption, mood and social interaction (Wolf,2017) • Information diet (McCormick, 2017) • Idea-tracking process (Chua, 2012) • Checks blood glucose levels in diabetics (e.g. Glooko) (Glooko, 2017) • Use of controller and rescue asthma medications through an inhaler sensor (e.g. Asthmapolis) (Asthmapolis, 2017) • Physical activity (e.g. FitBit; Jawbone Up, RunKeeper) (JawboneUp, 2017) • Diet (e.g. My Meal Mate) (Carter et al., 2013) • Psychological, mental and cognitive traits and states (e.g. MyCompass) (Harrison et al., 2011) • Sleep quality (e.g. Lark) (Lark, 2017) • Medication adherence (e.g. MyMedSchedule) (Dayer et al., 2013)
Location-based information	• Information based on Geographic Information Systems (GIS), Global Positioning Systems (GPS), in addition to other visualization projects and open source mapping. • Gives information on the social and environmental health determinants. • Monitors for the disease that outbreaks close to your location.	• Allergens, weather patterns, traffic patterns, pollution levels, walkability of neighborhood, water quality, in addition to access to fresh vegetables and fruit (for example supermarkets) (Cerin et al, 2013) • HealthMap(HealthMap, 2017)
Twitter (Note: a 2011 study has recommended that 8.5% of the English-language tweets are relating to illness, and 16.6% are relating to health (Paul & Dredze, 2012))	• Makes discourse easy on non-emergency healthcare (e.g. quantify medical misconception, broadcasts of public health messages) • Makes the crisis mapping easy (e.g. where eyewitness is reporting are planned on interactive maps. These data are able to assist objective areas for emergency services in addition to additional resources) • Makes the emergency services easy by permitting for the available resource wide-scale broadcast, enabling people destitute of medical help for locating help • Assesses moods and sentiments • Assesses disease extend in real-time	• Trends of resuscitation communication and cardiac arrest (Bosley et al., 2013) • Measure medical misconceptions (e.g. concussions) (Sullivan et al., 2011) • breast and Cervical cancer screening (Lyles et al.,2013) • The poor medical compliance spread (e.g., antibiotic use) (Scanfeld, Scanfeld& Larson, 2010) • 2010 Haitian cholera outbreak (Chunara, Andrews & Brownstein, 2012) • Postpartum depression (De Choudhury, Counts & Horvitz, 2013) • Boston marathon explosion Emergency situations (Chunara, Andrews & Brownstein, 2012) • Influenza A H1N1 outbreak (public concern and disease activity) (Chews & Eysenbach, 2010)
Health-related social networking sites	• Monitors the infectious diseases spread via the crowd surveillance • Makes easy of the sharing of personal health advice and data amongst consumers and patients.	• Disease surveillance locations that collect participant-reported symptoms in addition to utilize familiar online data supplies to map, disseminate and analyze, information about infectious disease outbreaks (e.g. Flu Near You, HealthMap, GermTracker, Sickweather) (HealthMap, 2017) • PatientsLikeMe (PatientsLikeMe, 2017)
Additional social networking sites (e.g. board Facebook, online discussion)	• Checks how patients are using social media for discussing their issues and concerns. • Gives awareness of what the ''person in the street'' says (Hill, Merchant &Ungar, 2013)	Associated medication adherence behaviors and Side effects (e.g. drug switching as well as discontinuation) (Mao et al., 2013)
Search queries plus Web logs	• ''Click'' stream navigational data as of web logs are establish to be educational of individual distinctiveness such as dietary preferences and mental health (West, White & Horvitz, 2013) • Search keyword choice has been critical to arrive at dependable curated health satisfied • Found to be extremely predictive for an extensive range of the population-level health behaviors	Yahoo and Google search questions have been applied for predicting epidemics of illnesses, for example: • Seasonality of depression, suicide and mental health (Ayers et al., 2013) • Influenza (Google 2013) • Lyme disease Prevalence (Seifter et al., 2010) • Prevalence of electronic cigarette use and smoking (Ayers, Ribisl& Brownstein, 2011) • Dengue fever (Chan et al., 2011)

Hill, Merchant &Ungar, 2013; Swan, 2013.

Consequently, as the volume of data develops, any technique, which needs considerably more than O (Nlog(N)) steps (that is to say greater than the time's order, which is a solitary pass in excess of the full data would demand) could be unreasonable. Whereas, some of the significant obstacles in practice with the solutions of O (Nlog(N)) are immediately concerning scalable (for example fast Fourier change), those of superior difficulty, positively involving the problems of NP-Complete class, would need help aid from the algorithmic strategies such as sampling, randomization, approximation, etc. Consequently, whereas the theory of classical complexity may think about the solutions of polynomial time the same as computational tractability's hallmark, the big data's world is required even more demanding (Fokoue, 2015).

For describing big data analytics, the same as dissimilar from the common data analysis, a particular individual could propose variety of principles, particularly if the obtainable analytical strategies are not enough to solve the obstacles in hand because of particular features of data. Such features may go beyond pure volume of data (Pyne, Rao & Rao, 2016). High velocity of data has the ability to represent unparalleled problems to the statistician who could not be used to the forgoing idea (more willingly than retaining) the points of data, the same as they stream out, to convince computational challenges like single pass (the constraint of time) as well as bounded storage (the constraint of space). The variety of High data possibly will need multidisciplinary imminent in order to enable a particular individual to make rational conclusion depending on incorporation of apparently unconnected datasets. From one side, such issues are supposed to view only as cultural gaps; whereas on the other side, they have the ability to stimulate the improvement of the essential formalisms, which has the ability to bridge those gaps. Thus, a superior understanding of the cons and pros of various algorithmic choices can aid any analyst decide concerning the most appropriate of the probable resolutions objectively (Chandrasekaran & Jordan, 2013).

Data Mining Perspectives

Data mining is broadly used within fields such as medicine, science, business and engineering. With this procedure, previously concealed insights have been discovered from large quantities of data to help the business community (Che, Safran & Peng, 2013). From the time of the organizations establishment in the present era, data mining has been practical within data recording. On the other hand, Big Data is collected of not just large data amounts but as well data during different formats. Consequently, large processing speed is required (Michael & Miller, 2013). For flexible data study, there are three projected principles (Begoli & Horey, 2012):

1. Architecture must support a lot of analysis methods, for example data mining, statistical analysis, visual analysis and machine learn in.
2. Diverse storage mechanisms ought to be used since every data is notable to fit within a single form of the storage area. In addition, the data ought to be processed in a different way at different stages.
3. Data ought to be accessed proficiently.

To consider Big Data, data mining algorithms which are computer exhaustive are utilized. Like algorithms require high-performance processors. In addition, the storage as well as computing requirements of the Big Data analysis are efficiently met through cloud computing (Talia, 2013).

The aims of large data mining methods go beyond attractive the demand ed information or even finding some hidden patterns and relationships between numeral restrictions. Analyzing massive and fast stream data can lead to novel theoretical concepts and valuable insights (Berkovich & Liao, 2012). Contrasting between the results based on mining the conventional datasets, presentation the large volume of consistent heterogeneous large data has the possible for maximizing our insights and knowledge within the target domain. However, this is bringing a series of novel challenges for the research community. Defeating the challenges will redesign the data mining technology future, resulting within a spectrum of the ground-breaking data in addition to mining algorithms and techniques (Che, Safran & Peng, 2013).

One feasible advance is for improving existing algorithms and techniques by exploiting extremely parallel computing architectures. Big data mining deals with velocity, heterogeneity, privacy, extreme scale, interactiveness, accuracy and trust which existing mining algorithms and techniques are incapable of. They require of implementing and designing very-large-scale parallel mechanism learning in addition to data mining algorithms (ML-DM) has extremely increased, that accompanies the appearance of powerful parallel as well as very-large-scale data handing out platforms, e.g., HadoopMapReduce. NIMBLE is a transferable infrastructure which has been exclusively designed to enable quick execution of parallel ML-DM algorithms, running on top of Hadoop (Ghoting et al., 2011).

Apache's Mahout is a library of data mining implementations and machine learning. Also, the library is applied on top of Hadoop by the MapReduce programming form. Some significant mechanism of the library is able to run stand-alone. The most important disadvantages of Mahout are that its learning cycle is very long as well as its need of user-friendly interaction hold up. In addition, it does not apply all the required machine learning algorithms and data mining. BC-PDM (Big Cloud-Parallel Data Mining), as a cloud-based data mining stage, as well based on Hadoop, is providing access to great telecom data in addition to business solutions to the telecom operators; it is supporting parallel ETL process (load, extract and transform), text mining, data mining and social network analysis (Yu et al., 2012).

BC-PDM attempted to defeat the problem of the single function of additional approaches also to be further applicable to the Business Intelligence. PEGASUS (Peta-scale Graph Mining System) and Giraph the tow implement graph mining algorithms employing parallel computing as well as they run on top of Hadoop (Kang, Tsourakakis & Faloutsos, 2009). GraphLab is a graph-based, scalable structure, on that a number of data mining algorithms and graph-based machine learning are executed. The reported disadvantage of GraphLab is that it is requiring all data appropriate into memory (Low et al., 2012).

Machine Learning Perspectives

Machine learning methods have been found extremely effective as well as relevant to many real world requests in bioinformatics, healthcare, network security, transportations as well as finance and banking. Eventually, health related and bioinformatics data are created as well as accumulated incessantly, resultant in an unbelievable data volume. Newer appearances of big data, such as 3D imaging, biometric and genomics sensor readings, are as well fueling this exponential increase. Future requests of real-time data, for example fast application of the suitable treatments and early discovery of infections/diseases and could decrease patient mortality and morbidity. Previously, real time flowing data monitors neonates in the ICU, infectious life-threatening diseases at real time. The capability for performing real-time analytics against like large stream data crosswise all specialties would transform healthcare. There lies data with variety, volume and velocity (Kashyap et al., 2015).

Machine learning is a computer science field which studies the computational techniques which learn from data (Anzai, 2012). There are mostly a couple of types of learning techniques in machine learning, viz., supervised as well as unsupervised learning techniques (Bhattacharyya & Kalita, 2013). Within supervised learning, a technique learns from a group of things with class label, frequently called the training set. The obtained knowledge is applied to give label to unidentified objects frequently called the test objects. Alternatively, unsupervised learning techniques do not rely on the availability of training instances or prior knowledge with class labels. Every one of these machine-learning techniques needs preprocessing of datasets for effectual results. Feature collection is one of the significant preprocessing tasks, which leads to enhanced result in addition to reduced time necessity. Hybrid learning techniques, for example Deep learning, have turned into popular during the current years as well as provide significantly large accuracy. Superior data capturing technologies have guided to accumulation of an extremely high data volume, growing quickly over time. Even though the computational technologies have enhanced over time, this development is not in proportion to the increase rate in data volume. The conventional machine learning techniques are found insufficient in treatment voluminous data by the present computational resources (Floridi, 2012). Figure 3 shows the contrast among traditional data mining as well as mining of big data.

Figure 3. Traditional data mining and mining of big data
Kashyap et al., 2015.

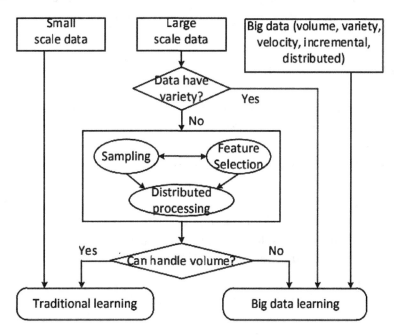

Supervised Learning

Within big data analytics, we require several advanced supervised advances for distributed and parallel learning for example divide-and-conquer SVM (Hsieh &Dhillon, 2014), Multi-hyper plane Machine (MM) classification form [49], and neural network classifiers. Amongst these SVM is one of the mainly widely and efficient used supervised learning technique and a number of modified SVM techniques have been initiated for big data analytics. Nie et al. suggest a customized SVM called New Primal SVM for big data classification (Djuric, 2013). The technique uses a new linear computational cost primitive SVM solver by two loss functions called L1-norm plus L2-norm in Augmented Lagrange Multipliers (ALM). Individual discovery of patients with Parkinson disease by SVM analysis was projected by Haller et al.,(2012).

Unsupervised Learning

Unsupervised learning does not employ the class labels of the substances for learning (Aggarwal& Reddy, 2013). Clustering is an unconfirmed technique, which is attempting to group objects for optimizing the criterion, which states that detachment among objects within the identical cluster is reduced and distance between objects in diverse clusters is exploited (Tan, Steinbach & Kumar, 2013). A most important issue within clustering is the calculation of the distance among two objects. Different proximity is measuring have been applied for this reason, such as city block distance, Euclidean and Cosine. In customary clustering, every feature is used as computing the distance among two objects. A cluster is a collection of objects, which are near to each other regarding to their common distance. That means they are alike in nature in excess of the entire set of features. However, in a number of applications, especially where number of obtainable features within a dataset is extremely large, researchers are paying attention in finding collections of objects, which are alike over division of the obtainable features (Cheng & Church, 2000). This necessity has guide to the appearance of another alternative of clustering called blustering, wherever every balusters related with a division of features (Kashyap et al., 2015).

Deep Learning

Deep learning tries to build high-level concepts in data by unsupervised or supervised learning algorithms to absorb from several abstractions levels. Deep learning utilizes data hierarchical representations for classification. Its methods are used in several applications, pattern recognition, viz., natural language processing, computer vision, besides speech recognition. Because of exponential data growth in the previous applications, this kind of learning is valuable for precise prediction from big data. Recently, academics have advanced scalable and effective parallel training deep models algorithms (Hinton et al., 2012). Several administrations use deep learning for the purpose of information retrieval, semantic indexing and decision making. The architecture of deep learning is presented in Figure 4. Input data are divided into data abstractions' multiple samples. The intermediary layers are for processing the multiple levels features for data prediction. The last prediction is done using the immediate upper layer outputs at the output layer (Kashyap et al., 2015).

DATA TYPES OF HIV/AIDS BIG DATA ANALYTICS

Biological Data

The elements of biological data characteristically addressed involve (Geoff & Jillian, 2015):

1.   The profiles of protein expression and RNA in diseased and healthy tissue at whole-organ, single cell, or regional levels
2.   Inherent information concerning disease and healthy-influenced individuals, characteristically in the wide single nucleotide polymorphism (SNP)'s form, which are whole –genome sequence data (WGS) or whole exome sequence data (WES)
3.   Epigenetic data on the modifications of site-specific DNA as well as his tone acetylation

This information possibly will be demanded from the models of cellular involving (iPS cells) which refers to induced pluripotent stem cells, and from vertebrate and invertebrate animal models. Moreover, it has the ability to be gained from the tissues of human, since in this case it is mostly connected to pseudononymised clinical data on cognitive function, diagnostic status, neuropath logical, neuroimaging, serological or biochemical information. Currently, this kind of compound clinical and biological data has been gathered for humble numbers of controls and cases. Instances of particular databases involve the GEO-PD, Alzheimer's Disease Genetics Consortium (ADGC), Alzheimer's Disease Neuroimaging Initiative (ADNI) in addition to different community repositories of protein expression data and cell type like Allen Brain Institute (Geoff & Jillian, 2015).

Figure 4. Deep leaning architecture
Kashyap et al., 2015.

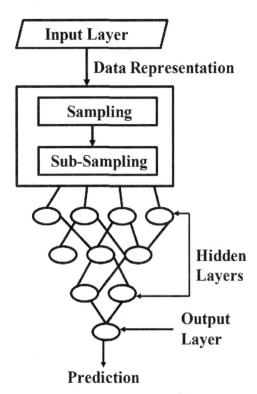

Medical and Clinical Data

Clinical data characteristically involve information concerning symptoms, diagnostic tests involving brain-imaging, CSF and blood tests; disease progression's rates, kind of treatment specified to interest's disease; the influence of that treatment, the attendance of other comorbid and illness factors; and such information concerning economic, social and physical environment. This information has the ability to be connected, within databases, to particular biological data as mentioned previously. it is predicted that, in the following one to five years, these kinds of multifaceted multimodal data will be obtained for superior numbers of controls and cases. Instances of these superior datasets involve the dementia platform of UK, Mayo clinic study of aging, DZNE Rhineland dementia project and UK 1000 Genomes projects. Several of these cohorts involve cross-sectional data and longitudinal data. Further potential resources of such detailed clinical and biological information are profitable databases taken place from trails of candidate diagnostics and new medicines (Haussleiter, Brüne & Juckel, 2009; Geoff & Jillian, 2015).

Other Types, Social, Psycho, and Demographic

Furthermore, Broad population-based information has the ability to be obtained on a great deal of persons from lasting care records, medical record as well as other population depended on epidemiological studies. even though these datasets do not typically coupled with deep biological classification, significant data has the ability to be gleaned from medical records, the recodes of lasting care institutions concerning socio-economic status, drug exposure, hospitalizations, diagnosis, exposure to different environmental risks like occupation, smoking, diet, the factors of lifestyle like exercise or cognitive engagement (Olsen & McGinnis, 2010). A number of these items (for instance, continuing cognitive engagement or early education of childhood) are already thought to the disease's progression as well as impact risk, it is predicted that, in excess of the next decade, the content of information concerning population-depended on datasets will radically develop throughout the low-cost DNA sequencing's acquisition that permits the enclosure of transcription profiling and genomics-wide sequence data on great numbers of persons (McKenzie, Neiger& Thackeray, 2016).

Other probable resources of data involve different kinds of profitable data such as social media usage, internet, mobile phone, and data on credit card. These commercial data possibly involve information about lifestyle (for instance exercise and cigarette, alcohol and diet consumption, etc) . Moreover, transformation through the time in the difficulty of such parameters like social engagement as well as shopping habits have the ability to reproduce transformations in the cognitive activities, which possibly depict the disease's early stages (Miller, Oldham & Geschwind, 2008). In addition, we are supposed to expect a more occupied public were sick individuals and healthy individuals who are sick will follow their own phenotypic data. Nowadays, there are several devices that permit sleep and exercise, blood pressure and heart rate, which present emerging instruments in order to connect the public at the same time as full partners in the diseases' developing models. Such information is probable to be produced throughout wearable devices and smart phones through three ways as the following (Zhang et al., 2013):

1. The activities of Passively-tracking like exercise utilizing the accelerometers
2. Prearranged tests wherever someone is frankly asked to perform a tests intended for properties like cognitive decline

3.   Questions and surveys that the individuals have the ability to answer in real-time multiple times for every day

FUTURE WORKS AND OPPORTUNITIES

Opportunities

In the previous two decades there was an explosion within Big Data all through the health-care value chain, and the start of novel platforms, tackles, in addition to methodologies in analyzing, storing and structuring Big Data. Significant developments comprise the genomic data use within drug discovery, the clinical-trial data sharing, the electronic healthcare records use (EHRs), and the improved availability of the data from social media, mHealth applications and patient registries (Szlezák et al., 2014). The data fusion concept is gaining additional significance as on top of the set of individual data basics increases the fusing jointly of several data sets (Howell, 2014). The enormous amount of new data being produced is by now making significant contributions within epidemiology, more especially in activist public health surveillance (Salathe et al., 2012).

In the satellite sensors era, a variety of epidemiologically appropriate environmental information is able to be sourced internationally at daily periods. Big Data is allowing a closer activist matching of the disease outbreaks through covariates which can improve the mapping models accuracy. The opportunity of seasonally modified geographic baselines definitely improves conventional temporal surveillance through facilitating early caution of epidemiologically appropriate environmental changes (Hay et al., 2013).

The quantified self-concept, in that individuals deploy monitoring and sensors devices for measuring their own behavior and health, has become a truth. If aggregated and expanded at level of population, will guide to a data-driven advance of wellbeing measurement and collective health (Barrett et al., 2013). The creation of new knowledge of the treatments effectiveness as well as the outcomes prediction are of two essential applications of the big healthcare data. That means Big Data is able to be practical in retrospective and prospective research. Prospective research is product focused (for example, improvement of the disease relation to other factors for example protection factor(s) or suspected risk) and has a small recall error when it is involving longitudinal observations eventually as well as results are composed at usual time intervals. In addition, Big Data is different from tradition choice support tools when it is allowing the collection also examination real-time patient data (Murdoch & Detsky, 2013).

Novel possibilities about the discovery of the innovative pharmaceuticals, improvement of more effectual treatment protocols in addition to the improvement of personalized medicine obtain play. Statistical algorithms and tools improve clinical experiment design as well as patient recruitment for better match actions to individual patients, decreasing trial failures as well as speeding novel treatments to market. The analysis of patient records and clinical trials is allowing the classification of follow-up suggestions and the finding of adverse results before products attain the market that ultimately will develop pharmaco-vigilance in addition to patient safety (Raghupathi & Raghupathi, 2014). The assure of personalized medicine led by a considerate of every individual's genome has been advanced through increasingly powerful plus economical methods for acquiring clinically appropriate information (Pulley et al., 2012). Big Data is helping translate personalized medicine to a clinical practice through offering the chance to apply analytical capabilities which can incorporate systems biology (such as, genomics) among data of EHRs (Murdoch & Detsky, 2013). The population science integration by individual genomic measurements will allow the personalized medicine practice (Altman, 2013).

Challenges

Currently, the high variety, volume and velocity of the data collection techniques available is possible to make the society of data driven to a point in that sampling will not be essential because the whole background population is obtainable. Through working with approximately all, the information of the phenomena there is a rising capacity for expanding research questions. Additionally, Big Data includes a high messiness level in the intellect that the raise in the information amount by orders of magnitude is meaning giving up the favorite for extremely curated data for the object of having a superior sample as well as effect size (Walker, 2014). The analysis of disorganized, unstructured and voluminous data has got important discoveries (Baker, 2013; Whiteet al., 2013). However, in the lack of causality in addition to strong assumptions, is society possible to fall blindly on associations? (Lazer et al., 2014).

Still, there are a standardization problems within the healthcare sector, when data is frequently generated or fragmented within IT systems through incompatible formats. Hospital services, research, education, clinical activities as well as administrative services are siloed, furthermore, in a lot of organizations, every silo maintains its possess separate organizational (also sometimes duplicated) information and data infrastructure. The need of cross-border coordination as well as technology integration is calling for standards for facilitating interoperability amongst the Big Data value chain components (Roney, 2012).

When the quantity of health related data in addition to global digital information is growing, therefore does the number of actors' admissions in addition to using this information. Assurances have to be given in order that personal data associated with health will be employed correctly, within the context of the projected uses in addition to consistent with the related laws. Still there is skepticism in view of (where the data goes to) and (by whom it is used) moreover (for what purpose) within the EU split and excessively multifaceted legal environment. In what worries to privacy, circumstances under that data are, 10 shared to research are being conversed under the planned Data Protection Regulation (File, 2012).

Future Directions

Based on the challenges and related issues that big data scientists need to address, the following present some future research directions that can be applied to the handling of big data (Anagnostopoulos, Zeadally & Exposito, 2016):

- Big Data Curation and Cleansing
- Sharing/Storage/Transfer of Big Data
- Analysis and Collection of Big Data Results
- Ethical Considerations of Big Data

CONCLUSION

Big data is a term that defines the large amount of structured and unstructured data that have the ability to enhance the performance of the various businesses on a day-to-day basis. In the health sector, incorporating big data has a great influence in the different treatment stages and public health. However, the opportunities that big data can provide are facing some challenges including the rapid changes in the information systems and unreliable infrastructures; therefore, there must be a new direction for future research and innovations.

REFERENCES

Aggarwal, C. C., & Reddy, C. K. (Eds.). (2013). *Data clustering: algorithms and applications*. CRC press.

Agrawal, M., Joshi, A. S., & Velez, A. F. (2017). *Best Practices in Data Management for Analytics Projects*. CTO Office, Persistent Systems Ltd.

Altman, R. B. (2013). Personal genomic measurements: The opportunity for information integration. *Clinical Pharmacology and Therapeutics*, *93*(1), 21–23. doi:10.1038/clpt.2012.203 PMID:23241835

Anagnostopoulos, I., Zeadally, S., & Exposito, E. (2016). Handling big data: Research challenges and future directions. *The Journal of Supercomputing*, *72*(4), 1494–1516. doi:10.100711227-016-1677-z

Anzai, Y. (2012). *Pattern recognition and machine learning*. Elsevier.

Asthmapolis. (2017). Available from: http://propellerhealth. com/

Ayers, J. W., Althouse, B. M., Allem, J. P., Rosenquist, J. N., & Ford, D. E. (2013). Seasonality in seeking mental health information on Google. *American Journal of Preventive Medicine*, *44*(5), 520–525. doi:10.1016/j.amepre.2013.01.012 PMID:23597817

Ayers, J. W., Ribisl, K. M., & Brownstein, J. S. (2011). Tracking the rise in popularity of electronic nicotine delivery systems (electronic cigarettes) using search query surveillance. *American Journal of Preventive Medicine*, *40*(4), 448–453. doi:10.1016/j.amepre.2010.12.007 PMID:21406279

Baker, E. W. (2013). Relational Model Bases: A Technical Approach to Real-time Business Intelligence and Decision Making. CAIS, 33, 23.

Barrett, M. A., Humblet, O., Hiatt, R. A., & Adler, N. E. (2013). Big data and disease prevention: From quantified self to quantified communities. *Big Data*, *1*(3), 168–175. doi:10.1089/big.2013.0027 PMID:27442198

Begoli, E., & Horey, J. (2012). Design principles for effective knowledge discovery from big data. In *Software Architecture (WICSA) and European Conference on Software Architecture (ECSA), 2012 joint working IEEE/IFIP conference on* (pp. 215-218). IEEE.10.1109/WICSA-ECSA.212.32

Berkovich, S., & Liao, D. (2012). On clusterization of big data streams. In *Proceedings of the 3rd International Conference on Computing for Geospatial Research and Applications* (p. 26). ACM.

Bhattacharyya, D. K., & Kalita, J. K. (2013). *Network anomaly detection: A machine learning perspective*. CRC Press.

Big Data Solutions. (2017). *Harnessing the Power of Big Data for Trade and Competitiveness policy*. World Bank Group.

Bosley, J. C., Zhao, N. W., Hill, S., Shofer, F. S., Asch, D. A., Becker, L. B., & Merchant, R. M. (2013). Decoding twitter: Surveillance and trends for cardiac arrest and resuscitation communication. *Resuscitation*, *84*(2), 206–212. doi:10.1016/j.resuscitation.2012.10.017 PMID:23108239

Bourne, P. E. (2014). What Big Data means to me. *Journal of the American Medical Informatics Association*, *21*(2), 194. doi:10.1136/amiajnl-2014-002651 PMID:24509599

Brown, B., Bughin, J., Byers, A. H., Chui, M., Dobbs, R., Manyika, J., & Roxburgh, C. (2011). *Big data: the next frontier for innovation, competition, and productivity*. McKinsey Global Institute.

Burghard, C. (2012). Big data and analytics key to accountable care success. *IDC Health Insights*.

Carter, M. C., Burley, V. J., Nykjaer, C., & Cade, J. E. (2013). Adherence to a smartphone application for weight loss compared to website and paper diary: Pilot randomized controlled trial. *Journal of Medical Internet Research*, *15*(4), e32. doi:10.2196/jmir.2283 PMID:23587561

Cerin, E., Lee, K. Y., Barnett, A., Sit, C. H., Cheung, M. C., & Chan, W. M. (2013). Objectively-measured neighborhood environments and leisure-time physical activity in Chinese urban elders. *Preventive Medicine*, *56*(1), 86–89. doi:10.1016/j.ypmed.2012.10.024 PMID:23137445

Chan, E. H., Sahai, V., Conrad, C., & Brownstein, J. S. (2011). Using web search query data to monitor dengue epidemics: A new model for neglected tropical disease surveillance. *PLoS Neglected Tropical Diseases*, *5*(5), e1206. doi:10.1371/journal.pntd.0001206 PMID:21647308

Chandrasekaran, V., & Jordan, M. I. (2013). Computational and statistical tradeoffs via convex relaxation. *Proceedings of the National Academy of Sciences of the United States of America*, *110*(13), E1181–E1190. doi:10.1073/pnas.1302293110 PMID:23479655

Chaorasiya, V., & Shrivastava, A. (2015). A survey on Big Data: Techniques and Technologies. *International Journal of Research and Development in Applied Science and Engineering*, *8*(1), 1–4.

Che, D., Safran, M., & Peng, Z. (2013). From big data to big data mining: challenges, issues, and opportunities. In *International Conference on Database Systems for Advanced Applications* (pp. 1-15). Springer. 10.1007/978-3-642-40270-8_1

Chen, X., Wang, S., Dong, Y., & Wang, X. (2015). Big Data Storage Architecture Design in Cloud Computing. In *National Conference on Big Data Technology and Applications* (pp. 7-14). Springer.

Cheng, Y., & Church, G. M. (2000). Biclustering of expression data. ISMB, 8, 93-103.

Chew, C., & Eysenbach, G. (2010). Pandemics in the age of Twitter: Content analysis of Tweets during the 2009 H1N1 outbreak. *PLoS One*, *5*(11), e14118. doi:10.1371/journal.pone.0014118 PMID:21124761

Chua, S. (2012). *Notes from the quantified self 2012 conference*. Available from: http://sachachua.com/blog/p/23723/

Chunara, R., Andrews, J. R., & Brownstein, J. S. (2012). Social and news media enable estimation of epidemiological patterns early in the 2010 Haitian cholera outbreak. *The American Journal of Tropical Medicine and Hygiene*, *86*(1), 39–45. doi:10.4269/ajtmh.2012.11-0597 PMID:22232449

Connolly, S., Wooledge, S., & Aster, T. (2013). *Harnessing the value of big data analytics*. Academic Press.

Cottle, M., Hoover, W., Kanwal, S., Kohn, M., Strome, T., & Treister, N. (2013). Transforming Health Care Through Big Data Strategies for leveraging big data in the health care industry. *Institute for Health Technology Transformation*. Retrieved from http://ihealthtran.com/big-data-in-healthcare

Courtney, M. (2012). Puzzling out big data. *Engineering & Technology, 7*(12), 56–60. doi:10.1049/et.2012.1215

Curry, L. (2005). The Future of the Public's Health in the 21st Century. *Generations (San Francisco, Calif.), 29*(2), 82.

Dayer, L., Heldenbrand, S., Anderson, P., Gubbins, P. O., & Martin, B. C. (2013). Smartphone medication adherence apps: Potential benefits to patients and providers. *Journal of the American Pharmacists Association: JAPhA, 53*(2), 172–181. doi:10.1331/JAPhA.2013.12202 PMID:23571625

De Choudhury, M., Counts, S., & Horvitz, E. (2013). Predicting postpartum changes in emotion and behavior via social media. In *Proceedings of the SIGCHI Conference on Human Factors in Computing Systems* (pp. 3267-3276). ACM. 10.1145/2470654.2466447

Djuric, N. (2013). *Big data algorithms for visualization and supervised learning*. Temple University.

Durairaj, M., &Ranjani, V. (2013). Data mining applications in healthcare sector: A study. *International Journal of Scientific & Technology Research, 2*(10), 29-35.

Edmunds, M., Thorpe, L., Sepulveda, M., Bezold, C., & Ross, D. A. (2014). The future of public health informatics: Alternative scenarios and recommended strategies. *EGEMS (Washington, DC), 2*(4), 3. doi:10.13063/2327-9214.1156 PMID:25848630

Erdman, A. G., Keefe, D. F., & Schiestl, R. (2013). Grand challenge: Applying regulatory science and big data to improve medical device innovation. *IEEE Transactions on Biomedical Engineering, 60*(3), 700–706. doi:10.1109/TBME.2013.2244600 PMID:23380845

Fan, J., Han, F., & Liu, H. (2014). Challenges of big data analysis. *National Science Review, 1*(2), 293–314. doi:10.1093/nsr/nwt032 PMID:25419469

Fan, J., & Liu, H. (2013). Statistical analysis of big data on pharmacogenomics. *Advanced Drug Delivery Reviews, 65*(7), 987–1000. doi:10.1016/j.addr.2013.04.008 PMID:23602905

Fan, W., &Bifet, A. (2013). Mining big data: current status, and forecast to the future. *ACM SIGKDD Explorations Newsletter, 14*(2), 1-5.

File, I. (2012). *Proposal for a Regulation of the European Parliament and of the Council on the Protection of Individuals with Regard to the Processing of Personal Data and on the Free movement of Such Data*. General Data Protection Regulation.

Floridi, L. (2012). Big data and their epistemological challenge. *Philosophy & Technology, 25*(4), 435–437. doi:10.100713347-012-0093-4

Fokoue, E. (2015). *A taxonomy of Big Data for optimal predictive machine learning and data mining.* arXiv preprint arXiv:1501.00604

Forsyth, C. (2012). *For big data analytics there's no such thing as too big.* The compelling economics and technology of big data computing. White Paper.

Geoff, A., & Jillian, O. (Eds.). (2015). *Dementia Research and Care Can Big Data Help? Can Big Data Help?* OECD Publishing.

Ghoting, A., Kambadur, P., Pednault, E., & Kannan, R. (2011).NIMBLE: a toolkit for the implementation of parallel data mining and machine learning algorithms on mapreduce. In *Proceedings of the 17th ACM SIGKDD international conference on Knowledge discovery and data mining* (pp. 334-342). ACM.10.1145/2020408.2020464

Glooko. (2017). Available from: http://www.glooko.com/

Groves, P., Kayyali, B., Knott, D., & Kuiken, S. V. (2016). *The'bigdata'revolution in healthcare: Accelerating value and innovation.* McKinsey& Company.

Gupta, S., Kumar, D., & Sharma, A. (2011). Performance analysis of various data mining classification techniques on healthcare data. *International Journal of Computer Science & Information Technology, 3*(4).

Halevi, G., & Moed, H. (2012). The evolution of big data as a research and scientific topic: Overview of the literature. *Research Trends, 30*(1), 3–6.

Haller, S., Badoud, S., Nguyen, D., Garibotto, V., Lovblad, K. O., & Burkhard, P. R. (2012). Individual detection of patients with Parkinson disease using support vector machine analysis of diffusion tensor imaging data: Initial results. *American Journal of Neuroradiology, 33*(11), 2123–2128. doi:10.3174/ajnr.A3126 PMID:22653326

Harrison, V., Proudfoot, J., Wee, P. P., Parker, G., Pavlovic, D. H., & Manicavasagar, V. (2011). Mobile mental health: Review of the emerging field and proof of concept study. *Journal of Mental Health (Abingdon, England), 20*(6), 509–524. doi:10.3109/09638237.2011.608746 PMID:21988230

Haussleiter, I. S., Brüne, M., & Juckel, G. (2009). Psychopathology in multiple sclerosis: Diagnosis, prevalence and treatment. *Therapeutic Advances in Neurological Disorders, 2*(1), 13–29. doi:10.1177/1756285608100325 PMID:21180640

Hay, S. I., George, D. B., Moyes, C. L., & Brownstein, J. S. (2013). Big data opportunities for global infectious disease surveillance. *PLoS Medicine, 10*(4), e1001413. doi:10.1371/journal.pmed.1001413 PMID:23565065

HealthMap. (2017). Available from: http://healthmap.org/

Hill, S., Merchant, R., & Ungar, L. (2013). Lessons learned about public health from online crowd surveillance. *Big Data, 1*(3), 160–167. doi:10.1089/big.2013.0020 PMID:25045598

Hinton, G., Deng, L., Yu, D., Dahl, G. E., Mohamed, A. R., Jaitly, N., & Kingsbury, B. (2012). Deep neural networks for acoustic modeling in speech recognition: The shared views of four research groups. *IEEE Signal Processing Magazine, 29*(6), 82–97. doi:10.1109/MSP.2012.2205597

Howell, D. R. (2014). *An examination of motor and cognitive recovery following concussion* (Doctoral dissertation). University of Oregon.

Hsieh, C. J., Si, S., & Dhillon, I. (2014). A divide-and-conquer solver for kernel support vector machines. *International Conference on Machine Learning*, 566-574.

JawboneUp. (2017). Available from: https://jawbone.com/up

Jewell, D., Barros, R. D., Diederichs, S., Duijvestijn, L. M., Hammersley, M., Hazra, A., & Portilla, I. (2014). *Performance and capacity implications for big data*. IBM Redbooks.

Jokonya, O. (2014). Towards a Big Data Framework for the prevention and control of HIV/AIDS, TB and Silicosis in the mining industry. *Procedia Technology*, *16*, 1533–1541. doi:10.1016/j.protcy.2014.10.175

Kaisler, S., Armour, F., Espinosa, J. A., & Money, W. (2013). Big data: Issues and challenges moving forward. In *System Sciences (HICSS), 2013 46th Hawaii International Conference on* (pp. 995-1004). IEEE.

Kale, D. C., Gong, D., Che, Z., Liu, Y., Medioni, G., Wetzel, R., & Ross, P. (2014).An examination of multivariate time series hashing with applications to health care. In *Data Mining (ICDM), 2014 IEEE International Conference on* (pp. 260-269). IEEE. 10.1109/ICDM.2014.153

Kang, U., Tsourakakis, C. E., & Faloutsos, C. (2009).Pegasus: A peta-scale graph mining system implementation and observations. In *Data Mining, 2009.ICDM'09. Ninth IEEE International Conference on* (pp. 229-238). IEEE. 10.1109/ICDM.2009.14

Kashyap, H., Ahmed, H. A., Hoque, N., Roy, S., & Bhattacharyya, D. K. (2015). *Big data analytics in bioinformatics: A machine learning perspective.* arXiv preprint arXiv:1506.05101

Kum, H. C., Krishnamurthy, A., Machanavajjhala, A., Reiter, M. K., & Ahalt, S. (2014). Privacy preserving interactive record linkage (PPIRL). *Journal of the American Medical Informatics Association*, *21*(2), 212–220. doi:10.1136/amiajnl-2013-002165 PMID:24201028

Lane, J., Stodden, V., Bender, S., & Nissenbaum, H. (Eds.). (2014). *Privacy, big data, and the public good: Frameworks for engagement.* Cambridge University Press. doi:10.1017/CBO9781107590205

Laney, D. (2001). *3-d data management: Controlling data volume, velocity and variety.* META Group, Research Note, February 2001.

Lark. (2017). Available from: http://lark.com/

LaValle, S., Lesser, E., Shockley, R., Hopkins, M. S., & Kruschwitz, N. (2011). Big data, analytics and the path from insights to value. *MIT Sloan Management Review*, *52*(2), 21.

Lazer, D., Kennedy, R., King, G., & Vespignani, A. (2014). The parable of Google Flu: Traps in big data analysis. *Science*, *343*(6176), 1203–1205. doi:10.1126cience.1248506 PMID:24626916

Lee, C. H., & Yoon, H. J. (2017). Medical big data: Promise and challenges. *Kidney Research and Clinical Practice*, *36*(1), 3–11. doi:10.23876/j.krcp.2017.36.1.3 PMID:28392994

Lin, J., & Ryaboy, D. (2013). Scaling big data mining infrastructure: The twitter experience. *ACM SIG-KDD Explorations Newsletter, 14*(2), 6–19. doi:10.1145/2481244.2481247

Lomotey, R. K., & Deters, R. (2014). Towards knowledge discovery in big data. In *Service Oriented System Engineering (SOSE), 2014 IEEE 8th International Symposium on* (pp. 181-191). IEEE. 10.1109/SOSE.2014.25

Low, Y., Bickson, D., Gonzalez, J., Guestrin, C., Kyrola, A., & Hellerstein, J. M. (2012). Distributed GraphLab: A framework for machine learning and data mining in the cloud. *Proceedings of the VLDB Endowment International Conference on Very Large Data Bases, 5*(8), 716–727. doi:10.14778/2212351.2212354

Lyles, C. R., López, A., Pasick, R., & Sarkar, U. (2013). "5 mins of uncomfyness is better than dealing with cancer 4 a lifetime": An exploratory qualitative analysis of cervical and breast cancer screening dialogue on Twitter. *Journal of Cancer Education, 28*(1), 127–133. doi:10.100713187-012-0432-2 PMID:23132231

Manyika, J., Chui, M., Brown, B., Buhin, J., Dobbs, R., Roxburgh, C., & Byers, A. H. (2011). *Big Data: The Next Frontier for Innovation, Competition, and Productivity.* McKinsey Global Institute.

Mao, J. J., Chung, A., Benton, A., Hill, S., Ungar, L., Leonard, C. E., & Holmes, J. H. (2013). Online discussion of drug side effects and discontinuation among breast cancer survivors. *Pharmacoepidemiology and Drug Safety, 22*(3), 256–262. doi:10.1002/pds.3365 PMID:23322591

McCormick, T. (2012). *Video of my healthier information talk.* Available from: http://tjm.org/2012/04/17/videoof-my-healthier-information-talk/

McKenzie, J. F., Neiger, B. L., & Thackeray, R. (2016). *Planning, implementing & evaluating health promotion programs: A primer.* Pearson.

Michael, K., & Miller, K. W. (2013). Big data: New opportunities and new challenges. *Computer, 46*(6), 22–24. doi:10.1109/MC.2013.196

Miller, J. A., Oldham, M. C., & Geschwind, D. H. (2008). A systems level analysis of transcriptional changes in Alzheimer's disease and normal aging. *The Journal of Neuroscience, 28*(6), 1410–1420. doi:10.1523/JNEUROSCI.4098-07.2008 PMID:18256261

Mitchell, I., & Wilson, M. (2012). *Linked Data: Connecting and exploiting big data.* White paper. Fujitsu UK, 302.

Mukherjee, S., & Shaw, R. (2016). Big Data–Concepts, Applications, Challenges and Future Scope. *International Journal of Advanced Research in Computer and Communication Engineering, 5*(2).

Murdoch, T. B., & Detsky, A. S. (2013). The inevitable application of big data to health care. *Journal of the American Medical Association, 309*(13), 1351–1352. doi:10.1001/jama.2013.393 PMID:23549579

Nguyen, T., Khosravi, A., Creighton, D., & Nahavandi, S. (2015). Classification of healthcare data using genetic fuzzy logic system and wavelets. *Expert Systems with Applications, 42*(4), 2184–2197. doi:10.1016/j.eswa.2014.10.027

Niakšu, O., &Kurasova, O. (2012). Data mining applications in healthcare: research vs practice. *Databases Inform Syst Baltic DB&IS, 58.*

Nitrd, N. (2016). *The Federal Big Data Research and Development Strategic Plan.* Networking and Information Technology Research and Development.

Olsen, L., & McGinnis, J. M. (2010). *Evidence Development for Healthcare Decisions: Improving Timeliness.* Reliability, and Efficiency.

PatientsLikeMe. (2013). Available from: http://www.patientslikeme.com/

Patil, R. D., & Jadhav, O. S. (2016). Some Contribution of Statistical Techniques in Big Data: A Review. *International Journal on Recent and Innovation Trends in Computing and Communication, 4*(4), 293–303.

Paul, M. J., & Dredze, M. (2012). A model for mining public health topics from Twitter. *Health, 11,* 16–6.

Pulley, J. M., Denny, J. C., Peterson, J. F., Bernard, G. R., Vnencak-Jones, C. L., Ramirez, A. H., & Crawford, D. C. (2012). Operational implementation of prospective genotyping for personalized medicine: The design of the Vanderbilt PREDICT project. *Clinical Pharmacology and Therapeutics, 92*(1), 87–95. doi:10.1038/clpt.2011.371 PMID:22588608

Pyne, S., Rao, B. P., & Rao, S. B. (2016). Big Data Analytics: Views from Statistical and Computational Perspectives. In Big Data Analytics (pp. 1-10). Springer India.

Raghupathi, W., &Raghupathi, V. (2014). Big data analytics in healthcare: Promise and potential. *Health Information Science and Systems, 2*(1), 3.

Roney, K. (2012). *If Interoperability is the Future of Healthcare, What's the Delay. Becker's Hospital Review.*

Rumsfeld, J. S., Joynt, K. E., & Maddox, T. M. (2016). Big data analytics to improve cardiovascular care: Promise and challenges. *Nature Reviews. Cardiology, 13*(6), 350–359. doi:10.1038/nrcardio.2016.42 PMID:27009423

Russom, P. (2011). Big data analytics. *TDWI Best Practices Report, 19,* 40.

Sabia, S. K., & Kalra, S. (2014). Applications of big Data: Current Status and Future Scope. *SSN (Print), 3*(5), 2319–2526.

Sagiroglu, S., & Sinanc, D. (2013).Big data: A review. In *Collaboration Technologies and Systems (CTS), 2013 International Conference on* (pp. 42-47). IEEE. 10.1109/CTS.2013.6567202

Salathe, M., Bengtsson, L., Bodnar, T. J., Brewer, D. D., Brownstein, J. S., Buckee, C., & Vespignani, A. (2012). Digital epidemiology. *PLoS Computational Biology, 8*(7), e1002616. doi:10.1371/journal.pcbi.1002616 PMID:22844241

Savel, T. G., & Foldy, S. (2012). The role of public health informatics in enhancing public health surveillance. *MMWR. Surveillance Summaries, 61*(Suppl), 20–24. PMID:22832993

Scanfeld, D., Scanfeld, V., & Larson, E. L. (2010). Dissemination of health information through social networks: Twitter and antibiotics. *American Journal of Infection Control, 38*(3), 182–188. doi:10.1016/j. ajic.2009.11.004 PMID:20347636

Seifter, A., Schwarzwalder, A., Geis, K., & Aucott, J. (2010). The utility of "Google Trends" for epidemiological research: Lyme disease as an example. *Geospatial Health, 4*(2), 135–137. doi:10.4081/ gh.2010.195 PMID:20503183

Sharma, V., Joshi, N. K., & Manisha. (2015). Big Data Introduction, Importance and Current Perspective of Challenges. *International Journal of Advances in Engineering Science and Technology, 4*(3), 221–225.

Shivade, C., Raghavan, P., Fosler-Lussier, E., Embi, P. J., Elhadad, N., Johnson, S. B., & Lai, A. M. (2013). A review of approaches to identifying patient phenotype cohorts using electronic health records. *Journal of the American Medical Informatics Association, 21*(2), 221–230. doi:10.1136/amiajnl-2013-001935 PMID:24201027

Shoenbill, K., Fost, N., Tachinardi, U., & Mendonca, E. A. (2013). Genetic data and electronic health records: A discussion of ethical, logistical and technological considerations. *Journal of the American Medical Informatics Association, 21*(1), 171–180. doi:10.1136/amiajnl-2013-001694 PMID:23771953

Stone, M. L. (2014). *Big data for media. Reuters Institute For The Study Of Journalism.* University of Oxford.

Sullivan, S. J., Schneiders, A. G., Cheang, C. W., Kitto, E., Lee, H., & Redhead, J. (2011). What's happening? A content analysis of concussion-related traffic on twitter. *Br J Sports Med.* Available from: http://www.academia.edu/1037228/Whats_happening_A_content_analysis_of_concussion-related_traffic_on_Twitter

Swan, M. (2013). The quantified self: Fundamental disruption in big data science and biological discovery. *Big Data, 1*(2), 85–99. doi:10.1089/big.2012.0002 PMID:27442063

Szlezák, N., Evers, M., Wang, J., & Pérez, L. (2014). The role of big data and advanced analytics in drug discovery, development, and commercialization. *Clinical Pharmacology and Therapeutics, 95*(5), 492–495. doi:10.1038/clpt.2014.29 PMID:24642713

Talia, D. (2013). Clouds for scalable big data analytics. *Computer, 46*(5), 98–101. doi:10.1109/MC.2013.162

Tan, P. N., Steinbach, M., & Kumar, V. (2013). Data mining cluster analysis: basic concepts and algorithms. *Introduction to Data Mining.*

Tasse, D. (2012). *Quantifiedself 2012: Some cool things. Tales 'n' ideas.* Available from: http://talesnideas.blogspot.com/2012_09_01_archive.html

Tenenbaum, J. D., Sansone, S. A., & Haendel, M. (2013). A sea of standards for omics data: Sink or swim? *Journal of the American Medical Informatics Association, 21*(2), 200–203. doi:10.1136/amiajnl-2013-002066 PMID:24076747

Ularu, E. G., Puican, F. C., Apostu, A., & Velicanu, M. (2012). Perspectives on big data and big data analytics. *Database Systems Journal, 3*(4), 3–14.

Unit, E. I. (2012). The deciding factor: Big data &decision making. *Capgemini Reports*, 1-24.

Ventura, A., Koenitzer, M., Stein, P., Tufano, P., & Drummer, D. (2015).The Future of FinTech: A Paradigm Shift in Small Business Finance. *World Economic Forum, Global Agenda Council on the Future of Financing and Capital.*

Walker, S. (2014). *Big data: A revolution that will transform how we live, work, and think.* Academic Press.

West, R., White, R. W., & Horvitz, E. (2013). From cookies to cooks: Insights on dietary patterns via analysis of web usage logs. In *Proceedings of the 22nd international conference on World Wide Web* (pp. 1399-1410). ACM. 10.1145/2488388.2488510

White, R. W., Tatonetti, N. P., Shah, N. H., Altman, R. B., & Horvitz, E. (2013). Web-scale pharmacovigilance: Listening to signals from the crowd. *Journal of the American Medical Informatics Association, 20*(3), 404–408. doi:10.1136/amiajnl-2012-001482 PMID:23467469

Wolf, G. (2012). The data-driven life. *The New York Times* Available from: http://www.nytimes.com/2010/05/02/magazine/02self-measurement-t.html

Yau, N. (2011). A year of food consumption visualized. *FlowingData*. Available from: http://flowingdata.com/2011/06/29/a-year-of-food-consumption-visualized/

Yoo, C., Ramirez, L., & Liuzzi, J. (2014). Big data analysis using modern statistical and machine learning methods in medicine. *International Neurourology Journal, 18*(2), 50. doi:10.5213/inj.2014.18.2.50 PMID:24987556

Yu, L., Zheng, J., Shen, W. C., Wu, B., Wang, B., Qian, L., & Zhang, B. R. (2012). BC-PDM: data mining, social network analysis and text mining system based on cloud computing. In *Proceedings of the 18th ACM SIGKDD international conference on Knowledge discovery and data mining* (pp. 1496-1499). ACM. 10.1145/2339530.2339764

Zhang, B., Gaiteri, C., Bodea, L. G., Wang, Z., McElwee, J., Podtelezhnikov, A. A., & Fluder, E. (2013). Integrated systems approach identifies genetic nodes and networks in late-onset Alzheimer's disease. *Cell, 153*(3), 707–720. doi:10.1016/j.cell.2013.03.030 PMID:23622250

Zicari, R. V. (2014). Big data: Challenges and opportunities. *Big Data Computing, 564.*

This research was previously published in Big Data Analytics in HIV/AIDS Research; pages 81-116, copyright year 2018 by Medical Information Science Reference (an imprint of IGI Global).

Section 5
Organizational and Social Implications

Chapter 73
Big Data and IoT Applications in Real Life Environment

Anjali Chaudhary
Noida International University, India

Pradeep Tomar
 https://orcid.org/0000-0002-7565-0708
Gautam Buddha University, India

ABSTRACT

Big data and the Internet of Things (IoT) are the recent innovations in this era of smart world. Both of these technologies are proving very beneficial for today's fast-moving lifestyle. Both technologies are connected to each other and used together in many real-world applications. Big data and IoT have their uses and applications in almost every area from homes to industries, from agriculture to manufacturing, from transportation to warehousing, from food industries to entertainment industry, even from our shoe to robotics. This chapter discusses various applications of big data and IoT in detail and also discusses how both the technologies are affecting our daily life and how it can make things better.

INTRODUCTION

Nowadays human life is very much affected by scientific advancement; internet of things has a great role in making human life more comfortable and has potentials to provide a smart environment around by establishing communication between man, machines & objects or machine to machine transmission/communication. IoT symbolizes a system which comprises things in the material world where sensors dedicated to these IoT things that are connected to the internet in a network structure whether wired or wireless. IoT sensors can be connected by using various technologies like GPRS, RFID, Wi-Fi, GSM, Bluetooth, ZigBee, 3G, and LTE. IoT-empowered devices will share the info about the situation of the surroundings with persons, systems & other machines. IoT makes the world smarter in each aspect; IoT will lead to smart cities, smart homes, smart healthcare, smart transportation smart buildings, smart

DOI: 10.4018/978-1-6684-3662-2.ch073

energy management and smart waste management. Millions of dollars have been spending on research of IoT, worldwide.

In this era of digitization, the use of big data is not only to store massive amount of heterogeneous data but also it includes the analysis of the data which is commonly known as big data analytics. Big data can be beneficial for an organization in such a way that big data analytics uses different analytical and mining tool to extract useful information from the huge data which can be very useful for the progress of the organization (Mohsen et al, 2017; Kwon et al, 2014). In many domains big data has brought a tremendous change. The major goal of big data applications is to analyze the large data with the various tools and to help companies or organizations to predict what can happen in future and then take decisions according to the situations. Along with the private sectors public sectors are also benefited with big data. Big data applications store data by servers, internet click streams, social media mobile phone records, sensors, etc. Nowadays various domains are hiring big data analytics to analyze the big data to know the hidden pattern, risks, relations between data, customer choice or priority and much other business information.

IoT and big data are connected with each other. Even both the technologies have almost same applications. While we are using IoT devices and network everywhere in future world, the data that is produced by these sensors is heterogeneous big-data files required to be stored to process in future to predict potential solutions to modern world problems.

Government has also embraced the arena of "Big Data" and "Internet of Things" as a National Digital Mission to attain their aim to be a prominent country in the field of hyper connected domain with a promotional scheme of strengthening the affordability in software sensor devices; also providing training to produce specialists that will internalize security for IoT services and big data analytics so that data can be analyzed.

Some major applications of IoT and big data are explained in detail in this chapter that will help to learn the use of IoT and big data in real world.

Figure 1. Big Data applications

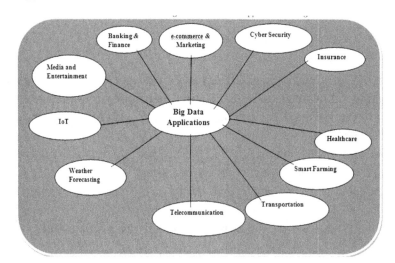

BIG DATA APPLICATIONS

Figure 1 represents various domains of big data.

Let us discuss various domains of big data applications:

Banking and Finance

Banking is the most prominent area which is benefited by data science or big data. Nowadays almost every person has bank account, and while someone opens his or her account bank demands a lot of information and thus this process produce a large amount of digital data that is big data. The aim of banks is not only to store this data but also to analyze the data. This big unstructured and heterogeneous data can be analyzed using several techniques and very useful information can be extracted as per the need of the bank. Big data is also useful in financial market as it can be used to track illegal trading activities. But keeping the records of customers safe is the most concern as distributing data among various departments and applying analytics techniques makes data more prone to leak or breach (Sravanthi & Reddy, 2015).

Some common actions which can be taken by banks using big data can be concluded as follows:

- **Fraud Detection:** Using big data analytics and machine learning banks and financial firms can differentiate between a normal and abnormal transaction based on the historical statistics of a customer. For example, if some unusual high transaction occurs from a customer's account and if bank's fraud detection system analyzes it, immediately transaction can be abort until customer verifies it.
- **Regular Monitoring:** Financial firms perform regular monitoring of the financial activities for example shares and stocks and they are also supposed to maintain report of the data. Moreover, with the help of data a pattern for example closing, lows or high stocks or shares within a period of time can be identified. This analysis can be useful in prediction and can reduce various financial risks.
- **Customer Division & Personalized Marketing:** Customer segmentation is to divide customers into different sets depending on their age, income, region, online transactions, and frequency of transactions. This type of segmentation is to understand the customers which can definitely improve promotions and marketing campaigns since we can know which type of promotions and marketing campaigns is needed for which segment of customer.
- **Risk Management:** Financial firms are always critical to various types of risks for example credit risk, market risk, operational risk, liquidity risk, reputational risk etc. Risks can be monitored and controlled using the analysis of data.
- **Customer Support:** For any type of organization the key of success is excellent customer support. Data science makes this process better automated, more accurate, personal, direct, and productive, and less costly concerning employee time.
- **Life Time Value Prediction:** Big data helps to predict or determine the future marketing strategies based on user data, it also helps to maintain good customer relations during each customer's lifetime which gives opportunity of growth and profit.

Electronic: Commerce and Marketing

Buying or selling things electronically is a very common trend nowadays due to the easy availability of internet and electronic devices for example smart phones and laptops. The large volume data that is produced during e-commerce acting a very important role in determining, assessing the interest of the customers. This data is analyzed using analytical tools and provide very meaningful information about what customer wants and thus improves business strategy.

Social media analytics that is analysis of data produced by social sites playing an acute role in the growth of e-commerce. Social media is such type of platform where users interact and exchange views with each other and affects each other thus can influence a brand. E- Commerce vendors uses social media analytics to gain knowledge about what people talking about, what are their likes and opinions. Using this data vendors advertise their product accordingly and enhance the business.

Real life examples of E-commerce business are Amazon, Myntra, Jabong, etc. These shopping websites analyzes cookies (a text piece, stored by web server in user's hard disk) to identify either the customer has visited website before or he/she is an existing customer, number of customers who visited the website, the frequency of a customer to visit the website, to identify the preferences of the customer. Moreover, cookies are helpful to track what customer has in her/his bag. So, by using such type of information it can be easily identified what a customer is browsing, what are his/her preferences, etc., and thus a better service and advertising policy can be made Edosio, 2014).

Many industries are now adopting big data analytics to optimize their profit and to achieve their goals. Data analysis helps industrialists to take decisions. It saves time and money. Data analytics helps marketers to investigate valuable customers. Digital customers keep producing lots of data with each click by using mobile phones, laptops and internet. This information can cultivate very useful information to improve the manufacturing process, can be helpful to predict failures, and also can be helpful to analyze right time to launch a product.

Big data analytics can also work as predictive insight which can be useful to predict demand of a particular product. This will directly impact to transportation and logistics industries (Elgendy & Elragal, 2014).

Cyber Security

Easy availability and accessibility of internet has made our life easier but on the other hand it brought a lot of cyberattacks. There are many cyber security solutions available but due to the production of large amount of data over internet that is increasing day by day than before solely traditional cyber security solutions are not feasible. To solve this problem cyber security analytics comes into the picture that is analyzing the data present on network.

Combination of traditional cyber security solutions and big data tools has given birth to the term 'Big Data Cybersecurity Analytics' that is the analysis of massive amount of data collected from various sources for example social sites, clouds, servers, databases, networks, firewalls, applications etc.

Big data cyber security analytics system of a particular company or organization monitors the activities of the concerned people of the company and other details like IP addresses to which or from they communicate. This analysis gives a pattern usage network. For instance, if an IP address is found that is trying to connect with the company server that IP ca n be considered suspicious and appropriate action can be taken (Mahmood & Afzal, 2013)·

Insurance

Data is a centric part of insurance company. Data has always been advantageous for the insurers as insurers analyze the data to give more profit and policies to the customer, identify and remove the risks, and make financial model which can ensure growth. But in this era of digitization the nature of data has been changed. Data is now large in volume then before, it is heterogeneous and increases rapidly. In older days the only method for the insurance agents was to meet their customers personally but nowadays, agents use real time methods to collect information about the customer, for example real-time climate feeds, geospatial data, public records, social media, cookies and click streams along with the traditional structured data. With the help of analytical tools this data can be analyzed and more precise information can be gathered from this massive data, which can be helpful to mitigate risk, to generate more detailed reports, more satisfied users and business enhancement.

Some common actions which can be taken by insurance companies using big data can be concluded as follows:

- **Risk or threat Assessment:** The primary concern of insurers is to determine the policy premium. When a customer comes to the insurance company, before giving insurance insurers want to know what the adverse things possible with the customer for which customer wants to make a claim. Big data makes this task of policy setting easier as it provides a lot of data of the customer. For example, if a customer wants an insurance for a car then insurance company can analyze that in which areas car travels most, how much that area is vulnerable to the road accidents and damage etc. So, keeping all these points in mind insurance company can decide the policy premium without any losses.
- **Fraud Detection:** fraudulency is a very common practice in insurance. It is undesirable for the insurers. Big data can help in this case in a very broad way. For example, if a customer demands an insurance, company can check the post claims of the person and can predict the probability of fraud and can take appropriate action.
- **Gaining satisfied customers:** With the use of big data in insurance, information about a customer can be collected from different sources. This data can be helpful to predict which policy would be most beneficial for the customer, and policy agents would be able to give more satisfied answers to the customers because they know the history (policies held by the customer, earning, etc.) and requirement of the customer in advance. Thus in this way big data can help insurance agencies to meet their objectives because more satisfied users leads to more profit for an organization.
- **Marketing:** After analyzing the customer data insurance agents can understand what exactly customer need and can suggest appropriate services or product. Moreover, agents can give special offers to the customer according to the circumstances (home. Health, vehicle insurance).
- **Smarter Work and Finance:** With the advance use of big data, machine learning, and data mining insurers can save his/her time and can prioritize policies according to the customer.

Healthcare

Big data is a technical sensation nowadays. Even healthcare sector is not untouched with big data. Nowadays hospitals maintain the patients record electronically, and by using analytics tools desired information can be extracted. Hospitals can collect massive amount of unstructured and different data from different sources like patient health record, test result, electronic medical equipment, social media, health insurance data, drug research, genome research, clinical outcome, transaction. Data analytics can manage this data using analytics tool and can extract meaningful information (Ojha & Mathur, 2016).

One of the favorable areas where big data can be useful is healthcare. Many countries are also using big data in this area to make the things easier. Since healthcare professionals also produces lots of data on daily basis this data can be helpful in various ways. Even some of the countries have also been adopted big data in health sector.

Few hospitals in Paris are analyzing data gathered from different sources and predict number of customers on daily and hourly interval. This solves the problem of staff size. By predicting number of customers in advance staff size can be increased or decreased which is beneficial for both patients as it optimizes the service and for the management as it can reduce the cost.

Moreover, data scientists are working on "time series analysis technique" in which old record of patient admission is analyzed and patient rate can be predicted in different weathers. Using machine algorithm an algorithm can be made which can forecast future admission patterns.

The next application which is using big data is Electronic Health Record (EHR). US has installed EHR in about 90 percent hospitals, however many countries are struggling for this. EHR is a digitized collection of patients. It contains all the information about a customer for example medical history, allergies detail, medication, age, weight, lab test details etc. details of EHR can be shared among healthcare. One modifiable file is also attached along with the record, this file can be modified by the doctor. Thus, EHR reduces the paper work and gives correct and unambiguous detail of a patient.

America and Canada used big data analytics to tackle the problem of misused opioids. With the help of big data, information about chronic disease and population can be gathered. It can also be predicted which region don't have sufficient health facility. Big data can also help to bio researchers to study about chronic diseases for example cancer, tumors etc. Researchers can study tumor samples stored in bio banks linked with patient treatment records. This research can give unexpected results.

Smart Farming

Big data is playing a very important role in smart farming. Smart farming is a phenomenon which uses IoT, Cloud Computing and AI in farming. These all technologies are surrounded by big data as smart farming uses smart devices, which are basically an extension of traditional devices with sensors and intelligence. Machine sensors can collect various type of data like temperature, water levels of a particular area, historical weather, soil and water consumption, growth, gene sequencing of a particular plant and this information can be used to know desired conditions for a particular plant (Wolfert, Ge, Verdouw et al., 2015). Moreover, this information can help to predict feasible amount of fertilizers and seeds for a crop.

Not only traditional area of farming even livestock economy is also affected by digitization. Livestock plays a very important role in the economy. It is a great source of milk, meat, eggs which gives employment to many people. Sensors and robots are being used in a very smart way (Schönfeld, Heil & Bittner (2017).

A smart farm uses GPS to collect information about a particular region or the position of the animals in the farm. This data is fed in to the computers and based on the data and programs computer analyze what should be the feasible composition of seeds and fertilizers for a specific area. Even researchers are doing research on robots that can maintain the farms and can take decisions (Schönfeld, Heil & Bittner, 2017) Drones are also being used for the surveillance of the farm. Drones are used to take images to gather data about the field. This data (Collected by the drones) and sensors help to gain information for example to create digital map of a specific area (Schönfeld, Heil & Bittner, 2017).

Big data is helpful in farm animals too. Microchips and sensors can be put in the collars of the animals which can measure the temperature and other important data. Analysis of data can be helpful in regular monitoring of the animals. Farmers and doctors can be notified for the same (Schönfeld, Heil & Bittner, 2017; Poppe, Wolfert & Verdouw, 2015).

Transportation

In transportation big data brought lots of possibilities by which we can make our transportation system as smart transportation system which will be efficient to solve many problems we face in our daily routine. A smart transportation system is a system which contains information about accidents, road congestion and route suggestions.

A smart transportation system collects a large amount of data from social signals, drivers' GPS coordinates, mobile phones' billing records to messages post on social media, record spatial, temporal and emotional information and establish the data foundation for social transportation research (Zheng, Chen, Wang et al., 2015; Wang, 2014). For example, if we talk about social signals, people are very active on social sites e.g.: Facebook, Twitter, etc. it is a virtual community where people keep sharing their location, information about accidents, traffic congestion, this data works as an input data to the smart transportation system. Many applications using this data for example the Waze app, which is a GPS navigation app, works on smartphones and tablets. Another example of SMT is Google map which takes data from the sensors and uses GPS coordinators to guide the user for the destination, also suggest path which leads to minimum traffic and helps passenger to reach the destination in minimum time. Moreover, while we travel in public transport for example metro millions of passengers daily generate massive amount of data by using cards. These social signals record temporal information of passengers is being used by the researchers to optimize transportation system (Zheng, Chen, Wang et al., 2015). With the help of big data government can understand the need of the people and can map the route accordingly. Government can use this data to identify which type of transportation can make people life simpler, number of buses or trains for a route and the size of the vehicle. By analyzing the data collected by the sensors (implemented in the vehicles) it can be predicted in advance which part of the vehicle need maintenance before the failure of the part. It is also beneficial for the safety of the passengers. Many private transportation industries for example uber, Ola are also based on big data. These industries maintain the database of all the drivers of all the covered cities, and when a passenger asks for a ride they provide a driver after analyzing the database. With the help of data collected by sensors and GPS fare is calculated.

Telecommunication

In the telecommunication sector, big data is helping operators in a very broad way. Using big data analytics operators can understand the demand of the customers and can get more satisfied users and with a big profit. Because of internet and mobile devices telecommunication sector need to store various type of information in bulk which keeps changing rapidly. Telecommunication sector collets a big amount of data such as call detail, user online data usage, user location data, network performance data, server log data, billing data etc.

Figure 2. Big Data in telecommunication

The analysis of data can help operators in different ways, for example operators can examine a new plan that how much it is being liked by the customers and hence they can get more satisfied users, fault detection can be done before failure, they can predict how much bandwidth is needed in advance, they can identify the problems of customers and can resolve them and even they can give more secured network to their customers (Su & Peng, 2016) Figure 2 represents how big data can be useful in telecommunication sector.

Media and Entertainment

For media and entertainment companies, big data has been proven as an asset to attract more and more customers and producing more revenue. Companies are analyzing the data collected from various sources to identify what customer need what for example music, video, sows etc. moreover it can also be predicted what is the favorable time for a show. Media is adopting big data in a very broad way because big data has given an opportunity to media market for digital revolution as big data analysis gave the opportunity to use data not even within the organization but also from outside the organization (Lippell, 2016). Now media owners know what their customers want more precisely than before.

Media companies which are using big data are more capable in marketing or publishing their content more intelligently (Lippell, 2016). Many companies, for example, Netflix, Amazon, etc., use big data to understand their customers more precisely.

IoT

IoT, the Internet of Things, is a network of smart devices which can interact with each other without human interaction. Smart city and smart home are prominent applications of IoT. A city becomes smart when it has smart workplaces, smart farming, smart banking, smart transportation, smart cultivation and smart energy, etc., (Al Nuaimi, Al Neyadi, Mohamed et al, 2015; Gubbi, Buyya, Marusic et al., 2013) and a home becomes smart when it has smart devices like sensors which are able to communicate. Big data and IoT can be thought as two sides of a coin. Big data and IoT both are affecting all the fields of technologies and providing large scope and opportunity of growth. Due to the increased use of IoT the use of big data has also grown, as sensors collect and deal with the data by taking input data from other sensors and at the same time by providing input to other sensors in the IoT environment. By analyzing this huge amount of data organizations and individuals may get more profit by taking right decisions on right time.

Figure 3. Relationship between Big Data and IoT

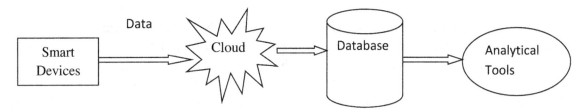

In figure 3 (Marjani, Nasaruddin, Gani et al., 2017) the relationship between big data and IoT is shown. This figure can be partitioned into three parts; first part depicts the communication between smart sensor devices such as CCTV cameras, smart traffic lights, and smart home devices etc. This data can be stored on cloud which is big and heterogeneous and increases rapidly. In second part this huge data known as big data is stored in big data files in shared distributed fault- tolerant databases. In last part comprises analytics tool which can analyze the data generated due to IoT (Marjani, Nasaruddin, Gani et al., 2017).

Weather Forecasting

Predicting weather has always been a tough task. Scientist is trying hard to predict it. Since, to predict whether it is important to analyze data becomes very advantageous for weather forecasting. So it will be useful for saving lives, improving the quality of life, reducing risks, enhancing profitability and humanity. Some examples of these domains include Forecasting Solar Power for Utility Operations, large-scale crop production forecasts for global food security (Jain & Jain, 2017). Example: IBM's Deep Thunder was developed by IBM which forecast the weather for a specific location and identifies how weather will influence the people and communications there. It is focused on much more short-term forecasts. Deep Thunder was used during the 1996 Atlanta Olympic Games to precisely forecast that there would be no rain during the closing ceremony. It was also used for the 2016 Summer Olympics in Rio de Janeiro. To predict the weather deep thunder takes data from public satellites, historic statistic data and many other private sources as well as local sensors and data a location may have.

APPLICATIONS OF IOT

IoT in Homes

Smart Homes is a technology that was started decades back by introducing the idea of interacting devices and networking equipment in the houses. The best description of smart homes is: the combination of technology and amenities in home network for an enhanced quality of existence. Most of the equipment that are commonly used in computer can also be assimilated in Smart Homes. In this topic, we will study the tools & Technologies that can be applied in Smart Home structures.

Smart Home Systems

Smart home is the phenomena generally used to describe a home that uses a home automation controller system. Generally, most prevalent home controller systems are connected to a computer system all through program design only, and left to accomplish the home controller system responsibilities unconnected. Assimilating the home controller system devices permits them to interconnect with each other via the controller system, thus empowering one single particular button and speech controller of the different controller systems all together, in already programmed set-ups or operational modes. This field is escalating promptly as electronic tools unite.

Smart Home Technology

PCS technology (Powerline Carrier Systems) is used to send signals in a home controller system's electrical system to programmed outlets (Robles & Kim, 2010). These signals commands those connected devices how to operate corresponding to that location. PCS transmitter send the signal via home connections and the receiver device plugged in home will receive that signal and then perform the required operation on the appliances plugged with it. PCS has a common protocol X10 to control remotely plugged device by using short radio frequency. European countries use *InstaBus* to install home controller devices. This control protocol consists of a 2-wire bus line installed with normal wiring system which connects all appliances in the home to a decentralized transmission system and operates as an old telephone line system which in turns controls all the appliances. Except these other technologies are also present like Z-wave, ZigBee, insteon, etc. In smart home automation technology commonly connected appliances and some famous services of IoT are controlling curtains, garage shutters, kitchen appliances, garden sprinkles, managing lighting, security, eCAMs, etc.

Installation of Home Automation System

- Manufacturers and industries have produced various smart home appliances with systems like X10, Z-wave, Zig Bee etc. some illustrations of smart home appliances are presented here for better understanding of the topic.
- E-CAM that can capture pictures of exterior of home even at night.
- Motion sensors that can sense movement around home and that can differentiate between pets and burglars.
- Video doorbell in which your visitors can be checked before opening the door.
- Door locks with code or door handles with fingerprint sensors.
- Smart equipment to make physically handicapped people's life easy.

The requirements for smart home controller technologies: smart home networks must have provision for varied technologies to be able to run several services simultaneously. The server installed for home network is the soul of the Network that supports most of the applications. Third party services run on a distinct virtual machine (VM) that is connected to the server with the help of a typical interface. Some other server attributes that have to be considered are security& safety, maintenance and its ability to upgrade (Das, 2013).

Some noticeable features of home servers are the following:

- IP set-top box and servers have a virtualized design.
- Operating system used is Linux.
- Virtual Machines are focused on the top most layer of Linux.
- Virtual Machines construction is done in Security Layer according to the service application it runs.
- Virtual machines are isolated by the Security Layer that is built on Fuzzy Logic.

IoT in Transportation

Transportation is essential for the relocation of goods, animals and, humans; for transportation various kind of vehicles and modes are used by humans. A manageable and ecological transportation system permits fundamental and development requirements of public and societies to be met. Therefore, the interest of public in internet of things (IoT) potential is growing to see potential changes in transportation. The approach of internet of things in the form of connected appliances, devices and new technologies emerging rapidly signifies the emerging hyper-connected world. With the help of IoT we can modifies the advantages of steady internet to constantly connected controlled remote devices and goods in real world. IoT makes everything in this world accessible and connected with wireless sensors to make transportation more convenient for everybody even for physically challenged peoples. Government division of transportation plays a pivot role to implement up-to-date and well equipped, IoT enabled mode of transportation and to make it available to public instead of regular public transport. In this topic we will see what benefits can be there by adopting new technologies in transportation; the problem here is: "What would be the part of IoT in attaining feasibility in transportation supervision and control." The aim of IoT in transportation would be:

- To recognize the areas where we can apply IoT in the field of transportation.
- To identify the probable contribution of IoT to be applied in transport management.

The domains recognized for IoT enabled transportation were highway network regulation, road safety, aeronautics management, traffic supervision, naval facilities, and train services. These domains are further divided into sub domains to ease the administration of transport department (NomusaDlodlo, 2015). Here we have included some diagrams to make things clear.

In route network management, some sub domains have to be considered as shown in figure 4 like roadway management, quick reaction to emergency, observing and managing of road conditions etc. highways and route network is the most important resources in the development of any country. Roadways management or footpath management is the policy of maintaining and repairing the paved facilities and enforcing laws for the safety of public. IoT enabled small electric vehicles with the help of GPS system can help in route network management; it will collect data about the road conditions and will send the data directly to the maintenance department.

In road security management, important sub domains to be considered as shown in figure 5 are security awareness, load bearing capacity of roads and bridges, importance of traffic rules and regulations, control on speed of vehicles and pollution. Road security generally refers to various measures that ensure safety of public travelling on roads and highways including pedestrians, animals, cyclists, bikers, private vehicles, commercial vehicles and public transport. Visibility on roads is sometimes not clear, may be because of bad lighting, dark, bad weather; in that case IoT can help in detecting other vehicles and pedestrians on roads with the help of sensors. IoT enabled devices can also help in controlling "drink and drive cases" with help of the equipment that can detect alcohol in blood. IoT devices can also detect the speed of the moving vehicles that help police in managing over speed traffic in roads; that will also reduce road accident cases. IoT enabled devices also help in calculating the load bearing capacity of any road, bridge, train rails and infrastructure of subways, over crossing buildings. These sensors can generate early warning about changing potential conditions or about the need of repair, renovation and inspection. IoT enabled vehicles can generate alarm for the need of engine, fuel and other maintenance issues. Emergency sensors will automatically send emergency call and data directly to the help centre instead of manually calling for help; this will reduce the risk of sudden engine failure on highway.

IoT is helpful in traffic management also. Sub-domains of road traffic management are shown in figure 6. IoT is helpful in accident investigation, road networking policing, communications and route management etc.

Figure 4. Sub-domains of route network management

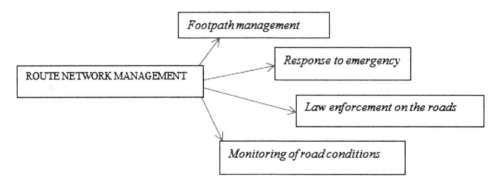

Figure 5. Sub-domains of road security management

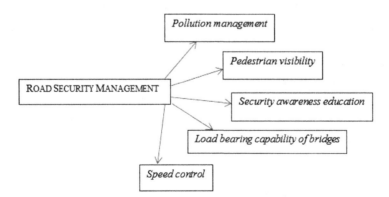

Figure 6. Sub-domains of road traffic management

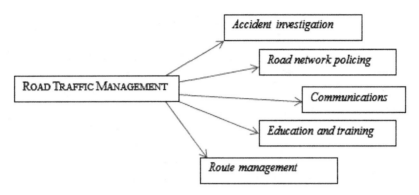

Similarly, in the aircraft management and marine vehicles management as shown in figure 7 and figure 8 IoT devices can help in security, tracing and managing the movement of aircraft and ships. Database management and wireless communication is used to trace and rescue of any lost ship with the help of GPS & GIS enabled vehicles in ocean. To make the safety inspection effective and efficient metal detectors and sensors are used for Safety at port and airports as well as parking of airplanes and ships can be easily managed with the help of IoT devices. Passengers can check their schedule on their smart phones and laptops; Google also provide 3D simulation of flight; *Google Earth Flight Simulators*, passengers can feel the experience of flight while sitting in their living rooms. IoT enabled devices also help in monitoring the weather to avoid any unfortunate incident, collisions or mishaps during air travel and in the ocean. Pollution in oceans can be traced and managed with the sensors that can detect their surrounding objects, oil spills, seepages; garbage dumping etc. that data will be stored and used in pollution control as well as in Collison control.

Figure 7. Sub-domains of aviation management

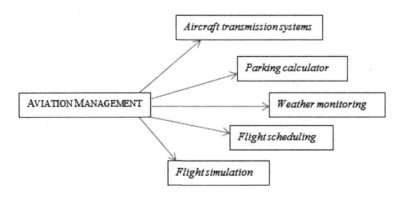

Figure 8. Sub-domains of maritime services management

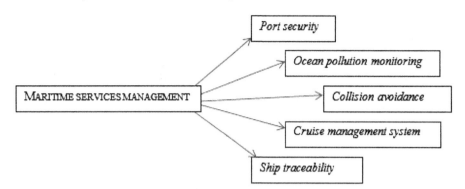

IoT in Agriculture: Smart Agriculture

Farming till now is done by mundane, manual ways in India. Most of the farmers do not have proper knowledge about the modern methods. A huge percentage of agricultural activities depend on the predictions, due to this Farmers generally bear enormous losses and their loss forces them to commit suicide. Since it is known that benefits of appropriate soil moisture, irrigation etc.; these parameters can't be overlooked while growing harvests.

Therefore, in this topic we will study about the new ideas of monitoring the crops and uses of IoT in agribusiness; it will provide reliability &distant monitoring. Digitalizing agricultural activities enable farmers to check the requirements of their harvest and precisely predict growth of their crops. This notion of IoT in agriculture will certainly speed up the agribusiness to attain new heights; its success basically depends on the responsiveness and attentiveness among farmers.

Internet of things is the term that refers to a world where every object is connected with every other objects of our daily use; every machine transmit data continuously just like man to man communication. Similarly, agriculture appliances and tools can also be connected via IoT, various sensors like temperature sensor, crop quality checking tools; humidity sensors etc. can be installed in fields to collect the data to be processed and to send recommendation to the farmers so that their harvest growth can be improved. Every sensor sends data after a particular time interval to the IoT based server where this data is examined by agriculture experts and scientists; for e.g. soil sensor collects data about the soil conditions on a regular basis in every season, with the help of this data experts calculates the effect on nutrients in soil, humidity variance in soil, pesticides effects etc. which help scientists to make decisions. Similarly, other sensors and appliances sends their data, various information was then combined into one database set, this database is processed using machine learning techniques by the IoT based agriculture expert systems. Different IoT expert systems have been generated for rabbi crops, kharif crops and other various crops based on their required conditions for growth; like wheat crop require different condition than sugarcane, rice paddy require different condition than Aloe-Vera plant. All IoT based agriculture expert systems generally works on some common modules as discussed here moreover communication among these modules is shown in figure 9 (Shahzadi, Ferzund, Tausif et al., 2016):

- User interface
- Knowledge base

- Storage memory
- Trained algorithms
- Database set

Recommendations are sending to the farmers on their mobile phones for the accessibility of uneducated farmers; some android applications are also developed for the use of farmers in various local languages. The server sends the predicted results to the farmers in their convenient languages.

Figure 9. Various parameters of smart agriculture

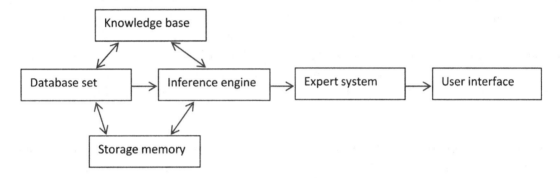

IoT in Healthcare

Real-time monitoring of health for elderly people provides improved life care in countryside areas. This technology was used to cut down the cost of treatment for population; this will improve the life quality of aged population living hood. Implanted sensors collect the data for detecting the ups and downs in individual's health. Recognizing the problematic changes in beginning phase will makes the cure easy comparatively. This technology is more useful for citizens above 60 years; this technology ensures consistent and healthy aging. This method is for monitoring pulse and body temperature of the patient regularly for self-regulating living.

IoT enabled devices are used to generate, assemble, compile and then for uploading the code for input from the installed sensors, sending data to server & storing and for connecting the hardware devices to internet. Whenever the nursing staff clicks the button on webpage then a query is triggered, and a request for data will be directed to the Server via internet, System there get that request and establish a connection to webpage of user, and instantly start collecting data from the assimilated sensors, the data collected is sent to server over the internet. This information will be shown on webpage after every 5 sec the data is updated and shown in a bar graph to make it easy to read. These embedded sensors help in monitoring the patient from home for gathering data about changes in his health condition (Kumar & Prabu, 2016). This calculation helps in capturing real-time health pattern. These results are shown to the experts who are helpful for medical examiners and the IoT system delivers spontaneous health alerts to recognize various health issues in the beginning phase for the potential treatment. This technology is very useful in monitoring patients with IoT enabled devices especially in those rural areas where the doctor cannot be available physically. Doctor can easily analyze patient continuously using web browser, moreover the biggest advantage of IoT devices is that it makes the treatment cost effective and also diminish casualties.

IoT devices has made senior citizens life better while it has also improved the living conditions of physically & mentally challenged people. Nowadays, we see so advanced devices like smart watches which keep track of individuals heart rate, calories burned, distance covered walking, body temperature etc. some small IoT devices used by patients at their homes to keep a check on their blood pressure, blood sugar, cholesterol. Earlier patients have to visit hospitals and labs for every small test but now most of the thing are available at the comfort of their home. Except these small devices there are some major appliances or tools; you can say, that help physically challenged person. Artificial body parts which are developed with the help of these IoT appliances, successfully gave a new life to many people. New modern IoT enabled wheel chairs which the patient himself or herself operate, made the movement of bed-ridden individual life beautiful and easy. Not just humans, animals are also getting advantage of IoT technology, veterinary scientist and experts has worked a lot to provide better treatment to their patients; as a result now artificial legs for animals taking the market to sky high. IoT Embedded sensors can also be very beneficial in keeping track of wild animal in wild life reserves and bird sanctuaries; tracking the movement of birds, animals and the tourist will be very useful in avoiding any life threating danger for both animals as well as humans.

Not only healthcare sector but the insurance sector is also not untouched by IoT, and are also getting benefits of the internet of things; although the use of IoT in insurance sector is not as much as in healthcare sector. The database that is generate by smart homes, smart vehicles, smart home and garden appliances, smart watches, smart medical equipment will be used by the insurance companies to check the health risk, vehicles breakdown risk, appliances failure risk etc. before ensuring the demanded insured amount. In the USA an insurance company uses a special IoT technique known as uses-based-insurance (UBI) to monitor how the customer drives its vehicle. With the help of machine learning and data analytics, the insurer can efficiently judge a driver's performance on each of his journey. This technique ensures a more accurate price to all individuals and this also boots safe driving with bargain premiums. Till now the organization has done 1.7 trillion observations of drivers based on this technique rather than traditional factors.

The participation of Internet of Things in insurance industry will propagate now as insurers are becoming more technically adequate, with this technology insurers will be having a huge amount of data to cope with. Insurers are looking forward to leveraging this money to expand their business by rewarding their customers believed to be better and safe than others. The future is possibly be affected by increasing machine-to-machine transmission network, artificial intelligence, data analysis and cloud computing, with various algorithms shaping our activities and actions.

IoT in Industries

Industrial IoT is a term which refers to the coming era of industrial uprising, also known as "industry 4.0." Industrial IoT has more sounding potential of proficiencies over automation, connectivity and analytics. Concentration of industrial IoT is on those sectors where the use of IoT can increase the production and take the business forward in a more efficient way. Some industries which are using IoT are related to agriculture, logistic, production, construction, manufacturing, engineering, supply and mining, airbus, warehousing, robotics etc. *Digitally connected factories:* IoT enabled machine transmits operative data to the company associates and field engineers about original equipment and producers. This technique enables process managers and industrial unit heads to distantly monitor the manufacturing and enable them to yield benefits of development automation, mechanization and optimization. Along with it, a digitally linked division establishes better commands and categorizes key result zones.

Managing flow of manufacture: IoT in production enables managers to monitor the production process initially from refining method to packaging ultimate goods. This whole monitoring process in real world offers prospect to end or reduce alterations in procedures for improved supervision of operational expenses. Additionally, this kind of close supervision enables managers to overcome lags in manufacture, eliminating excessive workload in progress. *Security and safety in factories*: IoT with data analysis improves the safety of the workers in organization. By supervising Key Indicators of health and safety, like the frequency of getting injured, near-misses, illness, type of illness, absences, vehicle accidents, property loss or any other loss during working hours; because operational supervision ensures enhanced safety methods. IoT indicators and sensors ensure proper well-being, protection, and surroundings issues. Industrial IoT is also useful in getting information about real time supply and tracking goods. This technique enables manufacturers and other parties associated with the organization to keep track of interdependencies, production cycle time, delivery time, goods flow and other data. This data is very helpful for managers, manufacturers, cuts prediction issues, & reduces capital requirements.

Quality controller: IoT sensors gather goods data and third-party information of various phases in a production cycle. This information checked in alignment of raw material, employee's working environment, temperature and trashes, transportation etc. on the finalized goods. Besides, IoT devices make information available about the client sentiments after using company goods. Later, all this information is analyzed for detection and correction of quality concerns. *Capacity management:* IoT devices and sensors in engineering equipment permits maintenance alerts based on situations. Now-a-days many vital IoT machines specifically developed to operate in specific temperature and trembling ranges. IoT Sensors efficiently observe these IoT enabled machines and send warning when the installed tools & equipment differs from pre-set parameters. IoT also helpful in reducing cost, saving energy, eliminating downtime of machines and for increasing working efficiency. As more and more consumers are shifting to online shopping now days, E-commerce is also getting benefited by IoT. 60-70% of the sellers have opted for IoT to improve their customer shopping experience. Latest IoT devices have captured the market for e.g. smart mirrors in stores for trial of dresses virtually; that means anybody can try different clothes virtually without actually wearing those clothes. Amazon has opted for a new IoT technique which allows users to reorder their desired items with just a click; IoT has entirely changed the shopping experience.

IoT in City Administration

With emerging technology of IoT homes, vehicles, medical facilities, retail, industries have already opted for latest IoT technologies and it's time to change cities into smart cities. A smart city is the municipal area that has various technologies, devices and sensors for collecting electronic data to stream info that can be used to manage resources efficiently. This data collection is done from various devices, citizens and resources. This info is processed and examined to monitor public transport, water supply network, power plants & industries, waste management, law implementation, universities, schools, public library, medical facilities etc. The concept of smart cities incorporates info and transmission technology, various other physical devices are also linked to the IoT network to enhance the productivity of city services which connect the citizens. This expertise permits city bureaucrats to interrelate directly with the community for monitoring how the development of the city is progressing. IoT technique is used to improve the worth, performance and inter-mutuality of the services in urban area, to lessen the costs and the consumption of various resources and for increasing the interaction between the government and the citizens. So, smart cities must be more equipped to handle the challenges.

Currently, so many initiatory moves have been intended at investigating the beginning procedure, positioning approaches or consequences of Smart City ventures with the help of IoT network; established in numerous areas. Since its beginning, Smart City concept has progressed from the implementation of some specific missions to the execution of worldwide stratagems to tackle varied city disputes and defiance. Any Smart City should respond to the actual challenges of the cities in 21st century; like availability of parking space, monitoring traffic, controlling pollution, reducing crime rate, better administration within city and improved public transportation, medical and other basic facilities etc. it offers a wide-ranging outline of the accessible opportunities. Initiatives in this direction will be offered for establishing relations among the 'known city challenges' & 'actual solutions' provided by IoT network to support smart city venture. A Project Escort has established for the execution of Smart City ventures that professionally handle various complex urban problems without bargaining their progress as well as improving life quality of citizens. The objectives of smart city ventures are (Monzon, 2015):

- To outline the concept of smart city with the help of IoT devices and to find out how this project can help in achieving urban development main concerns.
- To establish a procedure to evaluate and prioritize better economy and flexible governance in these Smart City ventures.
- To set guidelines for implementing and managing environmental conditions and affordable housing in Smart Cities.
- To improve unemployment and exchangeability strategies for Smart Cities.

Problems in today's metropolitan cities specifically in Asian cities are categories in six major sections namely administration of the city, economy, transportation, environmental conditions, population and living conditions which are further explained with sub sections for better understanding; that are shown here in a table. In spite of the IoT technologies discussed above in this chapter like smart homes, smart transportation, smart industries etc. IoT can help in reducing the challenges which are discussed in the given table to achieve the goal of smart cities. This table gives a wide overview of the area where the IoT devices can be beneficial to turn a city into smart city.

Poverty, unemployment and uncertainty in safety are the major issues to tackle. Living standards in these cities are not so attractive, that has also affected the capability of attracting fresh innovative businesses. Instability of government sometimes invites fierceness and bribery. By refining these social conditions founds the grounds for constructing a better future.

IoT and Animal Husbandry

Animal husbandry and dairy farming are the branches of science that are related to animals that are up-raised to fulfill human necessities like milk and milk products, fiber, eggs, wool, meat etc. It comprises everyday care of animals and selective breeding. Modern husbandry production depends on the availability of land type, for example cattle that are kept for beef; they require high concentration feedlots, where as thousands of hens and chickens might be raised up in very confined battery houses. Sometimes in such cases animal health gets ignored although various laws has been made for animal rights but technology can also help in managing health of animals. IoT sensors use for managing animal's health, are gaining popularity very fast in international market. Some sensors are produced for animal fitness at various stages; these sensors generate precise health status and sickness prediction which are relevant to humans. Correct animal breeding practice include a widespread extent of superior technology applied, like sound analyzers, location detector, micro fluidics, sweat sensors, salivary sensing strategy etc.

There generated a need to assimilate these available sensing technologies to create a proficient gadget for on-line monitoring in order to monitor animal health in real time. In this topic we will discuss the possibility of various wearable gadgets for animals and Nano molecular sensors with superior diagnose technique for many infections in cattle. IoT not only propose the apparatus for data collection in stream-lined manner, but also provides interpretable, relevant and meaningful data. Nowadays, farming does not depend on conventional knowledge; sensor-driven information in farming permits great tracking of crucial factors for great profit. As population is increasing day by day demand for is also increasing, it is predicted that this increasing demand for dairy products and livestock can be fulfilled efficiently with IoT; it enables us to breed more livestock per farm with modern technique for feeding, milking and other tasks. Small IoT chip attached to an animal's legs or ear gives exact data about their health, age, growth rates, meat quality, etc., which can be used to predict the best time to slaughter the livestock to get maximum profit and to reduce cost of drugs and veterinary care.

The structure of unstable natural compounds in inhaling can be very helpful in understanding the glucose level in blood; these organic Compounds are computed for the same cause. Normally, blood-glucose level is associated with ketone, ethanol, and exogenous mixes in animal's body. Besides, hazardous configuration of exhaled air used for analysis of the breath—a forward technique for critical diagnosis in which puncturing animal's body is not required. These ailments involve many circulatory and chronic breathing diseases. The composition of respiration shows the configuration of blood-stream; a whole frame of animal's digestion. Cattle tuberculosis is a sickness in livestock with universal health impact. The capability to find out unstable organic compounds formed by means of microorganisms has developed the curiosity in veterinary scientist for diagnosing this illness. Many software Applications has been established to strengthen the link between veterinaries and pet owners. Engineers nowadays are busy in developing computer-generated peer group to mollify the desires of puppy owners, dairy owners, cattle managers and farmers.

Pharmacological firms use software applications for their medication manufacture items portfolio for providing transparency in health status of each and every animal at any point of time in its lifecycle. Governing bodies and strategy planers have also understood the benefits of IoT, nowadays some of the European countries involve this data collected by IoT sensors on antibiotic use. The IoT for animal health will generate an innovative level of translucency and turn into a requirement for international research initiatives. With these latest IoT technologies, there is a communal accountability also to use this data in optimistic manner to make the most of the production sequence, whereas defending the constitutional rights of animals. The usage of this sensor generated data in seclusion does not achieve its possible benefits: better translucency in food chain, enhanced traceability, further advances to animal welfare. This big-data is also vital when describing legislative policies, classifying trends and cultural swings in population.

CONCLUSION

This chapter first gives general idea about big data and IoT, and further discusses the various applications of big data and IoT in various fields of today's life. Big Data and IoT are the technology booming rapidly now a day. The biggest resource of big data is IoT applications. Both are connected in some or the other way. Big data and IoT applications have huge scope in every major field of human life as well as everyday life chores. Many applications of both the technologies are discussed in this chapter but there are many more applications like controlling traffic on highways, training robots, developing artificial intelligence applications, inventing voice commanding devices etc. Every new smart technology invented to make human life easy is either related to big data or IoT. These two technologies are also proving beneficial for animals and environment as well for e.g. stopping deforestation, to stop poaching, in poultry farming, reducing human intervention in animal reserves, to stop hunting, saving under extinction animals etc. The future of Big data and IoT is very Enthralling than this where billions of devices will be talking to each other, these technologies will bring macro shift in the way we live and work.

REFERENCES

Al Nuaimi, E., Al Neyadi, H., Mohamed, N., & Al-Jaroodi, J. (2015). Applications of big data to smart cities. *Journal of Internet Services and Applications*, 6(1), 25. doi:10.118613174-015-0041-5

Das, S. (2013). Technology for Smart Home. In *Proceedings of International Conference on VLSI, Communication, Advanced Devices, Signals & Systems and Networking (VCASAN-2013)* (pp. 7-12). Springer, India. Retrieved from http://www.springer.com/978-81-322-1523-3

Dlodlo, N. (2015). The internet of things in transportation in south Africa. In *2015 International Conference on Emerging Trends in Networks and Computer Communications*. IEEE.

Edosio, U. Z. (2014). Big data Analytics and its Application in E-commerce. *E-Commerce Technologies*, 1. Retrieved from https://www.researchgate.net/publication/264129339_Big_Data_Analytics_and_its_Application_in_E-Commerce

Elgendy, N., & Elragal, A. (2014, July). Big data analytics: a literature review paper. In *Industrial Conference on Data Mining* (pp. 214-227). Springer, Cham.

Gubbi, J., Buyya, R., Marusic, S., & Palaniswami, M. (2013). Internet of Things (IoT): A vision architectural elements and future directions. *Future Generation Computer Systems*, 29(7), 1645–1660. doi:10.1016/j.future.2013.01.010

Jain, H., & Jain, R. (2017, March). Big data in weather forecasting: Applications and challenges. In *2017 International Conference on Big Data Analytics and Computational Intelligence (ICBDAC)* (pp. 138-142). IEEE.

Kumar, R., & Prabu, S. (2016). Smart healthcare monitoring system for rural area using IoT. *International Journal of Pharmacy & Technology*, 8(4), 21821–21826.

Kwon, O., Lee, N., & Shin, B. (2014). Data quality management, data usage experience and acquisition intention of big data analytics. *International Journal of Information Management, 34*(3), 387–394.

Lippell, H. (2016). Big Data in the Media and Entertainment Sectors. In *New Horizons for a Data-Driven Economy* (pp. 245–259). Cham: Springer.

Mahmood, T., & Afzal, U. (2013, December). Security analytics: Big data analytics for cybersecurity: A review of trends, techniques and tools. In *2013 2nd national conference on Information assurance (NCIA)* (pp. 129-134). IEEE.

Marjani, M., Nasaruddin, F., Gani, A., Karim, A., Hashem, I. A. T., Siddiqa, A., & Yaqoob, I. (2017). Big IoT data analytics: Architecture, opportunities, and open research challenges. *IEEE Access: Practical Innovations, Open Solutions, 5*, 5247–5261.

Monzon, A. (2015, May). Smart cities concept and challenges: Bases for the assessment of smart city projects. In *2015 International Conference on Smart Cities and Green ICT Systems (SMARTGREENS)* (pp. 1-11). IEEE.

Ojha, M., & Mathur, K. (2016, March). Proposed application of big data analytics in healthcare at Maharaja Yeshwantrao Hospital. In *2016 3rd MEC International Conference on Big Data and Smart City (ICBDSC)* (pp. 1-7). IEEE.

Poppe, K., Wolfert, S., & Verdouw, C. N. (2015). A European Perspective on the Economics of Big Data. *OECD*. Retrieved from https://www.oecd.org/tad/events/Autumn15_Journal_Poppe.et.al.pdf

Robles, R. J., & Kim, T. H. (2010). Applications, systems and methods in smart home technology. *Int. Journal of Advanced Science And Technology, 15*.

Schönfeld, M., Heil, R., & Bittner, L. (2017). Big Data in a Farm- Smart Farming. In *Big Data in Context* (pp. 109–120). Springer.

Shahzadi, R., Ferzund, J., Tausif, M., & Suryani, M. A. (2016). Internet of Things based Expert System for Smart Agriculture. *International Journal of Advanced Computer Science and Applications, 7*(9), 341–350.

Sravanthi, K., & Reddy, T. S. (2015). Applications of Big data in Various Fields. *International Journal of Computer Science and Information Technologies, 6*(5), 4629–4632.

Su, F., & Peng, Y. (2016). The research of big data architecture on telecom industry. In *2016 16th International Symposium on Communications and Information Technologies (ISCIT)*. IEEE. doi:10.1109/ISCIT.2016.7751636

Wang, F. (2014). Scanning the Issue and Beyond; Parallel driving with software vehicular robots for safety and smartness. *IEEE Transactions on Intelligent Transportation Systems, 15*(4), 1381–1387. doi:10.1109/TITS.2014.2342451

Wanichayapong, N., Pruthipunyaskul, W., Pattara-Atikom, W., & Chaovalit, P. (2011, August). Social-based traffic information extraction and classification. In *2011 11th International Conference on ITS Telecommunications (ITST)* (pp. 107-112). IEEE.

Wolfert, S., Ge, L., Verdouw, C., & Bogaardt, M. J. (2017). Big data in smart farming–a review. *Agricultural Systems*, *153*, 69-80. Retrieved from https://www.sciencedirect.com/science/article/pii/S0308521X16303754

Zheng, X., Chen, W., Wang, P., Shen, D., Chen, S., Wang, X., ... Yang, L. (2016). Big data for social transportation. *IEEE Transactions on Intelligent Transportation Systems*, *17*(3), 620–630.

This research was previously published in the Handbook of Research on Big Data and the IoT; pages 1-21, copyright year 2019 by Engineering Science Reference (an imprint of IGI Global).

Chapter 74
Amelioration of Big Data Analytics by Employing Big Data Tools and Techniques

Stephen Dass
Vellore Institute of Technology, India

Prabhu J.
Vellore Institute of Technology, India

ABSTRACT

This chapter describes how in the digital data era, a large volume of data became accessible to data science engineers. With the reckless growth in networking, communication, storage, and data collection capability, the Big Data science is quickly growing in each engineering and science domain. This paper aims to study many numbers of the various analytics ways and tools which might be practiced to Big Data. The important deportment in this paper is step by step process to handle the large volume and variety of data expeditiously. The rapidly evolving big data tools and Platforms have given rise to numerous technologies to influence completely different Big Data portfolio.In this paper, we debate in an elaborate manner about analyzing tools, processing tools and querying tools for Big datahese tools used for data analysis Big Data tools utilize numerous tasks, like Data capture, storage, classification, sharing, analysis, transfer, search, image, and deciding which might also apply to Big data.

INTRODUCTION

Current advancement in the field digital information improves the data which are exceptional to both software and hardware. About 70% unstructured data deals with multimedia data, in that 60% of them are from internet traffic (Boyd & Crawford, 2012; Hartmann et al., 2014; Jagadish et al., 2014; Katal, Wazid, & Goudar, 2013; Purcell, 2013). Unexpectedly huge data creates stints multi-media data semantic definitions searched by conventional methods are difficult to any set of forms. Unsorted raw data are complicated to deal directly so few easy and machine processing forms are made to design semantic

DOI: 10.4018/978-1-6684-3662-2.ch074

data. This type of data works on content-based retrieval methods from which data are restored. This phenomenon is known as Feature Extraction (Katal, Wazid, & Goudar, 2013). Miloslavaskaya and Tolstoy (2014) state "…big data concept are the datasets of such size and structure that exceed the capabilities of traditional programming tools (databases, software, etc.) for data collection, storage and processing in a reasonable time and a-fortiori exceed the capacity of their perception by a human…"

In General, Big Data is exported as data wealth peculiarize as high volume, velocity, and variety to get particular technology and analytical methods to change to value. Since from the invention of the internet in the early 1990s, the growth of the data has been increasing steadily. In Past Decade data generation growth is massively high which become a great challenge in storing, managing and process of data. This set a path to the new concept of Big Data, a concept that concerns with all generated data that are analyzed and processed in the day to day tools (Fayyad, Piatetsky-Shapiro, & Smyth, 1996). Jeong and Shin (2016) posted a security management scheme that allows users to easily access Big Data from different network environments. For implementing security management using key management, they added furthermore as future research as to Design and operate a model that can integrate and manage the stratified properties of the security awareness information sent and received between users and servers (Bakshi, 2012).

RELATED WORK

Literature Survey

Liu et al. (2014) proposed a mining system with Big Graph analysis by performing in bulk synchronous parallel (BSP) naming it as BSP based Graph Mining (BSPGM). This System inferred is compared with Hadoop Map-Reduce concept in processing Massive Data and it is developed based on Cloud platform. The drawback of this system often it restricts the graph data in the processing phase.

Meng et al. (2014) suggested keyword-Aware service recommendation method using Hadoop when customer service is growing rapidly with online information generation is difficult to use traditional service recommendation system for large scale data. This lacks scalability and inefficiency in processing the massive data. Usually recommending system uses same rating and ranking of service but here the author uses frequently used keyword for search of particular word and they are analysed. The author uses MapReduce framework.

Chen, Mao, and Liu (2014) put forth system as privacy aware cross cloud service for Big Data application using MapReduce. This paper uses medical data as dataset in large scale for analysis the data. They propose Hiresome-II (History record based service optimization method). Cloud uses QaS for history records. Complexity of the cloud system is resolved using Hiresome-II.

Jamshidi et al. (2015) discuss how Big Data and system of service (SoS) works together. Big Data analytics tools used in this paper are Principal Component analysis (PCA), fuzzy logic clustering and K means. These tools of Big Data help in handling (a) Extract information. (b) Build acknowledge from derived data. (c) Develop model for Big Data.

Elgendy and Elragal (2014) explain the Large data graph analyzing by Big Data. Graph processing is implemented using the shortest path of the data. Map Reduce is used to determine the graph processing.

Boyd and Crawford (2012) discuss the question raised by various different field of technology where huge data are generated, processed and handled. The author discusses the varies tools from which Big

Data are processed and studied. Furthermore, author an intimate user who uses Big Data and its provocation about its mystery.

Alexender Boicen et al. (2013) present the difference between SQL and NoSQL database management system and explains about the feature, architecture, restriction and integrity of both oracle and MongoDB. He concluded in context with database management system as if we need fast and flexible, MongoDB is the best option. Otherwise Oracle is the best for its rapidness and tables collection and relation with classic solution.

Vithal Yenkar and Mahip Bartere (2014) explain the major domain of Data Mining with Big Data. How Big data analysis is implemented in data Mining. Author explains the tough issues in Big Data and data driven model. They elaborate as heterogeneous mixture learning technology implementing in Big Data analysis.

Demchek et al. (2014) discussed all about big data used in technology, industries with defining an architecture and operational models such as Big Data management and security, Big Data infrastructure (BDI), Big Data Architecture Framework (BDAF), Big Data lifecycle management (BDLM)and Big Data Cloud based Infrastructure. The author initiates to discuss about the Big Data Tools more intensively.

COMPARATIVE ANALYSIS

Based on the functionality Big Data is classified into three categories such as Big Data Storage management, Big Data Processing and Big Data Streaming.

Big Data Storage Usage

Big Data nowadays usually deals with very large unstructured data sets, and relies on fast analytics, with answers provided in seconds. For instance, Facebook, Google or Amazon analyse users' statuses or search terms to trigger targeted advertising on user pages. However big data analytics aren't restricted to those internet giants. All type of organisations, and not essentially large ones, will take pleasure in finance houses inquisitive about analysing stock exchange behaviour, to police departments getting to analyse and predict crime trends. In this section we compare Big Data Storage tools MongoDB, CouchDB and Big Table and traditional database Structure Query Language like MySql, Oracle and SQL server. Table 1 elaborately describes the Storage management. MongoDB and MySql Database System.

Limitations of RDBMS Over Big Data

First, the data size has accumulated hugely to the vary of petabytes—one petabyte = 1,024 terabytes. RDBMS finds it difficult to handle such immense data volumes. to deal with this, RDBMS extra more central processing units (or CPUs) or more memory to the direction system to rescale vertically. Second, the bulk of the data comes in an exceedingly semi-structured or unstructured format from social media, audio, video, texts, and emails. However, the second drawback concerning unstructured data is outside the view of RDBMS as a result of relational databases simply can't reason unstructured data. They're designed and structured to accommodate structured information love weblog device and money information. Also, "big data" is generated at a really high speed. RDBMS lacks in high velocity as a result of it's designed for steady data retention instead of rapid climb. Even if RDBMS is employed to handle and store "big data," & nbsp; it'll prove to be terribly dear. As a result, the lack of relational databases to handle "big data" led to the emergence of latest technologies.

Table 1. Comparative analysis of MongoDB and MySql

Name	MongoDB	MySql
Description	Most popular document store	Used in relational database base
Primary Database model	Document store	Relational RDBMS
Initial release	2009	1995
Implementation language	C++	C and C++
Server operating System	Linux, OS X, Soloris, Windows	Free BSD, Linux, Windows
Data Scheme	Scheme free	Yes
SQL	No	Yes
Server-side Scripts	Java Script	YES
Map Reduce	YES	NO
Consistency concepts	Eventual consistency and Immediate consistency	Immediate consistency
Advantage	1. Non-Relational means table-less 2. Less expensive and open source 3. Easier scalability in order to support for Map Reduce 4. No detailed database model is required	1. derives with standard schema 2. Support is instantly available whenever is required 3. developed according to Industry Standard
Disadvantage	1. Community not as well defined 2. Lack of standardization	1. Mysql Suffers From Relatively Poor Performance Scaling 2. Development Is Not Community Driven – and Hence Has Lagged 3. Its Functionality Tends To Be Heavily Dependent On Add-ons 4. Developers May Find Some Of Its Limitations To Be Frustrating

DATA ANALYSIS

All data associated with big data is generated every second by second and are available from completely different sources; it's exactly the good diversity of data varieties what complicates the storage and analysis as a result of the combination of data with different structures because it has been mentioned (Liu et al., 2014). As a result of this, big data classified in 3 main operations: storage, analytics, and integration, through that solutions are display so in an efficient manner the size of this tool is often scaled. There are totally different techniques for big data Analysis; some of these tools are.

Need for Big Data Analytics

Big data Analysis resolved many issues related to a real-time application which is shown in a different structure such as graphical structure (Meng et al., 2014). They set an example in optimizing the railway paths, disease prediction, and analysis related to social media network, genome constraint analysis, Information network and semantic analysis etc.

Figure 1. Need for Big Data analytics

Big Data Processing

Big data are processed in two ways

1. Integrated processing
2. Distributed processing

Integrated Processing

Data is collected and stored in one integrated location where storage and processing are done on the single machine. This integrated processing machine is computed by the very high processor, storage has high configuration. This type of processing structure is defined too small organization where storage and processing are done on the single machine. It promotes to be as Supercomputing system.

Distributed Processing

The collection, storage, and processing are done in the different architecture of distributed processing. Peer to peer architecture and clustering architecture are a prominent example of distributed processing.

BIG DATA ANALYSIS STEP

Big data uses a very large data set which cannot be processed by classical tools and techniques (Sánchez et al, 2008). Steps involved in making our material into a finite data are as follows:

Figure 2. Big Data processing

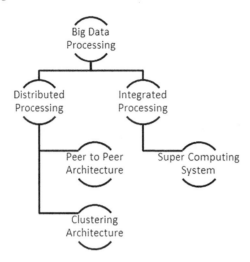

1. **Data Collection:** Data collection is gathering the raw data from real time generating data resources then stored in storage device. Data collection process is done in high concern from which it fails leads to inaccurate and inappropriate results. Tools used for data collections are Chekwa, WebCrawler, pig, and flume.
2. **Data Partition:** Since large data are difficult to process there comes different partition techniques such as data tagging classification and clustering approaches.to reduce the complexity of processing a huge volume data, many clustering approaches are designed they are classified into algorithms like text mining, data mining, Mahout, scalable nearest neighbor algorithm and pattern processing.
3. **Data Coordination:** Coordination denotes the data move towards any data warehouse or any other Big data database technique. In common, it is denoted as the exchange of data from one format to another big data technique. Sqoop is a Big data technology used to exchange data from the relational database. Flume is the technology used in big data defined to hold and manage the huge amount of data from one system network to another efficiently. Zookeeper provides data synchronization which is used the configuration information programming language like java, python, was used in data coordination.
4. **Data Transformation:** Converting one data format from sources to another format refers to data transformation. Data migration tools help to convert the relational database to Hadoop repository.
5. **Data Storage:** In laymen terms, Big Data is defined to storage of data and how voluminous data are stored in the storage management. Data storage must perform retrieval, manipulation and data collection efficiently. Handling different types of data also plays a role in data storage. Tools used are HBase, NoSQL, cluster HDFS and GFS.
6. **Data Processing:** Till now, there is no defining and devise a tool for processing Big Data. Hadoop, NoSQL and apache-spark etc. helps in processing structured and unstructured data in various formats. QlikView is a perfect instance of in-memory data processing for big data which gives advanced reporting. Infinispan is scalable and available grid platform data processing.
7. **Extract Data:** Extracting required files or data from the database and resulted in output preferred in different result reports such as visualization, integration, and reporting. Two methods used in

data extract. Data query tools-using query language like Hive helps in fetching the data. Big Data search – using parallel or distributing processing with clustering fetching data.

8. **Data Analysis:** Data Analysis is defined as checking, investigating or analyzing and inspecting the data and then modeling according to the goal set by the client's expectation by making useful data. Rapid Miner is open sources software where the text is mining for using the data for predictive analysis. Pentaho- is business intelligence software where video; data OLAP, Service, ETL are used. Talend and Spago BI- are the tools which are used in many managerial organizations. Weka- is machine learning tool where data mining algorithm is implemented for data analysis.

9. **Data Visualisation:** DIVE & Orange are Big data Visualisation tools used for formatting the huge data to structure format are inadequate. It works in order to solve the inadequate issue.

Big Data Analytics Processing

For analytics processing of Big Data, four critical requirements are suggested (Bakshi, 2012): 1. Fast data loading 2. Fast query processing, 3. High efficient utilization of storage space 4. Strong adaptivity to high dynamic workload.

Hadoop

MapReduce

MapReduce is a processing model used in Hadoop. The word "MapReduce" itself denotes, "Map" and then "Reduce". These type of processing is suitable for Big Data. It performs both analytics and processing function (Chen, Mao, Liu, 2014). MapReduce is a process by which, it adds additional system or resources rather than increasing the storage space of individuals systems. The main idea of MapReduce is breaking the job into many phases and executing each phrases parallel in which it reduces the processing time and completes the job before its scheduled time.

Two jobs are performed in MapReduce. They are

1. Map-job
2. Reduce Job

Map job is setting Map input value to the output value. This Map function computes huge jobs into little jobs and issue a required set of input keys to map output keys. Reduced function is implemented to collect and combine all key values, which are shared, to get the final computation. When MapReduce and Hadoop meet, they perform two different nodes. First, Job Tracker takes care of distributing Map and Reduce function and monitor them. It schedules the work for the execution of Map job. Second, Task tracker runs related to jobs and get backs the result of the task monitor and the work of the reduce functions. We explain MapReduce functions in four steps

Step 1: Data collection in massive volume including log files, sensors data etc.
Step 2: Job tracker defines and executes the MApjobs and reduce job and send the both
Step 3: Job Tracker allows jobs to task tracker it runs mapper provide output then it is stored in HDF file system.

Step 4: Data are mapped, and it reduces jobs to get the result.

Principal Component Analysis

Principal Component Analysis (PCA) is a statistical system to identify a pattern in the dataset in order to find the similarities and dissimilarities which are reduced to a set of value according to the client desire. It highlights the specific attributes accordingly to client's choice (Hinton, Osindero, & Teh, 2006). It helps in compressing the data PCA is implemented and solved by both numerical and also image data. It eliminates the unrelated set of value. The simple steps to perform PCA is as follows steps

Step 1: Fetch a data set
Step 2: Find the mean value and the then eliminate each data value
Step 3: Covariance matrix is calculated
Step 4: Finding Eigen values and Eigen vectors for covariance matrix
Step 5: Forms feature vector.

This Eigen values & Eigenvectors values are necessarily useful for Big Data concepts which become a little disadvantage to PCA in analytics of Big Data.

Fuzzy Logic

The concept of fuzzy logic was initially developed by Zadeh in 1965. Fuzzy logic mainly focuses on two terms fuzzy sets and fuzzy system. It is a problem-solving system which consists of methodology to lead and implement network embedded system or work station based on data acquisition and control system. *Fuzzy set*-It deals with knowing and probability in truth table and it's analyzing like human reasoning. Two problems are developed in fuzzy logic is fuzzy set theory finds the vacuum in semantic. Fuzzy measure theory evaluating the nature which has many sets of analyzing points. *The fuzzy system is* reasoning methods based on the almost accurate collection. Fuzzy consist of fuzzy mathematics, fuzzy operating, fuzzy clustering are few examples of fuzzy systems. Fuzzy systems are eliminated because of it low tolerance and experience in nature. The fuzzy system is implemented using if-then conditional operator methods. Each and every parameter in fuzzy logic have definite and individual operations and context.

Fuzzy C- Mean Clustering

Fuzzy clustering is an unsupervised learning method implemented in many other domains such that machine learning, bioinformatics, data mining and pattern recognition. Fuzzy clustering is used in application-oriented domains such as processing medical imaging and Image partition. Clustering analysis is defined as a grouping similar type of feature attributes (Elgendy & Elragal, 2016). Fuzzy c means clustering algorithms is denoted in the following function.

$$F_m = \sum_{a=1}^{N}\sum_{b=1}^{c} U_{ab}^m \left\| x_a - C_b \right\| 2, 1 < M < \infty$$

where

U_{ab} = degree of ownership of x_a in the cluster b
x_a = the pa[th] of the d dimensional meaning data
C_b = the d- dimensional center of cluster
$\|*\|$ = the norm expressing the similarity between measured data and the center

Ownership of U_{ab} and cluster centers C_b is denoted as

$$U_{ab} = \frac{1}{\sum_{k=1}^{C} \frac{\|x_{i-c_j}\|}{\|x_i - c_k\|} {}^2\!/m - 1}$$

where

$$C_b = \frac{\sum_{i=1}^{N} U_{ab}^m x_a}{\sum_{i=1}^{N} U_{ab}^m}$$

Traditional Artificial Neutral Network

The idea of the artificial neural network is initially incorporated from computation model of human brains of the human neuron. This traditional artificial neural network is data formulating system which carries a certain set of data in it. Signals are generated by neurons from other neurons or outside layer that is interlinked. The important concept Multilayer perception (MLP) comprises of three layers:

1. One input layer
2. Hidden layer
3. Output layer

Functions are manipulated in a hidden layer so hidden layers are also greater in number than Input layer which gives high threshold. From this MLP we learn layered feedforward network trained with back propagation method. This type of network has static pattern classification. The main advantage of MLP is that learn to use and mapping of input and output approximation is popular.the main disadvantage is when the data are one in process of training it takes much time to train data. The acceleration of learning decreases when a lot of training data are in processing so, the traditional artificial neural network will not much applicable to big data and deep architecture. But they are in the field of information technology for more than 30 yrs (Hinton, Osindero, The, 2006). From this point the algorithms yet to be established to prove the best of knowledge discovery

Traditional Genetic Algorithm

Genetic algorithms are the very voluminous class of data processing method called evolutionary computations. GA is inquisitive search method which imitates the technique of natural selection and survival of fittest. This GA adds with genetic programming concept from which text data, symbolic representation is improved with evolutionary computations (Ho Chi Minh City University of Technology, n.d.). After many generations, inheritance, mutation, and selection are obtained. In GA, population is initiated in initial stage as such denoted by 0 and 1 bits. Each and every pair of the chromosome is exchanged and modified after the process of selection. When a new population is obtained, they are commended withhold chromosome and compared for the survival of the chromosome. The life cycle of Genetic Algorithm is shown in Figure 3.

Figure 3. Life cycle of Genetic Algorithm

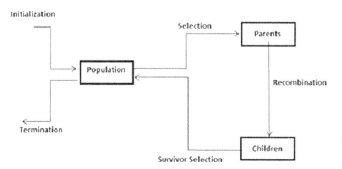

Tools Used for Data Analytics: From Storage Management Perspective

The complying dividing put forth the several numbers of tools which are presently in use of storage, management, and analysis of data which tends to form Big Data.

- **Hadoop (HDFS):** Stands for distributed file system projected to be performed by the commodity hardware (Gilbert, Lynch, 2012; Kamat, Singh, 2013).
- **Hardware:** Hadoop is interconnected with several hundreds of cluster of nodes which store and perform user's job. Failure occurrence in the commodity hardware is high, therefore if the only Master node fails in its task which leads to failure of whole clusters failure. Moreover, the Hadoop platform unremittingly has an assertive percentage of inactivity (Jagadish et al., 2014; Gilbert, Lynch, 2012).
- **Transmission:** The data performed by Hadoop are not in general for usage since the set of data is processed by the user without any connection.
- **Data:** Generally, applications performed during this kind of tool are of huge in size; Hadoop incorporate in supporting it with a handsome variety of nodes that distributed for data. This handling brings as a profit the rapid growth in the information measured is obtainable in many nodes, A fair performance within the access to data and its continuous presentation (streaming).

- **Computation:** One of the advantages of Hadoop when comparing with other tools is that both storage and processing of data done in the same system from which, data transmission, collision is avoided in the network.
- **Portability:** Many of Open Source application is developed with easy of diaspora with different platforms. Hadoop is also designed in such a way.
- **Accessibility:** Java programming merges with web sources to give an access and browsing structure of the data in which its data nodes are carried out.

MongoDB

MongoDB is a NoSQL database from which data manager of a documental sort of non-relational database. Exchange of data is performed by means of BSON. For a text file, data structuring and Mapping are implemented using binary representation (Yenkar, Bartere, 2014). NoSQL data manager is written in C++ programming. Characteristics structures are as follows:

- Lithe Data Storage is supported by JSON and does not need any priority scheme
- Many numbers of indexes are initiated in order to use it however, it is not essential to use or define MapReduce or parallel processes
- MongoDB performs the replication and scalability for highly efficient processing. this property is continued when there is an increasing number of the machine.
- In query conceptive, they have high performance with updating and processing. The query is based on documents.

Big Data Analytics Tools and Methods

Big- Data, Analytics, and Decision (B-DAD) are supported by big data tools and methods in the decision-making process. This framework is categories big data into few such as Storage, management and processing tools which help the methods to visualize and evaluate in different levels of decision making. These methods have three main levels such as Big Data Storage and architecture, Data and analytics processing, Big data analysis Kamat, Singh, 2013). These levels incorporate from knowledge discovery where a still lot of research is needed in finding suitable tools in developing the big data tools.

BIG DATA STORAGE AND MANAGEMENT

When dealing with big data the foremost time in the process is handling the data to be placed in correct storage or acquired. A relational database, data marts, and data warehouse are traditional methods to store and retrieve the structured data. Data admitted in big data storage using the general phenomenon of Extract, Transform, Load (ETL) or Extract, Load, Transform (ELT) data are added from the resources. This is done in order to clean and then been fatigued before the data mining and online analytical functions (Katal, Wazid, Goudar, 2013).

Traditional enterprise data warehouse (TDW) have a lot of disadvantage in admitting new data sources of different forms (unstructured and semi-structured data) so Big data introduces Magnetic, Agile, Deep (MAD) analysis to clear all disadvantage to the traditional relational database. This resource attracts by all data sources by its storage quantity and requires the agile database to help in data evolution. Massive Parallel Processing (MPP) database gives a solution to distributing system where it provides rapid query performance with respect to the velocity of the data transferred. To solve this type of issues with semi-structured and unstructured data, NoSQL (Not only SQL) is developed in storing the different types of data. The main aim is to store massive data, with scaling, flexibility in data models.

Big Data Storage Concepts

The most important concepts in Big Data tools is Big data storage. When there is a massive generation of data, leads to a large volume of data storage, so here come the Big Data storage concepts. Some key concepts involved in Big Data storage are Data Models, Data partitioning, Data Replication, and Data Persistence.

1. **Data Models:** For accessing and manipulation of data in Big Data technology uses various data models such as Relational model, NoSQL database model, Graph based model and Schema based model. Relational model (Chen, Mao, Liu, 2014) is ancient and widely used model proposed in 1960 by Edgar F Codd. He suggested in the model as represented in terms of tuples (or records), group (table) connected with a specific key, database combined with relational model lead to outcome and usage of Structured Query Language (SQL) to define and access data. Consequently, Big Data technologies support database model which does not relate to the relational model. They are defined as NoSQL database. They pertain attribute key, key based model support to all data type (integer, character, byte). Another important data model supporting Big Data Technologies is graph data model. They are denoted by nodes and links or edges. Graph data model solves many different problems like computing line is, getting cycle like a relationship supporting the connection etc. Graph model has much application used in real life Use cases when we compare to other models. Some of the real-life applications are customer network, social media, and payment transaction networks etc.

Big Data Technologies are developed on a new concept known as 'Schema and Read' which is based on run time models definition. When data are available in the data store, they moved into data models getting into reading mode. This concept is best game changer when we compared with traditional DB Technologies reading a data to be well defined.

2. **Data Partitioning:** All data in the data store cannot be stored in the single system so partition concept can be implemented. In Big Data technologies, some approaches methods to partition the data are implemented across various nodes. Accessing and data modeled are done by value/ or key for partition by key. The following table explains the various type of scheme in Data partition.

Data partition in data node is typically identifying in following approaches such as the First Approach- writing on the node which is local to the client program. This approach is used by Block partition. Second Approach- Identifying the key node. This approach is applicable to hash partition, Round Robin partition, and random partition. The third Approach- they are used by Range Partition, List partition, Tag partition. The fourth Approach- data is allocated with selected data with the same node based on reference key/Foreign key.

Table 2. Types of data partitioning

S. No.	Types	Description
1	Range Partition	Partition based on range of an attribute key
2	Hash Partition	Hash function applied to one or more attribute
3	Random Partition	Assigning keys in a random manner
4	Round Robin Partition	Assigning keys to node in round robin mechanism
5	Tag based partition	Based on tag or data, keys are grouped in logical partition
6	Block based Partition	Data stored and accessed in bulk without any predefined schema.

3. **Data Replication:** Data replication is a common characteristic of all methods in Big Data Technologies. Replication gradually increased the data availability and provides redundancy when it is different, and many copies of data are stored in nodes. This helps in increasing the availability and locality of data in query processing in distributed systems. There are three types of replica that take care of most of the failure in data replication. The first replica is defined putting in a rack from one replica into another same partition. Second replica- data required in emergency and recovery put into the different data center.

4. **Data Compression:** The basic problem arises in Big Data are storing and processing of large volume of data, thus compression technique has been considered even before the data are in large. Many different ways are introduced to data compression techniques initially it reduces the volume/size of the data. This denotes low storage needs lower time to read and write the data from disk. Secondly, use of network bandwidth which large data process needs to move from one to other. Compression which is also defined as split and define ability in reading and writing the data. Traditionally compression technology has lot of limitation when Big Data Technology is processing by the compression Technique (Kamat, Singh, 2013).

5. **Data Persistence:** Data persistence is one of the substantial features of Big Data Technologies as for network involving the system for high performance and processing and also for disk input and output data in accessing large data. Data Persistence is implemented in two dominant ways. First Approach Data persistence is used to store the data in the local hard disk of each data node. The second Approach holds Distributed Filesystem APIs for implementing the generic set of distributed files and also ensure all product/ vendor in Quality of service. This approach gives vital solution for Big data. Implementation is done in two types for Distribution file system. In a traditional database system, data are stored in a shared local disk of the data node.

OTHER BIG DATA PROCESSING TOOLS AND METHODS

Apache Group established Apache Software Foundation (ASF) in June 1999 held in Delaware, U.S. ASF is an open source form for software developers. They started developing in terms of Apache Free license providing distribution open source (Apache Software Foundation, n.d.). Projects of Apache are characterized by consumer-based development, collaborative and an open and pragmatic software license. Apache Software Foundation is denoted as a second generation open source organization providing security working without any risk to the platform. Each and every project in ASF is organized by a team of experts with good sound of knowledge. There are some volunteers who dedicatedly working in Apache project who contribute in large number.

The quick time stamp of Apache software foundation in related with Apache HTTP server which is established in early 1993. A small group of eight developers working to strengthen NCSA HTTP Daemon are the ones who designed Apache group on March 25, 1999. Early a members of Apache Software Foundation (ASF) projects are Behlendorf, KenCoar, Mignel Gonzales, Mark Cox, Lars Eilebrecht, Ben Hyde, Ralf S. Engelschall, Roy T. Fielding, Dean Gaudet, Ben Hyde, Jim Jagielski, Alexi Kosut, Martin Kraemer, Sameer parekh, Cliff Skolnick, Marc Slemko, William Stoddord, Paul Sutton, Randy Terbush and Dirk-Willen Van Gulik. They conducted a first official meeting on April 13, 1999. Later after a serial of the meeting, the elected board members formed a legal board committee as Apache Software Foundation as a corporation on June 1, 1999. The name "Apache" is selected from an American native people who were well known for greater skills in the strategy of wars and endurance (Apache Airvata, n.d.). ASF started releasing so many softwares and started calling themselves as Apache Group.

Table 3 shows a list of Apache Software tools developed for Dealing with Big Data Technologies.

Table 3. Detailed description about Apache software developed for Big Data

S. No.	Apache Tools	Short Description	Category	Data File	Programming Language	Release Year	Latest Version
1	Airavata (Apache Airvata, n.d.)	Airavata is a software framework, mini- service architecture used to implement and manage the flow of work and reckoning job. They use distributed computing resources.	Cloud, Big data and network-server	DOAP RDF (json)	Java	2014	V 0.11
2	Ambari (Apache Ambari, 2015)	Software Framework to process Hadoop cluster and other data processing domains.	Big data	DOAP RDF (json)	Java, Python and JavaScript	2014	V 1.5.0
3	Apex (Apache Apex, n.d.)	Batch processing Search engine	Big-Data	DOAP RDF (json)	Java	2016	V 3.7.0
4	Avro (Apache Avro, 2015)	Data Serialization System	Library, Big-Data	DOAP RDF (json)	C, C++, C#, Java, PHP, Python, Ruby	2012	V 1.7.2
5	Beam (Apache Beam, n.d.)	Programming model runs with data processing pipelines	Big-Data	DOAP RDF (JSON)	Java, Python	2014	V 2.0.0
6	Bigtop (Apache BigTop, n.d.)	Community- driven BigData management platform	Big-Data	DOAP RDF (json)	Java	2016	V 1.2.0
7	BookKeeper (Apache BookKeeper, n.d.)	Authentic Log service	Big-data	DOAP RDF (json)	Java	2014	V 4.3.0
8	Calcite (Apache Calcite, n.d.)	Dynamic data Management Framework	Big-Data, Hadoop, SQL	DOAP RDF (JSON)	Java	2013	V1.13.0
9	Couch DB (Apache Couch DB, n.d.)	NoSQL- Database using JSON and MapReduce and HTTP	Database, Big-data	DOAP RDF (json)	JavaScript, Erlang, C++,C	2014	V 1.6.1
10	Crunch (Apache Crunch, n.d.)	The framework used to implement writing, testing and running MapReduce pipelines.	Big-Data Library	DOAP RDF (json)	Java and Scala	2011	V 0.5.0

continues on following page

Table 3. Continued

S. No.	Apache Tools	Short Description	Category	Data File	Programming Language	Release Year	Latest Version
11	DataFu (Apache DataFu, n.d.)	Consist of two library- pig and hourglass. This works for data mining and statistics	Big-Data Incubating	DOAP RDF (JSON)	Java	2015	V 1.3.0
12	Drill (Apache Drill, 2015)	Query language as distributed SQL MPP with Hadoop and NoSQL	Big- data	DOAP RDF (json)	Java	2014	V 0.7.0
13	Edgent (Apache Edgent, n.d.)	It is programming model used for streaming process to execute analytics	Big-Data, Library, Mobile network client	DOAP RDF (JSON)	Java, JavaScript	2016	V 1.0.0
14	Falcon (Apache Falcon, 2015)	Platform for Data management and processing	Big-Data Incubating	DOAP RDF (json)	Java	2014	V 0.7.0
15	Flink (Apache Flink, 2015)	Rapid and trustworthy for voluminous scale data processing	Big-Data	DOAP RDF (JSON)	Java and Scala	2017	V 1.2.7
16	Flume (Apache Flume, 2015)	Flume is trustworthy, distributed, efficient, aggregation to store data in a centralized manner	Big-Data	DOAP RDF (JSON)	Java	2014	V 1.5.0
17	Giraph (Apache Giraph, 2015)	Giraph is developed to high scalability and iterative graph processing	Big-Data	DOAP RDF (JSON)	Java	2016	V 1.2.0
18	Hama (Apache Hama, n.d.)	Hama consist of BSP computing engine	Big-data	DOAP RDF (json)	Java	2014	V 0.6.4
19	Helix (Appache Helix, n.d.)	Framework uses clustering analysis for data partition and replication data resources	Big-Data	DOAP RDF (JSON)	Java	2016	V 0.6.8
20	Ignite (Apache Ignite, 2015)	Ignite is In-Memory Data providing processing, querying components	Big-Data, SQL, Cloud, OSGi IoT	DOAP RDF (JSON)	Java, C#, C++, SQL, JDBC, and ODBC	2015	V 1.5.0
21	Kafka (Apache Kafka, 2015)	Open source programming provides distributed fault tolerance	Big-Data	DOAP RDF (JSON)	Scala, Java	2011	V 0.10.2.1
22	Knox (Apache Knox, n.d.)	API gateway to Hadoop service	Big-Data, Hadoop	DOAP RDF (JSON)	Java	2014	V 0.4.0
23	Lens (Apache Lens, n.d.)	Provides Unified Analytics interface	Big-Data	DOAP RDF (JSON)	Java	2015	V 2.6.1
24	MetaModal (Apache MetaModal, n.d.)	Put forth uniform connector, query API to various Datastore Types	Database, Big-Data library	DOAP RDF (JSON)	Java	2014	V 4.3.1
25	Oozie (Apache Oozie, 2015)	Workflow scheduler to access Hadoop jobs	Big-Data	DOAP RDF (JSON)	Java, JavaScript	2014	V 4.3.0
26	ORC (Apache ORC, n.d.)	Columnar File format for Hadoop jobs	Big-Data, Database, Hadoop library	DOAP RDF (json)	Java, C++	2016	V 1.2.1
27	Phoenix (Apache Phoenix, 2015)	Provides OLTP and operational analytics for Sql	Big-Data, Database	DOAP RDF (json)	Java, SQL	2016	V 4.7.0

continues on following page

Table 3. Continued

S. No.	Apache Tools	Short Description	Category	Data File	Programming Language	Release Year	Latest Version
28	REEF (Apache REEF, n.d.)	Retainable Evaluator Execution framework(REEF) is Framework to control for scheduling and coordination	Big-Data	DOAP RDF (json)	Java, C#, C++	2016	V 0.15.0
29	Parquet (Apache Parquet, 2015)	Parquet is a columnar storage format	Big-Data	DOAP RDF (json)	Java	2015	V 1.6.0
30	Samza (Apache Samza, n.d.)	Samza executes Stream processing task.	Big-Data	DOAP RDF (json)	SCALA	2014	V 0.8.0
31	Spark (Apache Spark Streaming, 2015)	Spark is rapid speed and efficient in handling data stream processing for large-scale data	Big-Data	DOAP RDF (JSON)	Java. Scala, Python	2014	V 2.1.1
32	Sqoop (Apache Sqoop, 2015)	Sqoop is tools which help to process and transfer a massive amount of data in Hadoop and relational database.	Big-Data	DOAP RDF (json)	Java	2014	V 1.4.5
33	Storm (Apache Storm, n.d.)	The storm is framework used for doing distributed real-time computation system through batch processing.	Big-Data	DOAP RDF (json)	Java	2015	V 0.9.5
34	Tajo (Apache Tajo, n.d.)	It is an open source big data Warehouse system	Big-Data, Database	DOAP RDF (JSON)	Java	2013	V0.11.3
35	Tez (Apache Tez, 2015)	Framework to develop generic application to process Direct Acyclic Graph (DAG)	Big-Data	DOAP RDF (JSON)	Java	2014	V 0.8.5
36	VXQuery (Appache VXQuery, n.d.)	VXQuery is XML query processor to evaluate massive data collection	Big data, XML	DOAP RDF (json)	Java	2015	V 0.6
37	Zeppelin (Zeppelin, 2015)	Zeppelin is visualization tool for data analytics to exploration of data	Big data	DOAP RDF (JSON)	Java, JavaScript, and Scala	2015	V 0.7.1
38	Chukwa (Apache Chukwa, n.d.)	Chukwa is an open source programming framework for surveillance the large dataset	Hadoop	DOAP RDF (JSON)	Java, JavaScript	2012	V 0.5.0
39	Pig (Apache Pig, 2015)	Pig is framework to evaluate large data set on Hadoop	Database	DOAP RDF (json)	Java	2008	V0.16.0
40	Accumulo (Apache Accumulo, n.d.)	Accumulo is based in Google Big Table which stores distributed key values at various data management system	Database	DOAP RDF (json)	Java	2011	V 1.8.1
41	Cassandra (Apache Cassandra, 2015)	Cassandra helps in scalability, high availability without any adjustment.	Database	DOAP RDF (json)	Java	2008	V 3.10
42	ZooKeeper (Apache ZooKeeper, n.d.)	ZooKeeper is framework used for data coordination	Database	DOAP RDF (json)	Java	2015	V3.4.10
43	Curator (Apache Curator, n.d.)	Java libraries additional to ZooKeeper in executing	Database	DOAP RDF (json)	Java	2016	V 3.5.0
44	Gora (Apache Gora, n.d.)	Gora supports column based support and helps in In-memory data model	Database	DOAP RDF (JSON)	Java	2014	V 0.5

continues on following page

Table 3. Continued

S. No.	Apache Tools	Short Description	Category	Data File	Programming Language	Release Year	Latest Version
45	Hbase (Apache Hbase, 2015)	HBase is a Hadoop Database for big data storage processing	Big-Data Database	DOAP RDF (JSON)	Java	2010	V 1.2.6
46	Hive (Apache Hive, n.d.)	Hive is a framework to process querying and maintain the large datasets in distributed system.	Big-Data, Database	DOAP RDF (json)	Java	2013	V 2.1.1

PROGRAMMING FOR BIG DATA

There are various programs helpful for big data processing the foremost distinguished and powerful languages are R, Python, Java, Storm, etc. Python is extremely helpful to programmers for doing statistics and economic manipulation of applied mathematics data. This includes usually vectors, lists, and data frames that represent data sets organized in rows and columns, Whereas R, outshines in the range of applied mathematics libraries it compromises. Most applied mathematics tests/methods area unit a part of associate degree R library. It's terribly straightforward to be told language with an enormous quantity of inherent methods. NumPy library in Python encompasses homogenized, a two-dimensional array that gives numerous ways for information manipulation. it's many functions for activity advanced arithmetic and statistics Java and Storm additionally play a major role in massive information programming.

RESEARCH GAP

The research gap in of big data Tools and Platforms is ever-changing speedily. It's not solely obtaining oil-fired by the innovations happening within the open supply world however additionally having support from the licensed product world in maturing those innovations for the mainstream use. The prevailing technologies are becoming richer in terms of options and stability quarterly. At the same time, the frequent emergence of latest tools and frameworks fostering different paradigms in big data computation is creating the prevailing ones stale. In NoSQL database gap technologies like Foundation dB and cockroach DB are to be watched for. The support for acid and multiple data models will create Foundation dB selection for numerous use cases. On the opposite hand cockroach, dB is double-geared to resolve real distributed transaction issues alongside different NoSQL options.

On the opposite hand, the Spark from Berkeley Data Analytics Stack is rising out as a robust contestant to varied Distributed processing components (and corresponding Application Components) in the Hadoop system. At identical time industry has also seen Flink, the contestant to Spark. Flink is still less matured compared to Spark and only time can say which one is going to win during this area. Tachyon is another promising technology happening in Berkeley Data Analytics Stack.

CONCLUSION

A modified paradigm of contemporary business and are advancement in communication and technology has given a brand-new face to the analytics. Just like the light-weight fastening in computers, currently people would like super-fast deciding and it's attainable with big data analytics. Advancement in tools and technologies created it attainable. Best practices have emerged to assist huge data processing. a stimulating truth is that a lot of those practices are the new empowered, versatile extensions of the old one. the biggest issue behind the recognition of big data analysis is that it helps a company to require corrective actions and helpful choices while not a lot of data processing latency. Thus, big data allows call capability, nearly in run time setting.

REFERENCES

Apache O.R.C. (n.d.). the smallest, fastest columnar storage for Hadoop workloads. Retrieved from https://orc.apache.org/

Apache REEF. (n.d.). Apache REEF™ - a stdlib for Big Data. Retrieved from http://reef.apache.org/

Apache Accumulo. (n.d.). Apache Accumulo. Retrieved from https://accumulo.apache.org/

Apache Airavata. (n.d.). Apache Airavata. Retrieved from https://airavata.apache.org/

Apache Ambari. (2015, August). Apache Ambari. Retrieved from https://ambari.apache.org

Apache Apex. (n.d.). Apache Apex. Retrieved from https://apex.apache.org/

Apache Avro. (2015, August 6). Welcome to Avro. Retrieved from http://avro.apache.org/docs/1.3.0/

Apache Beam. (n.d.). Apache Beam: An advanced unified programming model. Retrieved from https://beam.apache.org/

Apache BigTop. (n.d.). Apache Bigtop. Retrieved from http://bigtop.apache.org/

Apache BookKeeper. (n.d.). Apache BookKeeper. Retrieved from http://bookkeeper.apache.org/

Apache Calcite. (n.d.). The foundation for your next high-performance database. Retrieved from https://calcite.apache.org/

Apache Cassandra. (2015, August 6). Manage massive amounts of data, fast, without losing sleep. Retrieved from: http://cassandra.apache.org/

Apache Chukwa, (n.d.). Overview. Retrieved from: https://chukwa.apache.org/docs/r0.8.0/

Apache Couch DB. (n.d.). Data Where You Need It. Retrieved from http://couchdb.apache.org/

Apache Crunch. (n.d.). Getting Started. Retrieved from https://crunch.apache.org/getting-started.html

Apache Curator. (n.d.). Welcome to Apache Curator. Retrieved from: http://curator.apache.org/

Apache DataFu. (n.d.). Apache DataFu. Retrieved from https://datafu.incubator.apache.org/

Apache Drill. (2015, August 6). Apache Drill. Retrieved from http://drill.apache.org/

Apache Edgent. (n.d.). Apache Edgent a Community for Accelerating Analytics at the Edge. Retrieved from http://edgent.apache.org/

Apache Falcon. (2015, August 6). Falcon - Feed management and data processing platform. Retrieved from http://falcon.apache.org/index.html

Apache Flink. (2015, August 6). Introduction to Apache Flink. Retrieved from https://flink.apache.org/

Apache Flume. (2015, August 6). Welcome to Apache Flume. Retrieved from https://flume.apache.org/

Apache Giraph. (2015, August 6). Welcome to Apache Giraph. Retrieved from http://giraph.apache.org/

Apache Gora, (n.d.). Welcome to the Apache Gora project. Retrieved from: https://gora.apache.org/

Apache Hama, (n.d.). Apache Hama. Retrieved from https://hama.apache.org/

Apache Hbase. (2015, August 6). Welcome to Apache HBase. Retrieved from: http://hbase.apache.org/

Apache Helix, (n.d.). Helix A cluster management framework for partitioned and replicated distributed sources. Retrieved from http://helix.apache.org/

Apache Hive, (n.d.). Home. Retrieved from: https://cwiki.apache.org/confluence/display/Hive/Home

Apache Ignite. (2015, August 6). Database and Caching Platform. Retrieved from https://ignite.incubator.apache.org/

Apache Kafka. (2015, August 6). Documentation. Retrieved from http://kafka.apache.org/documentation.html

Apache Knox, (n.d.). REST API and Application Gateway for the Apache Hadoop Ecosystem. Retrieved from https://knox.apache.org/

Apache Lens, (n.d.). Welcome to Lens. Retrieved from https://lens.apache.org/

Apache Metamodal, (n.d.). Apache MetaModel. Retrieved from http://metamodel.apache.org/

Apache Oozie. (2015, August 6). Apache Oozie Workflow Scheduler for Hadoop. Retrieved from http://oozie.apache.org/

Apache Parquet. (2015, August 6). Parquet. Retrieved from http://parquet.apache.org/

Apache Phoenix. (2015, August 6). Overview. Retrieved from http://phoenix.apache.org/

Apache Pig. (2015, August 6). Welcome to Apache Pig. Retrieved from: https://pig.apache.org/

Apache Samza, (n.d.). What is Samza? Retrieved from http://samza.apache.org/

Apache Software Foundation. (n.d.). Apache Software Foundation. Retrieved from http://en.wikipedia.org/wiki/Apache_Software_Foundation

Apache Spark Streaming. (2015, August 6). Apache Spark Streaming. Retrieved from https://spark.apache.org/streaming/

Apache Sqoop. (2015, August 6). Apache Sqoop. Retrieved from http://sqoop.apache.org/

Apache Storm. (n.d.). Storm Distributed and Fault-Tolerant Realtime Computation. Retrieved from: http://storm-project.net/

Apache Tajo. (n.d.). Apache Tajo: A big data warehouse system on Hadoop. Retrieved from http://tajo.apache.org/

Apache Tez. (2015, August 6). Introduction. Retrieved from http://tez.apache.org/

Apache VXQuery. (n.d.). Apache VXQuery. Retrieved from: https://vxquery.apache.org/

Apache Zeppelin. (2015, August 6). Apache Zeppelin. Retrieved from: https://zeppelin.incubator.apache.org/

Apache ZooKeeper. (n.d.). General Information. Retrieved from: https://cwiki.apache.org/confluence/display/ZOOKEEPER/Index

Bakshi, K. (2012, March). Considerations for big data: Architecture and approach. In *Proceedings of 2012 IEEE Aerospace Conference*. IEEE. 10.1109/AERO.2012.6187357

Borthakur, D. (2007). The hadoop distributed file system: Architecture and design. *Hadoop Project Website*, *11*, 21.

Boyd, D., & Crawford, K. (2012). Critical questions for big data: Provocations for a cultural, technological, and scholarly phenomenon. *Information Communication and Society*, *15*(5), 662–679. doi:10.1080/1369118X.2012.678878

Chen, M., Mao, S., & Liu, Y. (2014). Big data: A survey. *Mobile Networks and Applications*, *19*(2), 171–209. doi:10.100711036-013-0489-0

Demchenko, Y., Ngo, C., de Laat, C., Membrey, P., & Gordijenko, D. (2013, August). Big security for big data: Addressing security challenges for the big data infrastructure. In *Workshop on Secure Data Management* (pp. 76-94). Springer.

Dou, W., Zhang, X., Liu, J., & Chen, J. (2015). HireSome-II: Towards privacy-aware cross-cloud service composition for big data applications. *IEEE Transactions on Parallel and Distributed Systems*, *26*(2), 455–466. doi:10.1109/TPDS.2013.246

Elgendy, N., & Elragal, A. (2014, July). Big data analytics: a literature review paper. In *Industrial Conference on Data Mining* (pp. 214-227). Springer, Cham. 10.1007/978-3-319-08976-8_16

Elgendy, N., & Elragal, A. (2016). Big Data Analytics in Support of the Decision Making Process. *Procedia Computer Science*, *100*, 1071–1084. doi:10.1016/j.procs.2016.09.251

Fayyad, U., Piatetsky-Shapiro, G., & Smyth, P. (1996). From data mining to knowledge discovery in databases. *AI Magazine*, *17*(3), 37.

Gilbert, S., & Lynch, N. (2012). Perspectives on the CAP Theorem. *Computer*, *45*(2), 30–36. doi:10.1109/MC.2011.389

Hartmann, P. M., Zaki, M., Feldmann, N., & Neely, A. (2014, March 27). Big data for big business? A taxonomy of data-driven business models used by start-up firms. *A Taxonomy of Data-Driven Business Models Used by Start-Up Firms*.

Hinton, G. E., Osindero, S., & Teh, Y. W. (2006). A fast learning algorithm for deep belief nets. *Neural Computation*, *18*(7), 1527–1554. doi:10.1162/neco.2006.18.7.1527

Jagadish, H. V., Gehrke, J., Labrinidis, A., Papakonstantinou, Y., Patel, J. M., Ramakrishnan, R., & Shahabi, C. (2014). Big data and its technical challenges. *Communications of the ACM, 57*(7), 86–94. doi:10.1145/2611567

Jamshidi, M., Tannahill, B., Yetis, Y., & Kaplan, H. (2015). Big data analytic via soft computing paradigms. In *Frontiers of higher order fuzzy sets* (pp. 229–258). Springer New York. doi:10.1007/978-1-4614-3442-9_12

Jeong, Y. S., & Shin, S. S. (2016). An Efficient Authentication Scheme to Protect User Privacy in Seamless Big Data Services. *Wireless Personal Communications, 86*(1), 7–19. Retrieved from http://web.a.ebscohost.com/abstract?direct=true&profile=ehost&scope=site&authtype=crawler&jrnl=09296212&AN=111455684&h=7IFKiKh0Lg%2fy2FHp%2b55gtkcsVzZJxAEGRQ15KxUutmue2vo481ON7i1qe1jDHwu%2fkZg0y%2b7wVoBerrtIukr5PQ%3d%3d&crl=c&resultNs=AdminWebAuth&resultLocal=ErrCrlNotAuth&crlhashurl=login.aspx%3fdirect%3dtrue%26profile%3dehost%26scope%3dsite%26authtype%3dcrawler%26jrnl%3d09296212%26AN%3d111455684 doi:10.100711277-015-2990-1

Kamat, G., & Singh, S. (2013). Comparisons of compression. In: Hadoop Summit 2013. Retrieved from http://www.slideshare.net/Hadoop_Summit/kamat-singh-june27425pmroom210cv2

Katal, A., Wazid, M., & Goudar, R. H. (2013, August). Big data: issues, challenges, tools and good practices. In *2013 Sixth International Conference on Contemporary Computing (IC3)* (pp. 404-409). IEEE. 10.1109/IC3.2013.6612229

Liu, Y., Wu, B., Wang, H., & Ma, P. (2014). Bpgm: A big graph mining tool. *Tsinghua Science and Technology, 19*(1), 33–38. doi:10.1109/TST.2014.6733206

Mazumder, S. (2016). Big Data Tools and Platforms. In Big Data Concepts, Theories, and Applications (pp. 29-128). Springer International Publishing. doi:10.1007/978-3-319-27763-9_2

Meng, S., Dou, W., Zhang, X., & Chen, J. (2014). KASR: A keyword-aware service recommendation method on mapreduce for big data applications. *IEEE Transactions on Parallel and Distributed Systems, 25*(12), 3221–3231. doi:10.1109/TPDS.2013.2297117

Miller, J. A., Ramaswamy, L., Kochut, K. J., & Fard, A. (2015, June). Research directions for big data graph analytics. In *2015 IEEE International Congress on Big Data (BigData Congress)* (pp. 785-794). IEEE. 10.1109/BigDataCongress.2015.132

Miloslavskaya, N., & Tolstoy, A. (2016). Big Data, Fast Data and Data Lake Concepts. *Procedia Computer Science, 88*, 300–305. Retrieved from https://ac.els-cdn.com/S1877050916316957/1-s2.0-S1877050916316957-main.pdf?_tid=4d5629d4-ff7f-11e7-bdfe-00000aab0f6c&acdnat=1516630968_7bf0960c12ee94bb5d00caa036126bfc doi:10.1016/j.procs.2016.07.439

Purcell, B. (2013). The emergence of" big data" technology and analytics. *Journal of technology research, 4*, 1.

Sánchez, D., Martín-Bautista, M. J., Blanco, I., & de la Torre, C. J. (2008, December). Text knowledge mining: an alternative to text data mining. In *IEEE International Conference on Data Mining Workshops ICDMW '08* (pp. 664-672). IEEE. 10.1109/ICDMW.2008.57

Sánchez, D., Martín-Bautista, M. J., Blanco, I., & de la Torre, C. J. (2008, December). Text knowledge mining: an alternative to text data mining. In *IEEE International Conference on Data Mining Workshops ICDMW '08* (pp. 664-672). IEEE.

Smith, L. I. (2002). A tutorial on principal components analysis. *Cornell University, 51*(52), 65.

Tannahill, B. K. (2014). Big Data Analytic Techniques: Predicting Renewable Energy Capacity to Facilitate the Optimization of Power Plant Energy Trading and Control Algorithms.

Yenkar, V., & Bartere, M. (2014). Review on "Data Mining with Big Data". *International Journal of Computer Science and Mobile Computing, 3*(4), 97–102.

This research was previously published in Applications of Security, Mobile, Analytic, and Cloud (SMAC) Technologies for Effective Information Processing and Management; pages 212-232, copyright year 2018 by Engineering Science Reference (an imprint of IGI Global).

Chapter 75
Understanding the Determinants of Big Data Analytics Adoption

Surabhi Verma
NMIMS, Navi Mumbai, India

Sushil Chaurasia
(iD) https://orcid.org/0000-0003-0747-8907
NMIMS, Navi Mumbai, India

ABSTRACT

This article aims to empirically investigate the factors that affects the adoption of big data analytics by firms (adopters and non-adopters). The current study is based on three feature that influence BDA adoption: technological context (relative advantage, complexity, compatibility), organizational context (top management support, technology readiness, organizational data environment), and environmental context (competitive pressure, and trading partner pressure). A structured questionnaire-based survey method was used to collect data from 231 firm managers. Relevant hypotheses were derived and tested by partial least squares. The results indicated that technology, organization and environment contexts impact firms' adoption of big data analytics. The findings also revealed that relative advantage, complexity, compatibility, top management support, technology readiness, organizational data environment and competitive pressure have a significant influence on the adopters of big data analytics, whereas relative advantage, complexity and competitive pressure have a significant influence on the non-adopters of big data analytics.

1. INTRODUCTION

Emerging economies had witnessed dramatically changing business environment and severe market competition (Paley, 2017). Given this competitive landscape firms have still prompted to adopt various state-of-the-art Information Technologies (IT) to improve their business operations and performance

DOI: 10.4018/978-1-6684-3662-2.ch075

(Pan and Jang, 2008; Faizi et.al., 2017). Technologies have also changed in this decade. The term "big data analytics (BDA)" has been critical in the world of IT. BDA, or the analysis of structured and unstructured data of consumers and devices to conduct business, is recognized as an important area for IT innovation and investment (Manyika et al., 2011; Zomaya and Sakr, 2017). BDA has been spread out through the main areas related to information systems (IS) and technologies, such as databases, analytical tools and visualization techniques for firms (Chen and Zhang, 2014; Zomaya and Sakr, 2017). In other words, BDA is a kind of data capturing, storing and analyzing tools and techniques that is similar to data warehousing and business intelligence (Faizi et.al., 2017). BDA also uses ubiquitous data from various sources like cloud, social media, geo-location and more for generating insights which could be used by the business employees for decision making (Labrinidis and Jagadish, 2012; Zomaya and Sakr, 2017). Thus, BDA enable firms to utilize huge amount of structured and unstructured data for (near) real-time decision making. Advanced IT devices, social media services, and corporate information system are continuously churning out vast amount of data. Businesses today are increasingly facing challenges in managing and capitalizing them to their advantages. Using BDA, a firm perform better in monitoring acceptance of products/services in the marketplace and in understanding its business environment by potentially fueling competitive advantages (Davenport, 2014; Thuemmler and Bai, 2017; Verma, 2018). Already there is no shortage of evidence that BDA, if adequately utilized, can unleash major impacts on reducing business costs, kindling business insights, and unraveling strategic information, and subsequently boosting quality and effectiveness of corporate decision making (Chen and Zhang, 2014; McAfee and Brynjolfsson, 2012; Zomaya and Sakr, 2017). Thus, BDA provides the opportunity of improving the performance and business processes to firms (Paley, 2017).

From a business point of view, firms are increasingly attempting to integrate business processes into the existing information systems (IS) applications and build fact-based technologies for making decisions in real-time (Gandomi and Haider, 2015; Verma et.al., 2018). Industries are getting ubiquitous amount of data from various customers' touch points, geo-location, social media and sensors have become one of the key aspects for improving operation efficiency (Paley, 2017). To enhance competitive advantage, developing BDA capability is an important undertaking because it is rapidly changing the way that enterprises' understanding of their customers, and also thus becoming a more integral part of enterprises' business tactics (LaValle et al., 2013; Paley, 2017). BDA diffusion becomes a significant topic because it enables firms to execute data analytics along value chain activities (e.g. manufacturing, distribution, sales, finance, information sharing, customer service and collaboration with trading partners) (Russom, 2011; Paley, 2017).

While BDA has been discussed as a new technology development that can provide several advantages, at strategic, tactical and operational level, to its adopters, the BDA adoption rate is not growing as fast as expected (Tien, 2013; Paley, 2017). In fact, LaValle et al., (2011) surveyed different companies from different industries that have built analytics applications using big data and analyzed how BDA affected companies' operational and strategic decisions. The future of analytics lies in BDA, whose major goal is to increase the operational efficiency, information of strategic direction, development of better customer service, identification and development of new products and services, identification of new customers and markets, etc. (Chang and Zhang, 2014; Paley, 2017). Many firms began carefully examining the possibility of utilizing big data analytics and are actively considering its adoption (Rosati and Lynn, 2017; Guarisco and Langabeer, 2017). Owing to the lack of exploratory studies that explain the diffusion and adoption of BDA (Kwon et al., 2014; Rosati and Lynn, 2017), the current study aim is to understand the process of adoption of the technology and to identify factors affecting the BDA adoption decision in organization.

2. THEORIES AND LITERATURE REVIEW

2.1. Prior Research on BDA Adoption

BDA can revolutionize the business scenario through various technological disruptions and techniques, and facilitate the access of different types of real time data for decision making (Chen et al., 2012; Zomaya and Sakr, 2017; Verma, 2017). Many previous studies in the field of BDA had addressed the areas of new technologies, security requirement, privacy concerns and expectations in these emerging environments (Rosati and Lynn, 2017). Pavolotsky and Seirmarco (2012) built different types of business models that can be exploited for companies (BDA users) keen on BDA services adoption. Additionally, many recent big data business model capture and analyze data streams, such as social media feeds etc. (Russell, 2013). The transaction cost in such big data adoption may be based on data processing units (DPUs). Many other business models include the analysis of various analyze structured and unstructured data in real time (Gandomi and Haider, 2015). The techniques of BDA to analyze structured and unstructured data in real time have been categorized in five sub-categories (Table 1) by Gandomi and Haider (2015):

For successful adoption of big data technologies as an analytic capability, Moore (2014) developed a big data roadmap and maturity model to understand the ecosystem of the domains of the technology infrastructure, data management, analytics, governance, monitoring and governance. Quality of data and interoperability of BDA was found to be suitable for BDA adoption in different types of firms (Moore, 2014; Shin, 2015; Rosati and Lynn, 2017; Guarisco and Langabeer, 2017). Kwon et al., (2014) study reveals that a firm's intention for BDA can be positively affected by its competence in maintaining the quality of corporate data. The big data adopter firm's favorable experience (i.e., benefit perceptions) in utilizing data could encourage their future financial investment. Perceived benefits of BDA have a positive effect on the adoption behavior of BDA (Esteves and Curto, 2013; Rosati and Lynn, 2017).

Prior studies have examined the link between Big Data use and competitive advantage (Paley, 2017). Kamioka and Tapanainen (2014), found that management involvement and understanding was connected to competitive advantage using BDA. The cross-functional activities of employees who are tasked with analyzing Big Data was found as the antecedent factors which were connected with systematic Big Data use (Kamioka and Tapanainen, 2014). The availability of information systems for BDA processing, the IT use abilities of users, and the power of the IS division had a positive effect on the organizational use of BDA (Rosati and Lynn, 2017). The positive attitudes of the users, the sufficiency of human resources, user IT skills and the secure management of data were found to have an influence on the extent of BDA use (Thuemmler and Bai, 2017).

In summary the above-mentioned BDA adoption research can be concluded in two perspectives:

1. Although various factors effects BDA adoption in prior researchers' findings, all these factors can be classified in technological, organizational or environmental contexts. Thus, it is feasible to apply the Technology-Organization-Environment (TOE) framework to explore the BDA adoption issue;

2. Most studies explored the importance of the technological factors affecting BDA adoption. However, the adoption intention of BDA could also be influenced by environmental and organizational factors. Therefore, there is a need to analyze the organizational and environmental determinants to acquire a better understanding of BDA adoption.

Table 1. Tools, techniques and applications for Big Data

Techniques of BDA Analysis	Description	Tools and Techniques	Applications	Reference(s)
Text analytics	It enables businesses to convert large volumes of human-generated text into meaningful summaries by involving statistical analysis, machine learning and computational linguistics (Chung, 2014).	IBM Watson Analytics Information extraction techniques Natural Language Processing (NLP) techniques Question answering techniques Sentiment analysis Tableau Software Text summarization techniques	Create infographics Extract structured information such as drug name, dosage and frequency from medical prescriptions Obtain valuable information about different features of the product Predict stock market based on information extracted from financial news Share analytics in cloud to create custom charts	Herschel et al. (2015), Rackley (2015), Faizi et.al, 2017
Audio analytics	it analyzes and extracts information from unstructured audio data (call center, health care and such others) (Hirschberg et al., 2010).	Automatic speech recognition algorithms Behavioral Analytics Harmony Suite Praetorian Voice Recorder Qfiniti Explore	Analyses customer interactions across multiple communication channels and languages Analyze an infant's cries, which contain information about the infant's health and emotional status Call monitoring and reporting Recording functionality for quality monitoring Support diagnosis and treatment of certain medical conditions that affect the patient's communication patterns (e.g. depression)	Khan et al. (2014), Faizi et.al., 2017
Video analytics	it refers to techniques to monitor, analyze and extract meaningful information from video stream (Panigrahi et al., 2010).	Google Analytics Vimeo Analytics YouTube Analytics	An analytics suite to find total views, number of comments, likes and dislikes based on channel subscriber changes and demographics Automated security and surveillance systems; and buying behavior of groups Event tracking	Topps et al. (2013), Agneeswaran (2014), Knapp (2009)
Social media analytics	It refers to the analysis of unstructured and structured data from social media channels and user-generated content (such as sentiments, videos, images and bookmarks) (Barbier and Liu, 2011; Gundecha and Liu, 2012)	Community detection Content-based analytics Facebook Insights Link prediction LinkedIn analytics for businesses Structure-based analytics	Discover links in biological networks Provide an overview of all the posts on business page Track a number of different companies and compare performance Uncover potential collaborations in terrorist or criminal networks Uncovering behavioral patterns Viral marketing	Russell (2013), Faizi et.al., (2017), Paley (2017)
Predictive analytics	Techniques that predict future outcomes by uncovering patterns and predicting relationships from current and historical data (Fan et al., 2014)	Kount complete Asset Archive Regression techniques (e.g. logit models) Machine learning techniques	SaaS solution for fraud management Examine and audit loan trends Predict the failure of jet engines based on the stream of data from several thousand sensors predict customers' moves	Albrechet et al. (2007), Faizi et al., (2017), Paley (2017)

2.2. TOE Framework

A theoretical model for BDA diffusion needs to consider the weakness in the adoption and diffusion technological innovation, which are caused by the specific technological, organizational and environmental contexts of the firm. Several studies (Chong and Ooi, 2008; Oliveira and Martins, 2010; Kuan and Chau, 2001; Shrivastava and Teo, 2010; Chau and Tam, 1997; Zhu et al., 2004; Lin and Lin, 2008; Pan and Jang, 2008; Hsu and Yeh, 2017; Sun et.al., 2018) have been credited with proposing the TOE framework, developed by Tornatsky and Fleischer (1990), to analyze IT adoption by firms. The TOE framework identifies three context groups: technological, organizational and environmental. The technological context refers to internal and external technologies applicable to the firm. Organizational context refers to several indexes regarding the origination, such as firm size and scope, centralization, formalization, and complexity of managerial structure and the quality of human resources. Environmental context refers to a firm's industry, competitors and government policy or intention. The TOE framework is consistent with Rogers' (1983) theory of innovation diffusion (Pan and Jang, 2008; Srivastava and Teo, 2010; Wang et al., 2010; Ngah et. al, 2017), which recognises the following five technological characteristics as precedents for any adoption decision: relative advantage (RA), complexity (CX), compatibility (CM), observability, and trialability. Therefore, the TOE framework explains the adoption of innovation and a considerable number of empirical studies have focused on various IS domains.

Firm's faces challenges in making a decision about whether BDA would be appropriate for firms with already existing and functional technology. The organization must decide to both develop and invest in its own recourses or to make changes based on consideration of the environmental situation (Hsu and Yeh, 2017). Based on the literatures that supported TOE framework for the examination of IT and IS innovations, including open systems, e-business, e-commerce, ICT, ERP, and RosettaNet standard technology adoption and performance (Chau and Tam, 1997; Kuan and Chau, 2001; Zhu et al., 2004; Shrivastava and Teo, 2010). The current study is based on following three features influence BDA adoption: technological context (RA, CX, and CM), organisational context (TMS, TR and ODE), and environmental context (PA and CP). Table 2 summarizes the relevant studies based on the TOE framework.

3. RESEARCH MODEL AND HYPOTHESES

In this study, the research model incorporates technological, organizational, and environmental contexts as important determinants of BDA adoption. As shown in Figures 1-4, this incorporation of the three contexts posited eight predictors for BDA adoption, and adoption was considered as a binary variable, with non-adopter firms assigned the value of 1 and adopter firms assigned the value of 0. Logistic regression analysis is used to test the hypotheses, and these factors are hypothesized to have a direct effect on firm adoption of BDA services; the relationships among the eight factors were outside the scope of our research.

Table 2. Model constructs from the TOE framework

Technology/Dependent Variable	Source	Rel. Advantage	Constructs						
			Complexity	Compatibility	Top Mgmt. Support	Tech. Readiness	Org. Data Environment	Trading Partner Pressure	Comp. Pressure
Data warehousing adoption	Ramamurthy et al. (2008)	X	X		X		X		
Electronic data interchange (EDI) adoption	Kuan and Chau, 2001					X			X
e-commerce adoption	Ghobakhloo et al., 2011	X		X	X	X			X
Cloud computing adoption	Abdollahzadegan et al., 2013	X	X	X	X	X			X
RFID adoption	Wang et al. (2010)	X	X	X	X	X		X	X
Enterprise application adoption	Ramdani et al. (2013)	X	X	X	X	X			X
Cloud computing adoption	Low et al. (2011)	X	X	X	X	X		X	X
Business intelligence systems	Puklavec et al., 2014	X	X	X	X	X	X	X	X
Open systems adoption	Chau and Tam (1997		X						
B2C e-commerce	To and Ngai (2006)	X				X			X
Internet-based ICT	Tan et al. (2008)	X	X	X					
E-business	Oliveira and Martins (2010)					X		X	X
ERP	Pan and Jang (2008)					X			X

Figure 1. Proposed research model

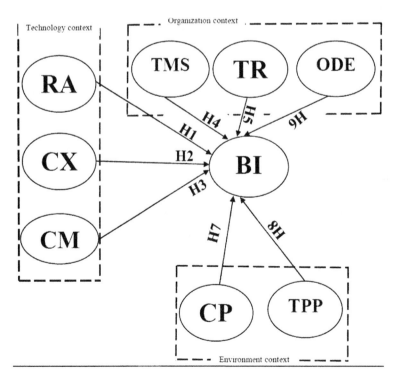

Figure 2. Proposed research model (full sample)

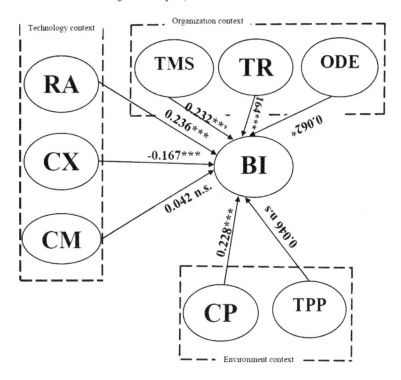

Figure 3. Proposed research model (adopter sub-sample)

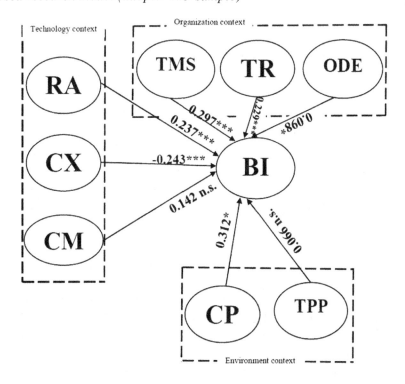

Figure 4. Proposed research model (non-adopter sub-sample)

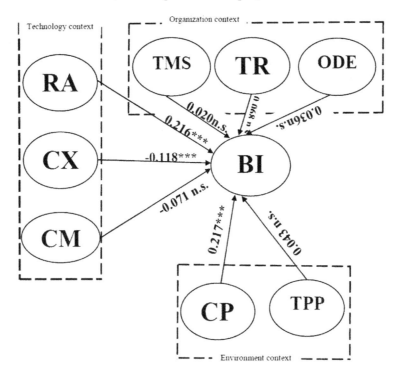

3.1. Technology Context

The technological factors are based on the IDT (Rogers, 2003). Rogers identified five technological characteristics as antecedents to any adoption decision: relative advantage (RA), compatibility (CM), complexity (CX), trialability, and observability (Rogers, 1983). Many studies, including the meta-analysis of 75 diffusion articles conducted by Tornatzky and Klein (1982), found that only RA, CM, and CX are consistently related to innovation adoption. Observability and trailability, both are correlated to risk and can increase the uncertainty about the innovation among the adopters (Fichman and Kemerer, 1993). Measuring these attributes to specific technology innovation is difficult because in all the cases, they may not be the key perceived characteristics for adopter. Grover (1983) and Lee and Kim (2007) directly excluded the trialability and observability constructs in their research models. Therefore, three technological characteristics –RA, CX, and CM – are included in the model.

3.1.1. Relative Advantage (RA)

RA is defined as the degree to which a technological factor is perceived as benefit for firms than the idea it supersedes or the status quo (Rogers, 1983). It is reasonable that firms take into consideration the advantages that well comprehend adopting innovations (To and Ngai, 2006; Paley, 2017). BDA services, which allow data management, risk management, business process optimization and more in (near) real-time, can substitute for or complement business intelligence and data warehousing software. The expected benefits of BDA services include the following (Russom, 2012; LaValle et al., 2013; Labrindis and Jagadish, 2012; Paley, 2017; Zomaya and Sakr, 2017): enabling effective decision support and business intelligence solutions; facilitating OLAP; ensuring data integrity, accuracy, security, and availability; easing the setting and enforcing of standards, facilitating data sharing, and improving customer service, market segmentation. Therefore, BDA is expected to be able to give organizations greater competitive advantage (Davenport, 2014). Therefore, hypothesis is:

Hypothesis H1: Relative advantage will have a positive effect on BDA adoption.

3.1.2. Complexity (CX)

CX is the extent to which an innovation is perceived as relatively difficult to understood and to be used (Rogers, 1983). It acts like an inhibitor for successful implementation of an innovation and usually negatively associated with the adoption of innovation (Tornetzky and Klein, 1982; Premkumar et al., 1994; Premkumar and Roberts, 1999; Rosati and Lynn, 2017). People may not have confidence in the BDA services because it is relatively new to them (Manyika et al., 2011; Paley, 2017). The security and privacy of data, availability of architecture, and protocols and the diversity of the techniques and technology, time to comprehend makes BDA implementation a very complex task (Labrindis and Jagadish, 2012; Gandomi and Haider, 2015; Broeders et. al., 2017; Zhang et. al., 2017). Therefore, the hypothesis is:

Hypothesis H2: Complexity will have a negative effect on BDA adoption.

3.1.3. Compatibility (CM)

CM refers to the degree to which an innovation is perceived as being consistent with the potential adopters' needs or the existing practices (Tornatzky and Klein, 1982). High CM has been considered as a facilitator for innovation adoption (Cooper and Zmud, 1990; Wang et al., 2010; Rosati and Lynn, 2017; Guarisco and Langabeer, 2017). If implementation of BDA system requires similar technology infrastructure relative to the extant technology base, it will facilitate the adoption of BDA in a firm (McAfee and Brynjolfsson, 2012; Guarisco and Langabeer, 2017). Therefore, CM may be an important determinant of BDA adoption, so the hypothesis is:

Hypothesis H3: Compatibility will have a positive effect on BDA adoption.

3.2. Organization Context

The functional perspective of top managers (Wang et al., 2016; Paley, 2017), the data management perspective of a firm (Ramamurthy et al., 2008; Zomaya and Sakr, 2017) and the capability perspective of a firm (Gangwar et al., 2014), top management support, organizational data environment and technology readiness are identified as important organizational factors.

3.2.1. Top Management Support (TMS)

TMS is an important factor for creating a supportive climate and for providing adequate resources for the adoption of new technologies (Lin and Lee, 2005; Wang et al., 2010; Paley, 2017). As the complexity and sophistication of technologies increase, top management can provide a vision, support and commitment to create a positive environment for innovation (Lee and Kim, 2007; McAfee and Brynjolfsson, 2012). TMS is more critical for BDA technologies since the BDA implementation requires adequate resources, integration of data and architectures and user coordination. Therefore, the hypothesis is:

Hypothesis H4: TMS will have a positive effect on BDA adoption.

3.2.2. Organizational Data Environment (ODE)

ODE refers to reducing errors and increasing the ability to access previously unavailable information (Ramamurthy et al., 2008). An organization's data environment is responsible for data planning and developing and enforcing policy, data dictionary standards, data integrity and security policies in large organizations. An effective ODE offers a number of benefits such as reducing errors reduction and increase in the ability to access previously unavailable information (Jain et al., 1988; Goodhue et al., 1992; Zomaya and Sakr, 2017). Big data are heterogeneous data from very diverse set of sources with differing formats and semantics extracted from different source systems. There is need to clean, transform, combine, and format before analyzing these data (Kimball, 1998; Wixom and Watson, 2001). A data environment that is not properly managed is likely to suffer from problems relating to quality, reliability, security, availability, integrity, and standards. Such an environment would pose greater challenges for the adoption of BDA. Therefore, following hypotheses is proposed:

Hypothesis H5: Quality of existing ODE will have a positive effect on BDA adoption.

3.2.3. Technology Readiness (TR)

The readiness concept is defined as a belief, intention, and attitude regarding the extent to which change is needed (Rafferty and Simons, 2006). This concept connects with the employees either to be supportive or resistant which shows the individual's behavioral aspects of change. Parasuraman (2000, p. 308) defined technology readiness as "people's propensity to embrace and use new technologies for accomplishing goals in home life and at work." Technology readiness includes four dimensions: optimism, innovation, discomfort, and insecurity (Parasuraman, 2000; Kuan and Chau, 2001; To and Ngai, 2006; Zhu et al., 2006; Pan and Jang, 2008; Wang et al., 2010; Oliveira and Martins, 2010). Resource at IT implementation provide the knowledge and skills to implement BDA (Wang et al., 2010). BDA services can become part of value chain activities only if firms have the required behavioural competence. Therefore, firms with greater TR are in a better position to adopt BDA (Cunningham, 2014), so the hypothesis is:

Hypothesis H6: Technology readiness will have a positive effect on BDA adoption.

3.3. Environment Context

Inspired by the broader perspective of competitive bandwagon pressure (Wang et al., 2016), competitive pressure and trading partner pressure are identified as potential environmental factors.

3.3.1. Competitive Pressure (CP)

Zhu et al. (2004) and Kuan and Chau (2001) identified CP as an important determinant of IT adoption. As market competition increases, managers might feel the need to seek competitive advantage through innovations. By adopting BDA, firms may benefit from better understanding of customers and market, inventory visibility, greater operation efficiency, and more accurate data-driven decision making (Chen and Zhang, 2014; LaValle et al., 2013; Mourtzis et al., 2016; Borkar et. al., 2016). Therefore, the hypothesis is:

Hypothesis H7: Competitive pressure will have a positive effect on BDA adoption.

3.3.2. Trading Partner Pressure (PA)

Studies have found that pressure from trading partners may influence innovation adoption (Teo et al., 2003; Gibbs and Kraemer, 2004; Iacovou et al., 1995). Recommendation from powerful partners (ones that generate a large proportion of sales) are a critical factor in adoption of an innovation. When a firm's dominant customers or suppliers have adopted an innovation, the firm may adopt the innovation to demonstrate its seamlessness as a business partner (To and Ngai., 2006). Firms engaged in such supply chain relationship, rely on trading partners for their IT implementation tasks (Pan and Jang, 2008).) and big data adoption (Lai et.al., 2018; Pan and Jang, 2008). The classic porter's five-force competitive model also indicates that competitive pressure (e.g. from trading partners) is an important external driver to initiate the deployment of IOS (inter-organizational innovation (Porter, 1980).

Therefore, the hypothesis is:

Hypothesis H8: Trading partner pressure will have a positive effect on BDA adoption.

4. RESEARCH METHODOLOGY

Most of the technology adoption research has been conducted in developed countries (Alshamila et al., 2013; Ramamurthy et al., 2008; Low et al., 2011). Research in a developing country context is limited (Saffu et al., 2007; Dubey et al., 2015). Developing countries have been projected to have bigger economies than developed countries and are driving global growth (World Economic Outlook, 2014). Therefore, it is necessary to understand the usage and adoption of BDA in developing economies also. According to a survey conducted by Ernst & Young, India has been identified as a country where digital information has been growing twice as fast as other worldwide rates. India already has 900 million plus mobile connections. There are approximately 100 million plus active mobile data users in India. Currently, the enterprises in India are implementing the BDA project to harness these data from consumers and devices to gain competitive advantages (Agrawal, 2013; Dubey et al., 2015). Big data analytics sector in India is expected to reach $16 billion (Economic Times, 2017). However, according to a survey conducted by International Data Corporation (IDC) for 250 Indian enterprises, it was found that only 15 percent of surveyed enterprises have adopted or deployed BDA technology. So the scope of current study was confined to Indian firms.

4.1. Measurement

A structured survey was conducted on Indian firms to evaluate the theoretical constructs. A structured survey questionnaire was developed by experts in the field of data analytics and business processes. Items used in the survey questionnaire were based on previously published literature (Table 3). The constructs (relative advantage, complexity, compatibility, top management support, technology readiness, organizational data environment, competitive pressure, and trading partner pressure) were measured using a five-point Likert (1 to 5) scale on an interval level ranging from "strongly agree" to "strongly disagree". Likert scale has been used in several previous information systems research studies similar to big data analytics (Gangwar et al., 2015; Wang et al., 2010). The turnover volume and number of employees are used as measures of the firm size (Wang et al., 2016; Oliveria et al., 2014). The questionnaire was pre-tested by seven industry experts and academician. A pilot test was conducted among 42 business managers of firms to test the instrument. These companies were not included in the main survey. The results of pilot test provided evidence that the scales are valid, reliable and have translation equivalence (Brislin, 1970).

4.2. Data

An online version of the structured survey questionnaire was emailed to qualified respondents i.e. CIOs, CTOs, directors, senior business and IS managers at 1600 firms in India. Majority of organizations, which make up the largest part of the economy, are not yet conversant with big data (Sanders, 2016). Even many of those organizations who understand and operate in data-rich environments, they do not understand how to exploit that data (Ross et.al., 2013). So, the firms listed in the Indian industries directory were non-probabilistically selected. This study utilized the key informant approach for data collection (Warheit et.al., 1978) in order to identify the individuals in the firm who are most involved in and knowledgeable about big data analytics. To qualify respondents, they were briefed about BDA and asked to self-qualify as adopter or non-adopter. BDA was conceptualized for the study as, as a suite of data management and analytical techniques for handling very large (from terabytes and exabytes) and complex (from sensor to social media) data. Additionally, Respondents were also asked to categorize themselves based on Gandomi and Haider's (2015) five big data characteristics, namely, volume, velocity, variety, veracity and value.

In order to increase the response rate, follow up emails were sent to the respondents. Total, 257 responses was received. However, out of 257 responses, 231 responses were considered valid (26 responses were unusable). The overall response rate was 14.4%, which is comparable to other research studies of similar scale (Verma, 2017). Of the valid responses, 40.7% (94 firms) were received from the adopter firms, and 59.3% (137 firms) were received from the non-adopter firms. The profile of the sample is shown in Table 4. The nonresponse bias was tested by comparing the sample distribution of the early and late respondent groups using the Kolmogorov-Smirnov (K-S) test (93). The K-S test shows the absence of response bias as the sample distributions of the early and late respondent groups did differ statistically. As shown in Table 4 the respondents were qualified individuals indicating a good quality of data. Harman's one-factor test was used for examining the common method bias (Podsakoff et.al, 2003). In the data set no significant common method bias was found. Table 5 summarizes the mean and standard deviation of all the constructs from the full and sub-samples (manufacturing and service).

Table 3. Measurement items

Variables		Measurement Items	Sources
Relative advantage	RA1	Usage of BDA, could facilitate better understanding of the nature of customers' demands.	Ramamurthy et al. (2008); Gangwar et al. (2015); Tan et al. (2008), To and Ngai (2006), Wang et al. (2010); Low et al. (2011)
	RA2	Usage of BDA, could enhance the scope for customized offerings.	
	RA3	BDA could prevent fraudulent events in (near real time).	
	RA4	BDA enhances granularity which improves personalization of services by analyzing individual customer or customer group data.	
	RA5	BDA could help in developing strategies based on user generated content on social media.	
	RA6	BDA have capabilities to monitor markets on (near) real time basis to increase sales opportunities.	
	RA7	BDA could increase revenue on (near) real time basis by pricing products by matching market conditions.	
	RA8	BDA could reduce business operational costs by automating process.	
	RA9	BDA could reduce maintenance costs by monitoring the devices/appliances on real time basis.	
Complexity	CX1	It is difficult to normalize huge amount of unstructured data from multiple sources to make it compatible with structured data.	Wang et al. (2010); Ramamurthy et al. (2008); Ramdani et al. (2013)
	CX2	After analysing big data, interpretation of results to extract actionable knowledge has been difficult.	
	CX3	It is difficult to integrate data, across multiple incompatible databases among various stakeholders.	
	CX4	It is difficult to integrate data across silos.	
Compatibility	CM1	CM1. BDA provides flexible architecture, which is compatible to various analytical tasks.	Tan et al. (2008), Oliveira and Martins (2010), Wang et al. (2010), Low et al. (2011)
	CM2	BDA architecture are compatible to schemas used for storing data.	
	CM3	BDA is compatible with existing technological architecture.	
	CM4	It is easy to synchronize external data with organization's internal data.	
Top management support	TS1	Top management has generally being likely to take risks involved in the adoption of the BDA.	Wang et al. (2010); Low et al., (2011); Gangwar et al. (2015)
	TS2	Top management is likely to consider the adoption of BDA which is strategically important.	
	TS3	Top management have policies that encourages usage of BDA initiatives to streamline, monitor and maintain enterprise's data flow.	
	TS4	Top management have strong positive views on how BDA could transform business.	
Technology readiness	TR1	Presently, it is difficult to find data scientists with the domain knowledge in the field in which analysis is to be done.	Kuan and Chau (2001), Pan and Jang (2008), Wang et al. (2010), Low et al. (2011)
	TR2	Presently people skills in handling (cleaning and organizing) large data sets are hard to find.	
	TR3	It is difficult to get analysts for interpretation of data to generate actionable information.	
Organizational data environment	ODE1	Big data is fragmented and dispersed among various stakeholders.	Ramamurhty et al. (2008), Puklavec et al. (2014)
	ODE2	Lack of metadata across different silos exists presently.	
	ODE3	Usage of BDA could increase the vulnerability of sensitive data to be exposed.	
	ODE4	A clear agreement on a common set of big data definitions and business rules is required in my organizations.	
Trading partner pressure	TPP1	My business partners encourage the usage of BDA.	Pan and Jang (2008), Zhu et al. (2004); Low et al. (2011)
	TPP2	My business partners request to use BDA.	
Competitive pressure	CP1	CP1. There is a trend in industry to enhance the utilization of BDA for business-related activities and decision making.	Oliveira and Martins (2010), To and Ngai (2006), Zhu et al. (2004)
	CP2	Company could lose customers to their competitors if they do not adopt new technologies.	
	CP3	I feel it is necessary to use BDA to compete in the marketplace.	
Adoption intention	BI1	I intend to use BDA for future decision making in the next 2 years.	Oliveria et al., 2014)
	BI2	I think that using BDA is advantageous for beating competitors by better responding to market.	
	BI3	My organization uses big data analytics.	

Table 4. Sample characteristics (N = 231)

Characteristics	Number	Percentage (%)
Employee number		
• <=400 *(Small)*	43	18.5%
• 400-800 *(Medium)*	54	23.2%
• >800 *(Large)*	134	58.3%
Company age (years)		
• <10	49	21.3%
• 10-19	68	29.3%
• 20-39	82	35.5%
• >=40	32	13.9%
Capital (in million of INR)		
• Turnover<= 750 *(Small)*	50	21.8%
• 750< Turnover<= 3,000 *(Medium)*	57	24.6%
• Turnover>3,000 *(Large)*	124	53.6%
BDA adoption		
• Yes	94	40.7%
• No	137	59.3%
Industry		
Service	133	57.58%
Manufacturer	98	42.42%

5. RESULTS

Partial Least Square-Structural Equation Modelling (PLS-SEM) method was used to empirically assess the research model. PLS-SEM advantage is that it does not require a normal distribution (Oliveria et al., 2014). The minimum sample size required for PLS estimation should satisfy any one of the following conditions:

- Ten times the largest number of formative indicators used to measure one construct (Hair et al., 2011);
- Ten times the largest number of structural paths directed at a particular latent construct in the structural model (Wu et al., 2011).

The sample of this study consists of 231 Indian firms, therefore meeting the necessary conditions for using PLS. SmartPLS version 3.0 software was used to assess the validity and reliability of the measurement model before testing different structural models (Hair et al., 2011). The proposed research model was evaluated through a two-fold analysis approach. To understand the key determinants of big data analysis adoption, this research study conducted a quantitative assessment of the full sample. Furthermore, to investigate how the determinants vary, this study also analyzed the sub-samples of the data for the adopters and non-adopters of big data analytics.

Table 5. Mean and standard deviation of full and sub-samples

Independent Variables	All	Mean (SD)		Diagnosing Multicollinearity	
		Adopter	Non-Adopter	VIF	C.I
RA	3.77 (0.89)	3.64 (1.03)	3.83 (0.80)	1.122	1.01
CX	3.17 (0.90)	3.31 (0.80)	3.09 (0.95)	1.057	9.55
CP	3.58 (0.83)	3.41 (0.81)	3.67 (0.83)	1.120	12.69
TS	3.71 (0.78)	3.61 (0.91)	3.56 (0.69)	1.092	13.21
TR	3.63 (0.93)	3.65 (0.94)	3.59 (0.91)	1.210	15.46
ODE	3.32 (0.85)	3.34 (0.84)	3.29 (0.86)	1.048	19.48
TPP	3.62 (1.03)	3.90 (0.99)	3.27 (0.97)	1.060	21.93
CP	2.06 (0.86)	1.75 (0.75)	2.65 (0.77)	1.183	26.02

RA = Relative advantage; CX = Complexity; CM = Compatibility; TMS = Top management support; TR = Technology readiness; ODE = Organization data environment; CP = Competitive pressure; TPP = Trading partner pressure; BI = Big data analytics adoption intention

5.1. Measurement Model

Table 6 and 7 depicts the measurement model results, i.e. reliability, validity, correlations and factor loading. In this study, the reliability of the scales was tested using Cronbach's alpha and Composite Reliability (CR) (Table 6). The results are higher than recommended value of 0.6 for Cronbach's alpha and 0.7 for CR for the full sample and the sub-samples of adopter and non-adopter. This suggests that scales used in this study are reliable (Henseler et al., 2009). A sufficient degree of convergent validity could be ensured if the average variance extracted (AVE) value is greater than 0.50 (Hair et al., 2014). Measurement models for full sample and adopter and non-adopter sub-sample demonstrate convergent validity (Table 6). The loadings of all items for both the full sample as well as the sub-samples have loadings greater than 0.7. Also, all items are statistically significant at the 0.01. Thus, all items are retained. Furthermore, the discriminant validity of constructs was evaluated using two measure including Fornell-Larcker criteria and cross-loadings. The first criteria suggest that the loading of each factors should be greater than all cross-loadings (Lowry and Gaskin, 2014). However, the second criterion needs that the square root of AVE should be greater than the correlations between the constructs (Henseler et al., 2009). The square root of AVE all factors is greater than the correlation between each of the pair factors, therefore, the second criterion is satisfied (Table 7). Therefore, both measures fulfilled the criteria for the full sample and the sub- samples.

5.2. Structural Model

The correlation table and the Variance Inflation Factors (VIF) were examined for finding the multi-collinearity among exogenous constructs. Table 7, 8 and 9 depicts that the highest correlation between exogenous constructs is 0.565, 0.4993 and 0.409. As depicted in Table 5, the VIF values was examined for all constructs are lower than 3, which is less that the recommended conservative threshold value of 5 (Low et al., 2011). These two results suggest that there is no concerns of multi-collinearity.

Table 6. Reliability indicators for full sample and sub-samples

Constructs	Full Sample			Adopter Sub-Sample			Non-Adopter Sub-Sample		
	AVE	CR	Cronbach's Alpha	AVE	CR	Cronbach's Alpha	AVE	CR	Cronbach's Alpha
Relative Advantage	0.657	0.822	0.815	0.694	0.901	0.862	0.638	0.870	0.843
Complexity	0.651	0.851	0.841	0.613	0.841	0.772	0.592	0.831	0.827
Compatibility	0.748	0.809	0.759	0.658	0.837	0.809	0.597	0.875	0.774
Top management support	0.663	0.818	0.741	0.649	0.853	0.801	0.567	0.847	0.748
Technology readiness	0.562	0.794	0.692	0.589	0.815	0.724	0.564	0.846	0.743
Organizational data environment	0.714	0.839	0.816	0.745	0.907	0.862	0.691	0.871	0.863
Competitive pressure	0.617	0.829	0.743	0.569	0.871	0.753	0.562	0.825	0.771
Trading partner pressure	0.588	0.810	0.725	0.673	0.869	0.814	0.562	0.860	0.761
BDA Adoption	0.762	0.876	0.827	0.783	0.896	0.862	0.749	0.895	0.826

Table 7. Correlations and AVEs (full sample)

	1	2	3	4	5	6	7	8	9
BDA Adoption	**0.873**								
Compatibility	0.336	**0.865**							
Complexity	0.254	0.514	**0.801**						
Competitive pressure	-0.165	0.035	0.035	**0.786**					
Organization data environment	0.494	0.321	0.331	-0.022	**0.845**				
Relative advantage	0.061	0.192	0.141	0.165	0.092	**0.811**			
Technology readiness	0.119	0.202	0.191	0.162	0.098	0.242	**0.750**		
Top management support	0.536	0.524	0.436	-0.147	0.390	0.177	0.205	**0.815**	
Trading partner pressure	0.392	0.384	0.535	0.018	0.433	0.230	0.275	0.565	**0.767**

*Bold diagonal values are square root of AVE

Table 8. Correlations and AVEs (adopter sample)

	1	2	3	4	5	6	7	8	9
BDA Adoption	**0.884**								
Compatibility	0.2225	**0.813**							
Complexity	0.2891	0.0481	**0.789**						
Competitive pressure	0.2287	0.077	0.0883	**0.760**					
Organization data environment	0.4993	0.0667	0.2645	0.0469	**0.863**				
Relative advantage	0.3386	0.1313	0.29	0.0905	0.1963	**0.833**			
Technology readiness	0.1833	0.0838	0.0082	0.1374	0.2403	0.148	**0.768**		
Top management support	0.1645	0.0055	0.4327	0.0441	0.1289	0.2514	0.1498	**0.805**	
Trading partner pressure	0.3076	0.0534	0.2322	0.0269	0.3147	0.2693	0.1211	0.1641	**0.820**

*Bold diagonal values are square root of AVE

Table 9. Correlations and AVEs (non-adopter sample)

	1	2	3	4	5	6	7	8	9
BDA Adoption	**0.762**								
Compatibility	-0.3055	**0.773**							
Complexity	0.2884	0.064	**0.77**						
Competitive pressure	0.3275	-0.061	-0.114	**0.750**					
Organization data environment	0.3056	-0.0709	0.3794	0.153	**0.823**				
Relative advantage	0.2378	-0.2031	0.2893	0.1059	0.2439	**0.799**			
Technology readiness	0.1188	0.0713	0.02	-0.0787	0.1236	0.1988	**0.751**		
Top management support	0.1921	0.015	0.2067	0.0136	0.2397	0.2393	-0.1608	**0.753**	
Trading partner pressure	0.409	-0.1492	0.3079	-0.0541	0.3655	0.3929	0.1055	0.2482	**0.750**

*Bold diagonal values are square root of AVE

The hypothesis used in this study was analyzed by examining the standardized paths. The path significance levels between independent and dependent variables were estimated using the bootstrapping method (500 re-samples). The results of hypothesis analysis are summarized in Table 10 and Figure 2, 3 and 4.

For the full sample, an examination of R^2 as a descriptive measure shows that the technology, organization and environment factors explain 63.5% of big data analytics adoption intention. For the full sample, the hypotheses for relative advantage ($\beta = 0.236$, $p < 0.01$), complexity ($\beta = -0.167$, $p < 0.01$), top management support ($\beta = 0.232$, $p < 0.01$), technology readiness ($\beta = 0.164$, $p < 0.01$), organizational data environment ($\beta = 0.062$, $p < 0.10$) and competitive pressure ($\beta = 0.228$, $p < 0.01$) as a predictor of the BDA adoption are confirmed for the full sample. However, Compatibility ($\beta = 0.042$, $p > 0.10$) and trading partner pressure ($\beta = 0.046$, $p > 0.10$) are not statistically significant for the full sample. The findings indicate that the research model of this study is significant in explaining the adoption of BDA firms. The examination of R^2 as a descriptive measure for the sub-samples demonstrates that the technology, organization and environment factors explains 65.8% and 52.1% of the adoption of BDA.

For the non-adopter sub-sample, the findings of this study are noteworthy. Hypotheses relative advantage ($\beta = 0.216$, $p < 0.05$), complexity ($\beta = -0.118$, $p < 0.05$) and competitive pressure ($\beta = 0.217$, $p < 0.01$) (H8) for are confirmed. While, compatibility ($\beta = -0.071$, $p > 0.10$), technology readiness ($\beta = 0.068$, $p > 0.10$), top management support ($\beta = 0.020$, $p > 0.10$), organizational data environment ($\beta = 0.036$, $p > 0.10$) and trading partner pressure ($\beta = 0.043$, $p > 0.10$) are not statistically significant. The research mode explains 52.1% of big data analytics adoption among non-adopters firms. For the adopter sub-sample, relative advantage ($\beta = 0.237$, $p < 0.01$), complexity ($\beta = -0.243$, $p < 0.01$), top management support ($\beta = 0.297$, $p < 0.01$), technology readiness ($\beta = 0.229$, $p < 0.01$), organizational data environment ($\beta = 0.098$, $p < 0.01$) and competitive pressure ($\beta = 0.312$, $p < 0.01$) are confirmed are confirmed. However, Compatibility ($\beta = 0.142$, $p > 0.10$) and trading partner pressure ($\beta = 0.066$, $p > 0.10$) are not statistically significant for the adopter sample. The research model explains 65.8% of BDA adoption among firms in the services sector.

Table 10. Relevant constructs for the structure model

Constructs	Full Sample (n=231)		Adopter Sub-Sample (n= 94)		Non-Adopter Sub-Sample (n=137)	
	Path Coeff.	T-Value	Path Coeff.	T-Value	Path Coeff.	T-Value
Technological factors						
Relative Advantage	0.236	4.014***	0.237	2.149***	0.216	1.972**
Complexity	-0.167	3.485***	-0.243	2.192**	-0.118	1.787**
Compatibility	0.042	0.092	0.142	0.894	-0.071	0.254
Organizational factors						
Top management support	0.232	3.467***	0.297	5.262***	0.020	0.125
Technology readiness	0.164	3.525***	0.229	5.295***	0.068	1.043
Organizational data environment	0.062	1.736*	0.098	3.217***	0.036	0.312
Environmental factors						
Competitive pressure	0.228	4.115***	0.312	4.671***	0.217	3.418***
Trading partner pressure	0.046	0.861	0.066	1.412	0.043	0.251
	R^2=0.635		$R^2 = 0.658$		$R^2 = 0.521$	

*Significance at $p < 0.10$
**Significance at $p < 0.05$
**Significance at $p < 0.01$

5. DISCUSSION

The nature of the BDA is more closely related to core business processes. Therefore, BDA adoption enables firms to perform critical tasks along value chain activities. The goal of this study was to extend understanding of BDA adoption, by identifying factors that distinguish adopters from non-adopters. This study demonstrated the value of the TOE framework and the empirical results indicated that there were significant determinants in each context of the TOE framework. Thus, determinants affecting the adoption of BDA in industries should include not only the characteristics of the technology itself, but also factors related to the internal organization and the external environment. Therefore, this study estimated the full and the adopter and non-adopter sub-samples with all the identified constructs as predictors of big data analytics adoption intention. Of the six variable, relative advantage, complexity, top management support, technology readiness, organizational data environment and competitive pressure are confirmed as the important driver to explain the big data analytics adoption intention. This result is consistent with studies that have found relative advantage (Muhammad et.al., 2018), top management support (Gunasekaran et.al., 2017), technology readiness (Popovič et.al., 2018), organizational data environment and competitive pressure (Alshamaila et al., 2013) to be a strong driver of the adoption of big data-based solutions in industries like technology, supply chain, logistics, manufacturing, finance and services (Gangwar et al., 2015; Paley, 2017). Complexity is confirmed as the important inhibitor to big data analytics adoption. This is consistent with the work of Wang et al. (2016) and Low et al. (2011).

Technology context: RA was found as a significant factor in the decision to adopt BDA. According to Premkumar and Roberts (1999), managers adopt technology only if they perceive a need for the technology to overcome a perceived performance gap or exploit a business opportunity. According to adopters, BDA adoption would improve their insights in fulfilling an unmet need, improve quality of a product or service, enhance customer segmentation, improve demand forecasting in their organizations and reduce customer acquisition and retention costs (Paley, 2017; Thuemmler and Bai, 2017). It helps in providing better and timely information which could further help to lower operational costs, improve business process, increase customer satisfaction levels and innovate (Miller and Mork, 2013; Paley, 2017). Further, for non-adopters the value of BDA advantages is relatively less significant or the costs of BDA adoption outweigh the benefits of BDA adoption in the present context.

CX was observed to have a significantly negative influence on BDA adoption in firms. The notion of CX associated with BDA is no different than other disruptive technologies and appears to be a significant determinant for BDA (Shin, 2015). In investigating the role of the complexity of BDA, it was found that, complexity was more important inhibitor for adopter firms than for non-adopter firms to explain the BDA adoption intention. It is certainly more complex to implement BDA than data warehousing and business intelligence (Chen et al., 2012). The immaturity of the BDA technologies, the lack of common standards, and the difficulty of integrating BDA with the existing enterprise information systems and business processes contribute to the CX of BDA adoption and are inhibiting non-adopter firms from adopting BDA. Therefore, the CX of BDA implementation can be an important barrier to BDA adoption.

In contrast, compatibility is found to be not significant for BDA adoption intention. Integration of BDA would not be an issue for adopter as well as non-adopter firms. However, compatibility is identified as important facilitator of new innovation in several studies (Wang et al., 2010; Ghobakhloo et al., 2011). If firms' existing experiences with IT are compatible with BDA development, BDA applications match existing information infrastructure, and the changes introduced by BDA will be consistent with existing architecture. In that case, a positive impression of BDA is likely to occur and favorably facilitate BDA implementation. For non-adopter discordant CM acts as drag in BDA adoption.

Organisational context. Wang et al. (2010) and Low et al. (2011) had indicated that the characteristics of a firm should play an important role in the decision-making process. In this study, TMS, TR and ODE were significantly influence BDA adopters but did not influenced non-adopters of BDA. The vision of decision makers in adopter firms determined the level of support for BDA adoption. TMS becomes more important for BDA since it involves third party data and a wide portfolio of technologies to handle these data and establishing standards, privacy and security policies.

TR was observed to have a significantly positive influence on BDA adoption intention. This finding is inconsistent with previous studies (Wang et al., 2010; Low et al., 2011; Ramdani et al., 2013). This finding implies that top managers of adopter firms must realize the benefits of applying BDA with IS applications, helps in creating high level of physical infrastructure and intangible skills. One possible reason is, BDA is a new technology. BDA requires complex mechanisms for handling complex data from various sources (Labrandis and Jagadish, 2012; Chen and Zhang., 2014; Rosati and Lynn, 2017; Guarisco and Langabeer, 2017). The non-adopter firms might face difficulty in finding professionals and data scientists with business domain knowledge and BDA skills. Another significant organisational factor is ODE, suggesting that the quality of the existing data environment defines a firms' maturity level in managing and analysing data (Humphrey, 1988; Weber et al., 1994). It is facilitator of BDA adoption in firms, which is inconsistent with the previous study of Ramamurthy et al. (2008). One possible explanation could be that, with sufficient agreement, protocols and architecture, firms could easily adopt BDA. Thus, BDA need a robust IT infrastructure, a large portfolio of IT applications and a platform that could leverage BDA value. It is possible that many non-adopter firms may not possess a robust infrastructure or a large base of applications to leverage the potential of BDA.

Environmental context. CP was significant for BDA adoption. The results indicate that adopters of BDA perceived higher CP than non-adopter firms. This finding is consistent with those of previous IT adoption studies such as Wang et al. (2010) and Low et al. (2011) and inconsistent with the study of Lin and Lin, 2008. CP is an environmental stimulator and adopters of BDA respond more quickly in the competitive environment. When competitor firms implement BDA as a competitive initiative, managers would be pressurized and be more receptive to BDA. Thus, BDA adopters are more concerned about the competitive differentiation than non-adopters.

Unexpectedly, the trading partner pressure did not significantly impact BDA adoption. This finding is inconsistent with previous studies (Low et al., 2011; Wang et al., 2011; Oliveira and Martins, 2010). Nevertheless, this inconsistency does not mean that the firms think BDA adoptions do not have trading partner pressure. As reflected in Table 4 and 5, the average of BDA adopters and non-adopters are both above 3.0 (natural assessment), but are slightly different. One possible explanation for this being insignificant is that the BDA is still in its infancy and common standards, architecture, protocols, data privacy and security regulations are lacking (Labrindis and Jagadish, 2012). Given this uncertainty, non-adopter firms may prefer to wait and watch how well and in what direction BDA technology is developing. They would require more business use cases and validation before recommending it to their business partners than adopter firms. Thus, PA would be insignificant discriminator of business BDA adoption in the early stage of BDA industry development.

6. CONCLUSION

While BDA has been regarded an important technology that can provide strategic, tactic and operational advantages, it has yet to see significant rates of adoption in industries (Paley, 2017). Hence, it is necessary to understand what determines firms' adoption decision of BDA adoption. Based on the TOE theoretical framework, this study developed and validated a research model to examine the influence of eight contextual factors on BDA adoption. The contributions of this study are fourfold.

First, the study obtains several key findings and implications about the determinants of BDA adoption. These key findings are as follows:

- A firms' decision to implements BDA, depends on the firm's technological, organizational, and environmental contexts;
- Selected variables (i.e., relative advantage, complexity, top management support, technology readiness, organizational data environment and competitive pressure) were found to be significant determinants of BDA adoption among adopters. While, only relative advantage, complexity and competitive pressure were found to be significant determinants of BDA adoption among non-adopters;
- Among the determinants, competitive pressure was observed to be the most influential factor affecting a firm's BDA adoption. Technology readiness was the second most influential predictor of BDA adoption among adopter and relative advantage was the second most influential predictor of BDA among non-adopters.

Second, this study empirically verifies and supports the applicability of the TOE framework in understanding business IT adoption (i.e., BDA). The TOE framework provides a good starting point for analyzing and considering suitable factors that can influence innovation-adoption decisions. Third, this study found one significant determinant of BDA adoption (i.e., ODE), which was seldom explored in the prior IT adoption research. And fourth, compared with prior BDA adoption research, this study empirically uses a large and representative sample which consists of several BDA adoption decision makers in enterprises. Thus, the findings of this study are valuable and provide several important implications for BDA adoption research and practice.

7. THEORETICAL IMPLICATIONS

This study contributes to the extant literature of BDA research by identifying and investigating BDA adoption factors in technological, organizational and environmental context. The extant literature on BDA has paid insufficient attention to organizations' adoption of BDA. In order to bridge this knowledge gap, this study specifically investigates TOE variables influencing BDA adoption. The TOE framework is implied in this study to integrate various perspective into a proposed BDA adoption model. Based on the IDT, this study proposes RA and CX as technological characteristics that would influence BDA adoption. Building upon the functional perspective of top managers (Wang et al., 2016; Paley, 2017; Thuemmler and Bai, 2017), the data management perspective of a firm (Ramamurthy et al., 2008) and the capability perspective of a firm (Gangwar et al., 2008), this study proposes that TMS, ODE and TR comprise the organizational aspects that would influence BDA adoption. Finally, inspired by the perspective of competitive bandwagon pressures, this study proposes that CP (Wang et al., 2016) serve as the environmental features that may influence BDA adoption. The proposed TOE model theoretically integrates several TOE variables from various perspectives. The different findings and dissimilar interpretations denote the newness of this study.

8. PRACTICAL AND SOCIAL IMPLICATIONS

The findings of this study provide important implications for BDA users and service provides. Firstly, both RA and CM in the technological context have significant effect on BDA adoption. But the complexity associated with the BDA systems inhibits its adoption in firms. Therefore, in order to facilitate organizational adoption of BDA, service provides may need to ensure that systems could provide benefits to the firm, compatible with firm's existing IT infrastructure. Service providers and user should work collaboratively to reduce the complexity associated with the adoption of BDA. For BDA adoption detailed standards and policies should be developed by the users and service providers. They should also attempt to integrate BDA with the extant IT infrastructure. Secondly, top management support, technology readiness, organizational data environment and competitive pressure have a significant positive effect on the adoption of BDA. Firms are more likely to adopt BDA if the top management believes in the benefits of BDA and make strategies and policies related to BDA and encourage their employees to adopt BDA. But the skills required to manage and analyse BDA and the lack of data definitions and standards inhibits the adoption process of BDA. Therefore, BDA service providers should provide standard data storage and management platforms and training to the users of BDA systems. Further, firms should create a dedicated team which is empowered to take decisions for fast adoptions of BDA while interacting with the various organizational user departments. BDA helps in understanding customer need and tune it with organizational response faster than traditional IT. This would improve the quality of life of customers and create a positive public perception for a firm adopting BDA.

9. LIMITATIONS AND FUTURE SCOPE

As in most empirical studies, this study also has several limitations that also represent opportunities for future research. First, the sample is based on only one country and it may not be sufficient to generalize to the entire population of industries in the world. Furthermore, because the sampling frame of this study was the list random 1600 firms in India, these firms might have more resources and capabilities to be able to afford BDA investments and risks. For this reason, the BDA adoption rate in this sample may be higher than the BDA adoption rate in Indian businesses. Thus, caution needs to be exercised in generalizing the findings to the entire industry population in India or other countries. Therefore, samples from different nations or industries should be collected to validate or refine this model. As the data was collected from diverse industry and settings, the practical applicability of the results in a specific industry is limited. Second, this study employed the partial least square technique to identify the predictors that distinguish between adopters and non-adopters of BDA services. The interrelationships among the independent variables (e.g. TR may affect RA and CX), influence of control variables and moderators, were not analyzed in this study. Future research can simultaneously examine a series of variable dependence relationships. Finally, the TOE framework may not explicitly point out that what are the major constructs in the model and the variables in each context. To solve this limitation, future research should consider that for more complex new technology adoption it is leading to combine more than one theoretical model to express a better understanding of the IT adoption phenomenon. Besides, many other variables in the TOE model, such as quality of big data and security and privacy concerns may be potential determinants of BDA adoption. Future research may incorporate these variables into a predictive model to enhance our understanding of the causality and interrelationships between the predictors.

REFERENCES

Abdollahzadegan, A., Hussin, C., Razak, A., Moshfegh Gohary, M., & Amini, M. (2013). The organizational critical success factors for adopting cloud computing in SMEs. *Journal of Information Systems Research and Innovation*, 4(1), 67–74.

Agneeswaran, V. S. (2014). *Big Data Analytics Beyond Hadoop: Real-Time Applications with Storm, Spark, and More Hadoop Alternatives*. Upper Saddle River, NJ: Pearson FT Press.

Agrawal, K. P. (2013). The assimilation of Big Data Analytics (BDA) by Indian firms: a technology diffusion perspective. In *3rd Biennial Conference of the Indian Academy of Management (IAM)*, December 12-14.

Alain, C. Y. L., & Ooi, K. (2008). Adoption of interorganizational system standards in supply chains: An empirical analysis of RosettaNet standards. *Industrial Management & Data Systems*, 108(4), 529–547. doi:10.1108/02635570810868371

Albrecht, S., Lübcke, M., & Hartig-Perschke, R. (2007). Weblog campaigning in the German Bundestag Election 2005. *Social Science Computer Review*, *25*(4), 504–520. doi:10.1177/0894439307305628

Alshamaila, Y., Papagiannidis, S., & Li, F. (2013). Cloud computing adoption by SMEs in the north east of England: A multi-perspective framework. *Journal of Enterprise Information Management*, *26*(3), 250–275. doi:10.1108/17410391311325225

Borkar, D., Mayuram, R., Sangudi, G., & Carey, M. (2016). Have your data and query it too: From key-value caching to big data management. *Paper presented at the ACM SIGMOD International Conference on Management of Data*, June 26 (pp. 239-251). 10.1145/2882903.2904443

Brislin, R. W. (1970). Back-translation for cross-cultural research. *Journal of Cross-Cultural Psychology*, *1*(3), 185–216. doi:10.1177/135910457000100301

Broeders, D., Schrijvers, E., van der Sloot, B., van Brakel, R., de Hoog, J., & Hirsch Ballin, E. (2017). Big data and security policies: Towards a framework for regulating the phases of analytics and use of big data. *Computer Law & Security Review*, *33*(3), 309–323. doi:10.1016/j.clsr.2017.03.002

Chau, P. Y. K., & Tam, K. Y. (1997). Factors affecting the adoption of open systems: An exploratory study. *MIS Quarterly: Management Information Systems*, *21*(1), 1–20. doi:10.2307/249740

Chen, H., Chiang, R. H. L., & Storey, V. C. (2012). Business intelligence and analytics: From big data to big impact. *MIS Quarterly: Management Information Systems*, *36*(4), 1165–1188. doi:10.2307/41703503

Cooper, R. B., & Zmud, R. W. (1990). Information technology implementation research: A technological diffusion approach. *Management Science*, *36*(2), 123–139. doi:10.1287/mnsc.36.2.123

Cunningham, S. (2014). Big data and technology readiness levels. *IEEE Engineering Management Review*, *42*(1), 8–9. doi:10.1109/EMR.2014.2300254

Davenport, T. (2014). *Big data at work: dispelling the myths, uncovering the opportunities*. Harvard Business Review Press. doi:10.15358/9783800648153

Dijcks, J. P. (2012). Oracle: Big data for the enterprise. *Oracle*. Retrieved from http://www.oracle.com/us/products/database/big-data-for-enterprise-519135.pdf

Dubey, R., Gunasekaran, A., Childe, S. J., Wamba, S. F., & Papadopoulos, T. (2016). The impact of big data on world-class sustainable manufacturing. *International Journal of Advanced Manufacturing Technology*, *84*(1-4), 631–645. doi:10.100700170-015-7674-1

Economic Times. (2017, July 02). Big data analytics to become $16 billion industry by 2025. Retrieved from https://economictimes.indiatimes.com/tech/ites/big-data-analytics-to-become-16-billion-industry-by2025/articleshow/59410695.cms

Esteves, J., & Curto, J. (2013). A risk and benefits behavioral model to assess intentions to adopt big data. *Journal of Intelligence Studies in Business*, *3*(3), 37–46.

Faizi, R., El Fkihi, S., El Afia, A., & Chiheb, R. (2017). Extracting business value from big data. *Paper presented at the 29th International Business Information Management Association Conference - Education Excellence and Innovation Management through Vision 2020: From Regional Development Sustainability to Global Economic Growth* (pp. 997-1002).

Fichman, R. G., & Kemerer, C. F. (1999). The illusory diffusion of innovation: An examination of assimilation gaps. *Information Systems Research, 10*(3), 255–275. doi:10.1287/isre.10.3.255

Gandomi, A., & Haider, M. (2015). Beyond the hype: Big data concepts, methods, and analytics. *International Journal of Information Management, 35*(2), 137–144. doi:10.1016/j.ijinfomgt.2014.10.007

Gangwar, H., Date, H., & Ramaswamy, R. (2015). Understanding determinants of cloud computing adoption using an integrated TAM-TOE model. *Journal of Enterprise Information Management, 28*(1), 107–130. doi:10.1108/JEIM-08-2013-0065

Ghobakhloo, M., Arias-Aranda, D., & Benitez-Amado, J. (2011). Adoption of e-commerce applications in SMEs. *Industrial Management & Data Systems, 111*(8), 1238–1269. doi:10.1108/02635571111170785

Gibbs, J. L., & Kraemer, K. L. (2004). A cross-country investigation of the determinants of scope of e-commerce use: An institutional approach. *Electronic Markets, 14*(2), 124–137. doi:10.1080/101967 80410001675077

Goodhue, D. L., Wybo, M. D., & Kirsch, L. J. (1992). The impact of data integration on the costs and benefits of information systems. *MIS Quarterly: Management Information Systems, 16*(3), 293–310. doi:10.2307/249530

Grover, V. (1993). An empirically derived model for the adoption of Customer-based interorganizational systems. *Decision Sciences, 24*(3), 603–640. doi:10.1111/j.1540-5915.1993.tb01295.x

Guarisco, J., & Langabeer, J. (2017). Big data: Use of analytics for operations management. In *Value and quality innovations in acute and emergency care* (pp. 215-222) doi:10.1017/9781316779965.028

Gunasekaran, A., Papadopoulos, T., Dubey, R., Wamba, S. F., Childe, S. J., Hazen, B., & Akter, S. (2017). Big data and predictive analytics for supply chain and organizational performance. *Journal of Business Research, 70*, 308–317. doi:10.1016/j.jbusres.2016.08.004

Hair, J. F., Anderson, R. E., Tatham, R. L., & Black, W. C. (1998). *Multivariate Data Analysis*. Upper Saddle River, NJ: Prentice-Hall.

Henseler, J., Ringle, C. M., & Sinkovics, R. R. (2009). The use of partial least squares path modeling in international marketing. doi:10.1108/S1474-7979(2009)0000020014

Herschel, G., Linden, A. and Kart, L. (2015). Magic quadrant for advanced analytics platforms. Gartner.

Hopkins, M. S. (2011). From the editor: Big data, analytics and the path from insights to value. MIT Sloan Management Review, 52(2), 21-22.

Hsu, C., & Yeh, C.-C. (2017). Understanding the factors affecting the adoption of the internet of things. *Technology Analysis and Strategic Management, 29*(9), 1089–1102. doi:10.1080/09537325.2016.1269160

Humphrey, W. S. (1988). Characterizing the software process: A maturity framework. *IEEE Software*, 5(2), 73–79. doi:10.1109/52.2014

Iacovou, C. L., Benbasat, I., & Dexter, A. S. (1995). Electronic data interchange and small organizations: Adoption and impact of technology. *MIS Quarterly: Management Information Systems*, 19(4), 465–485. doi:10.2307/249629

IMF. (2014, April 8). World Economic Outlook: Innovativeness, novelty IMF, recovery strengthens, remains uneven., available at: www.imf.org/external/pubs/cat/longres.aspx?sk=41120

Jain, H., Ramamurthy, K., Ryu, H. & Yasai-Ardekani, M. (1998). Success of data resource management in distributed environments: An empirical investigation. *MIS Quarterly: Management Information Systems, 22*(1), 1-22.

Kamioka, T., & Tapanainen, T. (2014). Organizational use of big data and competitive advantage - exploration of antecedents. Paper presented at the *Proceedings - Pacific Asia Conference on Information Systems, PACIS 2014*

Khan, M. A., Uddin, M. F., & Gupta, N. (2014). Seven V's of big data understanding big data to extract value. *Paper presented at the 2014 Zone 1 Conference of the American Society for Engineering Education - "Engineering Education: Industry Involvement and Interdisciplinary Trends", ASEE Zone 1 2014*, 10.1109/ASEEZone1.2014.6820689

Kimball, R. (1998). *The data warehouse lifecycle toolkit: expert methods for designing, developing, and deploying data warehouses.* John Wiley & Sons.

Knapp, S. (2009). Ooyala–accelerating the evolution of online video – an interview with Sean Knapp of online video publishing. *Journal of Digital Asset Management, 5*(5), 264–273. doi:10.1057/dam.2009.23

Kuan, K. K. Y., & Chau, P. Y. K. (2001). A perception-based model for EDI adoption in small businesses using a technology-organization-environment framework. *Information & Management, 38*(8), 507–521. doi:10.1016/S0378-7206(01)00073-8

Kwon, O., Lee, N., & Shin, B. (2014). Data quality management, data usage experience and acquisition intention of big data analytics. *International Journal of Information Management, 34*(3), 387–394. doi:10.1016/j.ijinfomgt.2014.02.002

Labrinidis, A., & Jagadish, H. V. (2012). Challenges and opportunities with big data. *Proceedings of the VLDB Endowment International Conference on Very Large Data Bases, 5*(12), 2032–2033. doi:10.14778/2367502.2367572

Lai, Y., Sun, H., & Ren, J. (2018). Understanding the determinants of big data analytics (BDA) adoption in logistics and supply chain management: An empirical investigation. *International Journal of Logistics Management, 29*(2), 676–703. doi:10.1108/IJLM-06-2017-0153

Lee, S., & Kim, K. (2007). Factors affecting the implementation success of internet-based information systems. *Computers in Human Behavior, 23*(4), 1853–1880. doi:10.1016/j.chb.2005.12.001

Lin, H., & Lee, G.-G. (2005). Impact of organizational learning and knowledge management factors on e-business adoption. *Management Decision, 43*(2), 171–188. doi:10.1108/00251740510581902

Lin, H., & Lin, S.-M. (2008). Determinants of e-business diffusion: A test of the technology diffusion perspective. *Technovation*, *28*(3), 135–145. doi:10.1016/j.technovation.2007.10.003

Low, C., Chen, Y., & Wu, M. (2011). Understanding the determinants of cloud computing adoption. *Industrial Management & Data Systems*, *111*(7), 1006–1023. doi:10.1108/02635571111161262

Lowry, P. B., & Gaskin, J. (2014). Partial least squares (PLS) structural equation modeling (SEM) for building and testing behavioral causal theory: When to choose it and how to use it. *IEEE Transactions on Professional Communication*, *57*(2), 123–146. doi:10.1109/TPC.2014.2312452

Manyika, J., Chui, M., Brown, B., Bughin, J., Dobbs, R., Roxburgh, C., & Byers, A. H. (2011). Big data: The next frontier for innovation, competition (p. 9). and productivity. *McKinsey Global Institute*. Retrieved from https://www.mckinsey.com/business-functions/digital-mckinsey/our-insights/big-data-the-next-frontier-for-innovation

McAfee, A., & Brynjolfsson, E. (2012). Big data: The management revolution. *Harvard Business Review, 90*(10), 60-66, 68, 128.

Miller, H. G., & Mork, P. (2013). From data to decisions: A value chain for big data. *IT Professional*, *15*(1), 57–59. doi:10.1109/MITP.2013.11

Moore, D. T. (2014). Roadmaps and Maturity Models: Pathways toward Adopting Big Data. In *Proceedings of the Conference for Information Systems Applied Research*, Baltimore, MD (Vol. 2167, p. 1508).

Mourtzis, D., Vlachou, E., & Milas, N. (2016). Industrial big data as a result of IoT adoption in manufacturing. *Procedia, 55*, 290-295. 10.1016/j.procir.2016.07.038

Muhammad, S. S., Dey, B. L., & Weerakkody, V. (2018). Analysis of factors that influence customers' willingness to leave big data digital footprints on social media: A systematic review of literature. *Information Systems Frontiers*, *20*(3), 559–576. doi:10.100710796-017-9802-y

Ngah, A. H., Zainuddin, Y., & Thurasamy, R. (2017). Applying the TOE framework in the halal warehouse adoption study. *Journal of Islamic Accounting and Business Research*, *8*(2), 161–181. doi:10.1108/JIABR-04-2014-0014

Oliveira, T., & Martins, M. F. (2010). Understanding e-business adoption across industries in european countries. *Industrial Management & Data Systems*, *110*(9), 1337–1354. doi:10.1108/02635571011087428

Paley, N. (2017). Leadership strategies in the age of big data, algorithms, and analytics. In *Leadership strategies in the age of big data, algorithms, and analytics* (pp. 1-285) doi:10.1201/9781315164977

Pan, M. -., & Jang, W. (2008). Determinants of the adoption of enterprise resource planning within the technology-organization-environment framework: Taiwan's communications industry. *Journal of Computer Information Systems*, *48*(3), 94–102.

Parasuraman, A. (2000). Technology readiness index (tri): A multiple-item scale to measure readiness to embrace new technologies. *Journal of Service Research*, *2*(4), 307–320. doi:10.1177/109467050024001

Pavolotsky, J. & Seirmarco, J. (2012). Big Data Business Models, New Matter. *State Bar of California Intellectual Property Section, 37*(3).

Philip Chen, C. L., & Zhang, C. (2014). Data-intensive applications, challenges, techniques and technologies: A survey on big data. *Information Sciences*, *275*, 314–347. doi:10.1016/j.ins.2014.01.015

Podsakoff, P. M., MacKenzie, S. B., Lee, J., & Podsakoff, N. P. (2003). Common method biases in behavioral research: A critical review of the literature and recommended remedies. *The Journal of Applied Psychology*, *88*(5), 879–903. doi:10.1037/0021-9010.88.5.879 PMID:14516251

Popovič, A., Hackney, R., Tassabehji, R., & Castelli, M. (2018). The impact of big data analytics on firms' high value business performance. *Information Systems Frontiers*, *20*(2), 209–222. doi:10.100710796-016-9720-4

Porter, M. E. (1980). *Competitive Strategy: Techniques for Analyzing Industries and Competitors*. New York: Free Press.

Premkumar, G., Ramamurthy, K., & Nilakanta, S. (1994). Implementation of electronic data interchange: An innovation diffusion perspective. *Journal of Management Information Systems*, *11*(2), 157–186. doi:10.1080/07421222.1994.11518044

Premkumar, G., & Roberts, M. (1999). Adoption of new information technologies in rural small businesses. *Omega*, *27*(4), 467–484. doi:10.1016/S0305-0483(98)00071-1

Puklavec, B., Oliveira, T., & Popovic, A. (2014). Unpacking Business Intelligence Systems Adoption Determinants : An Exploratory Study of Small and Medium Enterprises. *Economic and Business Review*, *16*(2), 185–213.

Rackley, J. (2015). *Marketing Analytics Roadmap*. New York City, NY: Apress. doi:10.1007/978-1-4842-0259-3

Rafferty, A. E., & Simons, R. H. (2006). An examination of the antecedents of readiness for fine-tuning and corporate transformation changes. *Journal of Business and Psychology*, *20*(3), 325–350. doi:10.100710869-005-9013-2

Ramamurthy, K., Sen, A., & Sinha, A. P. (2008). An empirical investigation of the key determinants of data warehouse adoption. *Decision Support Systems*, *44*(4), 817–841. doi:10.1016/j.dss.2007.10.006

Ramdani, B., Chevers, D., & Williams, D. A. (2013). SMEs' adoption of enterprise applications: A technology-organisation-environment model. *Journal of Small Business and Enterprise Development*, *20*(4), 735–753. doi:10.1108/JSBED-12-2011-0035

Rogers, E. M. (1983). *Diffusion of Innovation*. New York, NY: The Free Press.

Rosati, P., & Lynn, T. (2017). Challenges to technology implementation. In *The Routledge companion to accounting information systems* (pp. 272-291) doi:10.4324/9781315647210

Ross, J. W., Beath, C. M., & Quaadgras, A. (2013). You may not need big data after all. *Harvard Business Review*, (DEC)

Russell, M. A. (2013). *Mining the Social Web: Data Mining Facebook, Twitter, LinkedIn, Google+, GitHub, and More*. Sebastopol, CA: O'Reilly Media, Inc.

Russom, P. (2011). Big Data Analytics. TDWI Research. https://tdwi.org/research/2011/09/~/media/TDWI/TDWI/Research/BPR/2011/TDWI_BPReport_Q411_Big_Data_Analytics_Web/TDWI_BPReport_Q411_Big%20Data_ExecSummary.ashx

Saffu, K., Walker, J. H., & Hinson, R. (2007). An empirical study of perceived strategic value and adoption constructs: The Ghanaian case. *Management Decision*, *45*(7), 1083–1101. doi:10.1108/00251740710773925

Sanders, N. R. (2016). How to use big data to drive your supply chain. *California Management Review*, *58*(3), 26–48. doi:10.1525/cmr.2016.58.3.26

Shin, D. (2016). Demystifying big data: Anatomy of big data developmental process. *Telecommunications Policy*, *40*(9), 837–854. doi:10.1016/j.telpol.2015.03.007

Srivastava, S. C., & Teo, T. S. H. (2010). E-government, e-business, and national economic performance. *Communications of the Association for Information Systems*, *26*(1), 267–286.

Sun, S., Cegielski, C. G., Jia, L., & Hall, D. J. (2018). Understanding the factors affecting the organizational adoption of big data. *Journal of Computer Information Systems*, *58*(3), 193–203. doi:10.1080/08874417.2016.1222891

Swanson, E. B. (1994). Information systems innovation among organizations. *Management Science*, *40*(9), 1069–1092. doi:10.1287/mnsc.40.9.1069

Tan, K. S., Chong, S. C., Lin, B., & Eze, U. C. (2009). Internet-based ICT adoption: Evidence from malaysian SMEs. *Industrial Management & Data Systems*, *109*(2), 224–244. doi:10.1108/02635570910930118

Teo, H. H., Wei, K. K., & Benbasat, I. (2003). Predicting intention to adopt interorganizational linkages: An institutional perspective. *MIS Quarterly: Management Information Systems*, *27*(1), 19–49. doi:10.2307/30036518

Thuemmler, C., & Bai, C. (2017). Health 4.0: How virtualization and big data are revolutionizing healthcare. In *Health 4.0: How virtualization and big data are revolutionizing healthcare* (pp. 1-254) doi:10.1007/978-3-319-47617-9

Tien, J. M. (2013). Big data: Unleashing information. *Journal of Systems Science and Systems Engineering*, *22*(2), 127–151. doi:10.100711518-013-5219-4

To, M. L., & Ngai, E. W. T. (2006). Predicting the organisational adoption of B2C e-commerce: An empirical study. *Industrial Management & Data Systems*, *106*(8), 1133–1147. doi:10.1108/02635570610710791

Topps, D., Helmer, J., & Ellaway, R. (2013). YouTube as a platform for publishing clinical skills training videos. *Academic Medicine*, *88*(2), 192–197. doi:10.1097/ACM.0b013e31827c5352 PMID:23269305

Tornatzky, L. G., & Fleischer, M. (1990). *The Processes of Technological Innovation*. MA: Lexington Books.

Tornatzky, L. G., & Klein, K. J. (1982). Innovation characteristics and innovation adoption-implementation: A meta-analysis of findings. *IEEE Transactions on Engineering Management*, *EM-29*(1), 28–45. doi:10.1109/TEM.1982.6447463

Verma, S. (2017). Big data and advance analytics: Architecture, techniques, applications, and challenges. *International Journal of Business Analytics*, *4*(4), 21–47. doi:10.4018/IJBAN.2017100102

Verma, S. (2018). Mapping the intellectual structure of the big data research in the IS discipline: A citation/co-citation analysis. *Information Resources Management Journal*, *31*(1), 21–52. doi:10.4018/IRMJ.2018010102

Verma, S., Bhattacharyya, S. S., & Kumar, S. (2018). An extension of the technology acceptance model in the big data analytics system implementation environment. *Information Processing & Management*, *54*(5), 791–806. doi:10.1016/j.ipm.2018.01.004

Wang, H., Xu, Z., Fujita, H., & Liu, S. (2016). Towards felicitous decision making: An overview on challenges and trends of big data. *Information Sciences*, *367-368*, 747–765. doi:10.1016/j.ins.2016.07.007

Wang, Y., Wang, Y.-S., & Yang, Y.-F. (2010). Understanding the determinants of RFID adoption in the manufacturing industry. *Technological Forecasting and Social Change*, *77*(5), 803–815. doi:10.1016/j.techfore.2010.03.006

Ward, J. S., & Barker, A. (2013). Undefined by data: a survey of big data definitions. https://arxiv.org/pdf/1309.5821.pdf

Warheit, G. J., Buhl, J. M., & Bell, R. A. (1978). A critique of social indicators analysis and key informants surveys as needs assessment methods. *Evaluation and Program Planning*, *1*(3), 239–247. doi:10.1016/0149-7189(78)90079-4 PMID:10239083

Weber, C. V., Curtis, B., & Chrissis, M. B. (1994). *The capability maturity model: Guidelines for improving the software process* (Vol. 441). Reading, MA: Addison-wesley.

Wixom, B. H., & Watson, H. J. (2001). An empirical investigation of the factors affecting data warehousing success. *MIS Quarterly: Management Information Systems*, *25*(1), 17–41. doi:10.2307/3250957

Zhang, K., Wang, J., Jiang, C., Wei, Z., & Ren, Y. (2017). Big data driven information diffusion analysis and control in online social networks. *Paper presented at the IEEE International Conference on Communications*, Paris, France (pp. 1-6). 10.1109/ICC.2017.7996330

Zhu, K., Kraemer, K. L., & Xu, S. (2006). The process of innovation assimilation by firms in different countries: A technology diffusion perspective on e-business. *Management Science*, *52*(10), 1557–1576. doi:10.1287/mnsc.1050.0487

Zhu, K., Kraemer, K. L., Xu, S., & Dedrick, J. (2004). Information technology payoff in E-business environments: An international perspective on value creation of E-business in the financial services industry. *Journal of Management Information Systems*, *21*(1), 17–54. doi:10.1080/07421222.2004.11045797

Zomaya, A. Y., & Sakr, S. (2017). Handbook of big data technologies. In Handbook of big data technologies. doi:10.1007/978-3-319-49340-4

This research was previously published in Information Resources Management Journal (IRMJ), 32(3); pages 1-26, copyright year 2019 by IGI Publishing (an imprint of IGI Global).

Chapter 76
Human–Computer Interaction With Big Data Analytics

Gunasekaran Manogaran
VIT University, India

Chandu Thota
Albert Einstein Lab, India

Daphne Lopez
VIT University, India

ABSTRACT

Big Data has been playing a vital role in almost all environments such as healthcare, education, business organizations and scientific research. Big data analytics requires advanced tools and techniques to store, process and analyze the huge volume of data. Big data consists of huge unstructured data that require advance real-time analysis. Thus, nowadays many of the researchers are interested in developing advance technologies and algorithms to solve the issues when dealing with big data. Big Data has gained much attention from many private organizations, public sector and research institutes. This chapter provides an overview of the state-of-the-art algorithms for processing big data, as well as the characteristics, applications, opportunities and challenges of big data systems. This chapter also presents the challenges and issues in human computer interaction with big data analytics.

1. INTRODUCTION

1.1 Background and History of Big Data

Data generation speed and amount of data has increased over the past 20 years in different fields. A report published in 2011 from International Data Corporation (IDC) states that, the overall generated and stored data size in the globe was 1.8ZB ($\approx 1021B$), which enlarged by almost 9 times within 5 years (Lopez et al., 2014). Due to the enormous growth of world data, the name of big data is essentially used to

DOI: 10.4018/978-1-6684-3662-2.ch076

express massive datasets. In general, big data analytics is requires advance tools and techniques to store, process and analyze the huge volume of data. Big data consists of huge unstructured data that require advance real-time analysis (Lopez and Gunasekaran, 2015). Thus, nowadays many of the researchers are interested in developing advance technologies and algorithms to solve the issues when dealing with big data. In order to discover new opportunities and hidden values from big data, Yahoo developed the Hadoop based tools and technologies to store and process the big data. Nowadays, private organizations are also interested in the high prospective of big data, and numerous government agencies declared vital ideas to speed up the big data research and applications. Two leading scientific journals such as nature and science are also opened special issues to solve and discuss the challenges and impacts of big data. In recent years, big data plays a vital role in Internet companies such as Google, Facebook and Twitter. For example, Google handles nearly 100 Petabyte (PB) and Facebook produces log data of over 10 Petabyte per month. A popular Chinese company, Baidu, analyzes data of 10 Petabyte (PB), and Taobao, a subsidiary of Alibaba, produces data of 10 Terabyte (TB) for online trading per day. Sources of big data and the corresponding mining techniques are depicted in Table 1. State of-the-art tools and technologies to handle big data are depicted in Table 2.

1.2 Big Data and Its Market Value

Nowadays, Big Data has been playing a vital role in almost all environments such as healthcare, education, business organizations and scientific research. There is a strong relationship in Big Data and IoE (Internet of Everything). In general, IoE applications are used to capture or observe some specific values to find the hidden values and take better decisions. When the device is connected to the Internet, it always senses the specific metric and stores those metrics into a connected data stores. This would increase the size of the data stored in a data store. Hence, high end devices and scalable storage systems are needed to store such huge size of data. The amount of data to be stored and processed becomes an important problem in real life. Relational data base management system (RDBMS) is generally used to store the traditional data but day by day the volume, velocity and variety of sensor data is growing towards the Exabyte. This requires advanced tools and techniques to store, process and display such large amount of sensor data to the end users. Hence, Big Data tools are often used to process such huge amounts of data. This would increase the economy and market of the Big Data analytics. The report "Big Data Market by Component (Software and Services) states that "The Big Data market is expected to grow from USD 28.65 Billion in 2016 to USD 66.79 Billion by 2021 at a high Compound Annual Growth Rate (CAGR) of 18.45%". For the purpose of the report, 2015 has been considered as the base year and 2016 as the estimated year for performing market estimation and forecasting. 10V's of big data is shown in Figure 1. Various big data analytical algorithms are shown in Figure 4.

1.3 Big Data in Healthcare

In recent decades, big data analytics also impact more in healthcare (Lopez and Sekaran, 2016). Nowadays, health care systems are rapidly adopting clinical data, which will rapidly enlarge the size of the health records that are accessible, electronically (Shan et al., 2012). Concurrently, fast progress and development has achieved in modern healthcare management system (Hayes et al., 2014). A recent study expounds, six use cases of big data to decrease the cost of patients, triage, readmissions, adverse events, and treatment optimization for diseases affecting multiple organ systems (Feldman et al., 2013).

In yet another study, big data use cases in healthcare have been divided into number of categories such as clinical decision support (with a sub category of clinical information), administration and delivery, consumer behavior, and support services (Lopez and Manogaran, 2017). Jee et al. described that how to reform the healthcare system based on big data analytics to choose appropriate treatment path, improvement of healthcare systems, and so on (Parthasarathy et al., 2011; Fageeri et al., 2014; Manogaran et al., 2016). The above use cases have utilized the following big data in health care implementation. 1. Patient- centered framework produced based on the big data framework to approximate the amount of healthcare (cost), patient impact (outcomes), and dropping readmission rates (Tang et al., 2010). 2. Virtual physiological human analysis framework combined with big data analytics to create robust and valuable solutions in silico medicine (Sharma et al., 2015).

Figure 1. 10V's of big data

1.4 Cloud Computing With Big Data Analytics

Cloud computing has revolutionized the way software services and computing are delivered to the clients on demand. Cloud providers offered the components of cloud computing that includes Software as a Service (SaaS), Platform as a Service (PaaS) and Infrastructure as a Service (IaaS). Normally, cloud providers are named as cloud service providers or CSPs. Amazon Simple Storage Service (Amazon S3) is the first cloud service offered to the end users by Amazon in 2006. There after large number of cloud providers are developing variety of cloud services such as Apple, IBM, Joyent, Microsoft, Rackspace,

Google, Cisco, Citrix, Salesforce.com and Verizon/Terremark. Users are using cloud computing through networked client devices such as desktop computers, smart phones, laptops, tablets and any Ethernet enabled device such as Home Automation Gadgets. More number of cloud applications allows end users to access cloud without any definite applications and software. Web user interfaces such as HTML5 and Ajax can achieve a similar or even better look and feel to native applications.

Figure 2. Big data challenges

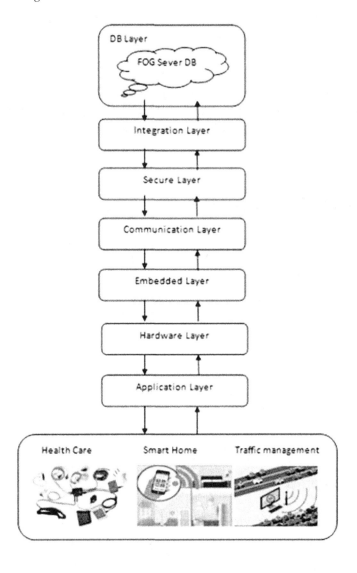

1.5 Big Data Applications

Big Data has gained much attention from many private organizations, public sector and research institutes. It is observed that, in recent decades, big data has been playing a major role in all fields (Varatharajan et al., 2017b). In this section explains how the real-time applications of big data are likely to grow in the future and how they will essentially shape our day-to-day environment. The push towards collecting and analyzing large amounts of data in diverse application domains has motivated us to use variety of applications such as Health and human welfare, Nature and natural processes, Government and the public sector, commerce, business and economic systems, social networking and the internet, and computational and experimental processes (Kambatla et al., 2014). Big Data Challenges are shown in Figure 2.

1.5.1 Hospitals and Healthcare Institutes

In general, Clinical data are classified as following types such as electronic medical records (EMRs), pharmaceutical data, imaging data, data on personal practices and preferences (including environmental factors, dietary habits and exercise patterns), and financial/activity records (Varatharajan et al., 2017a). Successfully combining all these data becomes Big Data, then it provides major development in well-being, delivery and interventions (Vayena et al., 2015). Recently, McKinsey Global Institute conducted a study in which it reports that healthcare analytics could produce more than $300 billion in value every year (Mckinsey.com, 2015). Data is collected at point-of-care, and is stored in distributed systems with huge access (Manogaran and Lopez, 2016). For example, imaging data (MRI, fMRI) is often accessed overseas by skilled radiologists to produce reports and diagnoses (Manogaran et al., 2017a).

1.5.2 Government and Public Sector Unit

Recently, Public sector and government also start using of big-data analytics to store and process the General Services Administration details (WIRED, 2016). Business cloud services have been created, such as AWS GovCloud, which entirely aim to transfer exhaustive workloads to the cloud (Amazon Web Services, 2016). Thus, Big Data based systems have extensively reduced processing and execution time (both upload and download) and operational costs (Chandrasekaran and Kapoor, 2011; Kim et al., 2014).

1.5.3 Social Networking

Social networking and the internet users are increases dramatically in worldwide. The latest report states that above 2 billion people are actively using social media each month (Kemp, 2014). Monitoring people emotions have been applied in many areas to solve big issues and doing sentiment analysis in social networking data is help to increase the high value business insights (Wang et al., 2012; Shah et al., 2015).

1.5.4 Computing Platforms

Nowadays computing platforms most often uses big data to get high value insight. For example, Astrophysical simulations, quantum-mechanical modeling (Pandey et al., 2015), Geospatial modeling (Mhlanga et al., 2015) are use Big Data computational platforms and Big Data tools to model the huge size of real time streaming datasets to bring in qualitative and quantitative changes in the near future (Reed et al., 2015).

1.5.5 Nature and Natural Processes

Big data also use to save nature and natural processes as copious data being collected linking to our environmental footprint and its noticeable impact. Natural related data is normally collected from satellite imagery, sensors and radars to monitor the extreme weather events, deforestation and urban encroachment. Thus, big data analytics has major impact in, including sustainable development (Gijzen et al., 2013), land and water resources management (Wang et al., 2013), environmental impact assessment (Howe et al., 2008), natural resource management (Hampton et al., 2013) and global warming and climate change (Jang et al., 2015; Manogaran and Lopez, 2017a).

1.6 Solving Big Data Storage Challenges With Private Cloud

Private clouds are used to store and share data for one organization and do not share physical resources to others (Manogaran and Lopez, 2017b). Resources of the private cloud can be provided externally or in-house. Private clouds is always use virtualized on-premises computing resources and storage to present a devoted cloud that a industry owns and operates. In general, due to regulatory or security limits Organizations requiring direct cloud environment control. An organization must maintain and handle infrastructure costs and technical or architectural issues that arise. As a result, organizations normally don't deploy Big Data on private clouds. A classic fundamental prerequisite of private cloud deployments are security regulations and requirements that require a strict partition of an organization's data storage and processing from malicious or accidental contact through shared resources.

In addition, private cloud setups are demanding because financial merits of scale are typically not possible within most projects and organizations despite the consumption of industry standards. The return of investment contrast to public cloud offerings is hardly ever acquired and the operational cost and risk of failure is also important. Nevertheless, users maintain private visualized isolated storage and processing methodologies. Security concerns, which attract a few to accept private clouds or custom deployments, are for the huge majority of users and projects unrelated (Manogaran et al., 2017a). Visualization is always used to access other customers' data tremendously tricky. Real time issues about public cloud computing are more ordinary similar to data lock-in and irregular performance of individual instances (Manogaran et al., 2017b). The data lock-in is a typical soft assess and works by assembly data inflow to the cloud provider open or extremely economical. The replication of data out to local systems or other providers is often more costly. This is not an impossible problem and in practice promotes to consume extra services from a cloud provider as an alternative of transferring data in and out for various processes or services. Typically, this is not reasonable anyway due to complexities and network speed around processing with many platforms (Manogaran et al., 2017c).

1.7 Solving Big Data Storage Challenges With Public Cloud

Public clouds that are offered by third-party providers is used to share and process physical resources and storage. As public cloud providers maintain numerous users, the processing platform is far more scalable and more than that of private cloud. To lower operating costs, unused resources are unconstrained once the processing job is ended. Public cloud provides a "utility" computing model, and is supreme for on-demand Big Data applications. Public clouds share physical resources for data storage, transfers and analyzing. It is approximately certain that in the cloud, data will be unencrypted. In addition, if public cloud uses a PaaS-based application or SaaS, unencrypted data will also approximately stored in the multitenancy platform (Manogaran et al., 2017d).

Recently, many organizations especially small and midmarket businesses promoters are use cloud based software applications from an external service provider to store their transactional data. If the organization maintains deep historical data in that cloud service, it might already have collected in Big Data levels. Value added analytics services such as marketing optimization, churn analysis, or off-site backup and archiving of customer data is provided by extending the cloud service provider functions; it might make intelligence to influence that rather than store it all in-house. Dedicated Hadoop cluster for huge size extract-transform-load (ETL) process on unstructured data sources is used to provide access to the public cloud applications such as multichannel marketing, geospatial analytics, social media analytics, elastic data-science sandboxing and query-able archiving. Public cloud providing might be the only possible alternative if the user need to process the data that include petabyte-scale, streaming, multi-structured and Big Data.

1.8 Solving Big Data Storage Challenges With Hybrid Cloud

Hybrid clouds combine public and private cloud, enabling services to drift between the two clouds using orchestration. In hybrid cloud, cloud bursting is known as the private cloud can use public cloud resources when additional compute is necessary. Private cloud manages basic workloads, whereas public cloud resources temporarily contain spikes in demand. This feature is used when the user processing Big Data in cloud. Nevertheless, organizations hardly ever use hybrid clouds for Big Data analytics since public cloud is effortless and takes benefit of any long-term cost allowances from the public cloud provider.

As hybrid cloud architecture combines public and private cloud deployments, there is a need to achieve the following features such as elasticity and security, provide cheaper base load and burst capabilities. Some business organizations experience small periods of enormously high loads. For example, as a result of online shopping offer and advertising events like sponsoring an admired television occasion. In general, these events can have massive economic impact to organizations if they are provided very worst service. In order to overcome this issue, hybrid cloud presents the opportunity to serve the base load with in-house services and lease for a short period. This needs a big deal of operational ability in the organization to effortlessly scale between the public and private cloud. Familiar tools and technologies for hybrid or private cloud deployments are already available such as Eucalyptus for Amazon Web Services. On the long-term extra expenditure of the hybrid cloud approach often is not reasonable since cloud providers present most important discounts for multi-year commitments. This would cause shifting base load services to the public cloud attractive since it is accompanied by an easier deployment policy.

1.9 Internet of Things

The Internet of Things (IoT) is a connection of physical objects such as devices, vehicles, buildings and other items-embedded with electronics, software, sensors, and network connectivity that enables these objects to collect and exchange data. 'Thing' refers to a device which connected to the internet and transfer the device information to other devices. An interesting trend contributing to the growth of IoT is the shift from consumer-based IPv4 Internet of tablets and laptops, that is, Information Technology (IT), to an Operational Technology (OT)-based IPv6 Internet of Machine-to-Machine interactions. This includes sensors, smart objects and clustered systems (for example, Smart Grid) (rank-watch, 2016). The

IPv6 Internet is one of the most important connectivity of the IoT, as it is not possible to add billions of devices to the IPv4 Internet. Layered Architecture of IoT is shown in Figure 3.

2. INTRODUCTION TO HCI

Human-computer interaction (HCI) provides services and features to interact between people and computers (Dix, 2009). Various Fields in HCI is shown in Figure 5.

Figure 3. Layered architecture of IoT

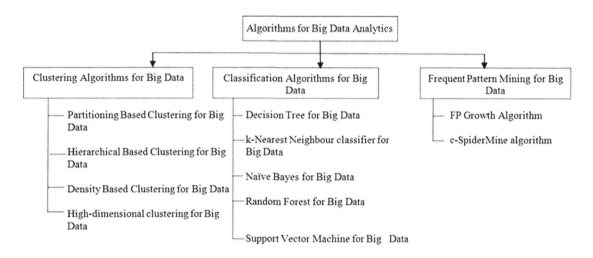

Table 1. Source of big data and the corresponding mining techniques

S.No	Sources of Big Data	Type of Data	Data Mining Technique/ Methodology	Reference
1.	Healthcare	Electronic Health Record (EHR)	Natural Language Processing (NLP)	(Byrd et al., 2014; Manogaran and Lopez, 2017e)
		Medical Imaging Data	Content based Image Retrieval System	(Müller et al., 2004)
		Genetic Data	Penalized Logistic Regression	(Wu et al., 2009)
2.	Social Networking	Text Data	Sentiment Analysis	(Feldman, 2013)
		Graph Data	Community Detection	(Parthasarathy et al., 2011)
			Social Influence Analysis	(Tang & Liu, 2010)
			Collaborative Filtering	(Sharma & Sethi, 2015)
3.	CCTV Surveillance	Video	Labor based Surveillance Systems	(Shan et al., 2012)
4.	Sensor Data	Unstructured Data	Contextual Anomaly Detection	(Hayes et al., 2014)
5.	Machine Generated Data	Log File	Frequent Pattern Mining	(Fageeri et al., 2014)

Figure 4. Various big data analytical algorithms

2.1 Human Computer Interaction Models

Human computer interaction models are developed based on various development models such as:

- Unimodal HCI system
- Multimodal HCI system

2.1.1 Unimodality HCI System

Unimodality based human computer interaction models are relies on numeral and variety of its inputs and outputs (Robertson, 1985). This type of human computer interaction interfaces based on only one modality is called unimodal. Unimodality based human computer interaction models are further divided based on the nature of different modalities such as:

- Audio-Based Interaction Models
- Sensor-Based Interaction Models
- Visual-Based Interaction Models

Table 2. State of-the-art tools and technologies to handle big data

S. No	Task	Tool	Description
1	Data Storage and Management	Hadoop	Hadoop implements a master–slave architecture that consists of a namenode and datanode. The namenode controls the access of all datanodes. The main responsibility of datanodes is to manage the storage of data on the nodes that are running. Hadoop splits the huge file into a number of blocks and these blocks are stored in the datanodes of the system.
		Cloudera	Cloudera has provides an integrated platform for big data named as Enterprise Data Hub. Cloudera offers a service to store, process, and analyze all their data, allowing them to enlarge the significance of existing investments while providing primary ways to obtain value from their data.
		MongoDB	MongoDB is a type of document-oriented database and freely available online. MongoDB does not follows traditional rows and columns format. Instead, it uses built in architecture of collections and documents. In general, documents in the MongoDB contain sets of key-value pairs.
		Talend	Talend is an open source software that offers number of services includes data quality management, data integration and data storage. Talend consists of Master Data Management (MDM) function, which combines applications, streaming data, and function integration with fixed data quality.
2	Data Cleaning	OpenRefine	OpenRefine is also called as GoogleRefine used to clean the messy data. OpenRefine freely available online to investigate large amount of data sets quickly and merely even if the data is not in structured format. OpenRefine wiki and Github are provided to solve the user issues.
		DataCleaner	DataCleaner is used to transforms the messy semi-structured data sets into clean readable data sets that many of the visualization organizations can read. In addition, DataCleaner also provides data management and data warehousing services for end users. Though, DataCleaner is not open source, the company provides a trial version for a specific period.
3	Data Mining	RapidMiner	RapidMiner is used to provide an integrated environment for text mining, machine learning, data mining predictive analytics and business analytics. RapidMiner offers APIs to integrate our own specialized algorithms. It is used for various data mining operations including data collection, data visualization, data validation and optimization.
		IBM SPSS Modeler	IBM SPSS Modeler is developed for performing data mining operations includes analyzing data and developing analytic assets. The term *analytic asset* represents the variety of features that solve a business issue. The analytic asset performs the following operations: combines data from three historical data sources, C5.0 decision tree algorithm is used to build the model and results are displayed as tables.
		Oracle Data Miner	Oracle data mining provides various services include make predictions, discover business insights and influence their Oracle data. Oracle data mining also provides user to discover most excellent customers, behavior of the customer, and build company profiles. The Oracle Data Miner GUI allows business analysts, data analysts and data scientists to work with data inside a database using a rather elegant drag and drop solution.
		Teradata	Teradata is used to consolidate data from variety of sources and make the data available for analysis. It also provides end-to-end services and solutions in big data and analytics, data warehousing and marketing services. Teradata also provides various services including business consulting, implementation and training and development.
4	Data Analysis	Qubole	Qubole is used to improve the speed and scalability of big data analytics operations against data stored on Google, Amazon Web Service or Microsoft Azure clouds. Qubole also supports Hive, Spark and Presto to process the data in different data centers.
		BigML	BigML is used to simplify the difficulties in traditional machine learning libraries. BigML provides a powerful Machine Learning service with simple graphical user interface to import data and find predictions out of it. It allows users to use their models for data processing and predictive analytics.

Figure 5. Various fields in HCI

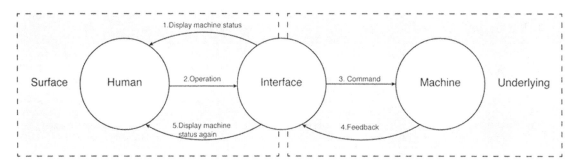

Drawbacks of Unimodal human computer interaction models are mentioned below:

- Interfaces and API developed in Unimodal human computer interaction models are not like nature
- Unimodal human computer interaction models are developed for very small average of users
- Unimodal human computer interaction models not applicable to a different group of users
- Disabled, untrained and illiterate people are not possible to use the unimodal human computer interaction models
- Universal interface is not provided in the unimodal human computer interaction models

2.1.2 Multimodal HCI System

Multimodal human computer interaction models use a variety of independent channel signals with multiple modalities to develop the interaction model between a user and a machine. More than one modes of input is used in the multimodal interface to develop the API and Interface for human-computer interaction model.

Advantages of Multimodal human computer interaction models are mentioned below:

- Interfaces and API developed in Multimodal human computer interaction models are visualized naturally and easy to use
- Multimodal human computer interaction models are used to a different group of users
- Illiterate and disabled people can use the multimodal human computer interaction models without any additional knowledge and study
- Example multimodal human computer interaction model is "Put That There" demonstration system

2.2 Cognitive Engineering

Cognitive engineering is a technology used to evaluate and design the complex systems of people and technology. The essential role of cognitive engineering is to combine the information and practice from human factors, cognitive science, human computer interaction models, and systems engineering. Cognitive style is widely used to process the information of personality for any individual.

2.3 HCI in Mobile Devices

Nowadays, many mobile devices are produced with small size. Hence, there is a need to develop an efficient human interaction model. In order to overcome this issue, touch screen display system is introduced with good touch input or a miniature keyboard. Text input method is also considered as an additional interaction model for communication between human and machine. In addition, BlackBerry has introduced miniature thumb keyboards to enhance the existing human computer interaction methods. Moreover, smart touch keyboards (STK) is inbuilt with the current generation of smart mobile phones.

2.4 Operating Systems for Mobile Devices

Nowadays, various types of operating systems have developed to run the mobile phones. Microsoft Windows Mobile uses Windows operating system originally developed by Microsoft Corporation. The version of Windows operating is system is updated regularly. It is observed that Microsoft has released Windows Mobile 6.1 version on April 1, 2008 with an extension of Windows Mobile 6 platform. The enhanced Windows mobile operating system solves various issues with the exiting Windows operating systems. The essential role of Windows Mobile 6.1 version makes it easier to stay linked and supervise our life from just about everywhere. The following devices use the Windows operating systems it include Pocket PCs, Transportable Media Centers, Smart phones, and onboard computers for convinced automobiles.

2.5 Challenges of HCI in Mobile Devices

Nowadays, the process of human computer interaction is increasing more and more complex. In order to catch up with the transitory and prompt transformation, various advance operating system, programming languages and more reliable human computer interaction models are required. In order to develop the market, the mobile and electronic development industries must solve the interface issues arise in the newly developed mobile phones and computers (Wang et al., 2007).

HCI challenges in mobile phone are classified into two types as follows:

- Hardware Challenges
- Software Challenges

2.5.1 Hardware Challenges

Mobile phone users require the mobile phones with very small size and small weight. Hence, there is a need to develop efficient mobile phones with less size and good human computer interaction model. Hence, it is difficult to develop an efficient human computer interaction model for small size of mobile devices.

2.5.2 Software Challenges

There is a need to develop an efficient algorithm as well as programming models to interact the device without need of any additional requirement. In order to overcome this issue, various advanced software's are used to enhance the existing development platform.

3. HCI WITH BIG DATA

Data visualization methods are used to visualize the results in understandable format. Human computer interaction models are widely used to develop the data visualization methods that efficiently visualize the big data. In general, x- and y- axes of graphs are widely applied to visualize any type of data. The users must identify when to use which types of visualization for visualizing big data with the help of human computer interaction models. The important issue with human computer interaction models is to identify the solutions when the data overloaded. It is important to use filtering methods to build meaningful knowledge from the raw data.

3.1 Data Visualization and Human Perception

Data visualization is an efficient method since it makes the stability between insight and cognition. Data visualization is also used in decoding the important information in a way that human eyes can distinguish and our brains can recognize. The main goal of the data visualization method is to interpret conceptual information into image representations that can be effortlessly, professionally, precisely, and significantly decoded.

3.2 HCI Architecture

HCI systems architecture is classified as follows:

- User inputs and machine outputs in the system
- Variety of inputs and outputs in terms of modality
- Interaction between the inputs and outputs

  Various HCI Systems Interfaces are listed below:

- Command Line Interface System
- Menu Driven Interface System
- Graphical User Interface System
- Natural Language Interface System

3.3 Human Interaction With Machines and Computers

3.3.1 Audio Based HCI

The audio based HCI systems are worked based on the data collected by diverse audio signals. The data collected from audio signals can be high reliable and cooperative. The following components are widely used to collect the audio signals such as Microphone, speech recognition instruments and natural language processing methods.

The classification of Audio based Human computer interaction models are listed below:

- Speech Recognition

- Auditory Sentiment Analysis
- Speaker Recognition
- Human Made Noise Detection
- Sign Detections
- Musical Communication

3.3.2 Visual Based HCI

Visual based human computer interaction models are use cameras to observe the machine vision. Various visual signals are identified from the cameras and transferred to the machine with the help of interaction models and interfaces.

The classification of Visual based Human computer interaction models are listed below:

- Facial Appearance Investigation
- Body association tracking
- Motion recognition
- Look recognition

3.3.3 Sensor Based HCI

Visual based human computer interaction models are use various sensors to observe the input from the human. The collected information from the sensor is transferred to the machine with the help of human computer interaction models and interfaces/API.

The classification of Sensor based Human computer interaction models are listed below:

- Motion Tracking Sensors
- Motion Tracking Digitizers
- Pen Based Interaction
- Haptic Sensors
- Force Sensors
- Mouse, Keyboard, Joysticks

CONCLUSION

Big data analytics requires advanced tools and techniques to store, process and analyze the huge volume of data. Big data consists of huge unstructured data that require advance real-time analysis. Thus, nowadays many of the researchers are interested in developing advance technologies and algorithms to solve the issues when dealing with big data. This chapter provides an overview of the state-of-the-art algorithms for processing big data, as well as the characteristics, applications, opportunities and challenges of big data systems. This chapter also presents the challenges and issues in human computer interaction with big data analytics.

REFERENCES

Byrd, R. J., Steinhubl, S. R., Sun, J., Ebadollahi, S., & Stewart, W. F. (2014). Automatic identification of heart failure diagnostic criteria, using text analysis of clinical notes from electronic health records. *International Journal of Medical Informatics*, *83*(12), 983–992. doi:10.1016/j.ijmedinf.2012.12.005 PMID:23317809

Dix, A. (2009). *Human-Computer Interaction. In L. Liu & M.T. Özsu (Eds.), Encyclopedia of Database Systems (pp.* 1327–1331). Springer.

Fageeri, S. O., & Ahmad, R. (2014). An efficient log file analysis algorithm using binary-based data structure. *Procedia: Social and Behavioral Sciences*, *129*, 518–526. doi:10.1016/j.sbspro.2014.03.709

Feldman, R. (2013). Techniques and applications for sentiment analysis. *Communications of the ACM*, *56*(4), 82–89. doi:10.1145/2436256.2436274

Hayes, M. A., & Capretz, M. A. (2014, June). Contextual anomaly detection in big sensor data. In *Proceedings of the 2014 IEEE International Congress on Big Data* (pp. 64-71). IEEE. 10.1109/BigData. Congress.2014.19

Lopez, D., & Gunasekaran, M. (2015). Assessment of Vaccination Strategies Using Fuzzy Multi-criteria Decision Making. In *Proceedings of the Fifth International Conference on Fuzzy and Neuro Computing (FANCCO-2015)* (pp. 195-208). Springer.

Lopez, D., Gunasekaran, M., Murugan, B. S., Kaur, H., & Abbas, K. M. (2014). Spatial Big Data analytics of influenza epidemic in Vellore, India. In Big Data (Big Data), 2014 IEEE International Conference on (pp. 19-24). IEEE.

Lopez, D., & Manogaran, G. (2016). Big Data Architecture for Climate Change and Disease Dynamics, Eds. Geetam S. Tomar et al. The Human Element of Big Data: Issues, Analytics, and Performance, CRC Press, USA.

Lopez, D., & Manogaran, G. (2017). Modelling the H1N1 influenza using mathematical and neural network approaches. *Biomedical Research*.

Lopez, D., & Sekaran, G. (2016). Climate change and disease dynamics-A Big Data perspective. *International Journal of Infectious Diseases*, *45*, 23–24.

Manogaran, G., & Lopez, D. (2016). Health Data Analytics using Scalable Logistic Regression with Stochastic Gradient Descent. *International Journal of Advanced Intelligence Paradigms*, *9*, 1–15.

Manogaran, G., & Lopez, D. (2017a). Spatial cumulative sum algorithm with big data analytics for climate change detection. *Computers & Electrical Engineering*.

Manogaran, G., & Lopez, D. (2017b). Disease surveillance system for big climate data processing and dengue transmission. [IJACI]. *International Journal of Ambient Computing and Intelligence*, *8*(2), 88–105.

Manogaran, G., & Lopez, D. (2017e). A Gaussian process based big data processing framework in cluster computing environment. *Cluster Computing*, 1–16.

Manogaran, G., Lopez, D., Thota, C., Abbas, K. M., Pyne, S., & Sundarasekar, R. (2017d). big data analytics in healthcare Internet of Things. In Innovative Healthcare Systems for the 21st Century (pp. 263-284). Springer International Publishing.

Manogaran, G., Thota, C., & Kumar, M. V. (2016). MetaCloudDataStorage Architecture for Big Data Security in Cloud Computing. *Procedia Computer Science, 87*, 128–133.

Manogaran, G., Thota, C., Lopez, D., & Sundarasekar, R. (2017c). Big data security intelligence for healthcare industry 4.0. In *Cybersecurity for Industry 4.0* (pp. 103–126). Springer International Publishing.

Manogaran, G., Thota, C., Lopez, D., Vijayakumar, V., Abbas, K. M., & Sundarsekar, R. (2017a). Big data knowledge system in healthcare. In *Internet of Things and Big Data Technologies for Next Generation Healthcare* (pp. 133–157). Springer International Publishing.

Müller, H., Michoux, N., Bandon, D., & Geissbuhler, A. (2004). A review of content-based image retrieval systems in medical applications—clinical benefits and future directions. *International Journal of Medical Informatics, 73*(1), 1–23. doi:10.1016/j.ijmedinf.2003.11.024 PMID:15036075

Parthasarathy, S., Ruan, Y., & Satuluri, V. (2011). Community discovery in socialnetworks: Applications, methods and emerging trends. In C. C. Aggarwal (Ed.), *Social network data analytics* (pp. 79–113). United States: Springer. doi:10.1007/978-1-4419-8462-3_4

Robertson, I. T. (1985). Human information-processing strategies and style. *Behaviour & Information Technology, 4*(1), 19–29. doi:10.1080/01449298508901784

Rogers, Y., Sharp, H., Preece, J., & Tepper, M. (2007). Interaction design: Beyond human-computer interaction. *netWorker. The Craft of Network Computing, 11*(4), 34.

Shan, C., Porikli, F., Xiang, T., & Gong, S. (Eds.). (2012). Video Analytics for Business Intelligence. In C. Shan, F. Porikli, T. Xiang et al. (Eds.), Video analytics for business intelligence (Vol. 1, pp. 309–354). Berlin: Springer.

Sharma, S., & Sethi, M. (2015). Implementing Collaborative Filtering on Large Scale Data using Hadoop and Mahout, *International Research Journal of Engineering and Technology, 2*(4).

Tang, L., & Liu, H. (2010). Community detection and mining in social media. *Synthesis Lectures on Data Mining and Knowledge Discovery, 2*(1), 1–137. doi:10.2200/S00298ED1V01Y201009DMK003

Varatharajan, R., Manogaran, G., Priyan, M. K., Balaş, V. E., & Barna, C. (2017b). Visual analysis of geospatial habitat suitability model based on inverse distance weighting with paired comparison analysis. *Multimedia Tools and Applications*, 1–21.

Varatharajan, R., Manogaran, G., Priyan, M. K., & Sundarasekar, R. (2017a). Wearable sensor devices for early detection of Alzheimer disease using dynamic time warping algorithm. *Cluster Computing*, 1–10.

Wang, L., & Sajeev, A. S. M. (2007, January). Roller interface for mobile device applications. In *Proceedings of the eight Australasian conference on User interface-* (*Vol. 64*, pp. 7-13). Australian Computer Society, Inc.

Wu, T. T., Chen, Y. F., Hastie, T., Sobel, E., & Lange, K. (2009). Genome-wide association analysis by lasso penalized logistic regression. *Bioinformatics (Oxford, England)*, *25*(6), 714–721. doi:10.1093/bioinformatics/btp041 PMID:19176549

Wu, X., Zhu, X., Wu, G. Q., & Ding, W. (2014). Data mining with big data. *IEEE Transactions on Knowledge and Data Engineering*, *26*(1), 97–107. doi:10.1109/TKDE.2013.109

ADDITIONAL READING

Curran, R. J., & Haskin, R. L. (2010). *U.S. Patent No. 7,840,995*. Washington, DC: U.S. Patent and Trademark Office.

Demchenko, Y., Zhao, Z., Grosso, P., Wibisono, A., & De Laat, C. (2012, December). Addressing big data challenges for scientific data infrastructure. In *Proceedings of the 2012 IEEE 4th International Conference on Cloud Computing Technology and Science (CloudCom)* (pp. 614-617). IEEE. 10.1109/CloudCom.2012.6427494

Fernández, A., del Río, S., López, V., Bawakid, A., del Jesus, M. J., Benítez, J. M., & Herrera, F. (2014). Big Data with Cloud Computing: An insight on the computing environment, MapReduce, and programming frameworks. *Wiley Interdisciplinary Reviews: Data Mining and Knowledge Discovery*, *4*(5), 380–409.

Gade, S., Pathan, A., Tomar, S., &Razdan, S. (2016). Big data on cloud using Hadoop. *Imperial Journal of Interdisciplinary Research, 2*(7).

Gai, K., Qiu, M., Zhao, H., & Xiong, J. (2016, June). Privacy-aware adaptive data encryption strategy of big data in cloud computing. In *Proceedings of the 2016 IEEE 3rd International Conference on Cyber Security and Cloud Computing (CSCloud)* (pp. 273-278). IEEE. 10.1109/CSCloud.2016.52

Gijzen, H. (2013). Development: Big Data for a sustainable future. *Nature*, *502*(7469), 38–38. doi:10.1038/502038d PMID:24091969

Hashizume, K., Rosado, D. G., Fernández-Medina, E., & Fernandez, E. B. (2013). An analysis of security issues for cloud computing. *Journal of Internet Services and Applications*, *4*(1), 1–13. doi:10.1186/1869-0238-4-5

Hongbing, C., Chunming, R., Kai, H., Weihong, W., & Yanyan, L. (2015). Secure big data storage and sharing scheme for cloud tenants. *Communications, China*, *12*(6), 106–115. doi:10.1109/CC.2015.7122469

Inukollu, V. N., Arsi, S., & Ravuri, S. R. (2014). Security issues associated with big data in cloud computing. *International Journal of Network Security & Its Applications*, *6*(3), 45–56. doi:10.5121/ijnsa.2014.6304

Kambatla, K., Kollias, G., Kumar, V., & Grama, A. (2014). Trends in big data analytics. *Journal of Parallel and Distributed Computing*, *74*(7), 2561–2573. doi:10.1016/j.jpdc.2014.01.003

Katal, A., Wazid, M., & Goudar, R. H. (2013, August). Big data: issues, challenges, tools and good practices. In *Proceedings of the 2013 Sixth International Conference on Contemporary Computing (IC3)* (pp. 404-409). IEEE. 10.1109/IC3.2013.6612229

Kim, G. H., Trimi, S., & Chung, J. H. (2014). Big-data applications in the government sector. *Communications of the ACM, 57*(3), 78–85. doi:10.1145/2500873

Kune, R., Konugurthi, P. K., Agarwal, A., Chillarige, R. R., & Buyya, R. (2016). XHAMI–extended HDFS and MapReduce interface for big data image processing applications in cloud computing environments. *Software, Practice & Experience.*

Lynch, C. (2008). Big Data: How do your data grow? *Nature, 455*(7209), 28–29. doi:10.1038/455028a PMID:18769419

Marchal, S., Jiang, X., State, R., & Engel, T. (2014). A big data architecture for large scale security monitoring. In *Proceedings of the 2014 IEEE International Congress on Big Data (BigData Congress),* (pp. 56-63). IEEE. 10.1109/BigData.Congress.2014.18

Pandey, A., & Ramesh, V. (2015). Quantum computing for big data analysis. *History (Historical Association (Great Britain)), 14*(43), 98–104.

Ranjan, R., Georgakopoulos, D., & Wang, L. (2016). A note on software tools and technologies for delivering smart media-optimized big data applications in the cloud. *Computing, 98*(1-2), 1–5. doi:10.100700607-015-0471-8

Reed, D. A., & Dongarra, J. (2015). Exascale computing and big data. *Communications of the ACM, 58*(7), 56–68. doi:10.1145/2699414

Sabahi, F. (2011). Virtualization-level security in cloud computing. In *Proceedings of the 2011 IEEE 3rd International Conference on Communication Software and Networks (ICCSN)*, Xi'an, China (pp. 250-254). IEEE. 10.1109/ICCSN.2011.6014716

Sharma, G., Arora, N., & Rai, A. (2016). Use and impact of big data in cloud computing. *Global Journal for Research Analysis, 4*(12).

Shmueli, E., Vaisenberg, R., Elovici, Y., & Glezer, C. (2010). Database encryption: An overview of contemporary challenges and design considerations. *SIGMOD Record, 38*(3), 29–34. doi:10.1145/1815933.1815940

Subashini, S., & Kavitha, V. (2011). A metadata based storage model for securing data in cloud environment. In CyberC (pp. 429-434).

Vayena, E., Salathé, M., Madoff, L. C., & Brownstein, J. S. (2015). Ethical challenges of big data in public health. *PLoS Computational Biology, 11*(2), e1003904. doi:10.1371/journal.pcbi.1003904 PMID:25664461

Wang, W., Chen, L., Thirunarayan, K., & Sheth, A. P. (2012). Harnessing twitter "big data" for automatic emotion identification. In *Proceedings of the 2012 International Conference on Privacy, Security, Risk and Trust (PASSAT), and 2012 International Conference on Social Computing (SocialCom)*, Amsterdam, Netherland (pp. 587-592). IEEE.

Wang, X., & Sun, Z. (2013). The design of water resources and hydropower cloud GIS platform based on big data. In *Geo-Informatics in Resource Management and Sustainable Ecosystem* (pp. 313–322). Springer Berlin Heidelberg. doi:10.1007/978-3-642-41908-9_32

Wu, X., Zhu, X., Wu, G. Q., & Ding, W. (2014). Data mining with big data. *IEEE Transactions on Knowledge and Data Engineering*, 26(1), 97–107. doi:10.1109/TKDE.2013.109

Chapter 77

The Components of Big Data and Knowledge Management Will Change Radically How People Collaborate and Develop Complex Research

Amitava Choudhury

iD https://orcid.org/0000-0001-5153-4449

University of Petroleum and Energy Studies, India

Ambika Aggarwal

University of Petroleum and Energy Studies, India

Kalpana Rangra

University of Petroleum and Energy Studies, India

Ashutosh Bhatt

Shivalik College of Engineering, India

ABSTRACT

Emerging as a rapidly growing field, big data is already known for promising success and having considerable synergies with knowledge management. The common goal of this collaboration is to improve and facilitate decision making, fueling the competition, fostering innovation, and achieving economic success through acquisition of knowledge to various applications. Knowledge in the entire world or inside any organization has already expanded itself in various directions and is exponentially increasing with time. To withstand the current competitive environment, an intensive collaboration of knowledge management with different approaches and algorithms of big data is required. Classical structuring is becoming obsolete with the increasing amount of knowledge components.

DOI: 10.4018/978-1-6684-3662-2.ch077

INTRODUCTION

By the advancement in technology, the life of people of present generation is very relaxing and they completely enjoy their life.While on the other hand, if we try to compare the lifestyle of the people living in 19th century or earlier, it was very poor, so here we can see the drastic change in the lifestyle of the people in a small amount of time, which is only possible because of the big data and knowledge management. We can also say that in the charming lifestyle of the present generation, there is a major role played by the big data and the knowledge management system. Over the years knowledge management has evolved to integrate information from multiple sources and perspectives. The data integration and manipulation paves the way for decision making. Decisions made by various organizations are not just based on single factor but it is the cumulative result of multiple driving forces. Considering the financial decisions of organization, dealing with revenues, salaries, interest rates alone would not be effective for deciding and predicting the solutions, Such factors must be comprehensively supported with the information of where and when to invest along with the proper consideration of the geographical locations of the market.

Data can exist in multiple forms, it simply has its existence and has no significance beyond that. Data that has some meaning is information. This information may be put to use or can just be stored without practically applying it to some area. Data gathering brings along with it all types of data or unstructured data which is to be separated, segregated and formalized to bring out something informative from the same. Unstructured data does not follow any specific format and cannot be put to use directly. It has to be organized and structured so that it can be put to use and can provide some valuable information within the resources. Structured data has defined length and has format specific. A document containing data with date and indexes is example of structured data in traditional databases. A recent survey (US San Diego, 2018) declares 20% out of 100% as the structured data, which is further categorized under machine generated, and human generated data. Sensor data, weblog data, point of sale data are typical examples of machine-generateddata gathered from web activities and product purchasing. Human generated data include input data such as online information; click stream data generated on clicking a website link. Another term coined for data that lies somewhere in between structured and unstructured data is semi-structured data. Semi-structured data can be understood as the data that has self-describing structure. It is the kind of data that does not conform to any data model typically associated with relational databases. Typical examples of semi-structured data can be XML and JSON files.

Figure 1. Approximate percentage distribution of digital data

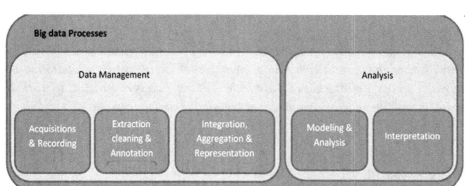

Knowledge Management

Nowadays data is considered as an important resource for business as compared to materialistic assets and intellectual capital. Organizations aspiring for sustainable growth deliberately require managing the information for innovations. One way to mediate the increasing load of information is application of knowledge management practices, which have their baseline in conventional approaches such as knowledge creation, innovation, sharing and transfer of knowledge, reusability of knowledge and applicability of knowledge. It does not end here but the conventional knowledge digs deep onto knowledge acquisition. Acquisition of knowledge is a complex area arising from competing disparate theories and calling for complications. One such complication is difficulty in predicting future needs of knowledge and skills as well. Another concern of knowledge imperatives is application of knowledge. Therefore, capturing knowledge and its application can be crucial for competitive and economic success of the firm. While knowledge management components include data identification, data capturing, and managing the data we have another emergent technology that deals with acquisition of data in huge volumes commonly referred to as raw data, mundane knowledge or unstructured data. This form of data is usually collected from social sites and analyzed for predictive insights. Though knowledge management covers a wide area of data processing, still the efficiency of knowledge management is restricted to structured data. The unstructured or semi structured data can be efficiently processed by collaborating knowledge management with big data approaches and algorithms.

Big Data Analytics

Big data Analytics covers the collection and connection of data extending to storage, manipulating, and presenting the vast data stores to the world. Big data can be defined precisely in dimensions of volume, variety and velocity. The solution isachieved by obtaining subsets of data, analyzing the subsets and aggregating the subsets to achieve results. Big data being the intensive change for IT has major implications for knowledge management. Business Analytics is one approach to use big data in collaboration with knowledge management that enables to store, process and retrieve information using business intelligence. Text analytics allows creation of data from enormous unstructured sources and helps in building sentiment scores. Speed at which the data is generated and communicated in various formats is also significantly taken into consideration in Big data analytics. The range of data from multiple sources and in multiple formats is yet another important aspect of big data analytics. It is possible to identify several features that can offer a wider perspective in understanding the impact of analyzing big data in an effective and influential contextual range covering knowledge management. The nature of sources from where the data is gathered, the understanding of individual and the language understood by humans also affect the concept of Big Data Analytics. The changing values of data that are captured from a source may reflect the change in subject and opinions of an individual over a short period of time. Large volume of data can be derived from changing perspectives but then there arises the question about degree of trust that can be placed on information so that it can be qualified as valid information. Thus, big data analytics can be critically evaluated as the impact of 10 V's for big data supported knowledge management (Crane, Lesley & Self, Richard., 2014).

1. Volume(size)
2. Velocity(speed)

3. Variety(format)
4. Variability(temporal)
5. Value (to whom?)
6. Validity(applicable)
7. Veracity(truth)
8. Volatility(temporal)
9. Verbosity(text)
10. Verification(trust)

Out of these, the first three are traditionally essential in determining the definition of Big Data. Volume, velocity and variety target the big data analytics challenging the surety of correct linkages made between objects and entities in different sources. Other social network accounts have more data that has to be structured and should have good linkages. Variety of sources henceforth brings forward a technical challenge and problem in veracity and validity of data questioning the reliability of the content. To gain correct linkages, Verification and validation approaches can be put to use before relying on analyzed information and knowledge. Changing values of data can be addressed under Variability and volatility. Data may be altered and affected by changing the demographic details. Verbosity deals with the nature of text sources since computer systems are not as good as humans in understanding the semantics of language. The value in data is correlated to extent to which it complies with 10 V's and analysis is not limited by pre-conceived ideas about data relation and connections.

With the time over 100 billion of mails are being received and sent per day that adds on the burgeoning volume created each day on social sites including LinkedIn, twitter, and Facebook (Falch, Morten, Henten, Anders, Tadayoni, Reza, Windekilde, Iwona, 2009). The huge metadata gives the tsunami like proportion view since the amount of data sent to the average person per year is enormously large. IBM reports have shown that major part of the data created in the world is not structured and if the trend continued, most of the data will turn out to be untrustworthy. By emerging as the technology that has revolutionized many service sectors big data permeated into every operative sector of business to gear up the competitive environment.

In the past years, the cost of data collection and storage limited the ability of the enterprises to obtain the required information to get a holistic view of the solution for information retrieval. The barriers in accessing the data have been removed by automated collection of digital information and cheap storage. Data is abundantly available these days but the relational databases limit the ability of retrieval of sensible information. Big Data has emerged as a new solution to deal with such problem.

Emergent applications including commercial are using big data for dealing with interrelated operational and transactional data thereby providing new dimensions to knowledge in directions of business operations, supply chain management, tracking the performance of distribution channels, predicting and analyzing the customer behavior for business intelligence.

There has been an explosive growth in amount of data streaming into businesses. There is no sign that this exponential growth will slow down in the near future. Several organizations will gain many benefits for their businesses by leveraging this data to their advantage to gain deeper insights in customer behavior, competitor tracking, operational efficiencies, and many more.The question that requires an answer here is - how are we going to manage and utilize this data to our advantage? A survey (J. N Dorlenas,Kassia Roberta Rodrigues de Souza,AméricoNobreAmorim2017)carried out in joint venture with the Outsourcing Center on the procedures of organizational data management and analysis of the proliferating data, application of big data for the benefit of their businesses came out with few findings. The survey resulted in identifying some general trends in emerging areas:

1. Big data platforms address the issue of managing future big data challenges in majority of organizations.
2. Organizations face difficulty in analyzing data sufficiency, handling external data and reporting data in real time.
3. Lack of formal organizational strategy in place to deal with and leverage big data.
4. Becoming more operationally efficient is considered the biggest benefit of implementing big data strategy.
5. The biggest roadblock to implementing a big data strategy is lack of measurable ROI.

The large amount of data, which can generate new and valuable information, beneficial for firms and organizations, as compared to traditional data sets and information obtained by trending knowledge management activities,can be called as big data. Thus, the concept of big data encompasses the amount of data, the tools, the technologies necessary to maintain vast amount of data in terms of variety, volume and velocity that cannot be achieved with traditional data management.

Why Big Data Analytics?

Digital data is growing at a huge pace of approximately 40% per annum and is expected to reach nearly 45ZB by the year 2020. Approximately 1.2 trillion GB of data was generated in 2010 itself which got doubled by the year 2012 and became 2.4 trillion GB. In the year 2014, the amount of data was approximated to be 5 trillion GB. The size of data is expected to be doubled in every 1.2 years across the globe (A. Cuzzocrea.,2014).

Approximately one million customer transactions are processed by Wal-Mart every hour. Every day its users post about 500 million tweets on twitter accounts. Facebook records approximately 2.7 billion 'Likes' and 'comments' per day. It is estimated that 2.5 quintillion bytes of data is created per day worldwide. It is also interesting to note that 90% of data worldwide was created in last two years itself.

The cost of storing data per gigabyte has dropped hugely and there a number of user-friendly tools available in the market for Big Data analytics.

CLASSIFICATION OF ANALYTICS

1. **Basic Analytics:** Basic analytics deals with classifying and categorizing data in order to obtain business insights. It primarily includes reporting based on historical data and basic data visualization, etc.
2. **Operationalized Analytics:** This kind of analytics becomes operationalized analytics when interlinked with the organization's business process.
3. **Advanced Analytics**: Advanced analytics majorly deals with future forecasting based on predictive and prescriptive modelling.
4. **Monetized Analytics**: This kind of analytics is used to derive direct revenues for business organizations.

COMPONENTS OF BIG DATA

- **HDFS (Hadoop Distributed File System):** It is component of big data, which is responsible for the storage layer. Because of this layer, we are able to get insights which enables to make the technology better. As without proper storage medium for data, we cannot store data and as a result, we will not be able to get some insights, which will help in directing us to our goal.

- **NoSQL Databases:** NoSQL databases are responsible for handling the data, whichis not structured, as it is not always possible that the insights we are getting are from structured data only, it may be unstructured or semi-structured data, which will be directing us towards our goal.

- **Real Time Processing:** It is another component of Big Data that allows to develop many modules of latest technology. By real time processing, we are able to answer or reply to the query raised within microseconds. This component will be very helpful in complex researches.

- **Fault Tolerant:** This component also plays a major role in complex researches and technology. Consider an important research, which is going on, on a system but what if the system fails; if the system is not fault tolerant then it will be very difficult to recover the progress.

- **Map Reduce:**It is very new concept for faster execution of huge amount of data, and to process distributed data.

COMPONENTSOFKNOWLEDGE MANAGEMANT

- **Functionality:** This component of knowledge management is responsible for enhancing and supporting the knowledge intensive applications/processes, their transformation, their maintenance, their structures, their evolution, the application of knowledge etc. This component is the backbone of the applications, which require complex researches.

- **Interface:** For the facilitation of knowledge or a service which manages knowledge, an interface is required, this interface could be technological, structural or a human itself. It doesn't matter what type of interface it is, but it should be there for the proper working of the systems.

- **Strategy:** It is very important component of knowledge management, as a strategy should be present to deal with the problem, or to gain proper benefit from a opportunity. In other words, to develop anything, to cope up with a problem, to run a business, or to perform complex researches we should have a strategy.

- **Persistent Improvement:** As we all know, that nothing is perfect, therefore we have to improve it and we should always try to improve a particular thing regardless of how good it is, it is possible that there may be some flaws which will be resolved by the continuous improvement. Therefore, persistent improvement is necessary.

Now, coming back to the original discussion, this chapter would like to say that with the help of the components of big data and knowledge management, there would be a drastic change we will see in the collaboration of the people and their development of complex research. Now after using the components of big data and knowledge management, collaboration of people will face a sharp turn or an interesting twist, as now they are already able to get insights from the big data, so, now they will collaborate smartly. The possible changes we will see in the collaboration of people will be:

- They will try to collaborate with people who are having same goals.
- They will collaborate in order to create creative conflict, which will be productive for them.
- The people who will collaborate will be selected carefully by considering their potential, their skills, their determination towards their work and what creative they can do in order to gain benefits. As only the people who can dig out some insights from the ocean of data and facilitate the information will not be sufficient to collaborate, some creative people will be needed to collaborate because for doing such type of tasks we already have big data and knowledge management components.
- Collaboration will be done on the basis of how good the people are in surfacing creativity and facilitation of techniques.
- Collaboration will be done on the basis of the engagement.

In development of the complex research, if we are provided with the services, which will automatically, do computation on data and facilitate information it will be very helpful for us in doing complex researches and also give us motivation to do more. This work is done by the components of big data and the knowledge management. It is not that without these components we are not able to do something but with the use of technology as a tool we are able to do complex researches fast and effective.

It is not that, that technology is our advantage; we are only smartly using the resources, which will accelerate our learning and will enhance our capabilities. Consider a research, which is very complex, and we are not able to perform it normally or we are facing difficulties in it.Now if we use services provided by the components of the big data and knowledge management system, we may able to perform it easily, here we are using technology in a smart way to get rid of the problems or converting a complex problem into a simple one. Use of components of big data and knowledge management are very helpful and beneficial for us, it will exceed all expectations if we are a well-structured organization which will follow collaboration protocols and regularly do researches. Example of this is Human Genome Project. As the complexity of scientific challenges is increasing constantly therefore we need to use the latest technology such as big data and knowledge management systems/frameworks and collaborate to tackle the challenges.

One thing we should always keep in our mind that excellence in education is the ultimate outcome, the more superior thing above excellence in education is our ability to learn. We should not think ability to learn as an individual achievement but it is a collective one, collective learning are the backbone of the great learning ecosystems.

So, we should learn every time to enhance technology and use it in complex researches or anywhere where it can be used, like we are using components of big data and knowledge management.

BIG DATA FOR SCIENTIFIC RESEARCH

In recent times, Big Data has rapidly evolved and has emerged as topic of great interest for researchers, academicians, industry experts and even government organizations all across the globe (Mayer-Schonberger & Cukier, 2013; Thomson, Lebiere & Bennati, 2014; Cuzzocrea, 2014). Big data has instigated the entire scientific community to re-evaluate its methodology of scientific research and has triggered a revolution in scientific thinking and methods.

Historically, the researches were based on experimental results. Then emerged the theoretical science, which involved the study of various laws and theorems. However, it was observed that theoretical analysis was becoming too complex and was not viable for solving practical problems, which eventually led researchers to opt for simulation based methods, and hence computational science was born.

The evolution of big data has given birth to a new research model. Now with big data in picture, researchers are able to extract and process only relevant information. The objects to be studied also do not need to be accessed directly. Jim Gray, the late Turing Award winner had illustrated in his last speech about the fourth paradigm of data-intensive scientific research (Hey, Tansley & Tolle, 2009), which separates data-intensive science from computational science. According to Gray, the fourth paradigm was the only possible systematic approach for solving some of the toughest global challenges faced today. In essence, the fourth paradigm was not merely a change in the way of scientific research, but also a change in the way that people think (Mayer-Schonberger & Cukier, 2013).

Figure 2. Big data processing model

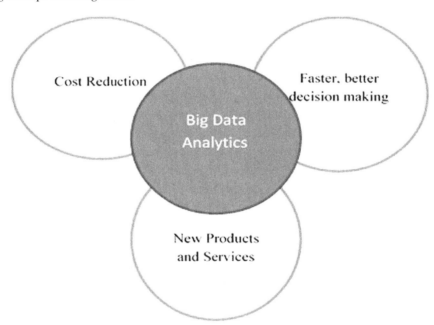

BIG DATA FOR EMERGING INTERDISCIPLINARY RESEARCH

An emerging interdisciplinary research area known as data science (Loukides, 2011) has eventually come into existence which is also taking advantage of the Big Data technology. The research objective of data science is big data which aims at generalizing knowledge extraction from data which eventually gives rise to the term knowledge management. The term data science is not restricted to any particular area or field; It rather expands across various disciplines, including mathematics, information science, network science, social science, system science, economics, and psychology (O'Neil & Schutt. 2013). It employs many theories and techniques from various fields, including machine learning, signal processing, statistical learning, probability theory, computer programming, pattern recognition, data engineering, visualization, data warehousing, uncertainty modeling, and high performance computing.

Big data has led towards establishment of numerous research centers and institutes in various Universities across the globe. Some of these Universities include New York University, University of California at Berkeley, Columbia University, Eindhoven University of Technology, Tsinghua University, and Chinese University of Hong Kong). Big Data tools and technologies are being used extensively by industry and academia to facilitate knowledge management and to create data science engineers.

NATIONAL DEVELOPMENT THROUGH BIG DATA

Currently, the world is entering into an era of information age. The extensive use of Internet, emergence of smart devices resulting in Internet of Things (IoT), evolution of cloud computing and various other data sources have resulted in huge amount of data which is mostly of unstructured type and is complex to process. Big Data processing and analytics will prove to be of great importance for enhancing competitiveness of companies hence promoting the economic growth of the nation.

The future of the world lies in Analysis as a Service (AaaS) and various IT giants like Google, Microsoft, IBM etc. have already started working towards it by employing Big Data analytics tools and technologies. In near future, the capacity and capability of a nation to store, process and analyze huge amount of data will become the new landmark of its strength.

Figure 3. Region specific data co-ordinates

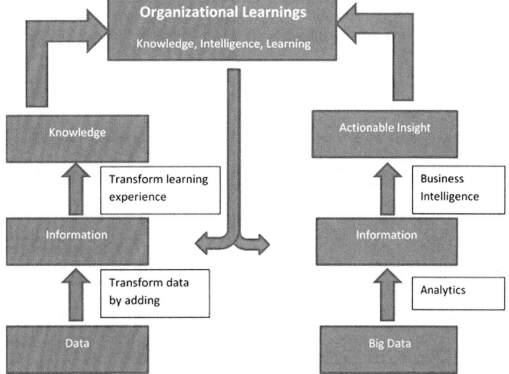

In China, a government report in China had proposed that cyberspace, as well as deep space and deep sea are the key areas of national core interests. A country lagging behind in the field of big data research and applications is not only an indication of the loss of its industrial strategic advantage, but it also indicates loopholes in its national security cyberspace. Considering this report, the Big Data Research and Development Initiative(RD. Williams, 2018), announced by the United States in March 2012, was not merely a strategic plan that promotes the US to continuously lead in the high-tech fields, but was also a strategy to shield its national security and enhance its social and economic development.

PREDICTING BETTER FUTURE WITH BIG DATA

Better prediction on future trends of various events can be made by achieving effective integration of big data and more accurate analysis of unstructured, heterogeneous big data. Big data analytics has made it possible to promote sustainable development of society by enhance its economic growth and providing opportunities to establish new industries based on data services. The ability of huge amount of data distributed over a network has been greatly developed and effectively implemented in the field of military and security. For example, the US released a report in 2010 (Louis, 2013) titled "Chinese Nuclear Warhead Storage and Handling System", stating that US had found Chinese nuclear bases in areas like Jiangxi, Shaanxi, and Sichuan. The names of the various cities and countries were also quoted by the report where the nuclear bases were located. This report immediately became a global sensation. The 2049 Project Institute of the United States, founded in 2008 in Washington, DC, got worldwide attention after the release of this report. The said institute analyzes and forecasts security issues related to economy and military in China by utilizing publically available data such as conference papers and journals. Another report was released by the institute in March 2013, based on China's Unmanned Aerial Vehicle (UAV) project (Easton & Hsiao, 2013) As per the report, a comprehensive analysis was conducted on equipment, research and development, and operational deployment of UAV in China.

Table 1. Various tools and platforms for big data analytics

Tool/Platform	Description
The Hadoop Distributed File System (HDFS)	HDFS provides the storage structures for HADOOP cluster. The data is divided into small segments and distributed across various nodes or servers for storage.
MapReduce	It acts as an interface that divides tasks into sub tasks and distributes them for processing and then collects various outputs and combines them. It also keeps track of the processing of various nodes or servers.
PIG and PIG Latin	PIG is a programming language which is configured to integrate any kind of data whether structured or unstructured. The two major modules of PIG are the language itself, known as PIG Latin, and the runtime environment in which its code is executed.
Hive	Hive is a runtime environment supported by Hadoop which is based on Structured Query Language(SQL). It allows programmers to write HQL (Hive Query Language) queries which are very similar to SQL.
Jaql	It is another functional and declarative query language which is designed for processing larger data sets. "High level queries" are converted into "low level queries" consisting of MapReduce tasks, in order to facilitate parallel processing.
Zookeeper	Zookeeper facilitates synchronization throughout a cluster of servers thus allowing a centralized infrastructure having various services. These services are being utilized by Big Data Analytics applications in order to coordinate parallel processing throughout big clusters.

Social issues such as public health and economic growth and development have also been addressed by applying big data predictive analysis techniques. Ginsberg, *et al.* concluded in one of their works that the number of influenza patients will increase eventually in the hospital emergency rooms of a particular region, if in the past few weeks, a high number of Google queries were submitted in that area with keywords like "flu symptom" and "flu treatment" (Ginsberg, Mohebbi, Patel, Brammer, Smolinski & Brilliant., 2009) Imagine the advantage of such predictive analysis in the area of public health. Hospitals and doctors can prepare themselves in advance with appropriate equipment, medicines and vaccines. In terms of economic growth and development, a project called Global Pulse (UN Global Pulse, 2012) was recently launched by the United Nations, which aims at utilizing big data technologies to promote and enhance global economic development.

Knowledge management (KM) is a collection of systematic approaches to help information and knowledge flow to and between the right people at the right time (in the right format at the right cost) so they can act more efficiently and effectively to create value for the organization. The term knowledge management is mainly deals with effectively deals with information within an organization. On the other hand, Big Data is used in process huge amount of data within or outside the organization. Big data is a broad term for data sets so large or complex that traditional data processing applications are inadequate. Challenges include analysis, capture, data curation, search, sharing, storage, transfer, visualization, and information privacy. The term often refers simply to the use of predictive analytics or other certain advanced methods to extract value from data, and seldom to a particular size of data set. Accuracy in big data may lead to more confident decision making. And better decisions can mean greater operational efficiency, cost reduction and reduced risk. Knowledge management is nothing but the process of data i.e. known as information, while recent days the computational data size is very huge. Traditional KM system may provide sufficient knowledge with in one commercial organization but it may fail in complex structure of data.

As noted before, knowledge management does not provide the solution very nicely in lower level of the data-information-knowledge hierarchy, which can be treated as knowledge management problem. Below figure, describe the process of data into information to knowledge management.

UNSTRUCTURED DATA PROCESSING PROBLEM IN KM

Commercial data is mainly applied in knowledge management (Lee, Ming-Chang.et al, 2009). Such data is unstructured in nature. In our traditional data process techniques, processing such kind of data was very challenging task. Big data supports knowledge management and extends its functionality by providing tool like Hadoop for analyzing unstructured data. Having the distributed storage capabilities and distributed processing framework, Hadoop enables working with huge volume of complex data.The design of Hadoop supports big data as it can accommodate the data that is too big for any traditional database technologies. Data is stored in files since Hadoop does not enforce schema or structure for data storage. Applications like Sqoop, HIVE, HBASE integrated with Hadoop enables import and export from various traditional and non-traditional database forms. This allows Hadoop to structure any unstructured data and explore semi-structured data for further analysis and decision-making. Expanding more, Hadoop is seen as a powerful tool for writing customized codes. Programmers can implement algorithms of any complexity exploiting the benefits of Hadoop features, framework to get efficient and reliable solutions. Thus, programmers gain flexibility for better understanding of data at crude level. Hadoop as an open

Figure 4. Organizational-learning process through big data analytics

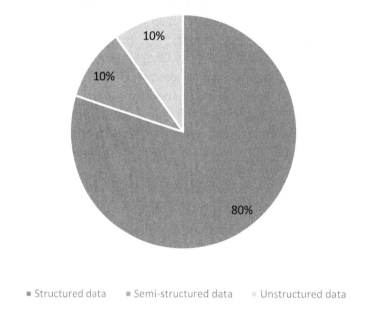

■ Structured data   ■ Semi-structured data   ▨ Unstructured data

source project has developed exponentially in the market since it has numerous applications including speech and image processing, file analysis, and text analysis pivoted with python.

MARITIME BUSINESS CASE: A CASE STUDY

Big data enabled knowledge management solutions can be applied to support maritime innovation capability. Big data driven knowledge management initiatives can be addressed in maritime organization in following areas

- Big data for Strategy and decision making in shipping industries
- Big data for competitive intelligence for knowing shipper supplier and competitors
- Big data for human capital development on board and ashore
- Data driven Culture from craftsmanship to knowledge and science orientation

Big Data for Strategy and Decision Making in Shipping Industries

Strategy formulation in shipping primarily addresses investment appraisal and portfolio management covering various elements of ship valuations and asset play,risk assessment for financing, market scanning and positioning or determining the exits.Strategic adjustment is considered as closest knowledge management system evolution approach using big data that provides possibility for new information services enabled by near time collection of multiple big data sources for both public and private, open andcorporateorganizations to support market interpretation and prediction.

Utmost research and development emphasis has been primarily laid on a) predictive maintenance applications to monitor ship health b) energy consumption/efficiency monitoring c) emission and environmental impact monitoring platform d) safety and security platform for monitoring piracy for critical incidence.WAVES and DANAOS are commonly used commercial platforms in shipping companies for monitoring vessel and fleet performance. Centralized policy orientation for operational authorities are currently emergent along with vessel tracking and trade route analysis functionality.

Big Data for Competitive Intelligence for Knowing Shipper Supplier and Competitors

Collection and analysis of available data resources to identify pattern of collaborators customers and competitor'sbehavioral patterns is the primary objective of maritime competitive intelligence. Predictive competitor behavior (like Liner shipping companies serving the same trade routes) allows future anticipation of strategic moves. Future behaviors of customers including shippers forwarder and charters can be analyzed with high confidence thus by strongly supporting the decision making of any maritime organization.

An unexplored area of knowledge management for maritime domain is unveiled to give impetus for driving maritime big data and business intelligence technology and development of applications. Related technologies range from doing sentimental analysis for inferring opinions to predict market trends and freight rate predictions.

Big Data for Human Capital Development on Board and Ashore

Human capital development needs assessment to necessitate reorientation in terms of soft skills in any maritime organization.Modern maritime education and training is required to fulfill current industry needs and complement future trends.New technical requirements pose new challenges for seafarers since they have to work with high speed equipment's on board as a part of unmanned mega ships.This requires more skilled workforce whichshould be technically literate and well equipped for problem solving and decision making along with high communication skill.Other marine professionals are continuously challenged to be trained and arecertified to retain their positions in maritime organization.Big data trends along with knowledge management e learning trends are likely to be influenced in maritime training sector for development of skill estimations and course recommendations.

Data Driven Culture From Craftsmanship to Knowledge and Science Orientation

Another major paradigm shift altering maritime industry these days is a new technological trajectory that is currently evolving with smart ships, smart ports and logistic infrastructure. Vessel and shipping company node are highlysupported by Big Data.Innovation orientated technology is gaining momentum in shipping environment and new strategies are also paving way for timely entering the profitable markets to develop and redesign decision support and operational support in maritime software. Inessence, of functionalities knowledge management is enabling systematic innovation capabilities of shipping companies.

It can be postulated that unless appropriately designed, visualized and dialogued knowledge management in big data era application for innovation support it's not possible to enhance innovative capabilities in a MARITIME INDUSTRY.

HANDLING BIG DATA IN AUTOMATIVE INDUSTRY

Big data is qualitatively different from previous data analytics technologies since it can cooperate with vast amount of different types of data. This data is real time data and can be tapped from multiple and large number of public and private resources. Big data will enhance the results and improve the supply chain and reduce the lean time of quality approaches like Six Sigma, design for Six sigma, lean manufacturing.

Big Data and Supply Chain Management

Supply chain is used to predict car demand and trends by using CRM (customer relationship management database or public data. SCM also provides for monitoring the dealers and end of line customer satisfaction. Various automotive industries apply Big Data in both economic and social aspects.

Big Data for End Customer Focus

Through big data customer becomes an eminent part of Control board of project decisions. The needs of customer influence the future improvement in car functionalities leading to production of new versions of the model. Customized driving Experience is gather to provide personalized driving tips and suggestions for improvement of driving style. Break warning, unnecessary acceleration, destination suggestions, alternative route suggestions message can inform drivers and answer their queries of common interest.

Big Data for Management Roles

Management requires future forecasting and business prediction. Client needs directly influence business decisions Client being the share manager,the power of decision-makingis harnessed directly from the former. This requires implementing Big Data decisions making algorithms to support CRM. Business profitability is increasing with growth of intangible resources. Big data supports this same by measuring the intellectual capital and knowledge management. Based on the processed data employee, records and performancecan be traced and the status can be measured for both the parameters. Big data platform is used to check "know –how" distribution inside companies and subdivisions. Changes can be implemented for efficient allocation of resources if the employee is well integrated inside the team. Big data answers the major question "what will the average growth in performance if the management is informed and prepared to deal with team issues and balance them without much problem." The big issue of employee inadaptability can be addressed using big data measurement technologies. Decisions can be madebased on suggestions provided by big data algorithms.Big data enables organization in data gathering data storage,management and manipulation of data at right speed and time that provides insights in decision-making.Finding new information has and patterns lead to new insights of knowledge management, which is valuable for the organization.Large volume of data helps to maintain knowledge functioning as foundation for decision-making constrained to few features like relevance of data,high quality of data, careful analysis and type of problem being addressed by it.

Big Data for Automotive Telematics

Globally and locally interconnected cars can save time, lives and money by avoiding accidents, traffic jams. Algorithms that map the personal driving behaviors can be used to get the above-mentioned results.Big data has a vital place in connected car environments to deliver real time solutions for traffic management and improve traffic efficiency .the concept of connected cars can revolutionize the cities to become Intelligent cities implementing intelligent infrastructures. There are several devices that can interpret the world around car and handle the exceptions, such devices lay foundation of automated driving solutions using big data and knowledge management.

Concluding the role of big data in automotive industry, big data will be higly effective in supply chain to perusecustomer-oriented policies to reduce warranty cost.Integrating big data solutions with government cities and agencies can support the safety system and revolutionize the traffic systems by collaborating with the traffic authorities. Big data allows combining the data between and among the organization to determine customer behavior and produce useful insights in numerous applications like public health and safety, frauddetection, cost reduction and much more.

Large quantities of raw and unstructured data can provide evolutionary leap to classical data handling and manipulating technologies.

BIG DATA IN HEALTHCARE

Healthcare is also another area where Big Data has been widely applied with rapid development in data and knowledge management. Analysis of prevalent diseases and the disease trends among population can be done using the clinical data. Clinal data analysis can be done to determine causality, effect and association between risk factors and diseases among the populations.

Big data can bring knowledge management in health science to reuse medical record data to aid medical research.Health science information can be manipulated to have positive impact on health science. Based on query placed google could predict the spread of flue that started in United states in 2009.The processing and the expertise power of google can provide public health care officials with valuable real time information. Google example shows what can be achieved with collaboration of Big Data and knowledge management in society for health services.Integration of patient information and the related data across entities and analysis of health care data can exponentially gear up the quality, efficiency and continuity of healthcare and outcome predictions.Being the most expensive sector within the nation,providing employment and services to people and costing high in terms of expenditure in an aging population, it'sa producer of enormous amount of data.This type of data includes health records, statistics which can be applied to enhance large operational efficiency, productivity to improvise the services provided.Healthcare executives and policy makers are also the implications of integrated big data knowledge management.

CONCLUSION

There's no wrong in saying that intellectual capital (IC), KM, and the escalating trend towards the use of big data processing and business analytics are all connected to each other. All of these are related to some sort of intangible asset, whether it is data, information, knowledge, or intelligence. A better understanding of how an organization can benefit from knowledge assets can be obtained by concentrating more on the strategic aspects of developing and protecting knowledge.

We can obtain an understanding of what kind of knowledge is appropriate to be developed in numerous industries by going through various variables such as the nature of knowledge. This perspective can be beneficial in obtaining an understanding about how and when contributions from big data might prove to be helpful. Further, such variables can provide an insight into whether data is at risk or not, and also give us guidelines regarding protection of intangible assets, and can even illustrate the need of protecting the data from competitive incursions if required.

REFERENCES

Crane, L., & Self, R. (2014). Big Data Analytics: A Threat or an Opportunity for Knowledge Management? *Lecture Notes in Business Information Processing, 185,* 25–34. doi:10.1007/978-3-319-08618-7_3

Cuzzocrea, A. (2014). Privacy and security of big data: current challenges and future research perspectives. *Proceedings of the First International Workshop on Privacy and Security of Big Data, PSBD '14.*

Easton, I.M., & Hsiao, L.R. (2013). The Chinesepeople's liberation army's unmanned aerial vehicle project: Organizational capacities and operational capabilities. Tech. rep., 2049 Project Institute.

Falch, M., Henten, A., Tadayoni, R., & Windekilde, I. (2009). Business Models in Social Networking. *Aalborg Universitet.* Retrieved from: http://vbn.aau.dk/files/19150157/falch_3.pdf

Ginsberg, J., Mohebbi, M. H., Patel, R. S., Brammer, L., Smolinski, M. S., & Brilliant, L. (2009). Detecting influenza epidemics using search engine query data. *Nature, 7232*(7232), 1012–1014. doi:10.1038/nature07634 PMID:19020500

Hey, T., Tansley, S., & Tolle, K. (2009). *The Fourth Paradigm: Data-Intensive Scientific Discovery.* Microsoft Corporation; doi:10.1145/2609876.2609883

Lee, M.-C. (2009). The Combination of Knowledge Management and Data mining with Knowledge Warehouse. *International Journal of Advancements in Computing Technology, 1.* doi:10.4156/ijact.vol1.issue1.6

Lewis, L. (2013). China's Nuclear Idiosyncrasis and Their Challenges. *Security Studies Center.* Retrieved from: https://www.ifri.org/sites/default/files/atoms/files/pp47lewis.pdf

Loukides, M. (2011). What Is Data Science? *O'Reilly Media, Inc.* Retrieved from: https://www.oreilly.com/ideas/what-is-data-science

Mayer-Schonberger, V., & Cukier, K. (2013). *Big Data: A Revolution That Will Transform How We Live, Work, and Think.* Houghton Mifflin Harcourt.

O'Neil, C., & Schutt, R. (2013). *Doing Data Science: Straight Talk from the Frontline.* O'Reilly Media, Inc.

Simião Dornelas, J., & Rodrigues de Souza, K. R. (2017, May/August). AméricoNobreAmorim Cloud Computing:Searching its Use In Public Management Environments. *JISTEM USP, Brazil, 14*(2), 281–306. doi:10.4301/S1807-17752017000200008

Thomson, R., Lebiere, C., & Bennati, S. (2014). Human, model and machine: a complementary approach to big data. *Proceedings of the Workshop on Human Centered Big Data Research, HCBDR '14.*

UNGlobal Pulse. (2012). *Big data for development: challenges & opportunities.* Available at: http://www.unglobalpulse.org/projects/BigDataforDevelopment

Williams, R. D. (2018). The 'China, Inc.+' Challenge to Cyberspace Norms. *Hoover Institution.* Retrieved from: https://www.hoover.org/research/china-inc-challenge-cyberspace-norms

ADDITIONAL READING

Angelo, T. A. (1999). Doing assessment as if learning matters most. *AAHE Bulletin, 51*(9), 3–6.

Erickson, S., & Rothberg, H. (2014). Big Data and Knowledge Management: Establishing a Conceptual Foundation. *Electronic Journal of Knowledge Management.*

This research was previously published in Big Data Governance and Perspectives in Knowledge Management; pages 241-257, copyright year 2019 by Information Science Reference (an imprint of IGI Global).

Chapter 78
Data Management and Big Data Analytics:
Data Management in Digital Economy

Vellingiri Jayagopal

Sree Vidyanikethan Engineering College, India

Basser K. K.

Sree Vidyanikethan Engineering College, India

ABSTRACT

The internet is creating 2.5 quintillion bytes of data, and according to the statistics, the percentage of data that has been generated from last two years is 90%. This data comes from many industries like climate information, social media sites, digital images and videos, and purchase transactions. This data is big data. Big data is the data that exceeds storage and processing capacity of conventional database systems. Data in today's world (big data) is usually unstructured and qualitative in nature and can be used for various applications like sentiment analysis, increasing business, etc. About 80% of data captured today is unstructured. All this data is also big data.

INTRODUCTION

Day by day the big world of internet is creating 2.5 quintillion bytes of data on regular basis according to the statistics the percentage of data that has been generated from last two years is 90%. This data comes from many industries like climate information collects by sensor, different stuff from social media sites, digital images and videos, different records of purchase transaction. This data is big data. The big data is the data that exceeds storage and processing capacity of conventional database systems. Data in today's world (Big Data) is usually unstructured and qualitative in nature that can be used for various applications like sentiment analysis, increasing business etc. About 80% of data captured today is unstructured and is being collected from various sources like sensors which are used to gather climate

DOI: 10.4018/978-1-6684-3662-2.ch078

information, posts on various social media websites like tweets from twitter, Digital pictures and videos uploaded on various websites like Facebook, Purchase transaction records and other similar data. All this data is also Big Data.

The systematic study of Big Data can lead to:

- Understanding target customers' better – Big data is used by business today for analyzing sentiments of the target customers and providing them better services to increase the business.
- Cutting down in expenditures in various sectors – Analysis of such huge volume of data has also helped business in cutting down their expenditures in various sectors wherever possible. Several billions of dollars being saved by improvements in operational efficiency and more.
- Increase in operating margins in different sectors – Big Data also helps industries in increasing operating margins in different sectors. With the help of Big Data, lot of manual labour can be converted into machine task and this helps in increasing operating margins.

Big data is a technology to transform analysis of data-heavy workloads, but it is also a disruptive force. It is fuelling the transformation of entire industries that require constant analysis of data to address daily business challenges. Big data is about broader use of existing data, integration of new sources of data, and analytics that delve deeper by using new tools in a more timely way to increase efficiency or to enable new business models. Today, big data is becoming a business imperative because it enables organizations to accomplish several objectives:

- Apply analytics beyond the traditional analytics use cases to support real-time decisions, anytime and anywhere
- Tap into all types of information that can be used in data-driven decision making
- Empower people in all roles to explore and analyze information and offer insights to others
- Optimize all types of decisions, whether they are made by individuals or are embedded in automated systems by using insights that are based on analytics
- Provide insights from all perspectives and time horizons, from historic reporting to real-time analysis, to predictive modelling
- Improve business outcomes and manage risk, now and in the future

Big data Use cases are:

1. IOT
2. Advertising analysis
3. Predictive Analysis
4. Customer churn Analysis
5. Aadhar project by govt of India
6. Telecom fault detection
7. Natural resource exploration

There are four major categories of big data.

1. Transactional & Application data

2.   Machine Data
3.   Social Data
4.   Enterprise Content

The social data is the major causes of veracity problems. The total no. of social media accounts exceeds the entire global population. This data is highly uncertain in both its expression and content. Social media data can be full of biases, abnormalities and it can be imprecise. Data is of no value if it's not accurate, the result of big data analysis is only as good as the data being analyzed. This is often described as junk in equals junk out. So, the evidence provided by data is only valuable if the data is of satisfactory quality. Quality of the data computed by accuracy of the data, reliability of the data source and hoe the data was generated.

Veracity issues arise due to:

1.   Process uncertainty
2.   Data uncertainty
3.   Model uncertainty

It is very important that companies get data quality right. To achieve improved efficiency, they need better quality data. Big data applications are thousands of times larger & require faster response time than traditional Business Intelligence applications.

So, we need to develop strong strategies to find the quality data which is undergoing the processing.

DATA MANAGEMENT IN DIGITAL ECONOMY

The Era of 'digital industrialization' is playing bigger role in our lives. The way data about people, places, product and process is generated, shared & consumed causes the growth of the data at rapid speed.

Due to rapid increase in the data for the enterprises it becomes extremely difficult to handle. Now our world is no longer data-centric one it becomes data-driven world. Nowadays without the use of data our life & lives will not move an inch.

Figure 1 gives an overview of the various data sources which from the core of digital industrialization. The social media data, IOT and machine to machine interaction, adds the new dimensions in data ecosystems. Because of everyone & everything is connected with Internet, the biggest challenges are to deal with volume, variety, velocity & veracity of the data. The effective data management is needed to turn the vast data into an organization asset.

DATA MANAGEMENT: ALIGNING CORPORATE SYSTEMS TO SUPPORT BUSINESS BETTER

Big Data: Simple Use

Are we able to imagine our life without smart phone? No one can. With smart phone in hand anyone in the world with the average application knowledge able to travel any part of the world. Best proof of this is, are you able to see the travelling guides in last three to four years as like before? Where are them? All become so simple with our smart phone. Before smart phone we need to depend on GPS device which is more costly one. Now with smart phone in hand we able to book tickets, select traffic free road path, nearby restaurant which have our favourite food and so on. Everything is possible because of the big data.

Figure 1. Digital industrialization and data management

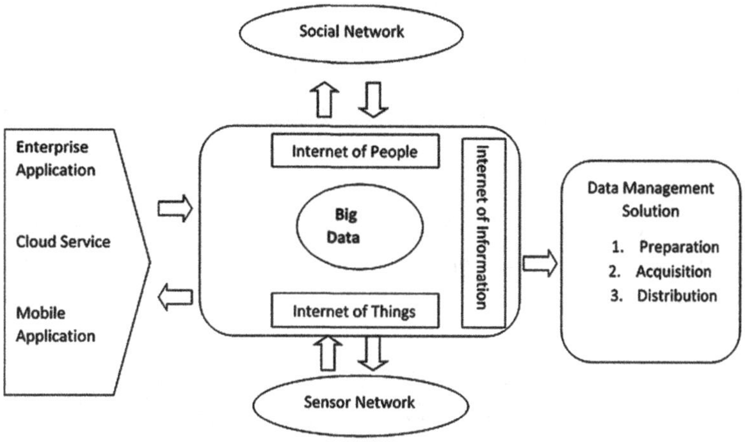

Big Data: Aligning Corporate Systems

Nowadays ERP systems getting lot changes in its implementation methodologies and usage of systems within the corporate. We have witnessing almost all the corporate companies upgrading their systems for fast data capturing and analysing. In online transaction if the amount is debited even though the transaction is declined, then the debited amount will return back to our account automatically. How this possible? This is all because of Big Data. Expanding the width and depth of ERP and every other relevant system for Big Data is a way to go. It's a small step of IT and a Giant leap for corporate.

DATA MANAGEMENT PLATFORM: CAPABILITIES, BUSINESS FUNCTIONS, AND SERVICES

A typical Data Management solution should aim at establishing Data foundation for the digital journey of the enterprise. The steps in data management part are:

1. **Data Acquisition:** To enable the acquisition of data from disparate sources by defining, sources of data, type of data, frequency and mode of acquisition.
2. **Data Preparation:** Enriching the quality of the data with primary focus on ensuring accountability and trustworthiness of the business data being managed.
3. **Data Distribution:** Sharing and protection of data within the enterprise and outside with ensuring Data privacy and Data security at each stage.

Big Data Analytics: Descriptive vs. Predictive vs. Prescriptive

What Is Big Data?

The term "big data" describes data sets that are growing exponentially and that are too large, raw, and unstructured for analysis using traditional database technology and techniques. Whether terabytes or petabytes, the precise amount of data is less the issue than how that data is used.

Definitions of Big Data (BD)

Big data is a term for data sets that are so large or complex that traditional data processing application software is inadequate to deal with them.

The term "big data" often refers simply to the use of predictive analytics, user behaviour analytics, or certain other advanced data analytics methods that extract value from data, and seldom to a particular size of data set (Wikipedia, n.d.).

Big data refers to extremely large data sets that may be analyzed computationally to reveal patterns, trends, and associations, especially relating to human behaviour and interactions (Beal, n.d.).

Big Data is a phrase used to mean a massive volume of both structured and\ unstructured data that is so large it is difficult to process using traditional database and software techniques (Beal, n.d.).

Big data is high-volume, high-velocity and/or high-variety information assets that demand cost-effective, innovative forms of information processing that enable enhanced insight, decision making, and process automation (Garter, 2018)

The big data revolution has given birth to different types of big data analysis. The big data industry is buzzing around with data analytics that offers enterprise-wide solutions for business success.

The key for any company that wants to successfully use big data is gaining the right information that delivers knowledge and gives businesses the power to gain a competitive edge. And this can be only be done by identifying and selecting from different types of big data analytics. Big data analytics should not be considered as a one-size-fits-all blanket strategy. What distinguishes the best data scientist or data analyst from others is that they have the ability to identify the kind of analytics that can be leveraged for gaining benefits for their particular business line.

There are three dominant types of analytics available today – descriptive, predictive, and prescriptive. These are interrelated solutions that are helping companies to make the most out of the big data that they have. Each of these analytic types offers organizations a different kind of insight. In this blog post, we will explore all of these three different types of for understanding what each type of analytics has got to offer to an organization's operational capabilities.

Definition of Big Data Analytics

The definition of big data holds key to understanding big data analysis. Like conventional analytics and business intelligence solutions, big data mining and analytics helps uncover hidden patterns, unknown correlations, and other useful business information. According to the Gartner IT Glossary, big data is high-volume, high-velocity, and high variety information assets that demand cost-effective, innovative forms of information processing for enhanced insight and decision making.

Types of Big Data Analytics: Descriptive

The descriptive analysis does exactly what the name implies; they summarize or describe raw data and make it something that is interpretable by humans. It analyzes past events, here past events refer to any point of time that an event has occurred, whether it is one minute ago, or one month ago. Descriptive analytics are useful as they allow organizations to learn from past behaviours, and help them in understanding how they might influence future outcomes.

Usually, the underlying data that gets analyzed is a count or aggregate of a filtered column of data. Descriptive statistics are useful in showing things like total stock in inventory or average dollars spent per customer. Organizations must use descriptive analysis when they want to understand, at an aggregate level, what is going on in their company.

Types of Big Data Analytics: Predictive

Predictive analytics has the ability of "Predicting" what might happen next. Predictive analytics is about understanding the future. Predictive analytics provides organizations with actionable insights based on data. Moreover, it also provides estimates of the likelihood of a future outcome. But, it is equally important to remember that no statistical algorithm can "predict" the future with 100% accuracy. Organizations can use these statistics for forecasting what might happen in the future. This is because the foundation of predictive analytics is based on probabilities obtained from data.

One common application of predictive analytics is to produce a credit score. These scores are used by financial institutions to determine the probability of customers making future credit payments on time.

Types of Big Data Analytics: Prescriptive

This relatively new field of prescriptive analytics facilitates users to "prescribe" different possible actions to implement and guide them towards a solution. Prescriptive analysis is all about providing advice. It attempts to quantify the effect of future decisions in order to advise on possible outcomes before those decisions are actually made. Prescriptive analytics not only predicts what will happen, but also tells why it will happen and thereby provide recommendations regarding actions that take advantage of these predictions.

Prescriptive analytics is complex to administer, and most companies are still not using it. However, when implemented correctly, prescriptive analytics can have a large impact on how businesses make decisions and thereby, help them in delivering the right products at the right time, consequently optimizing the customer experience.

Looking at all the different types of analytic options can be a daunting task. No one type of analytic is better than the other; rather they co-exist with, and complement each other.

CHARACTERISTICS OF BIG DATA ANALYTICS

BD Characteristics

The original three 'V' Dimension Characteristics of Big Data identified in 2001 are:

Volume

The quantity of data generated and stored every second, not only in Terabytes but also in Zettabytes or Brontobytes.

Size of the data = value + potential insight

Big data not deals with size of the data but it means that if any data beyond the capacity of a system exceeds and the data distributed across the network then the scenario is called Big Data. Remember until unless the data is distributed among the systems in the network it will not be a Big Data.

Variety

The type (structured, semi, unstructured and complex) and nature of the data (financial, social media, healthcare, cyber physical model, education etc) is said to be variety. With the help of big data technologies bring different types of data together for analyses.

Velocity

It refers to the speed at which the data is generated, stored, analyzed, processed and visualized to meet the demands and challenges that lie in the path of growth and development.

Figure 2 to 5 shows different dimensions of big data over a period of occurrences. Table 1 describes different types of Big Data Dimensions from 2001 to 2017 and in each year how many V's identified.

Characteristics of Big Data Analytics (BDA)

Figure 6 shows the important characteristics of big data analytics.

Figure 2. Three Vs dimensions of Big Data

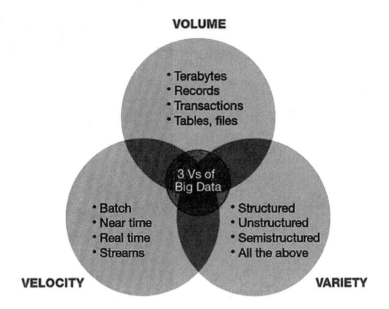

Figure 3. Four V's dimensions of Big Data

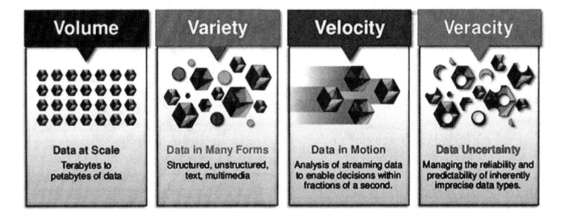

BIG DATA: HOW IT'S CAPTURED, CRUNCHED, AND USED TO MAKE BUSINESS DECISIONS

A staggering 2.5 Exabyte's of data are created daily; 90 percent of the data in the world today have been generated in the last two years alone. These data come from everywhere: sensors used to gather climate information, social media sites, digital pictures and videos, purchase transaction records, and cell phone GPS signals, to name just a few sources. Finding ways to turn the flood of data into useful information for business decisions is a growing challenge to the IT profession and C-level executives. That's where one of today's top tech buzzwords comes in: big data. And it isn't getting buzz for nothing. Big data has the power to change business in a big way. Here we'll take a look at how it works.

Figure 4. Five V's dimensions of Big Data

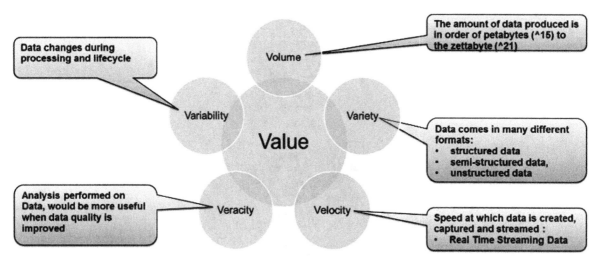

Figure 5. Six and Seven V's dimensions of Big Data

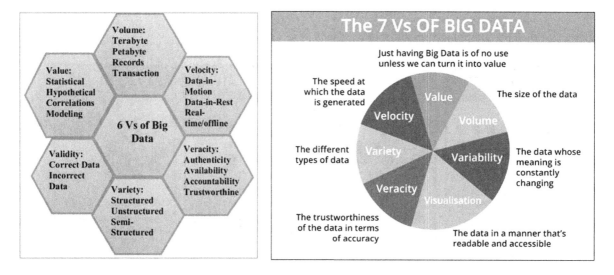

There are three dimensions to big data: volume, velocity and variety. Companies are awash in the amount of data, data are being created and processed at ever greater rates and the types of data, such as social media and context-aware mobile devices, are proliferating.

So how is any of this information useful? In fact, there are a number of ways that big data can create value for an organization. First, big data can unlock significant value by making information transparent and usable at much higher frequencies. Second, as organizations create and store more transactional data in digital form, they can collect detailed performance data on everything from product inventories to sick days. This is how companies are using data collection and analysis to conduct controlled experiments and make better management decisions. Others are using data for basic forecasting to high-frequency now casting to adjust their business levers just in time.

Table 1. Forty-two V's dimensions of Big Data

	Year					
	2001	**2012**	**2013**	**2014**	**2017**	
	Volume	Value	Veracity	Venue	Valor	Version Control
	Velocity		Variability	Vocabulary	Vane	Vet
	Variety		Visualization	Vagueness	Vanilla	Vexed
			Validity	Viscosity	Vantage	Vibrant
			Volatility	Virality	Varifocal	Victual
Big Data Dimensions			Viability		Varmint	Virtuosity
					Varnish	Visibility
					Vastness	Vivify
					Vatication	Vogue
					Vault	Voice
					Veer	Voodoo
					Veil	Voyage
					Verdict	Vulpine
					Versed	
	3 V's	**4 V's**	**10 V's**	**15 V's**	**42 V's**	

Figure 6. Characteristics of BDA

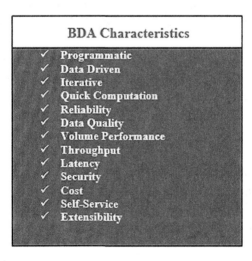

In addition, big data allows narrower segmentation of customers and more precisely tailored products or services. These sophisticated analytics can substantially improve decision making. What's more, big data can also be used to improve the development of the next generation of products and services. For instance, manufacturers are using data obtained from sensors embedded in products to create unique service offerings.

Capturing and Crunching Big Data

To capture and crunch big data, companies have to deploy new storage, computing and analytic technologies and techniques. The range of technology challenges and the priorities for tackling them will differ depending on the data maturity of the firm. However, legacy systems and incompatible standards and formats can prevent the integration of data and impede the more sophisticated analytics that create value. This means that big data also requires big technology.

Several new and enhanced data management and data analysis approaches assist with the effective management of big data and the creation of analytics from that data. The actual approach used will depend on the volume of data, the variety of data, the complexity of the analytical processing workloads involved, and the responsiveness required by the business. It will also depend on the capabilities provided by vendors for managing, administering and governing the big data environment. These capabilities are important selection criteria for product evaluation.

Big data technologies include open-source database management systems designed to handle huge amounts of data, including Cassandra and Hadoop, as well as business intelligence software designed to report, analyze and present data.

Making Use of Big Data for Business Decisions

Forrester Research estimates that organizations effectively use only five percent of their available information. That leaves a lot of room for optimization and improvement, which is why making use of large digital datasets for business decisions requires the assembly of a technology stack that consists of everything from storage and computing to analytical and visualization software applications. The specific technology requirements and priorities will vary based on the big data levers that are to be implemented and an institution's data maturity.

So is it worth the trouble? In a word, yes. The business benefits of using big data are clear. For example, the McKinsey Global Institute estimates that a retailer using big data effectively could increase its operating margin by more than 60 percent. When it comes to ROI, it just doesn't get much better than that.

To benefit from big data, McKinsey recommends that business leaders take the following steps:

1. Inventory all data assets
2. Identify value creation opportunities and risks
3. Build up internal capabilities to create a data-driven organization
4. Develop an enterprise information strategy to implement technology
5. Address data policy issues, such as privacy, security and intellectual property

Data policy issues are of particular concern when it comes to big data. Large databases often contain highly sensitive information, such as company secrets or data that must be protected by law. Plus, there is often a trade-off between the availability and confidentiality of data. If an organization wants data to be available and useful, there is often less security surrounding that data as a result. To process big data for real-time decision-making, centralization of the data is crucial. But as centralizing increases, the ability to sequester and secure confidential data declines.

In addition, the size of the data set can make implementing security and privacy controls unwieldy. Encrypting all those data for security reasons would be a time-consuming and expensive undertaking and would slow data processing, thus impeding rapid decision-making.

The key to dealing with the privacy and security challenges of big data is the first step identified above: inventory all data assets. Once the organization understands where the big data resides and what kind of data there are, it can take steps, such as investing in security technology capable of handling big data volumes, to secure its confidential information.

BIG DATA PROCESSING TECHNIQUES AND APPLICATIONS

Big Data is so massive in volume that it cannot be measured in terms of gigabytes or terabytes instead it is as large as peta bytes or zeta bytes (Davis, 2013). In addition to this the volume is still increasing on accelerated rate with every second. The Big Data is a blend of structured as well as unstructured data. Big Data is characterized by the five Vs which are variety, velocity, volume, veracity and value (Cardenas, Manadhata, & Rajan, 2013). And Big data is high-volume, high velocity and/or high variety information assets that demand cost-effective, innovative forms of information processing that enable enhanced insight, decision making, and process automation. Big data is massive dataset; its size is beyond the power of storage and processing capacity. Data increases exponentially from various application areas. Big data is a set of structured, unstructured and semi-structured datasets. It is not feasible to analyze this type of dataset using traditional database system because the challenges with the traditional database systems are: storage, processing, search, analysis, transfer, privacy and etc. Big data is being generated by almost every technology around us all the time. It is produced by social and digital process, transmitted by mobile devices and system sensors. So, there is a need of some new techniques to be discovered and analyzed, to process this erroneous amount of data.

Data increased by 90% in the last 2 to 3 years. Data is generated from various sources: Web, Social networking sites, Sensors, Geographic Information System, Weather forecasting, Bio-Informatics, and Medical science etc. A survey shows, in 2014, data generated every minute was: Facebook users share 2.5 million pieces of content, 3,00,000 tweets on Twitter, 2,20,000 new photos on Instagram, 72 hours of video content on you tube, 200 million messages over the Internet, 50,000 apps download son Apple, $80,000 online sales on Amazon etc., these all are un-structured data.

Big Data Application Areas

Big data has various applications in the field of Natural Language Processing, Human Behaviour Monitoring, GIS, Bio-informatics, Medical Science, Traffic Data Monitoring, Weather Forecasting, Cloud control system, Multimedia, Body Sensor Network and many more.

Use of BDA in Real Time Applications

- Errors within the organization are known instantly
- New strategies of your competition are noticed immediately
- Answer More Questions, More Completely
- Service improves dramatically, which could lead to higher conversion rate and extra revenue

- Fraud can be detected the moment it happens, and proper measures can be taken to limit the damage
- Introducing New Products & Services
- Become Confident in Your Accurate Data
- Cost savings
- Better sales insights, which could lead to additional revenue
- Keep up with customer trends (van Rijmenam, n.d.)
- Better Data Visualization
- Empower a New Generation of Employees
- Achieving Financial Efficiency
- Informed Decision Making

Big Data is generated from various application areas as discussed above. This section discusses about the application areas, how Big Data is generated from particular application, the benefit to handle Bid Data and which processing technique is used to handle it.

Natural Language Processing

It is a study of designing machines or programs that can understand verbal and written communications. The unstructured data like voice call, emails, text messages etc. is increasing exponentially and need to be analyzed accurately, which would lead to more insights and better predictive models.

Human Behavior Monitoring

Nowadays, human life is data centric. Emotions and sentiments, relationships and interactions, speech, offline and back-office activities, culture etc. generates huge set of data. By analyzing Big Data of human behavior, it can lead to a detailed insight and precise models.

Geographical Information System

It is designed for making better decision about location. It includes storing, manipulating, managing, collecting, selecting and storing of geographical data. Bid data will enable a number of transfomative societal applications. Societal applications in the context of understanding climate change, next-generation routing services and disaster response.

Bio-Informatics

It is a study of understanding the molecular mechanism of life on earth by analyzing genomic information. Genomic information includes genomic sequencing and expressed gene sequencing. Big data has a great impact on the bio-informatics field and a researcher in this field faces many difficulties in using biological Big Data to extract valuable information from the data easily thereby enhancing further advancement in the decision-making process related to diverse biological process, diseases and disorders.

Medical Science

The unstructured data generated by the field of medical science is huge. From genetic to genomic, internal imaging to motion picture, treatment to life course assessment etc. The easy and efficient analysis of Big Data benefits such as, detection of diseases can e done earlier, identification of health care deception can be done more quickly.

Traffic Data Monitoring

Detecting, diagnosing, fixing network problem, route profiling and capacity planning, congestion management etc. are the applications areas that generate huge amount of data. The analysis of this huge data will help in enhancing extensibility, easing-out programming, optimizing opportunities and efficiently process the data generated from routers, switches and from the website access log at fixed interval.

Weather Forecasting

Human has tried to get a better understanding of weather and forecast. Nowadays, satellite sensors and other resources are used by weather forecasting system to help general people for accurate predictions of weather. The volume of environmental data is increasing exponentially. So, there are needs of efficient Big Data techniques to manage, store and process this data.

Cloud Control System

It is to manage traffic hosting and delivery, video streaming services, network traffic monitoring, router log sand alerts etc. It is used to enable small scale teams to set up test environment for development and experimental purpose. Big data technology to deliver sufficient cost saving and scalability to business.

Multimedia

In today's digital world social networking applications are being used everywhere. They have multiplied fast and their uses have grown exponentially. Multimedia has become one of the largest application area that produces enormous amount of data at faster rate. The multimedia data include audio, video, texts, images, graphic objects, animation resources have grown so fast that is has brought the need for Big Data processing techniques.

Open source Tools for BD

Table 2. shows the list of big data open source tools for the implementation of big data concepts and also table shows different categories of tools with respect to the context.

BIG DATA ANALYTICS USING HADOOP

The processing of Big Data can be done by two processes: (i) Batch Processing, (ii) Non-Batch Processing.

Table 2. List of Big Data open source tools

Big Data Open Source Tools						
Platforms	**Business Intelligence**	**Databases**	**Mining**	**File System and Programming**	**Transfer and Aggregate**	**Miscellaneous**
• Apache Hadoop • Hadoop MapReduce • Grid Gain • Lumify • Apache Storm • HPCC Systems • Ikanow	• Talend • Jedax • Splunk • Jaspersoft • Pentaho • Spago BI • KNIME • BIRT	• Neo4j • Couch DB • Orient DB • Terrastore • Flock DB • Hibari • Riak • Hypertable • Blazegraph • Hive • ICE • Infinispan • Redis **NoSQL** • Mongo DB • Cassandra • HBase **SQL** • MySQL • MariaDB • Postgre SQL • Toku DB	• Rapid Miner • Mahout • Orange • Weka • Data Melt • KEEL • SPMF • Rattle • Elastic search • Apache Samoa	• Gluster • HDFS • Pig • R • ECL • Apache Drill • Dryad	• Lucene • Solr • Sqoop • Flume • Chukwa	• Terracotta • Avro • Oozie • Zookeeper

Batch Processing

In Batch processing, data is collected over a period of time, processed and then produces output. It uses MapReduce framework. MapReduce is a programming model which is used for distributed computed to process Big Data on a cluster of commodity hardware. The execution of MapReduce in two stages: Map and Reduce. In Map stage, input is given in to mapper in key/value pair. Map stage produces output also as key/value pair. The intermediate result generated by shuffling and sorting the data is also key/value pair. Reduce stage takes this intermediate key/value pair as input and gives final key/value as output.

Apache Hadoop Is an open source framework, used in distributed environment. It is used to process Big Data on a cluster of commodity hardware. It used two components; MapReduce and HDFS, to store and process Big Data respectively. Its strength are easy programming model, Non-linear speed-up, and fault tolerance.

Non-Batch Processing

It involves continual input of data and processed in small period of time. The problem with Hadoop is that it is inefficient in executing iterative jobs. If the complete input is not available before starting of job execution, then execution with Hadoop becomes inefficient. It can't execute iterative and streaming input queries. Solutions to this problem are In-Memory Computing.

In-Memory Computing

It is technique which is used to minimize the computation time of MapReduce. It makes computation faster and executes the jobs in less than seconds. To store and process Big Data, Distributed memory storage is used in In-Memory computing in two ways-

1. To execute iterative jobs which may have multiple iterations, catching layer for disk-based storages is used.
2. To handle streaming data generated from independent input source which can totally fit in distributed memory.

It can efficiently minimize execution time of jobs. Apache Spark is the one of the better tool used for in-memory computing.

Collecting and analyzing Big Data helps organizations for enhanced insight, decision making, and better process automation. Storing and analyzing Big Data is not possible using the traditional databases and programming languages. However, storing and analyzing big data effectively is possible using Hadoop. Hadoop is an open-source software framework for storing and processing large scale of data sets on clusters of commodity machines.

Hadoop provides Hadoop Distributed File System [HDFS] for storing huge amount of data. HDFS, the storage component of Hadoop, is a distributed file system that stores huge data sets in multiple machines. MAP Reduce Processing Unit is used for distributed computation. Hadoop ecosystem contains other tools like Pig, Sqoop, and Hive to address particular needs of users in an easy way.

Comparing Traditional Databases and Hadoop

The following are the main differences between traditional databases and Hadoop:

1. Hadoop uses Scale out instead of scale up
2. Hadoop uses key/value pairs instead of Relational Tables
3. Hadoop uses Map Reduce programming instead of relational programming
4. Hadoop supports offline batch processing instead of online transactions

Understanding Map-Reduce

Is a programming approach of Hadoop which is used for distributed computation? MapReduce splits the work submitted by client into small parallelized map and reduce tasks. The role of the user is to specify a map function which the Mapper class processes as a key/value pair and generates a set of intermediate key/value output pairs. The reducer class then aggregates the intermediate key/value output pairs produced earlier and generates a final key/value output pairs. Hadoop provides a set of API's to create Mapper and Reducer classes.

Figure 7. Hadoop ecosystem

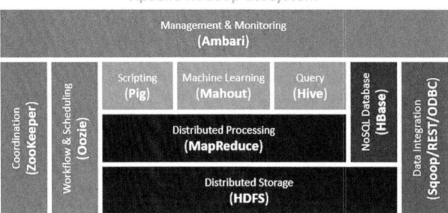

OVERCOMES PROBLEM OF BIG DATA

Increasing digitization and data complexities are continuously posing new challenges to enterprises in terms of managing it to derive business advantages over their competitors. The arrival of social media, Internet of Thing and Internet of Everything has added new dimensions to the velocity, variety and volume of data. Data capturing is become easy even though it originates from many new sources and in variety of forms. But the managing and analysis of these data become very difficult task. According to Meglena Kuneva, European Consumer Commissioner, Brussels, "Personal data is the new oil of internet and the new currency of the digital world" and is predicted that data is going to control / dictate economy on the same way oil is dictating the world economy (Shafer, n.d.). The significance of the data management increases rapidly as like the growth of the data. It has been widely reported that volume of data generated in the last two years is more than that generated in the last two decades (van Rijmenam, n.d.). Between now and 2020, the global volume of digital data is expected to multiply another 10 times or more (Cardenas, Manadhata, & Rajan, 2013; Shafer, n.d.).

Big Data Challenges and Issues

Table 3 shows the big data challenges and issues.

In recent report from Forbes, it is reported that there will be over 6.1 billion smart phone users by 2020 globally, and majority of them are embedded will many sensors that can collect various kind of data (Cardenas, Manadhata, & Rajan, 2013). According to the recent report by Gartner, "approximately 6.4 billion connected things will be in use worldwide in 2016, and will reach 20.8 billion by 2020" (Shafer, n.d.). This sudden rise in data puts all the enterprise off-guard to handle the volume, variety, velocity and veracity of data. These sudden forces, namely, the social media / connected devices / hand held devices from a very formidable base for a new economic model – Digital Economy, coined by Don Tapscott (van Rijmenam, n.d.).

Table 3. Big Data challenges and issues

Big Data		
Challenges	**Issues**	
Data Cleaning	Heterogeneity	System Complexity
Data Acquisition	Incompleteness	Inconsistent Data
Data Capture	Scale	Latency
Data Storage	Timeliness	Data Provenance
Data Sharing	Privacy	
Data Transfer	Human Collaboration	
Data Analysis / Results	Data Complexity	
Ethical Consideration	Computational Complexity	

The challenges in managing data in different formats and from varied sources are:

1. **Data Interoperability:** The ability of two or more systems or components to exchange information and to use the information that has been exchanged.
2. **Data Trustworthiness:** It includes traceability, reporting, utilization, speed and transparency of data.
3. **Data Security:** To ensure data is secure both at rest and in transit. Effective use of data could increase world income by $3 trillion each year in seven industries alone, these seven industries are education, transportation, consumer products, electricity, oil and gas, health care, and consumer finance (van Rijmenam, n.d.). The organizations are well aware of the fact that, for strategic decision making, merely in-house data will not be adequate, they also in need of social media data (their own data and competitor's data). So, the digital economy is not just transformation of face-to-face transactions of online, it includes all the interactions and transactions.

Comparing to other threats of Big Data, veracity is the biggest challenge.

Veracity == Quality (Validity, Volatility)

Data out is directly propositional to data in. Veracity of the big data refers to the quality of the data. It sometimes gets referred to as validity or volatility referring to the life time of the data. Veracity is very important for making big data operational. Because of big data can be noisy & uncertain, if the data is error-prone, the information that is derived from it is unreliable, & users lose confidence in the output. Trusting the data acquired goes a long way in implementing decisions from an automated decision-making system & veracity helps to validate the data acquired. Amassing a lot of data does not mean the data becomes clean & accurate. Data on customers must remain consolidated, cleansed, consistent & current to make right decisions.

It can be full of biases, abnormalities and it can be imprecise. Data is of no value if it's not accurate, the results of big data analysis are only as good as the data being analyzed. This is often referred as junk in equals to junk out. The evidence provided by data is only valuable if the data is of satisfactory quality.

Data Quality = Accuracy of the data + Reliability of the data source + How the data was generated. Unstructured data on the internet is imprecise and uncertain.

Veracity issues arise due to:

1. Process uncertainty
2. Data uncertainty
3. Model uncertainty

Truth Discovery

So, the data veracity problems lead to the 'Truth Discovery' Issue. Truth Discovery is finding the trustworthy information from conflicting data on the same object. Truth discovery is inferring the source reliability and the truth from the data. How to identify the source is a reliable one? If many pieces of correct information comes from the source than it is ranked as a reliable source. A piece of information is likely to be true if it is provided by many reliable sources. 'Confidence of the facts' is directly propositional to the 'Trustworthiness of Web sites'. Figure 8 shows different types of data veracity problems.

Figure 8. Types of data veracity

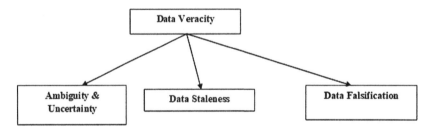

A common strategy to evaluate the reliability of the source is to take advantage of data redundancy & rely on majority voting heuristic, which simply assigns a true label to data that are claimed by the majority of the sources. So, veracity is the important problem in dealing with big data.

REFERENCES

Beal, V. (n.d.). *Big Data Definition*. Retrieved from https://www.webopedia.com/TERM/B/big_data.html

Cardenas, A., Manadhata, P. K., & Rajan, S. P. (2013). Big Data Analytics for Security. *IEEE Security and Privacy Magazine, 11*(6), 74–76. doi:10.1109/MSP.2013.138

Davis, B. (2013). *How much data we create daily*. Retrieved from http://goo.gl/a01mFT,2013

Gartner. (n.d.). *Big Data*. Retrieved from http://www.gartner.com/it-glossary/big-data

Shafer, T. (n.d.). *The 42 Vs of Big Data and Data Science*. Retrieved from http://www.kdnuggets.com/2017/04/42-vs-big-data-data-science.html

van Rijmenam, M. (n.d.). *The Advantages and Disadvantages of Real-Time Big Data Analytics*. Retrieved from https://datafloq.com/read/the-power-of-real-time-big-data/225

Wikipedia. (n.d.). *Definition of Big Data*. Retrieved from https://en.wikipedia.org/wiki/Big_data

This research was previously published in Optimizing Big Data Management and Industrial Systems With Intelligent Techniques; pages 1-23, copyright year 2019 by Engineering Science Reference (an imprint of IGI Global).

Chapter 79
Importance of Big Data and Hadoop in E-Servicing

Karthiga Shankar
Thiagarajar College of Engineering, India

Suganya R.
Thiagarajar College of Engineering, India

ABSTRACT

Consumers are spending more and more time on the web to search information and receive e-services. E-commerce, e-government, e-business, e-learning, e-science, etc. reflect the growing importance of the web in all aspects of our lives. Along with the tremendous growth of online information, the use of big data has become a vital force in growing revenues. Consumers are today shopping multiple products across multiple channels online. This transformation is substantial and many of the e-commerce companies have now turned to big data analytics for focused customer group targeting using opinion mining for evaluating campaign strategies and maintaining a competitive advantage, especially during the festive shopping season. So, the role of intelligent techniques in e-servicing is massive. This chapter focuses on the importance of big data (since there is a large volume of data online) and big data analytics in the field of e-servicing and explains the various applications, platforms to implement the big data applications, and security issues in the era of big data and e-servicing.

INTRODUCTION

E-Services

Typically the term e-services is used to describe a variety of internet based electronic interactions ranging from basic services, such as the delivery of news and stock quotes, to smart services, Products, clothes etc. These electronic-services involve various types, delivery systems, advanced information technologies, methodologies and applications of online services and they are provided by e-government, e-business, ecommerce, e-market, e-finance, and e-learning systems.

DOI: 10.4018/978-1-6684-3662-2.ch079

There services produce a large volume of data online. Where is this data stored and how this data is processed and analyzed to produce the useful information. The key is Big Data Analytics where the huge data data generated by this various applications over online is processed and analyzed. There is a need of some intelligent approaches to evaluate e-service systems, conduct web user classification, help users online trading and support users online decision making.

Big Data

Big Data is transforming healthcare, business, and ultimately society itself, as e-services becomes one of key driving features during the modernization process. Many business cases utilizing big data have been grasped in recent years; Facebook Twitter & LinkedIn are examples of companies in the social networking realm. Other big data use cases have focused on capturing of value from streaming of video movies, monitoring of network traffic or upgrading of processes in the manufacturing industry. With the e-services initiatives across the world especially in India, the transactional data is developing exponentially and it has become difficult to analyze such huge volume of data stored at multiple locations with conventional data mining algorithms. The alternative to analyze large data is to use Big Data analytical tools. The tools having capabilities of mining large data sets in distributed environment help in investigating and analyzing e-services projects.

The progresses in Information Technology (IT) services and hardware have led to the generation of huge amount of data referred to as Big Data. There are projects/systems in e-service where this big data needs to be processed and analyzed for better and effective decision making. Due to the fact that the data generated has unstructured and formats, it is difficult to analyze such huge data using traditional analyses tools. Big data analytics can manage this dynamic nature of Big data, keeping it secure by applying the correct analytical technique to use the information in an effective manner. It has the capacity to interact with huge Volume, Velocity, Veracity and Variety of data. With its scalable nature, it can expand the technologies that can correlate data and produce exploitable results. Big data analytics can help the government in providing its services directly to its citizens. It has the ability to recognize patterns in a set and make predictions regarding past experiences and provide results for taking future actions. Big Data Analytics refers to the use of advanced analytic techniques against very large and different data sets that include structured/semi-structured/unstructured data and of different sizes. Big data is the term applied to data sets whose size and type is beyond the ability of traditional relational databases to capture, manage and process the data. Big data is defined in terms of 3 V's i.e. Volume, Velocity and Variety [Gartner]. Analyzing Big data allows analysts, researchers, government and business users to make better and faster decisions using data that was previously inaccessible or unusable. Using advanced analytics techniques, government or business agencies can analyze previously unexploited data sources autonomous or together with their existing enterprise data to gain new imminent resulting in significantly better and faster decisions.

Quite simply, the Big data era is in full force today as the world is changing through instrumentation, we are clever to sense more objects, and if we can sense it, we tend to try and store it. Through advances in communications technology, people and things are becoming increasingly connected –and not just some of the time, but all of the time. This intersecting rate is a escape train. Generally referred to as machine-to-machine (M2M), interconnectivity is responsible for double digit year over year data growth rates. Finally, because small integrated circuits are now so cheap, we are able to add intelligence to almost everything.

Experiencing the Art of Big Data

Each day, 2.5 quintillion bytes of data are produced. These data come from digital pictures, videos, posts to social media websites, intelligent sensors, purchase transaction records, cell phones GPS signals etc. This is known as Big Data. In small, the term Big Data applies to information that can't be processed or analyzed using traditional processes or tools. Increasingly, organizations nowadays are facing more and more Big Data challenges. They have access to prosperity of information, but they don't know how to acquire value out of it because it is sitting in its most raw form or in a semi structured or unstructured format; and as a result, they don't even recognize whether it's merit keeping. There is no doubt that Big Data and particularly what we do with it has the probable to become a powerful force for innovation and value creation.

Data now stream from daily life: from phones and credit cards and televisions and computers; from the infrastructure of smart cities; from sensor-equipped buildings, trains, buses, planes, bridges, and factories.

Big Data Analytics

This outline of big data analytics will help you to know big data analytics, the e-service worth it gets to many corporate industries and government sector in the world, and how organizations across various industries are applying it to tackle their unique business requirements. Every big data source has different characteristics, including the occurrence, volume, velocity, type, and veracity of the data. When big data is developed and stored, extra dimensions come into play, such as governance, security, and policies. Choosing an structural design and constructing an appropriate big data solution is challenging because so many issues have to be considered

Big data analytics is the procedure of gathering and analyzing large sets of data (called big data) to find out patterns and other useful information. Big data analytics can assist organizations to better appreciate the information contained within the data and will also help recognize the data that is most important to the business and future business decisions. For most organizations, big data analysis is a challenge. Consider the huge volume of data and the different unstructured formats of the data that is collected across the entire organization and the many different ways diverse types of data can be joined, contrasted and analyzed to find patterns and other useful business information.

Big data, data is broken down into multiple data sets and accumulated on various nodes of a cluster environment. One of the nodes (Master node in Hadoop) keeps track of the data stored at various nodes (Slave node in Hadoop) by creating index of the data. When a request for data search appears, first index is checked and the based on that required data is found and fetched. This helps in making the search process faster even if data is too bulky and large. For example, twitter and facebook are using the concept of Big data. Data from any database management system like Oracle and MySql can be imported into Big data. Through data mining activities, data can be collected from various servers. Then data analytics techniques are applied on the data retrieved and reports are generated. After that reports are analyzed to find out the outcome or behavior in regard to a particular condition and the future action plans are prepared. According to various studies done, it has been observed that in the year 2008 enterprise servers had processed about $9.57 * 1021$ bytes and this number is doubled every couple of years. So, managing such huge volume of data using simple techniques is quite difficult. But if this big data is examined using Big data analysis techniques, the results produced would be much reliable and efficient and hence help in taking effective decisions. e.g. Walmart saves near about 2.5 peta byte of data every hour of its purchase history to do analysis for future using Big data analysis techniques.

Doug Cutting was the first developer who designed the structure for Nutch, a venture by Apache Software foundation. The program used MapReduce to split big data files into controllable areas which could be prepared by computer systems linked in similar.

A lot of people comprehend the importance of programming when they are to work with some applications. This is the result of the fact that they acknowledge the importance of knowing how to run the codes for the application. Apart from this, the code listings can furthermore trigger questions that deal with the possibility and operation of various business and games software. Hence, the latest hadoop framework serves as good business tools for each business operation to be a success. For leading search engines like Google, hadoop performance utilizes Map Reduce for indexing purposes. It comprises of the dynamic application that can improve the task of searching in at a faster rate than it had been done before.

Hadoop could run on current devices, which made it very practical. These days this is one of the most extensive alternatives or solutions to handle big data that are used by such significant organizations as Yahoo!, Facebook or Myspace. The achievements of the structure designed a big requirement for professionals who are dedicated to modifying and establishing up the several elements of the structure. A person operating in this area may be termed as a Hadoop developer or he may be called as a Hadoop consultant.

In addition to this, the usage of mobile phones has tremendously increased much beyond just sending or receiving the calls or text. Ranging from watching movies to booking movie tickets, listening to music to downloading every new song, drafting to sending email, and much more, mobile phones can carry out day-to-day activities easily and conveniently. All, this has become possible with the advent on internet on mobile phones. Due to this, windows and apps development took place. Looking all this, there are many companies which have introduced latest mobile windows & apps development, services Development, Android Application Development, gaming applications which includes iPhone Application Development, BlackBerry Applications Development, iPad Application development, Office/ Business Applications, Mobile Website Development, Productivity Applications, Networking applications and much more.

The growing role of Big data analytics in business is obvious. To survive in the frames of constant competition most organizations will need to support their business by having their own Big data analytics. If you already have an analytic idea you are welcome to visit Enterprise Mobility Service Provider Emorphis Technologies website and fill in the form with your requirements to help Emorphis team better understand and build your Enterprise Analytics solution for your business. We Enterprise mobility services provider company Emorphis Technologies have in-depth experience for creating engaging mobile apps for businesses. We are one of the premier Enterprise mobility Solution development company and have a long list of credentials and portfolio ranging from m-commerce solutions for retail services, Hadoop & Big data analytics, e-commerce web development, Cloud computing services, and outsourced web development. If you are on the lookout for a partner to help you leverage your online business through Mobile Applications, then do connect with Emorphis Technologies. Our proficient developers experienced in free source mobility and cloud computing applications will help you get the best solution for your company.

Benefits of Using Big Data Analytics for E-Servicing Projects

The major profits of introducing Big data platform in e-Governance projects are to assist government. These benefits are:

- Enhancement in online information and service delivery by government for business Analytics.
- Making practices open and apparent to endusers.
- Documenting and Visualizing government presentation through predictive policing.
- Producing insight for new business projects and improving business growth.
- Providing better Customer Services feedback

CHALLENGES OF USING BIG DATA ANALYTICS WITH E-SERVICING

Though analyzing Big Data using various analytical techniques has proved to be useful for e-Services projects but still there are some confronts that need to be handled to attain desirable results. Some of them are:

Privacy

Big data analytics refers to examining historical data. Each e-service project consists of a group of private information related to various end users. This data can be regarding UIDs of individuals, sales/ purchase information of a business firm, information of clients of an organization or records of patients of hospital. Such organizations may oppose in revealing their private information. If provided, such information should be preserved properly so that it is safe and beneficial.

Security

Big data generated from e-Governance projects is a combination of large data which is stored on various servers. Storage and security of this big data is one of the major challenges. Processing of this data using data analytics further produces more data in the form of reports. Managing this data and protecting it from unauthorized access and usage should be carefully done.

Lack of Technical Knowledge

Still it is very difficult to find skilled and qualified people who are proficient in using big data analytics techniques with e-Governance projects.

Unavailability of Appropriate Software Tools

Data generated by different e-Governance projects during analysis is of different types and different formats. Sometimes application of relevant software tools is not possible because of its unavailability or that technique/software is still under development.

Lack of Common Standards

No proper standards are defined of how data is to be represented using analytical techniques.

APPLICATIONS OF BIG DATA IN E-SERVICING

E-Health Services

In the context of e-Health, variety of flows have generated from various sources such as electronic medical records (EMR) systems, mobilized health records (MHR), personal health records, mobile health care monitors and predictive analytics as well as a large array of biomedical sensors and smart devices including IoT. The electronic medical record (EMR) initiative has resulted data streams from all types of patients at the hospital, insurance companies and doctor's office. A single patient stay generates thousands of data elements, including diagnoses, procedures, medications, medical supplies, digital image, lab results and billing. These need to be validated, processed and integrated into a large data pools to enable meaningful analysis. Multiplying this by all the patient-stays across the health processing systems and combining it with the large number of points where data is generated and stored and the scope of the big data challenge begins to emerge.

E- Government

Big data Applications have the potential to transform the digital Government services, communication between the Government, citizens and business sectors. The Government initiatives such as digital India and Smart City are some of the examples for the contribution of big data applications in the era of E-Government. Today there are lot of Government services available through online such as ration shop stocks (status of the ration items), e-certificates (community, birth certificate, etc), Applying aadhar cards online, etc.

E- Shopping

Internet shopping transactions have recently raised big concerns. But the problem on making businesses through internet is that it is impossible for the retailers to check whether the customer is the genuine or not who accept online payment mode transaction. Using Machine learning, a method of data analytics that iteratively learn from data and allows computers to find hidden insights without being any explicit programmed. Also there are algorithms to analyze the users previous transactions and purchases and it can predict what the customer's next purchase would be. It will be very useful for the retailers to promote the particular items with discounts so that they can increase the customer's buying.

PLATFORMS TO IMPLEMENT BIG DATA APPLICATIONS

Hadoop

Open source Hadoop is a cutting-edge device for harvesting big data. One of the most highly grade, and used, platforms, Hadoop's impact in Retail is as exciting as frontline. Hadoop has established itself as the go-to technology for Big Data management and data pipeline. What Hadoop does is extraordinary: it takes the dice-rolling out of sell business and allows the hub to shift to the individual consumer by providing a customized retail experience. The attractiveness of Hadoop is that there are tangible practical advantages to boast about. Enterprises are steadily moving to deploy Hadoop to increase returns.

Metascale is one such Hadoop solution which also has Big Data training as a service and helps enterprises speed up Hadoop implementation. MetaScale's key impact factor is in solving capacity and cost problems that accompany swelling data demands. With retail, viable storage and efficient processing capabilities are the top demands. Hadoop and NoSQL provide Big Data value to retail enterprises particularly when used to refine analytics along with brand monitoring, product perception, sentiment analysis and inventory management. Mitigating latency of voluminous data is another aspect where MetaScale outscores other Hadoop solutions. Processing data overnight for real-time application is a great Hadoop property which retailers use. Extract, Transform and Load (ETL) refers to a process in database usage. Software cost and management of ETL invariably are so large that projects often fail at launch. Moreover, with conventional ETL techniques it can be weeks before data created is utilized effectively.

Hadoop on HDFS

HDFS, the Hadoop Distributed File System, is a distributed file system designed to hold very large amounts of data (terabytes or even zetabytes), and provide high-throughput access to this information. Files are stored in a redundant fashion across multiple machines to ensure their durability to failure and high availability to very parallel applications. Hadoop Map/ Reduce is a software framework that process large amount of data, in parallel, in a fault tolerant manner. Map Reduce is highly efficient and scalable, and thus can be used to process huge datasets. HDFS has a master/ slave architecture.

An HDFS cluster consists of single Name Node, a master server that manages the file system namespace and regulates access to files by clients. In addition, there are a number of DataNodes, usually one per node in the cluster, which manages storage attached to the nodes that they run on. MapReduce programming consists of writing two function, a map function and a reduce function. The map function takes a key, value pair and outputs a list of intermediate values with the key. The map function takes a key, value pair and outputs a list of intermediate values with the key. The map function is written in such a way that multiple map functions can be executed at once, so it's the part of the program that divides up tasks. The reduce function then takes the output of the map functions, and does some process on them, usually combining values, to generate the desired result in an output file.

Since real-time data intelligence and processing is core to retail data's success, another great Hadoop use-case is the 'market basket analysis'. Popularly called MBA, market basket analysis, uses data mining algorithms to find similar patterns in consumer behavior on-site. This is much like predicting what a consumer will do in a current session bases on historic data patterns. The metrics here involve 'support' and 'confidence', which predict degree of interest a consumer has in buying in his, or her, active session. MBA thus is a useful indicator that can be used to devise new promotional initiatives and identifying optimal schemes. The fun part is that the MBA interface can be integrated with other standard business intelligence (BI) tools and can work independently for users as well as disparate data sets.

Spark

Spark is another platform to implement the Big data applications. It is the much advance cluster computing engine to process the online requests. It is mainly designed for fast computation. Spark is one of the favorite choices of data scientist and thus Apache Spark is growing very quickly and replacing Hadoop Mapreduce.

USE OF BIG DATA METHODOLOGIES AND ALGORITHMS IN E-SERVICING

Recommender Systems

Recommender system is very much helpful in the online websites for the users to obtain their exact search in the net surfing. The system learns the user's interests from their history and recommend desired items to purchase. For example in the e-shopping website, a user may buy a book and logs out. When the next time the same user comes in, the system recommends some of the books of same author or same topic of previously purchased book. Here the system learns and stores the users interests and accordingly recommending information. There are lot of algorithms available to enable recommender systems, some of the popular algorithms are,

- Collaborative filtering
- Content-based filtering
- Hybrid recommender systems
- Clustering
- Multi Criteria Recommender Systems

Sentiment Analysis

Sentiment analysis or Opinion Mining is the process of computationally identifying and categorizing opinions online that is expressed in a piece of text, especially in order to determine the user's attitude towards a particular topic or product, etc. and check whether it is a positive comment, negative or neutral comment. In many social networking services or e-commerce websites, users can provide text review, comment or feedback to the items. This will be helpful for the online retailers or distributors to check their product ratings and reviews and they can improve the product quality as well they can take up different solutions to make up the product better with the help of suggestions from the user's perspective. The most widely used Opinion Mining algorithms are

- Social Sentiment Analysis
- Sentiment by Term Algorithm
- Natural Language Processing
- Text Analytics Algorithms

FUTURE RESEARCH DIRECTIONS

The future research could be of comparative nature of the identified factors as barriers and drivers for ICT based e-services and the users satisfaction to use e-Service so as to indicate the aspects that need extra effort to enhance the usage of e-Services for all the societal needs. E-Services have better scope in all the domains like Medical where the patient can be monitored remotely by the doctors say E-Health, E-Certification, where the students write exams online and they can get certificates, E- Governance Project, etc. There is a wide range of challenges in all the fields and researchers can take up different problems and solve it with Big data technologies to experience the user friendly, interactive and intelligent E-Services.

CONCLUSION

The world is moving towards digitization. In India central and state governments are steadily moving towards digitizing all the government departments, scheme and services. Due to the awareness of people and availability of network access that emerges, use of e-servicing application has increased. Now a days all the basic requirements from Mobile recharge to Electricity bill payment, Shopping, Passport application and everything is seeking the help of E-Servicing. As a result data is getting more complex in size and its volume. Handling big data with huge volume is also a major challenge but however there are lot of research is being taken by various scientist to solve the issues with the Big Data Handling. Since Hadoop's prime functional advantage is making Big Data more viable, knowing how to select appropriate hardware is critical.

This research received no specific grant from any funding agency in the public, commercial, or not-for-profit sectors.

REFERENCES

Bertot & Choi. (n.d.). Big data and e-government: Issues, policies, and recommendations. *University of Maryland College Park.*

Chen, C. P., & Zhang, C. (2014). Data-intensive applications, challenges, techniques and technologies: A survey on big data. *Inf. Sci., 275,* 314–347. doi:10.1016/j.ins.2014.01.015

Clark, B. Y., Brudney, J. L., & Jang, S.-G. (2013). Coproduction of government services and the new information technology: Investigating the distributional biases. *Public Administration Review, 73*(5), 687–701. doi:10.1111/puar.12092

Coronel, C., Morris, S., & Rob, P. (2016). Database Systems: Design, Implementation, and Management (11th ed.). Cengage Learning.

Delena, D., & Demirkanb, H. (2017). Data, information and analytics as services. *Decision Support Systems, 55*(1), 359–363. doi:10.1016/j.dss.2012.05.044

Fan, S., Lau, R. Y., & Zhao, J. L. (2015). Demystifying big data analytics for business intelligence through the lens of marketing mix. *Big Data Res., 2*(1), 28–32. doi:10.1016/j.bdr.2015.02.006

Gandomi, A., & Haider, M. (2015). Beyond the hype: Big Data Concepts, Methods, and Analytics. *International Journal of Information Management, 35*(2), 137–144. doi:10.1016/j.ijinfomgt.2014.10.007

Hamed, T., Samshul, S., & Neda, J. (2015). *A Review paper on e-service technologies and concepts. 8th International Conference Interdisciplinary in Engineering*, Romania.

Holsapplea, C., Lee-Postb, A., & Pakath, R. (2014). A unified foundation for business analytics. *Decision Support Systems, 64*, 130–141. doi:10.1016/j.dss.2014.05.013

Inder Jit Singh, M., Vinod, K., Hanuv, M., & Uma, K. (2015). *Scope of City E-Government Initiative.* Sprott School of Business, Carleton University.

Mahesh Kumar, S., & Kunwar Singh, V. (2016). E-health for Rural Areas of Uttarakhand under Governance Service Delivery Model. *IEEE 1st International Conference on Recent Advances in Information Technology.*

Mahmud & Sattar. (2016). Deployment of Contextual E-healthcare System: A prospective e-service based on context aware conceptual framework and ICTization framework model. *IEEE 11th Conference on Industrial Electronics and Applications (ICIEA).*

Masatsugu, T. (2015). Analysis of the Long-run Effect of e-Health Intervention on Chronic Diseases: A DID-PSM Approach. *17th International Conference on E-health Networking, Applications& Services.*

Mashaqbeh. (2016). Computers and e-Health: Roles and New Applications. *IEEE Transactions.*

Minelli, M. Chambers, M., & Dhiraj, A. (2013). Big Data, Big Analytics: Emerging Business Intelligence and Analytic Trends for Today's Businesses. Wiley & Sons.

Nishant Srivastava, S., & Hashank, S. (2016). E- Business Scope and Challenges in India. *International Journal of Business and Management Invention.*

Poonam, M., & Priyanka, D. (2016). Challenges and Future Prospects for E-Governance in India. International Journal of Science, Engineering and Technology Research, 3(7).

Rina, D. (n.d.). Challenges and Future Scope of E-commerce in India. *International Journal of Emerging Trends & Technology in Computer Science.*

Sun, Z., Firmin, S., & Yearwood, J. (2012). Integrating online social networking with e-commerce based on CBR. *International Proceedings of the 23rd ACIS 2012, 3–5.*

Sun, Z., Strang, K., & Yearwood, J. (2014). Analytics service oriented architecture for enterprise information systems. International Proceedings of iiWAS2014, 506-518. doi:10.1145/2684200.2684358

Tan, O., Ng, J., Wong, A., & Koh, W. K. (2012). Bridging gaps between three generation family's Needs and Attitudes towards e-health technologies. *IEEE 14th International Conference on e-Health Networking, Applications and Services.*

Van der Meulen, R., & Rivera, J. (2014). *Gartner Says Worldwide Business Intelligence and Analytics Software Market Grew 8.* Academic Press.

Vesset, D., McDonough, B., Schubmehl, D., & Wardley, M. (2013). Worldwide Business Analytics Software. 2013–2017 Forecast and 2012 Vendor Shares.

KEY TERMS AND DEFINITIONS

Big Data: Large volume of data with vital characteristics such as volume, variety, and velocity.

Big Data Analytics: Techniques and algorithms to analyze large amount of data that comes from different sources over online.

E-Services: A variety of internet-based electronic interactions.

Hadoop: An open source platform for processing big data in a distributed environment.

HDFS: HDFS is a Hadoop-distributed file system to store data, gives high performance access to data across Hadoop clusters, and it is a data management layer in a Hadoop framework.

Intelligent E-Services: Various intelligent technologies like neural networks, fuzzy logic, expert systems, machine learning, data mining, etc. are being applied in various e-services approaches, so that these e-services will provide much higher quality of online information searching, presentation, etc.

Spark: Spark is the advanced technology in processing big data. It overcomes the drawbacks of Hadoop map reduce system, and it is mainly designed for fast computation.

This research was previously published in E-Manufacturing and E-Service Strategies in Contemporary Organizations; pages 39-52, copyright year 2018 by Business Science Reference (an imprint of IGI Global).

Chapter 80
Improving Forecasting for Customer Service Supply Chain Using Big Data Analytics

Kedareshwaran Subramanian
T. A. Pai Management Institute, India

Kedar Pandurang Joshi
T. A. Pai Management Institute, India

Sourabh Deshmukh
H. P. Inc., India

ABSTRACT

In this book chapter, the authors highlight the potential of big data analytics for improving the forecasting capabilities to support the after-sales customer service supply chain for a global manufacturing organization. The forecasting function in customer service drives the downstream resource planning processes to provide the best customer experience at optimal costs. For a mature, global organization, its existing systems and processes have evolved over time and become complex. These complexities result in informational silos that result in sub-optimal use of data thereby creating inaccurate forecasts that adversely affect the planning process in supporting the customer service function. For addressing this problem, the authors argue for the use of frameworks that are best suited for a big data ecosystem. Drawing from existing literature, the concept of data lakes and data value chain have been used as theoretical approaches to devise a road map to implement a better data architecture to improve the forecasting capabilities in the given organizational scenario.

DOI: 10.4018/978-1-6684-3662-2.ch080

INTRODUCTION

In any global manufacturing organization, as highlighted by Waller and Fawcett (2013), forecasting is an important dimension of interest from a big data analytics standpoint. From a business process perspective, forecasting using big data analytics can be applied to solve issues related to inventory management, transportation management & customer and supplier relationship management. A sample research question in the area of customer and supplier relationship management as cited in the paper by Waller and Fawcett (2013) include - How can more granular sales data from a wide variety of sources that exist be used to improve visibility and trust between trading partners?

The research question which the authors attempt to address in this book chapter is as follows:

How can a global manufacturing organization unlock the value hidden in its big data ecosystem to build better forecasting capabilities for its after-sales customer service supply chain?

This question is of great relevance to any global manufacturing organization which services customers across different parts of the world. From a business process perspective, the post-sales customer service function can be broadly sub-divided into the following operations:

1. Customer support contact center (over different channels – phone, web & service centers).
2. Spares management.
3. Field service technician organization.

In such global manufacturing organizations, more often than not, each of these three operations are managed as a separate entity with each operation creating its own set of planning processes and internal IT systems. Part of the reason being that global organizations are serving customers across different geographies - North & South Americas (NSA); Europe, Middle-East & Africa (EMEA) & Asia Pacific (APAC). Each geography would have its own strategic business units (SBU's) which have its localized operations and thereby creating its own systems to handle the post-sales customer support function. This eventually leads to having a fragmented view of the customer support function and poor forecasting capabilities for this customer service function as a whole.

From a technology standpoint as well, as discussed by Kumar and Deshmukh (2005), companies which followed the data mart bus architecture began by creating dependent data marts organized for each function such as customer service, procurement, finance, planning and quality.

As a result, today in most global organizations, every region and function has their own dedicated resources to extract the relevant data from their respective source systems and feed it into their forecasting models. Each of these teams is using their own set of tools and models creating many opportunities for data duplication and redundancy.

However, in reality, in order to service a post-sales customer need, query or issue, each of the three post-sales customer operations - namely customer support contact center, spares management & field service technician organization are inter-related and inter-dependent on each other. As pointed by Davenport (1998), fragmentation of information systems lead to a fragmented way of doing business. This argument is equally applicable in the current context. Fragmentation of SBU's and their information processing systems leads to sub-optimal forecasting capabilities with each region and operation creating its own independent forecast engine. This problem gets further compounded as these forecasts are built at different levels of granularity – forecast type (call –phone/web, spares, spares, field technicians); location (NSA/EMEA/APAC). Ultimately, these have a bearing on the quality of the post-sales customer support provided by the organization.

One of the significant recent developments in IT has been in area of 'Big data analytics'. Earlier, most global organizations developed Business Intelligence (BI) systems primarily relying on structured data residing in their internal systems. These BI applications have addressed managerial analytical queries by sifting through large data warehouses or data marts and presenting the results using interactive dashboards and visualizations.

A lot has changed with the arrival of big data. Today, organizations realize that much of the goldmine of information is present in semi-structured and unstructured data formats which can be used by different functions. In this book chapter, the authors illustrate the potential of big data analytics in developing more robust predictive forecasting models for the customer service supply chain. Waller and Fawcett (2013) characterize this form of analytics as 'SCM Predictive analytics'. However, one challenge is to identify the right source of data for a particular forecast type. Given the sheer size, diversity and complexity of data strewn across multiple data sources in structured, semi-structured and unstructured formats, there is a possibility that some of these data fields get duplicated in these different databases given that these databases are managed by different teams spread across different regions working within their own 'silos'.

It is also possible that some of these data fields may get completely ignored. This is mainly attributed to the cumbersome process of extracting the relevant data from the many databases and feeding it into the forecasting models. Both these problems of data duplication and data exclusion limit the reliability and accuracy of the forecasts and thereby limit its overall utility to the organization. Data governance challenges include maintaining completeness of data, accuracy of the source and target data systems and timely refresh rates to ensure reliable and relevant information to the various stakeholders involved in the customer service function.

This work attempts to do the following:

1. Examine the potential of big data in improving the forecasting models for the customer support function in the context of a global, manufacturing organization.
2. Address the data governance challenges inherent in any big data analytics project by adopting a research framework which help organizations manage their data better.

BACKGROUND: BIG DATA AND SERVICE SUPPLY CHAIN

This section describes two main strands of literature namely big data and service supply chain.

Big Data

Here, the various definitions of 'Big data' and its related terminology are reviewed to help define and differentiate big data from 'normal' data. This is followed by indicating the role of big data in a global manufacturing company context and reviewing the architectures and frameworks which can be applied in big data analytics applications.

'Big Data' when compared to 'normal' data has been often described by the 3 V's – Volume, Velocity and Variety. The earliest discussion on these 3-V's has been mentioned by Laney (2001) in his research note in a Gartner blog. The 3 V's were used by him in the context of the e-commerce industry. However, the general applicability of the 3 V's has been used to provide a generalized understanding of what characterizes a big data ecosystem.

Attempts have been made by several industry practitioners and researchers to provide a more detailed definition of big data. In the article by Adrian (2011), big data has been defined (and differentiated from 'normal' data) from an IT infrastructure standpoint, "Big data exceeds the reach of commonly used hardware environments and software tools to capture, manage and process it within a tolerable elapsed time for its user population." On similar lines, Madden (2012) prefers to define big data by qualifying it as too big or too fast or too hard for existing tools to process.

Another 'V'–'Veracity' of data is added in the info-graphic provided by IBM (2015) as depicted in Figure 1. Over time, sources of data have expanded beyond the traditional corporate data warehouses and data marts to include semi-structured and unstructured data sources such as social media content, sensors and so on. However, these new sources have their own set of challenges. The biggest being the issue of veracity or authenticity of the data given that most of this data is user generated on social media platforms. As a result, the data can be messy; yet it remains an important source of customer insight which is of importance to the organization.

Figure 1. IBM Infographic
Source: http://www.ibmbigdatahub.com/infographic/four-vs-big-data

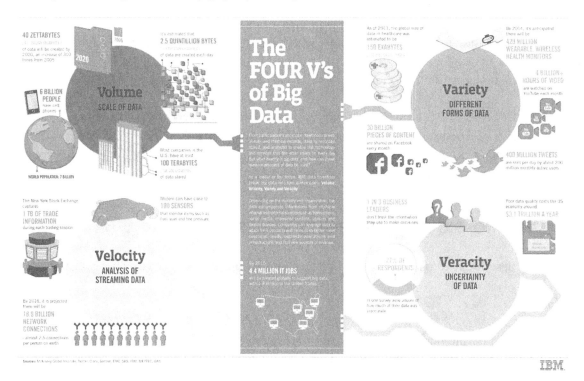

Waller and Fawcett (2013) argue that it is even more important in today's big data environment to pay a lot more attention to theory so that one does not end up making spurious connections based on unreliable (big) data. They state that theory is particularly important for preventing false positives[1]. Big data leads to an explosion of new variables and therefore there are far too many false positives generated when testing models on big data. These concerns are further supported by boyd and Crawford (2012) who argue that bigger data are not always better data. Cases of breach of privacy raise ethical concerns of the usefulness of big data analytics. These concerns again reinforce the importance of veracity of the data and results generated in a big data ecosystem.

In this literature review on how big data is understood today, the authors also come across one more 'V'–'Value'. Beulke (2011) argues that besides the other four V's (Volume, Velocity, Variety, Verifiability or Veracity), it is also extremely important for organizations to be able to assess the extent to which the four V's of data help you find more value or insights from the data. Otherwise, it is simply not worth the effort. Hence, this has also been added to make up a total of '5 V's' which are used to define big data and also differentiate it from normal data. The authors explore the different V's in the context of a global, manufacturing organization.

The variety of data comes from structured, semi-structured and unstructured data fields from different source systems. The description of the various data fields which are relevant for the forecasting model is shown in Table 1.

Table 1. Variety of data

Sr. No.	Data Field	Data Type	Data Format	Data Description
1	Install base	Structured, User-generated	RDBMS Tables	Contains the sales information of customers divided based on geography, type of customer (retail/corporate), what product they own, which location is product kept.
2	Service Bill of Material (SBOM)	Structured, User-generated	RDBMS Tables	Contains details of the components and kits that is used to repair the product. The supply chain stores and moves these components in SBOM.
3	Telemetry data	Semi-structured, machine generated	Machine specific	Generated by machines in form of logs and alerts that can be used to diagnose a problem and/or preempt it.
4	Spares demand	Structured	Excel	Users creating excel based forecasting models on a standalone basis to forecast spares demand.
5	Shipments forecast	Semi-structured	Excel	Users creating excel based forecasting models on a standalone basis to forecast shipments requirement.
6	Call logs	Unstructured	Text	Notes from interaction with customer support staff at call center to address customer queries.
7	Social media feedback	Unstructured	Web pages	Posts by customers regarding company's products on any of the widely used social media channels such as Twitter, Facebook or specific customer complaint forums/blogs.

This data is generated with high velocity by the respective source systems at different points in time. Telemetry data is created from millions of machines round the clock (24/7). Social media updates are also created round the clock. Table 2 provides a description of the frequency with which the various data fields relevant to the customer service function are updated.

Table 2. Velocity of data

Sr. No.	Data Field	Frequency
1	Social media feedback	Continuous, 24/7
2	Service Bill of Material (BOM)	Monthly refresh
3	Telemetry data	Continuous, 24/7
4	Spares demand	Daily updates
5	Shipments forecast	Monthly
6	Call logs	Continuous, 24/7
7	Social media feedback	Continuous, 24/7

High variety and velocity leads to high volume of data. There are millions of units of install base with about a billion service interactions over web, call center and field staff. These lead to thousands of engineering change notifications all resulting in terabytes of data generated every day. Table 3 shows the number of transactions generated in the system and the volume of data generated in supporting the customer service function in the organization.

Table 3. Volume of data

Sr. No.	Data Field	Volume Description
1	Install base	Millions of units globally with refresh in location, contracts
3	Telemetry data	Millions of Logs and alerts annually
4	Repair events	Millions of repair events annually
5	Shipments forecast	A few thousand line items refreshed monthly. Since this is forecast latest data replaces the previous data every month
6	Service interactions (web, call, field)	Billions of lines of data from calls, social media, web

However, as pointed in the introduction, there are challenges in identifying the 'right' sources of data suitable for a particular forecast function. The sheer size, diversity and complexity of data strewn across multiple data sources in structured, semi-structured and unstructured formats raises serious concerns regarding data quality and veracity. As pointed in Table 2, there are different velocities with which data is generated in the organization and ensuring that it is synchronized to ensure completeness and accuracy of data is a big challenge.

These data challenges impact operational decision making as well. Managers are never fully certain if their operational dashboards are showing the 'right' status of operations. These lead to misleading insights from the data affecting the overall customer service quality.

Service Supply Chain

This section describes the literature related to the service supply chain and its various aspects. Service supply chain refers to those supply chain system which does not include physical products rather "products" as pure services. For example, in many well-established service industries such as healthcare sector, financial consultancy, after sales service, etc. the respective supply chains are service supply chains. After-sales activities are recognized as a significant source of revenue as well as gaining competitive advantage in most manufacturing businesses (Ellram, Tate, & Billington, 2004; Saccani, Johansson, & Perona, 2007). In case of new products especially the after-sales service market is up to four or five times larger than the market. In their work, Saccani et al. (2007) addresses development of after-sales service supply chain through a case study approach of seven different firms. With special emphasis on durable consumer goods, and on three configuration choices: vertical integration, centralization, and decoupling of activities the study has been carried out. Three main after sales activities are compared across those seven firms viz. field technical assistance, spare parts distribution and customer care. The empirical evidence suggests that no one best way exists in configuring the after-sales supply chain.

Most service organizations understand that, in order to grow an efficient and effective service supply chain, service supply chain management needs to be measured for its performance. de Waart and Kemper (2004) envisage a roadmap toward gaining excellence in service supply chain management where five steps details highlights performance measurement is an important process. Cho, Lee, Ahn, and Hwang (2012) explore the performance measurement of service supply chains. A framework emphasizes on performance measures such as demand management, customer relationship management, supplier relationship management, capacity and resource management, service performance, information and technology management and service supply chain finance.

Recently, He, Xie, Wu, Hu, and Dai (2016) present a review of operational models in the context of service supply chain. The basic definition of service supply chain with specific examples also provided. Service Only Supply Chain (SOSC) is different than Product Service Supply Chain (PSSC). PSSC handles both the physical product as well as services while SOSC handles products (non-physical) and pure services. In reality, SOSCs are seen in industries such as financial services, travel & tourism, internet based services, mobile apps, and telecommunication.

Furthering in their study, He et al. (2016) present a model for an automobile Logistics Service Supply Chain (LSSC) which integrates Functional Logistics Service Provider (FLSP). Such integration brings challenges like forecasting spare parts because the data handled at both levels is of different nature. During this era the volume of data produced and transferred over the Internet is considerably growing. It also generates challenges for the organizations that would like to gain the profits from analyzing this immense advent of big data. Demand planning, is a crucial activity which analyzes various customer segments in terms of brands and product, down to the SKU level and develops models used to predict demand and generate revenue plans. This is the most fundamental step for collaborative planning and forecasting (CPFR) with major supply chain partners.

Syntetos, Babai, Boylan, Kolassa, and Nikolopoulos (2016) review forecasting aspect in supply chain with the emphasis on difficulty in extrapolating demand requirements at one echelon. This involves complex issues such as supply chain coordination and involvement of multiple stakeholders for information sharing. In a typical forecasting process, initial step is to identify the outputs to be forecast. The aggregated forecasts are better from minimizing error point of view. Therefore the aggregation level must be specified. In turn, three dimensions requires identifying the: Product: e.g. Stock keeping unit (SKU), item, family, etc.; Market / Location: customer, Point of Sale (POS), region, country, business area, etc.; Time: hour, day, week, month, year, etc. There is an emergence of studies related to frameworks related to service supply chain management.

Ramish, Azhar, and Rasheed (2017) build a comprehensive supply chain framework for service industry that includes engagement in purchasing of services, make of services and delivery the services, through the comparative analysis of models and conceptual frameworks in the earlier literature. This work offers basic understanding as to how service business can grow their performance systems to be converted into more effective service supply chains by focusing on newer dimensions. Their comparative analysis and theoretical framework would document the finding of the problems that surround result assessment within and transversely single supply chains. They also expand existing knowledge in the performance measurement in the service supply chain.

There is an interesting work by Sepúlveda-Rojas, Rojas, Valdés-González, and San Martín (2015), about forecasting in supply chain of Chilean companies. Their work presents an alternative methodology to assess the best-forecast model without the requisite to estimate all the forecast models or complement with any visual technique. Many studies are published with focus on forecasting in supply chain (Ali, Babai, Boylan, & Syntetos, 2017; van der Laan, van Dalen, Rohrmoser, & Simpson, 2016). Big data and forecasting is first compiled into a review work by Hassani and Silva (2015), in which challenges for forecasting with big data is detailed on various aspects like skills, noise, hardware, statistical significance and architecture of algorithms. In their work various applications like economics, finance, population dynamics, crime, energy, biomedical science and media has been covered. The authors of this book chapter have not come across prior studies where specific big data frameworks and architectures have been applied to improve the forecasting function in a global manufacturing company context. All these studies emphasize on various frameworks related to service supply chain and aspects like demand planning, forecasting without reference to big data environment. Therefore it is worth to research further to explore such issues in big data environment.

NEED FOR BIG DATA ANALYTICS

Big data analytics is deployed in several sectors of the economy. As per the seminal study conducted by Manyika et al. (2011) from the McKinsey Global Institute (MGI), big data can generate significant financial savings across different sectors such as healthcare, public sector, manufacturing, retail. In the manufacturing sector, they expect the benefits of big data analytics to decrease the cost of product development and assembly by half and reduction in working capital by up to seven percent. In their report, they develop two indices – 'Value potential index (VPI)' and 'Ease of capture index (ECI)' and different sectors have been evaluated based on these two indices. VPI refers to the extent to which the sector stands to gain by deploying big data analytics. The variables used to construct the value potential index include the amount of data per firm, firm relative performance, customer and supplier intensity, transaction intensity and sector turbulence. The ECI refers to possible constraints or barriers which may act as limitations to deploying big data analytics. These include talent pool, intensity/dependence on IT, data-driven mindset and data availability of data.

Data Lake and Big Data Architecture

Large manufacturing companies such as General Electric (GE) have been able to sell services to its customers based on a detailed analysis of data streaming from its equipment and the ability to predict failures and other key events as per Fitzgerald (2015). In the interview given by GE's CIO, Mr. Vince Campisi, he describes how they have used a '*data lake*' as the platform to develop their big data analytics applications. They ingest data from 25 airlines, 3.4 million flights into a data lake – a storage system to hold enormous amounts of raw data in its native format for future use.

The data is stored in raw format because they are not fully sure of what variables would be necessary to build their analytics application. Hence they prefer to collect the data first and then as they develop their analytical models, they extract the relevant data for the model. Since this is done in an iterative manner, more data is extracted from the data lake as they become clearer with the outcomes they are trying to arrive at.

This approach is diametrically opposite in its world-view as compared to the concept of data warehouses and data marts. In the latter, there is a predetermined set of data fields which need to be cleaned and loaded in a predetermined data format in order to enter into the data warehouse (or mart). The idea of a data lake is to collect all the data before it is potentially lost as per Watson (2015). This approach is more suited to a big data ecosystem where there is far more complexity attached with the dataset as compared to the traditional business intelligence system for which data warehouses or marts are a necessary precondition.

However, Violino (2015) argues that the concept of data lake is quite new. Like data warehouses, data lakes are a concept, not a technology. At its core, a data lake is a data storage strategy. The data lake does not require a predetermined schema. Data can be simply ingested and the schema gets created and applied when the data is read. The data lakes are not a replacement for existing analytical platforms or infrastructure. Instead, they complement existing efforts and supports the discovery of new (analytical) questions. Once these questions are solved, the insights can now be operationalized by shifting the data analytics solution from the data lake into the data marts or data warehouses.

Big data has not only brought new ways of storing data but also new frameworks and architectures. In the paper by Tekiner and Keane (2013), they attempt at defining a framework that captures all the stages of a Big data application with a strategic point of view. The framework consists of seven layers – systems layer, data layer, data collection layer, processing layer, modelling layer, access layer and visualization layer (Tekiner & Keane, 2013, pp. 1497). There are different tools being used to handle the operations in each of these layers.

For example, MapReduce developed by Google is being used to process and store large datasets on commodity hardware. Its main advantage is a programming paradigm which allows useable and manageable distribution of many computationally intensive tasks. Map-Reduce involves two main parts, a map operation where a simple function is used to emit key/value pairs in parallel similar to using primary keys in a relational database. Once the data to be processed is mapped into a key/value groups, then a reduce operation is used to apply the core processing logic to produce results in a timely manner as per McCreadie, Macdonald, and Ounis (2012). This simple concept of Map-Reduce removes many traditional challenges in High Performance Computing (HPC) to achieve fault tolerance and availability. Therefore, it paves the way for development of highly parallel, highly reliable and distributed applications on large datasets.

In the paper by Miller and Mork (2013), an alternative big data framework has been conceptualized. Based on Porter (1980) seminal book of industry value chain, the authors have developed a 'Data value chain'. This value chain consists of three stages – data discovery, data integration and data exploitation. Each of these stages have their own set of activities associated with it starting from creating an inventory of data sources to taking decisions based on which results are more appropriate and relevant within a given data analytics context (Miller & Mork, 2013, pp. 58).

The three key objectives to address using this data value chain approach is as follows:

1. Manage and coordinate data across the service continuum;
2. Form collaborative partnerships between the various data stakeholders to enable positive outcomes; and lastly
3. Establish a portfolio management approach to invest in people, process and technology that enhance the organization's performance by improved operations and lower costs.

In their article, Davenport, Barth, and Bean (2012) provide three recommendations which differentiate how organizations should undertake their big data analytics (as compared to their traditional business intelligence and data analysis environments). The first suggestion is to pay more attention to data flows as opposed to stocks. The second is to rely on data scientists and product and process developers rather than data analysts. Lastly, to move analytics away from the IT function into the core business functions. Storing data in its native format aids in shifting the attention from data stocks to flows.

In fact, Dutta and Bose (2015) follow a similar approach in developing a new framework for a big data analytics application. They integrate the widely adopted Cross Industry Standard Process for Data Mining (CRISP-DM)[2] with typical IT project management and create a new framework. They divide the lifecycle of any big data analytics project into three phases – strategic groundwork, data analytics and implementation. However, there are two limitations in applying this new framework to the current context. The first and primary limitation in the paper by Dutta and Bose (2015) is their claim that the Ramco Cements case study is an 'analytics' project.

As per the criteria given by Hardoon and Shmueli (2013), the case fits the description of a business intelligence project rather than an analytics project. They also raise concerns regarding the general lack of consensus of what differentiates a business intelligence project from an analytics project. As per their classification, projects can be treated as analytics project only if there is a machine-generated intelligence created based on some statistical or machine learning algorithm. Business Intelligence reports can at best provide intuitive aggregated data presented in an easy to understand graphical manner. But there is no native intelligence generated by the system. Hence, by applying this criteria, the case of Ramco Cements on which the big data framework is applied is not a good comparison to the big data context described here. The second limitation is that the framework follows a sequential process where one phase leads to another from business problem definition to training people in their framework for implementation of big data projects in firms (Dutta & Bose, 2015, pp. 295). However, in reality most analytics projects like any scientific experiment move back and forth between the various phases such as business under-standing, data understanding and so on. This has been rightly shown in the original CRISP-DM model (Figure 2). In this framework, there are inter-relationships between each and every phase of the data analytics project. Starting with business understanding till evaluation, it is quite natural to find that even after defining the problem and modeling the data, if the results of the model are not in agreement with

Figure 2. CRISP-DM framework
Source: Shearer (2000), pp. 14.

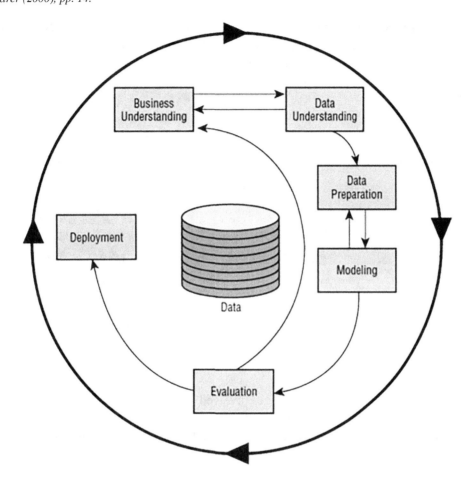

the business users, it can lead to redefining the problem again after exploring the results obtained from the data model and what business sense can be made from them.

Ultimately, the model can be deployed only after there is a happy marriage between the business users and data scientists in ensuring that requirements in terms of analytical queries from business side as well as model robustness in terms of reliability and validity are satisfied. Hence the authors believe that the model proposed by Dutta and Bose (2015) which makes an assumption of a linear approach appears unrealistic in terms of applicability to the given big data analytics case study and in general to most typical big data analytics projects.

Hence, based on the literature review, the authors conclude that the big data framework proposed by Miller and Mork (2013) is the most appropriate and hence is applied in the current case study. The authors have not come across any prior studies applying this framework to a big data analytics project and hence this is one of the key contributions of this book chapter. The following section describes the application of the data value chain framework in the customer service supply chain function in a global manufacturing organization.

APPLICATION OF DATA VALUE FRAMEWORK

Miller and Mork (2013) develop data value chain (Figure 3) specifically for big data analytics scenarios. Drawing inspiration from the seminal work of Porter (1980) which developed the concept of industry value chain, the authors have drawn parallels in the big data ecosystem. As per their framework, the value chain in a big data ecosystem consists of three parts – data discovery, data integration and data exploitation.

Figure 3. Big data value chain
Source: Miller and Mork (2013), pp. 58.

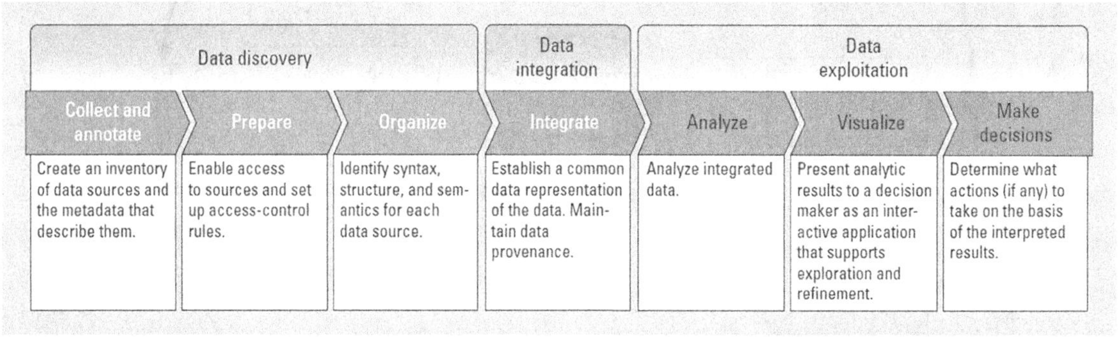

Data discovery primarily addresses the stages involved prior to model building and essentially examine the various aspects involved in deciding what data entities are required, the source of data and necessary pre-processing or data cleaning which is required in order to make it ready to be used in the analytical model. In specific terms, the tasks highlighted in their framework include – 'Collect and annotate', 'Prepare (the data)' and 'Organize (the data)'.

This stage is followed by the stage of 'Data integration' which addresses all issues related to data governance and access. This is followed by the 'Data exploitation' phase in which the analytical model is built using the data provided in the previous stages and results obtained based on which the analytical decisions are made. Specifically this stage includes tasks such as 'Analyze', 'Visualize and 'Make decisions'.

One of the central contributions of this book chapter is the application of the data value framework developed by Miller and Mork (2013) in the context of improving the forecasting capabilities in the service supply chain for a global manufacturing organization.

Data Discovery

This phase aims at addressing the challenges associated with disparate, dispersed & non-standard data granularity. Data across multiple systems which need to be used are identified. This data needs to be standardized and scalable across different regions and functions by creating a global meta-dictionary of forecasting variables with their definitions and nomenclature.

These variables need to be (a) flexible to "plug and play" for other downstream systems and with service providers (suppliers) as needed (b) accurate with right rate of refresh and (c) consistent in granularity and which enables availability of data at the right time.

To create such a solution will require working with the Subject Matter Experts (SME) across regions and global teams who run the process to gather their requirements and understand the current operations. The first step is to onboard the regional and functional teams in the project and initiate an assessment of their data requirements and current leading practices across. This provides key insights into creating a "best in class" data management process to ensure a level playing field for all.

In parallel, the project core team led by big-data architects initiate assessment of data sourcing options and big-data solution exploration to identify the right extraction point(s) and big data technology that aligns with the organization's IT strategy. Once all the SMEs align on the data management and provisioning process, extraction points are determined. Then big data solution architecture is defined and the solution development process is initiated.

The solution development includes creating Extract, Transform, Load (ETL) data capabilities, developing data structures in big data environment (linking data elements coming from diverse data sources at right level of granularity), and enabling data provision vehicles (reports, system feeds, Electronic Data Interchange(EDI)). One of the most critical activity after the solution development process is User Acceptance Testing (UAT), where the SMEs and users validate the availability of data per their requirements.

Data Integration

At the organizational level, in order to enable any changes to IT infrastructure and business processes the authors propose the idea of creating Centers of Excellence (COE) for achieving integrated planning and forecasting across the various organizational verticals. This organizational restructuring is necessary to ensure that there is uniformity in the process of planning and forecasting and also enables collaboration across different functions and regions.

As part of stages of organizational restructuring, first the COEs is created for each function (such as spares forecasting across regions) separately. Subsequently, an integrated COE is created to cover all functions and all regions enabling integrated cascading forecast across functions. This COE definitely needs to work closely with the regional supply chain stakeholders to fine-tune forecasts based on business context and market conditions. It is critical because every demand driver cannot be included in the forecast models and the 'tribal' knowledge of local business planners and stakeholders is crucial to ensure the forecast variable and values are appropriate for any given market.

Data Exploitation

This phase focuses on developing advanced forecasting models and enhancing the current processes & downstream interlocks to leverage the richer data (more demand drivers) that is now available for planners. Usually the legacy forecasting models that are usually being used are rudimentary such as moving averages or at best univariate (mostly hindsight based) forecasting models. With richer data, the project core team, led by analytics & modelling professionals, work with the planners and create multivariate data models to enhance the forecast accuracy.

Multiple forecasting models need to be developed to cater to regional nuances, business context across demand drivers, and also the lifecycle of the product. This is an iterative process and requires expertise in modeling and data science.

The accuracy of forecasts of multivariate models can be further improved by incorporating business variables like promotions working with the business SMEs. Once the new models are created it is important to incorporate them in forecasting and planning process, establish a governance to review forecast numbers and fine tune them in collaboration with regions and functions to ensure most current business context is considered and forecast numbers are realistic.

In parallel a team of automation experts should work on automating the activities and handoffs between sources of data, data mart, forecast generation tools (modeling tools) and their output into planning systems. This requires the project team working closely with the business and IT organizations and is a critical component in this big data analytics solution and the change management inherent in such an implementation.

FUTURE RESEARCH DIRECTIONS

This work is based on a single global manufacturing organization's customer support function. Hence there may be limitations in terms of generalizability in this approach and findings with other such comparable organizations. Industry specific contexts and prior data technology investments may also limit the applicability of this work to other organizational contexts. The authors provide below some considerations for such transformations as well as opportunities to further enhance the forecasting ecosystem.

The focus is first on creating a foundational capability to enable single source for forecasting data needs. In '*Data exploitation*' section, forecasting models have been developed based on unique '*demand drivers*' as variables. Identifying the right demand drivers and creating a forecasting model requires advanced use of analytics and very close integration with business and operations teams. Data lakes have made enhanced data available for analysis and modeling at one place. However the key challenge lies in making the best use of the data in improving business outcomes. It is an iterative process and should lead to significant improvements in accuracy of the forecast as well as downstream supply planning.

The technology and logic used to create the data lake depends on an organization's IT strategy. Incompatible technologies can lead to silos, gaps in data and significant costs. During such transformations, IT architects play a critical role in defining the solution that is aligned with current system constraints as well as long term IT strategy. Much of the big data analytics literature review includes newer ways of storing data (such as data lake) and processing data (using Hadoop). Further research may be undertaken to find the applicability of these new technologies in such organizational scenarios.

Further, every industry has its own unique industry constraints and characteristics. For example in the Food & Beverages (F&B) sector, the challenge is on managing the low shelf life of its products. Similarly, in the Computer Electronics industry, high rates of technological obsolescence makes its R&D operations and innovation its top priority. The authors view the role of foundational capabilities in building and managing data lakes in every industry to be critical. But the downstream application of the data and the nature of usage of data will vary depending on the industry requirements. Further studies may be undertaken to explore industry specific case studies which highlight the role of developing big data analytics solution to enhance business outcomes in those specific contexts.

In a globalized economy, any value chain consists of multiple organizations working in tandem. Partnerships between them is critical to ensure effective operations in areas such as design, manufacturing, distribution & customer support to the company's products and services. Sharing business signals through information across partnerships enable the value chains to work in the most optimal manner. In this book chapter, the authors have explored the aspects related to sharing information outside organizational boundaries to manage the service supply chain for a multinational enterprise. Further research may be conducted to explore aspects related to the service operations and supporting Information and Communication Technology (ICT) infrastructure to delve deeper into the process and technology. It may help tackle business concerns needed to answer questions such as "what to share" and "when to share" and "how to share". Specific areas of concern related to security and access management of data stored in data lakes have sufficient scope for further research.

CONCLUSION

In this book chapter, the authors begin by examining the V's of big data – volume, velocity, variety and veracity in the context of managing the post-sales customer support function in a global manufacturing organization. Using detailed descriptions, the authors argue how this scenario fits the description of a big data ecosystem. This is followed by examining the issues involved in the process of generating forecasting models which are currently being followed.

The authors find that there are significant limitations in terms of the reliability and accuracy of the current forecasting models which are hampering managerial decision making. The key reason for these limitations are the fragmented ways in which the forecasting function is being currently carried out. Using a big data value chain as the research framework, the authors propose a reorganization of the process followed in generating these forecasts. The value chain combines people, process and technology aspects in ensuring that there is a coordinated and standardized process followed in building these forecasts to ensure that there is a better data governance mechanism in place to support the global manufacturing organization in building its forecasting capabilities for handling its post-sales customer service support function.

REFERENCES

Adrian, M. (2011, January). Big Data: It's going mainstream, and it's your next opportunity. *Teradata Magazine, Q1*(5), 38–42.

Ali, M. M., Babai, M. Z., Boylan, J. E., & Syntetos, A. A. (2017). Supply chain forecasting when information is not shared. *European Journal of Operational Research, 260*(3), 984–994. doi:10.1016/j.ejor.2016.11.046

Beulke, D. (2011). *Big Data Impacts Data Management: The 5 Vs of Big Data.* Retrieved from http://davebeulke.com/big-data-impacts-data-management-the-five-vs-of-big-data/

boyd, d., & Crawford, K. (2012). Critical questions for big data. *Information, Communication & Society, 15*(5), 662-679. doi:10.1080/1369118X.2012.678878

Cho, D. W., Lee, Y. H., Ahn, S. H., & Hwang, M. K. (2012). A framework for measuring the performance of service supply chain management. *Computers & Industrial Engineering, 62*(3), 801–818. doi:10.1016/j.cie.2011.11.014

Davenport, T. H. (1998). Putting the enterprise into the enterprise system. *Harvard Business Review, 76*(4). PMID:10181586

Davenport, T. H., Barth, P., & Bean, R. (2012). How 'Big Data' Is Different. *MIT Sloan Management Review, 54*(1), 43–46.

de Waart, D., & Kemper, S. (2004). 5 steps to service supply chain excellence. *Supply Chain Management Review, 8*(1), 28–35.

Dutta, D., & Bose, I. (2015). Managing a Big Data project: The case of Ramco Cements Limited. *International Journal of Production Economics, 165*, 293–306. doi:10.1016/j.ijpe.2014.12.032

Ellram, L. M., Tate, W. L., & Billington, C. (2004). Understanding and Managing the Services Supply Chain. *Journal of Supply Chain Management, 40*(4), 17–32. doi:10.1111/j.1745-493X.2004.tb00176.x

Fitzgerald, M. (2015). Gone fishing -- for data. *MIT Sloan Management Review, 56*(3), 7–7.

Hardoon, D. R., & Shmueli, G. (2013). *Getting started with business analytics: insightful decision-making*. CRC Press.

Hassani, H., & Silva, E. S. (2015). Forecasting with big data: A review. *Annals of Data Science, 2*(1), 5–19. doi:10.100740745-015-0029-9

He, M., Xie, J., Wu, X., Hu, Q., & Dai, Y. (2016). Capability Coordination in Automobile Logistics Service Supply Chain Based on Reliability. *Procedia Engineering, 137*, 325–333. doi:10.1016/j.proeng.2016.01.265

IBM. (2015). *The Four V's of Big Data*. Retrieved from http://www.ibmbigdatahub.com/infographic/four-vs-big-data

Kumar, S., & Deshmukh, S. (2005). *Business intelligence: delivering business value through supply chain analytics*. Infosys White Paper. Retrieved from http://www.bcubeglobal.com/wp-content/uploads/supply-chain-analytics.pdf

Laney, D. (2001). *3D data management: controlling data volume, velocity, and variety*. Retrieved from http://www.blogs.gartner.com/doug-laney/files/2012/01/ad949-3D-Data-Management-Controlling-Data-Volume-Velocityand-Variety.pdf

Madden, S. (2012). From databases to big data. *IEEE Internet Computing, 16*(3), 4–6. doi:10.1109/MIC.2012.50

Manyika, J., Chui, M., Brown, B., Bughin, J., Dobbs, R., Roxburgh, C., & Byers, A. H. (2011). *Big data: The next frontier for innovation, competition, and productivity*. Retrieved from http://www.mckinsey. com/business-functions/business-technology/our-insights/big-data-the-next-frontier-for-innovation

McCreadie, R., Macdonald, C., & Ounis, I. (2012). MapReduce indexing strategies: Studying scalability and efficiency. *Information Processing & Management, 48*(5), 873–888. doi:10.1016/j.ipm.2010.12.003

Miller, H. G., & Mork, P. (2013). From Data to Decisions: A Value Chain for Big Data. *IT Professional, 15*(1), 57–59. doi:10.1109/MITP.2013.11

Porter, M. E. (1980). *Competitive strategy: technique for analyzing industries and competitors*. New York: Free Press.

Ramish, A., Azhar, T. M., & Rasheed, H. (2017). Building a comprehensive service supply chain conceptual framework: A step ahead, based on comparative analysis of previous frameworks. *International Journal of Services and Operations Management, 26*(1), 97–121. doi:10.1504/IJSOM.2017.080679

Saccani, N., Johansson, P., & Perona, M. (2007). Configuring the after-sales service supply chain: A multiple case study. *International Journal of Production Economics, 110*(1–2), 52–69. doi:10.1016/j. ijpe.2007.02.009

Sepúlveda-Rojas, J. P., Rojas, F., Valdés-González, H., & San Martín, M. (2015). Forecasting Models Selection Mechanism for Supply Chain Demand Estimation. *Procedia Computer Science, 55*, 1060–1068. doi:10.1016/j.procs.2015.07.068

Shearer, C. (2000). The CRISP-DM model: The new blueprint for data mining. *Journal of Data Warehousing, 5*(4), 13–22.

Syntetos, A. A., Babai, Z., Boylan, J. E., Kolassa, S., & Nikolopoulos, K. (2016). Supply chain forecasting: Theory, practice, their gap and the future. *European Journal of Operational Research, 252*(1), 1–26. doi:10.1016/j.ejor.2015.11.010

Tekiner, F., & Keane, J. A. (2013). *Big Data Framework*. Paper presented at the 2013 IEEE International Conference on Systems, Man, and Cybernetics, Manchester, UK. 10.1109/SMC.2013.258

van der Laan, E., van Dalen, J., Rohrmoser, M., & Simpson, R. (2016). Demand forecasting and order planning for humanitarian logistics: An empirical assessment. *Journal of Operations Management, 45*, 114–122. doi:10.1016/j.jom.2016.05.004

Violino, B. (2015, July 31). 5 Things You Need to Know about data lakes. *CIO, 28*(10), 17–17.

Waller, M. A., & Fawcett, S. E. (2013). Data Science, Predictive Analytics, and Big Data: A Revolution That Will Transform Supply Chain Design and Management. *Journal of Business Logistics, 34*(2), 77–84. doi:10.1111/jbl.12010

Watson, H. J. (2015). Data Lakes, Data Labs, and Sandboxes. *Business Intelligence Journal, 20*(1), 4–7.

ENDNOTES

[1]   A false positive is a result that indicates a given condition has been fulfilled, when it actually has not.

[2]   The CRISP-DM framework was conceived in 1996 and was elaborated by Shearer (2000). Till date, it remains the leading methodology used by industry for analytics, data mining or data science projects as per polls conducted by KDNuggets.

Chapter 81
Intelligent Big Data Analytics in Health

Ebru Aydindag Bayrak
🆔 https://orcid.org/0000-0002-2637-9245
Istanbul University – Cerrahpaşa, Turkey

Pinar Kirci
Istanbul University – Cerrahpaşa, Turkey

ABSTRACT

Intelligent big data analytics and machine learning systems have been introduced to explain for the early diagnosis of neurological disorders. A number of scholarly researches about intelligent big data analytics in healthcare and machine learning system used in the healthcare system have been mentioned. The authors have explained the definition of big data, big data samples, and big data analytics. But the main goal is helping researchers or specialists in providing opinion about diagnosing or predicting neurological disorders using intelligent big data analytics and machine learning. Therefore, they focused on the healthcare systems using these innovative ways in particular. The information of platform and tools about big data analytics in healthcare is investigated. Numerous academic studies based on the detection of neurological disorders using both machine learning methods and big data analytics have been reviewed.

INTRODUCTION

The concept of big data was first used by Michael Cox and David Ellsworth at Proceedings of the 8th Conference on Visualization held in 1997, entitled "Application Controlled Demand Paging for Out-of-core Visualization". In the same study, it was mentioned that the datasets were too big and the computer system filled up the memory, disks and even external disks, and this problem was called "Big Data Problem" (Aktan, 2018).

The term big data was used for using larger volumes of scientific data for visualization. Although there are a large number of definitions of big data in the literature, the most popular definition comes from IBM. Big data could be characterized by any or all of three "V" words as suggested by IBM. V means that volume, variety, and velocity (O'Leary, 2013).

DOI: 10.4018/978-1-6684-3662-2.ch081

2.5 quintillion bytes of data was created by people, that is to say ninety percent of data (%90) has just been created in the last two years. This data is generated social media posts, videos, cell phone GPS signals or sensors. Here it is, this data is called Big Data (IBM, n.d.a.).

According to Gartner Incorporation "Big data is high-volume, high-variety and/or high-velocity information assets that demand cost-effective, innovative forms of information processing that enable enhanced insight, decision making, and process automation" (Gartner IT Glossary, n.d.).

The concept of big data; can be defined as a problem that occurs when traditional database management systems are inadequate when the data is stored, analyzed and managed (Sağıroğlu, 2017).

Big data indicate to growing dataset that involves unstructured, structured and semi-structured data by contrast with traditional data. The term big data was defined using the three main characteristics (3V) by most scientists and experts (Oussous, Benjelloun, Lahcen and Belfkih, 2017).

- Volume: It means the size of data which is varying from different data unit (terabyte, petabyte). Digital devices and applications (smartphones, IoT, social networks, logs,…) are generate big volumes of digital data. According to the report of International Data Corporation (IDC) the volume of data will increase from 898 exabytes to 6.6 zettabytes between 2012 and 2020. In other words, data will grow more than % 25 per a year.
- Variety: Big data is a variety of different formats (logs, videos, sensors,…) and sources. So it means the diversity of datasets.
- Velocity: Data is generated in a fast way that is means speed of data change.

The three components of big data can be summarized as in Figure 1. In addition to the three 3V's, other dimensions of big data have also been mentioned. These include (Gandomi and Haider, 2015):

- Veracity: This concept was coined by IBM to represent the uncertainty in some sources of data. We can give example such as customer sentiments in social media that are uncertain and include personal opinion. Even so they are valuable for analyzing information.
- Variability: It refers to the variation in the data flow rates, was introduced by SAS (Statistical Analysis Software).
- Value: It is defined by Oracle to define attribute of big data. Clearly it can be explained creating a value to organizations using big data analysis in the decision-making.

When research is done in both academic and business literature Big Data has been identified four key themes to which refers: Information, Technologies, Methods and Impact (De Mauro, Greco & Grimaldi, 2015).

The evaluation of big data is explained that it is equivalent to the oil of 20th century and is the gold mine of the 21th century. It is valuable for organization, government and individual (Sun, 2017).

BACKGROUND

O'Leary (2013) have focused on some of the basic concern and uses of artificial intelligence for big data. About the integration of artificial intelligence and big data case studies were presented. As what is big data, the application of mapreduce and hadoop, the significance of structured data topics were explained. In the end of study, it is accepted that machine learning and artificial intelligence have a key role for providing enterprise with intelligent analysis of big data.

Ward and Barker (2013) have studied a survey of big data definitions between academia, industry and media. Definitions made by Gartner, IBM, Oracle, Intel and Microsoft etc. are included. Additionally the importance of big data and its progress were remarked and the concept of big data was defined following words: Big data is a term describing the storage and analysis of large and or complex data sets using a series of techniques including, but not limited to: NoSQL, MapReduce and Machine Learning.

Sagiroglu and Sinanc (2013) have reviewed an overview of big data's content, scope, samples, methods, advantages and handicap and discusses about the principle of privacy. They explained that have useful information is gained from big data analysis, take advantages for companies or organizations.

De Mauro et al. (2015) have reviewed the existing literature on big data and analyzed its previous definition. They have made out two suggestions about big data. Firstly, they offered a summary of the main research areas related to the concept of big data, trending and opportunities for future development. Secondly, they have provide a general definition for big data to synthesize common themes of previous definitions.

Yoo, Ramirez & Liuzzi (2014) have introduced modern statistical machine learning using big data analysis in medicine. Clinical, genomic and environmental datasets were collected from biomedical science that is too much and complex. To analyze these datasets, regression analysis and modern statistical model can be used. They have explained Linear and Logistic Regression and Bayesian Networks to analyze biomedical datasets. Bayesian Networks used big data sets that are more complicated data, have different type of huge data from clinical genomic and environmental data.

X. Wu, Zhu, G. Wu & Ding (2014) have studied data mining with big data sets. They have presented HACE theorem that models the key characteristics of the big data. This acronym means that huge with Heterogeneous and diverse data, Autonomous with distributed and decentralized control, Complex and Evolving relationships. Also data mining challenges with big data as data accessing, semantic and domain knowledge for different big data applications, algorithm designs were explained.

Singh and Reddy (2015) have studied a survey that is about different platforms for big data analytics, explains advantages and obstacle of data processing platforms. They have asserted a comparison of different platforms using rating, using parametrics for rating are scalability, data input/output performance, fault tolerance, real time processing, data size supported and iterative task support. Data size, speed and model development are specified important factors to choose platform for application.

Gandomi and Haider (2015) have worked on big data concepts, definitions of big data, using methods and big data analytics especially focused on analytics methods used for big data. Big data analytics were explained for using analyze and acquire intelligence from big data. They have reviewed analytics techniques for text, audio, video, social media and predictive analytics.

Özköse, Arı & Gencer (2015) have explained characteristic and classification of big data, big data process, usage areas of big data and methods used in big data in their study. In addition all these, they have mentioned yesterday, today and tomorrow of big data with some studies on big data in Turkey and all over the word.

Xu, Yue, L. Guo, Y. Guo & Fang (2015) have carried out privacy-preserving machine learning algorithms for big data systems. They have proposed a framework based on MapReduce to analyze big data. Additionally they have focused on support vector machines and explained two schemes for vertically and horizontally partitioned training data sets. The breast cancer data set, the Higgs bosons presence dataset and optical character recognition of handwritten digits dataset were used to test performance of their scheme.

Qui, Wu, Ding, Xu & Feng (2016) have presented a survey of machine learning for big data processing. They have reviewed advanced machine learning techniques such as representation learning, deep learning, distributed and parallel learning, transfer learning, active learning and kernel-based learning. The first purpose of their work is explaining current research efforts any challenges of big data. The other purpose is to analyze interaction between machine learning and modern signal processing for big data. In addition to these, different critical issues for machine learning applications on big data are explained.

Atalay and Çelik (2017) have discussed the use of artificial intelligence and machine learning technique in big data analysis. The general information about artificial intelligence and machine learning methods were given and some applications of these methods have been explained. They have suggested that artificial intelligence will be much more important in the future by means of technological developments.

Balasupramanian, Ephrem & Al-Barwani (2017) have purposed framework that is used big data analytics and machine learning technique to prevent online fraud detection before it happens.

Oussous et al. (2017) have prepared a survey about recent technologies developed for big data. They have explained big data definitions, applications and challenges in their study as the main title. Also they have studied different big data technologies and these technologies have been compared by capabilities and limits.

Zhou, Pan, Wang & Vasilakos (2017) have introduced a framework of Machine Learning on Big Data (MLBID). They have prepared an overview of opportunities and challenges of machine learning on big data. Big data, user, domain and system are components of MLBID framework. Also they have summarized open research issues in MLBID according to components of framework. At the end of study they have referred that machine learning is valuable for insights from big data.

Figure 1. The three components of big data (Adapted from Russom, 2011).

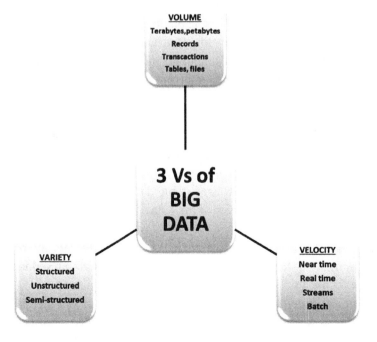

BIG DATA SAMPLES

We can use and find big data examples in the literature or different working areas. These areas can be sorted by respectively; astronomy, atmospheric science, genomics, biological science, natural science, health records, scientific research, private sector, military surveillance, financial services, retail. In addition, mobile phones, social networks, call detail records, web logs, photography-audio-video, click streams, search indexing, POS information, radio frequency identification (RFID) and sensor networks can be counted big data samples (Sagiroglu and Sinanc, 2013).

According to "Data Never Sleeps 6.0" project was prepared by Domo (2018), % 90 per of all data today has been created in the last two years. That means 2.5 quintillion bytes of data per a day. For example; approximately more than 4 million video views on YouTube, 2.083.333 snaps sharing on Snapchat, and users post 49.380 photos on Instagram. When we analyzed global internet population growth 2012-2017, the global internet population has grown 3.8 billion people as of 2017 (Domo, n.d.). If the growing continues at this rate, it is clear that the amount of data will continue to increase (Figure 2).

Big data samples can be grouped under three main headings: structural, semi-structural and non-structural data (Aktan, 2018):

1. **Structured Data:** Is expressed all data types that are easy for modeling, insertion as input, storage, interrogation, processing and visualizing.
2. **Semi-Structured Data:** Has various meta-models, such as tags and markers used to define certain items and hierarchical representations of different fields on the data, as well as models that define the structure data.
3. **Non-Structural Data:** Are types of records that are presented and stored and stored outside of defined format.

Big data is used many different working fields. Some of them are can be listed below (Özköse et al., 2015);

- High technology and industry,
- Medical field,
- Travel and transport sector,
- Education and research,
- Media and show business,
- Automotive industry,
- Financial services,
- Customer relationship management.

BIG DATA ANALYTICS

With the development of technology, the increasing number of smart devices, producing real-time log records via the help of sensors, increasing mobility and internet access social networks are becoming a part of our daily life have been increased the diversity, speed and volume of data surrounded. This situation brings with it the problems of obtaining, storing and processing big data. At this point, big data

Figure 2. A striking picture is shown related to the speed of the data. How much data is generated for every minute in 2018? (Adapted from Domo, n.d.).

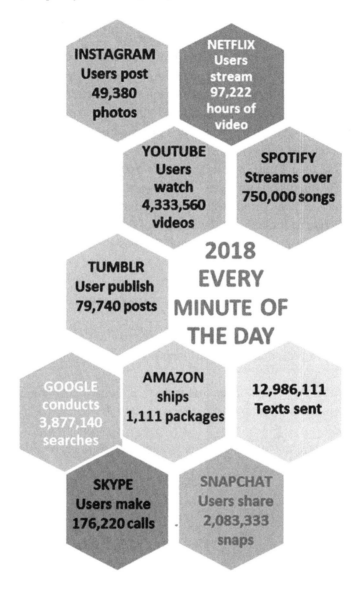

analytics provides access to information through selection, storage and processing of structured data (for example: corporate data) and unstructured data (for example: video, audio, text files, etc.) (Aktan, 2018).

Big Data Analytics can be described simply that using advanced analytic techniques operate on big data (Russom, 2011). In other words big data analytics is basically described as the process of collecting, structuring, analyzing and evaluating big datasets. The first goal is to find patterns and other hidden information from large data. Big data analytics assists to make sense of the data that is more significant for making decision and the business (Balasupramanian et al., 2017).

Big Data Analytics is an emerging science and technology involving multidisciplinary state-of-art information and communication technology, mathematics, operations research, machine learning and decision sciences for big data. Three main components of big data analytics include big data descriptive analytics, big data predictive analytics and big data prescriptive analytics (Z. Sun, L. Sun & Strang, 2018)

Big Data Analytics is described as the process of collecting, organizing, analyzing huge datasets to discover useful information and different patterns. Also it is formed techniques and technologies that require new forms of integration to disclose hidden values from large datasets. It is mainly focused on solving new problems or old problems with much better and impressive ways. The main goal of the big data analytics is sorted such as, helping future prediction and making better decision to organization, analyze organization transactions and update the organization data (Verma, Agrawal, B. Patel & A. Patel, 2016).

Technical components of big data analytics can be presented in Figure 3 that it is total of data warehouse, data mining, statistical modelling machine learning, visualization and optimization. Intelligent big data analytics is the core of data science and can be explained by the addition of the intelligent term to previous mention components. Besides big data, analytics and artificial intelligence are inseparable whole (Sun,2017).

Figure 3. The interrelationship of big data analytics (Adapted from Sun et al, 2018).

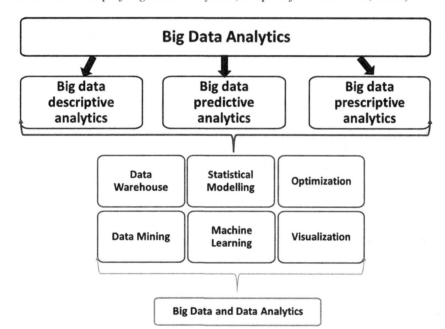

Big data analysis can give much more reason and prediction with the use of artificial neural networks, deep learning, natural language processing, image recognition and personalization technologies. On the other hand, artificial intelligence techniques that imitate the intelligent behaviours of living beings, create models that think and decide like human, are preferred resulting from gain advantages on big data analysis (Atalay and Çelik, 2017).

Big data analytics tools aim to obtain worthful information from data through analysis structured, semi-structured and non-structural data that are difficult to process using with traditional database techniques (Aktan, 2018).

Big data analytics is a technique used in the big datasets and can be viewed as a sub-process in the overall process of information extraction from big data. Big data analytics process can be explained five stages in the following words. The first three steps are called data management, while the last two steps are called analytics (Gandomi and Haider);

1. Data acquisition
2. Information extraction
3. Integration
4. Modeling and analysis
5. Interpretation

Transforming Data With Intelligence (TDWI) has asked many user organizations "In your organization, is big data considered mostly a problem or mostly an opportunity. Thirty percent of them said that they consider big data as a problem. The rest of organizations (%70) said that they consider big data an opportunity. The analyses of big data provide new facts to organizations about their customers, markets, partners, costs, and operations and then they can use these information for business advantage (Russom, 2011).

BIG DATA ANALYTICS IN HEALTHCARE SYSTEMS

The role of big data in the healthcare system is to guide datasets related to healthcare which are complicated and hard to manage using current management tools, software and hardware (Kumar and Singh, 2019).

The impact of big data on the healthcare system was defined in five pathways as following (Groves, Kayyali, Knott & Van Kuiken, 2013):

1. **Right Living:** Refers to living more healthier life for patients.
2. **Right Care:** Refers to having convenient treatment for patiens and is obtained same data and objectives.
3. **Right Provider:** Refers to provide better treatment options for patients using health data.
4. **Right Value:** Refers to increase the quality and value of health-related services.
5. **Right Innovation:** Refers to research and development activities about health as recognize new treatments and new medicine.

The process of big data analytic tool can be defined a data flow that provide worthful information from large dataset for decision making as following (Sahu, Jacintha & Singh, 2017);

- Collection of data
- Storage of data
- Processing
- Visualizing

The big health data sources are; Electronic Healthcare Records (EHRs), Biomedical images, Sensing data, Biomedical signals, Genomic data, Clinical text and Social media. EHRs refers a copy of patient's medical history. Biomedical images refers clinical imaging modalities as Magnetic Resonance Imaging (MRI), Positron Emission Tomography (PET), ultrasound, Computed Tomography (CT), etc. Sensing data refers such as Electrocardiogram (ECG) and Electroencephalogram (EEG) signals. Biomedical signals refers as blood pressure, brain activity, oxygen saturation levels etc. many sources. Genomic data refers relationships between genetic markers, mutations and disease. Clinical text refers clinical notes which are stored unstructured data. Social network refers various collected social media resources as Facebook, Twitter, web logs and social network sites (Ta, Liu & Nkabinde, 2016).

Wang, Kung & Byrd (2018) have aimed to identify big data analytics capabilities and explore the potential benefits of big data analytics in healthcare system in the study. They have explained the history of big data analytics from past to today, architecture of its in healthcare and the strategies for success with big data analytics.

Praveena and Bharathi (2017) have prepared a survey paper about big data analytics. They have examined various big data analytics and its operations, infrastructure, challenges and analysis algorithms of big data. Also they have investigated few of big data management tools which are used for different purpose.

Athmaja, Hanumanthappa & Kavitha (2017) have worked on advanced machine learning algorithms and techniques which are used to have solutions to big data analytic problems. They have analyzed some studies that is about different machine learning techniques and prepared literature survey.

Siuly and Zhang (2016) have reviewed medical big data analysis on neurological disease diagnosis. The difficulty of obtaining medical big data, medical big data analysis and computer aid diagnosis systems (CAD) have been explained on study. Also, they have surveyed developing CAD system for automatical diagnosis of neurological diseases.

Sun and Reddy (2013) have studied on big data analytics for healthcare. They have explained predictive models for clinical data analysis, scalable healthcare analytics platform and genetic data analysis. The overall goals of big data analytics in health have been mentioned.

The challenges of Big Data and Analytical process have been grouped as main topics; storage, data representation, the management of data life cycle, data confidentiality, data analysis, data reporting, energy management, redundancy reduction and data compression, expendability and scalability, cooperation and dimensionality reduction of big data (Praveena and Bharathi, 2017).

Platforms or Tools for Big Data Analytics in Healthcare

Apache Hadoop

Hadoop is an open source and parallel computing platform or tool that stores and process big data. The main component of Hadoop can be summarized as firstly, Hadoop Distributed File System (HDFS) secondly MapReduce and thirdly YARN. HDFS is file system distributed on cluster and has storage devices. MapReduce process the data that is stored on HDFS clusters. It has two steps on data. Map step is about divide of data into smaller, Reduce step is about produce a solution. As for, YARN is a resource management (Harerimana, Jang, Kim & Park, 2018).

A more general definition of the Hadoop ecosystem and framework is open source tools, methodologies and libraries for "big data" analysis in which lots of data sets are obtained from different sources (Kumar and Singh, 2019).

It is flexible and user friendly platform working with different data sources to use machine learning process (Praveena and Bharathi, 2017).

MapReduce

MapReduce is explained that is the heart of Apache Hadoop by IBM. It is programming paradigm that allow massive scalability between lots of server in Hadoop cluster. MapReduce term refers to have two different task in Hadoop program as map and reduce. The map task converts dataset into another set of data. The reduce task takes outputs from map and combines them to have reduced tuples (IBM, n.d.b.).

Apache Mahout

Mahout is another Apache project for generating free applications of distributed and scalable machine learning and data mining algorithms. It is used for big data analytics on the Hadoop platform (W. Raghupathi and V. Raghupathi, 2014).

Apache Pig

Apache Pig is open-source platforms for analyzing big data sets. It consists of high level language for identification of data analysis programs and it's infrastructure evaluates analysis programs. The most remarkable feature of Pig structure is that allows to handle very large data sets with parallelization (Apache Pig, n.d.).

Apache Hive

The Apache Hive is data warehouse software facilitates on Hadoop about reading, writing, and managing large datasets in distributed storage using SQL-like language (Apache Hive, n.d.).

Apache Spark

Spark is an open source and parallel computing platform for big data sources as Hadoop and also provides scalable data analytics paltform with in memory computing. When it was compared wih Hadoop, computing power is more power than Hadoop. Spark is planned for machine learning and natural language processing (Patel and Sharma, 2014).

It is programmed in Scala and programmable in Scala or Python. Spark's specific functionalities can be sorted as machine learning, graph analysis and data-streaming (Berral-Garcia, 2016). Spark is a heavily used platform for healthcare big data analytics because of performing more fast analysis using its stream computing capabilities (Harerimana et al., 2018).

MACHINE LEARNING SYSTEM

One of today's the fastest developing technical fields is machine learning and it is at the core of artificial intelligence and data science and also lying at the intersection of computer science and statistics. The study about mmachine learning is focused on the question about how to build computers that improve automatically through experience (Jordan and Mitchell, 2015).

Machine learning has been used both scientific and business study field to extract useful information from hidden pattern. Because it is not possible to analyze and process the data in very large quantities in the traditional way. For this reason, machine learning methods have been developed to analyze big data. This methods use old data to solve problem and predict the future. In addition to these advantages, machine learning methods contribute to decision making mechanism. Machine learning makes inference from the data using mathematical and statistical methods (Diri, n.d.).

Machine learning is defined by (Mithcell, 2006) as follows:" We say that a machine learns with respect to a particular task T, performance metric P, and type of experience E, if the system reliably improves its performance P at task T, following experience E".

For machine learning application generally dataset is divided into two groups and they called trainings set and testing set. The training set is used to teach for algorithm and discover the underlying structure in data. The testing set is used to calculate model accuracy (Altındal, 2006).

Machine learning has a significant role in big data systems due to discovering important knowledge and hidden information (Xu et al., 2015).

The some application of machine learning can sorted as pattern recognition, optical character recognition (OCR), face recognition, medical diagnosis, speech recognition, natural language processing, biometrics, knowledge detection and outlier detection (Alpaydın, 2014).

Especially along with the rising of big data, machine learning has become a key technique for solving problems in different areas; such as computational finance, energy production, automotive, aerospace and manufacturing (Mathworks, n.d.).

Machine learning is the one of most effective method used in big data analytics to predict with some models and algorithms. These analytical models give us a chance to produce reliable and acceptable results. In addition, machine learning algorithms allow to discover some hidden pattern and trends from big data (Angra and Ahuja, 2017).

The critical issue of machine learning for big data have been explained by Qui et al. (2016) with five different perspectives as below:

1. Learning for huge scale of data.
2. Learning for various types of data.
3. Learning for high speed of data stream
4. Learning for ambiguous and missing data.
5. Learning for data with low value density and meaning density.

Machine Learning Methods

The machine Learning methods aim to find the most suitable model for new data available by using the past data. To make this, two different methods are used as to be classification and clustering. Classification is used mostly as a supervised learning, while clustering is used for unsupervised learning.

But some clustering models are used for both supervised and unsupervised learning. Classification is purposed predictive, while clustering is descriptive (Rokach and Maimon, 2005).

Machine learning methods can be divided into three groups; they are called, supervised learning, unsupervised learning and reinforcement learning. In a few words, if we want to explain subdomains of the field of machine learning: Supervised learning requires training with labeled data which has inputs and expected outputs. Unsupervised learning does not require labeled training data and it only use inputs for training. Reinforcement learning provides learning from feedback (reward-penalty) via interactions with enviroment. The supervised and unsupervised learning techniques are preferred for data analysis process whereas reinforcement techniques are preferred for decision making process (Oiu et al., 2016).

Supervised Learning

Supervised learning is a machine learning technique which is used a function matching between preferred output and labelled data. When making a function it use training datasets. Function can be determined with classification and regression algorithms (Uzun, 2016).

It is known that input value corresponds to which output in supervised learning (Kartal, 2015).

Supervised learning is learned from our data when we determine a target variable. We approach to target variable as two cases: The first situation explains when the target variable can take only nominal or categorical values and this situation is called classification. For the second situation, the target variable can take infinite number of numeric and is called regression (Harrington, 2012).

Both of classification and regression are supervised learning problems that learning is carried out mapping from input to output. For example credit scoring, this is an example of classification problem because there are two classes: high risk customers and low risk customers. The customer information has been used an input to classify which customer is belong one of the two classes. The predict of car prices problem is regression problem which the output is numeric (Alpaydın, 2014).

The mostly used supervised learning methods in machine learning are explained as the following, e.g. support vector machines, artificial neural networks, decision trees, k-nearest neighbour, naive bayes classifier, random forest, linear regression, logistic regression and deep learning.

Support Vector Machines

The Support Vector Machines (SVM) is firstly called by Vapnik (1995). SVM is a machine learning method that tries to find optimal hyperplane to separate the classes by using support vectors, can be used for classification and regression. This technique aims to find optimal hyperplane to separate two classes of data. Two classes are to be separated when the margin between them is maximized as in Figure 4. If the problems cannot be separated a simple hyper-plane, the data is transferred to a new space which is higher dimensional space. And it aims to find hyperplane to separate data. (Burakgazi, 2017)

SVM is divided into two groups according to linear separation and non-linear separation dataset. The dataset can not be separated linearly, it can separate applying with kernel function. The most used kernel functions are; linear, polynomial, radial basis function and sigmoid function (Yahyaoui, 2017).

Figure 4. Architecture of support vector machine, using separate two classes with optimum hyperplane (Adapted from Alpaydın, 2014).

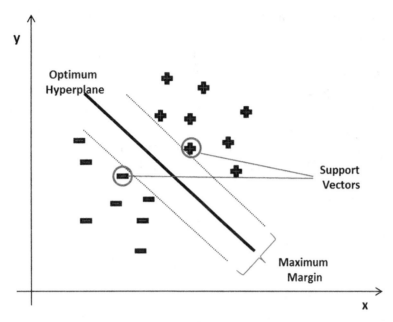

Artificial Neural Networks

Artificial neural networks (ANN) are trying to modelling of the human brain. It is aimed to training, learning and make a decision of machines by means of artificial neural networks (Kızrak, n.d.).

In engineering studies, the goal is not to model neural networks only in the brain. It is beneficial for us to make better computers using artificial neural networks. The brain is more than an engineering product in terms of its abilities such as image, speech, learning and recognition. These capabilities are crucial to implement artificial intelligence networks on computers (Alpaydın, 2013).

The main structure of ANN can be described basically as to be input, hidden and output layers in Figure 5.

Figure 5. The basic structure of artificial neural networks (Adapted from [Atalay and Çelik, 2017]).

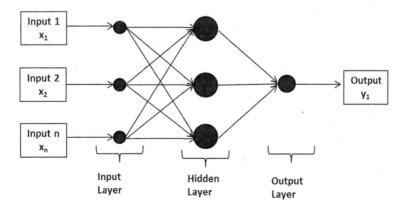

Decision Trees

The decision trees method is based on divide and rule strategy. It has a hierarchical structure consisting of decision nodes and leaves (Alpaydın, 2014).

To apply decision tree method, firstly you must make decision which feature is used to divide data. For the best results, every feature and measure should try and then you can split the datasets into subsets in Figure 6. The methods steps can be summarized as the followings: (Harrington,2012)

1. Firstly all of the dataset is used.
2. Dataset divided into two subsets according to value of a feature (the best feature that split).
3. The same procedure is applied for each subset until all of the feature are in same class. Otherwise you need to the splitting process.

Figure 6. The process of decision is represented by a tree structure (Adapted from Alpaydın, 2014).

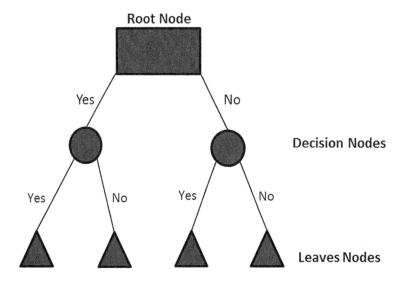

K Nearest Neighbour

The k-Nearest Neighbours (kNN) algorithm is a simple and effective but at the same time is powerful classification method. It uses the concept of distance measurement of classify items in Figure 7. kNN is a supervised learning methods so we have labels for all data and know what class each piece of the data should fall into. When we are given a new piece of data without a label, the classification steps can be summarized as follows (Harrington, 2012):

1. k parameter is determined. k is the number of neigbours closest to new data.
2. The distances between new data (testing) and existing data (training) are calculated.
3. The most closest distance values are selected (find the nearest neigbour)
4. New data falls into which class have highest number of similar data.

Figure 7. The architecture of k nearest neigbours algorithm. For k=1 new data (red circle) belongs to triangle class (right). For k=2 red circle belongs to square class, because two of the three nearest neighbours belong to the square class (Adapted from Ruan et al., 2017).

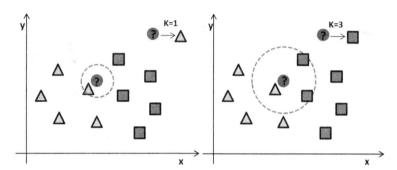

Naive Bayes Classifier

Naive Bayes Classifier is one of the most popular classification methods that based on the Bayesian theorem. Naive Bayes is very simple method, such that just small amount training data can be classify the given examples. The naive bayes algorithm which is used to calculate present and past frequency occurrences, can explain as follows (Umadevi and Marseline, 2017):

P(A \ B) = P(B \ A) * P(A) / P(B)

- Where P(A) is the prior probability of A. It counts only the occurrences of A.
- P(A\B) is the conditional probability of A, given B. It is also called as posterior probability which means A is derived from B.
- P(B\A) is the conditional probability of B, given A.
- P(B) is the prior probability of B.

Random Forest

The technique of Random Forest has been firstly improved by Leo Breiman in 2001. It is a classifier that is consisting of lots of tree-structure. Random forests are a combination of tree predictors and each tree depends on the values of a random vector. The classification is used the most popular or the best class according to input. At each node it selects the best of the randomly retrieved qualities and separates all nodes into branches (Breiman, 2001).

The method of Random Forest is based on a recursive approach in Figure 8. For every iteration, one random sample is chosen from sample size of N from data with replacement and another random sample is chosen from the predictors no replacement. After, acquired dataset is partitioned. The out-of-bag data is dropped and steps are repeated depending on how many trees we need. The classification is realized using majority vote over the decision trees (Bazazeh and Shubair, 2016).

Figure 8. The diagram showing how random forest works (Adapted from Bazazeh and Shubair, 2016).

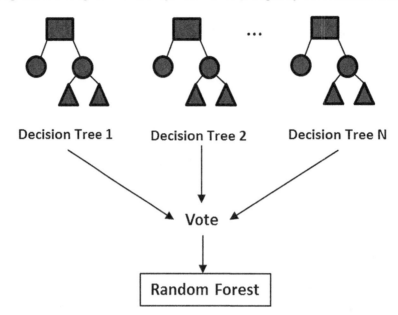

Linear Regression

Linear regression is a statistical method for modeling the relationship between a dependent variable and one or more independent variables. According to method, it supposes that outcome can be estimated via weighted sums of input variables (Yoo et al., 2014).

The linear regression model is represented by this formula:

$$Y = \beta_0 + \beta_1 X_1 + \beta_2 X_2 + \ldots + \beta_n X_n$$

where Y is dependent variable and X_i, $i=1,2,\ldots,n$ are independent variables and β_j, $j=1,2,\ldots,n$ are regression parameters. The equation enables us to predict the value of dependent variable Y from the independent variable X. The slope of equation is β_j where is called regression coefficent, R^2 is defined the coefficient of determination and is a measure of how well the regression model describes the observed data (Saritha and Abraham, 2017).

Logistic Regression

The Logistic Regression provides the relationship between the predictive attributes (independent variables) and the target attribute (dependent variable) if the target attribute is a categorical variable (Kartal, 2015).

Logistic regression has similarity in many aspects to linear regression, but actually they are very different due to one critical aspect (Figure 9). Logistic regression explains output can be expressed through weighted sum that is special mathematical transformation which is called logit. This transformation allows all weighted sum to be take a value in between 0 and 1 (Yoo et al., 2014).

The purpose of the logistic regression is to establish a model that can be identified the relationship between dependent variables and independent variables as having the best fit using the least variant. The most distinctive feature that separates the logistic regression from the linear regression is the result variable is binary or multiple in the logistics regression. This difference between logistic regression and linear regression have effected both parametric model selection and assumptions (Bircan, 2004).

Figure 9. The figure of linear regression and logistic regression model (Adapted from [Sayad, n.d.b.]).

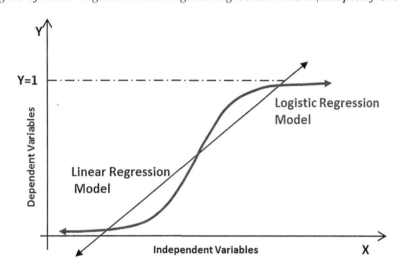

Deep Learning

Machine learning systems are used to transcribe speech into text, match news items, identify objects in images, posts or products with users interests. In the wake of technical developments, these applications make use of a class of techniques that is called deep learning (LeCun, Bengio & Hinton, 2015).

In 2006, deep learning has arisen as new field of machine learning research that uses multiple layers of information-processing in a hierarchical architecture for pattern classification and representation learning. The main advantage of deep learning can be explained as increasing chip processing abilities, having the much lower cost of computing hardware and the development in machine learning (Al-Jarrah, Yoo, Muhaidat, Karagiannidis & Taha, 2015).

Recently deep learning is one of the most attractive research interest in machine learning (Figure 10). It is different from most traditional learning techniques because of using shallow structured learning architectures. Deep learning can use together both supervised and unsupervised strategies in deep architectures to automatically learn hierarchical representations (Oui et al., 2016).

Unsupervised Learning

Unsupervised learning is a machine learning technique which use a function to predict unknown pattern through unlabeled data. In this method there is no training data. The algorithms group data and new data can be incorporated into the most suitable group (Uzun, 2016).

Figure 10. The relationship between deep learning, machine learning and artificial learning (Adapted from [Shorten, 2018]).

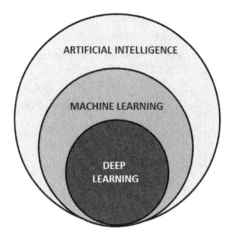

Bishop (2006) has explained unsupervised learning where the training data consist of input data without no mapping target values. The goal of unsupervised learning is to find groups of similar cluster within the data which is called clustering or see the distribution of data, known as density estimation, or reduce high dimension for visualization (Bishop, 2006).

In supervised learning, we do not have supervisor and we only have input data. The purpose is to find the pattern or regularities in the input data. The clustering purpose is to find clusters of input data. The customer segmentation is the best example for understanding clustering method. A company using demographic information and past transactions, can see the distribution of the customer profile and make customer grouping. Thus the company can manage customer relationship management better quality and could make better decide strategies, about services and products for different groups (Alpaydın, 2014).

The unsupervised learning is opposite of supervised learning, we do not have label or target value for given data. We can group similar items together which it is known clustering methods. In statistic, we can want to find values to describe data where it is called density estimation. As the other task, unsupervised learning is used for reducing dimensionality of data (Harrington, 2012).

If we need to give an example about unsupervised learning, we can say human and animal learning is largely unsupervised. The people discover the structure of the world by observing it, not by being told the name of every object (LeCun et al., 2015).

Hierarchical Clustering (HC)

The clusters are composed by iteratively dividing the patterns using bottom up or top-down approach in hierarchical clustering methods. As to be agglomerative and divise hierarchical clustering, hierarchical methods are subdivided two forms in Figure 11. The agglomerative hierarchical clustering is based on the bottom-up paradigm which clusters start with single object and then clusters merge larger clusters. Until all of the objects are lying in a single cluster, this process continue. The divise hierarchical clustering is based on top-down paradigm which firstly all of the objects belongs to only one cluster and then breaks up cluster as to be all objects will be smaller clusters (Saxena et al., 2017).

Figure 11. The hierarchical clustering dendogram (Adapted from Janssen, Walther & Lüdeke, 2012)

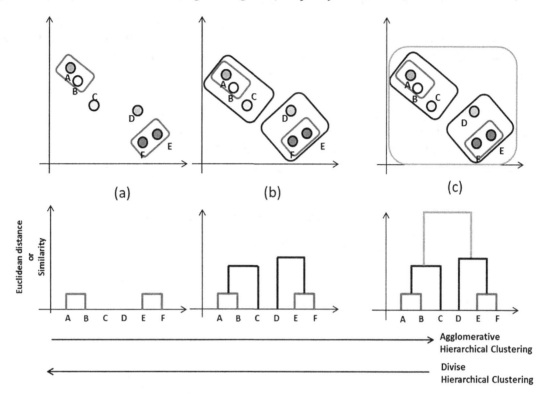

The hierarchical clustering methods can be divided into three groups according to similarity measures as following (Rokach and Maimon, 2005):

- **Single-Linkage Clustering:** Is also known as the connectedness or the neighbour method. In this method, two clusters are combined according to the distance or similarities between two cluster. The distance is defined that is shortest distances from any member of one cluster to any member of the other cluster.
- **Complete-Link Clustering:** Is also known as the diameter or the furthest neighbour method. The distance is the longest distance from any member of one cluster to any member of the other cluster. According to distance, clustering process is applied.
- **Average-Link Clustering:** Is also known as minimum variance method. According to this method, the distance between two clusters is determined by average distance from any member of one cluster to any member of the other cluster.

K-Means

K-Means is for finding the cluster inside the data. The clusters are represented by their corresponding centroids of origin. This process can also be used as a preprocessing step prior to the classification or regression (Alpaydın, 2013).

The K-Means algorithm partitions a set of n objects k cluster that is input parameter. As a result of partitioning intracluster, similarity is high but the intercluster similarity is low. Cluster similarity is measured in regard to the mean value of the objects in a cluster. The center of each cluster is represented by the mean value of the objects in the cluster. The algorithm proceeds can be explained as follows: (Han and Kamber, 2001). The summary of K-Means in Figure 12;

1.   Firstly k is choosen randomly from dataset as the initial cluster centroid.
2.   Each object is assigned to the cluster which the object is the most similar based on the mean values.
3.   The mean value of the objects is updated for each cluster.
4.   If the centroids change, 2 and 3 steps are repeated. Else, the process is terminated.

Figure 12. K-means clustering algorithm (Adapted from Chris Piech, n.d.)

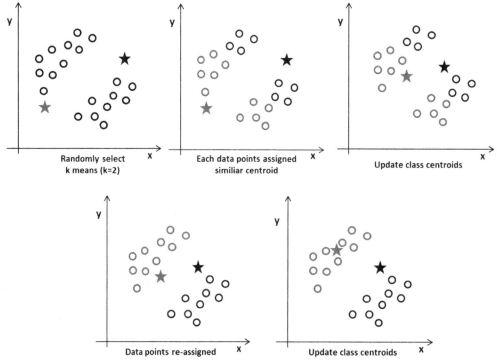

Self Organizing Maps

Around 1981–82 Teuvo Kohonen introduced a new non-linearly projecting mapping and he was called the Self-Organizing Map (SOM). The SOM models are identify with regular nodes such as two-dimensional grid. The SOM algorithm constructs the models like that: More similar models will be correlated nodes that are closer in the grid, on the contrary less similar models will be associated with nodes that are gradually farther away in the grid. The learning principles and mathematics of the SOM can be explain basically. Every input data unit will select the model that is best matching with input unit and this model, should be modified for much better matching (Kohonen, 2013).

Self-Organizing Map (SOM) is an unsupervised learning algorithm, and does not require a output vector since it learns to classify data without supervised. It is used for analysis of high-dimensional datasets and their visualization. SOM make easier the presentation of high dimensional datasets into lower dimensional ones. With using SOM, higher dimensional dataset can be reduced to two dimensional map. SOM is formed from a grid of nodes to which the input are presented. The algorithm process can be explained at below (Sayad, n.d.b.):

1. Initialization of each node's weights randomly between 0 and 1.
2. Choose a random input vector.
3. Calculate the Best Matching Unit (BMU) between input and weights nodes using Euclidean distance.
4. Calculate the size of the neighbourhood around the BMU.
5. Update nodes' weights of the BMU and neighboring nodes.
6. Repeat from step 2 for enough iterations for convergence.

The Self-Organizing Map was intended as a convenient alternative to more traditional neural network architectures. It has been used for tasks similar to those to which other more traditional neural networks have been applied: pattern recognition, process control, robotics and semantic processing (Kohonen, 1990).

Principal Component Analysis

Principal Components Analysis (PCA) is an unsupervised method because of no using the output information. In this method, main criterion is to be maximized is the variance and we aim to find a mapping from the inputs in the original space to a new lower dimensional space, with minimum loss of information (Alpaydın, 2014).

The Principal Component Analysis (PCA) is a method for dimensionality reduction as given in Figure 13. In PCA, the dataset is transfered from its original coordinate system to a new coordinate system. The new coordinate system is selected by using the data itself. The first new axis is chosen according to obtaining the most variance in the data. The second axis is orthogonal to the first axis and it is chosen by the largest variance. This procedure is iterated for as many features in dataset. Finally, we will see that the majority of the variance is contained in the first few axes. Therefore, we can keep out the rest of the axes, and we can reduce the dimensionality of dataset (Harrington, 2012).

Reinforcement Learning

In some applications, the output of the system is a sequence of actions and single action is not important. The first goal is to reach achievement. In this situation these systems learn from past action sequences which are called reinforcement learning. If we want to clarify what reinforcement learning is, we can give a good example as game playing. In playing, just a single move by itself is not that important; but it is the sequence of right moves that is good and important (Alpaydın, 2014).

Reinforcement Learning roots has based on control theory. It has a dynamic environment that results of state-action-reward triples as the data as shown in Figure 14. The strategy of learning algorithm must be determined so as to maximize expectation of reward. The most important point of reinforcement learning is to learn what to do in order to maximize a given reward, namely how we can plan situations according to actions (Camastra and Vinciarelli, 2008).

Figure 13. The principal component analysis (Adapted from Harrington, 2012)

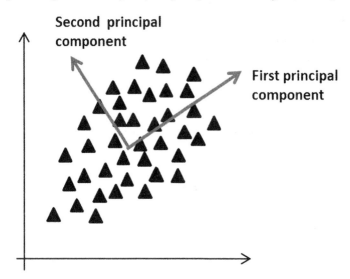

Figure 14. The summary of reinforcement learning (Adapted from Wang et al., 2012).

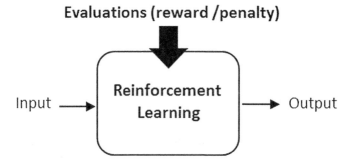

Reinforcement Learning has focused on the question of how an autonomous agent can learn to choose optimal actions to achieve with using senses and acts in its environment. According to the principle of working, trainer may give a reward or penalty to indicate the desirability of the resulting state that is true or not (Mitchell, 1997).

EARLY DETECTION OF NEUROLOGICAL DISORDERS USING MACHINE LEARNING SYSTEMS

Alzheimer Disease

Zhang, Wang & Mao (2018) have designed Alzheimer's Artificial Intelligence Technologies (AAIT) system to improve the quality lives of Alzheimer's patients. This system is consisted of lastest information technologies as Internet of Things services (IoT), big data and artificial intelligence. They have explained the solution architecture of the AAIT system and the designing and deployment of AAIT prototype system. Three categories of big data were collected, the first category of data is related to information of Alzheimer's patients, the second category of data is related to movement behaviour of patients and third category of data is consist of interactions with caregivers, control command for the IoT devices and triggering events.

Maity and Das (2017) were used Bayesian Inference to diagnose Alzheimer's disease based on historical patient data, cognitive test results and risk factors. They obtained historical patient data from the National Alzheimer's Coordinate Center, University of Washington. In the end of study approximately 80% accuracy has been obtained in the Bayesian inference model used to diagnose Alzheimer's disease.

Liu et al. (2014) have studied on early diagnosis of Alzheimer's disease and mild cognitive impairment with using deep learning because at the early stage the accurate diagnosis has important effect for on treatment. They have built a deep learning architecture with stacked auto enconders and a softmax regression on Matlab. Single and multi kernel support vector machine methods were chosen to compare their applied method.

Khedher et al. (2015) computer aided diagnosis for detection of early stages of Alzheimer's Disease. They analyzed tissue segmented brain images from Alzheimer's Disease Neuroimaging Initiative database (188 Alzheimer's disease patients, 401 Mild cognitive impairment patients and 229 Control subjects). For feature selection principal component analysis and partial least squares methods were used, for classification support vector machines with linear and radial basis function kernels were used.

Parkinson's Disease

Lahmiri, Dawson & Shmuel (2018) have compared the performance of machine learning methods to diagnosis Parkinson's Disease (PD) based on dysphonia symptoms in their study. They have studied on 195 voice records (147 PD patient, 48 healthy control) and Support Vector Machine (SVM), Linear Discriminant Analysis (LDA), Naive Bayes, Radical Basis Function Neural Network (RBFNN), Regression Trees (RT), k-Nearest Neighbours (kNN) and Mahalanobis Distance Classifier (MDC) were applied as machine learning methods. Their results have shown that SVM has the best performance compared to other machine learning classifiers.

Alhussein (2017) have studied on a Parkinson's Disease (PD) monitoring framework for using in smart cities. The speech signals from clients that is captured from various sensors were used. They have used two voice sample database from the University of California Irvine (UCI) Machine Learning Repository and Faculty of Medicine in İstanbul University. The proposed framework was based on clouds system for PD detection and its components are smart home, smart city, the cloud system, the doctors and the clients. Support Vector Machine (SVM), Extreme Learning Machine (ELM), Gaussian Mixture Model (GMM) and Random Forest tree algorithms were used. The best accuracy detection of PD was obtained with the combining ELM and SVM classifiers.

Sonu, Prakash, Ranjan & Saritha (2017) have proposed to predict Parkinson's disease from patients voice recording datasets using data mining algorithm. They have suggested that this system can bu used for early diagnosis of Parkinsons's disease and its early treatment. They have written a javascript program to analyze record voice of patients. Decision Trees, Naive Bayes, Support Vector Machines, Logistic Regression, Linear Discriminant Analysis and k-Nearest Neighbours were used in this study, but they have been more focused on decision tree algorithm. With feature selection and pruning, decision tree algorithm has give accuracy ratio 88% and 94% respectively.

Dinov et al. (2016) used model based and model free approaches for predictive analytics on Parkinson's disease data that is obtained from Parkinson's Progression Markers Initiative (PPMI). AdaBoost, Support Vector Machine (SVM), Naive Bayes, Decision Tree, k-Nearest Neighbour (kNN) and K-Means classifiers were used as model-free approaches. AdaBoost and SVM methods with high accuracy and precision have showed best performances.

Nilashi, Ibrahim & Ahani (2016) have proposed a new hbyrid intelligent system for the prediction of Parkinson's Disease (PD) using machine learning methods and they have studied on prediction techniques for PD progression. The dataset was obtained from Data Mining Repository of the University of California, Irvine (UCI) machine learning repository. Support Vector Regression (SVR) that is an extension of the support vector classifier and Adaptive Neuro-Fuzzy Inference System (ANFIS) are applied this dataset to predict of PD progression. Also, for data clustering Expectation Maximization (EM) was chosen and Principal Component Analysis (PCA) was used for dimensionality reduction and to solve multi-collinearity problem.

Schizophrenia

Madsen, Krohne, Cai, Wang & Chan (2018) have aimed to explain classification of machine learning methods on schizotypy research using Functional Magnetic Resonance Imagining data (fMRI), because these methods can be important for early diagnosis of disease process. They have described as statistical parametric mapping, seed-based analysis, complex network analysis and decomposition methods as feature extraction, also support vector classification and deep learning were focused on in their study.

Winterburn et al. (2017) have researched the accuracy of machine learning methods used in magnetic resonance images of schizophrenia patients and healthy controls classification studies They have used on three independently collected datasets that were used cortical thickness and two estimates of tissue density. These datasets are obtained from Centre for Addiction and Mental Health, Northwestern University Schizophrenia Data and Software Tool and National Institute of Neurology and Neurosurgery. The Logistic Regression, Support Vector Machines (SVM) and Linear Discriminant Analysis have been applied on three independently collected datasets. All machine learning analysis has performed R software. The best performance has gained with % 73.5 SVM on cortical thickness data.

Vyškovský, Schwarz, Janoušová & Kašpárek, (2016) have studied to make an improvement on computer-aided schizophrenia diagnosis, they have combined the classifier in ensembles. They have used random subspace enseble method and combined support vector machines and multi-layer perceptron. The magnetic resonance imaging (MRI) data of 52 schizophrenia patients and 52 healthy control subject were analyzed. They have gained that the performance accuracy of ensemble methods was not much quite a change from the accuracy of single classifier with high dimension feature vectors.

Depression

Mumtaz, Ali, Yasin & Malik (2018) have remarked accurate and early diagnosis of depression can be difficult in their study. They have aimed a machine learning framework involving electroencephalogram (EEG) based synchronization likelihood to diagnose major depressive disorder. They have used Naive Bayes, Logistic Regression and Support Vector Machine as classification methods to determine a model between EEG features and dataset (Major depressive disorder patient and health control). Classification accuracy, specificity, sensitivity and the F-measures have been calculated as classification performance metrics. The highest classification performance were provided by support vector machine as compared using other machine learning methods.

Sadeque, Xu & Bethard (2017) have presented a study that is the techniques employed for the University Arizone team's participations for early depression detection. For dataset, they used the user posts in Reddit website. They applied support vector machine and recurrent neural network these data. Also they have used ensemble methods to strengthen the best of each model. They have asserted that ensemble model is more better than individual models.

Schnyer, Clasen, Gonzalez & Beevers (2017) have applied support vector machine to magnetic resonance images of brain white matter to classify major depressive disorder patients and healthy controls. Fractional Anisotropy, Mean Diffusivity, Axial Diffusivity and Radial Diffusivity maps have been used for diffusion tensor processing. For the all brain fractional anisotropy mapping total classification accuracy has been calculated 70% with sensitivity of 68% and specificity of 80%. Total classification accuracy has been calculated 74% with sensitivity of 76% and specificity of 68%.

Stroke

Park, Chang & Nam (2017) have aimed to develop a Pronator Drift Test (PDT) tool using machine learning classifier. Signal processing and feature selection were applied to PDT features for classification of stroke patients. Also, Support Vector Machine, Random Forest and Radial Basis Function Network were performed to classify stroke patient from healthy controls. They have demonstrated that applying methods based on machine learning were classified with accuracy of 92.3% in PDT cases.

Arslan, Colak & Sarihan (2016) have studied medical data mining techniques to extract pattern from huge datasets. Different medical data mining approaches were examined for prediction of ischemic stroke patients data that is included 80 ischemic stroke patients and 112 healthy individuals. Support Vector Machines, Stochastic Gradient Boosting and Penalized Logistic Regression were used and they were compared based on some performance metrics. According to accuracy and area under the curve, support vector machine have showed the best performance for prediction. They have asserted that all the performance metrics of methods were high and could use for the classification of ischemic stroke.

Colak, Karaman & Turtay (2015) have made a study about application of knowledge discovery process on the prediction of stroke. They have performed Artificial Neural Network (ANN) and Support Vector Machine (SVM) methods for extracting pattern from dataset. The dataset is consist of 297 people that 130 of them are stroke patients and 167 of them are healthy individuals. Feature selection was applied and data was standardized before applying machine learning methods. ANN model is better than SVM for stroke diagnosis as compared to parametry of accuracy and area under the curve.

Cognitive Impairment

El-Gamal et al. (2018) have aimed to present a local based early diagnosis of Mild Cognitive Impairment (MCI). A set of PIB-PET scans that were collected from Alzheimer's Disease Neuroimaging Initiative (ADNI) database, have been used to exercise. They have discussed a personalize MCI diagnosis system. Support Vector Machine and a probabilistic version of SVM (pSVM) were used as two decision making levels. They have used linear-linear SVM based on classifier to build the computer aid diagnosis because of the best results in generally.

Khazaee, Ebrahimzadeh & Babajani-Feremi (2016) have studied to combine a graph theoretical approach with machine learning methods for mild cognitive impairment. They have exercised totaly 168 people who are Alzheimer disease (AD), mild cognitive impairment (MCI) and healthy controls, also the dataset is obtained from Alzheimer's Disease Neuroimaging Initiative (ADNI). The Support Vector Machines, k-Nearest Neighbour, Naive Bayes, Fisher Linear, Linear Discriminant, Quadratic Classifier and Decision Tree were used to classify and they compared them according to classification metrics. They have explained that the recommended method in their study that is about combining graph theory approach with machine learning had high accuracy to classify AD, MCI and healthy controls.

Seixas, Zadrozny, Laks, Conci & Saade (2014) have proposed a Bayesian network decision model to diagnose Mild Cognitive Impairment (MCI), Alzheimer's disease (AD) and Dementia. They have used Expectation maximization supervised learning algorithm on a dataset which includes patients and normal control from Duke University Medical Center and the Center for Alzheimer's Disease and Related Disorders. Five Bayesian Networks (BN) have been designed for classification in their study. They have explained that their aim is to develop a decision model for clinical diagnosis using BN. Besides, they have showed that the results of BN is better than other classification methods for diagnosing MCI, AD and dementia.

Stroke Rehabilitation

Lo and Tseng (2017) have purposed to study the relevance between power of rehabilitation and recurrence of stroke and set a model about stroke recurrence prediction using machine learning approach to help making decisions. They have performed classification methods so as C4.5 and CART Decision Trees and Logistic Regression to classify risk groups of stroke rehabilitation patients in Weka software. The C4.5 methods have been explained the best classifier for stroke recurrence between the patients with and without stroke recurrence chance.

Yang et al. (2017) have introduced IoT- enabled stroke rehabilitation system based on smart wearable armband and machine learning algorithms. The algorithm of machine learning were used to analyze and determine different hand movements. Linear discriminant analysis, Multi Layer Perceptron and Support Vector Machine algorithms were compared.

Harris et al. (2016) have proposed to explain a fall recognition system that is called mStroke, using wearable technologies and machine learning algorithms. mStroke is real time and mobile health system for stroke recovery and rehabilitation. The system design has been consisted of three wearable sensor and IOS applications. Random Forest, Linear Support Vector Machine, Logistic Regression and k-Nearest Neighbour algorithms were applied for fall recognition. Different machine learning methods applied in the study have achieved high accuracy approximately above 90%.

Stroke Management

Feng, Badgeley, Mocco & Oermann (2018) have reviewed deep learning based stroke management on clinical applications. They have explained which areas deep learning can be applied to stroke management. These areas have been sorted image segmentation, automated featurization and multi-model prognostication. They have asserted that deep learning tools could be used as customized medical process for patients with stroke.

Lee, Y. H., Kim, N., Kim & Kang (2017) have focused on artificial intelligence in stroke imagining and offered its technical principles, clinical application and future perspectives. They have explained that the analysis of stroke imagining must have been suffcient for correct store management. The development in both artificial intelligence techniques and big data can be hopeful in stroke disease were explained.

Medical Imaging and Signal Processing

De Bruijne (2016) has explained some machine learning approaches that are increasingly successful in medical imaging, diagnosis and prognosis and risk assessment. Also he has expressed three main challenges about machine learning techniques in medical imaging. They can be sorted varying imaging protocols, weak labels and interpretation and evaluation of results.

Gait Cycle Impairment

Carnevale et al. (2018) have studied on an alternative approach based on big data analytics using robotic rehabilitation devices to improve the patient's therapy. They have analyzed big data coming from sensors installed in Lokomat and proposed to find the best personalized treatment therapy. Lokomat is the most known advanced robotic technology available for gait training and neurological re-patterning. The used dataset is rehabilitation treatments performed in the period from 2012-2016 and is total 179 patients. The dataset has been analyzed with Python packages.

Shirakawa, Sugiyama, Sato, Sakurai & Sato (2017) have performed gait analysis on 113 young and healthy subjects in normal walking that are taken from National Defense Academy of Japan (NDA). They have aimed to classify walking pattern using machine learning classification techniques. The gait pattern were analyzed according to the accelerometry for pelvic movements of the subjects in normal walking. For classification, they have used cluster analysis and principal component analysis and the both of measurements were performed based on eight parameters. They have found no important difference between male and female subjects, also the correlation with age, training period, body height and body weight of subjects have not been determined for all parameter.

Mannini, Trojaniello, Cereatti & Sabatini (2016) have purposed a machine learning framework for gait classification. They have defined classification framework three steps, firstly is feature extraction using Hidden Markov Models, secondly is classification with Support Vector Machine and thirdly is majority voting classification was applied for summarizing the result of second step. Using leave-one-subject-out cross validation and majority voting the 90.5% of subjects have been classified.

Neurorehabilitation

Deng et al. (2018) have studied on comprehensive review about advances in automation technologies for lower extremity neurorehabilitation. They have examined last technological advances in wearable sensors, assistive robots and biofeedback devices. Also network technologies for the Wireless Body Area Network (WBAN) have been compared according to timing performance, reliability, scalability, privacy and security.

Lledo et al. (2015) have presented Adaptive Resonance Therapy (ART) that is based on neural networks combined with Fuzzy Logic systems, have classified user physiological reactions during rehabilitation therapied by a robot-assisted. This neuro-fuzzy method was called Supervised and Dynamic Fuzzy Adaptive System ART (S-dFasArt) by researchers. Although they have used nine machine learning algorithms, S-dFasArt approach has been obtained accuracy of 92.38 compared with other methods. The second highest accuracy 91.43% has been found out support vector machine with radial basis function kernel.

Motor Function Disorder

Crippa et al. (2015) have developed a machine learning method to determine between 15 pre-school children with Autism Spectrum Disorder (ASD) and 15 typically developing (TD) children. The machine learning method has been applied two steps, first step was feature selection and second step was classification process that separate ASD and TD children datasets from each other. For classification algorithm, support vector machine was used. The classification accuracy has been calculated 96.7%, furthermore the specificity and sensitivity have been achieved respectively 93.8% and 100%.

Stem Cells

Joutsijoki, Haponen, Rasku, Aalto-Setälä & Juhola (2016) have studied on automated identification of the quality of human Induced Pluripotent Stem Cell (iPSC) colony images. To solve the monitoring problem of iPSC colonies, they have asserted to use machine learning methods so as k-Nearest Neighbour (kNN) and Multiclass Support Vector Machines. Also they have used other classification methods as Classification Tree, Naive Bayes variant, Multinomial Logistic Regression and Linear Discriminant Analysis. Scaled Invariant Feature Transformation (SIFT) have been used for feature extraction. The best accuracy of 62.4% has been calculated by kNN method with Euclidean measure.

Shouval et al. (2014) have reviewed data mining approach in hematopoietic stem cell transplantation. They have examined some application of machine learning algorithms for clinical predictive modeling. When they prepare this study, they have aimed to increase data mining and machine learning studies in the field of stem cell transplantation. They have mentioned that better experience based on high technologies could improve patient and donor selection, advance transplantation outcome and decrease transplant-related mortality.

Drug Delivery

Bernick (2015) have studied about the role of machine learning in drug design and delivery system. Some machine learning applications in drug design and delivery have been discussed in the study. Especially, it have been explained that machine learning has several advantages in drug design. Furthermore, it have been highlighted, the importance of machine learning algorithms used in the design and optimization of the preformulation and formulation drug delivery system.

Li, Lenaghan & Zhang (2012) have developed a framework that is data driven predictive system for drug delivery using machine learning methods. This framework have been modelled in reference to the drug-pathogen dynamics. Fuzzy C-Mean clustering algorithm has been used to categorize the drug-pathogen interactions into a discrete set. They have explained that the framework could predict drug-pathogen dynamics according to observations, furthermore experimental training data has been used to determine efficiency on drug delivery method.

Epilepsy

Shen et al. (2013) have studied on the classification of Electroencephalography (EEG) signals for the diagnosis epilepsy. They have explained an EEG analysis systems of seizure detection which is based on cascade wavelet-approximate entropy for feature selection. Support Vector Machines (SVMs), k-Nearest Neighbour (kNN) and Radial Basis Function Neural Network (RBFNN) were used for classification and the results of classification methods were compared. For open source data, the overall accuracy has been achieved 99.97%. In addition, the performance of the system has been tested on clinical EEG data.

Siuly, Li & Wen (2011) have introduced feature extraction by sampling techniques from Electroencephalogram (EEG) signals. The EEG recording of healthy volunteers and the EEG record of epileptic patients during epileptic seizure activity were used for dataset in this study. Least Square Support Vector Machine (LS-SVM) toolbox was applied for classification of the EEG signals in Matlab. LS-SVM classifier has been achieved the accuracy of 80.31% for training data, while the accuracy of 80.05% for the testing data.

Autism

Heinsfeld, Franco, Craddock, Buchweitz & Meneguzzi (2018) have presented to apply deep learning algorithms for identification of autism disorder spectrum. The large brain imaging dataset has been obtained from multi-site database known as ABIDE (Autism Brain İmaging Data Exchange). In addition, Deep Learning, Support Vector Machine and Random Forest classifiers were used and all of the classifiers were compared with the results of accuracy, sensitivity and specificity.

Alhaddad et al. (2012) have studied on diagnosis of autism by Fisher Linear Discriminant Analysis (FLDA) based on autistic children Electroencephalogram (EEG) signal. They have used different preprocessing techniques, different ensemble averages and different feature extraction techniques. The average accuracy rate was calculated 90%.

Bosl, Tierney, Tager-Flusberg & Nelson (2011) have focused on showing Electroencephalogram (EEG) data can be used a biomarker for brain development using Modified Multiscale Entropy (mMSE). Multiclass Support Vector Machine was used for classification of control and High-Rish Autism (HRA). In addition, the classification by gender and age k-Nearest Neighbour, Support Vector Machine and Naive Bayes methods were used and compared. Infants were classified with over 80% accuracy into control and HRA groups at age 9 months with mMSE feature vector.

FUTURE RESEARCH DIRECTIONS

To be more useful for Alzheimer's patients, the Alzheimer's Artificial Intelligence Technologies (AAIT) system can be improved and applied to embedded system as wearable device for future (Zhang et al., 2018).

The division of patients according to pathologies will be analyzed for the improvement of customization therapy. Analytical models will be applied such as deep artificial neural networks for making statistical big data analysis (Carnevale et al., 2018).

Nilashi et al. (2018) have best result support vector regression (SVR)method on Parkinson's disease For reducing the computation time, they have plan to use incremental SVR. Furthermore, they have aimed to develop methods for incremental learning and apply them on big data sets.

Wang et al. (2018) have mentioned that future scientific studies should focused on efficient unstructured data analytical algorithms and major technological progression.

Crippa et al (2015) have explained that they will have work on neurodevelopmental conditions to verify autism spectrum disorder for their next research.

Any development in big data processing for bioinformatics, health informatics imaging and sensing will have show big effect on next clinical research (Perez et al., 2015).

Sexias et al. (2014) have expressed that they propose to revise Bayesian Network on more complete patients dataset comprising neuropsychological test in their future work.

Li et al. (2012) will have use Markov Decision Process on their machine learning framework to separate the dose into discrete actions based on pathogen population and it's effect. This system can be planned for determination of dosage.

CONCLUSION

In this chapter, big data analytics and machine learning systems have been introduced to explain for the early diagnosis of neurological disorders. A number of scholarly researches on big data about intelligent big data analytics in healthcare and machine learning system were used in healthcare system have been mentioned.

This work provides an opinion of how medical big data can be used by intelligent big data analytics and machine learning methods in neurological disorder diagnosis. The main aim behind this study is to assist the researchers or experts to provide an idea and understanding about intelligent big data analytics and machine learning methods in the diagnosis of neurological disorders.

In this survey, the researches about neurological disorder as Alzheimer's Disease, Parkinson's Disease, Schizophrenia, Depression, Stroke, Cognitive Impairment, Stroke Rehabilitation, Stroke Management, Medical Imaging and Signal Processing, Gait Cycle Impairment, Neurorehabilitation, Motor Function Disorder, Stem Cells, Drug Delivery, Epilepsy and Autism were summarized.

The intelligent big data analytics for healthcare system is in the early stage of development, similarly machine learning. Therefore, some challenges and problems can occurred in application areas. Any improvement of machine learning algorithms and big data analytics can be much better for good classification or diagnosis of disorders.

REFERENCES

Akın, M. (2012). *Kanserli hücrelerin mikroarray gen ifadelerinin incelenmesi ve veri madenciliği yöntemleri kullanarak sınıflandırılması*. Gazi Üniversitesi, Fen Bilimleri Enstitüsü, Yüksek Lisans Tezi,Temmuz.

Aktan, E. (2018). Büyük Veri: Uygulama Alanları, Analitiği ve Güvenlik Boyutu. *Bilgi Yönetimi*, *1*(1), 1–22.

Al-Jarrah, O. Y., Yoo, P. D., Muhaidat, S., Karagiannidis, G. K., & Taha, K. (2015). Efficient machine learning for big data: A review. *Big Data Research*, *2*(3), 87–93. doi:10.1016/j.bdr.2015.04.001

Alhaddad, M. J., Kamel, M. I., Malibary, H. M., Alsaggaf, E. A., Thabit, K., Dahlwi, F., & Hadi, A. A. (2012). Diagnosis autism by fisher linear discriminant analysis FLDA via EEG. *International Journal of Bio-Science and Bio-Technology*, *4*(2), 45–54.

Alhussein, M. (2017). Monitoring Parkinson's Disease in Smart Cities. *IEEE Access: Practical Innovations, Open Solutions*, *5*, 19835–19841. doi:10.1109/ACCESS.2017.2748561

Alpaydın, E. (2013). *Yapay öğrenme, 2*. Baskı, Boğaziçi Üniversitesi Yayınevi.

Alpaydın, E. (2014). *Introduction to Machine Learning*. MIT Press.

Altındal, T. (2006). *Machine Learning Algorithms in Classification and Diagnostic Prediction of Cancers using Gene Expression Profilling* (Master Dissertation). Ulusal Tez Merkezi. (No. 181232)

Angra, S., & Ahuja, S. (2017, March). Machine learning and its applications: a review. In *Big Data Analytics and Computational Intelligence (ICBDAC), 2017 International Conference on* (pp. 57-60). IEEE. 10.1109/ICBDACI.2017.8070809

Apache Hive. (n.d.). Retrieved December 23, 2018, from https://hive.apache.org/

Apache Pig. (n.d.). Retrieved December 23, 2018, from https://pig.apache.org/

Arslan, A. K., Colak, C., & Sarihan, M. E. (2016). Different medical data mining approaches based prediction of ischemic stroke. *Computer Methods and Programs in Biomedicine*, *130*, 87–92. doi:10.1016/j.cmpb.2016.03.022 PMID:27208524

Atalay, M., & Çelik, Ö. G. E. (2017). Artificial Intelligence and Machine Learning Applications in Big Data Analysis. *Mehmet Akif Ersoy University Journal of Social Sciences Institute*, *9*(22), 155–172.

Athmaja, S., Hanumanthappa, M., & Kavitha, V. (2017, March). A survey of machine learning algorithms for big data analytics. In *Innovations in Information, Embedded and Communication Systems (ICIIECS), 2017 International Conference on* (pp. 1-4). IEEE. 10.1109/ICIIECS.2017.8276028

Balasupramanian, N., Ephrem, B. G., & Al-Barwani, I. S. (2017, July). User pattern based online fraud detection and prevention using big data analytics and self organizing maps. In *Intelligent Computing, Instrumentation and Control Technologies (ICICICT), 2017 International Conference on* (pp. 691-694). IEEE. 10.1109/ICICICT1.2017.8342647

Bazazeh, D., & Shubair, R. (2016, December). Comparative study of machine learning algorithms for breast cancer detection and diagnosis. In *Electronic Devices, Systems and Applications (ICEDSA), 2016 5th International Conference on* (pp. 1-4). IEEE. 10.1109/ICEDSA.2016.7818560

Bernick, J. P. (2015). The Role of Machine Learning in Drug Design and Delivery. *Journal of Develop Drugs*, *4*(03), E143. doi:10.4172/2329-6631.1000e143

Berral García, J. L. (2016). A quick view on current techniques and machine learning algorithms for big data analytics. In *Proceedings of the 18th International Conference on Transparent Optical Networks (ICTON)* (pp. 1-4). Institute of Electrical and Electronics Engineers (IEEE). 10.1109/ICTON.2016.7550517

Bircan, H. (2004). Lojistik regresyon analizi: Tıp verileri üzerine bir uygulama. *Kocaeli Üniversitesi Sosyal Bilimler Enstitüsü Dergisi*, (8), 185-208.

Bishop, C. M. (2006). Pattern recognition and machine learning (information science and statistics). Academic Press.

Bosl, W., Tierney, A., Tager-Flusberg, H., & Nelson, C. (2011). EEG complexity as a biomarker for autism spectrum disorder risk. *BMC Medicine*, *9*(1), 18. doi:10.1186/1741-7015-9-18 PMID:21342500

Breiman, L. (2001). Random forests. *Machine Learning*, *45*(1), 5–32. doi:10.1023/A:1010933404324

Burakgazi, Y. (2017). *Identification of Breast Cancer Sub-types by Using Machine Learning Techniques* (Master Dissertation). Ulusal Tez Merkezi. (No. 459190)

Camastra, F., & Vinciarelli, A. (2008). *Machine Learning for Audio, Image and Video Analysis*. London: Springer. doi:10.1007/978-1-84800-007-0

Carnevale, L., Calabrò, R. S., Celesti, A., Leo, A., Fazio, M., Bramanti, P., & Villari, M. (2018). *Towards Improving Robotic-Assisted Gait Training: Can Big Data Analysis Help us? IEEE Internet of Things Journal*.

Carnevale, L., Calabrò, R. S., Celesti, A., Leo, A., Fazio, M., Bramanti, P., & Villari, M. (2018). *Towards Improving Robotic-Assisted Gait Training: Can Big Data Analysis Help us? IEEE Internet of Things Journal*.

Colak, C., Karaman, E., & Turtay, M. G. (2015). Application of knowledge discovery process on the prediction of stroke. *Computer Methods and Programs in Biomedicine*, *119*(3), 181–185. doi:10.1016/j.cmpb.2015.03.002 PMID:25827533

Crippa, A., Salvatore, C., Perego, P., Forti, S., Nobile, M., Molteni, M., & Castiglioni, I. (2015). Use of machine learning to identify children with autism and their motor abnormalities. *Journal of Autism and Developmental Disorders*, *45*(7), 2146–2156. doi:10.100710803-015-2379-8 PMID:25652603

De Bruijne, M. (2016). *Machine learning approaches in medical image analysis: From detection to diagnosis*. Academic Press.

De Mauro, A., Greco, M., & Grimaldi, M. (2015, February). What is big data? A consensual definition and a review of key research topics. In AIP conference proceedings: Vol. 1644. *No. 1* (pp. 97–104). AIP. doi:10.1063/1.4907823

Deng, W., Papavasileiou, I., Qiao, Z., Zhang, W., Lam, K. Y., & Song, H. (2018). Advances in Automation Technologies for Lower-extremity Neurorehabilitation: A Review and Future Challenges. *IEEE Reviews in Biomedical Engineering*, *11*, 289–305. doi:10.1109/RBME.2018.2830805 PMID:29994006

Dinov, I. D., Heavner, B., Tang, M., Glusman, G., Chard, K., Darcy, M., ... Foster, I. (2016). Predictive big data analytics: A study of Parkinson's disease using large, complex, heterogeneous, incongruent, multi-source and incomplete observations. *PLoS One*, *11*(8), e0157077. doi:10.1371/journal.pone.0157077 PMID:27494614

Diri, B. (n.d.). *Makine Öğrenmesine Giriş*. Retrieved from Lecture Notes Online Web site: https://www.ce.yildiz.edu.tr/personal/banud/file/2634/Makine+Ogrenmesi-ML-10.pdf

Domo. (n.d.). *Data Never Sleeps 6.0*. Retrieved January 1, 2019, from https://www.domo.com/learn/data-never-sleeps-6

El-Gamal, F. E., Elmogy, M. M., Ghazal, M., Atwan, A., Casanova, M. F., Barnes, G. N., ... Khalil, A. (2018). A Novel Early Diagnosis System for Mild Cognitive Impairment Based on Local Region Analysis: A Pilot Study. *Frontiers in Human Neuroscience*, *11*, 643. doi:10.3389/fnhum.2017.00643 PMID:29375343

Feng, R., Badgeley, M., Mocco, J., & Oermann, E. K. (2018). Deep learning guided stroke management: A review of clinical applications. *Journal of Neurointerventional Surgery*, *10*(4), 358–362. doi:10.1136/neurintsurg-2017-013355 PMID:28954825

Gandomi, A., & Haider, M. (2015). Beyond the hype: Big data concepts, methods, and analytics. *International Journal of Information Management*, *35*(2), 137–144. doi:10.1016/j.ijinfomgt.2014.10.007

Gartner I. T. Glossary. (n.d.) *Big data*. Retrieved December 12, 2018, from https://www.gartner.com/it-glossary/big-data

Groves, P., Kayyali, B., Knott, D., & Van Kuiken, S. (2013). The 'big data'revolution in healthcare. *The McKinsey Quarterly*, *2*(3).

Han, J., & Kamber, M. (2001). *Data Mining Concepts and Techniques* (2nd ed.). Morgan Kauffmann Publishers Inc.

Harerimana, G., Jang, B., Kim, J. W., & Park, H. K. (2018). Health Big Data Analytics: A Technology Survey. *IEEE Access: Practical Innovations, Open Solutions*, *6*, 65661–65678. doi:10.1109/ACCESS.2018.2878254

Harrington, P. (2012). *Machine learning in Action* (Vol. 5). Greenwich, CT: Manning.

Harris, A., True, H., Hu, Z., Cho, J., Fell, N., & Sartipi, M. (2016, December). Fall recognition using wearable technologies and machine learning algorithms. In *Big Data (Big Data), 2016 IEEE International Conference on* (pp. 3974-3976). IEEE. 10.1109/BigData.2016.7841080

Heinsfeld, A. S., Franco, A. R., Craddock, R. C., Buchweitz, A., & Meneguzzi, F. (2018). Identification of autism spectrum disorder using deep learning and the ABIDE dataset. *NeuroImage. Clinical*, *17*, 16–23. doi:10.1016/j.nicl.2017.08.017 PMID:29034163

IBM. (n.d.a). *What is big data? Bringing big data to the enterprise*. Retrieved May 5, 2018, from http://www-01.ibm.com/software/data/bigdata/

IBM. (n.d.b). *What is MapReduce?* Retrieved December 22, 2018, from https://www.ibm.com/analytics/hadoop/mapreduce

Janssen, P., Walther, C., & Lüdeke, M. (2012). *Cluster analysis to understand socio-ecological systems: a guideline*. Potsdam-Institut für Klimafolgenforschung.

Jordan, M. I., & Mitchell, T. M. (2015). Machine learning: Trends, perspectives, and prospects. *Science*, *349*(6245), 255–260. doi:10.1126cience.aaa8415 PMID:26185243

Joutsijoki, H., Haponen, M., Rasku, J., Aalto-Setälä, K., & Juhola, M. (2016). Machine learning approach to automated quality identification of human induced pluripotent stem cell colony images. *Computational and Mathematical Methods in Medicine*, *2016*, 1–15. doi:10.1155/2016/3091039 PMID:27493680

Kartal, E. (2015). *Sınıflandırmaya Dayalı Makine Öğrenmesi Teknikleri ve Kardiyolojik Risk Değerlendirmesine İlişkin Bir Uygulama* (Doctoral Dissertation). Ulusal Tez Merkezi. (No.394514)

Khazaee, A., Ebrahimzadeh, A., & Babajani-Feremi, A. (2016). Application of advanced machine learning methods on resting-state fMRI network for identification of mild cognitive impairment and Alzheimer's disease. *Brain Imaging and Behavior*, *10*(3), 799–817. doi:10.100711682-015-9448-7 PMID:26363784

Khedher, L., Ramírez, J., Górriz, J. M., Brahim, A., & Segovia, F. (2015). Early diagnosis of Alzheimer's disease based on partial least squares, principal component analysis and support vector machine using segmented MRI images. *Neurocomputing*, *151*, 139–150. doi:10.1016/j.neucom.2014.09.072

Kızrak, A. (n.d.). *Yapay Sinir Ağı Nedir?* Retrieved January 9, 2018, from https://medium.com/deep-learn-ing-turkiye/%C5%9Fu-kara-kutuyu-a%C3%A7alim-yapay-sinir-a%C4%9Flar%C4%B1-7b65c6a5264a

Kohonen, T. (1990). The self-organizing map. *Proceedings of the IEEE*, *78*(9), 1464–1480. doi:10.1109/5.58325

Kohonen, T. (2013). Essentials of the self-organizing map. *Neural Networks*, *37*, 52–65. doi:10.1016/j.neunet.2012.09.018 PMID:23067803

Kumar, S., & Singh, M. (2019). Big data analytics for healthcare industry: Impact, applications, and tools. *Big Data Mining and Analytics*, *2*(1), 48–57. doi:10.26599/BDMA.2018.9020031

Lahmiri, S., Dawson, D. A., & Shmuel, A. (2018). Performance of machine learning methods in diagnosing Parkinson's disease based on dysphonia measures. *Biomedical Engineering Letters*, *8*(1), 29–39. doi:10.100713534-017-0051-2 PMID:30603188

LeCun, Y., Bengio, Y., & Hinton, G. (2015). Deep Learning. *Nature*, *521*(7553), 436–444. doi:10.1038/nature14539 PMID:26017442

Lee, E. J., Kim, Y. H., Kim, N., & Kang, D. W. (2017). Deep into the brain: Artificial intelligence in stroke imaging. *Journal of Stroke*, *19*(3), 277–285. doi:10.5853/jos.2017.02054 PMID:29037014

Li, Y., Lenaghan, S. C., & Zhang, M. (2012). A data-driven predictive approach for drug delivery using machine learning techniques. *PLoS One*, *7*(2), e31724. doi:10.1371/journal.pone.0031724 PMID:22384063

Liu, S., Liu, S., Cai, W., Pujol, S., Kikinis, R., & Feng, D. (2014, April). Early diagnosis of Alzheimer's disease with deep learning. In *Biomedical Imaging (ISBI), 2014 IEEE 11th International Symposium on* (pp. 1015-1018). IEEE. 10.1109/ISBI.2014.6868045

Lledó, L. D., Badesa, F. J., Almonacid, M., Cano-Izquierdo, J. M., Sabater-Navarro, J. M., Fernández, E., & Garcia-Aracil, N. (2015). Supervised and dynamic neuro-fuzzy systems to classify physiological responses in robot-assisted neurorehabilitation. *PLoS One*, *10*(5), e0127777. doi:10.1371/journal.pone.0127777 PMID:26001214

Lo, C. L., & Tseng, H. T. (2017). Predicting rehabilitation treatment helpfulness to stroke patients: A supervised learning approach. *Artificial Intelligence Review*, 6(2), 1. doi:10.5430/air.v6n2p1

Madsen, K. H., Krohne, L. G., Cai, X. L., Wang, Y., & Chan, R. C. (2018). Perspectives on Machine Learning for Classification of Schizotypy Using fMRI Data. *Schizophrenia Bulletin*, 44(suppl_2), S480–S490. doi:10.1093chbulby026 PMID:29554367

Maity, N. G., & Das, S. (2017, March). Machine learning for improved diagnosis and prognosis in healthcare. In *Aerospace Conference, 2017 IEEE* (pp. 1-9). IEEE. 10.1109/AERO.2017.7943950

Mannini, A., Trojaniello, D., Cereatti, A., & Sabatini, A. M. (2016). A machine learning framework for gait classification using inertial sensors: Application to elderly, post-stroke and huntington's disease patients. *Sensors (Basel)*, 16(1), 134. doi:10.339016010134 PMID:26805847

Mathworks. (n.d.). *What is Machine Learning?* Retrieved May 6, 2018, from https://www.mathworks.com/discovery/machine-learning.html

Mitchell, T. M. (1997). Machine learning. Burr Ridge, IL: McGraw Hill.

Mitchell, T. M. (2006). *The discipline of machine learning* (Vol. 9). Pittsburgh, PA: Carnegie Mellon University, School of Computer Science, Machine Learning Department.

Mumtaz, W., Ali, S. S. A., Yasin, M. A. M., & Malik, A. S. (2018). A machine learning framework involving EEG-based functional connectivity to diagnose major depressive disorder (MDD). *Medical & Biological Engineering & Computing*, 56(2), 233–246. doi:10.100711517-017-1685-z PMID:28702811

Nilashi, M., Ibrahim, O., & Ahani, A. (2016). Accuracy improvement for predicting Parkinson's disease progression. *Scientific Reports*, 6(1), 34181. doi:10.1038rep34181 PMID:27686748

O'Leary, D. E. (2013). Artificial intelligence and big data. *IEEE Intelligent Systems*, 28(2), 96–99. doi:10.1109/MIS.2013.39 PMID:25505373

Oussous, A., Benjelloun, F. Z., Lahcen, A. A., & Belfkih, S. (2018). Big Data technologies: A survey. *Journal of King Saud University-Computer and Information Sciences*, 30(4), 431–448. doi:10.1016/j.jksuci.2017.06.001

Özköse, H., Arı, E. S., & Gencer, C. (2015). Yesterday, today and tomorrow of big data. *Procedia: Social and Behavioral Sciences*, 195, 1042–1050. doi:10.1016/j.sbspro.2015.06.147

Park, E., Chang, H. J., & Nam, H. S. (2017). Use of Machine Learning Classifiers and Sensor Data to Detect Neurological Deficit in Stroke Patients. *Journal of Medical Internet Research*, 19(4), e120. doi:10.2196/jmir.7092 PMID:28420599

Patel, J. A., & Sharma, P. (2014, August). Big data for better health planning. In *2014 International Conference on Advances in Engineering and Technology Research (ICAETR)* (pp. 1-5). Unnao: IEEE.

Piech, C. (n.d.). *K-Means*. Retrieved from Lecture Notes from Web site http://stanford.edu/~cpiech/cs221/handouts/kmeans.html

Praveena, M. A., & Bharathi, B. (2017, February). A survey paper on big data analytics. In *Information Communication and Embedded Systems (ICICES), 2017 International Conference on* (pp. 1-9). IEEE. 10.1109/ICICES.2017.8070723

Qiu, J., Wu, Q., Ding, G., Xu, Y., & Feng, S. (2016). A survey of machine learning for big data processing. *EURASIP Journal on Advances in Signal Processing, 2016*(1), 67. doi:10.118613634-016-0355-x

Raghupathi, W., & Raghupathi, V. (2014). Big data analytics in healthcare: promise and potential. *Health Information Science and Systems, 2*(1), 3.

Rokach, L., & Maimon, O. (2005). Clustering methods. In *Data mining and knowledge discovery handbook* (pp. 321–352). Boston, MA: Springer. doi:10.1007/0-387-25465-X_15

Ruan, Y., Xue, X., Liu, H., Tan, J., & Li, X. (2017). Quantum algorithm for k-nearest neighbors classification based on the metric of hamming distance. *International Journal of Theoretical Physics, 56*(11), 3496–3507. doi:10.100710773-017-3514-4

Russom, P. (2011). Big data analytics. *TDWI Best Practices Report, 19*(4), 1-34.

Sadeque, F., Xu, D., & Bethard, S. (2017, September). Uarizona at the CLEF erisk 2017 pilot task: Linear and recurrent models for early depression detection. In *CEUR workshop proceedings* (Vol. 1866). NIH Public Access.

Sağıroğlu, Ş. (2017). *Büyük Veri ve Açık Veri Analitiği: Yöntemler ve Uygulamalar* (Ş. Sağıroğlu & O. Koç, Eds.). Ankara: Grafiker Yayınları.

Sagiroglu, Ş., & Sinanc, D. (2013, May). Big data: A review. In *Collaboration Technologies and Systems (CTS), 2013 International Conference on* (pp. 42-47). Academic Press. 10.1109/CTS.2013.6567202

Sahu, S. K., Jacintha, M. M., & Singh, A. P. (2017, May). Comparative study of tools for big data analytics: An analytical study. In *Computing, Communication and Automation (ICCCA), 2017 International Conference on* (pp. 37-41). IEEE.

Saritha, K., & Abraham, S. (2017, July). Prediction with partitioning: Big data analytics using regression techniques. In *Networks & Advances in Computational Technologies (NetACT), 2017 International Conference on* (pp. 208-214). IEEE.

Saxena, A., Prasad, M., Gupta, A., Bharill, N., Patel, O. P., Tiwari, A., ... Lin, C. T. (2017). A review of clustering techniques and developments. *Neurocomputing, 267*, 664–681. doi:10.1016/j.neucom.2017.06.053

Sayad, S. (n.d.a). *Logistic Regression*. Retrieved May 9, 2018, from, http://www.saedsayad.com/logistic_regression.htm

Sayad, S. (n.d.b). *Self Organizing Map*. Retrieved May 7, 2018, from, http://www.saedsayad.com/clustering_som.htm

Schnyer, D. M., Clasen, P. C., Gonzalez, C., & Beevers, C. G. (2017). Evaluating the diagnostic utility of applying a machine learning algorithm to diffusion tensor MRI measures in individuals with major depressive disorder. *Psychiatry Research: Neuroimaging, 264*, 1–9. doi:10.1016/j.pscychresns.2017.03.003 PMID:28388468

Seixas, F. L., Zadrozny, B., Laks, J., Conci, A., & Saade, D. C. M. (2014). A Bayesian network decision model for supporting the diagnosis of dementia, Alzheimer's disease and mild cognitive impairment. *Computers in Biology and Medicine, 51*, 140–158. doi:10.1016/j.compbiomed.2014.04.010 PMID:24946259

Shen, C. P., Chen, C. C., Hsieh, S. L., Chen, W. H., Chen, J. M., Chen, C. M., ... Chiu, M. J. (2013). High-performance seizure detection system using a wavelet-approximate entropy-fSVM cascade with clinical validation. *Clinical EEG and Neuroscience, 44*(4), 247–256. doi:10.1177/1550059413483451 PMID:23610456

Shirakawa, T., Sugiyama, N., Sato, H., Sakurai, K., & Sato, E. (2017). Gait analysis and machine learning classification on healthy subjects in normal walking. *International Journal of Parallel Emergent and Distributed Systems, 32*(2), 185–194. doi:10.1080/17445760.2015.1044007

Shorten, C. (2018). *Machine Learning vs. Deep Learning.* Retrieved July 20, 2018, from https://towardsdatascience.com/machine-learning-vs-deep-learning-62137a1c9842

Shouval, R., Bondi, O., Mishan, H., Shimoni, A., Unger, R., & Nagler, A. (2014). Application of machine learning algorithms for clinical predictive modeling: A data-mining approach in SCT. *Bone Marrow Transplantation, 49*(3), 332–337. doi:10.1038/bmt.2013.146 PMID:24096823

Singh, D., & Reddy, C. K. (2015). A survey on platforms for big data analytics. *Journal of Big Data, 2*(1), 8.

Siuly, L., Li, Y., & Wen, P. (2011). EEG signal classification based on simple random sampling technique with least square support vector machine. *International Journal of Biomedical Engineering and Technology, 7*(4), 390–409. doi:10.1504/IJBET.2011.044417

Siuly, S., & Zhang, Y. (2016). Medical big data: Neurological diseases diagnosis through medical data analysis. *Data Science and Engineering, 1*(2), 54–64. doi:10.100741019-016-0011-3

Sonu, S. R., Prakash, V., Ranjan, R., & Saritha, K. (2017, August). Prediction of Parkinson's disease using data mining. In *2017 International Conference on Energy, Communication, Data Analytics and Soft Computing (ICECDS)* (pp. 1082-1085). IEEE. 10.1109/ICECDS.2017.8389605

Sun, J., & Reddy, C. K. (2013, August). Big data analytics for healthcare. In *Proceedings of the 19th ACM SIGKDD international conference on Knowledge discovery and data mining* (pp. 1525-1525). ACM.

Sun, Z. (2017). *Big Data Analytics and Artificial Intelligence.* UNITECH Research Committee Seminar, No. 7, PNG University of Technology.

Sun, Z., Sun, L., & Strang, K. (2018). Big data analytics services for enhancing business intelligence. *Journal of Computer Information Systems, 58*(2), 162–169. doi:10.1080/08874417.2016.1220239

Ta, V. D., Liu, C. M., & Nkabinde, G. W. (2016, July). Big data stream computing in healthcare real-time analytics. In *Cloud Computing and Big Data Analysis (ICCCBDA), 2016 IEEE International Conference on* (pp. 37-42). IEEE.

Umadevi, S., & Marseline, K. J. (2017, July). A survey on data mining classification algorithms. In *Signal Processing and Communication (ICSPC), 2017 International Conference on* (pp. 264-268). IEEE. 10.1109/CSPC.2017.8305851

Uzun, E. (2016). *Supervised ve Unsupervised Learning*. Retrieved January 01, 2018, from, https://www.e-adys.com/makine_ogrenmesi/hangisini-secmeliyim-supervised-ve-unsupervised-learning/

Verma, J. P., Agrawal, S., Patel, B., & Patel, A. (2016). Big data analytics: Challenges and applications for text, audio, video, and social media data. *International Journal on Soft Computing, Artificial Intelligence and Applications, 5*(1).

Vyškovský, R., Schwarz, D., Janoušová, E., & Kašpárek, T. (2016). Random subspace ensemble artificial neural networks for first-episode Schizophrenia classification. In *Computer Science and Information Systems (FedCSIS), 2016 Federated Conference on* (pp. 317-321). IEEE.

Wang, S., Chaovalitwongse, W., & Babuska, R. (2012). Machine learning algorithms in bipedal robot control. *IEEE Transactions on Systems, Man and Cybernetics. Part C, Applications and Reviews, 42*(5), 728–743. doi:10.1109/TSMCC.2012.2186565

Wang, Y., Kung, L., & Byrd, T. A. (2018). Big data analytics: Understanding its capabilities and potential benefits for healthcare organizations. *Technological Forecasting and Social Change, 126*, 3–13. doi:10.1016/j.techfore.2015.12.019

Ward, J. S., & Barker, A. (2013). *Undefined by data: a survey of big data definitions*. arXiv preprint arXiv:1309.5821

Winterburn, J. L., Voineskos, A. N., Devenyi, G. A., Plitman, E., de la Fuente-Sandoval, C., Bhagwat, N., ... Chakravarty, M. M. (2017). Can we accurately classify schizophrenia patients from healthy controls using magnetic resonance imaging and machine learning? A multi-method and multi-dataset study. *Schizophrenia Research*. doi:10.1016/j.schres.2017.11.038 PMID:29274736

Wu, X., Zhu, X., Wu, G. Q., & Ding, W. (2014). Data mining with big data. *IEEE Transactions on Knowledge and Data Engineering, 26*(1), 97–107. doi:10.1109/TKDE.2013.109

Xu, K., Yue, H., Guo, L., Guo, Y., & Fang, Y. (2015, June). Privacy-preserving machine learning algorithms for big data systems. In *Distributed Computing Systems (ICDCS), 2015 IEEE 35th International Conference on* (pp. 318-327). IEEE. 10.1109/ICDCS.2015.40

Yahyaouı, A. (2017). *Göğüs Hastalıklarının Teşhis Edilmesinde Makine Öğrenmesi Algoritmalarının Kullanılması* (Doctoral Dissertation). Ulusal Tez Merkezi. (No. 462917)

Yang, G., Deng, J., Pang, G., Zhang, H., Li, J., Deng, B., ... Xie, H. (2018). An IoT-Enabled Stroke Rehabilitation System Based on Smart Wearable Armband and Machine Learning. *IEEE Journal of Translational Engineering in Health and Medicine, 6*, 1–10. doi:10.1109/JTEHM.2018.2879085 PMID:29805919

Yoo, C., Ramirez, L., & Liuzzi, J. (2014). Big data analysis using modern statistical and machine learning methods in medicine. *International Neurourology Journal, 18*(2), 50. doi:10.5213/inj.2014.18.2.50 PMID:24987556

Zhang, A., Wang, K. J., & Mao, Z. H. (2018, August). Design and Realization of Alzheimer. In *2018 IEEE 6th International Conference on Future Internet of Things and Cloud (FiCloud)* (pp. 141-148). IEEE.

Zhou, L., Pan, S., Wang, J., & Vasilakos, A. V. (2017). Machine learning on big data: Opportunities and challenges. *Neurocomputing*, *237*, 350–361. doi:10.1016/j.neucom.2017.01.026

ADDITIONAL READING

Andreu-Perez, J., Poon, C. C., Merrifield, R. D., Wong, S. T., & Yang, G. Z. (2015). Big data for health. *IEEE Journal of Biomedical and Health Informatics*, *19*(4), 1193–1208. doi:10.1109/JBHI.2015.2450362 PMID:26173222

Belle, A., Thiagarajan, R., Soroushmehr, S. M., Navidi, F., Beard, D. A., & Najarian, K. (2015). Big data analytics in healthcare. *BioMed Research International*. PMID:26229957

Bhardwaj, R., Nambiar, A. R., & Dutta, D. (2017, July). A Study of Machine Learning in Healthcare. In *Computer Software and Applications Conference (COMPSAC), 2017 IEEE 41st Annual* (Vol. 2, pp. 236-241). IEEE. 10.1109/COMPSAC.2017.164

Bzdok, D., & Yeo, B. T. (2017). Inference in the age of big data: Future perspectives on neuroscience. *NeuroImage*, *155*, 549–564. doi:10.1016/j.neuroimage.2017.04.061 PMID:28456584

Chen, H., Chiang, R. H., & Storey, V. C. (2012). Business intelligence and analytics: From big data to big impact. *Management Information Systems Quarterly*, *36*(4), 1165–1188. doi:10.2307/41703503

Chen, M., Mao, S., Zhang, Y., & Leung, V. C. (2014). Big data: related technologies, challenges and future prospects. Springer Briefs in Computer Science, Springer, 2014. doi:10.1007/978-3-319-06245-7

Jatrniko, W., Arsa, D. M. S., Wisesa, H., Jati, G., & Ma'sum, M. A. (2016, October). A review of big data analytics in the biomedical field. In *Big Data and Information Security (IWBIS), International Workshop on* (pp. 31-41). IEEE.

Manyika, J., Chui, M., Brown, B., Bughin, J., Dobbs, R., Roxburgh, C., & Byers, A. H. (2011). *Big data: The next frontier for innovation, competition, and productivity*. McKinsey Global Institue. Retrieved from https://www.mckinsey.com/business-functions/digital-mckinsey/our-insights/big-data-the-next-frontier-for-innovation

Rahman, F., Slepian, M., & Mitra, A. (2016, December). A novel big-data processing framework for healthcare applications: Big-data-healthcare-in-a-box. In *Big Data (Big Data), 2016 IEEE International Conference on* (pp. 3548-3555). IEEE.

Ramesh, D., Suraj, P., & Saini, L. (2016, January). Big data analytics in healthcare: A survey approach. In *Microelectronics, Computing and Communications (MicroCom), 2016 International Conference on* (pp. 1-6). IEEE. 10.1109/MicroCom.2016.7522520

Reddy, A. R., & Kumar, P. S. (2016, February). Predictive big data analytics in healthcare. In *Computational Intelligence & Communication Technology (CICT), 2016 Second International Conference on* (pp. 623-626). IEEE. 10.1109/CICT.2016.129

KEY TERMS AND DEFINITIONS

Alzheimer's Disease Neuroimaging Initiative (ADNI): Provides database to researchers about the patient of Alzheimer's disease. The biomarkers are collected and analyzed for early diagnose and following the progression of Alzheimer's.

Big Data: Can be described large volume of data that are structural, semi-structural, and non-structural, and it provides valuable information for lots of research areas. It is often characterized by the 3V (volume, variety, and velocity), but it has continued to grow up with other characteristic components.

Big Data Analytics: Can be defined basically using analytics techniques on big data to explore worthful information. The analyzing of big data is pretty important for both prediction of future and decision making in all working areas.

Big Data Samples: Can be counted as social networks, health records, web logs, mobile phones, academic studies, sensors, and call records that surround us.

Machine Learning: Basically refers to the techniques for extracting useful information from hidden patterns. It can be defined a system consist of many methods that learn and improve from data.

Machine Learning Methods: Can be grouped as supervised learning, unsupervised learning, and reinforcement learning.

Neurological Disorder: Refers to any disorder on the nervous system. Alzheimer's disease, Parkinson's disease, autism, stroke, etc. are some neurological disorders explained in this study.

This research was previously published in Early Detection of Neurological Disorders Using Machine Learning Systems; pages 252-291, copyright year 2019 by Medical Information Science Reference (an imprint of IGI Global).

Chapter 82

The Strengths, Weaknesses, Opportunities, and Threats Analysis of Big Data Analytics in Healthcare

Chaojie Wang

https://orcid.org/0000-0001-8521-9420

The MITRE Corporation, McLean, USA

ABSTRACT

Improving the performance and reducing the cost of healthcare have been a great concern and a huge challenge for healthcare organizations and governments at every level in the US. Measures taken have included laws, regulations, policies, and initiatives that aim to improve quality of care, reduce costs of care, and increase access to care. Central to these measures is the meaningful and effective use of Big Data analytics. To reap the benefits of big data analytics and align expectations with results, researchers, practitioners, and policymakers must have a clear understanding of the unique circumstances of healthcare including the strengths, weaknesses, opportunities, and threats (SWOT) associated with the use of this emerging technology. Through descriptive SWOT analysis, this article helps healthcare stakeholders gain awareness of both success factors and issues, pitfalls, and barriers in the adoption of big data analytics in healthcare.

1. INTRODUCTION

The US healthcare system has both strengths and weaknesses. It enjoys a large-scale, well-trained, and high-quality workforce of clinicians, nurses, and specialists, robust medical research programs, and the world's best clinical outcomes in select medical services. Yet, it suffers from high expenditure, low performance, and disparity in health status, access to care, and outcomes of care (Barnes, Unruh, Rosenau, & Rice, 2018).

DOI: 10.4018/978-1-6684-3662-2.ch082

1.1. High Cost of the US Healthcare System

According to a recent report published by The Organization for Economic Co-operation and Development (2018), in 2017 the US spending on healthcare was the largest, measured by both the spending per capita and the percentage of the gross domestic product (GDP) among its 37 member nations. Figure 1 shows that the US spent over $10,000 per capita on healthcare that year, or about 17% of GDP.

Figure 1. 2017 health spending per capita as share of GDP (Organization for Economic Co-operation and Development, 2018, p. 2)

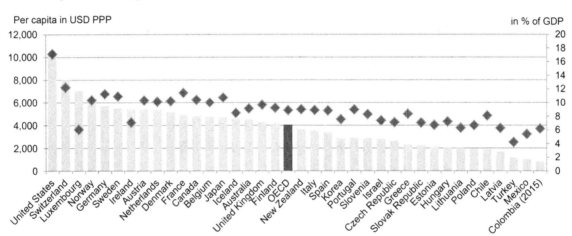

Even more alarming is the rapid growth in US healthcare spending. According to the Centers for Medicare and Medicaid Services (CMS), healthcare spending is projected to grow at an average rate of 5.8 percent from 2012-2022, 1.0 percentage point faster than the expected average annual growth in the GDP. By 2022, US healthcare spending is projected to be nearly 20% of GDP (Centers for Medicare and Medicaid Services, 2012).

1.2. Low Performance of the US Healthcare System

This extremely high spending is sharply contrasted with the low performance in the US healthcare system. In 2000, the World Health Organization (WHO) published a report that measured and ranked the health system performance of 191 countries. According to this report, the US healthcare system was unimpressively ranked at 37, below most industrialized countries including France, the UK, and Canada, and even below some less developed countries such as Colombia and Chile (Tandon, Murray, Lauer, & Evans, 2000). Almost two decades later, there has not been much improvement in the performance of the US healthcare system. According to a 2017 report from the Commonwealth Fund, the US is ranked last out of 11 high-income industrialized countries based on measures including care process, access to care, administrative efficiency, equity, and health outcomes (Schneider, Sarnak, Squires, Shah, & Doty, 2017). Figure 2 shows that the US healthcare system performs at the bottom on four of the five measures.

Figure 2. 2017 healthcare systems performance ranking (Schneider et al., 2017)

	AUS	CAN	FRA	GER	NETH	NZ	NOR	SWE	SWIZ	UK	US
OVERALL RANKING	2	9	10	8	3	4	4	6	6	1	11
Care Process	2	6	9	8	4	3	10	11	7	1	5
Access	4	10	9	2	1	7	5	6	8	3	11
Administrative Efficiency	1	6	11	6	9	2	4	5	8	3	10
Equity	7	9	10	6	2	8	5	3	4	1	11
Health Care Outcomes	1	9	5	8	6	7	3	2	4	10	11

1.3. Efforts to Improve the US Healthcare System

In 2007, the Institute for Healthcare Improvement (IHI) launched the Triple Aim initiative to improve the patient experience of care (including quality and satisfaction), improve the health of populations, and reduce the per capita cost of health care. The Triple Aim initiative directly targets the critical measures of healthcare performance including both quality of care and efficiency of care (Institute for Healthcare Improvement, 2007).

In 2008, Congress enacted the Medicare Improvements for Patients and Providers Act (MIPPA). As part of the implementation of MIPPA, CMS introduced the value-based purchasing (VBP) plan linking payments directly to the quality outcomes of the care provided. This pay-for-quality or pay-for-performance plan aims to move away from the traditional fee-for-service plan which provides no incentives for the providers to improve care quality and contributes to the high cost of healthcare (Terhaar, 2018).

In 2010, to address the disparity and inequity in healthcare and to increase access to care for tens of millions of uninsured and underinsured Americans, Congress enacted the Patient Protection and Affordable Care Act of 2010, also known as "Obamacare" ("Patient Protection and Affordable Care Act of 2010," 2010).

While healthcare initiatives, regulations, and policies may help drive the quality and performance improvement at the macro level, effective implementations require concerted efforts at the micro level by all stakeholders including policymakers, providers, payer, patients, and the public. In addition, these diverse stakeholders must be empowered and enabled by innovative solutions and technologies to deal with the complex problems in healthcare. Big data analytics as an emerging technology is one of many indispensable tools in the toolbox and can play an important role in improving healthcare. However, as with any new technology, benefits often come with limitations, opportunities with risks, and hopes with hypes. It is important to understand the full spectrum of this new technology so that it can be efficiently and effectively adopted and applied.

Motivated by the tremendous challenges facing the US healthcare system and the great potential big data analytics has in improving its performance, this paper presents a high-level analysis of the strengths, weaknesses, opportunities, and threats (SWOT) associated with the use of big data analytics in healthcare. The goal of this paper is to help policy makers, care providers, researchers, and the public gain broader and deeper understanding of the many dimensions of the use of this emerging technology in healthcare so that they can make informed and sensible decisions in their efforts to improve healthcare quality and performance.

2. BIG DATA ANALYTICS AS ENABLER TO IMPROVE HEALTHCARE

2.1. Big Data Analytics

During the past decade, big data emerged as a new technology trend thanks to the rapid innovation and advancement in information and communication technology (ICT). Big data was initially defined with three essential characteristics known as the Three V's – Volume, Velocity, and Variety. Since then, more V's have been added. A Six V's model widely used in healthcare adds three additional V's – Veracity, Variability, and Value (Senthilkumar, Rai, Meshram, Gunasekaran, & Chandrakumarmangalam, 2018). Data analytics is an umbrella term commonly used to reference business intelligence, business analytics, data mining, knowledge discovery in databases, and data science. As large volumes of data in wide varieties are collected and made available, the demand increases for extracting values from big data to improve business performance and drive organizational changes. Data analytics answers the challenge by integrating computer science, information technology, statistics, domain knowledge, and human collaboration in a streamlined process of knowledge discovery, creation, and application (Wang, 2018).

2.2. Applications of Big Data Analytics in Healthcare

Healthcare data analytics is the application of big data and data analytics to healthcare. Similar terms with minor differences also appear both in academia and industry. Among them are healthcare analytics, health analytics, healthcare big data analytics, big data analytics in health, and health informatics. Knowledge can be discovered, and insights can be gained from big data analytics to improve healthcare quality and performance. Based on the content analysis of 26 case studies, Wang, Kung, and Byrd (2016) identified five potential benefits of healthcare data analytics: IT infrastructure, operational, organizational, managerial, and strategic benefits. Lebied (2018) provided detailed accounts of twelve applications of big data analytics in healthcare such as prevention of opioid abuse, telemedicine, prevention of ER visits, and fraud detection. These serve as exemplars of the many applications currently recognized and many more innovative applications continuing to emerge.

The University of Pennsylvania Health System (UPHS)'s use of machine learning and Electronic Health Records (EHR) data to predict the onset of severe sepsis is an example of using big data analytics in healthcare. Sepsis is a life-threatening illness due to blood infection. According to the Center for Disease Control & Prevention (CDC), each year, 1.7 million American adults develop sepsis, 270,000 Americans die of sepsis, and one in three patients who die in hospitals has sepsis (Dantes & Epstein, 2018). Sepsis costs American hospitals $27 billion annually, making it the number one cost driver for hospitals (Reinhart, 2018). UPHS developed a predictive model by training a machine learning algorithm using historic patient data stored in its EHR including labs, clinical, and demographic data. The trained machine learning model was then used to predict severe sepsis 12 hours prior to the clinical onset by continuously pulling real-time patient data from the EHR. Alerts were sent to clinicians and nurses to enable additional monitoring and early intervention (Giannini et al., 2017).

2.3. The Adoption Model for Analytics Maturity (AMAM)

When it comes to the adoption and utilization of big data analytics, each organization is constrained by its unique organizational characteristics including size, financial resources, technical capability, and leadership and environmental characteristics such as geographical location, community, and patient populations. To help assess the maturity of healthcare organizations in adopting big data analytics, HIMSS Analytics, a wholly owned subsidiary of the Health Information and Management System Society (HIMSS), developed the Adoption Model for Analytics Maturity (AMAM) (HIMSS Analytics, n.d.). AMAM describes eight stages representing increasing levels of maturity. An organization typically starts out at stage zero in which it only uses analytics in sparse and siloed point solutions and gradually climbs up to stage seven, where analytics is used for prescriptive and personalized care for individual patients.

3. THE SWOT FRAMEWORK AND SUMMARY OF ANALYSIS

3.1. The SWOT Framework

Strengths-Weaknesses-Opportunities-Threats (SWOT) is a management science framework originally used for corporate strategic planning dating back to the 1960s. It is an analysis tool to assess a business's fitness as measured by how well its internal qualities (the strengths and weaknesses) match up with external factors (the opportunities and threats) (Hill & Westbrook, 1997).

Strengths and opportunities are considered positive, favorable, and synonymous to success factors while weaknesses and threats are considered negative, unfavorable, and synonymous to pitfalls, challenges or barriers. The objective of strategic planning is to mitigate or minimize the unfavorable factors and utilize or maximize the favorable factors. The SWOT framework has been applied to the use of big data analytics in general (Wang, Wang, & Alexander, 2015) and in a specific industry or domain (Collins, 2016). This paper applies SWOT analysis to the use of big data analytics in healthcare. Figure 3 shows the framework in four quadrants, known as a SWOT matrix.

3.2. Strengths and Weaknesses of the SWOT Framework

SWOT is a simple yet powerful model for analyzing a complex situation. It reflects the complexity of the reality and presents a dialectically balanced perspective for analyzing and dealing with complex problems. However, SWOT analysis is not considered a rigorous empirical research method. It is different from the qualitative method aiming at the generation of new theories or the quantitative method aiming at the confirmation or falsification of existing or proposed theories. SWOT provides a way of thinking akin to systems thinking or critical thinking. The definition and classification of what constitutes strengths, weaknesses, opportunities, and threats are subjective and reflect the researchers and practitioners' personal experience and understanding of the complex socioeconomic, cultural, and managerial problems. SWOT's power lies in its simplicity in dealing with complexity. It provides a simple frame of reference for analyzing and dealing with complex situations so that potential opportunities can be explored, po-

Figure 3. The SWOT matrix

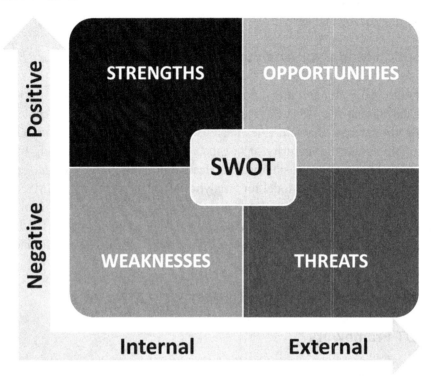

tential risks can be assessed, and potential outcomes (intended or unintended, desirable or undesirable) can be illuminated before interventions can be developed and actions can be taken.

3.3. SWOT Analysis of Big Data Analytics in Healthcare

This SWOT analysis was performed based on review of literature, industry reports, and expert opinions. The author also draws upon his professional experiences in systems engineering, health IT, data analytics, and healthcare quality management. Aligning with the four quadrants of the SWOT matrix, this paper sets out to answer the following four questions:

1.   What are the strengths of healthcare that make it favorable for the adoption of big data analytics?
2.   What are the weaknesses of healthcare that may hinder the adoption of big data analytics?
3.   What are the opportunities that favor the adoption of big data analytics in healthcare?
4.   What are the threats associated with the adoption of big data analytics in healthcare?

The extant literature on similar subjects tends to be at a lower level or with technical implementation details. Collins (2016) performed a SWOT analysis of big data and health economics in the UK with a focus on costs and included coverage of drugs, biomonitoring, and data repositories. Yang et al. (2016) performed a SWOT analysis of wearable devices in healthcare. While the flexibility of the SWOT framework allows for different levels of analysis, this paper focuses on the big picture (the forest) instead

Figure 4. Summary of the SWOT analysis on big data analytics in healthcare

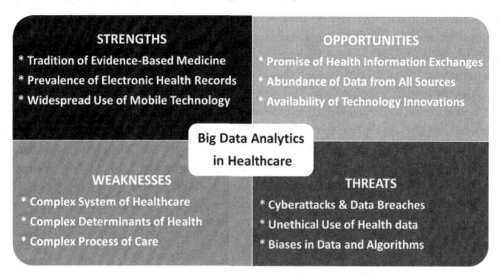

of low-level details (the trees). The results of the SWOT analysis are summarized in Figure 4. Detailed descriptions are provided in the following four sections.

4. STRENGTHS

4.1. Tradition of Evidence-Based Medicine

Western medicine has the tradition of applying science and technology in the prevention, control, diagnosis and treatment of diseases. From the development of medical devices such as Magnetic Resonance Imaging (MRI) and the Automated External Defibrillator (AED) to the use of experimental design and statistical inference in clinical trials, science and technology remain at the heart of modern medicine.

A spirited movement called Evidence-Based Medicine (EBM) began within the healthcare community in the early 1990s. EBM is defined as "the conscientious, explicit, and judicious use of current best evidence in making decisions about the care of individual patients. The practice of evidence-based medicine means integrating individual clinical expertise with the best available external clinical evidence from systematic research" (Sackett, Rosenberg, Gray, Haynes, & Richardson, 1996). EBM has become an essential code in the DNA of healthcare ever since. Its principles, processes, and practices are well aligned with those of big data and analytics. The increasing volume, variety, and availability of data along with the advancement of data storage, computing power, and analytics tools and techniques will make EBM more practical and powerful.

4.2. Prevalence of Electronic Health Records

Electronic Health Records (EHR) evolved from traditional Electronic Medical Records (EMR). While EMR was limited to medical records, EHR expands the scope to all records germane to health including medical, administrative, claim, and socioeconomic records. In 2009, the US Congress enacted the

Health Information Technology for Economic and Clinical Health (HITECH) Act as part of the American Recovery and Reinvestment Act (ARRA) after the 2008 global financial crisis. HITECH was created to promote the adoption of health IT and implementation of EHR to modernize technology infrastructure and capabilities of healthcare. Federal investment was provided to healthcare providers to incentivize health IT adoption and a federal certification process was put in place to ensure IT systems are developed according to technological, functional, and security requirements.

Since the enactment of the HITECH Act, more healthcare organizations have adopted health IT and implemented EHRs. According to the Office of the National Coordinator for Health Information Technology (2018), "In 2017, 96 percent of all non-federal acute care hospitals possessed certified health IT." The penetration of health IT and EHRs provides the technical foundation and data sources for the adoption of big data analytics to improve healthcare. At the same time, big data analytics aims to deliver the right amount of information to care providers at the right time in the right place and help realize the intended benefits of EHRs and alleviate the unintended burden associated with EHRs such as administrative overhead and information overload.

4.3. Widespread Use of Mobile Technology

The ubiquitous Internet coupled with Global Positioning Systems (GPS), mobile telecommunication networks, and cloud computing lead to the proliferation of mobile devices (including wearable fitness trackers) and mobile apps that are becoming an integral part of healthcare and our daily life. According to Statista (2018), as of January 2018 there were 3.7 billion mobile users worldwide. While the global mobile broadband subscription penetration rate is around 50%, the Americas and Europe have the highest rates, around 78.2 percent and 76.6 percent, respectively.

Among millions of mobile apps, health and wellness apps are becoming increasingly popular. There are close to 48,000 mobile health and wellness apps available from the Apple App Store alone (Statista, 2018). Mobile health and wellness apps not only change the way healthcare is delivered and how health is monitored and managed, but also provide additional biometrics and lifestyle data to the clinicians, researchers, and policymakers in their efforts to improve care for individual patients and populations at large.

5. WEAKNESSES

5.1. Complex System of Healthcare

The US healthcare delivery and payment system is complex with many interdependent, interacting stakeholders. As a complex adaptive system, it exhibits non-linear, dynamic, and indeterministic behaviors that are unpredictable and difficult to manage and control (Rouse, 2008). Figure 5 shows the many stakeholders and how each of them plays a different role in a complex relationship to deliver healthcare.

Improving healthcare requires the collaboration and concerted efforts of all stakeholders through consensus building. Government policymaking should be conducted by taking inputs from all stakeholders and any potential unintended adverse consequences should be evaluated and remedied. For example, CMS's bundled payment initiative intended to reduce cost of care may lead to care providers' discrimination in patient selection commonly known as "lemon dropping" and "cherry picking", where

Figure 5. Stakeholders and interests in health care (Rouse, 2008, p. 19)

Stakeholder	Risk Management	Prevention	Detection	Treatment
Public	e.g., buy insurance	e.g., stop smoking	e.g., get screened	
Delivery System			Clinicians[a]	Clinicians and providers[b]
Government	Medicare, Medicaid, Congress	NIH, Government CDC, DoD, et al.	NIH, Government CDC, DoD, et al.	NIH, Government CDC, DoD, et al.
Non-Profits		American Cancer Society, American Heart Association, et al.	American Cancer Society, American Heart Association, et al.	American Cancer Society, American Heart Association, et al.
Academia	Business schools	Basic science disciplines	Technology and medical schools	Medical schools
Business	Employers, insurance companies, HMOs		Guidant, Medtronic, et al.	Lilly, Merck, Pfizer, et al.

[a]The category of clinicians includes physicians, nurses, and other health care professionals.
[b]The category of providers includes hospitals, clinics, nursing homes, and many other types of testing and treatment facilities.

high risk patients are turned away in favor of low risk patients. Big data analytics can provide evidence and insights to help policymakers assess the intended benefits and unintended harm of health policies.

5.2. Complex Determinants of Health

While modern medicine has great success at treating symptoms and managing both acute and chronic conditions, it is not as successful in preventing and curing diseases. This is due to the complex nature of diseases and the multiple contributing factors including clinical, behavioral, and socioeconomic factors. There is a growing body of research linking socioeconomic factors, such as an individual's life condition and social standing, to his or her health status under the general scheme of social determinants of health (Barr, 2014; Marmot, 2005; McGovern, Miller, & Hughes-Cromwick, 2014). There is a myriad of factors that affect health and influence healthcare. Some are natural while others are cultural; some are measurable while others are not. Machine learning and artificial intelligence may be effective in analyzing natural or measurable factors but must rely on human intelligence and human judgement to deal with the cultural or unmeasurable factors.

5.3. Complex Process of Care

Healthcare is a team sport where multiple professionals must work together to deliver quality care to patients (Nancarrow et al., 2013). For example, the dialysis care for patients suffering from End-Stage Renal Disease (ESRD) requires coordinated efforts by administrative, medical, and social professionals including facility administrators, medical directors, nephrologists, nurses, dialysis technicians, dietitians, and social workers (Maryland Department of Health, n.d.). In addition, ESRD patients tend to have co-morbidities such as diabetes and hypertension and are vulnerable to hospitalizations and ER visits. Their quality of life depends on the coordinated care by dialysis facilities, hospitals, communities and their families. This process of care is complex and makes the quality of care much harder to quantitatively measure and analyze.

In addition, patient engagement plays a critical role in achieving optimal health outcomes in the patient-centered care process. Patients must be informed of how their treatment is being influenced by data, evidence, and analytics and be engaged in the healthcare decision making process. This requires ongoing patient education to improve both health literacy and data literacy.

The complexity articulated in the above three interrelated areas poses great challenges to the effectiveness of big data analytics. As much as we would like to use the insights gained from big data analytics to improve the performance of healthcare, actions cannot be taken solely based on the outputs of nondeterministic computer algorithms. For example, IBM Watson generated considerable buzz for its purported utility in helping doctors more rapidly and accurately diagnose illness, but a recent article revealed that Watson failed to live up to those expectations (Hernandez & Greenwald, 2018).

6. OPPORTUNITIES

6.1. Promise of Health Information Exchanges

While EHRs enable healthcare organizations to centralize the management of patient health data, the Health Information Exchanges (HIEs) go one step further by providing the technical infrastructure to connect these disparate and diverse EHRs so that patient health data can be exchanged, aggregated, and shared across the whole healthcare delivery system. "Electronic exchange of clinical information allows doctors, nurses, pharmacists, other health care providers, and patients to access and securely share a patient's vital medical information electronically - improving the speed, quality, safety, coordination, and cost of patient care" (The Office of the National Coordinator for Health IT, n.d.). HIEs make it possible to establish comprehensive, inclusive, and longitudinal patient and population health data for the effective application of big data analytics.

Since 2009, the Social Security Administration (SSA) has been using HIEs to automatically and timely request and obtain medical evidence records (MERs) from healthcare providers nationwide to support disability claims adjudication (Feldman & Horan, 2011). As of December 2018, over 18,000 healthcare providers represented by 150 healthcare organizations participated in the exchange of MERs with SSA. Compared to a paper process, the use of HIEs greatly speeds up medical evidence acquisition to support disability determination. Faster availability of benefits resulting from the expedited determination helps disability claimants pay for much needed healthcare services and supports healthcare providers in the delivery of healthcare (Social Security Administration, n.d.a). In addition, SSA uses the vast amount of electronic health data along with machine learning to provide data-driven decision support to its disability adjudicators. This use of big data analytics further speeds up the disability adjudication process and helps increase the accuracy and consistency of disability determination decisions. SSA established interoperability guidelines and a certification process to ensure participating organizations comply with industry interoperability standards (Social Security Administration, n.d.b).

6.2. Abundance of Data from All Sources

One of the many V's of big data is variety. For big data analytics to be effective, many kinds of data that are related and relevant to health and healthcare should be included, especially the socioeconomic data that measure the important social determinants of health. EHRs may contain individual patient's demographic data but lacks the macro socioeconomic data that can be obtained from government census and survey data.

For example, the American Community Survey data from the US Census Bureau contain rich sets of socioeconomic data about communities in the US and could be used in conjunction with clinical, administrative, and claims data to gain a better understanding of the state of health and healthcare. In addition, data from law enforcement, non-governmental organizations, and social media networks can also be leveraged for big data analytics in healthcare.

In January 14, 2019, President Trump signed into law the Foundations for Evidence-Based Policy-making (FEBP) Act. As part of the FEBP Act, the Open, Public, Electronic and Necessary (OPEN) Government Data Act requires all non-sensitive government data to be made available in open and machine-readable formats. The successful implementation of this federal law will help propel the adoption of big data analytics.

6.3. Availability of Technology Innovations

The past decade has seen a rapid advancement in computer science and information technology. The confluence of cloud computing, mobile computing, machine learning, artificial intelligence, and Internet of Things has given rise to a plethora of nascent tools, techniques, and platforms for performing productive and effective big data analytics. There are many readily available choices of both commercial-off-the-shelf (COTS) products and free open source software (FOSS) products. There are many virtual communities, blogs, forums, and tutorials available on the web. Data science has emerged as a burgeoning vibrant profession, and hundreds of data science programs have sprouted up in colleges around the world.

7. THREATS

7.1. Cyberattacks and Data Breaches

While big data analytics has the potential to help improve the quality and performance of healthcare, the risks of cyberattacks and data breaches are high and should not to be overlooked. According to a recent study over a five-year period from 2012 to 2017, there were 1,512 reported data breaches of protected health information affecting a total of more than 154 million patient records (Ronquillo, Erik Winter-holler, Cwikla, Szymanski, & Levy, 2018). These stolen data can be used for "identity theft, criminal impersonation, tax fraud, health insurance scams, and a host of other criminal offenses" (Goodman, 2016, p. 109).

The cyberattacks on healthcare IT systems not only put patients' privacy and security at risk, they also pose economic harms to healthcare providers, insurers, and tax payers. A 2016 study by the Ponemon Insfitute (2016) estimated that about 90% of the healthcare organizations represented in the study suffered data breaches in the past two years and the average cost of data breaches for covered entities surveyed was more than $2.2 million, while the average cost to business associates in the study was more than $1 million.

7.2. Unethical Use of Health Data

External malicious cyberattacks are certainly grave concerns, however insider threats and unethical use of health data to discriminate health insurance coverage and to boost corporate revenues and profits should not be overlooked. Big data analytics is a double-edged sword. When applied properly and ethically, it has the potential to do good; otherwise, it may cause harm to patients, providers, and tax payers. One emerging application is the use of predictive analytics to draw insights for profits without regard to privacy laws and protection of patients' personal and health information.

A 2017 report by The Century Foundation (Tanner, 2017) painted a gloomy picture of big data in healthcare. There exists a multi-billion-dollar industry that collects, mines, buys, and sells anonymized patient health data. The patient health data are traded routinely for profit. While the sharing and use of de-identified patient health data for secondary use in medical and policy research are allowed by the Health Insurance Portability and Accountability Act (HIPAA) (Cohen & Mello, 2018), there is a real danger for the patient health data to be re-identified through the process of data linking with additional data sources from social media networks and mobile health and wellness apps and the use of machine learning algorithms. This unethical for-profit data mining along with the upsurge in malicious hacking and data breaches can result in devastating impacts.

7.3. Biases in Data and Algorithms

Reality is complex and unknowable. As stated by Laozi in the 2500-year old Taoist text *Tao Te Ching*, "The tao that can be told is not the eternal Tao. The name that can be named is not the eternal Name. The unnamable is the eternally real" (Laozi, Mitchell, Roig, & Little, 1989). Echoing Laozi, statistician George Box (1976) was famously quoted for the maxim that "all models are wrong" because they are only approximations of true reality. Big data analytics is inherently biased since it relies on data as input, and algorithms as the enablers. Limitations and biases exist in both data and algorithms which can be traced back to the cognitive limitations and biases in human minds (Gianfrancesco, Tamang, Yazdany, & Schmajuk, 2018).

Whether collected through human observations or sensory devices, data are approximate measures of the actual properties of the observed entities. Even correctly measured and curated data cannot escape from the biases of those who define the measurement and those who design the data collection instruments. In addition, incomplete, inaccurate, and missing data are typical and can distort the outcome of the analytics (affectionately known as "garbage in, garbage out").

8. CONCLUSION

This paper presented a high-level analysis of the strengths, weaknesses, opportunities, and threats (SWOT) in the application of big data analysis in healthcare. While the strengths and opportunities are positive, desirable, and easier to comprehend, the weaknesses and threats are negative, undesirable, and demand diligence and vigilance. Although this paper provides even coverage of all four factors, it should be stressed that more attention must be paid to the weaknesses and threats. This is especially true in the era of rapid innovations in information technology which often give rise to an unrealistic expectation of a panacea with quick, autonomous, and magical cures for a complex social problem.

Technology such as machine learning and artificial intelligence have been effective in dealing with "hard" problems such as winning "Go" games, recognizing human voices and faces, and even translating languages. These problems have well-defined boundaries, well-understood rules of game or causal mechanisms, and can be simulated or programmed using software with high degrees of accuracy and certainty. However, social problems are much more complex with ill-defined boundaries and poorly-understood causal mechanisms (Kirk, 1995). Healthcare is a perfect example of a complex system with non-linear, dynamic, and indeterministic behaviors involving multiple stakeholders with conflicts of interests and under the influence of multitudes of intertwined natural and social forces. These weaknesses are inherent in healthcare and should be kept in mind when applying technologies such as health IT and big data analytics. There is no simple and straight-forward solution to the high cost and low-quality challenges facing the US healthcare system. Big data analytics is promising and can help uncover partial and limited knowledge from big data to inform clinical and policy decision making, but it does not provide the whole truth about healthcare and is not a silver bullet; overcoming the weaknesses requires the conscious and judicial use of political skills, business acumen, and collaborative spirit in addition to technical and analytical competency.

While this paper provides only cursory exposure to the subject of big data analytics in healthcare, one of its objectives is to draw attention to some of the many interrelated factors that must be considered when seeking to leverage big data analytics to improve healthcare quality and performance. A more detailed and deeper analysis on any of the factors mentioned in the above high-level analysis would represent a worthwhile research subject. For example, healthcare is a highly personalized process involving the coordination of multiple providers such as acute care hospitals, primary care physicians, and nurse practitioners. Care coordination is a known factor influencing such healthcare outcomes as unplanned hospital readmission (Fluitman et al., 2016). Quantitatively measuring health care coordination is a challenging task. Compared to readily-quantifiable clinical measures such as blood pressure or body mass index, individual human behaviors are much harder to quantify, and care coordination involves multiple parties. Moreover, fair and just attribution of quality measure scores to multiple providers is also a difficult task. This is further complicated by patient behaviors since patients are also part of the coordination process.

DISCLAIMER

The author's affiliation with The MITRE Corporation is provided for identification purposes only and is not intended to convey or imply MITRE's concurrence with, or support for, the positions, opinions or viewpoints expressed by the author. Approved for Public Release; Distribution Unlimited. Case Number 19-0249.

REFERENCES

Analytics, H. I. M. S. S. (n.d.). Adoption Model for Analytics Maturity. Retrieved from https://www.himssanalytics.org/amam

Barnes, A. J., Unruh, L. Y., Rosenau, P., & Rice, T. (2018). Health System in the US. In E. van Ginneken & R. Busse (Eds.), *Health Care Systems and Policies*. New York, NY: Springer. doi:10.1007/978-1-4614-6419-8_18-2

Barr, D. A. (2014). *Health disparities in the United States: Social class, race, ethnicity, and health*. JHU Press.

Box, G. E. (1976). Science and statistics. *Journal of the American Statistical Association, 71*(356), 791–799. doi:10.1080/01621459.1976.10480949

Centers for Medicare and Medicaid Services. (2012). *National health expenditure projections 2012-2020*. Retrieved from https://www.cms.gov/Research-Statistics-Data-and-Systems/Statistics-Trends-and-Reports/NationalHealthExpendData/Downloads/Proj2012.pdf

Cohen, I. G., & Mello, M. M. (2018). HIPAA and Protecting Health Information in the 21st Century. *Journal of the American Medical Association, 320*(3), 231. doi:10.1001/jama.2018.5630 PMID:29800120

Collins, B. (2016). Big data and health economics: Strengths, weaknesses, opportunities and threats. *PharmacoEconomics, 34*(2), 101–106. doi:10.100740273-015-0306-7 PMID:26093888

Dantes, R. B., & Epstein, L. (2018). Combatting Sepsis: A Public Health Perspective. *Clinical Infectious Diseases, 67*(8), 1300–1302. doi:10.1093/cid/ciy342 PMID:29846544

Feldman, S. S., & Horan, T. A. (2011). Collaboration in electronic medical evidence development: A case study of the Social Security Administration's MEGAHIT System. *International Journal of Medical Informatics, 80*(8), e127–e140. doi:10.1016/j.ijmedinf.2011.01.012 PMID:21333588

Fluitman, K. S., van Galen, L. S., Merten, H., Rombach, S. M., Brabrand, M., Cooksley, T., ... Nanay-akkara, P. W. B. (2016). Exploring the preventable causes of unplanned readmissions using root cause analysis: Coordination of care is the weakest link. *European Journal of Internal Medicine, 30*, 18–24. doi:10.1016/j.ejim.2015.12.021 PMID:26775179

Gianfrancesco, M. A., Tamang, S., Yazdany, J., & Schmajuk, G. (2018). Potential biases in machine learning algorithms using electronic health record data. *JAMA Internal Medicine, 178*(11), 1544–1547. doi:10.1001/jamainternmed.2018.3763 PMID:30128552

Giannini, H., Chivers, C., Draugelis, M., Hanish, A., Fuchs, B., Donnelly, P., ... Schweickert, W. (2017). D15 Critical Care: Do We Have A Crystal Ball? Predicting Clinical Deterioration and Outcome in Critically Ill Patients: Development And Implementation Of A Machine-Learning Algorithm For Early Identification Of Sepsis In A Multi-Hospital Academic Healthcare System. *American Journal of Respiratory and Critical Care Medicine, 195*.

Goodman, M. (2016). *Future crimes: Inside the digital underground and the battle for our connected world*. Random House.

Hernandez, D., & Greenwald, T. (2018). IBM Has a Watson Dilemma. *The Wall Street Journal*. Retrieved from https://www.wsj.com/articles/ibm-bet-billions-that-watson-could-improve-cancer-treatment-it-hasnt-worked-1533961147

Hill, T., & Westbrook, R. (1997). SWOT analysis: It's time for a product recall. *Long Range Planning*, *30*(1), 46–52. doi:10.1016/S0024-6301(96)00095-7

Institute for Healthcare Improvement. (2007). Triple Aim - The Best Care for the Whole Population at the Lowest Cost. Retrieved from http://www.ihi.org/Engage/Initiatives/TripleAim/Pages/default.aspx

Kirk, D. (1995). Hard and soft systems: A common paradigm for operations management. *International Journal of Contemporary Hospitality Management*, *7*(5), 13–16. doi:10.1108/09596119510090708

Laozi, M.S., Roig, J. V., & Little, S. (1989). *Tao teaching*. Kyle Cathie.

Lebied, M. (2018). 12 examples of big data analytics in healthcare that can save people. *Datapine*. Retrieved from https://www.datapine.com/blog/big-data-examples-in-healthcare/

Marmot, M. (2005). Social determinants of health inequalities. *Lancet*, *365*(9464), 1099–1104. doi:10.1016/S0140-6736(05)74234-3 PMID:15781105

Maryland Department of Health. (n.d.). Code of Maryland regulations: Sec. 10.30.02.04. freestanding dialysis facilities – staffing. Retrieved from http://mdrules.elaws.us/comar/10.30.02.04

McGovern, L., Miller, G., & Hughes-Cromwick, P. (2014). *The relative contribution of multiple determinants to health outcomes*. Project HOPE.

Nancarrow, S. A., Booth, A., Ariss, S., Smith, T., Enderby, P., & Roots, A. (2013). Ten principles of good interdisciplinary team work. *Human Resources for Health*, *11*(1), 19–19. doi:10.1186/1478-4491-11-19 PMID:23663329

Office of the National Coordinator for Health Information Technology. (2018). Percent of hospitals, by Type, that possess certified health IT. Retrieved from https://dashboard.healthit.gov/quickstats/pages/certified-electronic-health-record-technology-in-hospitals.php

Patient Protection and Affordable Care Act of 2010, 42 U.S. C § 18031. (2010). US Congress.

Ponemon Institute. (2016). *Six annual benchmark study on privacy & security of healthcare data*. Retrieved from https://www.ponemon.org/local/upload/file/Sixth%20Annual%20Patient%20Privacy%20%26%20Data%20Security%20Report%20FINAL%206.pdf

Reinhart, K. (2018). Sepsis: A global public health burden for hospitals. *Becker's Hospital Review*. Retrieved from https://www.beckershospitalreview.com/quality/sepsis-a-global-public-health-burden-for-hospitals.html

Ronquillo, J. G., Erik Winterholler, J., Cwikla, K., Szymanski, R., & Levy, C. (2018). *Health IT, hacking, and cybersecurity: national trends in data breaches of protected health information*. JAMIA Open.

Rouse, W. B. (2008). Health care as a complex adaptive system: Implications for design and management. *Bridge-Washington-National Academy of Engineering*, *38*(1), 17.

Sackett, D. L., Rosenberg, W. M., Gray, J. M., Haynes, R. B., & Richardson, W. S. (1996). Evidence based medicine: What it is and what it isn't. *BMJ: British Medical Journal*, *312*(7023), 71–72. doi:10.1136/bmj.312.7023.71 PMID:8555924

Schneider, E. C., Sarnak, D. O., Squires, D., Shah, A., & Doty, M. M. (2017). Mirror Mirror 2017: International Comparison Reflects Flaws and Opportunities for Better US Health Care. Retrieved from https://interactives.commonwealthfund.org/2017/july/mirror-mirror/

Senthilkumar, S., Rai, B. K., Meshram, A. A., Gunasekaran, A., & Chandrakumarmangalam, S. (2018). Big Data in Healthcare Management: A Review of Literature. *American Journal of Theoretical and Applied Business*, 4(2), 57–69. doi:10.11648/j.ajtab.20180402.14

Social Security Administration. (n.d.a). Health IT Partners. Retrieved from https://www.ssa.gov/hit/partners.html

Social Security Administration. (n.d.b). SSAgov/HealthIT. Retrieved from https://github.com/ssagov/healthit

Statista. (2018). Mobile Internet - Statistics & Facts. Retrieved from https://www.statista.com/topics/779/mobile-internet/

Tandon, A., Murray, C. J., Lauer, J. A., & Evans, D. B. (2000). *Measuring overall health system performance for 191 countries*. Geneva: World Health Organization.

Tanner, A. (2017). *Our bodies, our data: How companies make billions selling our medical records*. Beacon Press.

Terhaar, M. F. (2018). Value-Based Purchasing. *Clinical Analytics and Data Management for the DNP*, 1, 27.

The Office of the National Coordinator for Health IT. (n.d.). What is health information exchange? Retrieved from https://www.healthit.gov/faq/what-health-information-exchange

The Organization for Economic Co-operation and Development. (2018). *Spending on Health: Latest Trends*. Retrieved from http://www.oecd.org/health/health-systems/Health-Spending-Latest-Trends-Brief.pdf

Wang, C. (2018). Integrating data analytics & knowledge management: A conceptual model. *Issues in Information Systems*, 19(2), 208–216.

Wang, L., Wang, G., & Alexander, C. A. (2015). Big data and visualization: Methods, challenges and technology progress. *Digital Technologies*, 1(1), 33–38.

Wang, Y., Kung, L., & Byrd, T. A. (2016). Big data analytics: Understanding its capabilities and potential benefits for healthcare organizations. *Technological Forecasting and Social Change*. doi:10.1016/j.techfore.2015.12.019

Yang, Y., Yu, S., Hao, Y., Xu, X., & Liu, H. (2016). The SWOT Analysis of the Wearable Devices in Smart Health Applications. *Paper presented at the International Conference on Smart Health*.

Chapter 83

Cloud Computing Big Data Adoption Impacts on Teaching and Learning in Higher Education:
A Systematic Review

Fahad Nasser Alhazmi
King Abdulaziz University, Saudi Arabia

ABSTRACT

There is a rapid evolution in the purpose and value of higher education brought about by technological advancement and data ubiquity. Data mining and advanced predictive analytics are increasingly being used in higher education institutions around the world to perform tasks, ranging from student recruitment, enrolment, predicting student behaviour, and developing personalised learning schemes. This chapter evaluates and assesses the impact of big data and cloud computing in higher education. The authors adopt systematic literature research approach that employs qualitative content analysis to establish their position with regards to the impact, benefits, challenges, and opportunities of integrating big data and cloud computing to facilitate teaching and learning.

INTRODUCTION

The advancement in technology has impacted every facet of human endeavour and the higher education sector is consequently not left out. The impact of technology has infused the heart of higher education teaching and learning and contributes to providing and enhancing student experience and positive engagement. In today's world, technology has been cleverly infused in higher education teaching and learning to augment various elements, components, and processes like teaching, learning, curriculum design, and assessment. When associated with apt learning objectives and standards, the impact is overwhelming. For instance, some universities have already partnered with IBM to provide cloud-based access to the

DOI: 10.4018/978-1-6684-3662-2.ch083

emergent big data analytics platform – IBM's supercomputer Watson. Even though the service provided is only basic, it still provides an illustration of the impact of big data and cloud computing on teaching and learning in higher education. The paradigm of higher education is constantly evolving, therefore emphasizing the need for rapid and dynamic adaptation by higher education institutions. There are strict requirements from accrediting and regulatory agencies, government and parastatals, as well as other stake holders to explore new methods and techniques for enhancing and monitoring student success and experience.

Within the higher education, technology trends comprising data mining and predictive analytical techniques are progressively being adopted in higher education for the purpose of classifying students to categories based on performance, learning history, and future prospect. Higher education institutions that have seldom collaborated with commercial partners, have commenced the adoption of these methods to recommend courses, monitor student progress, customise learning curriculum, and even develop collaborative networks amongst students. Big data analytics is a critical component of business intelligence and industrial analytics and is fast becoming part of a revolutionary and disruptive technology for higher education in which the ability to forecast individual consequences completely transforms management and allows institutions to better understand their students (and their needs) by exploiting the vast amounts of data that higher education institutions generate in their day-to-day actions (Collins et al., 2018; Poonia et al., 2018; Wang et al., 2018).

On the other hand, the last two decades has witnessed the evolution of distributed computing, a disruptive technology that has altered the application of scientific and commercial applications. This progress has birthed several more recent and relevant applications. The most recent member of this family and consequence of the development of distributed computing is Cloud computing. Using Cloud environment, all the applications can be delivered as a web service (Ali, 2019; Ali et al., 2019, Ali et al., 2020). Cloud facilitates the delivery of applications, software development languages and server/hardware as a service. The concept of cloud computing relates to the delivery of IT services that typically run in a web browser as a service. These services range from modifications or enhancements of common applications, such as email, admin/secretarial and personal finance to innovative solutions such as virtual and physical social networks. A very critical and essential service provided by cloud computing is the storage of digital data. Therefore, cloud computing can be defined as a computing platform that is resident in a network provider's data centre and is able to randomly and rapidly give its numerous servers the capabilities to deliver a wide range of services to its clients (Dillon et al., 2010). The notion of 'cloud' is a metaphor that represents the internet. In other words, the cloud refers to a computing paradigm, one where tasks are allocated to a permutation of services, software and connections read over a network. This holistic network comprising the servers, client base, and connections is collectively referred to as the cloud. Performing computing on a large scale on the cloud creates opportunities for users to access computing resources at a clustered level. Rather than purchase, develop, maintain and administer their personal data centres, firms prefer to purchase this computing power and storage capacity as a service from a provider, typically on a 'pay-as-you-use' model, just as with regular bills of electricity or water. This model has also been described as "utility computing," in which the availability of computing resources is addressed as any other metered utility service (Jain and Bhardwaj, 2010).

Cloud computing serves many functions and can provide solutions to a myriad of challenges posed, even in the higher education institutions. Typical uses of cloud computing in the higher education sector include cloud computing as Personal Learning Environments (PLEs), which can substitute for organisation-wise Virtual Learning Environments (VLEs)/LMS, like blackboard, with various personalised functions to meet their personal needs and preferences. Second, it can enable ubiquitous computing and learning. For students, with the availability of cloud computing, there is the introduction of the element of flexibility, meaning that the students are no longer tied to their lecture classrooms or halls. Cloud computing offers live chat sessions, video conferencing facilities, collaboration for online assessments and virtual labs, which have actually expanded the borders of the classroom, and all but eradicated the limitation of geographical distance and time.

Consequently, this chapter aims to evaluate and assess the impact of big data and cloud computing in higher education. We adopt systematic literature research approach to establish our position with regards to the impact, benefits, challenges, and opportunities of integrating big data and cloud computing to facilitate teaching and learning. Adopting a systematic literature review process, this chapter aims to identify and discuss the impact of big data and cloud computing on higher education teaching and learning, as well as touch on the disadvantages and challenges of completely adopting these technologies in higher education.

LITERATURE REVIEW

This section presents a review of existing literature on big data analytics and cloud computing adoption by Higher Educational Institutions (HEIs). The aim is the identification of frameworks, models and architectures that have so far been proposed for establishing cloud computing services inside HEIs, as well as how these are integrated for big data analytics. The section commences with a basic description of concepts in the field of cloud computing and big data analytics. It then proceeds to review existing frameworks and academic articles.

BASIC DESCRIPTIONS OF CLOUD COMPUTING AND BIG DATA ANALYTICS

Cloud Computing

The concept of cloud computing as a term was first mentioned by John McCarthy in 1960s where he referred to it as the ability of providing computing facilities to the public as a service – like a utility. Although the business model of providing computing as a service is not novel and has been in used in the provision of essential amenities such as in the water, electric and telephone sectors, it is still in its beginning in computing. In the early 1990s, the term "cloud" was used in numerous perspectives and appeared in many articles' diagrams to signify large networks. However, the term 'Cloud Computing' really gained popularity after its use by then Google's CEO Eric Schmidt in 2006, where he used it to denote the business model for delivering services over the internet (Campbell-Kelly et al., 2008; Erl et al., 2013; Hwang et al., 2011; Jain and Bhardwaj, 2010).

There is no consensus standard definition for cloud computing and this ambiguity obviously creates misunderstanding about a clear, succinct and precise definition of this technology (Rittinghouse and Ransome, 2016). The authors in Vaquero et al. (2008) performed a critical and comparative analysis of many definitions from a variety of academic publications in order to formulate a standardised definition of cloud computing. Armbrust et al. (2010) presents an alternative approach, which differentiated between the definitions of the two terms – cloud and utility computing. In the paper, the authors defined the data centre components (i.e. hardware and software) as the "cloud" while the service being rendered as the "utility computing". In summary, the authors defined "cloud computing" as the accumulation of the implemented software services and utility computing (Ali et al., 2018).

However, the National Institute of Standards and Technology (NIST) presents a definition of cloud computing that is rapidly becoming the globally-accepted definition, both in literature and industry (Lee et al., 2014; Sokol and Hogan, 2013; Yang and Huang, 2013) . The description of cloud computing, according to NIST is "a model for enabling convenient, on-demand network access to a shared pool of configurable computing resources (e.g., networks, servers, storage, applications and services) that can be rapidly provisioned and released with minimal management effort or service provider interaction" (Lee et al., 2014). Furthermore, the International Organization for Standardization (ISO) and the International Electrotechnical Commission (IEC) have defined cloud computing in their respective standard documentation as "a paradigm for enabling network access to a scalable and elastic pool of shareable physical or virtual resources with self-service provisioning and administration on-demand" (Antonopoulos and Gillam, 2010).

Big Data Analytics

In conventional data analytics, extract, transform, and load (ETL) processes (Kelly, 2014) that are used to store structured data into data warehouses from enterprise software such as CRM, ERP, and financial database systems. Consequently, consistent reports run on the stored data are used to create dashboards and data visualizations that are often used as analytic and decision-making components. The advent of social networking sites (SNS) and media, smart phones, the internet, interconnected devices, and sensors have contributed to the evolving nature of big data. This precipitated the need for new methods, models, and techniques to manipulate big data, resulting in a field of research analytics known as big data analytics (BDA).

Big data refers to gigantic datasets with sizes ranging from thousands of gigabytes, terabytes to petabytes, exabytes, and beyond, coming from a variety of sources, therefore is heterogeneous (semi-structured or unstructured) and is generated at increasing velocity. It is important to note that big data should not be mistaken for a dataset that has expanded to the point that it can no longer be analysed on a spread sheet, nor is it a database that happens to be extremely large. Some characteristics differentiate big data from traditional data are tabulated in Table 1. As can be seen, the table distinguishes big data from conventional or traditional data on the basis of the listed characteristics. It is important to comprehend the nature of big data in order to decide on the methods, tools, and technologies to control and manage it effectively.

Big data is typically characterised by Vs, which appear to be increasing year-on-year. However, in (Katal et al., 2013), big data is characterised by three dimensions – Volume, Variety, and Velocity. Additional Vs including Veracity, Value, and Variability further refine the description and characterisation of the term big data. As Table 1 shows, big data is typically semi-structured and unstructured in nature and is mainly obtained from a range of sources, such as, sensor, computerised, device-generated data, social media and web data, etc. With big data, the data are generated at constantly increasing rates. Veracity relates to the inherent issues of ambiguity and authenticity of data, for instance being of low quality or lacking trust to enable it being used in decision-making. The dimension value explores big data using analytical techniques in order to provide essential insight from the data to allow businesses make more accurate and timely decisions for future prospects. The term variability, (Katal et al., 2013) refers to

Table 1. Comparative Analysis of Big and Conventional Data

Characteristic	Big Data	Conventional Data
Volume	Thousands of gigabytes, terabytes, petabytes, exabytes, and beyond	Megabytes to few hundred Gigabytes
Nature and Location	Typically, semi-structured or highly unstructured (text, likes, tweets, images, motion pictures, sound recordings, etc.)	Typically consists of highly structured and comprises a single discipline sub-discipline. The data is often in ordered and even records, such as an ordered spreadsheet or time series dataset
Reproducibility	Replication of big data is rarely feasible	Conventional data projects can easily be repeated
Analysis	Big data is typically analysed orderly in small incremental steps. In big data, the data can be extracted, examined, transformed, normalized, visualized, interpreted, and re-analysed with different analytical methods	Conventional data projects typically need to be analysed alongside the data
Frameworks and tools	HDFS, NoSQL, Hadoop, Storm, Spark	Relative DBMS, ETL tools and SQL
Data Preparation	Big data typically comes from diverse data sources and is organised by many people	In this data type, the data user formulates her own data for her use

data flow variations for heavy loads. For instance, an instance where numerous concurrent events on a social media platform cause a steep spike in the demand for/of the data.

Big Data Analytics and Cloud Computing Adoption in HEIs

In this section, qualitative content analysis methodology (Mayring, 2004) on the adoption of big data analytics and cloud computing services by HEIs is performed and a systematic review process is applied on this collection of academic articles. This process adopted to perform a Systematic Literature Review (SLR) followed the steps outlined below.

METHODOLOGY

The first step in this process involved a definition of the search terms in a manner that all the concerned research areas – adopting big data analytics and cloud computing in HEIs – were covered. Consequently, the proposed keywords include big data analytics, cloud computing, cloud computing services, information and communication technology services for higher education and big data and cloud computing for higher education. Next, each of these keywords were searched on popular online electronic databases – Google Scholar, Elsevier Science direct, IEEE Xplore and Web of Science. The search was constrained to articles published in English language. Furthermore, the search was constrained to only include articles from the last 10 years (i.e. 2010 to 2020). The contextual analysis was performed using the article title, abstract, and manuscript text. The outcome of the systematic literature review methodology described above resulted in 147 papers, which focused on adopting big data analytics and cloud computing technology in HEIs.

Aggregating the papers in terms of chosen methodology, of the 147 identified papers, 36 percent performed exploratory analyses that investigated the implementation and use of big data and cloud computing services respectively, while 19 percent applied quantitative survey methodology to obtain the analysed data about the adoption of this technology. Another 13 percent adopted literature survey methodology. 11 papers adopted case study methodology, which accounted to 8 percent of the papers as shown in Table 2.

The review process mainly focused on identifying frameworks, models and architectures that were used for adopting big data analytics and cloud computing in HEIs. The empirical analysis of the resultant dataset showed that only three papers of the identified papers proposed computing frameworks, while four papers described big data analytics and cloud computing models. Finally, five papers proposed cloud computing architectures.

Table 2. Summary of Methodologies used in the papers

Methodology	Percentage	Value
Exploratory analysis	36%	53
Quantitative Survey	19%	28
Systematic Literature Review	13%	19
Hypothesis	12%	17
Case Study	11%	16
Observation	9%	14

Frameworks for Cloud Computing Adoption in HEIs

Yang (2011) presents an enhanced framework for e-education that adopted open standards for cloud services. The framework is delineated into two parts – service and management phases. The service subsystem is further logically split into execution cloud, managing the virtual machines through service scheduler, core middleware, service monitor, hype visor and storage cloud merged, which are in the management subsystem and are provided according to the user's requests. The management subsystem accepts the user's requests through user-front-end and parses the same to the service subsystem stage after determining whether the service is satisfied locally, or it needs to be transmitted to alternative cloud locations. In Saidhbi (2012), a hybrid cloud computing framework for Ethiopian Universities Hybrid Cloud (EUHC) is presented. The framework comprises of four layers, including the user interface layer – which has three parts (user portal, service catalogue, and service repository) for accessing different services provided in the three other layers. The other three layers provide varying levels of cloud services (SaaS, PaaS, and IaaS).

Subramanian and Seshasaayee (2014) present three frameworks representing a roadmap for developing a best practice for the adoption of big data and cloud computing in Indian universities. The first framework proposes the hybrid cloud as a solution for security and capacity compromises. The second framework represents the workflow approach, which can be deliberated as a principled decision-making process concerning service provisioning on the basis of the scalable and 'pay as you use' model. The third framework provides an explanation of how the hybrid cloud works through all the universities and schools. The article presented in (Liu and Li, 2011) presents a cloud-based platform for digitalising a university campus, which adopts a Service Oriented Architecture (SOA) and virtualization technologies. The framework comprises three layers: (i) The infrastructure layer, (ii) the application layer, which provides the operational environment built around three requirements that define the required services, managing them and providing uniform access to various services as well as the convenience that comes with using them at a cloud platform. These requirements are met through the SOA architecture. The Third layer comprises the service offering layer which supports instant IT services provided through the network to satisfy the users' requests in various forms – IaaS, PaaS or SaaS.

Conghuan (2011) proposes a service computing model for communication between local campus clouds to manage the activities of universities and proposing the efficient sharing of resources. The model proposes multiple local campus clouds. Each campus cloud is programmed to provide given services by virtualising a set of resources. This set of virtualised resource is recorded in the service pool. Consequently, the service pool delivers the requisite incorporation of a learning platform and teaching environment for distributed resources under certain conditions, which provides the requested services.

The Adoption of Big Data Analytics in HEIs

As previously stipulated, big data provides higher education institutions an opportunity to strategically use their IT resources to improve the quality of educational services, guide students to provide student experience, deliver higher completion rates, and improve student persistence. Many business organisations around the world adopt big data analytics in business intelligence and areas including market and financial forecasting. Over the past decade, Big Data has attracted the interest of academia. Consequently, academic institutions are migrating to cloud architectures and, with the increased adoption of digital devices by users in these ecosystems, is resulting in a situation where more data is being generated in these institutions than ever before, therefore creating significant opportunities for using Big Data analytics techniques to find patterns in the data that can enhance decision-making.

Big Data presents a suitable framework for efficiently exploiting the enormous array of data in shaping the future of higher education (Görnerup et al., 2013). The adoption of Big Data application in higher education institutions (HEIs) is attributed to technological innovation and development, which have accelerated the growth of big data analytics in higher education institutions. According to Williamson (2017), Data Warehouses and Cloud Computing combined with greater proprietorship of digital devices by end users in the educational network make it possible to obtain, manage and sustain enormous amounts of data. These Information Technologies present critical resources that – when exploited by policy makers – are beneficial in compelling institutional strategy and policy making for the future. IT makes accessible sophisticated platforms that deliver computing power that is essential for analysing massive datasets and transforming these into important information. Data mining technologies, when applied, apply descriptive statistics to develop patterns from the massive amounts of collected data for actionable information (Eynon, 2013). Big Data Analytics is important in tackling a momentous amount of pressing issues for education systems. Such issues include (i) increasing effectiveness of HEIs, (ii) exploiting intuitions from learning experiences, (iii) delivering high-quality education for all, which may be tailored to individual learners' needs; and (iv) furnishing students with appropriate skills for their future.

CASES OF BIG DATA ANALYTICS AND CLOUD COMPUTING ADOPTION IN HEIS

For this section, let the assumption remain that big data analytics for higher education refers to the science of analysing institutional data from various sources using complex statistical, mathematical and machine learning-based quantitative models, and predictive models to enhance data-driven decision making. Big data analytics has been employed in higher education to provide academic, management and administrators the liberty to observe and obtain more insight about their respective institutions and learners and transform that knowledge into insight for informed decision-making. This section presents a practical application of big data analytics in higher education.

Case 1: Learning Analytics for Academic Student Tracking

The rapid advancement in the volume and veracity of data obtained by HEIs has resulted in a spike in the flow of data. Through learning analytics, HEIs can improve understanding of their learners' challenges and apply the resultant insight to emphatically enhance the improvement (Slade and Prinsloo, 2013). The ability to understand the learning needs of individual students should comprise the motivating factor for the adoption of learning analytics in HEIs. A successful case of implementing learning analytics in a HEI is the Rio Salado University in Arizona, which developed a learning analytics software for tracking student progress in courses, and the resultant analytics of the collected data in order to drive decision-making. The university enrols over 41,000 students in both online and in-campus courses. The application was developed to centre on personalisation, which involves providing assistance to non-traditional students to achieve academic goals through personalised intermediations (Crush, 2019).

Case 2: Cloud Computing in Higher Education

As stated in the preceding sections, cloud computing has the potential to increase flexibility and expose HEI users to a broad range of educational resources. This includes providing them with access to infrastructure, software, hardware, and platform at any time in any place provided there is internet access. Within HEIs, the users of cloud computing (i.e. students, lecturers, admin staff, developers, programmers and researchers) all adopt the overarching platform for delivery of the given service. Amongst the existent cloud service models (see Section 2.2.2), the software-as-a-service (SaaS) model is the most commonly applied service model in HEIs. The authors in Akande and Van Belle (2014) explored the adoption of SaaS cloud computing in South African HEIs, having the main motive of determining the viability of the adoption of SaaS in HEIs. The paper also articulated the benefits and limitations of SaaS in HEIs.

This findings from the study revealed that most South African HEIs were sensitive to the existence of SaaS and are typically employing public and hybrid cloud services, with none using community cloud services. Furthermore, in South African HEIs, SaaS is mainly applied towards student management (i.e. student recruitment, enrolment, financial disbursement, graduation, and alumni. SaaS is also employed for admin systems including human resource management (HR), customer relationship management (CRM), supply chain management, finance and payroll and asset management. In summary, the study supported the claim that cloud computing was beneficial to HEIs. To confirm this calls for an analysis of the benefits and challenges of cloud computing in HEIs.

BENEFITS OF BIG DATA AND CLOUD COMPUTING IN HEIS

As previously stated, Big Data typically integrates the research field of learning analytics (Siemens and Long, 2011), which is rapidly-growing area of research. However, rather than focus on the – rather peripheral – application of Big Data analytics in student tracking analytics, Big Data can provide opportunities and challenges for HEIs. Siemens and Long (2011) showed that Big Data presents an intriguing framework for efficiently exploiting the broad range of data and eventually moulding the future of higher education.

Analytics can be used to improve the quality of teaching in HEIs. Just as in businesses, the value of performance or monitoring dashboards applied towards improving teaching or course provision is also highlighted by the literature. For instance, in the University of Wollongong, Australia, analytics of social network data showed interaction patterns that surface in sections that are local. On the other hand, the learners themselves, particularly when in their early years of higher education, often have little or no idea of their performance in comparison with their peers, thereby having gaps in essential knowledge, lacking key study skills. Consequently, providing students with better information relating to their progression and what is required in order to meet their educational goals represents an important use of learning analytics for improving teaching and learning quality. This action has the potential to transform their learning and understanding of how they learn by providing frequent formative feedback as the students advance through their studies. It also enables them to compare themselves to their contemporaries, adding a competitive component and adding a check that enables them to keep up with the group or the progress of successful students in previous groups. Meanwhile, other universities use analytics systems to assist students choose future modules, building up on historical data about career picks, aptitudes and grades of previous modules to provide optimal pathways through their studies.

CHALLENGES OF BIG DATA AND CLOUD COMPUTING IN HEIS

The research field of Big Data Analytics is receiving increased interest in many HEIs with many scholars supporting its relevance for enhancing the success of higher education. To improve the quality of learning outcomes, it is critical that the massive amounts of data generated by educational systems should be effectively analysed to expedite suitable responses to emergent challenges. However, the challenges to the adoption of Big Data in Education typically include ethical aspects of tracking student data, failure to correlate vital business problems with big data solutions. Furthermore, users or executives are typically rooted in old technologies constitutes another challenge. Third, the cost of computational resource and manpower can also result in a challenge for the adoption of big data analytics and cloud computing.

More so, there is also the shortage of data warehouses and analytical methods and algorithms as well as issues with data quality, which basically leaves most data uncollected resulting in no analyses. It is observed in the literature that prevalent analytics use is limited mainly to the functional aspects of student enrolment administration, progress, and resource optimisation. This peripheral space of application of analytics is mainly due to the barriers of cost, data availability and quality, culture, know-how, and communication. In reality, attaining a well-structured and handy big data ecosystem with distinct encouragements for all parties poses challenges in many aspects. These are segments such as regulation, policy making, public administration and management. This calls for progress of practical models for big data. Big Data analytics in HEIs also faces the strict test of discovering the means to mine knowledge from the widespread datasets generated daily and the distillation of the extracted data into usable information for administrators, students, instructors, and the public. Tracking big data is costly, and therefore organisational managers must be persuaded that analysing such data will yield tangible results prior to investing in the technology.

Big Data also presents many analytical issues that require recurrent updating of instruments and expertise, meaning that HEIs need to have sufficient finances to accommodate these concerns. Furthermore, there also exist genuine concerns about privacy, especially given that the data is obtained from online sources. This, in combination with the 'digital divide' in many countries presents hindrances to fully exploiting the power of Big Data analytics and cloud computing for the benefit of the users of the educational systems (Dede et al., 2016). In summary, the challenges associated with the manipulation and analysis of Big Data using cloud computing are broadly due to its defining properties – volume, velocity, veracity, variety and value. The challenge is in the integration of heterogeneous data sources in this era. For instance, in HEIs, there is the need for the integration, synchronisation, and aggregation of data from sensors, cameras, social media, and legacy systems, all of which are in different formats, size, structure, etc. Table 3 provides a summary of the key opportunities and challenges of cloud computing stated above:

Table 3. Summary of Key Opportunities and Challenges of Cloud Computing

Opportunities	Challenges
Efficiency	Ethical issues regarding tracking student data
Improve the quality of teaching and course provision	User resistance from traditional system users
Improve the quality of teaching and course provision	High cost of computational resource and manpower
Provision of frequent formative feedback	Shortage of data warehouses and analytical methods
Supports future career development	Issues with data quality
	Lack of cloud competency
	Difficulties maintaining a well-structured and handy big data ecosystem
	Complex big data analytics in HEIs
	Privacy issues

CONCLUSION

A popular saying "knowledge is power" implies that the more one knows, the more control he/she has. In HEIs, when tutors are provided with insight into the individual progression of their students, they are able to take action if things are going in the wrong direction. Consequently, technology-based learning provides data that, when analysed can provide this intuition, illuminating what works and what does not work so that learning outcomes can be enhanced using informed mediation. Within HEIs, there is increasing data growth, although most of it is distributed across desktops in departments, faculties, or schools, and typically come in different formats, increasing the difficulty of retrieving nor consolidating it. On the other hand, notwithstanding the many critics and deterrents of the widespread adoption of cloud computing, it appears obvious that Cloud Computing is not going away anytime soon. Cloud computing guarantees a revolutionary migration in the provision of computing resources within an organisation. Currently, it is penetrating into many domains and areas of endeavour, from computer science to engineering, student recruitment to learning analytics; from research laboratories to enterprise IT infrastructures. Educational institutes are at the genesis of a changeover period during which they will encounter many challenges relating to cloud adoption. Despite the many benefits of adopting cloud computing and big data analytics in higher education, there will always be demerits that will impede adoption of the technology.

Limitations of the research is the lack of empirical support since a systematic approach was adopted. Cases were presented, but only for a select few HEIs. Other cases conducted through empirical enquiry may yield different findings since each University is different and thus cloud computing may not be the ideal fit for meeting their institutional goals. Empirical enquiry could help to rectify this issue. So this leads to conducting potential future studies. Future studies could the topic of cloud computing adoption in HEIs further to analyse the benefits and challenges from a wider lens. For example, a PESTLE analysis could be conducted to determine the political, economic, social, technological, legal and environmental determinants and barriers to cloud computing big data. This may provide a greater insight why HEIs may choose to adopt or not adopt ubiquitous technologies. Another study could also look at the benefits and challenges through a sociotechnical lens where interactions between HEI stakeholders and potential cloud technology may help to unravel further reasons for adoption and non-adoption of cloud computing. A comparison of cloud computing and other ubiquitous technologies such as Internet of Things could also help to reveal some interesting trends of ubiquitous technology adoption in HEIs to foster teaching and learning.

REFERENCES

Akande, A. O., & Van Belle, J.-P. (2014). Cloud computing in higher education: A snapshot of software as a service. In *2014 IEEE 6th International Conference on Adaptive Science & Technology (ICAST)*. IEEE. 10.1109/ICASTECH.2014.7068111

Ali, M. (2019). Cloud Computing at a Cross Road: Quality and Risks in Higher Education. *Advances in Internet of Things*, 9(3), 33–49. doi:10.4236/ait.2019.93003

Ali, M. B. (2019). Multiple Perspective of Cloud Computing Adoption Determinants in Higher Education a Systematic Review. *International Journal of Cloud Applications and Computing*, 9(3), 89–109. doi:10.4018/IJCAC.2019070106

Ali, M. B., Wood-Harper, T., & Mohamad, M. (2018). Benefits and challenges of cloud computing adoption and usage in higher education: A systematic literature review. *International Journal of Enterprise Information Systems*, 14(4), 64–77. doi:10.4018/IJEIS.2018100105

Ali, M. B., Wood-Harper, T., & Ramlogan, R. (2020). A Framework Strategy to Overcome Trust Issues on Cloud Computing Adoption in Higher Education. In Modern Principles, Practices, and Algorithms for Cloud Security (pp. 162-183). IGI Global. doi:10.4018/978-1-7998-1082-7.ch008

Antonopoulos, N., & Gillam, L. (2010). *Cloud computing*. Springer. doi:10.1007/978-1-84996-241-4

Armbrust, M., Fox, A., Griffith, R., Joseph, A. D., Katz, R., Konwinski, A., Lee, G., Patterson, D., Rabkin, A., Stoica, I., & Zaharia, M. (2010). A view of cloud computing. *Communications of the ACM*, *53*(4), 50–58. doi:10.1145/1721654.1721672

Campbell-Kelly, M., Garcia-Swartz, D. D., Aspray, W., & Ceruzzi, P. E. (2008). The rise, fall, and resurrection of software as a service: historical perspectives on the computer utility and software for lease on a network. In *The Internet and American Business* (pp. 201–230). MIT Press Cambridge.

Collins, C., Andrienko, N., Schreck, T., Yang, J., Choo, J., Engelke, U., Jena, A., & Dwyer, T. (2018). Guidance in the human–machine analytics process. *Visual Informatics*, *2*(3), 166–180. doi:10.1016/j.visinf.2018.09.003

Conghuan, Y. (2011). A service computing model based on interaction among local Campus Clouds. In *2011 6th International Conference on Computer Science & Education (ICCSE)*. IEEE. 10.1109/ICCSE.2011.6028668

Crush, M. (2019). Monitoring the PACE of student Learning: Analytics at Rio Salado Community University. *Campus Technology*.

Dede, C. J., Ho, A. D., & Mitros, P. (2016). Big data analysis in higher education: Promises and pitfalls. *EDUCAUSE Review*.

Dillon, T., Wu, C., & Chang, E. (2010). Cloud computing: issues and challenges. In *2010 24th IEEE International Conference on Advanced Information Networking and Applications*. IEEE. 10.1109/AINA.2010.187

Erl, T., Puttini, R., & Mahmood, Z. (2013). *Cloud computing: concepts, technology & architecture*. Pearson Education.

Eynon, R. (2013). *The rise of Big Data: what does it mean for education, technology, and media research?* Academic Press.

Görnerup, O., Gillblad, D., Holst, A., & Bjurling, B. (2013). *Big data analytics-a research and innovation agenda for Sweden*. The Swedish Big Data Analytics Network.

Hwang, K., Dongarra, J. J., & Fox, G. C. (2011). *Distributed and cloud computing: clusters, grids, clouds, and the future internet*. Morgan Kaufmann.

Jain, L., & Bhardwaj, S. (2010). Enterprise cloud computing: Key considerations for adoption. *International Journal of Engineering and Information Technology*, *2*, 113–117.

Katal, A., Wazid, M., & Goudar, R. H. (2013). Big data: issues, challenges, tools and good practices. In *2013 Sixth International Conference on Contemporary Computing (IC3)*. IEEE. 10.1109/IC3.2013.6612229

Kelly, J. (2014, Feb 5). *Big data: Hadoop, business analytics and beyond* [Blog post]. Wikibon.

Lee, K., Lee, S., & Yang, H.-D. (2014). Towards on cloud computing standardization. *International Journal of Multimedia & Ubiquitous Engineering*, *9*(2), 169–176. doi:10.14257/ijmue.2014.9.2.17

Liu, N., & Li, G. (2011). Research on digital campus based on cloud computing. In *International Conference on Computer Education, Simulation and Modeling*. Springer. 10.1007/978-3-642-21802-6_34

Mayring, P. (2004). Qualitative content analysis. *A companion to Qualitative Research, 1*, 159–176.

Poonia, P., Jain, V. K., & Kumar, A. (2018). Short Term Traffic Flow Prediction Methodologies: A Review. *Mody University International Journal of Computing and Engineering Research, 2*, 37–39.

Rittinghouse, J. W., & Ransome, J. F. (2016). *Cloud computing: implementation, management, and security*. CRC Press.

Saidhbi, S. (2012). A cloud computing framework for Ethiopian Higher Education Institutions. *IOSR Journal of Computer Engineering, 6*, 1–9.

Siemens, G., & Long, P. (2011). Penetrating the fog: Analytics in learning and education. *EDUCAUSE Review, 46*, 30.

Slade, S., & Prinsloo, P. (2013). Learning analytics: Ethical issues and dilemmas. *The American Behavioral Scientist, 57*(10), 1510–1529. doi:10.1177/0002764213479366

Sokol, A.W., & Hogan, M.D. (2013). *NIST Cloud Computing Standards Roadmap*. NIST.

Subramanian, S., & Seshasaayee, A. (2014). Review & Proposal for a Cloud based Framework for Indian Higher Education. *International Journal of Engineering and Computer Science, 3*, 3689–3694.

Vaquero, L.M., Rodero-Merino, L., Caceres, J., & Lindner, M. (2008). *A break in the clouds: towards a cloud definition*. Academic Press.

Wang, J., Ma, Y., Zhang, L., Gao, R. X., & Wu, D. (2018). Deep learning for smart manufacturing: Methods and applications. *Journal of Manufacturing Systems, 48*, 144–156. doi:10.1016/j.jmsy.2018.01.003

Williamson, B. (2017). Big data in education: The digital future of learning, policy and practice. *Sage (Atlanta, Ga.)*.

Yang, C., & Huang, Q. (2013). *Spatial cloud computing: a practical approach*. CRC Press. doi:10.1201/b16106

Yang, Z. (2011). Study on an Interoperable Cloud framework for e-Education. In *2011 International Conference on E-Business and E-Government (ICEE)*. IEEE. 10.1109/ICEBEG.2011.5887174

ADDITIONAL READING

Askari, S. H., Ahmad, F., Umair, S., & Khan, S. A. (2018). Cloud Computing Education Strategies: A Review. In Exploring the Convergence of Big Data and the Internet of Things (pp. 43-54). IGI Global. doi:10.4018/978-1-5225-2947-7.ch004

Feng, J., Yang, L. T., Gati, N. J., Xie, X., & Gavuna, B. S. (2019). Privacy-preserving computation in cyber-physical-social systems: A survey of the state-of-the-art and perspectives. *Information Sciences*.

Stergiou, C., Psannis, K. E., Gupta, B. B., & Ishibashi, Y. (2018). Security, privacy & efficiency of sustainable Cloud Computing for Big Data & IoT. *Sustainable Computing: Informatics and Systems, 19*, 174-184.

Tawalbeh, L. A., & Saldamli, G. (2019). Reconsidering big data security and privacy in cloud and mobile cloud systems. *Journal of King Saud University - Computer and Information Sciences*.

Wazid, M., Das, A. K., Hussain, R., Succi, G., & Rodrigues, J. J. P. C. (2019). Authentication in cloud-driven IoT-based big data environment: Survey and outlook. *Journal of Systems Architecture, 97*, 185–196. doi:10.1016/j.sysarc.2018.12.005

KEY TERMS AND DEFINITIONS

Adoption: The acceptance of technologies in an organisational setting.

Big Data: A large volume of structured and unstructured data that inundates an organisation.

Cloud Computing: The use of applications, storage, and processing facilities to deliver on-demand computing services over the internet on a pay-per-use basis.

Data Analytics: The process of probing datasets to determine what information they contain.

E-Learning: Learning via online applications and systems.

Higher Education: University taught education.

Pedagogy: The practice of teaching in a learning environment.

Section 6

Managerial Impact

Chapter 84
Big Data Technologies and Management

Jayashree K.
Rajalakshmi Engineering College, India

Abirami R.
Rajalakshmi Engineering College, India

ABSTRACT

Developments in information technology and its prevalent growth in several areas of business, engineering, medical, and scientific studies are resulting in information as well as data explosion. Knowledge discovery and decision making from such rapidly growing voluminous data are a challenging task in terms of data organization and processing, which is an emerging trend known as big data computing. Big data has gained much attention from the academia and the IT industry. A new paradigm that combines large-scale compute, new data-intensive techniques, and mathematical models to build data analytics. Thus, this chapter discusses the background of big data. It also discusses the various application of big data in detail. The various related work and the future direction would be addressed in this chapter.

1. INTRODUCTION

Big data is the new approach that is used for analyzing large amount of data-set. Data-set can be from different sources which includes both structured and unstructured data, be it a sensor data or emails or social media (Hiba et al., 2014). The standard method used for analyzing and processing the structured data using Relational Databases is no longer satisfactory due to several challenges. Big data deals with high Volume, Velocity, Variety, Veracity and Value of data.

As the amount of data grow day by day, the cost of storage and management became a vital aspect to be taken care. It was then the evolution of cloud computing that came into existence which provides the best methods to store data in a cost-effective way. The rapid progress of IT industries in different fields like medicine, engineering, business and research requires new technique for processing huge volume of data. Each of the specified field contains voluminous data which has to be managed and controlled

DOI: 10.4018/978-1-6684-3662-2.ch084

for processing. To process and manage the data in an effective way certain mathematical models, data-intensive techniques are required together. A new emerging approach that is used for processing multi-dimensional data which combines mathematical models, data-intensive techniques is termed as big data computing (Kune et al., 2016).

Big data keeps the data safe and secure by utilizing different software tools (Venkatesh et al., 2015). Since data are stored on cloud, the three major criteria like speed, scalability and capacity to process the data are achieved. New business opportunities emerge by using big data as it enables the users to visualize the data. Data analytics is another advantage where the datasets are examined, and information's are obtained.

Section 2 introduces the background of big data. Section 3 discusses big data challenges. Section 4 describes the related work. Section 5 explains the future research directions. The conclusion of the chapter is described in Section 6.

2. BACKGROUND

In day-to-day life millions and billions of data are created everyday by people be it on any social networking sites, finance, medicine, sensors, mobile applications and so on. To manage, analyze and process all these data new processing methodologies, techniques and tools must be used. The information's are being flooded and are beyond a range, in which it cannot to measure. A best example is Facebook, where 100 Terabytes of data are uploaded every day. The term "Big data" came into emergence to store and process huge amount of data in a simple way. There are various definitions of big data stated by researches. According to McKinsey, Big data is a huge amount of data in which the size of the data is beyond the size of regular databases. O'Reilly states that big data is nothing but the data that exceeds the limit of normal database where the data or information is large and processed quickly. Hence new approaches have to be followed to process the information. According to Gartner, Enormous data means high volume, rapid speed and variety of data resources which needs new procedures and techniques to handle the data. New approaches and techniques is difficult to apply on traditional databases by using simple software tools used in accessing the relational database. Data can be both structured as well as unstructured data collected from different resources. All the definitions lead to 5 V's which is Volume, Velocity, Variety, Veracity, Value.

Hence new approaches have to be followed to process the information. According to Gartner, Enormous data means high volume, rapid speed and variety of data resources which needs new procedures and techniques to handle the data. New approaches and techniques is difficult to apply on traditional databases by using simple software tools used in accessing the relational databases database. Data can be both structured as well as unstructured data collected from different resources (Sunny Sharma et al., 2016). All the definitions lead to 5 V's which is Volume, Velocity, Variety, Veracity, Value.

1. **Volume:** Large volume of data are collected from enterprises or organizations. These data are usually in form of terabytes ranges from 30-50 or even more TBs. The available storage cannot handle structure and unstructured data; this is an important challenge for organizations.
2. **Velocity:** Velocity describes the speed of data that an organization can handle and analyze to increase the profit of business before the value of information is lost.

3. **Variety:** Information can be structured, unstructured, semi structured or even the combination of all three. It comes in many forms like logs, tweets status, images, animations, audio, text files, PDF, click stream and so on.
4. **Veracity:** Data sources are of different qualities with differences accuracy, coverage and timeliness.
5. **Value:** The data collected are stored and has to reused whenever needed. Hence the data should not be outdated. The data has to be processed and produced quickly during analysis. The data are combined with other data-sets and reused for future reference. Based on the 5 V's big data can be classified under five categories:

   a. **Data Sources:** Includes internet data-for example social media, sensing data- example IoT, and transactional data- example financial data.

   b. **Content Format:** Since data are from different sources, they are of different format namely structured, unstructured and semi-structured data.

   c. **Data Stores:** The collected data are stored in either document database, column database, graph database, and key-value alternate to relational database.

   d. **Data Staging:** In staging the unwanted or incomplete data are identified, then the data are transformed for analysis and finally normalization is done for minimizing duplicate, redundant data.

   e. **Data Processing:** The collected data are processed by batch processing using Map-reduce techniques, and by certain big data tools (Ibrahim Abaker et al., 2015).

Since the huge amount of data collected are unstructured the concept of Big data emerged. A large amount of complex data, which can be captured, stored and analyzed in Real-Time. 570 new websites are developed every minute, 72 hours of video are uploaded in Youtube every second. Billions of data are added to Facebook every week and millions of tweets are created by user on each day. It is highly impossible. without big data for all these data to be stored, analyzed and managed.

As the amount of data grows, cloud computing is combined with big data technologies for managing and storing the large amount of data. In all the applications the information's are easily accessible. Hence the advantages of using cloud in the field of big data is in terms of Agility, Affordability, Data processing and feasibility (Ibrahim et al., 2015).

Agility: In organizations the normal databases is no longer compatible for storing and managing enormous data, as it is slower and is difficult to process the data. Hence cloud computing is used to provide resources to the organizations on demand. Storing information's on cloud database can enable the organization to have number of virtual servers which can manage, store and access data.

Affordability: Before cloud, the organizations invested huge amount of money to update the hardware and software they use. Now the resources are easily available on cloud and can be used by the organizations any time whenever need at any cost, that is they need to pay only for the resources they use, be it a storage space or power.

Data processing: Due to a drastic increase of data, processing became a little difficult. For example, Social media generates millions and trillions of data such as videos, photos, tweets, blogs, posts which cannot be analyzed and processed under a single class or category. Cloud computing makes use of map-reduce methodology on big data platform like Hadoop which helps to process the data in an easier and efficient way.

Feasibility: To increase the storage space and processing speed, large number of servers are required, whereas virtual characteristic of cloud helps to access the resources on demand, anywhere and at any time easily and quickly. Big data needs new methodologies for processing enormous data, hence cloud computing plays a vital role in providing the resources.

APPLICATIONS

The several areas of application where big data computing used are Education, Health care, sports, gaming, security, Financial and business analytics (Sabia et al., 2014).

In the Field of Education

Big data plays vital role in education. Educators can create an online forum for students be it a moodle or any online website. The educators or instructors can upload video, notes, lesson plan on all topics and activities can be given based on the topics related to video. The Students behavior such as their understanding of the topics can be evaluated by the activities done by the students. It can also identify the interest of student looking at time spent on online videos, notes, textbook. Smart classrooms are on board where the major base is big data.

Healthcare

The major goals in healthcare sectors is to enhance the quality and satisfaction of the patients experience in treatment, to reduce the cost, to use modern approaches to analyze and manage the patients records or information's. It is quite difficult to collect, store and manage the clinical data of all patients. Hence high-performance analytics and methods has to be used to manage the large amount data. Unstructured data can be extracted by performing text mining on patients record. Hence the data can be collected quickly and correctly without causing any difficulty to clinicians. In addition to it, making the information's regarding treatment of patients transparent, patients will be able to get their treatment through online health applications.

Network Security

Big data plays a vital role in security technologies. For example, credit card details given during online transactions can be hacked and used by an intruder. Big data makes use of fraud detection techniques to tackle the issue and prevents the intruder to access the personal card details. It is also being used in the field of forensics and SIEM.

Sports

Big data next interesting application is sports. Coaches, players and the leading minds in sports came together to discuss the potential of analytics and big data. For example, in athletics, the athletes are monitored frequently in terms of speed, performance, time, kilometers they run per day so on. The monitored data are stored on daily basis. Statistics of data collected are calculated to understand the capacity of the athletes. The benefit is, coaches can easily identify which player need additional support, training and guidance. This will surely help to increase the performance and progress of the player.

Gaming

Three main data such as game data, player data and session data are collected from the people playing video games. The volume of data that the players are generating every day is growing very quickly. To manage all these data a new big data technology which is "Hadoop" is used. It makes use of map-reduce concept to analyze collect and process the massive data. By analyzing the collected data like the user's behavior, rewards, activity, leader boards, character selections the game developers will be able to improve or upgrade the game options and versions. The up-gradation helps to improve the gaming experiences of the player.

Telecommunication

A very big challenge faced by telecommunication sector are volume, variety and complexity. To overcome this challenge "telcos" technology is used. It is actually the combination of ETL and traditional databases with big data technologies. Telcos combines huge volume of data generated by location sensors, IPv6 devices, clickstream, CDRs, 4G networks and machine to machine monitors information. It also handles multiple forms of unstructured data be it form mobile, web, mail and so on.

Emerging applications are continuously generating huge amount of structured and unstructured data hence advanced techniques like Hadoop has to be used to process and store the data. New tools and approaches has to adapted in near future to track, analysis share our personal data in a secure manner. All real-world applications are related to big data is one way or the other.

3. BIG DATA CHALLENGES

Several challenges need to be focused as big data deals with large amount of data. Based on the applications of big data the issues or challenges faced are broadly classified into two. The issues that are related to management activities like storage, scalability and efficiency are grouped under engineering category and the issues dealing with unstructured data are grouped under semantic challenges.

Since the application of big data ranges from Science to business, enormous amount of data needs to be stored analyzed and processed. As the result various challenges like Heterogeneity, Incompleteness, scalability, Timeliness, Privacy and Security are to be addressed.

Heterogeneity

Data collected are from various sources the major challenges lies on the format of data. Mostly the collected data will be in unstructured form. It may be in the form of email's, pdf file, graphics, audio, animations, medical x-rays, CT scans, voice mails and so on. Converting all these data into structured form is a major challenge where new technologies and methodologies has to be adopted to deal with the issues.

Incompleteness

Sometimes the data fields values entered would be missing. This creates uncertainty of data which is a major challenge to be addressed. The missing values can occur due to repair in sensor, system crash and so on. Incomplete data creates uncertainties during data analysis and it must be managed during data analysis. Various datamining algorithms are developed to deal with missing data or values. If the algorithms are not stated properly it would become a major drawback to collect and process the data correctly.

Scalability

Scalability is one of the serious issue which prevails for several years as big data deals with large amount data. Parallel data processing methods that were used in the past to maintain and process the data are no longer useful as the size of data keeps increasing rapidly day by day. New approaches have to be followed to maintain the growing size or elasticity of data.

Timeliness

The next serious issue is timeliness which means the request of the data has to processed much faster, but since the size of data is large it is difficult to scan the data and respond the query or request made by the user.

Security

Among all the issues the most serious issue that must be addressed is security. If security violation occurs, it will cause very serious damage and consequence on data that is stored and analyzed. In-order to maintain the data in a secured .way we need to follow techniques and algorithms related to encryption, logging, honeypot, and fraud detection.

Management Challenges

As big-data deals with enormous amount of data several challenges related to data management like accessing, processing and governing the data arises. The repository of data which are otherwise called as data warehouse stores large amount of sensitive data related to medicine, insurance, diagnosis, end user's personal data etc. Hence all the data must be kept in a secure manner by the organizations and each user has to be given privilege only to view relevant data. Certain privacy rules have to be followed by the management to monitor the security of data, which means only the relevant data can be viewed and accessed by the employees of the organization. Broadly all these data management issues are divided into seven fields namely privacy, data and information sharing, cost, operational expenditures, data governance and data ownership (Stephen et al., 2013).

Data and Information Sharing

Each and every agency and departments, maintain their own data center, and data are kept confidentially. Certain data cannot be shared due to some privacy conditions in such cases data sharing becomes a challenge in smart city as data has to be shared among different devices. Different approaches need to be followed to achieve proper information sharing and exchange among different devices and departments. In addition to it, large amount of data are updated, and stored in different format every second on real time applications. Hence it is difficult to create a general format of data and extract information, directly from real time application.

Cost

Even if huge investments are made on certain projects to maintain privacy, it still remains to be greater challenge. For example, in smart cities sensors are used to capture each and every individual activity, which are accessed by several government and security agencies. As the result location based data are transferred over the network which is an important privacy concern.

Security and Privacy

Next major concern in big data is security. If security issues are not properly taken care, then it may lead to attacks like malware or it can be hacked by any third-party user. In certain applications as confidential data about people and government are collected and stored in the database, more security policies and procedures should be followed to keep the data protected from unauthorized user and from virus attack or bugs. Privacy rights of organizations and individuals has to be clearly stated and protected. In certain cases, like medical records, bank and financial records are viewed by the individual which violates the privacy rights hence better techniques has to be followed to rectify this issue.

Governance

Data quality must be met as importance of big data is increasing day by day. The major three issues in maintaining the quality of data are how data are analyzed, accessed and stored. A good big data governance strategy must be followed to ensure the quality of the data.

In addition to it, certain key challenges have been identified in big data management related to the cloud. The challenges include Data security and privacy. Security issues causes a major threat to business and cloud providers nowadays. Mostly transactional data carry sensitive information like details of credit and debit cards like numbers, address and so on. The intruders find new ways to hack the details of the system and find out the card details. Other security issues like ransomware, Denial of Service attacks, Phising attacks, Cloud abuse are of major concern which has to be addressed. Weak APIs and interfaces allows the hackers to hack the information's and misuse them in anyway.

Certain cloud models are still in development stage. Data-Acts is another major issue where the cloud providers except the datacenter to be closer to the user so that the data can be accessed easily. The next issue is data replication- more data are collected from various resources and devices it is necessary to avoid the duplication of data, as duplication results affects the analysis stage. Other issues include approximate results, Data exploration to enable deep analytics; Enterprise data enrichment with web and social media, Query optimization; and Performance isolation for multi-tenancy (Stephen et al., 2013).

Since large amount of data are used for storage, the cost for storing the enormous amount of data is still a challenge for medium and small organizations. In traditional method the storage is based on network-attached storage. To collect and store information or data large number of NAS need to be interconnected with one another to form cluster, which requires NAS pods. Hence the best option for medium and small organizations is to make use of cloud. The resources on demand will be provided by an outside entity, hence only, little management effort and cost need to be put by the small and medium sized organizations. (Bernice, 2012)

The way to deal with all these challenges is to implement new next-gen technologies which can identify the issue before it could cause damage to the data. Algorithms like fraud detection, encryptions can be used to protect the data from intruders.

4. RELATED WORK

Sameer Agarwal et.al. presents a BlinkDB, an approximate query engine for running collaborative SQL queries on large volume of data which is massively parallel. BlinkDB uses two key ideas such as an adaptive optimization framework that builds and maintains a set of multi-dimensional stratified samples from original data over time, and a dynamic sample selection strategy that selects an appropriately sized sample based on a query's accuracy or response time requirements.

Yingyi Bu et.al. have used a new technique called HaLoop that allows iterative applications to be assembled from existing Hadoop programs without modification, and significantly improves their efficiency by providing inter- iteration caching mechanisms and a loop-aware scheduler to exploit these caches. He presents the design, implementation, and evaluation of HaLoop, a novel parallel and distributed system that supports large-scale iterative data analysis applications.

Swanson et.al develops a new MapReduce scheduling technique to enhance map task's data locality. He has integrated this technique into Hadoop default FIFO scheduler and Hadoop fair scheduler.

Albert Bifet et.al. Stated that streaming data analysis in real time is becoming the fastest and most efficient way to obtain useful knowledge, allowing organizations to react quickly when problem appear or detect to improve performance. The tools used for mining big data are apache Hadoop, apache big, cascading, scribe, storm, apache HBase, apache mahout, MOA, R, etc.

5. BIG DATA ANALYTICS

Big data analytics deals with analyzing, inspecting, transforming large amount of data in order to find useful information and also use the data for decision making purposes. To get valuable information from the data it has to processed in a timely manner. Analytics plays a vital role in the field of business. To process the data efficiently the combination of three major parameters namely people, process, technology have to be considered compulsorily. In addition to it explanatory and predictive models are used for processing statistical and quantitative data in order to achieve effectiveness. The major benefits of using analytics in big data is it optimizes the process, combines internal and external data, helps organizations to meet client's requests, manage market related risks and as a whole converts useful information or data to intelligent data. Analytics is a huge area where it can be divided as text analysis, audio, video analysis, social media analysis and so on. Big data deals with all these fields.

Text analysis deals with textual data like news feeds, surveys, call and message logs, blogs, social media updates and posts. All these data are analyzed and helps in evidence related decision making. Analyzing text data helps in prediction purpose for example prediction of stock market. Audio usually comes under unstructured data. Call centers and healthcare are two major application of audio analytics. In call centers each and every hour, minutes, seconds, the calls are recorded which improves customers' demands, increases the sales profit rates, identify sales turnover etc. Few organizations use Interactive Voice Response (IVR) platforms to identify and handle frustrated callers in the field of medicine, the psychological behavior of patients can be identified, and treatment can be given based on the disease predicted (Hadi et al., 2014).

In video analytics the information is gathered from video streams. The vital issue in video analytics is the size of data from which the information is extracted, analyzed and processed. Social media analytics contains both structured as well as unstructured data. Maintaining both these data is a major task, which is done in an easier way by data analytics.

Predictive analytics comprise a variety of techniques that predict future outcomes based on historical and current data predictive analytics seek to uncover patterns and capture relationships in data. Predictive analytics techniques are sub divided into two groups. Some techniques, such as moving aver-ages, attempt to discover the historical patterns in the outcome variable(s) and extrapolate them to the future. Others, such as linear regression, aim to capture the inter dependencies between outcome variable(s) and explanatory variables, and exploit them to make predictions. Based on the underlying methodology, techniques can also be categorized into two groups: regression techniques and machine learning techniques.

6. FUTURE RESEARCH DIRECTIONS

Big data has become a great technology that is used by all organizations to analyze, store data. The huge amount of data obtained or gathered from different resources like mobile devices, sensors, social media, satellites helps organization to improve their decision making and take their organization to a higher level. Few issues are addressed which have to be taken into account to improve the quality of information given to the customers. Bigdata makes use of Hadoop at present to handle large amount of data, but it is becoming insufficient. Effective techniques and tools should be developed to overcome the issues faced by big data.

Future scope of big data relies on: (Samiddha Mukherjee et al., 2016)

1. **Data Volume Increases Rapidly:** As new smart applications are evolving rapidly enormous amount of data, will be collected from various internet collected devices hence as the result the volume of data will grow rapidly.
2. **Improve the Ways to Analyze the Data:** Traditional SQL database will be outdated, and several tools like Spark will be rapidly evolving for analyzing the data.
3. **Real-Time Streaming of Data:** Users will be able to process the real-time data for decision making using programs like kafka and spark.
4. **Machine Learning:** The advent of machine learning, will be helpful for data preparation and prediction analysis of applications.
5. **Privacy:** Since, all the data are shared online, the major challenge will be privacy. Organizations has to find way through new policies and regulations to address privacy controls and procedures.
6. **Autonomous Agents:** Automatic agents and things like robots, autonomous vehicles, virtual personal assistants, and smart advisers will be a new trend for the people.
7. The data-as-a-service business model is growing rapidly used for predictions in whether forecast.

8.   New algorithms to support big data methodologies have to be developed. Existing algorithms like Algorithmia, Data Xu, and Kaggle can be expected to grow and multiply.

CONCLUSION

With the advent of the digital age, the amount of data being generated, stored and shared has been on the rise. The benefits and limitations of accessing the data are arguable in view of the fact that this analysis may involve access and analysis of medical records, social media interactions, financial data, government records and genetic sequences. The requirement of an efficient and effective analytics service, applications, programming tools and frameworks has given birth to the concept of big data Processing and Analytics. Big data analytics has found application in several domains and fields. Some of these applications include Education, Health care, sports, gaming, security, Financial and business analytics. Thus, this chapter describes a collaborative study on applications, general issues and challenges in big data and cloud computing and the future scope where this big data will take the organization in the near future.

REFERENCES

Abaker, I., Yaqoob, A., & Mokhtar, G. (2015). The rise of "big data" on cloud computing: Review and open research issues. *Information Systems, 47*, 98–115. doi:10.1016/j.is.2014.07.006

Abawajy, J. (2015). Comprehensive analysis of big data variety landscape. *International Journal of Parallel, Emergent and Distributed Systems, 30*(1).

Agarwal, S. (2013). *BlinkDB: Queries with Bounded Errors and Bounded Response Times on Very Large Data*. ACM. doi:10.1145/2465351.2465355

Bifet, A. (2013). Mining Big Data. In *Real Time*. Informatica.

Big data and privacy. (n.d.). Standard Law School-The center for internet and society.

Condie, T. (2010). *Online Aggregation and Continuous Query support in MapReduce. In SIGMOD*. ACM.

Eldawy, A. (2013). A Demonstration of Spatial Hadoop: An Efficient MapReduce Framework for Spatial Data. *Proceedings of the VLDB Endowment International Conference on Very Large Data Bases, 6*(12). doi:10.14778/2536274.2536283

Emani, C. K., Cullot, N., & Nicolle, C. (2015). Understandable Big Data: A survey. *Computer Science Review, 17*, 70–81. doi:10.1016/j.cosrev.2015.05.002

Gandomi, A., & Haider, M. (2015). Beyond the hype: Big data concepts, methods, and analytics. *International Journal of Information Management, 35*(2), 137–144. doi:10.1016/j.ijinfomgt.2014.10.007

Hadi, Shnain, Hadishaheed, & Ahmad. (2015). Big data and five v's characteristics. *International Journal of Advances in Electronics and Computer Science, 2*(1).

Harshawardhan, S., & Gadekar, P. (2014). A Review Paper on Big Data and Hadoop. *International Journal of Scientific and Research Publications, 4*(10).

Kaisler, S., & Armour, E. (2013). Big Data: Issues and Challenges Moving Forward. *46th Hawaii International Conference on System Sciences*. 10.1109/HICSS.2013.645

Kune, Konugurthi, Chillarige, & Buyya. (2016). *The anatomy of big data computing, Software: Practice and Experience*. Wiley Online Library.

Lee & Choi. (2011). Parallel Data Processing with MapReduce: A Survey. SIGMOD Record, 40(4).

Loshin, D. (2014). *Addressing Five Emerging Challenges of Big Data*. Progress Software.

Marcos, Calheiros, Bianchi, Nettoc, & Buyya. (2015). Big Data computing and clouds: Trends and future directions. *Journal of Parallel and Distributed Computing*, 79–80.

Mukherjee & Shaw. (2016). Big Data – Concepts, Applications, Challenges and Future Scope. *International Journal of Advanced Research in Computer and Communication Engineering, 5*(2).

Narooka. (2016). Paradigm Shift of Big-Data Application in Cloud Computing. *International Journal of Advanced Research in Computer and Communication Engineering, 5*(5).

Pansarel, N. (2011). *Online Aggregation for Large MapReduce Jobs*. ACM.

Phaneendra, V. S. (2013). Big Data- solutions for RDBMS problems- A survey. *12th IEEE/IFIP Network Operations & Management Symposium (NOMS 2010)*.

Purcell. (2012). Big data using cloud computing. *Journal of Technology Research*.

Purcell. (2013). The emergence of big data technology and analytics. *Journal of Technology Research*.

Sabia, S. K. (2014). Applications of big Data: Current Status and Future Scope. *International Journal on Advanced Computer Theory and Engineering, 3*(5).

Security and Privacy in the Era of Big Data. (n.d.). The SMW, a Technological Solution to the Challenge of Data Leakage, renci ncds.

Sivarajah, U., Kamal, M. M., Irani, Z., & Weerakkody, V. (2017). Critical analysis of Big Data challenges and analytical methods. *Journal of Business Research, 70*, 263–286. doi:10.1016/j.jbusres.2016.08.001

Swapnil, A. (2014). Understanding the big data problems and their solutions using hadoop and mapreduce. International Journal of Application or Innovation in Engineering & Management, 3, 3.

Troester, M. (2013). *Big Data Meets Big Data Analytics*. White Paper.

Umasri, M.L. (2014). *Mining Big Data: Current status and forecast to the future*. Academic Press.

Venkatesh, Perur, & Jaliha. (2015). A Study on Use of Big Data in Cloud Computing Environment. *International Journal of Computer Science and Information Technologies, 6*.

Ying Lu, C. H., & Swanson, D. (2010). Matchmaking: A New MapReduce Scheduling. *10th IEEE International Conference on Computer and Information Technology (CIT'10)*.

This research was previously published in Innovative Applications of Knowledge Discovery and Information Resources Management; pages 196-210, copyright year 2018 by Information Science Reference (an imprint of IGI Global).

Chapter 85
Managerial Controversies in Artificial Intelligence and Big Data Analytics

Kenneth David Strang
https://orcid.org/0000-0002-4333-4399
Multinations Research, USA

Zhaohao Sun
https://orcid.org/0000-0003-0780-3271
Papua New Guinea University of Technology, Papua New Guinea

ABSTRACT

This chapter discusses several fundamental and managerial controversies associated with artificial intelligence and big data analytics which will be of interest to quantitative professionals and practitioners in the fields of computing, e-commerce, e-business services, and e-government. The authors utilized the systems thinking technique within an action research framework. They used this approach because their ideology was pragmatic, the problem at hand, was complex and institutional (healthcare discipline), and they needed to understand the problems from both a practitioner and a nonhuman technology process viewpoint. They used the literature review along with practitioner interviews collected at a big data conference. Although they found many problems, they considered these to be already encompassed into the big data five V's (volume, velocity, variety, value, veracity). Interestingly, they uncovered three new insights about the hidden healthcare artificial intelligence and big data analytics risks; then they proposed solutions for each of these problems.

INTRODUCTION

Technological entrepreneur and UK-based venture capitalist Viktor Prokopenya (2018) pointed out that artificial intelligence applications like machine learning have many limitations especially that many tasks have too much data and are simply too complicated to program. Scholars already know about the major

DOI: 10.4018/978-1-6684-3662-2.ch085

challenges faced by big data analytics practitioners across all disciplines which are described as the five V's (Jovanovi et al., 2015, Terry, 2015) or sometimes more (Sun et al., 2016). The big data five V's are commonly phrased as high volume (Chen and Zhang, 2014), complex variety (Kessel et al., 2014), large velocity (Ekbia et al., 2015), strategic value (Gandomi and Haider, 2015), and more recently veracity (Strang and Sun, 2016). Value in big data can be viewed as a constraint because it can be challenging to derive a benefit from analytics that is worth the investment time and cost to accommodate the other factors. Big data veracity can refer to ethics, accuracy, validity, or truthfulness (Vajjhala et al., 2015) as well as social-cultural relevance (Vajjhala and Strang, 2017). In addition to the above characteristics, each discipline and industry has unique big data analytics issues.

In the healthcare discipline researchers have posited that privacy is one of the biggest problems associated with the big data paradigm (Thorpe and Gray, 2015, Hoffman and Podgurski, 2013, Kshetri, 2014, Filkins et al., 2016, Rothstein, 2015). Most countries have legislation to uphold the privacy of individuals, such as the *Health Insurance Portability and Accountability Act* in USA (Brown, 2008). However, we propose there are important hidden big data analytics issues in the healthcare industry that are not documented in the literature. In this study we review the literature and collect information from practitioners about tacit problems associated with healthcare big data analytics and then summarize the results in a visual model.

The big data paradigm is relatively new since it formally commenced in 2011 (Salleh and Janczewski, 2016, Burrows and Savage, 2014, Strang and Sun, 2017) so there is roughly half a decade of research at the time of writing. Most of the published big data research has been focused on technology-related keywords like data mining, cloud computing, machine learning, electronic data processing, algorithms and others (Strang and Sun, 2017). According to a recent meta-analysis of the big data literature only 2% of peer-reviewed publications examined privacy and security topics including healthcare during 2011-2016 that that decreased to 1% for the first three months of 2017 (Strang and Sun, 2017). Many researchers have called for more studies about big data privacy (van Loenen et al., 2016, Eastin et al., 2016, de Montjoye and Pentland, 2016, Salleh and Janczewski, 2016, Chen and Zhang, 2014), and particularly in healthcare (Jungwirth and Haluza, 2017, Filkins et al., 2016). This is strong evidence that more research about healthcare big data analytics is needed. This also implies there may be unseen risks that practitioners know exist in healthcare big data analytics. We attempt to articulate these obscure issues in healthcare big data analytics through a literature review and from discussions with other practitioners.

LITERATURE REVIEW

Overview of Big Data Literature

Chen and Zhang (2014) reviewed the literature several years ago and came to the conclusion that privacy was not adequately investigated within the big data body of knowledge. However, in addition to being dated, they did not perform a longitudinal structured review of the literature. Therefore we conducted a thorough review of the big data literature published during the last decade.

We start with a summary of the literature before we review the relevant healthcare data analytics papers. Using "big data" as the search term, we closely examined 13,029 manuscript titles, abstracts and keywords published in journals during 2011-2017 (only the first three months of 2017 were included). We used the title, abstract and keywords to a dominant theme for every article. We counted the frequencies of the themes which resulted in 49 topics consisting of 1-3 words like 'data mining', 'artificial intelligence' and 'online social networks'. We then factored the journal big data from 2011-2017 into a displayable short-list of 10-15 dominant themes using the frequency, and grouped all remaining low-count topics into a new category called '<1%'.

The results revealed that the most frequent big data topic published in journals was data mining (N=1186) at 9.1%. The next three topics were similar in frequency, namely data analytics (N=979, 7.5%), cloud computing (N=808, 6.2%), and literature reviews (N=784, 6.0%). For reference purposes we could classify the current study as either a big data literature review (or under the others topic). Machine learning (N=493, 3.8%) and social media (N=466, 3.6%) came next but were a third less frequent than data mining. The following seven big data topics were somewhat equivalent in frequency: electronic data processing (N=455, 3.5%), algorithms (N=388, 3.0%), databases (N=360, 2.8%), map reduce (N=358, 2.7%), research methods (N=302, 2.3%), human behavior (N=282, 2.2%) and privacy & security (N=280, 2.1%). As shown in figure 1, the remaining articles generated frequencies at or less than 1% so all were grouped into the '<1%' category which amounted to 6752 or 51% of the manuscripts in the meta-analysis. This other category included 36 topics like information technology, concepts or frameworks, hadoop, acquisition of data, computer algorithms, as well as healthcare.

These 13 dominant topics represented 49% of the big data body of knowledge production in scholarly journals during the literature review sample time frame. Only a very small proportion of the privacy & security articles were grounded in the healthcare discipline. Thus, it was clear that published research about privacy in big data was scarce (at 2.1%) and this included all disciplines not just healthcare. This shows that there was a shortage of big data analytics research about privacy.

In our literature meta-analysis of big data we grouped privacy and security together because researchers often did that despite that they meant one or the other term. To clarify, privacy in big data is the claim of individuals to have their data left alone, free from surveillance or interference from other individuals, systems or organizations (Kessel et al., 2014, Kshetri, 2014). In the healthcare discipline privacy can be further defined as an individual's right to control the acquisition, use, or disclosure of his or her identifiable health-related data even if it does not contain personal identifiers. In contrast, big data security refers to the technology, software, policies, procedures, and technical measures used to prevent unauthorized access, alternation, theft of data or physical damage to devices and systems (Gandomi and Haider, 2015, Jovanovi et al., 2015). In the healthcare discipline, security is further refined as the physical, technological, or administrative safeguards or tools used to protect identifiable health data from unwarranted access or disclosure. In this study we focus on healthcare big data privacy and not security – not that the latter is any less critical but it is beyond the scope.

Positive Impact of Big Data in Healthcare

Notwithstanding the five or more challenges with big data (volume, velocity, variety, value, veracity), there are many positive benefits for healthcare practitioners and researchers. Detailed big data on people can be used by policymakers to reduce crime or terrorism, improve health delivery, and better manage cities (Strang and Alamieyeseigha, 2015, Terry, 2015). Organizations and nations can benefit from big data because research indicates that data-driven businesses were 5% percent more productive and 6% more profitable than their competitors (Chen and Zhang, 2014, Burrows and Savage, 2014). The macro-economic impact is that the gross domestic product of a country could increase due to big data analytics (Gandomi and Haider, 2015).

We have seen big data analytics used to help combat global and domestic terrorism (De Zwart et al., 2014, Strang and Sun, 2016). The American military has tapped into big data to uncover and mitigate terrorist plots (Strang, 2015a). For example geo-location smart phone big data was helpful for investigating the Boston bomber and his accomplices (Strang and Alamieyeseigha, 2017) and many other terrorist plots have been foiled (Lichtblau and Weilandaug, 2016).

Big data analytics can assist with decision making in all disciplines and industries, from commercial entities to government policy makers (Eastin et al., 2016, Kessel et al., 2014). Big data is valuable to commercial businesses to improve target marketing and thereby increase effectiveness on a microeconomics level but the benefits go further to the macroeconomic environment as a cost reduction and increased goods production using the same scarce resources (de Montjoye and Pentland, 2016).

The benefits of big data analysis for improving healthcare medical research are well-known (Lusher et al., 2014, Thorpe and Gray, 2015). These benefits include facilitating evidence-based medical research to detect diseases at the earlier stages (ADA, 2015, Rothstein, 2015), minimizing drug surpluses and inventory shortfalls in pharmaceutical (Zhong et al., 2015), and better tracking of viruses through location-enriched social media big data (Vaidhyanathan and Bulock, 2014). As with the other disciplinary benefits, this has a positive domino effect by improving microeconomics and macroeconomics (Chen and Zhang, 2014).

Environmental monitoring has generated useful big data that can help to identify virus and disease spreading patterns through global position system (GPS) location-coding (Leszczynski, 2015, Zhong et al., 2015) and from patient symptom-related messages in social media posts (Jungwirth and Haluza, 2017, Hogarth and Soyer, 2015). Hospital executives and management have used administrative big data to monitor patient quality and staff feedback, which affords information that may not otherwise be forthcoming (Hoffman and Podgurski, 2013). Interestingly, when individual patient data is aggregated together for an entire hospital or facility, fluctuations in vitals could indicate a major problem such as poor air quality or a pandemic like pneumonia (Jungwirth and Haluza, 2017, Kshetri, 2014).

Healthcare researchers have gained the most from big data because this has become another rich data collection avenue providing more volume, velocity, variety, and potential value, as compared with surveys, observation, and physical vitals capture (Kshetri, 2014, Lusher et al., 2014). Healthcare big data tends to be categorized into two streams: Vitals and social. The vitals are the obvious value-laden form of big data in healthcare. However, social big data can also be useful to the healthcare industry by allowing practitioners to detect attitudes through sentiment analysis (Zikopoulos et al., 2011, Gandomi and Haider, 2015).

Unintended Healthcare Big Data Access

The literature is ripe with the benefits of big data but there are also some unadvertised pitfalls. In these next three sections we will examine the three hidden problems of healthcare bug data analytics. Wireless micro-technology advances have given healthcare professionals insights into diseases and medical conditions. What puts wireless healthcare technology into the big data analytics domain is that micro-technology implants and devices can generate huge volumes of high velocity and a wide variety of valuable 'personal data'. Personal data generated by healthcare devices and implants may contain date of birth, social security number or other healthcare patient identification, gender, address with geo-location coordinates, along with the high volume high velocity probe readings such as blood pressure, counts, etc. (Lusher et al., 2014, Ward, 2014).

Wireless healthcare devices and implants are similar to SCADA systems used for environmental monitoring in that a huge amount of readings are generated – more big data than could possibly be stored or analyzed (Strang and Sun, 2016). Likewise in healthcare wireless devices or implants, there are so many probe readings that only a small number are processed by the receiving station (Filkins et al., 2016). The personal identification data is more extensive during the initiation sequence with a receiving station (to authenticate the connection), and while this may be encrypted, it is transmitted either randomly or at specific intervals to maintain a connection with a receiving station (Lusher et al., 2014).

Healthcare wearable devices or internal implants are generally connected to servers through a pervasive computing application, with the purpose to monitor a patient from sensor readings so as to warn physicians if a pattern changes for the worst or for the better (Lusher et al., 2014). Sensors are not new technology because they have been used with pervasive computing applications to gather data from the physical environment such as binary (1=on or 0=off) sensors attached to household objects or infrastructure like movement detectors, door sensors, contact switch sensors and pressure pads (Shen and Zhang, 2014). Healthcare specific devices or implants tend to collect readings on body temperature, blood pressure, pulse, blood–oxygen ratios, heart ECG or glucometers, movement (e.g., a fall), and chemical presence (Vaidhyanathan and Bulock, 2014). Radio frequency identification data (RFID) chip tags or Quick Response (QR) codes can be used to uniquely identify and locate tagged objects (e.g., a medical device presence), or to store (a link to) relevant information such as medication instructions (van Otterlo, 2014). Similarly, Bluetooth or modulated illumination-based beacons deployed throughout the user's environment can be used to transmit unique location identification codes, which a hand-held device or wearable badge can detect in order to locate the user through GPS coordinate (van Otterlo, 2014).

Some type of personal identification is included in every healthcare wireless broadcast to ensure that a receiving station does not confuse the patient's device device/implant with another close by patient. Although the identification in pure data reading transmissions may be a unique number generated for the patient, it is nevertheless linked to the patient as well as to the location of the patient. This is what makes wireless healthcare personal big data subject to the veracity or viability characteristic – many people do not want their wireless-transmitted personal data to be captured by anyone other than the intended receiving station. Unfortunately, the nature of wireless transmissions is that even encrypted data could be easily intercepted and decoded with currently available software (Al-Ameen et al., 2012).

The capability of identifying individuals in big data even when personal attributes have been removed is a risk. There are several well-known cases in the literature. Likelihood algorithms have been used to link big data streams without personal identifiers to a master file based on information that could estimate age, gender, location, and employment characteristics (Angiuli et al., 2015, Wang et al., 2015. Winkler, 2005). If the social media big data include even a few direct identifiers, like names, address, cell phone numbers, social security numbers, or company numbers, the risk is high that a match could be made with organizational or government data (Wang et al., 2015, Zikopoulos et al., 2011).

Most healthcare devices or implants have physical machine addresses (MAC's) and Internet Protocol (IP) addresses if they are online. The MAC address is hard-coded at the factory and is detectable in cellular data networks or on the Internet, while IP addresses are usually active only when on the Internet but they can still be read with the appropriate software (Wang et al., 2015). These addresses are necessary for the device/implant to connect to a peer or network receiver in order to transmit their data (Wang et al., 2015). The problems is that since these network addresses can be accessed, they can be linked to location and device owner so that when combined with the transmitted data it could identify an individual including financial and other confidential information. There are free open software applications that can track cell phone locations and social media user names through the MAC and GPS big data which are being used for malicious reasons (Shen and Zhang, 2014, Shull, 2014).

At the other end of the situation is the informed consent presented to the healthcare patient and/or physicians. Usually a healthcare device/implant will contain a privacy policy declaration that must be signed before surgery or application. Secondly, any mobile software being used in conjunction with the device/implant, such as a smartphone application would contain a privacy policy that would require patient consent. However, the Internet generation of people are accustomed to seeing software agreements due to downloading applications on smartphones, laptops, and other products so there is a tendency to hastily recklessly agree out of frustration or habit. Therefore, more attention must be given to informed consent when wireless healthcare big data collection is being authorized.

Most developed countries have legislation to protect individual privacy in healthcare big data, such as the Health Insurance Portability and Accountability Act (HIPAA) regulations under the Privacy Rule of 2003 in USA (Brown, 2008). HIPAA requires healthcare providers to remove 18 types of identifiers in patient data, including birthdate, vehicle serial numbers, image URLs, and voice prints (Brown, 2008). However, even seemingly innocuous information makes it relatively easy to re-identify individuals through wireless healthcare big data, such as finding sufficient information that there is only one person in the relevant population with a matching set of unique conditions (van Loenen et al., 2016).

Data generated by interacting with recognized professionals, such as lawyers, doctors, professors, researchers, accountants, investment managers, project managers or by online consumer transactions, are governed by laws requiring informed consent and draw on the Fair Information Practice Principles (FIPP) legislation (Brown, 2008, Terry, 2015). Despite the FIPP's explicit application to protect individual data, the rules are typically confined to personal information such as social security number and do not encompass the large-scale data-collection issues that arise through location tracking and online social media postings or Internet site visits (Terry, 2015).

Ultimately, the major drawback of wireless healthcare big data is that it takes place in the open public domain outside of a healthcare provider jurisdiction, and therefore it is not covered by privacy legislation (Brown, 2008). Two practitioner examples from colleagues of the first author illustrate the extreme risk of what can happen. In one case a licensed medical physician from Sydney Australia specializing in pediatric immunology (children allergies, asthma, rhinitis, sinusitis, atopic dermatitis, urticarial, anaphylaxis and immune disorders) missed two days of the IEEE Big Data conference. When he was pulled aside for a detailed interview at the Dulles Washington International airport immigration he did not realize that his foreign passport contained a readable electronic passive chip that contained his place of birth, which happened to be Tehran but his parents had emigrated from Iran to Australia when he was one year old. It is easy to sympathize with anyone held up in immigration-customs especially in his predicament where he was asked "so prove to me that you are a doctor in Australia." After several hours of interrogations he was able to produce several of his journal papers stored on his laptop and by later in the evening EST the Sydney clinic had opened for their early morning so they were able to confirm his identity through a Skype call. During immigration apparently humans are guilty until proven innocent.

A piping engineer in the oil-gas industry was living in Houston, TX while completing his doctorate at an American university under the guidance of the first author. Since he travelled frequently for work and university the engineer used a wireless pass card for toll roads and he had an enhanced driver license that facilitated his passing through land and water borders between USA and Mexico. When he was finishing his dissertation he took several months off and became annoyed at receiving what he thought were scam collection letters in the mail. After a visit with his bank and discussions with a credit counselor, he found that his identity had been stolen and over $20,000 in debt had been incurred in his name in addition to his student loan. Investigators believed that the wireless passive chip in his driver license had been read to furnish his birth date, citizenship information and address, and some credit card data along with other vehicle identifiers were somehow captured from the toll-pass-card and their billing system. The culprits were professionals because there was no evidence to charge them so he was forced to declare bankruptcy.

The prevalence of multiple digital devices of the sample person being connected to the Internet has resulted in personal information being inadvertently collected by legitimate providers, which when combined across sources can become powerful big data. For example, as Ohm (2010) proved, a marketing specialist or a hacker could re-identify more than 80% of Netflix clients using an individual's zip code, birthdate, and gender along with viewing history. Netflix is a popular entertainment site but it is unlikely that high ranked officials would necessarily want their viewing information or other online behaviors revealed to the world. Another example of big data caveats occurred when Target was able to predict a teenage girl was pregnant due to her online browsing activity and sent baby coupons to her house which were not well-received by her father (Duhigg, 2014). The same problems can occur in the healthcare discipline because professionals may have their online Internet behavior linked to their personal identity, or patients may have their Internet activity, location, and other personal details connected together using big data analytics (Lusher et al., 2014, Leszczynski, 2015).

METHODS

We utilized the systems thinking technique popularized by Checkland (1999) which Strang (2015b) classifies as an action research method where practitioners apply a pragmatic ideology towards a study. "The action research method starts by the researcher reviewing the literature either before or after the analysis, so as to validate or improve upon existing theories" (Strang, 2015b, p. 59). This systems thinking technique differs from the critical analysis method in that the latter attempts to find gaps or inaccuracies in the literature using only the literature with deductive reasoning, but the former also collects practitioner or process data and attempts to find a solution to an institutional problem (Strang, 2015b). An advantage of the systems thinking approach over other traditional research methods is that it helps to "understand group and nonhuman processes" (Strang, 2015b, p. 403) such as in healthcare informatics. This approach is ideal for examining the complicated hidden big data analytics problems in the healthcare discipline which is dominated by subject matter specialists and leading edge technology.

A pragmatic ideology is pluralistic in that a study "begins with research questions focused on a problem, with a process improvement unit of analysis and a community of practice level of analysis", using mixed data types interpreted by the researcher and participants (Strang, 2015b, p. 23). This may be contrasted to a positivistic worldview where the data is fact-driven and hypothesis testing is often employed, or at the other philosophical extreme point is a constructivist ideology where participants provide rich data and communicate their own socio-cultural meaning reported verbatim by the researcher (Strang, 2015b).

In this study we do not make any cause-effect, correlation, deductive or inductive propositions, nor do we merely report practitioner opinions – we interpret what we discover in an open-minded practical manner. We first review scholar perspectives from the literature, we collect big data analyst practitioner opinions, and then we integrate results produced by statistical techniques. The practitioner opinions were collected through two channels. The first was direct interviews and discussions during the IEEE

Big Data Conference held at Washington DC December 3-5, 2016. The second was also from direct discussions with practitioners through emails and using discussions on the Research Gate scholar social network system during the first six months of 2017.

According to Checkland (1999), after the literature review and subsequent knowledge assessment are completed, the key output of the systems thinking method is a visual model of the proposed critical real-world and tacit processes needed to solve the problem(s). The systems thinking model has two areas separating the known practices from the uncertain issues or processes with strategic links intended to bridge the gap or reduce risks. The model does not replace a discussion, but rather it summarizes the findings in a systematic diagram. A visual model will assist in communicating the findings to the healthcare discipline stakeholders as well as to researchers in this or any related discipline.

A pragmatic action research systems-thinking type of project does not necessarily follow the introduction-literature-method-results-discussion paper sequence. The rationale for choosing a pragmatic ideology is that proven techniques must often be adapted to accomplish the research goal(s) because formal methods do not necessarily accommodate messy problems or the complex mixed data collected (Strang, 2015b). Our research design is pragmatic, with a manuscript containing an introduction to the problem(s), methodology explanation, literature review, subject matter expert discussions, synthesis and assessment of data, recommendations to solve problem(s), conclusions and reference listing. Here we integrate our discussion into the literature review and close with a combined recommendations-conclusions section.

DISCUSSION

Earlier we stated that there are many benefits to having wireless healthcare big data but if it used unethically or outside of a personal privacy stipulation, the result can be harmful to individuals. For example, high blood pressure and other poor health indicators could trigger higher insurance premiums or prevent being hired. Inadvertent release of personal healthcare information such as a patient's mental illness, dementia, or other cognitive impairments could result in losing a job, losing their driver license, failing to obtain a mortgage/loan, losing friends, and at the extreme it could lead to depression, premature forfeiture of independence to caretakers or even suicide.

We will overlook the pure technology related issues with healthcare big data problems. For example, electromagnetic interference could scramble some or all of the data, a natural or anthropogenic disaster could compromise the device/implant or server, and device or server could simply overheat and fail. These problems are beyond the scope of our healthcare big data privacy study – but these risks do exist and they ought to be examined by other researchers.

We will categorize the above risks associated with wireless/remote healthcare device/implant big data being available and usable outside of its intended purpose as the hidden problem of unintended healthcare big data access. Although we found most unintended access was through wireless technology, this definition should also encompass other media, such as inadvertent use or covert theft of a clinic's data files along with other big data in ways that were not originally authorized.

The first proposed solution to this 'unintended healthcare big data access' problem seems intuitive. Strong public or private key encryption could be added as a security layer, and actually this is already being done. As software becomes more powerful encryption algorithms will run fast enough to permit more real-time use. Additionally, a government managed security clearing network could be built to serve as an intermediary between healthcare devices/implants and the outside connection to another

other system. That is obviously a monolithic costly suggestion if implemented at the national or global level. The other potential solution is simple: Eliminate factory-coded MAC addresses and instead use temporary ones. Actually that is more difficult to achieve in practice due to the dependencies of the MAC address. Another constraint associated with MAC addresses is that they are useful to investigate criminal activity as well as domestic and global terrorism (Strang and Alamieyeseigha, 2015, Strang, 2015a). More research into this problem and these proposed solutions will be needed.

Healthcare Big Data Statistical Sampling Violations

Healthcare big data and big data in general tends to measure patterns in behavior (physical or mental), not internalized states like attitudes or beliefs that would be captured through other collection methods such as interviews, surveys, observations, or literary records. Healthcare big data is near-real-time and has a high granularity of details, owing to the high volume, velocity and variety.

Healthcare big data are usually high in volume and velocity but at any given point there are very few variables or fields transmitted. Social media big data often contains only a GPS location code and a text message (Strang and Sun, 2016). In healthcare big data it is typical to see four fields, an identifier, a timestamp, a GPS coordinate and some sensor reading (Strang and Sun, 2016). Some sensor readings contain several numbers but others are simplistic, such as a decimal 1 or 0 meaning yes or no, on or off, ok or not ok, etc. In a technical sense, a single byte has 8 bits which could each be a code. In a simple example, let's say a medical device transmitted a patient number, the time, their location, and their body temperature, every second, which would result in 3600 records per hour 86,400 per day and 31,536,000 per year, for every device per patient. This is why healthcare devices/implants generate big data. Let's say that researchers want to determine if there is a correlation or a cause-effect between the drugs administered to their 100 patients and their body temperatures during the year, and that an equally sized data was generated per patient for the drug administration processes. This would conceptually require 6,307,200,000 records which we can round up to 6.4 billion.

The problem is that it is difficult for healthcare researchers to perform statistical analysis on healthcare big data because even without the addition of the drug information for this anecdote, the desktop version of one of the most powerful statistical software programs SPSS can hold only 2 billion cases in a dataset since the file format includes a count of the cases in a 32-bit signed integer with the high order bit devoted to the sign (IBM, 2013); thus, the largest record number that can be stored is $2(31)-1 = 2,147,493,647$. Thus, we could not store all the healthcare big data even for a simple drug-temperature analysis! No problem though, IBM have a mainframe version of SPSS without these big data file size constraints that can be purchased with hardware facilities for a few million USD.

Actually, several researchers had already pointed out that a barrier to performing big data analytics was that most statistical software could not handle the large file sizes (Vajjhala et al., 2015). However, researchers have found ways around the big data five V's – at least the volume, velocity and variety attributes – by using could-based and distributed software such as Hadoop along with sampling techniques to reduce the five V's (Couper, 2013, Varian, 2014, Strang and Sun, 2016). Nonetheless, this is where another hidden healthcare big data problem lurks. There are several tacit issues that revolve around research design assumptions and statistical sampling assumptions.

Social media big data was once criticized for being focused on the young generation but paradoxically the modern products like Facebook and Twitter are now used older baby-boom adults whereas Instagram and Snapchat tend to be preferred by the younger generation (Ekbia et al., 2015). In the healthcare industry medical devices/implants that generate wireless big data are used by people with injuries, viruses, diseases or illnesses (Rothstein, 2015). Additionally the popular social media products with big data available are predominately in English (Filkins et al., 2016). In laymen terms, researchers of social media big data do not know who in the population is excluded, who is not texting or responding, or even the true extent of the underlying population. Thus it is clear there is a sampling bias beyond nonresponse in the entire big data paradigm (Couper, 2013, Varian, 2014). Almost an entire global generation and many world-wide non-English speaking cultures could be missing in popular social media big data files, depending on the situation.

Obviously if only sick people are included in most healthcare big data analytics this would be a biased very small sample of humans. More so, it could be difficult to convince a significant sample of healthy people to have medical devices implanted to participant without offering a huge monetary incentive and even if they agreed it could present a new obstacle of statistical self-selection bias. Additionally, healthcare big data usually represents a large volume of readings collected from a very small number of patients in close proximity at a medical facility (Al-Janabi et al., 2016). For example, in the anecdote above the healthcare big data collection of body temperature reading records at 86,400 is well beyond the minimum statistical sample size of 30 but it is useless for estimating correlations or cause-effect predictions to the underlying population. Likewise, when social media big data is applied for healthcare research, generational, language and socio-cultural barriers would likely confound the statistical sampling principles. Therefore it is likely that all healthcare big data collected violates the statistical sampling principles of randomness and population representation (Strang, 2015b). There are exceptions to this problem in healthcare big data analytics because some medical devices are used for single patient emergency monitoring and decision making such as spatiotemporal sensing to alert staff when a patient falls or if vitals abruptly change – there is no logical reason to improve sampling of this type of healthcare big data.

The difference between primary and second research collection is that primary research data collection involves conducting research oneself, or using the data for the purpose it was intended for. Secondary research data, on the other hand, was collected by a third party or for some other purpose (Couper, 2013). An advantage of using primary data is that researchers are collecting information for the specific purposes of their study. In essence, the questions the researchers ask are tailored to elicit the data that will help them with their study (Couper, 2013, Varian, 2014) such as to test hypotheses or answer complex research questions. Researchers collect the data themselves, using surveys, interviews, direct observations or from records (namely reports or transaction files designed to capture information specific to the study). This is called the research design, that is, the articulation of the study goals, unit of analysis, generalization targets (Strang, 2015b). In the healthcare discipline, most scholarly research takes place in the field – the hospital or clinic – using primary data collection techniques like observations (of physical vitals included), visual observations, interviews, and sometimes surveys if controlled experiments are conducted. The hidden problem is that healthcare big data is being used as a replacement for accessing secondary data but the issue is the secondary data was not collected as a proper research design.

There are substantial risks associated with replacing traditional data collection methods, such as a misallocation of resources. For example, there have been many social media big data studies to improve emergency management practices during natural disasters like hurricanes (Strang, 2013) and tornados (Strang, 2012). On the other hand there has been an overreliance on Twitter data in deploying resources in the aftermath of hurricanes which has led to the misallocation of resources toward young, Internet-savvy people with cell phones and away from elderly or impoverished neighborhoods lacking in social medial access and literacy (Ohm, 2010). A famous example of poor survey methodology led the Literary Digest to incorrectly predict the 1936 presidential election results (Ohm, 2010). Inadequate understanding of sample coverage, incentive, and the lack of a comparison control group when analyzing administrative criminal big data records unfortunately led to incorrect inferences being made that a death penalty policy reduces state crime (Ohm, 2010).

One of the main reasons for applying statistical techniques and the *Central Limit Theorem* is for inferential thinking, that is, to show there is a link between variables or a predictive cause-effect trend in the entire underlying population by using an efficient cost-effective sample (Couper, 2013, Varian, 2014). Therefore, much work must be done to adapt statistical techniques that can exploit the richness of healthcare big data but preserve inference principles (Varian, 2014). We will categorize the above risks associated with wireless/remote healthcare device/implant big data collection as 'statistical sampling violations'. A straightforward solution to this 'statistical sampling violations' is to correct the research design using stratification, systematic or other generally-accepted sampling technique to collect a more representative sample. Due to the big data five V's, this will likely require sampling from multiple sources and combining the results as a single input to parametric or nonparametric statistical techniques. Strang and Sun (2016) discussed how this could be done with global terrorism big data so this could be applied to healthcare big data analytics.

There may be other solutions to the 'statistical sampling violations' healthcare big data analytics problem. Much of our discussion in this section has been positivist but a pragmatic approach could also be taken. Healthcare big data could be collected about each patient from multiple sources so as to achieve data triangulation. Healthcare big data could be collected to sample the entire context of the patient including the room conditions, nearby patient readings, atmospheric radiation, and so on. A constructivist approach could also supplement healthcare big data by adding qualitative patient feelings and physician opinions into the file to be analyzed.

Healthcare Big Data Statistical False Positives

We found more hidden problems with healthcare big data. Other researchers have articulated the data quality issues with big data, such as missing or incomplete data, errors due to technical interference like delays or magnetic fields, and duplicated values (Ekbia et al., 2015, Hoffman and Podgurski, 2013).

A common error with healthcare big data is inaccurate or erroneous labeling of the column data (Couper, 2013, Chen et al., 2014). As an example of this error consider a hospital register may include a column labeled 'number of employees' defined in the data dictionary as the number of persons in the company that received a payroll check in the preceding month but instead the column contains the number of persons on the payroll whether they received a check last month or not, including persons on leave without pay. Other types of big data healthcare errors could rest with the analysts if they perform manipulation or transformation of the values. For example, perhaps changing a timestamp signed integer into a character field representing a calendar day, or transforming ordinal data into a low-medium-high scale. Transformation of data is acceptable for some types of regression and categorization analysis, but since it is literally impossible to see the big data, care must be taken when researchers are transforming values. Additionally, traditional content errors use for master files in a healthcare big data analysis could cause errors, such as keying, coding, or editing of drug or patient characteristics in a master file which is linked to the healthcare big data sensor stream. However, these errors are not unique to healthcare big data – the problem of data entry errors and incomplete inaccurate data is widespread with all manual or machine coded data.

On the other hand there is potentially a new hidden problem associated with healthcare big data. A well-known example of this healthcare big data risk was the error produced by the Google Flu Trends series, which used Google searches on flu symptoms, remedies, and other related keywords to provide near-real-time estimates of flu activity in the United States and 24 other countries worldwide (Lazer et al., 2014). The USA Center for Disease Control (CDC) regularly predicts the flu trends in order to ensure there will be enough vaccinations and healthcare facilities to accommodate the need. According to Lazer, Kennedy, King and Vespignani (2014), Google Flu Trends provided a remarkably accurate indicator of the flu cases in the United States between 2009 and 2011, which was significantly more accurate than the CDC predictions. However, Google Flu Trends was inaccurate thereafter for 2012–2013, more than twice as high as the CDC predictions of which the latter were accurate (Lazer et al., 2014). Thus, Google Flu Trends used healthcare big data analytics to incorrectly forecast future flu trends resulting in more than double the proportion of vaccinations and doctor visits scheduled.

The Google Flu Trends healthcare big data incident may have been caused by social media herd-behavior and commercial search engine manipulation. Apparently the healthcare big data-generating engine at Google was modified in such a way that the formerly highly predictive search terms eventually failed to work, for example, when a user searched on fever or cough, Google's other programs started recommending searches for flu symptoms and treatments, which had a domino impact on other user searches because they would be redirected to flu sites which was counted in the predictor variable (Lazer et al., 2014). These types of problems are programming errors made by Google. There have been similar problems reported by other social media platforms like Twitter, Facebook, and Microsoft Bing in their attempt to improve the user experience (Lazer et al., 2014).

Fan, Han, and Liu (2014) stood out in the literature as researchers that identified several legitimate hidden healthcare big data problems, which they referred to as (1) noise accumulation; (2) spurious correlations; and (3) incidental endogeneity. To illustrate noise accumulation suppose a practitioner is comparing patients in two hospital wards A and B based upon the values of 1,000 features (or variables) in a healthcare big data file but unknown to that researcher the mean value for participants in A is 0 on all 1,000 features while participants in B have a mean of 3 on the first 10 features and a value of 0 on the other 990 features. A big data machine learning classification rule based upon the first $m \leq 10$ features performs quite well, with little classification error, but as more and more features are included in the rule, classification error increases because the uninformative features (i.e., the 990 features having no discriminating power) eventually overwhelm the informative signals (i.e., the first 10 features). We agree with this if you are using contemporary big data machine learning algorithms. We suggest that big data algorithms be used in parallel with other recognized statistical techniques as methodical triangulation (Strang, 2015b).

Fan, Han, and Liu (2014) describe spurious correlations as healthcare big data files that have many unrelated features but which may be highly correlated simply by chance, resulting in false discoveries and erroneous inferences. For example, using simulated populations and relatively small sample sizes, Fan, Han, and Liu (2014) proved that with 800 independent features, there was 50% chance of observing an absolute correlation that exceeded R=0.4 which would be statistically significant (p<.05) and amount to a small effect size of 16% (r^2=0.16). Their results suggest that there are considerable risks of false inference associated with a purely empirical approach to predictive analytics using high-dimensional data. We agree and we will explore this in more detail later.

Thirdly, Fan, Han, and Liu (2014) assert that endogeneity is a problem when performing regression analysis on big data that results in a model with covariates correlated with the residual error. For high-dimensional models, with many factors, this can occur purely by chance. We agree this is possible but statistically it is an extension of the same spurious correlation phenomenon identified above. Regarding all he above potential hidden problems, we suggest that all but the spurious correlations could be avoided by following the 'statistical sampling violations' solution of improving the research design through rigorous sampling collection plans. Additionally the recommendations of Hair, Black, Babin, Anderson and Tatham (Hair et al., 2006) should be reviewed when designing complex multiple or multivariate regression models in any discipline regardless of whether they are healthcare big data sourced.

The third category of hidden healthcare big data analytics problems is also statistical in nature. When Dr. Gauss invented the student t-test using the normal distribution he probably did not envision the large sample sizes characteristic of the big data five V's. The root of this problem stems from the sample size which is used in many nonparametric as well as parametric formulas (Strang, 2015b). For example, the well-known formula for standard deviation is shown in equation 1 where X is the big data value, μ is the mean, and N is the total sample size.

$$\sqrt{\sum \frac{\left(X - \mu\right)^2}{N}} \tag{1}$$

Going back to the patient temperature anecdote, let's say that we received 30 readings in a small sample and 3600 readings in a small big data sample over the span of one hour (60 seconds * 60 minutes). All the temperature readings were 97F except that last 15 readings were 50F to simulate patient going into a serious medial trauma. In the big data file all the values were 97F except for the last 15. Any practitioner or researcher could easily reproduce the data in this anecdote. Table 1 lists the descriptive statistics of these two samples (all estimates rounded for display).

Table 1. Descriptive statistics of anecdotal healthcare small and big data samples

	Small Sample	**Big Data Sample**
N	30	3600
Mean	73.5	96.804
SD	23.902	3.027
Median	73.5	97
Correlation	-0.867	-0.112

The anecdotal descriptive statistics in table 1 illustrates the fallacy of healthcare big data. By the way each has the same minimum and maximum readings. In the small sample, the mean (M) is 73.5F with a huge standard deviation (SD) of 23.902, which is a coefficient of variation of 33% (SD/M*100). The median is also 73.5F. This clearly indicates the patient is in medical trauma distress. Unfortunately, the healthcare big data descriptive statistics shows that despite recording data for an hour, that the mean temperature is 96.8F with a minor SD of 3.027 which is a small effect size of about 3% (SD/M*100).

The healthcare big data makes us believe the patient is doing well, maybe feeling a bit chilly so they could use a sweater. The median is 97F which is further misleading. Actually, having more data would only further obscure the medical emergency for this healthcare patient.

Additionally, going back to the table 1 anecdote, how could we be sure that the temperature of 50F was not created through imputation, with the remaining 50 values being created by copying the change from 97 to 50, or maybe simple duplication, or perhaps a spurious value of 50 created by wireless network electromagnetic interference. Of course the same arguments could be made against the small sample too.

Another problem with healthcare big data is that parametric statistics will be unknowingly impacted by the sheer sample volume, velocity and variety. In the anecdote, assume we have the time sequence number for each reading and we performed a correlation of the temperature against the time sequence. In the small sample of table 1, the correlation was significant between time and temperature with $R=-0.867$, $p<.05$ (two-sided). The effect size of the small sample correlation of temperature with time was 75% ($r^2 =0.751$, $N=30$) which shows a significant negative correlation between temperature and time, meaning that temperature is quickly falling as time progresses. This is valuable to know because the healthcare staff could be alerted and the patient could be treated in order to save their life.

Unfortunately, based on the table 1 anecdote with the healthcare big data sample, the correlation between temperature and time sequence was -0.112 ($p>.05$) which was insignificant. This could be interpreted that there is no statistically significant relationship between patient temperature falling and time. Perhaps the big data value in this would be that the hospital will soon have an extra bed available in their facility. The same phenomenon occurs when using more advanced parametric statistical techniques such as regression to estimate cause-effect predictions on healthcare big data.

As further test we used random sampling on the 3600 healthcare big data records in the table 1 anecdote, and after 360 iterations (10% of the data) all values were 97F. Thus, even random sampling of healthcare big data is not reliable for parametric statistics. The fallacy of healthcare big data should now be obvious. Therefore, even if the earlier 'statistical sampling violations' hidden problem was not present, the large sample size of healthcare big data could present a type I error or rejecting the null hypothesis when in fact it was true there was no statistically significant result, which is known as a false positive (Strang, 2015b). We will classify this hidden healthcare big data problem as 'statistical false positives'.

The solution we propose to the hidden healthcare big data problem of 'statistical false positives' is to use nonparametric techniques. This advice has been applied to analyze terrorism big data (Strang & Alamieyeseigha, 2017) as well as financial market collapse portfolio manager behavior big data (Strang, 2015b). To prove our point we applied nonparametric techniques in SPSS and Minitab software to test a medical-related hypothesis that the anecdotal patient temperature is no different than an expected average of 97F. The distribution free one-sample Wilcoxon signed rank test on the small sample from table 1 verified as anticipated that the patient temperature was significantly different than the benchmark median of 97F, based on the results of $W(30)=15$, $p=.001$ (two-sided). The interesting result was the same finding from the healthcare big data sample in table 1, with a $W(3600)=15$, $p=.001$ (two-sided). Thus, the nonparametric test on the healthcare big data sample was able to correctly identify that the patient temperature was significantly different than the expected median. We ought to disclose though that parametric one-sample t-tests on the same data produced the same results. Nonetheless, we highly recommend nonparametric statistical techniques become the norm when analyzing healthcare big data.

CONCLUSION

Our literature review of 79,012 journal articles from 2011-2016 confirmed the astonishing situation that healthcare privacy and security related topics accounted for only 2% of the total research production, and this rate had fallen to 1% during the first three months of 2017. Healthcare big data analyst practitioner interviews were therefore used to supplement our research.

The results of our literature review and practitioner interviews verified that the healthcare discipline suffers from the same problems endemic to any type of statistical analysis, namely data entry, coding, mislabeling, missing/inaccurate values, and poor research design. Additionally, healthcare big data suffers from electromagnetic interference, network delays or outages, and the same factors which impact any technology. The same cautions would thus apply to mitigate against those risks. Additionally, the healthcare big data faces the big data five V's: high volume, complex variety, large velocity, strategic value tradeoffs, and more recently veracity (accuracy, ethics, privacy, socio-cultural meaning).

Healthcare big data analytics in particular is prone to veracity privacy violations, perhaps more so than other disciplines. Although most countries have legislation to protect patients against inappropriate use of their data, this only forces providers within the healthcare domain to avoid recording certain identifying attributes. Even the HIPAA in USA allows a hospital to override the rules if they have a justifiable reason – which seems hard to fathom for a healthcare big data collection context. Additionally, informed consent may not be getting the scrutiny it deserves from patients or physicians. Healthcare medical devices/implants transmit wireless readings which could be intercepted. For example a patient driving through a weight station, toll bridge, parking lot, border entry could have their personal data read without their knowledge or consent. Encryption may be a solution to this common big data privacy problem when software and hardware improve to make it faster and affordable in the healthcare industry.

Although there were many issues found, we considered these to be already encompassed into the big data five V's. We uncovered several insights about the hidden healthcare big data analytics risks. We grouped these new hidden problems into three logical categories, and we also provided recommended solutions for each. Furthermore, we applied the action research systems thinking technique to organize the insights into a diagram, as summarized in figure 1. This diagram will facilitate communicating the information to other stakeholders such as healthcare practitioners, researchers, decision makers and policy administrators. The three hidden healthcare big data analytic problem categories are briefly enumerated below.

1. Unintended healthcare big data access – inadvertent or intentional wireless eavesdropping – this could be mitigated by using strong public or private key encryption once software becomes more powerful and affordable for the healthcare industry/patients;
2. Statistical sampling violations – non-coverage, lack of random selection, nonresponse, self-selection bias caused by lack of a research design – this could be fixed by a research design using stratification, systematic or other generally-accepted sampling technique to collect a more representative multiple-sourced sample (pragmatic and constructivist approaches were also mentioned);
3. Statistical false positives – caused by mathematical formulas that use sample size in calculations resulting in spurious relationships, correlations, and other inaccurate estimates (a healthcare big data simulation was used to prove this) – this risk could be reduced by applying nonparametric statistical techniques and methodological triangulation (use of multiple parametric, distribution free and qualitative methods).

Figure 1. Hidden healthcare big data analytics problems

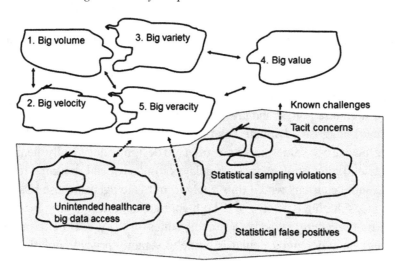

We feel we uncovered several insights about the fundamental and managerial controversies associated with big data analytics and artificial intelligence that will be of interest to quantitative professionals and practitioners in the fields of computing, e-commerce, e-business services, and e-government. The goal of this chapter was to explain contemporary managerial and conceptual problems concerning big data analytics. We utilized the systems thinking technique within an action research framework. The methodology that we applied was unique and worth considering by other researchers. We utilized the systems thinking technique popularized within an action research framework. We used this approach because our ideology was pragmatic, the problem at hand was complex and institutional (healthcare discipline), and we needed to understand the problems from both a practitioner group and nonhuman process (technology). We used the literature review summarized above along with practitioner interviews collected at a big data conference. According the systems thinking methodology, after the literature review and subsequent knowledge assessment were completed, we organized the key results into a visual model of the proposed critical real-world and tacit processes that could identify and solve the problems.

In conclusion, big data and artificial intelligence privacy is an important topic that was not adequately covered in the existing literature, so more research is needed. Additionally, while our findings that the traditional five big data challenges also impact the healthcare discipline, we identified three new tacit issues that are essential to address in future studies. We could not locate any other publication that identified and explained these three new hidden problems in healthcare data analytics so we feel this is a worthy contribution to the community of practice literature. In closing we will make our data available to anyone by request to the corresponding author.

REFERENCES

ADA. (2015). Harnessing Big Data to Help Stop Diabetes. *The American Journal of Managed Care*, *9*(1), 1–4.

Al-Ameen, M., Liu, J., & Kwak, K. (2012). Security and privacy issues in wireless sensor networks for healthcare applications. *Journal of Medical Systems*, *36*(1), 93–101. doi:10.100710916-010-9449-4 PMID:20703745

Al-Janabi, S., Al-Shourbaji, I., Shojafar, M., & Shamshirband, S. (2016). *Survey of main challenges (security and privacy) in wireless body area networks for healthcare applications*. Egyptian Informatics Journal.

Angiuli, O., Blitzstein, J., & Waldo, J. (2015). How to De-Identify Your Data. *Communications of the ACM*, *58*(12), 48–55. doi:10.1145/2814340

Brown, B. (2008). HIPAA Beyond HIPAA: ONCHIT, ONC, AHIC, HITSP, and CCHIT. *Journal of Health Care Compliance*, *10*(41), 1–21.

Burrows, R., & Savage, M. (2014). After the crisis? Big data and the methodological challenges of empirical sociology. *Big Data & Society Journal*, *12*(2), 1–6.

Checkland, P. (1999). *Systems Thinking, Systems Practice*. Chichester, UK: John Wiley & Sons Ltd.

Chen, C. L. P., & Zhang, C. Y. (2014). Data-intensive applications, challenges, techniques and technologies: A survey on big data. *Information Sciences Journal*, *275*(1), 314–317. doi:10.1016/j.ins.2014.01.015

Chen, M., Mao, S., Zhang, Y., & Leung, V. C. (2014). Open issues and outlook in big data. In Big Data: Related Technologies, Challenges and Future Prospects (Vol. 1, pp. 81-89). Springer.

Couper, M. P. (2013). Is the sky falling? New technology, changing media, and the future of surveys. *Survey Research Methods Journal*, *7*(1), 145–156.

de Montjoye, Y.-A., & Pentland, A. S. (2016). Response to Comment on "Unique in the shopping mall: On the reidentifiability of credit card metadata". *Science Journal*, *351*(6279), 1274.

De Zwart, M., Humphreys, S., & Van Dissel, B. (2014). Surveillance, big data and democracy: Lessons for Australia from the US and UK. *The University of New South Wales Law Journal*, *37*(2), 713–747.

Duhigg, C. (2014). *The power of habit: Why we do what we do in life and business*. New York: Penguin Random House.

Eastin, M. S., Brinson, N. H., Doorey, A., & Wilcox, G. (2016). Living in a big data world: Predicting mobile commerce activity through privacy concerns. *Computers in Human Behavior*, *58*(1), 214–220. doi:10.1016/j.chb.2015.12.050

Ekbia, H., Mattioli, M., Kouper, I., Arave, G., Ghazinejad, A., Bowman, T., ... Sugimoto, C. R. (2015). Big data, bigger dilemmas: A critical review. *Journal of the Association for Information Science and Technology*, *66*(8), 1523–1545. doi:10.1002/asi.23294

Fan, J., Han, F., & Liu, H. (2014). Challenges of Big Data Analysis. *National Science Review Journal*, *1*(1), 293–314. doi:10.1093/nsr/nwt032 PMID:25419469

Filkins, B. L., Kim, J. Y., Roberts, B., Armstrong, W., Miller, M. A., Hultner, M. L., ... Steinhubl, S. R. (2016). Privacy and security in the era of digital health: What should translational researchers know and do about it? *American Journal of Translational Research*, *8*(3), 1560–1580. PMID:27186282

Gandomi, A., & Haider, M. (2015). Beyond the hype: Big data concepts, methods, and analytics. *International Journal of Information Management, 35*(2), 137–144. doi:10.1016/j.ijinfomgt.2014.10.007

Hair, J. F., Black, W. C., Babin, B. J., Anderson, R. E., & Tatham, R. L. (2006). *Multivariate data analysis* (6th ed.). Upper Saddle River, NJ: Prentice-Hall.

Hoffman, S., & Podgurski, A. (2013). Big Bad Data: Law, Public Health, and Biomedical Databases. *The Journal of Law, Medicine & Ethics, 41*(1), 56–60. doi:10.1111/jlme.12040 PMID:23590742

Hogarth, R. M., & Soyer, E. (2015). Using Simulated Experience to Make Sense of Big Data. *MIT Sloan Management Review, 56*(2), 49–54.

IBM. (2013). IBM SPSS Statistics for Windows (21st ed.). International Business Machines Corporation (IBM).

Jovanovi, U., Stimec, A., & Vladusi, D. (2015). Big-data analytics: A critical review and some future directions. *International Journal of Business Intelligence and Data Mining, 10*(4), 337–355. doi:10.1504/IJBIDM.2015.072211

Jungwirth, D., & Haluza, D. (2017). Information and communication technology and the future of healthcare: Results of a multi-scenario Delphi survey. *Health Informatics Journal*. doi:10.1177/1460458217704256 PMID:28438103

Kessel, P. v., Layman, J., Blackmore, J., Burnet, I., & Azuma, Y. (2014). *Insights on governance, risk and compliance: Big data, changing the way businesses compete and operate*. Ernest and Young.

Kshetri, N. (2014). Big datas impact on privacy, security and consumer welfare. *Telecommunications Policy, 38*(11), 1134–1145. doi:10.1016/j.telpol.2014.10.002

Lazer, D. M., Kennedy, R., King, G., & Vespignani, A. (2014). The parable of Google Flu: Traps in big data analysis. *Science Journal, 343*(1), 1203–1205. doi:10.1126cience.1248506 PMID:24626916

Leszczynski, A. (2015). Spatial big data and anxieties of control. *Environment and Planning. D, Society & Space, 33*(6), 965–984. doi:10.1177/0263775815595814

Lichtblau, E., & Weilandaug, N. (2016). Hacker Releases More Democratic Party Files, Renewing Fears of Russian Meddling. *New York Times*, pp. A12-A14.

Lusher, S. J., McGuire, R., van Schaik, R. C., Nicholson, C. D., & de Vlieg, J. (2014). Data-driven medicinal chemistry in the era of big data. *Drug Discovery Today, 19*(7), 859–868. doi:10.1016/j.drudis.2013.12.004 PMID:24361338

Ohm, P. (2010). Broken promises of privacy: Responding to the surprising failure of anonymization. *UCLA Law Review Journal, 57*(1), 1701–1818.

Prokopenya, V. (2018). *Truths, half-truths and lies about artificial intelligence*. The European Financial Review. Available http://www.europeanfinancialreview.com/?p=25629

Rothstein, M. A. (2015). Ethical Issues in Big Data Health Research: Currents in Contemporary Bioethics. *The Journal of Law, Medicine & Ethics, 43*(2), 425–429. doi:10.1111/jlme.12258 PMID:26242964

Salleh, K. A., & Janczewski, L. (2016). Technical, organizational and environmental security and privacy issues of big data: A literature review. *Procedia Computer Science Journal, 100*(1), 19–28. doi:10.1016/j.procs.2016.09.119

Shen, Y., & Zhang, Y. (2014). Transmission protocol for secure big data in two-hop wireless networks with cooperative jamming. *Information Sciences, 281*(1), 201–210. doi:10.1016/j.ins.2014.05.037

Shull, F. (2014). The True Cost of Mobility? *IEEE Software, 31*(2), 5–9. doi:10.1109/MS.2014.47

Strang, K. D. (2012). Logistic planning with nonlinear goal programming models in spreadsheets. *International Journal of Applied Logistics, 2*(4), 1–14. doi:10.4018/jal.2012100101

Strang, K. D. (2013). Homeowner behavioral intent to evacuate after flood warnings. *International Journal of Risk and Contingency Management, 2*(3), 1–28. doi:10.4018/ijrcm.2013070101

Strang, K. D. (2015a). Exploring the relationship between global terrorist ideology and attack methodology. *Risk Management Journal, 17*(2), 65–90. doi:10.1057/rm.2015.8

Strang, K. D. (2015b). *Palgrave Handbook of Research Design in Business and Management*. New York: Palgrave Macmillan. doi:10.1057/9781137484956

Strang, K. D., & Alamieyeseigha, S. (2015). What and where are the risks of international terrorist attacks: A descriptive study of the evidence. *International Journal of Risk and Contingency Management, 4*(1), 1–18. doi:10.4018/ijrcm.2015010101

Strang, K. D., & Alamieyeseigha, S. (2017). What and Where Are the Risks of International Terrorist Attacks. In Violence and Society: Breakthroughs in Research and Practice. IGI Global. doi:10.4018/978-1-5225-0988-2.ch026

Strang, K. D., & Sun, Z. (2016). Analyzing relationships in terrorism big data using Hadoop and statistics. *Journal of Computer Information Systems, 56*(5), 55–65.

Strang, K. D., & Sun, Z. (2017). Scholarly big data body of knowledge: What is the status of privacy and security? *Annals of Data Science, 4*(1), 1–17. doi:10.100740745-016-0096-6

Sun, Z., Strang, K. D., & Li, R. (2016). Ten bigs of big data: A multidisciplinary framework. *Proceedings of 10th ACM International Conference on Research and Practical Issues of Enterprise Information Systems (CONFENIS 2016), 1*, 550-661.

Terry, N. (2015). Navigating the Incoherence of Big Data Reform Proposals. *The Journal of Law, Medicine & Ethics, 43*(1), 44–47. doi:10.1111/jlme.12214 PMID:25846163

Thorpe, J. H., & Gray, E. A. (2015). Law and the Public's Health: Big data and public health - navigating privacy laws to maximize potential. *Public Health Reports, 130*(2), 171–175. doi:10.1177/003335491513000211 PMID:25729109

Vaidhyanathan, S., & Bulock, C. (2014). Knowledge and Dignity in the Era of Big Data. *The Serials Librarian, 66*(1-4), 49–64. doi:10.1080/0361526X.2014.879805

Vajjhala, N. R., & Strang, K. D. (2017). Measuring organizational-fit through socio-cultural big data. *Journal of New Mathematics and Natural Computation, 13*(2), 1–17.

Vajjhala, N. R., Strang, K. D., & Sun, Z. (2015). Statistical modeling and visualizing of open big data using a terrorism case study. *Open Big Data Conference*, 489-496. 10.1109/FiCloud.2015.15

van Loenen, B., Kulk, S., & Ploeger, H. (2016). Data protection legislation: A very hungry caterpillar: The case of mapping data in the European Union. *Government Information Quarterly*, *33*(2), 338–345. doi:10.1016/j.giq.2016.04.002

van Otterlo, M. (2014). Automated experimentation in Walden 3.0: The next step in profiling, predicting, control and surveillance. *Surveillance & Society*, *12*(2), 255–272. doi:10.24908s.v12i2.4600

Varian, H. R. (2014). Big data: New tricks for econometrics. *The Journal of Economic Perspectives*, *28*(2), 3–27. doi:10.1257/jep.28.2.3

Wang, H., Jiang, X., & Kambourakis, G. (2015). Special issue on Security, Privacy and Trust in network-based Big Data. *Information Sciences*, *318*(1), 48–50. doi:10.1016/j.ins.2015.05.040

Ward, J. C. (2014). Oncology Reimbursement in the Era of Personalized Medicine and Big Data. *Journal of Oncology Practice / American Society of Clinical Oncology*, *10*(2), 83–86. doi:10.1200/JOP.2014.001308 PMID:24633283

Zhong, R. Y., Huang, G. Q., Lan, S., Dai, Q. Y., Chen, X., & Zhang, T. (2015). A big data approach for logistics trajectory discovery from RFID-enabled production data. *International Journal of Production Economics*, *165*(1), 260–272. doi:10.1016/j.ijpe.2015.02.014

Zikopoulos, P., Eaton, C., DeRoos, D., Deutsch, T., & Lapis, G. (2011). *Understanding Big Data: Analytics for Enterprise Class Hadoop and Streaming Data*. McGraw-Hill Osborne Media.

This research was previously published in Managerial Perspectives on Intelligent Big Data Analytics; pages 55-74, copyright year 2019 by Engineering Science Reference (an imprint of IGI Global).

Chapter 86
Improving Project Management Decisions With Big Data Analytics

George Leal Jamil
Informações em Rede C e T Ltda., Brazil

Luiz Fernando Magalhães Carvalho
Banco Itaú, Brazil

ABSTRACT

A relationship between project management and knowledge management was observed with a detailed level of analysis in this chapter, as analytics tools and methods were presented to define new perspectives for these dynamics. After a theoretical review that advanced the level reached by a previous paper on the same topic a new theoretical background was completely worked, resulting in a base where a deeper way of analysis allowed, at the end, to study practical cases of rich association for PM and KM in practical, ready to apply situations. As a trend for next competitive cycles, tools, methods, and techniques that focus knowledge production for decision making are to be increasingly defined and applied, on one hand enabling organizations to propose new competitive structures and positioning, and on the other hand, presenting a more aggressive, faster, and demanding competitive environment.

BACKGROUND

This chapter was produced adopting Jamil and Carvalho (2015) as a base, producing a review of its findings, adding studies from big data and analytics perspectives.

Project management (PM) is a remarkably dynamic area, where data, information and knowledge are systematically and empirically produced and, as well, demanded, in fast-change scenarios. As projects are to be detailed, proposed, negotiated, executed and maintained, several contents of these fundamental assets are to be faced by the project manager and his associated team, users and other project stakeholders, as decisions need to be produced with precision every time. Poor decisions, taken from indefinite or problematic data and information, will lead to more risky and precarious implementations.

DOI: 10.4018/978-1-6684-3662-2.ch086

This chapter reviews the previous findings of Jamil and Carvalho (2015), detailing how big data and analytics, as a potential trend to produce more qualified and applicable knowledge, can result in better decisions, producing a challenging, but worthy picture for project management.

PROJECTS, STRATEGIC DECISIONS, AND DEMANDS FOR KNOWLEDGE

The basic definition of a project already motivates to think about knowledge and its strategic applications. It is possible to check, from PMBoK (2013), that projects are ways to achieve organizational strategic goals. By analyzing this initial concept, it is possible to understand that a view of the future for this organization was projected, configuring goals to be achieved. As this new situation is faced from organizations, knowledge can be one of the most critical assets to be applied to produce the design of this reachable description. But it is also relevant to understand the role of projects in this process, how its execution and implementation, as final results, were based on data, information and knowledge, as these contents were also generated during the project management phases. It is an important relationship, which defines the background of this research.

It is important to remind that strategy is a discipline oriented to coherently propose future positions for one organization in its social, business and competitive environment. One strategy is stated through a set of consistent decisions, expressed in a base that constitutes the organizational strategic plan, as a coherent path of subsequent decisions (Porter, 2008). In this context, strategic planning is a process that continuously study organizational resources, capabilities, perspectives and competencies, with addition of determination of internal and external factors, aiming to monitor and design implementable actions to reach established goals (Kotler & Keller, 2005; Porter, 2008; Mintzberg, Ahlstrand & Lampel, 2009).

Jamil *et al.* (2012) conceptualized strategic planning, as the main organizational process, as it is a "knowledge demanding" cohesive set of tasks, which needs, for its success, some factors, components and contents, such as:

- Studies of external business environment, considering data and information from competitors, suppliers, customers, legal aspects, business rules, market reactions to events, etc. (Porter, 2008).
- Internal business environment analysis, observing corporate resources, motivations and restrictions and its correlated control and management perspectives, competitive advantage positioning, etc. (Mintzberg, Ahlstrand & Lampel, 2009).
- Data and information about a market history, as a "knowledge base of best practices", which can be revoked for simulations, business models and dynamic studies for competitive design (Choo, 2005; Nonaka, 2008).
- Details of connected and interrelated projects, assuming they are data, information and knowledge producers, as the practices cited above and other productions, that will enable favorable conditions to plan and execute a new project.
- Definition of measurements and methods to measure, or "indicators", as financial quantitative demonstrations, reputation, performance and many other factors that can be set by strategy staff and followed through a plan execution for strategic monitoring that will allow its following and management in the workplace (Kaplan & Norton, 2007).

It is opportune, from the definitions pointed above, to notice the importance of data, information and knowledge sources. This fact is fundamental to comprehend how Big Data contents, as announced in the following text, are relevant for internal, external and historical studies to serve as bases for strategic planning, as it results in goals prediction for new reachable and challenging points.

Among typical strategic planning tasks conducted during the phases of project, planning and execution, it is possible do describe:

- Definition of strategic goals and correspondent ways of monitoring, defining a reachable scenario as a success for the specific planning process;
- Intermediate and final results evaluation or plan monitoring;
- Project resources management methods and goal reaching perspectives.

In these cases, strategic planning and its associated execution demand data, information and knowledge to plan, review, modify and design business dimensioning and positioning. The "meaning" or "sense" about competitive scenarios, which will result in more precise strategic propositions are affirmed by various authors as intermingled with structured knowledge availability (Choo, 2003; Kearns & Lederer, 2003; Prado, 2006).

KNOWLEDGE MANAGEMENT FOR PROJECT MANAGEMENT-AN IMPORTANT RELATIONSHIP

The relationship of PM and knowledge management (KM) must be observed initially for the proposed objective of this study. As defined by Project Management Institute (PMI, 2014), projects are a *temporary group of activities designed to produce a unique product, service or result*. As an additional conceptualization from the same source, project management is:

… the application of knowledge, skills and techniques to execute projects, effectively and efficiently. It's a strategic competency for organizations, enabling them to tie project results to business goals — and thus, better compete in their markets.

Project, project management and its associated perspectives produce an interesting research object to understand its correspondence with organizational knowledge.

Reich, Gemino and Sauer (2008; 2012) tell that knowledge management (KM) practices have a contributive interaction with project management planning capabilities, which result in production of knowledge for strategic advantage, as projects can be related to strategic planning, as its goals executive plans and procedures. The analysis held by the authors, which evolved from one approach to the older, through information and knowledge contents, shows a detail level further explored in this section when considering the cooperation of KM practices to PM planning. From these works, also, it is possible to understand the complexity and richness of project management contexts when observing these tasks as critical consumers and producers of organizational knowledge, interacting with all organizational levels. It is important to address this relevant aspect, as analytics tools, as dynamic processors of data and information in all organizational contacts, will help decisively to produce knowledge that will be managed in advance, according to the perspectives of a continuous process, the knowledge management activities. It will, for example, refer to the major definition at PMBoK (2013) for "knowledge areas", such as financial, risk, executive and operational communication, human resources, acquisition, cost, time and quality project management.

It is possible to explore this critical relationship of KM and PM, as it was observed in several theoretical and practical analysis. For example, in Landaeta (2008) we find an evaluation on how the transfer of knowledge among projects can benefit its design and management. In this study, there is an observation on how a set of KM practices can improve a project portfolio management, serving as an important strategic tool for companies that compete in several markets or with diversified product lines that always demand new projects for its marketing and commercial positioning.

Recurring to Reich, Gemino and Sauer (2012), it is possible to understand how risks management practice, another critical PM task, is improved by the relation with applied KM actions, findings that are consolidated on the final model presented by these authors. Gasik (2011) researched a model that also sought to associate KM and PM principles, resulting in an analysis of the importance of knowledge assets in the project management organizational roles, from the planning according to strategy to implementation. For Müller *et al.* (2013), it is possible to understand how the modern approaches of project management correspond to some observed through the KM conceptual and theoretical base. For example, project management offices (PMOs) propositions and actions, along with management tasks distributed over companies' networks are approached by these authors as evidences of these interactions.

Regarding to the works of Barney (1991) and Porter (2008), it is possible to affirm that PM and KM practices alignment appear as a critical strategic relation, with clear potential to generate competitive advantage, as a valuable, rare and irreplaceable resource (Barney, 1991). Projects can be defined as methodological ways to produce results according to strategic planned goals and actions, and it is opportune to understand how knowledge is applied on decisions taken during its planning and execution (Barney, 1991; Porter, 2008; Nonaka, 2008). In addition, the association of a corporative and inter-company projects, known as project management *portfolio* (PMBoK, 2013), brings another level of demand for knowledge, with additional degree of complexity to produce it, as those contexts where these projects are held also reveal, produce and apply data, information and knowledge.

As these and other works reviewed, it is possible to affirm the perception of KM and PM integration, and the role of analytics in its development in modern contexts as the rationale for this chapter. This proposition constitutes a valid and opportune research objective. The introduction of new fronts of study, such as risk management, financial project structure, project portfolio management, among many others, represent new trends for applied studies. It is possible also to think Big Data and its associated phenomenon, analytics, as new areas to be studies, producing several essential, opportune and trending perspectives for this potential integration. For project management base, as it was also approached by PMI (2013), the potentials for data analysis, information and knowledge generation are immensely opportune at this moment, facts that will be explored in the forthcoming analysis.

DATA, INFORMATION, AND KNOWLEDGE

The relationship and conceptualization for these basic concepts is interesting, as they are useful components for business activities and plans. Nowadays, the comprehension of the dynamics of these contents constitutes in opportunities to offer services and products, as they present opportunities by themselves and in business plans that relate to each other, as information systems, information technology applications and implementations, among several others. With the insertion of new technology-based services and new methods of industrial production, dynamical collaborations among companies and events, such as the Analytics and Big Data phenomena, this integrative and complementary view demands more study (Ohata & Kumar, 2012; McAfee & Brynjolfsson, 2012; SAS, 2017).

It is possible to understand data, information and knowledge as isolated concepts, but also in terms of their relationships, which already advance on the perspective of information and knowledge management (Jamil, 2005). Davenport and Prusak (2000) affirmed a set of definitions and contours for these concepts that will contribute for the theoretical base adopted in this chapter. For them, these basic concepts keep its definition, but also reveal relationships with each other, a dynamic characteristic. Tuomi (2000) studied the producing of data from knowledge conception. It is an apparent opposite way as usually treated by literature, but it indeed reinforces the concepts of each item and its correspondent relationship. Also from Lucas Jr. (2005), Turban, Mc Lean, and Wetherbee, 2002, Turban, Rainer and Potter, 2007 and Stair and Reynolds (2009), it is possible to understand how Information Technology (IT) and communication resources applied such concepts in themes as technological infrastructure, information systems design and web-based applications development, nowadays impacting the design of applications, or, as it is commercially described, the "apps".

Jamil (2005) consolidated these definitions, producing a conceptual base that states data as an absolute value that can be obtained directly from a measurement, observation or collected from an automated source and is expressed in usual measuring standards (as currency, metering system units, etc.). Although showing flexibility and easiness to generate, storage and communication, data lacks context, or immediate support for more complex decisions, being an understandable building block for more consistent concepts.

Information was conceptualized as a collection of homogeneous, correlated data, added with notions from the context where it was produced. With this wider conception, it is possible to expect results of better contribution for predictions, as decision-making, planning activities, prospection and several others with more complex managerial results. Information increases organizational decision prospects, but it demands more resources to be precisely applied, as the support from information systems and its linked infrastructure, demanding investments and adequate planning abilities (Turban, Rainer & Potter, 2007; Stair & Reynolds, 2008).

Based on these concepts, knowledge can be produced from a collection of homogeneous information, including definitions of the processes that generated that set of information. Knowledge allows the maximum level of decision capabilities, description and analysis. For example, it enables even competitive predictions such as market dynamics, product negotiation evolutions, demands, etc. (Davenport, 2000; Akbar, 2003; Jamil, 2005; Nonaka, 2008). But on the other hand, knowledge shows many challenges for its management, as to store, convert, communicate and share, are not simple, straightforward activities, resulting in the need of a specific process to treat it, as it is defined by authors as knowledge management (Choo, 2003; Kearns & Lederer, 2003; Jamil, 2005; El-Bashir, Collier & Sutton, 2011).

To conclude this initial conceptualization about these fundamental concepts, it is relevant to point out, from the authors cited above and many others (for example, for those that study marketing relationships such as customer-behavior knowledge and strategic planning implementations), that it is possible to obtain knowledge from data and from information, as it is also possible to develop information from data. This relationship prescribes a managerial cycle, where the contents are applied to produce each other, eventually resulting in a process description that can be found and evidenced in productive actions, chains and organizational trivial tasks. This result is adequate to define how knowledge management practice is more frequent and simpler than it appears when approaching the theme just for strictly theoretical origin.

BIG DATA AND ANALYTICS

Some years ago, it was possible for any Internet web-based service manager to understand how interactive his service was: a lot of commercial, interactions, customer data flown through servers, web transactions, orders and other simple dynamics. Lately, these findings called attention when data mining services were offered in simple, cheap way, aiming to decipher behaviors, reactions and preferences, enabling web-site and electronic commerce managers to understand and even to predict some trends – as positive reactions by customers, how he will potentially react to an offer, what are the reasons that will take him to analyze a competitor´s offer and so forth. Then, we reached the "big data" wave, as unstructured communication tools invaded our lives forever (Dodge, 2010).

Although not new, "Big data" phenomenon has been perceived by entrepreneurs and socio-political actors, as a process of "knowledge generation from data". This new wave of scientific and practical evidences proves how important is to observe data, information and knowledge in organizational and competitive context for decisions, such as strategic planning (Ohata & Kumar, 2012; Park, Huh, Oh & Han, 2012; SAS 2017). It is a new area of scientific and applied research, which must be adopted for future studies about information and knowledge management, along with several other contributive fields. It calls special attention due to the huge amounts of data generated randomly and spontaneously throughout the world, in numberless ways. It is also supported by the fast introduction of technology and the continuous reduction of IT infrastructural costs, such as storage, transmission, and many other components. Along with these remarkable features, it is possible to observe how big companies, such as Google, Microsoft and Facebook, or small, fast-action, innovative ones, reacted to this data production, offering easy-to-access tools for analysis, scenario detailing and prediction, known as "analytics" (Rayome, 2016).

As a referential source, McKinsey (2011) described big data as *datasets whose size is beyond the usual ability of typical database software tools to capture, store, manage, and analyze*. Obviously, as it seems, to use these data sets, huge computing resources, optimized algorithms and other technologic resources and structures must be applied in a planned way to extract knowledge from big data. IT market and scientific communities have been studying tools and associated techniques to capture, collect, store, classify, analyze and produce deeper results or applicable outcomes from datasets (McKinsey, 2011; Chen, Chiang & Storey, 2012; Ohata & Kumar, 2012; Courtney, 2013; SAS, 2017).

Additionally, analytics emerged as both a demand from market agents, regarding that massive data generation and technology availability, as new resources are presented everyday by IT players (De Roche, 2016; Jain, 2016; SAS, 2017). As typical analytics services, it is possible to identify big players offers, such as Google and Facebook, when they put available for this service customers, solutions as:

- Number of users on-line and their geographical distribution.
- Information technology infrastructure used for access.
- Frequent sites accessed, based on user groups.
- Some typical customer reactions, as, for example, to marketing advertisements, announcements and offers.

- Conversion Rates: How many users advanced negotiation with refer to offer announcements.
- Selling performances, for each offer through internet.
- Segmentation information, as customer identifications and definitions can be used to analyze their adjustments to each offer (Mehmod, 2017).

As a typical analytics application, one business analyst can evaluate how a product offer prescribed a trend, aiming to understand its perspective adjustment to statistical models and projections, which may allow adjust better this offer. As a comprehensible detailing from this commercial study, several small and medium projects can be started, as commercial points of sales promotions and discounts, commercial campaigns, logistics operations, human resources training and preparation, among several others. It is a simple, clear way to relate the conceptual base, the practical context that motivate this chapter writing: projects and project management that emerge from analysis produced from big data generation and analytics projections.

Informational products can now be regarded as definitions presented by Manyika *et al.* (2011) and IBM (2014), as they are created from big data and analytics, when authors cited contents to produce strategic and tactical plans for various industries around the world, and how they connect to strategic project management, enabling projects that will not only follow, but execute strategy actions on the field. This factor allows pondering the effort trying to relate such production of knowledge to strategic marketing planning, and perceive it as critical tasks conducted by competitive firms specially when applied for long time plans. In one of these cases, it is opportune to refer about market intelligence as one process improved by such a correlation of data treatment and knowledge generation for critical tactical and strategic decisions, more specifically, for strategic marketing planning (Jamil, 2013).

As one of the interesting organizational processes to understand, taken as an example of a knowledge producer of sectorial data, market intelligence (MI) is exposed by Jamil *et al.* (2012) as a cyclic set of activities coordinated to provide strategic marketing plan knowledge for a group of companies who compete in the same sector. MI has a proposed structure of phases such as value chain modelling, knowledge demands diagnosis, data and information availability and a cycle of collection, validation, classification, processing, communication and end-cycle review. MI is a process oriented to produce knowledge for market sectors, as any of the companies who receive this produced knowledge take advantage of it in its specific strategic and tactical plans – such as marketing, logistics, project management, etc. MI deals directly with data, encompassing those huge sets identified as Big Data, as it is treated properly through any analytical process (Jamil, Santos, Alves, & e Furbino, 2012; Johnson, 2012; De Man, 2012; Dimitrios, Sakas & Vlachos, 2013).

Big data and analytics studies and practical applications brought a new way to observe how knowledge can be produced and applied in new entrepreneurial contexts, such as those put available by systems interconnectivity, new software design and social media applications, as they can be used to collect and treat some customer, citizens, agent reactions to any event. Classical and new methods, such as statistical and heuristics, has been suggested for studies that will allow, for example, the precise application for information technology. This way, it is possible to define that we have a specific condition to depict precise targets and reachable goals for future projects. As this section of literature review showed, these concepts can define already perspectives of the basic relationship sought in this chapter, where project management is benefited by knowledge management which, in its way, is produced and processed through new processes and services, as big data and analytics.

KNOWLEDGE MANAGEMENT, BIG DATA, AND ANALYTICS

Knowledge management is conceptualized as a process, a continuum, composed by a set of predicted and manageable tasks that deal with organizational knowledge (Jamil, 2005). Clearly, it is a simple definition, also supported by an objective concept of knowledge, as exposed earlier, presenting the perspective referring to practical aspects, allowing further discussions about the KM goal and practices.

Nonaka (2008) defined knowledge management as a more complex process, with wider results, designed to answer several organizational needs for planning and execution. As this process is approached as a more complex theoretical construction, it was consolidated in reviews produced by Christea and Capatina (2009) and Haslinda and Sarinah (2009), where, typically, several KM research models were described and analyzed. Jamil (2005) studied basic knowledge oriented activities, taking business organizations as examples and its correlation, resulting in a composed set of tasks, such as searching, generating, registering, sharing, valuating and strategic application monitoring, which was proposed also as an integrative KM process model, designed to receive additional contributions in future studies.

Clark Jr., Jones and Armstrong (2007) and El-Bashir, Collier and Sutton (2011) also studied knowledge management systems in an integrative perspective. These and other studies that adopt integrative focus propose KM process integration to other organizational factors and processes, becoming not only a function, but a set of principles which can be applied to improve knowledge application in all organizational activities. From these sources is also observed the importance of information and technological systems as components of such processes, to allow understanding and corroboration of the intended conceptual relationship between knowledge and project management practices. This implementation-oriented contribution allows us to understand how IT can be a supporting technology for information systems, which, by this way, can also encompass social media, big data and analytics processing for project management perspectives.

As we aim to discuss how knowledge management can occur in this new scenario of massive data generation, it is also important to relate classical concepts, as the organizational business intelligence (BI) (Cao, Zhang & Liu, 2006). It was defined as an important set of tools, its related methods and analytical procedures exposed mainly by information technology (IT) market. Defining this way, BI is now a receptive conceptual and practical field for the application of big data and analytics resources (Inmon, Strauss & Nishloss, 2008; El-Gayar & Timsina, 2014). These peculiarities encompass technological issues and information generation concept, when the first group of authors dedicate a special effort to identify BI as a set of components, such as data warehouses (as storing resources), "mining" tools (specifically for pattern recognition processes, relationship and frequency analysis) and result production, as customized report tools facilities.

As Kimball and Ross (2010) detail, BI depends not only on the definition of this set of components, but also in its integration, planned application and overall conditions to be used in organizational situations to produce its complex and usually synthetic results. Taking their definition of pre-requisites for a BI effective application, it is useful to recall, from studies of information systems as from Stair and Reynolds (2009) that, among these basic elements to be used, an organization needs skilled, prepared people with fair conditions to interpret results and implement the BI outcomes for decisions, as those discussed earlier in this text. For project management, for instance, as it will be better debated in the following text, a BI-oriented set of IT tools can produce several results as simulations for risk management, financial values, human resources allocation, etc., allowing a deeper study for PM planning and execution.

BI tools and associated techniques assume a relevant situation in this study, as they represent a set of organized components to process data to produce a synthetic, specific knowledge for decision-making, exactly aligned to what is observed for a conceptual relationship between project and knowledge management practices, which will be expanded in this study, regarding the introduction of big data, analytics. Interestingly, it will perform an integrated informational environment, as presented by information system researchers.

Finally, it is important to discuss information systems. Information systems (IS) are arranged sets of several components oriented to treat information to produce desired results for pre-defined organizational goals (Stair & Reynolds, 2009; Jamil, Santos, Alves, & e Furbino, 2012). This concept represents an important functional and strategic arrangement of IT hardware, software, interconnection infrastructure and skilled people, which will implement processes, tasks and methods that solve information-driven organizational problems. Several authors from project management area exemplify ISs that impact expressively works as financial, risk, people, logistics and other administrative PM tasks.

Information systems, as a theoretical objective, is an opportune way to understand in a broader perspective, how information will be dealt in one organizational arrangement, how it can be treated to be applied in its value-aggregation chain and, finally, how information is processed and flows through organizational networks. IS will also be a connection point for the present study, relating some of our theoretical contexts in one complete, dynamic and interrelated research scenario.

THEORETICAL BACKGROUND

As an integrated approach is adopted for this chapter, an opportunity to study several concepts arise and will be, at least partially, addressed in this section. Among these concepts, as a focus, we can explore big data, project management, knowledge management and information systems theoretical references. This study intends to set a first level of relationship, allowing to understand this immense potential and enabling further discussions about KM, Big Data and PM practices.

APPROACHING KNOWLEDGE DISCOVERY AS A PERSPECTIVE OF KNOWLEDGE PRODUCTION FROM PROJECTS

Projects can be regarded, firstly, as a source of knowledge. As PMI (2013) conceptualized project management as a continuous process, there is a potential arena where data and information are continuously processed and will allow, by consequence, the possibility to produce knowledge. In these terms, the theoretical delimitation of knowledge discovery in databases (KDD) can be an essential base to propose the relationship among big data, analytics and project management (Fayad, Patesk-Shapiro & Smyth, 1996).

As stated by (Fayad, Patesk-Shapiro & Smyth, 1996; Yonce, Taylor, Kelly, & Gnau, 2017), the generation of potential value for users and customers of information and knowledge systems depend or are related to analysts' abilities on extracting useful answers from datasets, as, for example, business reports, trends, sales reports, customer-oriented driver's information and many others. This view relates the main value, not exactly to the amount of data, but in users´ ability and conditions to analyze it, according to final business rules and applications. These abilities can be significantly improved, if analytics and big data tools and resources can be applied. In the following, we aim to discuss some resources, as examples.

From Chapman et al. (2000), SEMMA, and from Hampton (2011) and SAS(2014), CRISP-DM are proposed solutions of methodologies for knowledge discovery processes, which became almost industrial standards, as they are widely applied for knowledge generation from datasets, such as those that compose the functional array of big data assets and resources. It is also notable the popularization of tools which enable knowledge discovery in massive data, such as the MapReduce models and techniques, cited by Jeffrey and Ghemawat (2008) and the Hadoop framework, presented by White (2009). According to Azevedo and Lourenço (2008), each step of CRISP-DM and SEMMA can be mapped to KDD steps and, by this way, regarded as actions of a typical KM process. Dodge (2010) and Chen, Roger and Storey (2012) studied also the application of mining techniques over big data contents, discussing how the adaptation of the classical mining methods for knowledge generation in this new environment can produce applicable knowledge for business decisions.

As Berry and Linoff (1997) defined that data mining as the analytical step of the KDD process in which prepared data is used to generate applicable knowledge, it is possible to understand how this opportune process is reaffirmed in SAS (2014) and SAS (2017), this last reference clearly connecting to project management actions and plans. This production of knowledge can be performed using various approaches and algorithms for purposes, such as marketing support (Rygielskk, Wang, & Yen, 2002; Hu & Liu, 2004; Yonce, Taylor, Kelly, & Gnau, 2017), stock marketing perspectives (Enke & Thawornwong, 2005; Bollen, Mao & Zeng, 2011) and fraud detection (Chan, Fan, Prodromidis, & Stolfo, 1999; Phua, Lee, Smith, & Gayler, 2010). Kremer, Mantin and Ovchinnikov (2013) showed how a process that could coordinate and prepare information and knowledge about the external competitive environment favors strategic marketing planning, connecting it to the organizational strategic process.

As cited before, a critical aspect for information management is customer behavior. Various authors described how an alignment of internal resources could occur to fulfill customers' expectations, attributing the term "myopia" to identify the correspondent difficulty for a company to understand correctly its market. A strategic alignment, for example, using an information system, will define a relationship of internal forces and resources to this external context, to implement effective strategic marketing. This perspective integrates big data datasets, processed through KDD resources, through an information system, to allow project management tasks implementations.

Approaching, generally, KDD alternatives, we find from the sources cited: Classification, Regression, (cluster) analysis, rules generation and outlier detection. Summarizing these possibilities, we can describe *Classification task* as labeling a set of data using a decision model created from a set of known data that can allow prediction of new data generated through the same system. *The regression task* is also based on known records, but besides "labeling" new records, as it was proposed by Classification, approximated numerical values could be calculated, or inferred, another trend or prospective prediction possibility.

Big contents of datasets can be split using *Cluster analysis* or *clustering*. Dividing the data into groups, can minimize instances (or occurrences) differences, maximizing the analytical views of several groups, understanding how data can reveal evidences from a big sample, which may vary from one situation to another. This way, it is possible to generate *association rules* to verify the co-occurrence between observations from data generated from past activities. Finally, *Outlier detection* is related to identifying patterns in data that do not conform to expected behavior (Varun, Banerjee & Kumar, 2009).

RELATING KNOWLEDGE MANAGEMENT, ANALYTICS, BIG DATA AND PROJECT MANAGEMENT

It is possible to understand several proposals that examine project management as a dynamic context, where knowledge can potentially flow among its activities, being expressively understood as a knowledge management evolution. Considering the SECI model, discussed by Nonaka (2008), allow to stress the relation and definitions for KM practices for project management tasks. From this study, it is opportune to define that there is a big comprehension of knowledge management contribution for PM, also that this contribution was not sufficiently addressed at the time of its writing. In this analysis, producing explicit knowledge from tacit level, and then combining it to other explicit knowledge, resulting in a permanent cycle condition where new tacit can be absorbed, reminds completely situations of projects being proposed, planned and executed, starting from improvised, practical compositions to more structured, explicit, process-oriented basics, illustrating how knowledge management processes can be investigated in this example.

For Reich and Wee (2006), several explicit knowledge-based components for these basal directives for project management, such as the project charter, project scope statement and the project plan can be depicted as KM. In this work, the authors also call attention to the knowledge production and demands for the 44 processes defined by PMI for PM, calling a special attention for tacit knowledge management needs.

It is possible to extend Landaetta (2008) findings to project portfolios, where a set of projects can be managed together, in one level, and then be observed in further detail. His conclusions showed the relevant impacts on the fostering of this knowledge flow among projects, implicating in better project execution performance. He also obtained some results, which may lead to better levels of capabilities formation, starting a positive cycle of knowledge management. Alternatively, Paramkushan and Gordon (2013) analyzed the inhibiting factors for this knowledge flow. It was studied a group of six information technology projects, where authors also reported their findings to project performance, but this time observing how the lack of the flow will impact negatively on the project final and significant factors. As those studies show, knowledge production, coming from expressive sets of data, impacts positively, when efficiently managed, in various project aspects, as those critical final-user points, such as performance, quality and communication.

As it was defined for analytics, it is opportune to understand that, nowadays, its propositions arise from commercial, simple offers, as those produced by analysis of popular, public platforms, as Google apps – Mehmod (2017) – to more sophisticated and complex solutions, that allow planners and strategists to develop additional comprehension regarding business decisions, trends and contributions (Deloitte, 2017; Linke, 2017). This way, analytical studies, arising from big data contents, populated and shared through project management activities, could result in potential knowledge to improve further decisions for PM planning actions. This opportune cyclic process will be approached in the last section, where some study cases will be analyzed. It can, initially be perceived from the findings of Müller *et al.* (2013), where authors concluded that earlier collaborators play a decisive role in knowledge management for projects, when considering organizational clusters.

With all these examples of association of KM and PM, it is interesting to appreciate how big data sources are generated, stored, managed and applied in the context of projects. Approaching those references cited before, this association is explored in the following. From these studies, it was noticed that:

- Sometimes, data is not predicted and organized in the dynamic environment of projects. It is always available and intensively produced, resulting in a perception of an almost unlimited source of signals linked to all project management events. Informal datasets are also produced, as it can be identified as tacit knowledge sources.
- Knowledge is intuitively produced also, sometimes, through informal processes related to cultural aspects of each organization, being applied without any structured perception, as tacit knowledge contents. This situation produces a continent that is difficult to apply in new situations, as it is related to environmental aspects – such people´s conditions, organizational tacit communication, competitive pressures, etc.
- Knowledge demands also grow in the field, on the application situations, as projects usually are proposed in such an evolving, more complex ways, to achieve new and higher value goals.
- On the strategic level, it is also interesting to point out that the generated knowledge can be further applied for KM itself improving, as it also receives more structured knowledge production to improve PM practices as well.
- Knowledge is managed in contexts of multiple projects and various organizations, the *portfolios,* bringing the complexity described as those scenarios related by the literature with big data.

This last observation identifies the situation where it is possible to understand big data as referring to contexts of huge amounts of available data in dynamic conditions. Additionally, the need of knowledge production from this data and the correlated need for knowledge management process for the production itself potentially implies in better project management practices and results.

Some aspects important to assess, from this broad conceptual relationship perceptions are:

- It is possible to describe a cycle, where, progressively, organizations that improves KM practices can improve their PM practices also allowing, in result, better KM practices. It recalls a "spiral" model, as that announced by Nonaka (2008), generally identified as SECI model.
- Big data contents can be analyzed and treated by some tools, methods and techniques, as those exemplified above and many others. It can be recognized as those sets produced by interactions in multiple, concurrent projects in any organizational contents.
- KM practices remain very challenging for organizations, as efficient and coherent application of IT tools, infrastructure, information systems projects and implementations, planned managerial tasks and skills.
- There are several models and recommendations proposed by the literature at this time, with no predominant trend at all, as this context is still new to the market, various practices and empirical research are in exercise now, that must be investigated further for a potential description for this relationship.
- Big data contexts, as projects for strategic purposes and knowledge management practices are continuously being proposed, studied and applied. In their way to be precisely, conceptually affirmed, they enable to better implement tools - as information systems, for example.

Rajamaran and Ullman (2011) present an interesting provocation, announcing that instead of "supercomputers", these new approaches demand also a technological infrastructure specially customized to produce knowledge in an effective and objective way, where, for example, resides project management usual demands. This factor is sometimes forgotten in theoretical approaches and practical applications, as immense amount of data – characterized as Big Data – must be continuously processed, sometimes, under the application of complex algorithms, providing knowledge results to be further used in plans and associated actions. Along with these processing capabilities, storage is also an infrastructural issue that must be considered in information systems projects, and its related implications. Distributed file systems tools are techniques to be applied for efficient performances in these contexts of knowledge production.

Some authors, as Boyd and Crawford (2011), argue about the application of "networked datasets", allowing the adaptation of technological infrastructure methods for knowledge production. For them, these new technologies can improve knowledge management, as *Ford changed the way we made cars*. It must be recalled, eventually, that Toyota process-driven and oriented systems and production design also modified Ford initial ideas on manufacturing.

The following section produces some study cases, to exemplify how this conceptual network can really be applied.

CASE STUDIES

The dynamic conceptual relationship among data generation, big data-based knowledge production, decision making, overall performing knowledge management in project management contexts is to be approached in this section, oriented to produce a practical view that elaborates the final composition for the intended goal of this chapter. As it happens in multidisciplinary observations, this consolidation could be produced in various ways, adopting several techniques and different methodological propositions. Here, it was adopted a genuine multidisciplinary observation, supported by the previous theoretical background developed in the previous sections of this text, regarding practical cases of infrastructure, industrial and services projects.

For the first case, a usual infrastructure project is to be analyzed. It is a basic study, adapted from a real case, which is an intention of a local government to improve a traffic interstate road in a region of an emerging country. It is a complex decision, as it contemplates two different views for the results of this project, after the cited road and its associated supporting structures – bridges, tunnels, services areas, etc. – are delivered to the population:

- For some citizens, it is a real opportunity of economic growth, presenting the improvement of passengers and load transportation, along with jobs created along the road, both to keep it working and others derived from its main objectives. These additional jobs could correspond to the service people, hired for food catering, hotels, transportation itself, etc. As the local government impose some transportation taxes, the public budget can also be benefited from business improvement.
- On the other hand, a significant part of the population will prefer not to have this road system increment, as more traffic will go through their cities and region. Pollution, heavy traffic, potential occurrences of accidents and other facts would be possible, bringing new security issues. Along with these unwished events, this part of population argues about heavy public investments on an old-fashioned system, which should be effectively replaced by modern systems, such as electrical trains (clean energy), for example.

As it happened to some private companies, the govern, with the help of their Public Relation and Communications secretariat, starts a campaign in social media, radio and television to inform citizens about their intention on improving, augmenting this traffic system, implementing some benefits and increments to the old one. This campaign is not merely informative, as several monitoring services, based on an information system, created specifically to follow citizens reaction (which be a base to be applied in the future for other processes, as elections, other public projects, overall public relations with citizens, international government actions, etc.) through some channels – social media, mainly, but also from manifests, newspapers publications, political reactions, among many others – intending to develop a "trend topic" model, that shows, in practical terms, how local citizens react, influence each other, etc.

Data is collected from structured sources – as, for example, money spent for some citizens and political parties' movements in advertisements pro or against the project, number of reactions – by type, projections of investment and return or payback values – and from unstructured, mainly characterized by social media reactions – Facebook posts, tweets, blogs interactions, public services answers to citizens – to compose a big data content, which will be analyzed. This analysis, which typically produces knowledge from heterogeneous data (as big data promises), will return the first level of analysis to local government managers.

As we are thinking about an information system, analytics are applied, in a continuous way, to understand how people will react to some simulations produced by local authorities, testing practical hypothesis. In some tests, local government managers inform that only a part of the road will be expanded – it is not a technical recommendation, indeed, but a test to produce another level of communications exchange, interaction. These new, unstable announcements generate some additional events which will be analyzed, producing new waves of knowledge from data and information, designing specific decision scenarios, where it is possible to identify main groups of citizens that want to react, how they react, what are their preferences and how they will potentially think about the final governmental decision, if the negotiations for this project are to be started.

In this case, big data and analytics are to be applied to understand citizens´ reactions to one initiative from the local government, as is to be inserted in a real process of one information system. This IS, which involves information technology, people, data collected and compared, organizational structure, communication resources and process designed, will result not only for this specific decision, which is already important, but in an information and knowledge process that can be repeated or adapted for other public and private projects, reinforcing our conceptions over the richness for this interaction in practical cases. It can generate, for instance, some public governmental actions and plans, based on predictions made over citizens previous behavior. More knowledge, methodologically generated, applied to better decision about projects.

In another practical case, an industrial food processing corporation wants to adopt an "industry 4.0" based system in one of its plants and distribution line. The alternative of industry 4.0 is a modern, competitive investment, which proposes to automatize production lines, with the implementation of robots, adjusted production schemes based on knowledge generated from the commercial fronts and, overall, optimizing industrial production. As it usually happens in projects of this size and impacts, it also presents an irreversible situation where human jobs will be lost forever, as operators are to be changed by these programmable machines and optimized level of process controlling.

This project contemplates a decision scenario, as it also will take a long time – typical estimated for some years – to payback the complete investment made in this change. As this company has to replace human operators and managers for automatized infrastructure, optimization must be achieved faster, at the beginning of this new working business model, assuring this modernization to return the investment as fast as it is possible.

Thinking this way, the company starts a research about its production lines, using social media contents and customer face-to-face promotions in supermarkets, to understand several issues regarding customers preferences and habits. Some tests and researches to be conducted will try to measure satisfaction levels, brand retention, product lines diversification potential strategies, customer expectations, etc. These tests results are to be analyzed consolidating two types of data – structured, formal, defined and unstructured, informal, spontaneous – as it will be collected from commercial documents, spreadsheets, invoices, budgets and schedules (structured) and blog posts, interviews, reactions perceptions (unstructured). For this, first, a big data processing system is implemented, receive these contents and depicting some details about customers´ reactions. This system is so added by analytics processing, where a comprehension about the evolution of these reactions can occur if some changes are to be implemented in the productive chain.

It is important to say that we have several different signals coming from customers reactions. At a first glance, it can show, in a similar way as we understood the first case, of the traffic road project, the continuity of the customer satisfaction, even if the processed food package he or she is acquiring now was produced by a robot, not by a human operator. But in another level, it can show, objectively, how products are really acquired by customers, how we develop our preferences towards a specific purchase – ways, information needed, amount paid, etc. – allowing this company to precisely decided what production line will be automatized and when. This is a typical strategic decision for project management, which will impact directly on the investment plan for its food processing plant automatization, industry 4.0, project.

So, this way, big data and analytics will produce knowledge allowing the first level of adjustment for this project, or an association of smaller projects, a *portfolio*, which can be coordinated. It is not a one-way knowledge generation for project management indeed, but a continuous cycle, a knowledge management market intelligence scenario, where commercial data is produced to adjust projects implementation in a period.

In another typical case, that are impacting a complete sector nowadays, it is analyzed how a communication agency can implement all this informational infrastructure to bring more automation to its daily routines of process and works. Analyzing in a simple way, just observing its more typical service for a regular customer, one agency has the goal to provide an advertising campaign for a customer – typically a commercial company – as to inform the final customer about an added value in a product or service. This is a frequent relevant part of the communication plan, which is an indispensable service for a marketing strategic and tactical plan.

Thinking "digitally", this agency, in the future, could receive a draft document from its customer, as the business owner will fill a form, through internet, with its potential demands. After automatically identified – by a big data tool – basic key-words detailed in that document are to be analyzed by analytics software and systems in Internet, identifying usage, frequency, trends, resulting in some pictures that will inform the publisher about scenarios for efficient advertising.

For example, we can consider the agency customer if it is a clothe shop, which mainly sells sports materials and related items, from worldwide known brands, as a multi-brand strategy. From this analysis, the agency can react to an intention from the shop owner, as he informed, in his draft document, that he wants to open a new space in his shops, focusing new sports modality (for example, as it happened few years ago in Brazil, where NFL was not well known – now, it is a successful case in this country).

The agency, producing a big data analysis, can research internet contents, data collected from press agencies channels and other structured and unstructured ways, producing a picture about the actual market situation, future trends, expected transaction volumes, customer segments that will be candidates for promotions, etc. These knowledge components will generate a series of marketing – related project plans, to be detailed, developed and implemented in the future.

Interestingly, the first level of advertisement can also be digitally produced and digitally disseminated, using social media channels, communicating with potential customers, associated to press and institutional channels of that specific sportive modality (local confederation, clubs, fans clubs) about their offers of sports materials.

As additional marketing strategies, customers can have "loyalty" and other retention marketing strategies applied, when – maybe automatically – studying their consumption levels, media reaction, interactions, integration to the advertisements, to evolve and improve their participation and levels of adhesion to marketing campaigns. Maybe this more sophisticated agency performance can reach other level of service, transforming it into a marketing agency, who will produce, with the help of this information system (big data, analytics, social media and related infrastructure) in an effective advisor on customer capture, development and retention strategies, in typical service-sector projects.

CONCLUSION

Project management emerges as a turbulent, dynamic, controversial context where data, information and knowledge are generated massively and demanded for better decision processes and structures. In this chapter, aiming to expand previous developments, regarding a publication where it was studied the relationship of project management and knowledge management, new components for these potential contributions were addressed: analytics and information systems architecture. As these two concepts prescribe modern possibilities to produce knowledge for application in organizational decisions, the association of PM and KM is improved, together with its perspectives of new competitive forces.

A theoretical review was conducted, to define how analytics will compose with big data, as the former work assessed this important resource as a trend of knowledge production. After this, knowledge management and project management were proposedly studied together, to observe their correlation. Interestingly, this relation appears both as a dynamic process, oriented to solve business issues and complex situations, but also as a potential generator for new strategic positioning, to be structured by strategic planning process in organizations. Information systems, a concept that composes with every informational source, regarded to align several active elements – such as people, organizational structure, process definitions and so for – promote the final key part to be added to the theoretical background.

As we discussed final examples for this dynamic challenging solution, attention has been called for its complete integration when simple, frequent actions of actual market competitive methods are observed with more detail. Finally, it is possible to affirm that this chapter observed and promoted a study where knowledge management and project management expressive relationship can be improved in modern value-aggregated chains, enhancing their abilities, perspectives of modern trends adoption (such as automation, for example) and strategic solutions, with the quick responses demanded by nowadays market competition.

REFERENCES

Azevedo, A., & Lourenço, A. (2008). *KDD, SEMMA and CRISP-DM: a parallel overview*. Available at http://hdl.handle.net/10400.22/136

Barney, J. (1991). Firms Resources and Sustained Competitive Advantage. *Journal of Management, 17*(1), 99–120. doi:10.1177/014920639101700108

Berry, M. J., & Linoff, G. (1997). *Data mining techniques: for marketing, sales and customer support.* New York: John Wiley and Sons, Inc.

Bollen, J., Mao, H., & Zeng, X. (2011). Twitter mood predicts the stock market. *Journal of Computational Science, 2*(1), 1–8. doi:10.1016/j.jocs.2010.12.007

Boyd, D., & Crawford, K. (2011). Six provocations for Big Data. *Annals of "A decade in Internet time: Symposium on the dynamics of the internet and society".*

Cao, L., Zhang, C., & Liu, J. (2006). Ontology-based integration of business intelligence. *Web Intelligence and Agent Systems. International Journal (Toronto, Ont.), 4,* 313–325.

Chan, P. K., Fan, W., Prodromidis, A. L., & Stolfo, S. F. (1999). Distributed data mining in credit card fraud detection. *IEEE Intelligent Systems and their Applications, 14*(6), 67-74.

Chapman, P., Clinton, J., Kerber, R., Khabaza, T., Reinartz, T., Shearer, C., & Wirth, R. (2000). *Step-by-step mining guide*. SPSS.

Chau, M., & Xu, J. (2012). Business intelligence in blogs: understanding consumer interactions and communities. MIS Quarterly, 36(4), 1189-1216.

Chen, H., Chiang, R. H. L., & Storey, V. C. (2012). Business intelligence and analytics: from big data to big impact. MIS Quarterly, 36(4), 1165-1188.

Choo, C. W. (2005). *The knowing organization: how organizations use information to construct meaning, create knowledge and make decisions.* Oxford, UK: Ed. Oxford University Press. doi:10.1093/acprof:oso/9780195176780.001.0001

Chou, J. S., & Yang, J. G. (2012). Project management knowledge and effects on construction projects outcomes: An empirical study. *Project Management Journal, 43*(5), 47–67. doi:10.1002/pmj.21293

Clark, T. D. Jr, Jones, M. C., & Armstrong, C. P. (2007). The dynamic structure of management support systems: Theory development, research, focus and direction. *Management Information Systems Quarterly, 31*(3), 579–615. doi:10.2307/25148808

Courtney, M. (2013). Puzzling out Big Data. Engineering & Technology, 7(12), 56-60.

Cristea, D. S., & Capatina. (2009). *A. Perspectives on knowledge management models*. Analls do "Duranea de Jos". *Universidade de Galati, 15*(2), 355–366.

Davenport, T. H., & Prusak, L. (2000). *Working knowledge: how organizations manage what they know* (2nd ed.). Harvard Business Press.

David, E., & Thawornwong, S. (2005). The use of data mining and neural networks for forecasting stock market returns. *Expert Systems with Applications*, *29*(4), 927–940. doi:10.1016/j.eswa.2005.06.024

De Man, D. (2012). A platform for market intelligence. *International Trade Forum*, (4), 21-21.

De Roche. (2016). Five critical aspects to applying data analytics. *Teammate solutions*. Available at http://www.teammatesolutions.com/five-critical-steps-to-applying-data-analytics.aspx

Dean, J., & Ghemawat, S. (2008). MapReduce: Simplified data processing on large clusters. *Communications of the ACM*, *51*(1), 107–113. doi:10.1145/1327452.1327492

Deloitte. (2017). *Five questions about applying analytics to risk management*. Available at https://www2. deloitte.com/content/dam/Deloitte/au/Documents/risk/deloitte-au-risk-risk-angles-applying-analytics-risk-management-250215.pdf

Dimitrios, N. K., Sakas, D. P., & Vlachos, D. S. (2013). The role of information systems in creating strategic leadership model. *Procedia: Social and Behavioral Sciences*, *73*, 285–293. doi:10.1016/j.sbspro.2013.02.054

Dodge, J. (2010). Mining for Gold. *Information Management*, *10*(5), 38-40.

El-Bashir, M. Z., Collier, P., & Sutton, S. G. (2011). The Role of Organizational Absorptive Capacity in Strategic Use of Business Intelligence to Support Integrated Management Control Systems. *The Accounting Review*, *86*(1), 155–184. doi:10.2308/accr.00000010

El-Gayar, O., & Timsina, P. (2014). Opportunities for Business Intelligence and Big Data Analytics In Evidence Based Medicine. In *Annals of 47th Hawaii International Conference on System Science*. IEEE. 10.1109/HICSS.2014.100

Fayyad, U., Piatetsky-Shapiro, G., & Smyth, P. (1996). The KDD process for extracting useful knowledge from volumes of data. *Communications of the ACM*, *39*(11), 27–34. doi:10.1145/240455.240464

Gasik, S. (2011). A model of project knowledge management. *Project Management Journal*, *42*(April), 23–44. doi:10.1002/pmj.20239

Hampton, J. (2011). *SEMMA and CRISP-DM: Data mining methodologies*. Available at http://jesshampton.com/2011/02/16/semma-and-crisp-dm-data-mining-methodologies/

Haslinda, A., & Sarinah. (2009). A review of knowledge management models. *The Journal of International Social Research*, *2*(9), 187-198.

Hu, M., & Liu, B. (2004). Mining and summarizing customer reviews. In *Proceedings of the tenth ACM SIGKDD international conference on Knowledge discovery and data mining (KDD '04)*. ACM. Retrieved from http://doi.acm.org/10.1145/1014052.1014073

Inmon, B., Strauss, D., & Neushloss, G. (2008). *DW 2.0: The Architecture for the Next Generation of Data Warehousing*. Morgan Kaufmann.

Jain, C. L. (2016). How to Use Big Data and Predictive Analytics to Improve the Success of New Products. *Review of Business*, *37*(1), 48-55.

Jamil, G. L. (2005). *Gestão da Informação e do conhecimento em empresas brasileiras: estudo de múltiplos casos*. Belo Horizonte: Ed. Con / Art.

Jamil, G. L. (2013). Approaching Market Intelligence concept through a case analysis: Continuous knowledge for marketing strategic management and its complementarity to competitive intelligence. *Annals of Centeris 2013 – Conference on Technology and Information Systems.*

Jamil, G. L., Santos, L. H. R., Alves, M. L., & Furbino, L. (2012). A design framework for a market intelligence system for healthcare sector: a support decision tool in an emergent economy. In *Handbook on research of ICTs for Social Services and Healthcare: developments and applications*. Hershey, PA: IGI Publishing.

Johnson, J. E. (2012, July). Big data + Big Analytics + Big opportunity. *Financial & Executive*, 51-53.

Kaplan, R., & Norton, D. (2007). *The execution premium: linking strategies to operation for competitive advantage*. Harvard Business School Press.

Kearns, G. S., & Lederer, A. L. (2003). A resource based view of IT alignment: How knowledge sharing creates a competitive advantage. *Decision Sciences*, *34*(1), 1–29. doi:10.1111/1540-5915.02289

Kimball, R., & Ross, M. (2010). *Relentlessly Practical Tools for Data Warehousing and Business Intelligence*. John Wiley and sons.

Kotler, P., & Keller, K. (2005). *Marketing Management* (12th ed.). Prentice Hall.

Kremer, M., Mantin, B., & Ovchinnikov, A. (2013). *Strategic consumers, Myopic retailers*. Darden School of Business at University of Virginia. Available at http://www.darden.virginia.edu/web/uploadedFiles/Darden/Faculty_Research/Research_Publications/Ovchinnikov_StrategicConsumer_MyopicRetailers.pdf

Landaetta, R. R. (2008). Evaluating benefits and challenges of knowledge transfer across projects. *Engineering Management Journal*, *20*(1), 29–38. doi:10.1080/10429247.2008.11431753

Linke, R. (2017). Applying analytics – Ideas and examples from leading companies and researches. *MIT Management Newsroom*. Available at http://mitsloan.mit.edu/newsroom/articles/reading-list-applying-analytics/

McAfee, A., & Brynjolfsson, E. (2012). Big data: The management revolution. *Harvard Business Review*, *90*(10), 60–68. PMID:23074865

Mehmod, H. (2017). *A big list of what Google Analytics can and can not do*. Available at http://marketlytics.com/blog/list-of-things-google-analytics-can-and-cannot-do

Mintzberg, H., Alhstrand, B., & Lampel, J. (2009). *Strategy Safari: the complete guide through the wilds of strategic management* (2nd ed.). Pearson Education Limited.

Müller, R., Glücker, J., Aubry, M., & Shaun, J. (2013). Project management knowledge flows in network of project managers and project management offices: A case study in the pharmaceutical Industry. *Project Management Journal*, *44*(2), 4–19. doi:10.1002/pmj.21326

Nonaka, I. (2008). *The knowledge creating company*. Harvard Business Review Classics.

Ohata, M. & Kumar, A. (2012, September). Big Data: A Boom for Business Intelligence. *Financial Executive.*

Paramkusham, R. B., & Gordon, J. (2013, Fall). Inhibiting factors for knowledge transfer in information technology projects. *Journal of Global Business and Technology, 9,* 2.

Park, S. H., Huh, S. Y., Oh, W., & Han, S. P. (2012). A social network-based inference model for validating customer profile data. MIS Quarterly, 36(4), 1217-1237.

Phua, C., Lee, V., Smith, K., & Gayler, R. (2010). *A comprehensive survey of data mining-based fraud detection research.* Available at http://arxiv.org/ftp/arxiv/papers/1009/1009.6119.pdf

PMBoK. (2013). *Project Management Body of Knowledge* (5th ed.). Project Management Institute.

Porter, M. (2008). *On Competition.* Harvard Business School Press.

Prado, D. (2006). *Gerenciamento de programas, portfólios e projetos nas organizações.* Belo Horizonte: INDG.

Rajamaran, A. & Ullman, J. D. (2011). *Mining of massive datasets.* Cambridge Editors.

Rayome, A. D. (2016). *Seven ways to build trust and analytics at your company.* Tech Republic Blog. Available at https://www.techrepublic.com/article/infographic-7-ways-to-build-trust-in-data-and-analytics-at-your-company/

Reich, B., Gemino, A., & Sauer, C. (2008). A temporary model of information technology project performance. *Journal of Management Information Systems, 24*(3), 9–44.

Reich, B., Gemino, A., & Sauer, C. (2012). Knowledge management and Project-based knowledge in its projects: A model and preliminary results. *International Journal of Project Management, 30*(6), 663–674. doi:10.1016/j.ijproman.2011.12.003

Reich, B., & Wee, S. W. (2006). Searching for knowledge in the PMBoK Guide. *Project Management Journal, 37*(2), 11–27.

Rygielski, C.; Wang, J. C. & Yen, D. C. (2002). Data mining techniques for customer relationship management. *Technology in Society, 24*(4), 483-502. doi:10.1016/S0160-791X(02)00038-6

SAS. (2017). *What is Analytics?* Available at https://www.sas.com/en_us/insights/analytics/what-is-analytics.html

SAS. (n.d.). *SAS Enterprise Miner – SEMMA.* Available at http://www.sas.com/technologies/analytics/datamining/miner/semma.html

Stair, R., & Reynolds, G. (2009). *Principles of information systems.* Course Technology.

Tuomi, I. (2000). Data is more than knowledge: Implications of the reversed knowledge hierarchy for knowledge management and organizational memory. *Journal of Management Systems, 16*(3), 103-117.

Turban, E., Mc Lean, E., & Wetherbee, J. (2002). *Information technology for management: transforming business in the digital economy* (3rd ed.). Hoboken, NJ: John Wiley and Sons.

Turban, E., Rainer, R. K. Jr, & Potter, R. E. (2007). *Introduction to information systems*. Hoboken, NJ: John Wiley and Sons.

Varun, C., Banerjee, A., & Kumar, V. (2009). Anomaly detection: A survey. *ACM Computing Surveys*, *41*(3), 2–15.

Yonce, C., Taylor, J., Kelly, N., & Gnau, S. (2017). BI Experts´ perspective: Are you ready for what´s coming in Analytics. *Business Intelligence Journal, 22*(3), 36-42.

This research was previously published in the Handbook of Research on Expanding Business Opportunities With Information Systems and Analytics; pages 45-65, copyright year 2019 by Business Science Reference (an imprint of IGI Global).

Chapter 87
Management of Big Data Projects:
PMI Approach for Success

A. Aylin Tokuç
Cerebro Software Services Inc., Turkey

Zeynep Eda Uran
Cerebro Software Services Inc., Turkey

Ahmet Tezcan Tekin
İstanbul Technical University, Turkey

ABSTRACT

Big data is an emerging area of research that is of interest to various fields; however, studies in the literature and various sources claim that failure rates for big data projects are considerably high. There are different reasons for failure; varying from management processes to the use of wrong technologies. This study investigates how the project management framework proposed by Project Management Institute (PMI) can be effectively adapted to big data projects to reduce failure rates. The application of processes as mentioned in this study can help to eliminate the causes of failure in the early stages of the project; thus, increasing the successful completion rate of such projects.

INTRODUCTION

Big data became a hot topic, attracting the extensive attention of academia, industry, and government across the world. Due to the rapid development of the Internet, the Internet of Things and Cloud Computing, data generated and stored in almost every industry and business area grow significantly in recent years. (Jin, Wah, Cheng, & Wang, 2015). Specifically, big data concept is also fundamental and prevalent in the area of Industry 4.0. Data and analytics are core capabilities of Industry 4.0 and contributing digital technologies; namely cloud computing, mobile devices, IoT platforms, Location detection technologies,

DOI: 10.4018/978-1-6684-3662-2.ch087

advanced human-machine interfaces, authentication and fraud detection, 3D printing, smart sensors, multilevel customer interaction and customer profiling, augmented reality and wearables (PWC, 2016).

Big Data analytics tools and techniques are rising in demand due to the use of Big Data in businesses. Organizations can find new opportunities and gain new insights to run their business efficiently. These tools help in providing meaningful information for making better business decisions (Verma, 2018). So, the number of projects which are in Big Data business increasing every year and these projects are becoming crucial for companies.

According to a Gartner report, it predicts \$2.5 M per minute in IoT spending and 1 M new IoT devices will be sold every hour by 2021. It is a testament to the speed with which digital connectivity is changing the lives of people all over the world (Riddle, 2017). Because of Big Data is part of Industry 4.0, the need for processing of the data which will be generated from these devices and the number of big data projects will increase exponentially year by year.

Big data technologies provide project managers to find opportunities for making corporate decisions for creating successful projects. By analyzing the narrowed scope of data, the company can make better-informed decisions leading to higher success projects and profits. Also, data analysis leads to reducing project complexity. Having inadequate knowledge of information to make decisions is determinant to any business. Many managers must deal with uncertainty and complex problems, but if they can uncover digital material using the right tools to comprehend the project's problems, then they can reduce the intricacy of the project (McAllister, 2018).

Analysis methods that utilize big data groups in production increase the quality of production, save energy and facilitate equipment maintenance. From the perspective of Industry 4.0, collection and analysis of data from various systems such as enterprise and customer-based management systems as well as production systems, and real-time decision-making systems will become the standard in the future (TÜSİAD, 2016). Integrated systems will analyze data to predict errors, define parameters and adapt to changing conditions; thereby increasing productivity. That is why "Big Data Analytics" is one of the nine principles of Industry 4.0.

Handling big data requires additional constraints about volume, variety, velocity, and veracity. In this context;

- **Variety** refers to different types of data collected via smartphones or social media such as images, text, and audio.
- **Volume** refers to large amounts of any data from many different sources, including mobile digital data creation devices and digital devices.
- **Velocity** refers to the speed of data transfers. As mentioned in the *variety* concept, there are different forms of streamed data from multiple sources. So, new algorithms and methods are needed to process and analyze the online and streaming data adequately.
- **Veracity (Complexity)** is related to the correctness and accuracy of information. Behind any information management practice lie the core doctrines of data quality, data governance, and metadata management, along with considerations of privacy and legal concerns (Bello-Orgaz, Jung, & Camacho, 2016).

Considering the constraints above, management of big data application projects demand an understanding of additional requirements given with processing of big data, as well as working with multidisciplinary teams. Development teams focus more on the technology and architecture for processing the data whereas business teams focus more on how to visualize meaningful business insights for the customer. Data scientists use techniques such as data mining, machine learning, and artificial intelligence to generate better insights and make decisions out of raw data. This work will discuss the required skill sets of a project manager to manage such a team in the following sections successfully.

This chapter considers all of those reasons above; it compiles and discusses the recommended project management approach of the Project Management Institute (PMI) for application to big data projects.

WHY DO BIG DATA PROJECTS FAIL?

In literature, various sources report that 65-100% of Big Data Analytics projects fail. Gartner, a research and advisory company, claims that 60% of big data projects would fail to move past preliminary stages in 2017 (Gartner Inc., 2015). In 2017, Nick Heudecker, who is an analyst at Gartner, said that they were overly optimistic about the forecast and the actual failure rate is closer to 85% (Heudecker, 2017). The primary cause for the failure is not the technology but integrating with existing business processes and applications, management resistance, internal politics, lack of skills, and security and governance policies.

The list of challenges in big data projects includes a combination of the following issues:

- Lack of appropriately scoped objectives
- Lack of required skills
- The size of big data
- The non-clearly defined structure of much of the big data
- The difficulty of enforcing data consistency
- Privacy
- Data management/integration
- Rights management
- ETL
- Data discovery (how to find high-quality data from the web?)
- Data veracity (how can we cope with uncertainty, imprecision, missing details?)
- Data verification
- Technical challenges for big data analytics when data is in motion rather than at rest (Zicari, et al., 2016)

Lack of appropriately scoped objectives is one of the most common problems encountered in Big Data projects. In this context, a big data project, as in any project, should also have a clearly defined business objective. The problem to be solved must be identified. New insights can be discovered through data analysis, but to uncover meaningful insights, the data should be collected and analyzed keeping the main problem in mind. As mentioned before, the whole system should be designed around the main problem and during the development phase should avoid using experimental development with new technologic features. Because those experimentations can result in project delays and getting the project away from the main problem.

Lack of required skills is also one of the most common problems for Big Data projects. It is essential to employ people with required skills during a big data project. As is known, big data is a rapidly evolving field of technology; an inexperienced project staff may be lost in this bottomless technology. This situation can cause severe time delays or project failures.

Management failures and lack of required skills can have disastrous consequences. In 2013, UK National Health Service abandoned NHS patient record system project. The project was initially expected to be completed with a £6.4 billion, had a cost of £10 billion when the government decided to shut it down (Syal, 2013). The project is described to be "the biggest IT failure ever seen" and the failure ultimately came down to human error. The system was left in the incapable hands of successive ministers, and civil servants who saw the costs continue to spiral as the new systems were badly managed, as well as data management issues and patient confidentiality problems.

In big data projects, the size of big data is very critical. Some specifications should be set according to the size of the data, and some of them should set at the beginning of the project. Planning of needs such as server capacity, database settings, selection of the algorithms is essential. On April 30, 2014, In the Los Angeles International Airport (LAX), all computers crashed, and this situation caused hundreds of delayed or canceled flights. The reason of the crash is the bug in the En Route Automation Modernization (ERAM) system which developed by Lockheed Martin Corp and worth 2.4 billion dollars. In that day, a U-2 spy plane was flying through to the airspace of LAX, ERAM notices the plane and trying to set altitude information in the airplane's flight plan. During this process, the system got many errors. An air traffic controller noticed the problem and entered the estimated altitude of the plane manually. After that, the system started to work on the calculating possibility of flight paths with other planes for avoiding crashes. As a result of this enormous calculation, the system fell short in memory and blocked every other flight process at the airport. The reason of ERAM's system failure was about limiting the size of data that planes send. Most planes have a simple flight plan, but that day, the U-2 spy plane had a complex one. As a result, faced with the unexpected size of data caused physical damage via delayed and canceled flights (Hamrouni, 2017).

Another major cause of a big data project to fail is poor data quality or having inaccurate, incomplete or outdated data to analyze. To be able to influence business actions, data analysis should lead to insights. Although there are some commonly accepted tools and techniques to increase the quality of data; the initial dataset should be consistent and have enough volume depending on the needs of the project.

In 2014, a credit card offer was sent to a journalist known as Lisa McIntire who lives in California. The offer was from Bank of America but posted by Golden Key International. Mail sent to Lisa's mother's address and addressed to "Lisa is a Slut McIntire". After her mother sent the picture of it, the journalist posted photos of the offer via social media. As a result, the dirty data problem caused failure and loss of prestige. Through this example, it is seen that data quality and veracity are significant factors for project success (Reddy, 2014).

Most of these reasons, which cause the failure of a project would disappear through the adaptation of project management processes as described by PMI. Next section focuses on the importance of big data project management and adaptation of project management processes to big data projects.

PMI APPROACH TO MANAGE BIG DATA PROJECTS

Big Data projects are specific IT projects. One should consider the following impacts of big data in the project management efforts, addressing the challenges summarized above, to successfully manage and finalize a project. The following table summarizes common phases of a big data project and the relation of each process to challenges and domains. Each process step has particular challenges in different domains, related to unique properties of big data.

ETL phase in Table 1 includes processes to prepare raw data for processing. Analytics phase is to extract information from the big data. Decision making phase is to evaluate the outcome of the analytics phase for insights. These phases are minimum for a big data project; other phases might be needed depending on the planned output of the project.

Project Management Body of Knowledge (PMBOK) Guide divides the project management process into five process groups and ten knowledge areas. Project management knowledge areas focus on areas of specialization for a project manager. PMBOK Guide is based on The Standard for Project Management and provides details about key concepts, trends, and considerations for project management processes and applies to projects from all industries and sectors (Project Management Institute, 2017a). This section investigates how one would answer the issues faced during the management of a big data project. The points to be noted are listed for each knowledge area, namely: Project Integration Management, Project Scope Management, Project Schedule Management, Project Cost Management, Project Quality Management, Project Resource Management, Project Communications Management, Project Risk Management, Project Procurement Management, and Project Stakeholder Management.

Table 1. Big Data Project phases, processes, challenges and domains

Phase	Process Step	Challenge	Domain			
			People	Process	Technology	GEIT
ETL	Capture and storage	Volume, Velocity, Variety	X	X	X	X
	Conversion and transformation	Variety, Velocity		X	X	X
	Cleansing and enrichment	Veracity, Volume	X	X	X	X
Analytics	Data profiling	Variety, Volume	X	X	X	
	Statistical modeling	Variety, Veracity	X	X	X	
	Algorithm / query development	Variety, Velocity, Veracity			X	X
Decision Making	Visualization	Variety, Veracity	X	X	X	
	Interpretation	Variety, Volume, Veracity	X			
	Automation	Volume, Variety, Velocity, Veracity		X	X	X

Source: (Voges, 2014)

PMI's Pulse of the Profession Report (2017) suggests that organizations become more mature with their project management practices distinguish more successful project performance. Champions of the study have 80% or more of the projects completed on time and budget and meeting original business goals (Project Management Institute, 2017c).

1. Project Integration Management

Project Integration Management knowledge area includes the processes and activities to identify, define, combine, unify and coordinate various activities. This knowledge area contains Develop Project Charter, Develop Project Management Plan, Direct and Manage Project Work, Manage Project Knowledge, Monitor, and Control Project Work, Perform Integrated Change Control and Close Project or Phase processes (Project Management Institute, 2017a). Project Integration Management is the coordination of all elements within a project. From the perspective of a big data-oriented software development project, the following processes have a crucial impact on the outcome.

Develop project charter process binds the project to a business case. Some big data projects fail due to lack of a business problem as described above. Hence, clearly defining a business objective is a crucial part of a successful big data-oriented project.

Manage project knowledge process uses existing knowledge to contribute to organizational learning. Assets such as lessons learned from similar projects help to define clear objectives and apply relevant techniques in a big data project. Use of new technologies brings new knowledge to the organization, which makes transferring of knowledge a crucial point. Knowledge can be transferred in a written form as in documentation, knowledge base or best practices document, as well as internal training or coaching. PMI's 2015 report states that effective knowledge transfer increases the chance of project success by over 20% (Project Management Institute, 2015).

Close project or phase process finalizes a contract, a phase or a project. The team updates organizational process assets, and lessons learned register, thus enabling big data related know-how to propagate within the organization.

Integration of big data technology with existing tools and techniques within the company is also an issue of a big data related project that should be solved within Integration Management processes. Various big data integration tools facilitate the integration of big data processing solutions, applications, and databases. The complete ecosystem for the project must be planned.

2. Project Scope Management

Project Scope Management knowledge area processes are required to make sure the project includes all the necessary work to complete the objectives. This knowledge area contains Plan Scope Management, Collect Requirements, Define Scope, Create WBS, Validate Scope and Control Scope processes. (Project Management Institute, 2017a). One should consider the scalability and performance needs of a big data project, as well as other business and functional requirements. Also, additional steps for collecting and preparing big data should be included in the scope. Common steps for big data management are listed below:

- **Data Generation:** Identifying data sources and collecting data.
- **Data Acquisition:** Aggregate information in a digital form for further storage and analysis. This step includes pre-processing the data; such as conversion and cleansing operations.
- **Data Storage:** Organizing the collected information in a convenient format for analysis and value extraction.
- **Data Analysis:** Applying tools and techniques on data, to extract information enabling decision making (Hu, Wen, Chua, & Li, 2014).

Project scope management is crucial for all the project's lifecycle. According to PMI's 2017 Pulse of the Profession (Project Management Institute, 2017c), only 69% of projects meet their original goals and business intent. This statistic shows that enough importance is not given to scope management. In addition, various sources indicate that lots of projects could fail or over budget for this reason. Because of the reasons above and the complexity of big data projects, it is critical to qualify the scope carefully and thoroughly.

3. Project Schedule Management

Project Schedule Management knowledge area processes are required to make sure the project is completed within an estimated period. This knowledge area contains Plan Schedule Management, Define Activities, Sequence Activities, Estimate Activity Durations, Develop Schedule and Control Schedule processes (Project Management Institute, 2017a).

The team might not be able to use expert judgment to define required activities or estimate activity durations clearly if the current know-how level of the company is insufficient for the big data project during the planning phase. Therefore, Define Activities and Estimate Activity Durations processes should require the use of iterative techniques such as rolling wave planning or progressive elaboration. Both methods start with an overview and then give a higher level of detail as the project evolves.

In the literature, there are some proposed best practices for IT project estimation. These practices also apply to Big Data Projects. Some critical points for estimation are:

- Create a higher-level plan and estimate large tasks in a range
- Involve people doing the work in estimation processes
- Bring in experts and use Delphi Method
- Construct the estimates based on the application's architecture, modules and programming language (Trotsyuk, 2009)

Paying particular attention to automated testing, security and backup procedures eliminates some potential flaws from the beginning and reduces the risk of schedule overrun in a big data project. After choosing the time management method, a project manager should clarify the expectations of stakeholders. Setting priorities and adjusting the project schedule plan when necessary helps to keep the project on the plan. Periodical time tracking activities and review sessions ensure the project is progressing as planned (Tremel, 2016).

4. Project Cost Management

Project Cost Management knowledge area includes processes that are required to make sure the project is completed within the planned budget. This knowledge area contains Plan Cost Management, Estimate Costs, Determine Budget and Control Costs processes (Project Management Institute, 2017a).

Project scope, schedule, and costs are all related. A change in scope affects both project schedule and cost. The term "triple constraint" is widely used to refer to these three main restrictions of a project. Big Data projects often have hidden cost and complexity, which makes planning and controlling costs throughout the project harder.

In the estimation process, historical values for a similar project might not be present for a big data project. Using expert judgment also might not be an option is the team lacks the required know-how for a big data project. Reserves should be carefully planned with buy-in from the management. Thus, rolling wave and progressive elaboration techniques should be preferred for work with high uncertainty when possible.

As raw data is increasing in size, traditional data warehousing solutions become inadequate. Companies turn to cloud storage solutions, which increase the costs of additional integration requirement and usage license fees. As data privacy becomes an issue and several countries have strict regulations about data privacy; organizations also need to invest in data security. Proper licensing options should be considered according to the needs of the project. The project managers need to identify and review these costs to keep the project on budget.

Human resource costs have a big part in a big data project budget. Such projects mostly deploy staff with different expertise such as database analyst, data scientist, software architect, software engineer, system administrator, QA and test engineer, and project manager. A small delay in a milestone would lead to a big cost increase. Hence, scope and schedule management have a greater impact on project cost management for a big data project.

5. Project Quality Management

Project Quality Management knowledge area processes support continuous process improvement activities while ensuring the organization's quality policy applies to the project. This knowledge area contains Plan Quality Management, Manage Quality and Control Quality processes (Project Management Institute, 2017a).

Since big data projects mostly involve high uncertainty, producing frequent and small deliverables for inspection makes it easier to meet the business needs and stakeholder objectives.

Field expertise is required to identify special quality requirements of a big data project such as data usability and system resource allocation, which is also in the scope of Quality Management. Tao and Gao summarize the quality factors for a big data application project to be:

- System Performance
- System Data Security
- System Reliability
- System Robustness (Tao & Gao, 2016)

Domain-specific quality metrics should be defined, including both data validation and system performance to assure quality.

6. Project Resource Management

Project Resource Management knowledge area includes processes to ensure that the resources needed for the completion of the project are available when needed. This knowledge area contains Plan Resource Management, Estimate Activity Resources, Acquire Resources, Develop Team, Manage Team, and Control Resources processes (Project Management Institute, 2017a).

The project manager should plan license and server needs as well as team resources for a successful big data project when estimating activity resources. Team development should be planned including big data related education needs for project team members depending on the team expertise level. Note that, selected team members have a more significant impact on project plan than usual. Tom Deutsch, Program Director on IBM's Big Data team, claims to "select the people before the technology" (Deutsch, 2012). Managing the team also differs from the usual software development projects, as the team consists of people with different background and expertise from various areas. There should be resources with the right blend of talent and skill sets already available, or management should have a training plan, ensuring the readiness of resources with the right skill set for the project.

7. Project Communications Management

Project Communications Management knowledge area processes ensure effective information exchange throughout the project. This knowledge area contains Plan Communications Management, Manage Communication, and Monitor Communications processes (Project Management Institute, 2017a). Project communication should be carefully planned, considering the needs and expectations of stakeholders. Because big data is a new and complex field, project communication management is critical for big data projects. Also, internal policies causing resistance encountered during big data projects can be minimized by applying communications management processes.

PMI's *The Essential Role of Communications report* (2013) finds that effective communication is the most crucial success factor in a project. Due to ineffective communications, 56% of each dollar spent on projects is at risk. The same report recommends the following strategies to improve communication in a project:

- Close the communications gap around business benefits
- Tailor communications to different stakeholder groups
- Acknowledge the value of project management, including project management communications
- Use standardized project communications practices, and use them effectively (Project Management Institute, 2013)

As stated before, big data projects are developed by cross-functional, multi-disciplinary teams. Project managers with both technical and business understanding are required to successfully run projects including people from different fields.

8. Project Risk Management

Project Risk Management knowledge area processes aim to enhance the chance of project success and decrease the probability and impact of negative risks. This knowledge area contains Plan Risk Management, Identify Risks, Perform Qualitative Risk Analysis, Perform Quantitative Risk Analysis, Plan Risk Responses, Implement Risk Responses and Monitor Risks processes (Project Management Institute, 2017a).

The team should consider additional risks raised from big data infrastructure, security constraints and lack of know-how in the field. Mark Vael summarizes the process to address risk and improve the organization's ability to use big data so that it can meet its business objectives as:

- Provide insight by monitoring all data that runs in the company; analyze and then take action based on the results if the organization's big data security policies and procedures are still under construction.
- For data to be used productively, the organization needs to consider a corporate data lifecycle process, including big data systems.
- Organizations should seek advice and guidance of external data experts when needed.
- Organizations must get a proper insight into the performance of their data handling processes to minimize the risks.
- Make sure that the organization's employees, data, networks, partners, and customers are protected end-to-end.
- Ensure future-proof systems by not only using the right systems, but also the right tools and processes are implemented for big data today and can cope with the inevitable data growth in the future.
- Implement logical and physical access security controls to prevent unauthorized access to sensitive and valuable data. (Vael, 2013).

9. Project Procurement Management

Project Procurement Management knowledge area includes processes to purchase or acquire products, services or results needed from outside the project team. This knowledge area contains Plan Procurement Management, Conduct Procurements and Control Procurements processes (Project Management Institute, 2017a).

The project team needs to decide the infrastructure required for the solution addressing the business needs first. Although cloud solutions are popular and easy to access, regulations should force on-premise solutions. Hybrid solutions should also be considered. All three infrastructure solutions require different procurement process. The project team should consider the technologies to be used and address needed procurement steps in the planning phase.

Vendor management is a troublesome issue for big data projects, as it is for many IT projects. Vendors may not have required qualification or expertise. According to Ron Bodkin, many legacy consultants and system integrators have positioned themselves as experts, despite their lack of skills. In addition to that, many established product vendors are marketing their products as "big data" when they are in fact not (Bodkin, 2013). Vendor selection should be carefully planned and executed to minimize possible vendor related problems.

10. Project Stakeholder Management

Project Stakeholder Management knowledge area processes are required to identify and manage stakeholders affected by the project. This knowledge area contains Identify Stakeholders, Plan Stakeholder Engagement, Manage Stakeholder Engagement, and Monitor Stakeholder Engagement processes (Project Management Institute, 2017a).

A primary reason for big data projects to fail is lack of support from the management. Managers of big data projects should focus on gaining support from all project stakeholders, based on their needs and expectations from the project. Inaccurate stakeholder analysis or failing to understand the needs of the most critical stakeholders based on a power/interest grid are other main reasons why a big data project may fail. The project manager also needs to understand the different needs of stakeholders from various fields. Both the data required by the data scientist and a business requirement set up by the client are all significant and require special attention.

To sum up, the effective use of project management processes as described in PMBOK (Project Management Institute, 2017a) increases the overall project success rate. Application of proven project management practices leads to less waste and greater success according to PMI's Pulse of the Profession 2018 report. The report also states that success is no driven by a single factor (Project Management Institute, 2018). Project managers need to apply suggested processes through initiation to closure phase for a successful outcome.

FUTURE RESEARCH DIRECTIONS

Organizations are going through changes in the era of digitalization and Industry 4.0. Companies seeking competition should adapt to the changing world, taking actions to meet changing customer and market demands. As the world trend is changing, project managers should embrace change. Companies worldwide are going through a set of changes; which is called "digital transformation". Digital transformation involves using digital technologies to redesign a process, aiming to transform that service into a significantly better experience. More and more real-time data will be available as a result of such transformations. Research areas such as big data, cloud computing, Internet of Things, machine learning and artificial intelligence will come into prominence.

Initial research in digital transformation project management field concludes that management of projects requires new ways of managerial thinking (Hassani, El Bouzekri El Idrissi, & Abouabdellah, 2017). Mark A. Langley; President and CEO of PMI states that digital transformation projects have unique challenges and proper project management is required to ensure that the organizations take critical steps to achieve desired results with digital transformation (Langley, 2018).

Project managers are expected to embrace the digital transformation of their company and lead the change. The role of a project manager in digital transformation and the obstacles a company faces during the transformation phase is an emerging research area, which requires further investigation.

Another emerging research and application area are the use of agile practices in project management. Although the Agile Manifesto for software development (Beck, ve diğerleri, 2001) expressing definitive values and principles of agile was published decades ago, effective use of agile and delivery of immediate value to customers become a hot topic in recent years. PMI extended the PMBOK Guide with Agile Practices Guide in 6th edition, only last year. PMI claims that organizations need to shift their focus from internal to outward customer experience, to stay competitive and relevant (Project Management Institute, 2017b). Therefore, further investigation on the use of agile practices for big data projects is a field which requires further research.

CONCLUSION

With the increasing of big data usage, organizations will have more opportunities to manage their businesses better, and the importance of big data projects will increase. Especially in the Industry 4.0 era, a number of IoT devices and big data projects are expected to be mounted. In addition, big data tools will positively affect project management periods like reducing complexity, and they will help in creating successful projects.

In the big data concept, data is large, complex and grows exponentially in a short time. Because of these facts and reasons which will be mentioned in the sections above, managing big data projects are challenging. In this context, various sources report that 65-100% of Big Data Analytics projects fail every year.

There are many reasons for Big Data projects to fail; such as lack of binding the project to a well-defined business objective, management problems or stakeholder engagement. This study investigated how the PMI approach can be effectively adapted to big data projects. With the application of processes in the knowledge areas of Project Integration Management, Project Scope Management, Project Schedule Management, Project Cost Management, Project Quality Management, Project Resource Management, Project Communications Management, Project Risk Management, Project Procurement Management and Project Stakeholder Management, it is proven that possible causes of failure would be eliminated in the early stages of the project, increasing the success rate.

ACKNOWLEDGMENT

This research is supported by Cerebro Software Services, Inc.

REFERENCES

Beck, K., Beedle, M., van Bennekum, A., Cockburn, A., Cunningham, W., Fowler, M., . . . Sutherland, J. (2001). Manifesto for Agile Software Development. *Agilemanifesto*. Retrieved from http://agilemanifesto.org/

Bello-Orgaz, G., Jung, J. J., & Camacho, D. (2016). Social big data: Recent achievements and new challenges. *Information Fusion*, *28*, 45–59. doi:10.1016/j.inffus.2015.08.005

Bodkin, R. (2013, September 14). The big data Wild West: The good, the bad and the ugly. *Gigaom*. Retrieved from https://gigaom.com/2013/09/14/the-big-data-wild-west-the-good-the-bad-and-the-ugly/

Deutsch, T. (2012, July 30). Selecting your first big data project. *IBM Big Data & Analytics Hub*. Retrieved from http://www.ibmbigdatahub.com/blog/selecting-your-first-big-data-project

Gartner Inc. (2015, September 15). *Gartner Says Business Intelligence and Analytics Leaders Must Focus on Mindsets and Culture to Kick Start Advanced Analytics*. Retrieved from https://www.gartner.com/newsroom/id/3130017

Gilchrist, P. (n.d.). The Project Manager's Guide to Big Data. *FreePMStudy*. Retrieved from http://www.freepmstudy.com/BigData/BigDataPMKnowledgeAreas.cshtml

Hamrouni, W. (2017, August 1). 5 of the Biggest Information Technology Failures and Scares. *Exoplatform*. Retrieved from https://www.exoplatform.com/blog/2017/08/01/5-of-the-biggest-information-technology-failures-and-scares

Hassani, R., El Bouzekri El Idrissi, Y., & Abouabdellah, A. (2017). *Software Project Management in the Era of Digital Transformation. In NETYS 2017: Networked Systems* (pp. 391–395). Cham: Springer.

Heudecker, N. (2017, November 9). We were too conservative. The failure rate is closer to 85%. And the problem isn't technology. *Twitter*. Retrieved from https://twitter.com/nheudecker/status/928720268662530048

Hu, H., Wen, Y., Chua, T.-S., & Li, X. (2014). Toward scalable systems for big data analytics: A technology tutorial. *IEEE Access: Practical Innovations, Open Solutions, 2*, 652–687. doi:10.1109/ACCESS.2014.2332453

Jin, X., Wah, B. W., Cheng, X., & Wang, Y. (2015). Significance and Challenges of Big Data Research. In *Big Data Research* (pp. 59-64).

Langley, M. A. (2018, January 29). Leveraging project management for successful digital transformation. *Business Reporter*. Retrieved from https://www.business-reporter.co.uk/2018/01/29/leveraging-project-management-for-successful-digital-transformation/

McAllister, J. (2018, June 22). How to Leverage Big Data in Project Management. *Project Insight*. Retrieved from https://www.projectinsight.net/blogs/project-management-tips/how-to-leverage-big-data-in-project-management

Project Management Institute. (2013). *The Essential Role of Communications*. Newtown Square, PA: Project Management Institute.

Project Management Institute. (2015). *Pulse of the Profession: Capturing the Value of Project Management*. Newtown Square, PA: Project Management Institute.

Project Management Institute. (2017a). *A guide to the project management body of knowledge (PMBOK guide)*. Newton Square, PA: Project Management Institute.

Project Management Institute. (2017b). *Agile Practice Guide*. Newton Square, PA: Project Management Institute.

Project Management Institute. (2017c). *Pulse of the Profession 2017*. Newtown Square, PA: Project Management Institute.

Project Management Institute. (2018). *Pulse of the Profession 2018*. Newtown Square, PA: Project Management Institute.

PWC. (2016, April 1). *2016 Global Industry 4.0 Survey*. Retrieved from https://www.pwc.com/gx/en/industries/industries-4.0/landing-page/industry-4.0-building-your-digital-enterprise-april-2016.pdf

Reddy, T. (2014, October 22). 7 Big Data Blunders You're Thankful Your Company Didn't Make. *Umbel*. Retrieved from https://www.umbel.com/blog/big-data/7-big-data-blunders/

Riddle, C. (2017, August 10). The importance of big data and analytics in the era of digital transformation. *ITProPortal*. Retrieved from https://www.itproportal.com/features/the-importance-of-big-data-and-analytics-in-the-era-of-digital-transformation/

Syal, R. (2013, September 18). Abandoned NHS IT system has cost £10bn so far. *The Guardian*. Retrieved from https://www.theguardian.com/society/2013/sep/18/nhs-records-system-10bn

Tao, C., & Gao, J. (2016). *Quality Assurance for Big Data Applications: Issues, Challenges, and Needs.* California, USA: SEKE.

Tremel, A. (2016, March 21). *Last-Minute Project Rescue: Time Management Tips for Project Teams.* Retrieved from ProjectManagement.com: https://www.projectmanagement.com/articles/323565/Last-Minute-Project-Rescue--Time-Management-Tips-for-Project-Teams

Trotsyuk, M. (2009, August 11). 7 Things You Need to Know About Development Project Estimations. *ProjectManagement.* Retrieved from https://www.projectmanagement.com/blog-post/1562/7-Things-You-Need-to-Know-About-Development-Project-Estimations

TÜSİAD. (2016). *Türkiye'nin Küresel Rekabetçiliği için Bir Gereklilik Olarak Sanayi 4.0: Gelişmekte Olan Ekonomi Perspektifi.* İstanbul: TÜSİAD.

Vael, M. (2013, June). How to manage big data and reap the benefits. *Computer Weekly.* Retrieved from http://www.computerweekly.com/opinion/How-to-manage-big-data-and-reap-the-benefits

Verma, A. (2018, March 19). Why is Big Data Analytics So Important? *WhizLabs.* Retrieved from https://www.whizlabs.com/blog/big-data-analytics-importance/

Voges, D. (2014, November 11). *Quality assurance on Big Data & analytics.* Amsterdam, Netherlands: Vrije Universiteit Amsterdam.

Zicari, R. V., Rosselli, M., Ivanov, T., Korfiatis, N., Tolle, K., Niemann, R., & Reichenbach, C. (2016). Setting up a Big Data project: Challenges, opportunities, technologies and optimization. In Big Data optimization: Recent developments and challenges (pp. 17-47). Switzerland: Springer.

KEY TERMS AND DEFINITIONS

Big Data: Big data is data that contains huge, variable and growing data.

Big Data Analytics: Big data analytics is the process of analyzing big, complex and variable data.

Big Data Analytics Projects: Projects that related to big data analytics.

Big Data Projects: Projects that focus on big data.

Data Analytics: Data analytics is a process that examines, clears, converts and models data to explore useful information, draws conclusions and supports decision making.

ETL: Short for "Extract, Transform, Load", ETL is a process in database usage to prepare data for analysis.

GEIT: Short for "governance of enterprise IT", GEIT is a framework which ensures that the IT resources of an organization are used in an effective way to fulfill stakeholder needs.

Progressive Elaboration: A project management technique, which involves continuously improving and detailing the plan as more detailed and specific information becomes available.

Project Management: Project Management is the planning, reporting, and control of project activities to reach the project goals.

Project Management Body of Knowledge (PMBOK): PMBOK is a book which published by PMI that contains world's well-known project management standards.

Project Management Institute (PMI): PMI is a not-for-profit association that accept professional membership for project and program managers.

Rolling Wave Planning: A project management technique that plans the project in waves, as the project proceeds and details become clearer.

This research was previously published in Agile Approaches for Successfully Managing and Executing Projects in the Fourth Industrial Revolution; pages 279-293, copyright year 2019 by Business Science Reference (an imprint of IGI Global).

Chapter 88
Big Data Analytics in Supply Chain Management

Nenad Stefanovic

ⓘD https://orcid.org/0000-0002-0339-3474

Faculty of Science, University of Kragujevac, Serbia

ABSTRACT

The current approach to supply chain intelligence has some fundamental challenges when confronted with the scale and characteristics of big data. In this chapter, applications, challenges and new trends in supply chain big data analytics are discussed and background research of big data initiatives related to supply chain management is provided. The methodology and the unified model for supply chain big data analytics which comprises the whole business intelligence (data science) lifecycle is described. It enables creation of the next-generation cloud-based big data systems that can create strategic value and improve performance of supply chains. Finally, example of supply chain big data solution that illustrates applicability and effectiveness of the model is presented.

INTRODUCTION

During the last several years there was an amazing progression in the amount of data produced within the supply chain information systems, but also externally. This poses many challenges related to data analysis specifically in terms of know-how, technology, infrastructure, software systems and development methods. The current business climate demands real-time analysis, faster, collaborative and more intelligent decision making.

The current approach to supply chain intelligence has some fundamental challenges when confronted with the scale and characteristics of big data. These include not only data volumes, velocity and variety, but also data veracity and value (Arunachalam, 2018).

The best way to effectively analyze these composite systems is the use of business intelligence (BI). Traditional BI systems face many challenges that include processing of vast data volumes, demand for real-time analytics, enhanced decision making, insight discovery and optimization of supply chain pro-

DOI: 10.4018/978-1-6684-3662-2.ch088

cesses. Big Data initiatives promise to answer these challenges by incorporating various methods, tools and services for more agile and flexible analytics and decision making. Nevertheless, potential value of big data in supply chain management (SCM) has not yet been fully realized and requires establishing new BI infrastructures, architectures, models and tools (Marr, 2016).

Supply chain BI system proved to be very useful in extracting information and knowledge from existing enterprise information systems, but in recent years, organizations face new challenges in term of huge data volumes generated through supply chain and externally, variety (different kind of structured and unstructured data), as well as data velocity (batch processing, streaming and real-time data). Most of the existing analytical systems are incapable to cope with these new dynamics (Larson & Chang 2016).

On the other hand, we have seen tremendous advancements in technology like in-memory computing, cloud computing, Internet of Things (IoT), NoSQL databases, distributed computing, machine learning, etc. Big data is a term that underpins a raft of these technologies that have been created in the drive to better analyze and derive meaning from data at a dramatically lower cost and while delivering new insights and products for organizations in the supply chain.

The key challenges for modern supply chain analytical systems include (Wang et al., 2016):

§   Data explosion – supply chains need the right tools to make sense of the overwhelming amount of data generated by a growing set of data internal and external sources.

§   Growing variety of data – most of the new data is unstructured or comes in different types and forms.

§   Data speed – data is being generated at high velocity which makes data processing even more challenging.

§   Real-time analysis - in today's turbulent business climate the ability to make the right decisions in real-time brings real competitive advantage. Yet many supply chains do not have the infrastructure, tools and applications to make timely and accurate decisions.

§   Achieving simplified deployment and management – despite its promise, big data systems can be complex, costly and difficult to deploy and maintain. Supply chains need more flexible, scalable and cost-effective infrastructure, platforms and services, such as those offered in cloud

In this chapter, challenges and new trends in supply chain big data analytics are discussed and background research of big data initiatives related to SCM is provided. The chapter also describes the main technologies, methods and tools for big data analytics. The methodology and the unified model for supply chain big data analytics which comprises the whole BI lifecycle is presented. Architecture of the model is scalable and layered in such a way to provide necessary agility and adaptivity. The proposed big data model encompasses supply chain process model, data and analytical models, as well as insights delivery. It enables creation of the next-generation cloud-based big data systems that can create strategic value and improve performance of supply chains. An example of supply chain big data solution that illustrates applicability and effectiveness of the model is presented. Finally, future trends, directions and technologies are presented.

BACKGROUND

As the globalized business environment is forcing supply chain networks to adapt to new business models, collaboration, integration and information sharing are becoming even more critical for the ultimate success. Supply chains enterprise systems are experiencing a major structural shift as more organizations rely on a community of partners to perform complex supply chain processes. While supply chains are growing increasingly complex, from linear arrangements to interconnected, multi-echelon, collaborative networks of companies, there is much more information that needs to be stored, processed and analyzed than there was just a few years ago (Tiwari et al., 2018).

Supply chain business intelligence is a collection of activities to understand business situations by performing various types of analysis on the organization data as well as on external data from supply chain partners and other data sources (devices, sensors, social networks, etc.) to help make strategic, tactical, and operational business decisions and take necessary actions for improving supply chain performance. This includes gathering, analyzing, understanding, and managing high volumes of variety data about operation performance, customer and supplier activities, financial performance, production, competition, regulatory compliance, quality controls, device data and Internet (Stefanovic & Milosevic, 2018).

Over the past few decades, the way in which companies need to collate, analyze, report and share their data has changed dramatically. Organizations need to be more adaptive, have increased access to information for decision-making, and effectively deal with a rapidly growing volume of data. Today's business environment demands fast supply chain decisions and reduced time from raw data to insights and actions. Typically, supply chains are capturing enormous data volumes - including vast amounts of unstructured data such as files, images, videos, blogs, clickstreams and geo-spatial data, as well as data coming from various sensors, devices, and social networks (Stefanovic & Milosevic, 2017).

During the past two decades organizations have made large investments in SCM information systems in order to improve their businesses. However, these systems usually provide only transaction-based functionality and mostly maintain operational view of the business. They lack sophisticated analytical capabilities required to provide an integrated view of the supply chain. On the other hand, organizations that implemented some kind of enterprise business intelligence systems still face many challenges related to data integration, storage and processing, as well as data velocity, volume and variety. Additional issues include lack of predictive intelligence features, mobile analytics and self-service business intelligence capabilities (Harvey, 2017).

Sixty-four percent of supply chain executives consider big data analytics a disruptive and important technology, setting the foundation for long-term change management in their organizations (Renner, 2016). Ninety-seven percent of supply chain executives report having an understanding of how big data analytics can benefit their supply chain. Nonetheless, only 17 percent report having already implemented analytics in one or more supply chain functions (Accenture, 2014).

Another survey shows that 68% of supply chain leaders believe that supply chain analytics are critical to their operations. However, a key ingredient for the success of supply chain analytics is consolidating data from all participants and flows in the system, essentially breaking the boundaries between them. 66% of supply chain leaders say advanced supply chain analytics are critically important to their supply chain operations in the next 2 to 3 years. While 94% of supply chain leaders say that digital transformation will fundamentally change supply chains in 2018, only 44% have a strategy ready (Columbus, 2018).

Running a global supply chain demands intricate planning, sourcing, delivery and measurement. This requires big data strategy and governance, as well as investing in education of supply chain professionals. The general guidelines include (Morley, 2017):

§ Starting with business objectives
§ Break down the communication silos between different teams
§ Define reasonable and achievable goals
§ Plan globally, but start with small projects
§ Prioritize and streamline analytical reports
§ Turn data into concrete decision
§ Evaluate and improve

The current approaches to BI have some fundamental challenges when confronted with the scale and characteristics of big data: types of data, enterprise data modeling, data integration, costs, master data management, metadata management, and skills (Chen et al., 2016).

The big data phenomenon, the volume, variety, and velocity of data, has impacted business intelligence and the use of information. New trends such as real-time and predictive analytics and data science have emerged as part of business intelligence (Schoenherr & Speier-Pero, 2015). In its essence, Data Science is simply a new term for Business Intelligence. It is a multi-disciplinary field that uses scientific methods, processes, algorithms and systems to extract knowledge and insights from structured and unstructured data (Frankenfield & Banton, 2019). is the concept that utilizes scientific and software methods, IT infrastructure, processes and software systems in order to gather, process, analyze and deliver useful information, knowledge and insights from various data sources.

Some of the supply chain challenges that data science is helping to solve include (Prokle, 2019):

§ Making the supply chain greener to minimize the environmental impact of global sourcing (e.g., shorter distances or consolidated shipments)
§ Increasing visibility into the supply chain and response time (e.g., through blockchain)
§ Adapting to demographic changes and customer expectations (e.g., free same day deliveries)
§ Allowing manufacturers to decrease their product life-cycle times (e.g., through better market insights and smart sourcing) to react to trends and demand more quickly
§ Increasing the product portfolio to serve not only the mass market but the entire demand curve (e.g., through mass-customization)

While data science, predictive analytics, and big data have been frequently used buzzwords, rigorous academic investigations into these areas are just emerging. Even though a hot topic, there is not many researches related to big data analytics in SCM. Most of the papers deal with big data potential, possible applications and value propositions.

Fosso Wamba and Akter (2015) provide a literature review of big data analytics for supply chain management. They highlight future research directions where the deployment of big data analytics is likely to transform supply chain management practices. Waller and Fawcett (2013) examine possible applications of big data analytics in SCM and provide examples of research questions from these applications, as well as examples of research questions employing big data that stem from management theories.

Identifying specific ways that big data systems can be leveraged to improve specific supply chain business processes and to automate and enhance performance becomes crucial for ultimate business success. The information and analytics delivered would be used to improve supply planning, vendor negotiations, capacity planning, warehousing and transportation performance, productivity, shop floor performance, materials requirements planning, distribution and customer service.

Organizations can apply big data and BI in the following supply chain areas (Stefanovic, 2014):

§ Plan Analytics — balancing supply chain resources with requirements.
§ Source Analytics — improving inbound supply chain consolidation and optimization.
§ Make Analytics — providing insight into the manufacturing process.
§ Deliver Analytics — improving outbound supply efficiency and effectiveness.
§ Return Analytics — managing the return of goods effectively and efficiently.

Big Data technologies are opening a range of possibilities for capitalizing on big data in logistics, and the use cases, as well as the benefits, continue to roll in (Feliu, 2019). These efforts can be classified into the following categories: visibility improvement, better form of demand and supply synchronization, optimization of fulfillment channels, building a smart and connected products, increased asset intelligence, and better work safety and productivity (Lopez, 2017).

Logistics companies such as DHL, are using big data analytics for flexible routing and optimization, as well as for capacity planning. Others use data-collecting sensors within vehicles to track the status of every vehicle to provide updates and make optimal decisions. Some airline companies are using big data analytics to improve the bottom line by predicting demand and performing dynamic pricing strategies (Eleks, 2019).

The supply chain economy is a web of multiple industries, and big data analytics has made an impact on most of them. McDaniel (2019) describe practical application of big data analytics in manufacturing (i.e. collecting telemetry data for predictive equipment maintenance, gathering contextual intelligence to eliminate bottlenecks for high throughput, or forecasting demand), consumer goods (i.e. plan for what-if scenarios and answer questions on whether strategies, such as marketing spends, are bringing in expected returns), and agriculture (i.e. combining past and real-time data to enhance operational efficiencies and reduce delivery cycles).

Some of the most important data-driven supply chain management challenges can be summarized as follows (Columbus, 2015):

§ Meet rising customer expectations on supply chain management.
§ Increase costs efficiency in supply chain management.
§ Monitor and manage supply chain compliance & risk.
§ Make supply chain traceability and sustainability a priority.
§ Remain agile and flexible in volatile times and markets.

Supply chains which implemented certain big data systems have achieved the following benefits (Howard, 2016):

§ Improvement in customer service and demand fulfillment.
§ Faster and more efficient reaction time to supply chain issues.

§   An increase in supply chain efficiency.
§   Integration across the supply chain.
§   Optimization of inventory and asset productivity.

Leading SCM and ERP solution vendors have incorporated analytical features into their latest information systems. There are many companies offering various software systems, platforms and services

As data analytics becomes critical in supply chain operations and management, supply chain analytics software solutions and tools have become must-have technologies. Many supply chain analytical tools feature improved forecasting and sales and operations planning to give supply chain managers the business intelligence they need to streamline operations, lower costs, and improve customer service. Leading SCM and ERP solution such as SAP, Microsoft, Oracle, and others, have incorporated some analytical features into their latest SCM information systems (Pontius, 2019). However, these analytics solutions usually relay on the own databases and data sources, thus requiring additional systems, services and tools to integrate and process large volumes of data from various departments and organizations across the supply network.

Despite new business requirements and technology innovations, big data methods, models and applications in SCM still need to be researched, studied and developed. In the subsequent sections, the supply chain big data model, software architecture and example of big data analytical system are presented.

BIG DATA AND SUPPLY CHAIN MANAGEMENT

Big data analytics uncovers patterns in a wide variety of data and associates the patterns with business outcomes. Analysts use analytical techniques and tools to detect unusual, interesting, previously unknown, or new patterns in data. Big data is a result of interaction of four dimensions of scale (increasing data volumes, high velocity of data creation, increasing complexity of data types, and extreme time sensitivity of data diminishing its value if not treated at that moment) thereby posing different challenges to manage, not to mention applying analytics techniques to find new insights. Big data does not behave the same as other data. The challenges associated with analytics on big data require a different approach from traditional data analytics processes (Nguyen et al., 2018).

Big data analytics has to do more with ideas, question and value, than with technology. Therefore, the big data analytics methodology is a combination of sequential execution of tasks in certain phases and highly iterative execution steps in certain phases.

The big data analytics process lifecycle is a combination of sequential execution of tasks in certain phases and highly iterative execution steps in certain phases. Because of the scale issue associated with supply chain big data system, an incremental and agile approach is recommended, which include modifying and expanding processes gradually across several activities as opposed to designing a system all at once (Mohanty, 2013).

In this section, an agile, iterative big data analytical process model to deliver supply chain predictive analytics solutions and intelligent applications efficiently is presented. The complete process model should encompass the lifecycle (phases, tasks, and workflows), roles, infrastructure, tools, and artifacts produced.

The proposed model is comprised of the following key components:

§ A big data lifecycle.
§ A standardized project structure.
§ Infrastructure and resources for big data projects.
§ Tools and utilities for project execution.

Figure 1 shows a proposed analytical lifecycle that can used to structure and execute various big data analytics projects (Ericson et al., 2017).

Figure 1. Big Data Analytic Lifecycle

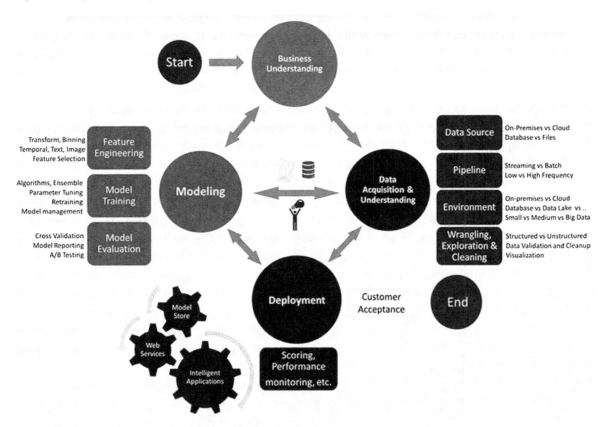

The lifecycle outlines the steps, from start to finish, that projects usually follow when they are executed. The process model includes the following stages that analytical projects typically execute, often iteratively:

1. Business understanding
2. Data acquisition and understanding
3. Modeling

4. Deployment
5. Customer acceptance

The lifecycle defines goals, tasks, and documentation artifacts for each stage of the lifecycle. These tasks and artifacts are associated with project roles such as: project manager, solution architect, data scientist, project lead, IT manager, business analyst, DevOps specialist, application developer, tester, etc.

The goal of the business understanding phase is to specify the key variables that are to serve as the model targets and whose related metrics are used determine the success of the project, and to identify the relevant data sources that the supply chain has access to or needs to obtain.

The second phase includes the three main tasks:

§   Data ingestion from various supply chain data sources into the target analytic environment.
§   Data exploration in order to determine if the data quality is adequate to answer the question.
§   Solution architecture development of the data pipeline that refreshes and scores the data regularly.

The modeling phase addresses the following tasks:

§   Feature engineering - Create data features from the raw data to facilitate model training.
§   Model training - Find the model that answers the question most accurately by comparing their success metrics.
§   Model evaluation - Determine if the model is suitable for production.

Deployment phase refers to deploying the models with a data pipeline to a production or production-like environment for final user acceptance and application usage. The final phase includes system validation (confirming that the deployed model and pipeline meet the customer's needs) and project delivery (hand the project off to the entity that's going to run the system in production.

The model also includes the standardized project structure so that projects share a common directory structure and use templates for project documents. This makes it easy for the team members to find information about their projects. All code and documents are stored in a version control system to enable more effective and efficient team collaboration. Tracking tasks and features in an agile project tracking system allows closer tracking of the code for individual features. The standardized structure for all projects helps build institutional knowledge across the supply chain.

The proposed big data process model also provides recommendations for managing shared analytics and storage infrastructure such as: cloud file systems for storing datasets, databases, big data (Hadoop or Spark) clusters, machine learning service, etc. Tools provided to implement the big data process and lifecycle help lower the barriers to and increase the consistency of their adoption. They are used to provision the shared resources, manage them, and allow each team member to connect to those resources securely. Tools also helps automate some of the common tasks in the data science lifecycle such as data exploration and baseline modeling.

The real users of the analytics outcomes are business users, but they often do not understand the complex mathematical formulae, statistical analysis models, etc. Therefore, it is extremely important to equip the business users with easy-to-understand and highly intuitive tools through which they will understand what actions are to be performed.

The proposed model and the lifecycle offer several advantages over existing supply chain analytical systems. They take into account the specifics of the big data analysis and provide unified framework for designing, developing, and deploying big data analytical solutions. The model can be applied to various analytical projects, regardless of technology and platforms. This enables faster development and implementation with high level of agility comparing to existing approaches.

SOLUTIONS AND RECOMMENDATIONS

In order to overcome main challenges of modern analytics and deficiencies of existing BI supply systems we propose a comprehensive multi-layered supply chain big data BI model that utilizes cloud-based big data services and tools for data extraction, transformation and loading (ETL), analysis, and reporting. Figure 2 shows the architecture with layers and services.

Figure 2. Supply chain analytical lifecycle model

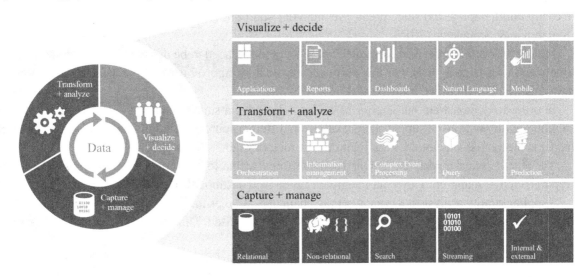

The proposed big data model unifies processes, methodologies and tools into a single business solution. The model has been developed in such a way to seamlessly integrate within overall BI and collaboration framework (Stefanovic et al., 2011). It is process-centric, metrics-based and modular. It introduces the new supply network and data modeling approaches, as well as layered application architecture which enables creation of composite BI systems.

The data integration layer supports various data types (relational, unstructured, streaming, OLAP, etc.) via cloud ETL services. The data management layer is based on the Hadoop engine but with additional services which provide more flexible data models and querying. The analytical layer hosts various analytical models and schemas. These can be exploration, data mining, or performance monitoring models. The final insights layer provides insights to all users such as self-service BI, data search, collaboration and performance monitoring. The central component of this layer is specialized supply chain BI portal as the unifying component that provides integrated analytical information and services, and also fosters collaborative decision making and planning (Stefanovic & Stefanovic, 2011).

This approach utilizes various cloud data management services such as ETL jobs for data extraction, cleansing and import, as well as event hubs that acts as a scalable data streaming platform capable of ingesting large amounts of high-velocity data form sensors and IoT devices throughout supply chain.

Additionally, the supply chain-wide data catalog was created in the cloud. It is fully managed cloud service that enables users to discover, understand, and consume data sources. The data catalog includes a crowdsourcing model of metadata and annotations, and it allows all supply chain participants to contribute their knowledge to build a various data models which can be integrated into specific applications and services.

In order to provide more flexibility, two big data stores are designed: supply chain enterprise multi-dimensional data warehouse and special in-memory tabular model for processing large amount of data. Combined with specific cloud analysis services, it is possible to design different analytical models. For example, stream analytical services can be used to set up real-time analytic computations on data streaming from devices, sensors, e-commerce sites, social media, information systems, infrastructure systems, etc. Another example is cloud machine learning service that enables supply chain participants to easily build, deploy, and share predictive analytics solutions (i.e. forecasting sales or inventory data) (Stefanovic & Stefanovic, 2015).

Finally, information derived from such analytical models need to be delivered to decision makers in timely and user-friendly way. For this purpose, a special web portal is used. It acts as a single point of data analysis, collaborative decision making.

In order to demonstrate our approach, we have designed a supply chain BI solution for analysis of supplier quality within the supply chain. Data from different sources (relational database, files, and web feeds) is integrated via cloud ETL job into the in-memory tabular data store.

Various analytical reports are designed using different technologies and services. All these BI artifacts (reports, charts, maps, etc.) are than integrated in the web dashboards as shown in Figure 3.

Supplier quality analysis is a typical supply chain task. Two primary metrics in this analysis are: total number of defects and the total downtime that these defects caused. This sample has two main objectives:

- Understand who the best and worst supply chain suppliers are, with respect to quality.
- Identify which plants do a better job finding and rejecting defects, to minimize downtime.

Each of the analytical segments on the dashboard can be further investigated by using various drill-down reports. For example, if user wants to analyze how plants deal with defective materials and the downtime, by clicking on the map segment, it opens supplier analysis dashboard that can be used for deeper analysis and filtering in order to derive meaningful knowledge about supplier management processes and take corrective actions.

The presented solution demonstrates the effectiveness and applicability of the proposed big data analytical model and the lifecycle. It encompasses the complete analytical lifecycle, from data capture and transformation, to storage, processing and visualization. This innovative approach enables better supply chain integration and coordination, as well as more informed decision making based on the advanced analytical services based on machine learning and visualization.

Figure 3. Supplier quality dashboard page

FUTURE RESEARCH DIRECTIONS

Supply chain management has been a highly researched area during the past twenty years, and it was seen as the key approach and enabler for organizational success and sustainability. Today's increased globalization, market pressures, uncertainty, shorter product lifecycles, tough competition and technological advancement make SCM critical in the years to come. Efficient decision making based on produced information and knowledge derived from vast supply chain data sources is the key for successful supply chain management (Pettey, 2019).

The impact of advanced analytics on supply chain is significant. Big data analytics is increasingly being deployed in real time or near-real time in various supply chain areas, from planning, sourcing and making, to delivery and return. The growth of data analytics has been particularly dramatic. In 2018 alone, big data adoption increased to 59% from 17% in 2015 (Keary, 2019).

The research show that supply chain leaders are using advanced analytics and artificial intelligence (AI) to augment and automate supply chain decision making. Within advanced supply chain companies, defined as those using two or more of the three advanced analytics techniques — predictive analytics, prescriptive analytics and artificial intelligence — 96% of respondents use predictive analytics, 85% use prescriptive analytics and 64% use AI (Van der Meulen, 2018).

Big data will certainly continue to play a crucial role in supply chain analytics and SCM in overall. Besides advancements directly related to big data systems, it is expected that big data will be combined with other technologies such as IoT, blockchain, augmented reality, cloud computing and many others. The main big data trends and research directions will be related to (Elliot, 2019):

§   Cloud analytics
§   Internet of Things (IoT)
§   Predictive analytics
§   Augmented analytics
§   Artificial Intelligence
§   Quantum Computing
§   Digital assistants and chatbots
§   Visualization and user experience
§   Mobile analytics

CONCLUSION

During the last several years there was an amazing progression in the amount of data produced within the supply chain information systems, but also externally. This poses many challenges related to data analysis specifically in terms of technology, infrastructure, software systems and development methods. The current business climate demands real-time analysis, faster, collaborative and more intelligent decision making.

The current approach to supply chain intelligence has some fundamental challenges when confronted with the scale and characteristics of big data. These include not only data volumes, velocity and variety, but also data veracity and value. One of the key aspects of leveraging big data is to also understand where it can be used, when it can be used, and how it can be used - how the value drivers of big data are aligned to supply chain strategic objectives.

Big data is starting to make inroads into logistics and supply chain management – large steps have certainly been taken over the past several years – but there is still a long way to go. Opportunities to create efficiency and savings through smart use of data are evident and concerted effort is being put into finding them. Big data and advanced analytics are being integrated successfully as logistics management solutions such as: optimization tools, demand forecasting, integrated business planning, supplier collaboration and risks analytics.

The proposed layered supply chain big data model and architecture allows construction of the next-generation loosely-coupled analytical systems that combine different services, data sources, analytical models and reporting artifacts into a unified analytical. This will enable collaborative, efficient, responsive, and adaptive supply chains.

ACKNOWLEDGMENT

Research presented in this paper was supported by Ministry of Science and Technological Development of Republic of Serbia, Grant III-44010, Title: Intelligent Systems for Software Product Development and Business Support based on Models.

REFERENCES

Accenture. (2014). *Big Data Analytics in Supply Chain: Hype or Here to Stay?* https://www.accenture.com/t20160106T194441__w__/fi-en/_acnmedia/Accenture/Conversion-Assets/DotCom/Documents/Global/PDF/Digital_1/Accenture-Global-Operations-Megatrends-Study-Big-Data-Analytics-v2.pdf

Arunachalam, D., Kumar, N., & Kawalek, J. P. (2018). Understanding big data analytics capabilities in supply chain management: Unravelling the issues, challenges and implications for practice. *Transportation Research Part E, Logistics and Transportation Review*, *114*, 416–436. doi:10.1016/j.tre.2017.04.001

Chen, D. Q., Preston, D. S., & Swink, M. (2016). How the Use of Big Data Analytics Affects Value Creation in Supply Chain Management. *Journal of Management Information Systems*, *32*(4), 4–39. doi:10.1080/07421222.2015.1138364

Columbus, L. (2015, July 13). *Ten Ways Big Data Is Revolutionizing Supply Chain Management*. Retrieved from https://www.forbes.com/sites/louiscolumbus/2015/07/13/ten-ways-big-data-is-revolutionizing-supply-chain-management/#3edf715f69f5

Columbus, L. (2018, January 15). *Analytics Will Revolutionize Supply Chains In 2018*. Retrieved from https://www.forbes.com/sites/louiscolumbus/2018/01/15/analytics-will-revolutionize-supply-chains-in-2018/#342dc94b6127

Eleks. (2019, October 13). *3 Winning Use Cases for Big Data in Logistics and Transportation*. Retrieved from https://eleks.com/blog/use-cases-for-big-data-in-logistics-and-transportation/

Elliot, T. (2019, January 29). *Top 10 Analytics Trends For 2019*. Retrieved from https://www.digitalist-mag.com/cio-knowledge/2019/01/29/top-10-analytics-trends-for-2019-06196108

Ericson, G., Rohm, W. A., Martens, J., Sharkey, K., Casey, C., Harvey, B., … Schonning, N. (2017, October 20). *Team Data Science Process*. Retrieved from https://docs.microsoft.com/en-us/azure/machine-learning/team-data-science-process

Feliu, C. (2019, October 14*). 4 relevant Big Data case studies in Logistics*. Retrieved from https://blog.datumize.com/4-relevant-big-data-case-studies-in-logistics#smooth-scroll-top

Fosso Wamba, S., & Akter, S. (2015). Big Data Analytics for Supply Chain Management: A Literature Review and Research Agenda. In Enterprise and Organizational Modeling and Simulation. Springer. doi:10.1007/978-3-319-24626-0_5

Frankenfield, J., & Banton, C. (2019, May 30). *Data Science*. Retrieved from https://www.investopedia.com/terms/d/data-science.asp

Harvey, C. (2017, June 5). *Big Data Challenges*. Retrieved from https://www.datamation.com/big-data/big-data-challenges.html

Howard, F. (2016, July 13). *Top Challenges for Big Data in the Supply Chain Management Process*. Retrieved from http://en.advancedfleetmanagementconsulting.com/2016/07/13/1199/

Keary, T. (2019, March 26). *A look at data analytics trends for 2019*. Retrieved from https://www.information-age.com/data-analytics-trends-2019-123481163/

Larson, D., & Chang, V. (2016). A review and future direction of agile, business intelligence, analytics and data science. *International Journal of Information Management*, *36*(5), 700–710. doi:10.1016/j.ijinfomgt.2016.04.013

Lopez, E. (2017, February 13). *How do supply chains use Big Data?* Retrieved from https://www.supplychaindive.com/news/how-big-data-application-supply-chain-Deloitte-digital-stack/435866/

Marr, B. (2016, April 22). *How Big Data And Analytics Are Transforming Supply Chain Management*. Retrieved from https://www.forbes.com/sites/bernardmarr/2016/04/22/how-big-data-and-analytics-are-transforming-supply-chain-management

McDaniel, S. (2019, August 22). *Big Data for Supply Chain Management*. Retrieved from https://www.talend.com/resources/big-data-supply-chain/

Mohanty, S., Jagadeesh, M., & Srivatsa, H. (2013). *Big Data Imperatives - Enterprise Big Data Warehouse, BI Implementations and Analytics*. Apress.

Morley, M. (2017). Supply Chain Analytics. John Wiley & Sons.

Nguyen, T., Yhou, L., Spiegler, V., Ieromonachou, P., & Lin, Y. (2018). Big data analytics in supply chain management: A state-of-the-art literature review. *Computers & Operations Research*, *98*, 254–264. doi:10.1016/j.cor.2017.07.004

Pettey, C. (2019, April 22). *Gartner Top 8 Supply Chain Technology Trends for 2019*. Retrieved from https://www.gartner.com/smarterwithgartner/gartner-top-8-supply-chain-technology-trends-for-2019/

Pontius, N. (2019, October 21). *Top Supply Chain Analytics: 50 Useful Software Solutions and Data Analysis Tools to Gain Valuable Supply Chain Insights*. Retrieved from https://www.camcode.com/asset-tags/top-supply-chain-analytics/

Prokle, M. (2019). *How data science is disrupting supply chain management*. Retrieved from https://www.northeastern.edu/graduate/blog/data-science-supply-chain-management/

Renner, A. (2016, February 19). *Overcoming 5 Major Supply Chain Challenges with Big Data Analytics*. Retrieved from https://www.computerworld.com/article/3035144/data-center/overcoming-5-major-supply-chain-challenges-with-big-data-analytics.html

Schoenherr, T., & Speier-Pero, C. (2015). Data Science, Predictive Analytics, and Big Data in Supply Chain Management: Current State and Future Potential. *Journal of Business Logistics*, *36*(1), 120–132. doi:10.1111/jbl.12082

Stefanovic, N. (2014). Proactive Supply Chain Performance Management with Predictive Analytics. *The Scientific World Journal*. doi:10.1155/2014/528917

Stefanovic, N. (2015). Collaborative predictive business intelligence model for spare parts inventory replenishment. *Computer Science and Information Systems*, *12*(3), 911–930. doi:10.2298/CSIS141101034S

Stefanovic, N., & Milosevic, D. (2017). Model for Big Data Analytics in Supply Chain Management. In M. Zdravkovic, Z. Konjovic, & M. Trajanovic (Eds.), *Proceedings of the 7th International Conference on Information Society and Technology*. Belgrade: Society for Information Systems and Computer Networks.

Stefanovic, N., & Milosevic, D. (2018). A Review of Advances in Supply Chain Intelligence. In M. Khosrow-Pour, D.B.A. (Ed.), Encyclopedia of Information Science and Technology, Fourth Edition (pp. 5538-5549). Hershey, PA: IGI Global. doi:10.4018/978-1-5225-2255-3.ch481

Stefanovic, N., & Stefanovic, D. (2011). Supply Chain Performance Measurement System Based on Scorecards and Web Portals. *Computer Science and Information Systems*, *8*(1), 167–192. doi:10.2298/CSIS090608018S

Stefanovic, N., Stefanovic, D., & Radenkovic, B. (2011). Integrated Supply Chain Intelligence through Collaborative Planning, Analytics and Monitoring. In S. Mohhebi, I. Mahdavi, & N. Cho (Eds.), *Electronic Supply Network Coordination in Intelligent and Dynamic Environment: Modeling and Implementation* (pp. 43–92). IGI Global. doi:10.4018/978-1-60566-808-6.ch003

Tiwari, S., Wee, H. M., & Daryanto, Y. (2018). Big data analytics in supply chain management between 2010 and 2016: Insights to industries. *Computers & Industrial Engineering*, *115*, 319–330. doi:10.1016/j.cie.2017.11.017

Van der Meulen, R. (2018, July 13). *Improve the Supply Chain With Advanced Analytics and AI*. Retrieved from https://www.gartner.com/smarterwithgartner/improve-the-supply-chain-with-advanced-analytics-and-ai/

Waller, M. A., & Fawcett, S. E. (2013). Data Science, Predictive Analytics, and Big Data: A Revolution That Will Transform Supply Chain Design and Management. *Journal of Business Logistics*, *34*(2), 77–84. doi:10.1111/jbl.12010

Wang, G., Gunasekaran, A., Ngai, E. W. T., & Papadopolous, T. (2016). Big data analytics in logistics and supply chain management: Certain investigations for research and applications. *International Journal of Production Economics*, *176*, 98–110. doi:10.1016/j.ijpe.2016.03.014

ADDITIONAL READING

Moshirpour, M., Far, B., & Alhajj, R. (2018). *Highlighting the Importance of Big Data Management and Analysis for Various Applications*. Springer International Publishing AG. doi:10.1007/978-3-319-60255-4

Pyne, S., Rao, P., & Rao, S. B. (2016). *Big Data Analytics: Methods and Applications*. Springer India.

KEY TERMS AND DEFINITIONS

BI Portal: A specialized web portal that provide a range of analytical services and which enables collaborative decision-making.

Big Data: The evolving term that describes a large volume of structured, semi-structured and un-structured data that has the potential to be mined for information and used in machine learning projects and other advanced analytics applications.

Business Intelligence: A set of processes, technologies and tools comprising data warehousing, On-Line Analytical Processing, and information delivery in order to turn data into information and information into knowledge.

Cloud Analytics: Cloud analytics is a type of cloud service model where data analysis and related services are performed on a public or private cloud.

Data Science: The concept that utilizes scientific and software methods, IT infrastructure, processes, and software systems in order to gather, process, analyze and deliver useful information, knowledge and insights from various data sources.

Machine Learning (Data Mining): Set of knowledge discovery techniques for intelligent data analysis in order to find hidden patterns and associations, devise rules and make predictions.

Supply Chain: Dynamic, interconnected, and collaborative group of companies working jointly on planning, management and execution of cross-company business processes spanning from the first-tier suppliers to the end-customers.

Supply Chain Intelligence: Process of integrating and presenting supply chain information in order to provide collaborative planning, monitoring, measurement, analysis and management of the supply network.

This research was previously published in the Encyclopedia of Organizational Knowledge, Administration, and Technology; pages 2443-2457, copyright year 2021 by Business Science Reference (an imprint of IGI Global).

Chapter 89

Big Data Adoption:
A Comparative Study of the Indian Manufacturing and Services Sectors

Hemlata Gangwar
Pune Institute of Business Management, India

ABSTRACT

This study inspects how big data is comprehended by IT experts and the difficulties that they have in respect to the reception of big data examination. The study also looks into the contributing factors of big data adoption within the manufacturing and services sectors in India. The data were analyzed using exploratory and confirmatory factor analyses, and relevant hypotheses were derived and tested by SEM analysis. The findings revealed that relative advantage, compatibility, complexity, organizational size, top management support, competitive pressure, vendor support, data management, and data privacy are the factors that are important for both industries. Through a comparison of the industries, statistically significant differences between the service and the manufacturing sectors were found; in other words, it has been noted that the relative importance of all factors for big data adoption differs between the industries, with the only exception being its complexity – it was found to be insignificant for the manufacturing sector.

INTRODUCTION

The development of Big Data has changed the manner in which organizations work and contend. The approach of Big Data has as of now and will further modernize numerous fields, including organizations, logical research, open organization, genomics, social insurance, operations management, the industrial internet, finance, etc. Big Data may be defined as a collection of massive and diverse data sets requiring advanced techniques and technologies to enable the capture, storage, distribution, management, and analysis of the information (Gandomi & Haider, 2015). In other words, it is a collection of huge and complex amalgamation of data sets that make it difficult to process using traditional data processing platforms. Big Data analytics (BDA) refers to the process and techniques used to analyze massive data in order to obtain value from that data.

DOI: 10.4018/978-1-6684-3662-2.ch089

Pragmatically, Big Data brings many attractive opportunities, such as increasing operational efficiency, enhanced strategic directions, developing better customer service, identifying and developing new products, services, new customers and markets. Use of BDA examines geospatial information and stock use on distributions, which gives bits of knowledge to manufacturing and service firms. These experiences could empower firm leaders to get request gauge continuously, mechanize substitution choices and distinguish main drivers of cost wastefulness (Dubey et al., 2016; Verma, Bhattacharyya, & Kumar, 2018). These measures could lessen lead times, costs, deferrals and procedure interferences, along these lines at last making worth. Besides, from the provider side, the quality or value aggressiveness can be improved by examining the provider's information to screen execution (Ren et al., 2017).

BDA can likewise limit execution fluctuation and avert quality issues by diminishing piece rates and diminishing an opportunity to advertise. In social insurance, BDA can make an incentive by improving quality and proficiency of administrations, and by coordinating patient information crosswise over various divisions and establishments (Gandomi & Haider, 2015). BDA can likewise give different constant data on perspectives, for example, traffic and climate. BDA can make an incentive for the financial area by empowering measurement of different operational dangers. BDA can even be utilized to recognize systems of teaming up fraudsters, or find proof of deceitful protection or advantages claims. This may at last lead to the revelations of until now unnoticed fake exercises (Elgendy & Elragal, 2014). However, despite these advantages of Big Data, evidence suggests that not all companies are rushing to adopt Big Data, or for that matter, Big Data analytics (Kwon, Lee, & Shin, 2014).

The purpose of this study is to understand the factors of the adoption of Big Data and its relative advantage to organizations. Most of the earlier studies on Big Data have focused solely on the technical and operational issues (Chen & Zhang, 2014; Lee, Kao, & Yang, 2014). Only a few studies have addressed the quintessence of adopting Big Data from an organizational perspective. As a matter of fact, no study has conducted a comprehensive evaluation of the factors on Big Data adoption. This study thereby looks to develop a research model based on technological, organizational and environmental framework in an attempt to lend more clarity. Further, two new constructs specific to Big Data have been added: data management and addressing privacy concerns. This study presents therefore, a more holistic assessment of the factors of Big Data by splitting them in two sectors – the manufacturing and the service sectors; in the process, this study contributes to a wider body of scientific knowledge that has so far not been studied. Further, this study highlights the importance of systematically evaluating the factors of Big Data at the industry level; and through the literature review provides the background on Big Data and related research. Further the study discusses the theoretical foundations for the research model and proposes hypotheses. The research methodology and the results are then presented, followed by a discussion of the major findings. The study concludes with implications of the findings and the scope for future study.

BACKGROUND

The term Big Data is used to describe unstructured enormous data that require more real-time analysis. Manyika et al. (2011) defined Big Data as "datasets whose size is beyond the ability of typical database software tools to capture, store, manage, and analyze" (p. 1). According to Hashem et al. (2015), Big Data is "a set of techniques and technologies that require new forms of integration to uncover large hidden values from large datasets that are diverse, complex, and of a massive scale" (p. 100). Thus, Big Data develops new methods or technologies for massive data that are difficult to store, process, and analyze through traditional database technologies (Tao et al., 2017; Zhong et al., 2016). This study regards Big Data as the infrastructure and technologies of the organization to collect store and analyze various types of data. Thus, Big Data can create value using advanced analytical techniques that could not be processed using a traditional database.

Big Data and "regular-sized" data can be distinguished based on the characteristics commonly referred to as the four 'Vs': i.e., volume, variety, velocity, and veracity (Abbasi, Sarker, & Chiang, 2016; Gandomi & Haider, 2015; Goes, 2014; Wang, Gunasekaran, Ngai, & Papadopoulos, 2016). There's no universal benchmark for volume, variety, velocity, veracity for defining Big Data; it depends upon the size, sector and location of the firm. Big Data and its four Vs clearly change how organizations store and manage data. Definitely Big Data and its four V characteristics have had a huge impact on the people, processes, and technologies related to the information value chain.

Big Data Analytics

Over the past two decades Big Data analytics has increased in importance in both academic and business communities alike. Big Data analytics could be referred as the techniques, technologies, systems, methodologies, tools and applications that analyze excessive variety of critical business data to make timely efficient and effective decision making (Gandomi & Haider, 2015; McAfee & Brynjolfsson, 2012). Some of the Big Data techniques include text analysis, audio analysis, video analytics, social media analytics, and predictive analytics. Even though some leading companies are actively adopting Big Data analytics to enhance decision making, understanding process optimization, strengthening market competition and thereby opening up new business opportunities, many companies are still at a nascent stage as regards the adoption of Big Data due to their lack of understanding and experience as regards this disruptive technology.

Big Data Adoption

Even though some leading companies have actively adopted Big Data analytics to enhance decision making and reducing business costs, many companies are still at an early stage regarding the ad option of big data due to their lack of understanding and experience regarding this disruptive technology (Verma, 2018). Many studies have addressed the technical and operational issues related to Big Data, including issues such as creating value from Big Data (Chen, Chiang, & Storey, 2012; Chen & Zhang, 2014; Jagadish et al., 2014), data processing framework for data storage and analysis (Chen et al., 2012), issue related to data transformation, data quality/heterogeneity, security, privacy and legal/regulatory issues (Hashem et al., 2015; Hu & Vasilakos, 2016). Only few study evaluated big data adoption from organizational perspective. Sun, Cegielski, Jia, and Hall (2016) developed a conceptual framework to identify the factors affecting organizational adoption of Big Data. Their framework is not extensive as the factors are explored from a theoretical perspective based on content analysis of IT adoption literature. Thus empirical research is needed for a better explanation of the adoption of Big Data at an organizational level.

Kwon et al. (2014) developed a research model using the resource view and isomorphism theories to explain the adoption intention of big data analytics. The result concluded that data quality and data usage benefits as the important indicator for Big Data adoption. Chaurasia and Rosin (2017) examined the applicability of Big Data in higher education institutions. Using qualitative methodology four major application areas that is reporting and compliance; analysis and visualization; security and risk mitigation; and predictive analytics were identified in their study. Verma and Bhattacharyya (2017) identified the factors that influence Big Data usage and adoption in the context of emerging economies. They used a qualitative exploratory study using face-to-face semi-structured interviews to collect data from 22 enterprises in India. Also they have not considered key factors such as data management and privacy concerns that are critical to the firm's adoption of Big Data.

Verma et al. (2018) investigated the effects of system characteristics on the attitude of managers toward the usage of Big Data analytics. The finding shows that Big Data characteristics have significant direct and indirect effects on the benefits of Big Data and perceived usefulness, attitude, and adoption. No study has taken a holistic approach to empirically validate the technology context, organization context, and environment context perspective for effective usage of Big Data. This study extended Technology Organization Environment (TOE) framework to study the effect of technology context, organization context, environment context, and security context on big data adoption. Also this study compares result in manufacturing and service industry. Big Data solutions are able to help organizations in every industry. Big Data in manufacturing can decrease product development and assembly costs by and can cause a reduction in working capital (Mourtzis, Vlachou, & Milas, 2016).

Adoption Models

There are many adoption behavior models/theories being developed in the information system to study technological adoption both at an organizational and an individual level. Some prominent theories used to understand technology adoption at an individual level include innovation diffusion theory (IDT) (Rogers, 1962), theory of reasoned action (TRA) (Fishbein & Ajzen, 1975), the technology acceptance model (TAM) (Davis, 1989), theory of planned behavior (TPB) (Ajzen, 1991), and the unified theory of acceptance and use of technology (UTAUT) (Venkatesh, Morris, Davis, & Davis, 2003). At an organizational level, theories such as diffusion of innovation (Rogers, 2003) and technology organization environment framework (TOE) have been widely applied to studies considering how innovations are actually adopted and diffused. Although Rogers' (2003) diffusion of innovation has solid theoretical foundation, is found to have consistent empirical support, and appears to be most applicable to study the innovation process, researchers are still searching for other contexts influencing the adoption process for better and smoother adoption (Moore & Benbasat, 1991; Zhu, Dong, Xu, & Kraemer, 2006; Zhu, Kraemer, & Xu, 2006).

Technology Organization Environment (TOE) Framework

Tornatzky and Fleischer (1990) proposed the Technology Organization Environment (TOE) framework, where technology and organization contexts are identical to the IDT construct. In fact, compared to the IDT framework, the TOE framework includes an environmental context, which offers both constraints and opportunities for technological innovation. According to Zhu, Kraemer, and Xu (2003), the TOE framework is more significant than IDT as it includes new constructs as well. Moreover, the TOE framework has been used to examine various technology adoption issues in order to distinguish adopters from non-adopters (Low, Chen, & Wu, 2011). Further Rui (2007) and Maduku, Mpingamjira, and Duh (2016) advocated that the TOE framework coasts up the inherent limitation of the dominant technical perspective, and suggests a useful analytical tool to differentiate between the intrinsic characteristics of innovation and drivers, capabilities, along with wider environmental circumstances of the adopting organization. Thus in order to better understand the Big Data adoption process, a conceptual model for BDA was developed based on the technology–organization–environment framework from the technology innovation and information systems (IS) literature (Tornatzky & Fleischer, 1990).

The TOE framework states that adoption to the technology innovation process is influenced by three contexts in an organization: technological context, organizational context and environmental context (Tornatzky & Fleischer, 1990). Technological context refers to the internal and external technologies relevant to the organization, both for technologies that are already in use, as well as those that are available in the market but not currently in use (Oliveira, Fürlinger, & Kranzlmüller, 2012). Organizational context refers to descriptive measures such as firm size, managerial structure, organizational structure etc. (Alsaad, Mohamad, & Ismail, 2017; Tornatzky & Fleischer, 1990). Environmental context refers to arenas in which firms conduct their businesses, typically in the context of market elements, competitors the regulatory environment etc. (Alshamaila, Papagiannidis, & Li, 2013; Oliveira & Martins, 2010a; Tornatzky & Fleischer 1990).

The technological context of the TOE framework will determine whether the technological readiness of the firm will restrain or facilitate the adoption of Big Data. It includes five innovation attributes including relative advantage, compatibility, complexity, triability, and observability, which put together influence the likelihood of adoption (Alsaad et al., 2017; Rogers, 2003). Relative advantage, compatibility, and complexity have been consistently reported to be the most important factors and therefore they've been considered in this study (Alsaad et al., 2017; Alshamaila et al., 2012; Gangwar, Date, & Ramaswamy, 2015; Hung, Hung, Tsai, & Jiang, 2010; Tornatzky & Klein, 1982).

Relative Advantage

The relative advantage of an innovation over its existing technologies and other alternatives shows imperative role in its adoption. Rogers (2003) defines relative advantage as "the degree to which a technology perceived as providing greater benefit for organizations" (p. 229). The valid role of relative advantage is well recognized in IT adoption literature (Alshamaila et al., 2013; Low et al., 2011; Ramdani, Kawalek, & Lorenzo, 2009; Tornatzky & Klein, 1982; Wang & Wang, 2016). Thus it is perceived that the likelihood of adoption will increase when organizations perceive a relative advantage in an innovation. Big Data allows organizations to reduce cost, improve decision making and have competitive offerings, implementing new strategies business models along with higher transparency of information. Although Big Data Analytics tools are expensive at the outset, but eventually it saves a lot of money, as it accesses massive amount of data at incomparable speeds and thereby results in a cost-effective strategy in the long run (Murdoch & Detsky, 2013). BDA offers organizations a data-driven decision making process based on data and analysis, rather than experience and intuition for a more informed decision making process, improved profitability and efficiency (Waller & Fawcett, 2013). It also delivers greater opportunities for having a competitive advantage by collating and analyzing information across organizations and industries in order to improve the overall operational efficiency, develop marketing strategies, support business growth and, create the "distinguishing factor". Further, BDA helps organizations to understand how others perceive their products, by analyzing the market and its customers, which in turn goes on to provide crucial insights to develop and improve new versions of the product; it allows higher transparency of information within organizations. These findings contribute to the development of H1.

H1: Relative advantage has positive effect on Big Data adoption.

Figure 1. TOE framework for big data adoption

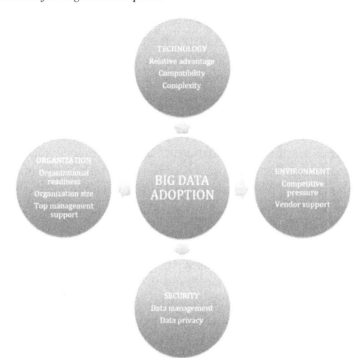

Compatibility

According to Rogers (2003), compatibility means "the degree to which an innovation is perceived as consistent with the existing values, past experiences, and needs of potential adopters" (p. 170). The role of compatibility is widely recognized in IT adoption literature (Alsaad et al., 2017; Gangwar et al., 2015; Low et al., 2011; Peng, Xiong, & Yang, 2012; Ramdani et al., 2009; Wang, Wang, & Yang, 2010). Compatibility takes into account organizational environment, considers business structures, business strategy, existing values, experience, work practice, organizational needs, information systems' environment and finally the employee, who are all in the reconcilability of a new technology. Further, Big Data adoption may require change in existing technological infrastructure, data environment, organizational process and culture, capabilities and skills. Building and supporting technology infrastructure for Big Data adoption requires infrastructure for storage, analytics software, processing and networking capacity. In addition to technological infrastructure, new data environment must accommodate existing methods to extract data from multiple sources. It is important to note that Big Data strategy should also be compatible with the existing organizational processes and culture, which in turn is ensured by inculcating changes in business processes, having managerial support and commitment, encourage a knowledge-sharing culture including a drive for innovation, experimentation and integration. Big Data adoption may also require special knowledge and skills, such as analytical and statistical skills in order to manage Big Data projects or assess how Big Data tools might help the organizations. The more compatible is the Big Data strategy with the existing development environment, the less effort would be required in actually adopting it, leading to H2.

H2: Compatibility has positive effect on Big Data adoption.

Complexity

Rogers (2003) describes complexity as the extent to which an innovation is difficult to use or understand. It is believed that easier to integrate and using the technology into business environment, the more the chance of its adoption (Alshamaila et al., 2013; Chaudhury & Bharati, 2008; Igbaria, Guimaraes, & Davis, 1995). However, Big Data strategy can be challenging to companies that lack technological expertise, and therefore specialized IT professional related to tools and technologies such as Apache Hadoop, Apache Spark, NoSQL, Machine Learning and Data Mining, Statistical and Quantitative Analysis, SQL and Data Visualization would be required. These tools are typically used and measured in terms of dealing with: ingesting data, storing data, transforming data, moving data, analyzing data, and visualizing data. Hence, organizations are more likely to adopt and use Big Data analytics if it does not require additional technical skills and greater efforts to implement and use it. So, the following hypothesis is proposed:

H3: Complexity has negative effect on Big Data adoption.

Organizational Context

Organizational context indicates the characteristics of the firm that facilitate or constrain the adoption and implementation of the innovation. It typically includes a firm's size, degree of centralization, degree of formalization, managerial structure, leadership behavior, the resources that the firm has including financial capital, technological resources and human resources, amount of slack resources, the distribution of power and control, information links, and linkages among employees (Kuan & Chau, 2001, Low et al., 2011; Tornatzky & Fleisher, 1990; Zhu, Dong et al., 2006). Of these, organizational readiness, management support, and the firm size are the most important factors for assessing the adoption of Big Data (Wang et al., 2010).

Organizational Readiness

Organizational readiness can be defined as having technological resources, financial resources and IT human resources (Zhu, Dong et al., 2006). Technological resources refer to possessing the right tools and technologies, platform, databases, architectural standard for storing, analyzing data in the Big Data environment. Financial resources refer to financial readiness to install, maintain, and upgrade the company's information systems and for ongoing expenses during its usage. IT human resources provide the knowledge and skills to implement Big Data-related IT applications. Big Data can become part of the value chain if organizations have sufficient resources and IT personnel. Therefore, firms that have organizational readiness are more prepared for the adoption of Big Data, leading to the following hypothesis:

H4: Organizational readiness has positive effect on Big Data adoption.

Organizational Size

Organizational size defines the number of employees in an organization, is one of the most commonly studied factors of IT adoption (Gangwar et al., 2015; Jeyaraj, Rottman, & Lacity, 2006; Lee & Xia, 2006; Oliveira & Martins, 2010b). However, literature indicates that the effect of organizational size varies and isn't clear yet. Some empirical studies indicate that there is a positive relationship between the two variables (Bose & Luo, 2012; Hsu, Kraemer, & Dunkle, 2006; Low et al., 2011; Pan & Jang, 2008; Premkumar, Ramamurthy, & Crum, 1997; Ramdani et al., 2009; Wang et al., 2010; Zhu, Kraemer et al., 2003); whereas some report a negative correlation (Zhu & Kraemer, 2005; Zhu, Kraemer et al., 2006). Further, it is believed that larger organizations have more ability to absorb risk so they are more innovative; on the other hand, small firms can be more innovative, they are flexible enough to adapt quick changes in their environments (Oliveira & Martins, 2010b; Zhu & Kraemer, 2005). In the case of Big Data adoption, the authors expect that large organizations have more resources and may be better able to take on risk and provided the basis of the following hypothesis.

H5: Organizational size has positive effect on Big Data adoption.

Top Management Support

Top management support refers to the degree to which top management understands the strategic importance of IS innovation and the extent to which it is involved in IS activities (Gangwar & Date, 2016; Miller & Toulouse, 1986). Top management support refers to the extent to which senior executives provide the necessary technological and financial resources, vision, support, authority for the innovative implementation, cultivation of favorable organizational climate, higher assessments of individual self-efficacy, support in overcoming barriers and resistance to change, along with a commitment to create a positive environment for innovation at large (Alsaad et al., 2017; Jang, 2010; Ramdani et al., 2009; Teo, Lin, & Lai, 2009; Wang & Wang, 2016; Wang et al., 2010). Top management support is more critical for Big Data adoption because it not only means integrating an information system but also requires addressing issues of organizational alignment, change management, business process reengineering, coordination, and communication (Wang & Wang, 2016). Accordingly, the following hypothesis is thus proposed:

H6: Top management support has positive effect on Big Data adoption.

Environmental Context

The environmental context in the TOE framework refers to the arena in which an organization conducts its business, wherein it may have a direct effect on organizational decision-making process. It includes factors such as external and internal pressure, trading partner pressure, vendor support, commercial dependencies, environmental uncertainty, information intensity, network intensity and government regulations (Alshamaila et al., 2013; Gangwar et al., 2015; Low et al., 2011; Wang et al., 2010). Of these, the factors that have an impact on Big Data are the organization's competition/competitors and vendor support (Alsaad et al., 2017; Alshamaila et al., 2013; Gangwar et al., 2015).

Competitive Pressure

The role of competitive pressure is widely recognized in IT adoption literature (Lian, Yen, & Wang, 2014; Low et al., 2011; Oliveira & Martins, 2010a; Ramdani et al., 2009; Zhu, Dong et al., 2006). Competitive pressure can be described as the amount of pressure a company experiences from competitors (Zhu & Kraemer, 2005). Ramdani et al. (2009) reported that when technology affects competition, it exerts pressure on an organization's ability to adopt new technologies to compete in the market. Adoption of Big Data can therefore lead to greater capacity utilization, accurate forecasting, operational efficiency, better market visibility, decision making and more accurate access to real-time data (Gandomi & Haider, 2015). Accordingly, the following hypothesis is proposed:

H7: Competitive pressure has positively effect on Big Data adoption.

Vendor Support

Vendor support is very important because most of the Big Data tools and technologies are open source and organizations want to make sure about support and availability at the time when they need it (Alshamaila et al., 2013). Organizations can develop innovation-related capabilities by tapping into the experiential learning of its supplier and may influence the firm's innovation adoption. Further, support is the key demand for problem resolution, offering technical solutions, customizing various apps, swift response to patches, fixes and bug detection in Big Data; it can thereby be inferred that support from the vendor can affect adoption as it ensures data availability, reliability and completeness. This contributes to the following hypothesis:

H8: Vendor support has positive effect on Big Data adoption.

Security Concern

The five 'Vs' of data changed the landscape including capturing and storing data, data storage devices, data storage architecture, and data access mechanism (Chen & Zhang, 2014; Oliveira et al., 2012). Big Data phenomenon arises from collecting and processing massive amounts of information from various sources including the internet. Thus ensuring security is more vital in the case of Big Data, as it deals with innumerable and limitless data. Risk areas that need to be considered include data ownership and classification, data creation and the collection process, data security protection, protection of intellectual property, personal privacy, commercial secrets and protection of financial information. These security challenges could be broadly categorized under two aspects of security – data management and data privacy.

Data Management

Big Data management is the process of ensuring accuracy, availability, accessibility, and quality of large stores of data by allocating right people, policies and technologies in place. It is an assortment of old and new best practices for administration, management and governance of large volumes of data. Al Nuaimi, Al Neyadi, Mohamed, and Al-Jaroodi (2015) define Big Data management as the development and execution of architectures, policies, practices and procedures for ensuring the availability, usability, integrity and security of data. Data availability issue arises when data is accessed by a large number of users from a huge pool of applications, wherein the user wants information available all the time or at the time when they need it. Reliability of data for decision making can be attained through high data quality. Appropriate data management allows an organization to improve availability, efficiency, accuracy and quality based on thorough cleansing of data regularly, integrating data across departments, normalizing user-specific data and have built-in high availability features. Moving to the Big Data adds new layers of complexity for managing data and thus influences an organization's decision to adopt the innovative tool. Thus proper Big Data management can result in higher availability, reliability and accessibility of data. Based on this argument, the following hypothesis is proposed:

H9: Data management has positive effect on Big Data adoption.

Data Privacy

Data privacy is related to an issue of data storage from various human studies as well as hosting of data sets on publicly accessible servers (Schadt, 2012). Big Data privacy includes protection of personal privacy during data acquisition and protection of personal privacy data during storage, transmission, and usage. The challenge here is ensuring citizens' rights of privacy while collecting and using Big Data. The objective of data privacy is on the use and governance of individual data such as setting up policies in place to ensure that consumers' personal information is being collected, shared and utilized in appropriate ways. The existing non-Big Data security solutions are not designed to handle the scale, speed, variety and complexity of Big Data. So, organizations need to embed specific data privacy and data protection measures into their processes and systems. Ensuring privacy through efficient protection mechanism will result in greater security, leading to the next hypothesis:

H10: Data privacy has positive effect on Big Data adoption.

RESEARCH METHODOLOGY

A survey was conducted in India from the manufacturing and service industries in order to evaluate the theoretical constructs of Big Data and Big Data analytics. A questionnaire was developed based on the literature. The questionnaire went through an evaluation process before it was administered. At first, pre-testing was carried out with an expert panel including two researchers, two local professors, and one external professor. The questionnaire was refined according to the comments/suggestions made by this panel for survey pre-testing and feedback from three well-known exponents of Big Data. Since there were no major comments received, the questionnaire was considered ready for data collection. The questionnaire had two parts including a cover letter, which explained the objective of this study and briefly described the concept of Big Data. The first part contained questions about business background information. The second part included items that assessed the ten factors affecting Big Data adoption. To be consistent with the sources, the constructs (relative advantage, compatibility, complexity, organizational readiness, top management support, competitive pressure, vendor support, data management data privacy) were measured using a five-point Likert scale from "strongly disagree" to "strongly agree".

Further, responses on the questionnaire were collected from the top and middle-level IT professionals of companies who were in the process of adopting Big Data (potential adopters).

Survey Administration

An online version of the questionnaire was emailed to qualified individuals (IS managers) at 1500 manufacturing and service companies in India. The company and contact data were accessed from the Bombay Chamber of Commerce and of Industry of India. Data were collected using an online questionnaire between November 2016 and July 2017. The survey was completed by IT staff or managers in the organization because they were in a better position to understand the current IT operations and future trends of the firms. This should contribute to content validity. The responses were collected from organizations that were in the process of adopting Big Data (potential adopters). In the first stage, 379 valid responses were received. A follow-up email was sent in the second stage to those who did not respond in the first stage. In this second stage, 99 valid responses were obtained, for a combined total of 478 usable responses. The overall response rate was 31.86%, which is comparable to other studies of similar scale in technology adoption (McCole & Ramsey, 2005). Of these valid responses 43.9 percent were received from manufacturing sector whereas 56.1 were received from service sector. Table 1 displays the categorization of firms with respect to size and Table 2 displays the categorization of firms by industry type.

A series of statistical tests for nonresponse bias were computed by comparing early responses with late responses in terms of item responses. The sample distributions of the two groups did not differ statistically, indicating an absence of nonresponse bias. Therefore, nonresponse bias does not appear to be a concern.

Table 1. Categorization of firms with respect to size

Size	Number of Employees	N
Small	< 400	164
Medium	400 - 800	137
Large	> 800	177
Total		478

Table 2. Categorization of firms by industry type

Manufacturing	n	Service	n
Electrical machinery	44	Hotel, banking, real estate	89
Food and beverages	53	Health	76
Motor vehicles	37	Commerce	64
Base metals	19	Information and communication	39
Chemicals	23	Total service	268
Textiles apparel	34		
Total manufacturing	210		

Validity and Reliability Assessment

To test the instrument, a pilot study was conducted among 34 firms, which were not included in the main survey. Reliability analysis revealed Cronbach's α value as 0.821, which is comparable with the reliabilities reported in earlier studies. Construct validity was evaluated using principal component analysis and Varimax rotation. The result for Bartlett's test of Sphericity was 0.000 and the KMO value 0.686. This value is more than 0.5 that shows high measure of sampling adequacy and ensures factorability of data. Items were retained based on the following criteria: (i) items with loading of 0.50 or more; (ii) items with loading of less than 0.50 were removed; and (iii) items with loading beyond 0.50 on two or more components were removed. From a total of 47 items, 3 of the items were dropped in the exploratory factor analysis. The reliabilities of sub-scales varied between 0.620 and 0.947; which exceeded the recommended level of 0.6. The variables were grouped in ten factors and all together accounted for 76.23% of the total variance. This value of total variance explained that the set of factors extracted from the data explain the adoption intention to a very high extent, and a lesser part of the adoption remains unexplained.

Confirmatory Factor Analysis

To test the stability of the scale, confirmatory factor analysis was employed on the sample using structural equation modeling (SEM). A measurement model was developed using of partial least squares (PLS); PLS can be used when data is distributed normally. The Kolmogorov–Smirnov test showed that none of the items were distributed normally ($p < 0.001$). The minimum sample size for using is obtained from the following formula: (1) ten times the largest number of formative indicators used to measure one construct or (2) ten times the largest number of structural paths directed at a particular latent construct in the structural model. The sample consisted of 478 firms, which fulfill the necessary conditions for using PLS. Smart PLS software was used for confirmatory factor analysis and hypothesis testing. Analyses were conducted utilizing the full sample for identifying the key factors of Big Data adoption and then sub-samples of the data for the manufacturing and services sectors to examine how the factors vary across different industries. The composite reliability for each construct ranged higher than 0.7 for the full sample, and the industry specific samples suggesting acceptable levels of reliability. The average variances extracted (AVEs), were greater than 0.50 for the full sample and the industry specific samples. All the indicators had significant loading greater than .50 for both full and industry specific value. Thus, measurement models for both industries ensure convergent validity. Discriminant validity was assessed by comparing the correlation between factors with average variance, which was extracted from the individual factors. Analyses showed that the square root of AVE is greater than the correlation between each of the pair that supports the discriminant validity of the construct.

HYPOTHESIS TESTING

To test proposed hypotheses, the measurement model was converted to structural model in PLS; results were interpreted using the regression weight table. Relative advantage was found to be significant on adoption for both the full sample and industry specific sample. Therefore, this supports the prior work of Wang and Wang (2016) that found relative advantage to be the most influential determinant of technology adoption. This is also in concurrence with the findings of Maduku et al. (2016) who found a positive relationship of relative advantage for mobile marketing adoption. These findings actually allow users to recognize that Big Data can certainly contribute to the efficiency and effectiveness of organizations, and thereby organizations are more likely to implement and adapt Big Data.

Compatibility is found to be a significant facilitator of Big Data adoption for both the full sample and industry specific sample. This is inconsistent with prior studies by Grandon and Pearson (2004), Lin and Chen (2012), Alshamaila et al. (2012), Gangwar et al. (2015), Wang and Wang (2016), Alsaad et al. (2017), and lastly Maduku et al. (2016). Complexity is also found negatively to affect adoption for full sample and service sector and insignificant for manufacturing sector. This is in consistent with Ramdani et al. (2009), Alshamaila et al. (2012), Tsai et al. (2013), Gangwar et al. (2015), and Wang and Wang (2016). The results show that there is no significant negative relationship between perceived complexity and Big Data adoption intention for the services sector. This finding is consistent with the earlier finding of Low et al. (2011) and Maduku et al. (2016).

Organizational readiness does not have any significant effect on organizations' decision to adopt Big Data for both the full sample and industry specific sample. This finding is consistent with Grandon and Pearson (2004), Wang et al. (2010), and Low et al. (2011). Organizational size is found to have a positive effect on adoption for both full sample and industry specific sample. The results are similar to those of Lee and Xia (2006), Zhu, Kraemer et al. (2003), Teo et al. (2003), Lippert and Govindarajulu (2006), and Hung et al. (2010). In addition, top management support shows a significant positive relationship with Big Data adoption for both full sample as well as industry specific sample. The importance of top management support is consistent with studies of Premkumar and Roberts (1999), Lewis, Agarwal, & Sambamurthy (2003), Teo et al. (2009), Sila (2013), and Alsaad et al. (2017).

Competitive pressure is supported to positively effect on adoption of Big Data for both the full sample and industry specific sample. The results are similar to those of Lin and Lin (2008), Oliveira and Martins (2010a), Low et al. (2011), and Alsaad et al. (2017). Vendor support does have significant effect on organizations' decision to adopt Big Data for both the full sample and industry specific sample. The results are similar to those of Gangwar and Date (2016) and Alshamaila et al. (2013).

Big Data adoption is more influenced by other factors such as data management. It ensures availability, quality and security of data. This finding is consistent with Gustin, Daugherty, and Stank (1995), Alshawi, Farouk, and Irani (2011), and Gangwar et al. (2015). Data Privacy is also found to have an impact on Big Data adoption for both the full sample and industry specific sample; this finding is consistent with Oliveira, Thomas, and Espadanal (2014) and Alsaad et al. (2017). The results are summarized below.

DISCUSSION AND RECOMMENDATIONS

Findings of the study show that relative advantage has a positive impact on Big Data adoption for both the full sample and industry specific sample. Positive relationship between relative advantage and adoption intention indicates that organizations which have an overall positive perception of the benefits of Big Data are likely to have a positive intention to go on to adopt it. Advantages identified by the study include improving the decision making process, cost reduction, competitive offerings, implementing new strategies and new business models, and providing new business opportunities. The relative advantage of Big Data leads to greater result, such as improved customer services, greater operational efficiency, reduced operating costs and improved business strategy and business plans. Advanced understanding

Figure 2. SEM result

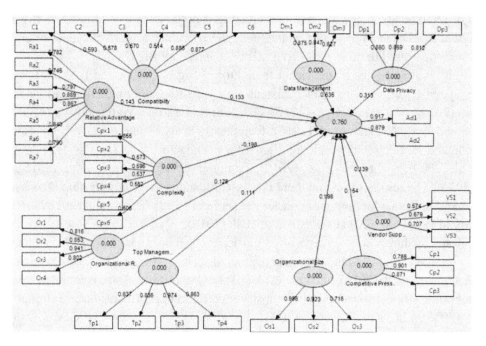

of the advantages of Big Data over existing technology helps managers in their management processes to build policies, and also improves relationship with customers. Thus it may be said that more the opportunity, easier would the technology become in terms of its day-to-day use. Moreover, the marginal effects are different between manufacturing and service industries. Relative advantage is more important in the service sector the possible reason might be because in the manufacturing sector the organizations are more informed of the perceived benefits of Big Data.

Compatibility between Big Data and an organization's existing technological architecture, techniques, and preferred work practices was also found to be an influential factor in this study. Organizations have positive attitudes and agreement about technological innovation when there is a good fit between a technological innovation, the people, processes, practices of the organization at large. Big Data should also be compatible with the organization's policies, IT development environment, and business needs (Lin & Chen, 2012). To enhance compatibility, organizations should make necessary contributions to make the Big Data system compatible with the organization's internal processes and policies. On the flip side, providers may customize Big Data services to the needs of individual organizations, wherein they need to understand the existing business processes, IT infrastructures, and organizational cultures in order to meet the compatibility parameters of Big Data solutions. Thus, if Big Data functions are consistent with the work styles, data format structural data, business needs, and practices of organizational activities, a positive impression of Big Data is likely to occur and this in turn, can facilitate Big Data implementation at a larger scale and mass.

The service sector reveals a statistically significant higher relative importance of compatibility for Big Data adoption when compared with manufacturing. One possible explanation is that as service sector firms have higher levels of compatibility in terms of existing IT infrastructure, practices and structure of the organization, skill and knowledge required working with Big Data, only these firms can take ad-

Table 3. SEM coefficients

Construct	Full Sample		Manufacturing		Service	
	Path Coeff.	T-Value	Path Coeff.	T-Value	Path Coeff.	T-Value
Relative Advantage -> Adoption	0.143	2.1825*	0.125	1.999*	0.134	2.001*
Compatibility -> Adoption	0.133	3.0827**	0.103	2.034*	0.146	2.283*
Complexity -> Adoption	-0.198	2.3509*	-0.122	1.0675	-0.21	3.356**
Organizational Readiness -> Adoption	0.128	1.336	0.121	1.456	0.128	1.088
Top Management Support -> Adoption	0.111	2.421*	0.11	2.345*	0.122	2.872**
Organizational Size -> Adoption	0.198	3.554**	0.123	3.012**	0.213	3.679**
Competitive Pressure -> Adoption	0.154	3.172**	0.145	2.346*	0.163	2.967**
Vendor Support-> Adoption	0.139	2.349*	0.114	1.998*	0.141	2.619**
Data Management-> Adoption	0.635	6.3819**	0.6004	5.867**	0.638	6.9019**
Data Privacy -> Adoption	0.313	4.304**	0.278	3.929**	0.324	4.656**

** Significance at p < 0.01

* Significance at p < 0.05

vantage of Big Data integration to the existing environment, i.e. improving the decision making process, improving customer service, and lowering inventory costs. Managers in the manufacturing industry in particular need to improve compatibility by introducing changes in existing practices and policies in order to customize to avail the Big Data services and thereby take its full advantage.

Organizations did not perceive Big Data technology to be intrinsically more complex in the services sector. They are not more complex for those who have expertise to integrate existing applications to Big Data and the skill set to develop customized solutions. This study has described the complexity in terms of efficiency of data transfer, data analysis, visualizing data etc. Big Data is found to be easy to learn, thereby taking lesser time in performing tasks of employees. The complexity of Big Data by its characteristics of volume, velocity, and variety is eased when service providers offer easy to use development and analytic tools. These tools, developed over a period of time, allow users to mine valuable information from Big Data. It has therefore been identified that lesser the complexity in using Big Data, more is the likelihood of their adoption and usage. Technology complexity is a statistically insignificant facilitator only in the manufacturing sector. One possible explanation is that manufacturing organizations perceive Big Data as complex technology because they don't have the expertise and skills needed to integrate and work with Big Data analysis (Zhong et al., 2015).

Organizational readiness is statistically insignificant factor for Big Data adoption for both full sample and industry specific sample. However, this may be because of organizations adopting Big Data may have already made requisite sophisticated technological changes including hardware, software, and overall expertise. Another possible explanation might be when organizations believe in the benefit of technology, they are able to manage the technological, financial and specialized IT skills better. Thus organizational readiness may not influence the initial part of Big Data adoption, but rather the extent of its usage.

Firm size is statistically significant for Big Data adoption in full sample as well as industry specific sample; this finding is consistent with extant literature suggesting that larger companies have more resources to cover the cost and have higher risk taking capability in terms of changing processes, practices and policies that have emerged because of this technological innovation. The results can help managers to predict the possibility of the adoption of Big Data by assessing the size of their organization. Notably, there is no size-fit relationship between organizational size and Big Data adoption; but managers must recognize the advantages and disadvantages of their size while adopting Big Data.

The study provides empirical evidence that top management support is significant in explaining the adoption of Big Data for full sample and industry specific sample. It demonstrates support of committing financial and organizational resources, development of IS/IT capabilities, reducing resistance, resolving conflicts, improving communications, convincing employees, and lastly overcoming the implementation barriers. Technology adoption should be carried out using a top down approach. First, organizations should realize the strategic importance of technology, it's only then they will take the initiative to adopt a technology per se. Top management support can encourage and motivate people to use Big Data and then influence the decision making process for adopting it by harping on the enhanced efficiency of the organization post implementation. Thus, top managers should take the initiative to convince one and all for the effective and efficient use of new technology.

This study determines that competitive pressure is a significant factor for Big Data adoption both in organizations in the full sample and the industry specific sample. Competitive pressure measured by market structure, imports pressure of adopting Big Data so as to maintain a competitive edge. It is important to understand that stiff competition drives organizations to switch from other technologies to Big Data without investing sufficient time in infusing a holistic innovation approach that is required within the organizations (Zhu, Dong et al., 2006). In other words, the greater the competition among similar organizations, the more likely organizations adopts Big Data in order to gain a competitive edge.

Findings also indicate that adoption of Big Data is largely influenced by vendor support for both full sample and industry specific sample. It is supported by the fact that supplier support in the form of reinforcement, assistance, information sharing and problem resolution can directly impact adoption of Big Data in an organization. Thus managers for Big Data should develop strong and transparent relations with suppliers through effective communication, cooperation, coordination, and service level agreements. On the other hand, vendors should provide data and advance data analytic driven solutions to the organizations in order to maximize revenue.

Findings also support that Big Data adoption is essentially driven by data management and associated requirements. It is related to the blend of old and new best practices, skills, teams, data types, tools and technologies along with vendor built-in functionality, so that businesses at large can fully leverage Big Data availability, quality, efficiency and effectiveness. Further high availability of Big Data and their support is ensured by Big Data providers by employing multiple network providers so that even if one of them experiences difficulties or a complete failure, the provider services will not be jeopardized due to the immediate availability of another network provider. Also, they adopt high availability architecture, test platforms and applications, and maintain on-premises storage backup, or use a cloud backup, or simply not store mission-critical data on any of the Big Data platforms. Data quality can be ensured through data profiling, data normalization, semantic data management and data quality firewall. The analysis indicates a statistically significant higher magnitude of data management for Big Data adoption in the service industry as compared to the manufacturing industry. One possible explanation is that the data management techniques are less active in the manufacturing industry vis-a-vis the service industry.

Privacy concerns have been found to have a significant negative effect on Big Data adoption for both full sample and industry specific sample. Privacy concern in Big Data indicates that lesser the privacy risk in using Big Data analytics, higher the trust developed on the privacy and integrity part of Big Data. Thus in order to secure Big Data from privacy and security threats, various privacy-enhancing techniques, monitoring mechanisms, identity management standards, access control, configuration management monitoring mechanisms, and encryption schemes to ensure confidentiality, integrity, and the security are incorporated into Big Data techniques. The higher magnitude of privacy concern in service sector may be because of the lack of concern regarding security and privacy when considering a Big Data analytics as compared to manufacturing sector.

CONCLUSION

Big Data is an important evolution of information systems because of the cost-effective capture of information in a timely manner. Thus it is important to understand what contributes to BDA adoption in the enterprises. Given the TOE framework, this study created and approved an exploration model to look at the impact of nine logical variables on BDA adoption in firms.

There were four major contributions of this study:

1. This study is an early endeavor to investigate and build up a BDA adoption model. This model is created to recognize the variables that impacts the appropriation of BDA hypothetically supported into the TOE framework:
    a. The study identified key findings and suggestions about the determinants of BDA selection in the enterprises of India that relies on the company's technological, organizational and environmental contexts;
    b. This study introduces an increasingly comprehensive evaluation of the components of Big Data by partitioning them in two segments – the manufacturing and service sectors;
    c. Nine relevant factors (i.e., relative advantage, compatibility, complexity, top management support, along with firm size, competitive pressure, vendor support, data management, and privacy concerns) impact the appropriation goal of BDA; organizational readiness does not have any huge impact on selection for both full example and industry explicit example;
    d. Among the nine determinants, complexity was the inhibitors of BDA, while remaining determinants alongside data security and data management of BDA were the facilitators of BDA adoption;
2. This study quantitatively analyzed the applicability of the three settings (technological, organizational, and environmental) of the TOE framework and confirms that there are measurably noteworthy differences between the service and manufacturing industries;
3. This study discovered two determinants that impacted the BDA appropriation (data privacy and organizational data environment), however were rarely investigated in the earlier IT adoption research;

4. Finally, compared with prior BDA adoption research, this quantitative study used a large and representative sample that consists of numerous BDA decision makers. Thus the findings of this study are valuable and provide several important implications for BDA adoption research and practice.

IMPLICATIONS

The findings of this study are important to managers, Big Data providers and researchers in developing better strategies for Big Data adoption. It provides relevant recommendations to achieve a conducive implementation environment for Big Data adoption. The proposed model can help organizations assess the possible Big Data adoption and increase awareness about factors that influence adoption. The findings offer Big Data users with a better understanding of how technology, organizational, environmental and security challenges affect Big Data adoption. Adopters can increase their understanding for extracting maximum benefits from Big Data adoption; prospector and non-adopters can increase knowledge on challenges and prerequisite to the uptake of Big Data increasing knowledge on impediments to the uptake of new technology.

The proposed model can help Big Data providers increase their understanding of why some organizations choose to adopt Big Data, while others facing similar market conditions do not. Thus Big Data providers may need to improve their interaction with the organizations that are involved in Big Data experience, in order to create healthy environment for Big Data adoption and to remove any ambiguity surrounding the Big Data adoption. However Big Data providers need to be aware of common concerns that organizations experience when they make adoption decision, such as complexity, security etc. The proposed framework can help managers in identifying the firm's situation in terms of strength and weakness for the possible adoption of Big Data. The findings can lead managers to improve their insight in balancing decisions concerning adoption of Big Data in the future. In general, the advantage of the TOE framework is that it can include many different contextual factors, which other models may not. Therefore, the TOE model has the potential to contribute to firm managers' decision making.

CURRENT RESEARCH TRENDS

Organizations continuously investing in analytics to support digital transformations so confirming that the organization is adopting the analytics strategies are crucial to be top of the latest trends. Even though adoption of Big Data within the industry is occurring but there is gap to clearly find the pros and cons for organizations to invest in Big Data. The outcome of this study is a comprehensive model that combines technology, organization, environment and security dimension but there is need to formulate a distinct model for each industry. Thus future research could build on this study by examining big data adoption in different in sector and industries and in different countries. Also future study can test another wide range of variables that are not included in this study.

ACKNOWLEDGMENT

A prior version of this manuscript appeared in the *Information Resources Management Journal*.

REFERENCES

Abbasi, A., Sarker, S., & Chiang, R. H. L. (2016). Big data research in information systems: Toward an inclusive research agenda. *Journal of the Association for Information Systems, 1*(2), 3. doi:10.17705/1jais.00423

Ajzen, I. (1991). The theory of planned behavior. *Organizational Behavior and Human Decision Processes, 50*(2), 179–211. doi:10.1016/0749-5978(91)90020-T

Al Nuaimi, E., Al Neyadi, H., Mohamed, N., & Al-Jaroodi, J. (2015). Applications of big data to smart cities. *Journal of Internet Services and Applications, 6*(1), 1–15. doi:10.118613174-015-0041-5

Alsaad, A., Mohamad, R., & Ismail, N. A. (2017). The moderating role of trust in business to business electronic commerce (B2B EC) adoption. *Computers in Human Behavior, 68*(1), 157–169. doi:10.1016/j.chb.2016.11.040

Alshamaila, Y., Papagiannidis, S., & Li, F. (2013). Cloud computing adoption by SMEs in the north east of England: A multi-perspective framework. *Journal of Enterprise Information Management, 26*(3), 250–275. doi:10.1108/17410391311325225

Alshawi, S., Farouk, M., & Irani, Z. (2011). Organizational, technical and data quality factors in CRM adoption – SME perspective. *Industrial Marketing Management, 40*(3), 376–383. doi:10.1016/j.indmarman.2010.08.006

Barton, D., & Court, D. (2012). Making advanced analytics work for you. *Harvard Business Review, 90*(1), 79–83. PMID:23074867

Bose, R., & Luo, X. (2012). Green IT adoption: A process management approach. *International Journal of Accounting & Information Management, 20*(1), 63–77. doi:10.1108/18347641211201081

Chaudhury, A., & Bharati, P. (2008). IT outsourcing adoption by small and medium enterprises: A diffusion innovation approach. *Proceedings of the Americas Conference on Information Systems (AMCIS)*, 14-17.

Chaurasia, S., & Rosin, A. F. (2017). From big data to big impact: Analytics for teaching and learning in higher education. *Industrial and Commercial Training, 49*(7/8), 321–328. doi:10.1108/ICT-10-2016-0069

Chen, C. P., & Zhang, C.-Y. (2014). Data-intensive applications, challenges, techniques and technologies: A survey on big data. *Information Sciences, 275*(10), 314–347. doi:10.1016/j.ins.2014.01.015

Chen, H., Chiang, R., & Storey, V. (2012). Business intelligence and analytics: From big data to big impact. *Management Information Systems Quarterly, 36*(4), 1165–1188. doi:10.2307/41703503

Chung, B. Y., Skibniewski, M. J., Lucas, H. C. Jr, & Kwak, Y. H. (2008). Analyzing enterprise resource planning system implementation success factors in the engineering – construction industry. *Journal of Computing in Civil Engineering, 22*(6), 373–382. doi:10.1061/(ASCE)0887-3801(2008)22:6(373)

Cukier, K. (2010). Data, data everywhere: A special report on managing information. *The Economist, 394*, 3-5. Retrieved from https://www.economist.com/node/15557443

Davis, F. D. (1989). Perceived usefulness, perceived ease of use, and user acceptance of diffusion perspective. *Technovation, 28*(3), 135–145.

Dubey, R., Gunasekaran, A., Childe, S. J., Wamba, S. F., & Papadopoulos, T. (2016). The impact of big data on world-class sustainable manufacturing. *International Journal of Advanced Manufacturing Technology*, *84*(1-4), 631–645. doi:10.100700170-015-7674-1

Elgendy, N., & Elragal, A. (2014). Big data analytics: A literature review paper. *Lecture Notes in Computer Science Industrial, 8557*, 214–227. 10.1007/978-3-319-08976-8_16

Fishbein, M., & Ajzen, I. (1975). *Belief, Attitude, Intention and Behavior: An introduction to theory and research*. Reading, MA: Addison-Wesley.

Gandomi, A., & Haider, M. (2015). Beyond the hype: Big data concepts, methods, and analytics. *International Journal of Information Management*, *35*(2), 137–144. doi:10.1016/j.ijinfomgt.2014.10.007

Gangwar, H., & Date, H. (2016). Understanding cloud computing adoption: A model comparison approach. *Human Systems Management*, *35*(2), 93–114. doi:10.3233/HSM-150857

Gangwar, H., Date, H., & Ramaswamy, R. (2015). Understanding factors of cloud computing adoption using an integrated TAM-TOE model. *Journal of Enterprise Information Management*, *28*(1), 107–130. doi:10.1108/JEIM-08-2013-0065

Goes, P. (2014). Editor's comments: Big data and IS research. *Management Information Systems Quarterly*, *38*(2), 3–8.

Grandon, E., & Pearson, J. M. (2004). E-commerce adoption: Perceptions of managers/owners of small and medium sized firms in Chile. *Communications of the Association for Information Systems*, *13*(1), 81–102. doi:10.17705/1CAIS.01308

Gustin, C. M., Daugherty, P. J., & Stank, T. P. (1995). The effects of information availability on logistics integra. *Journal of Business Logistics*, *16*(1), 1–13.

Hashem, I. A. T., Yaqoob, I., Anuar, N. B., Mokhtar, S., Gani, A., & Khan, S. U. (2015). The rise of big data on cloud computing: Review and open research issues. *Information Systems*, *47*, 98–115. doi:10.1016/j.is.2014.07.006

Hazen, B. T., Boone, C. A., Ezell, J. D., & Jones-Farmer, L. A. (2014). Data quality for data science, predictive analytics, and big data in supply chain management: An introduction to the problem and suggestions for research and applications. *International Journal of Production Economics*, *154*, 72–80. doi:10.1016/j.ijpe.2014.04.018

Hsu, P. F., Kraemer, K. L., & Dunkle, D. (2006). Factors of e-business use in US firms. *International Journal of Electronic Commerce*, *10*(4), 9–45. doi:10.2753/JEC1086-4415100401

Hu, J., & Vasilakos, A. V. (2016). Energy big data analytics and security: Challenges and opportunities. *IEEE Transactions on Smart Grid*, *7*(5), 2423–2436. doi:10.1109/TSG.2016.2563461

Huang, Z., Janz, B. D., & Frolick, M. N. (2008). A comprehensive examination of internet-EDI adoption. *Information Systems Management*, *25*(3), 273–286. doi:10.1080/10580530802151228

Hung, S. Y., Hung, W. H., Tsai, C. A., & Jiang, S. C. (2010). Critical factors of hospital adoption on CRM system: Organizational and information system perspectives. *Journal of Decision Support Systems*, *48*(4), 592–603. doi:10.1016/j.dss.2009.11.009

Ifinedo, P. (2011). An empirical analysis of factors influencing internet/e-business technologies adoption by SMEs in Canada. *International Journal of Information Technology & Decision Making*, *10*(4), 731–766. doi:10.1142/S0219622011004543

Igbaria, M., Guimaraes, T., & Davis, G. B. (1995). Testing the determinants of microcomputer usage via a structural equation model. *Journal of Management Information Systems*, *11*(4), 87–114. doi:10.1080/07421222.1995.11518061

Jagadish, H. V., Gehrke, J., Labrinidis, A., Papakonstantinou, Y., Patel, J. M., Ramakrishnan, R., & Shahabi, C. (2014). Big data and its technical challenges. *Communications of the ACM*, *57*(7), 86–94. doi:10.1145/2611567

Jang, S.-H. (2010). An empirical study on the factors influencing RFID adoption and implementation. *Management Review. International Journal (Toronto, Ont.)*, *5*(2), 55–73.

Jeyaraj, A., Rottman, J. W., & Lacity, W. C. (2006). A review of the predictors, linkages, and biases in IT innovation adoption research. *Journal of Information Technology*, *21*(1), 1–23. doi:10.1057/palgrave.jit.2000056

Koltay, T. (2015). Data literacy: In search of a name and identity. *The Journal of Documentation*, *71*(2), 401–415. doi:10.1108/JD-02-2014-0026

Kuan, K. K. Y., & Chau, P. Y. K. (2001). A perception-based model for EDI adoption in small businesses using a technology-organization-environment framework. *Information & Management*, *38*(8), 507–521. doi:10.1016/S0378-7206(01)00073-8

Kwon, O., Lee, N., & Shin, B. (2014). Data quality management, data usage experience and acquisition intention of big data analytics. *International Journal of Information Management*, *34*(3), 387–394. doi:10.1016/j.ijinfomgt.2014.02.002

Lee, G., & Xia, W. (2006). Organizational size and IT innovation adoption: A meta-analysis. *Information & Management*, *43*(8), 975–985. doi:10.1016/j.im.2006.09.003

Lee, J., Kao, H.-A., & Yang, S. (2014). Service innovation and smart analytics for Industry 4.0 and big data environment. *Procedia CIRP*, *16*, 3–8. doi:10.1016/j.procir.2014.02.001

Lewis, W., Agarwal, R., & Sambamurthy, V. (2003). Sources of influence on beliefs about information technology use: An empirical study of knowledge workers. *Management Information Systems Quarterly*, *27*(4), 657–678. doi:10.2307/30036552

Lian, J., Yen, D., & Wang, Y. (2014). An exploratory study to understand the critical factors affecting the decision to adopt cloud computing in Taiwan hospital. *International Journal of Information Management*, *34*(1), 28–36. doi:10.1016/j.ijinfomgt.2013.09.004

Lin, A., & Chen, N.-C. (2012). Cloud computing as an innovation: Perception, attitude, and adoption. *International Journal of Information Management*, *32*(6), 533–540. doi:10.1016/j.ijinfomgt.2012.04.001

Lin, H.-F., & Lin, S.-M. (2008). Factors of e-business diffusion: A test of the technology diffusion perspective. *Technovation*, *28*(3), 135–145. doi:10.1016/j.technovation.2007.10.003

Lippert, S. K., & Govindarajulu, C. (2006). Technological, organizational, and environmental antecedents to web services adoption. *Antecedents to Web Services Adoption*, *6*(1), 146–158.

Low, C., Chen, Y., & Wu, M. (2011). Understanding the factors of cloud computing adoption. *Industrial Management & Data Systems*, *111*(7), 1006–1023. doi:10.1108/02635571111161262

Maduku, D. K., Mpinganjira, M., & Duh, H. (2016). Mobile marketing adoption intention by South African SMEs: A multi-perspective framework. *International Journal of Information Management*, *36*(5), 711–723. doi:10.1016/j.ijinfomgt.2016.04.018

Manyika, J., Chui, M., Brown, B., Bughin, J., Dobbs, R., Roxburgh, C., & Byers, A. H. (2011). *Big Data: The next frontier for innovation, competition, and productivity*. Washington, DC: McKinsey Global Institute.

McAfee, A., & Brynjolfsson, E. (2012). Big data: The management revolution. *Harvard Business Review*, *90*(10), 60–68. PMID:23074865

McCole, P., & Ramsey, E. (2005). A profile of adopters and non-adopters of ecommerce in SME professional service firms. *Australasian Marketing Journal*, *13*(1), 36–48. doi:10.1016/S1441-3582(05)70066-5

Miller, D., & Toulouse, J.-M. (1986). Chief executive personality and corporate strategy and structure in small firms. *Management Science*, *32*(11), 1389–1409. doi:10.1287/mnsc.32.11.1389

Moore, G. C., & Benbasat, I. (1991). Development of an instrument to measure the perceptions of adopting an information technology innovation. *Information Systems Research*, *2*(3), 173–191. doi:10.1287/isre.2.3.192

Moura, J., & Serrão, C. (2015). Security and privacy issues of big data. In N. Zaman, M. Seliaman, M. Hassan, & F. Marquez (Eds.), *Handbook of Research on Trends and Future Directions in Big Data and Web Intelligence* (pp. 20–52). Hershey, PA: Information Science Reference. doi:10.4018/978-1-4666-8505-5.ch002

Mourtzis, D., Vlachou, E., & Milas, N. (2016). Industrial big data as a result of IoT adoption in manufacturing. *Procedia CIRP*, *55*, 290–295. doi:10.1016/j.procir.2016.07.038

Murdoch, T. B., & Detsky, A. S. (2013). The inevitable application of big data to health care. *Journal of the American Medical Association*, *309*(13), 1351–1352. doi:10.1001/jama.2013.393 PMID:23549579

Oliveira, S. F., Fürlinger, K., & Kranzlmüller, D. (2012). Trends in computation, communication and storage and the consequences for data intensive science. *Proceedings of the IEEE 14th International Conference on High Performance Computing and Communication & 2012 IEEE 9th International Conference on Embedded Software and Systems*, 572-579. 10.1109/HPCC.2012.83

Oliveira, T., & Martins, M. F. (2010a). Firms patterns of e-business adoption: Evidence for the European Union-27. *The Electronic Journal Information Systems Evaluation*, *13*(1), 47–56.

Oliveira, T., & Martins, M. F. (2010b). Understanding e-business adoption across industries in European countries. *Industrial Management & Data Systems, 110*(9), 1337–1354. doi:10.1108/02635571011087428

Opresnk, D., & Taisch, M. (2015). The value of big data in servitization. *International Journal of Production Economics, 165*, 174–184. doi:10.1016/j.ijpe.2014.12.036

Pan, M.-J., & Jang, W.-Y. (2008). Factors of the adoption of enterprise resources planning within the technology-organization-environment framework: Taiwan's communications industry. *Journal of Computer Information Systems, 48*(3), 94–102.

Pei-Fang, H., Soumya, R., & Li-Hsieh, Y.-Y. (2014). Examining cloud computing adoption intention, pricing mechanism, and deployment model. *International Journal of Information Management, 34*(4), 474–488. doi:10.1016/j.ijinfomgt.2014.04.006

Peng, R., Xiong, L., & Yang, Z. (2012). Exploring tourist adoption of tourism mobile payment: An empirical analysis. *Journal of Theoretical and Applied Electronic Commerce Research, 7*(1), 21–33. doi:10.4067/S0718-18762012000100003

Premkumar, G., Ramamurthy, K., & Crum, M. (1997). Determinants of EDI adoption in the transportation industry. *European Journal of Information Systems, 6*(2), 107–121. doi:10.1057/palgrave.ejis.3000260

Premkumar, G., & Roberts, M. (1999). Adoption of new information technologies in rural small pricing mechanism, and deployment mode. *International Journal of Information Management, 34*, 474–488.

Ramdani, B., Kawalek, P., & Lorenzo, O. (2009). Predicting SMEs' adoption of enterprise systems. *Journal of Enterprise Information Management, 22*(1/2), 10–24. doi:10.1108/17410390910922796

Ren, S. J., Wamba, S. F., Akter, S., Dubey, R., & Childe, S. J. (2017). Modelling quality dynamics, business value and firm performance in a big data analytics environment. *International Journal of Production Research, 55*, 1–16.

Rogers, E. M. (1962). *Diffusion of Innovations* (1st ed.). New York: Free Press.

Rogers, E. M. (2003). *Diffusion of Innovations*. New York: Free Press.

Rui, G. (2007). *Information Systems Innovation Adoption Among Organizations: A match-based framework and empirical studies*. Singapore: National University of Singapore.

Schadt, E. E. (2012). The changing privacy landscape in the era of big data. *Molecular Systems Biology, 8*(1), 612. doi:10.1038/msb.2012.47 PMID:22968446

Schillewaert, N., Ahearne, M. J., Frambach, R. T., & Moenaert, R. K. (2005). The adoption of information technology in the sales force. *Industrial Marketing Management, 34*(4), 323–336. doi:10.1016/j.indmarman.2004.09.013

Sila, I. (2013). Factors affecting the adoption of B2B ecommerce technologies. *Electronic Commerce Research, 13*(2), 199–236. doi:10.100710660-013-9110-7

Srivastava, U., & Gopalkrishnan, S. (2015). Impact of big data analytics on banking sector: Learning for Indian banks. *Procedia Computer Science, 50*, 643–652. doi:10.1016/j.procs.2015.04.098

Sun, S., Cegielski, C. G., Jia, L., & Hall, D. J. (2016). Understanding the factors affecting the organizational adoption of big data. *Journal of Computer Information Systems*, *58*(3), 193–203. doi:10.1080 /08874417.2016.1222891

Tao, F., Cheng, J., Qi, Q., Zhang, M., Zhang, H., & Sui, F. (2017). Digital twin-driven product design manufacturing and service with big data. *International Journal of Advanced Manufacturing Technology*, *94*, 1–14.

Teo, H. H., Wei, K. K., & Benbasat, I. (2003). Predicting intention to adopt interorganizational linkages: An institutional perspective. *Management Information Systems Quarterly*, *27*(1), 19–49. doi:10.2307/30036518

Teo, T. S. H., Lin, S., & Lai, K.-H. (2009). Adopters and non-adopters of e-procurement in Singapore: An empirical study. *Omega*, *37*(5), 972–987. doi:10.1016/j.omega.2008.11.001

Tornatzky, L. G., & Fleischer, M. (1990). *The Processes of Technological Innovation*. Lexington, MA: Lexington Books.

Tornatzky, L. G., & Klein, K. J. (1982). Innovation characteristics and innovation adoption-implementation: A meta-analysis of findings. *IEEE Transactions on Engineering Management*, *29*(1), 28–45. doi:10.1109/TEM.1982.6447463

Tsai, M. C., Lai, K. H., & Hsu, W. C. (2013). A study of the institutional forces influencing the adoption intention of RFID by suppliers. *Information & Management*, *50*(1), 59–65. doi:10.1016/j.im.2012.05.006

Venkatesh, V., Morris, M. G., Davis, G. B., & Davis, F. (2003). User acceptance of information technology: Toward a unified view. *Management Information Systems Quarterly*, *27*(3), 425–478. doi:10.2307/30036540

Verma, S. (2018). Mapping the intellectual structure of the big data research in the IS discipline: A citation/co-citation analysis. *Information Resources Management Journal*, *31*(1), 21–52. doi:10.4018/ IRMJ.2018010102

Verma, S., & Bhattacharyya, S. S. (2017). Perceived strategic value-based adoption of big data analytics in emerging economy. *Journal of Enterprise Information Management*, *30*(3), 354–382. doi:10.1108/ JEIM-10-2015-0099

Verma, S., Bhattacharyya, S. S., & Kumar, S. (2018). An extension of the technology acceptance model in the big data analytics system implementation environment. *Information Processing & Management*, *54*(5), 791–806. doi:10.1016/j.ipm.2018.01.004

Waller, M. A., & Fawcett, S. E. (2013). Data science, predictive analytics, and big data: A revolution that will transform supply chain design and management. *Journal of Business Logistics*, *34*(2), 77–84. doi:10.1111/jbl.12010

Wang, G., Gunasekaran, A., Ngai, E. W. T., & Papadopoulos, T. (2016). Big data analytics in logistics and supply chain management: Certain investigations for research and applications. *International Journal of Production Economics*, *176*, 98–110. doi:10.1016/j.ijpe.2016.03.014

Wang, Y., & Wang, Y. (2016). Factors of firms' knowledge management system implementation: An empirical study. *Computers in Human Behavior*, *64*(1), 829–842. doi:10.1016/j.chb.2016.07.055

Wang, Y., Wang, Y., & Yang, Y. (2010). Understanding the factors of RFID adoption in the manufacturing industry. *Technological Forecasting and Social Change*, *77*(5), 803–815. doi:10.1016/j.techfore.2010.03.006

Zhan, Y., Tan, K. H., Li, Y., & Tse, Y. K. (2018). Unlocking the power of big data in new product development. *Annals of Operations Research*, *270*(1/2), 577–595. doi:10.100710479-016-2379-x

Zhang, Y., Ren, S., Liu, Y., & Si, S. (2016). A big data analytics architecture for cleaner manufacturing and maintenance processes of complex product. *Journal of Cleaner Production*, *142*(2), 626–641.

Zhong, R. Y., Huang, G. Q., Lan, S., Dai, Q. Y., Chen, X., & Zhang, T. (2015). A big data approach for logistics trajectory discovery from RFID-enabled production data. *International Journal of Production Economics*, *165*, 260–272. doi:10.1016/j.ijpe.2015.02.014

Zhong, R. Y., Lan, S. L., Xu, C., Dai, Q. Y., & Huang, G. Q. (2016). Visualization of RFID enabled shop floor logistics big data in cloud manufacturing. *International Journal of Advanced Manufacturing Technology*, *84*(1), 5–16. doi:10.100700170-015-7702-1

Zhu, K., Dong, S. T., Xu, S., & Kraemer, K. L. (2006). Innovation diffusion in global contexts: Factors of post-adoption digital transformation of European companies. *European Journal of Information Systems*, *15*(9), 601–616. doi:10.1057/palgrave.ejis.3000650

Zhu, K., & Kraemer, K. L. (2005). Post-adoption variations in usage and value of e-business by organizations: Cross-country evidence from the retail industry. *Information Systems Research*, *16*(1), 61–84. doi:10.1287/isre.1050.0045

Zhu, K., Kraemer, K. L., & Xu, S. (2003). Electronic business adoption by European firms: A cross-country assessment of the facilitators and inhibitors. *European Journal of Information Systems*, *12*(4), 251–268. doi:10.1057/palgrave.ejis.3000475

Zhu, K., Kraemer, K. L., & Xu, S. (2006). The process of innovation assimilation by firms in different countries: A technology diffusion perspective on e-business. *Management Science*, *52*(10), 1557–1576. doi:10.1287/mnsc.1050.0487

KEY TERMS AND DEFINITIONS

Big Data: A dataset that is larger than a typical dataset that requires unique tools, techniques, and technologies to store, manage, and analyze data.

Big Data Analytics: Techniques, technologies, systems, methodologies, tools, and applications used to analysis for decision making.

Compatibility: The extent to which an innovation aligns with an organization's current values and/ or needs.

Competitive Pressure: Amount of pressure an organization experiences from competitors that may in turn affect big data adoption.

Complexity: The extent to which an innovation is difficult to use or understand.

Data Management: Process of ensuring accuracy, availability, accessibility, and quality of large stores of data by allocating people, policies, and technologies.

Data Privacy: Protection of personal privacy during data acquisition, storage, transmission, and usage.

Environmental Context: Refers to the context in which the organization functions which may impact the decision making.

Four Vs: The four Vs refer to volume, variety, velocity, and veracity; characteristics used to describe big data.

Organizational Context: Characteristics of an organization that can facilitate or constrain adoption and implementation of an innovation.

Organizational Readiness: Term used to refer to organizational resources—technological, financial, and IT human resources/personnel—necessary for big data adoption.

Organizational Size: Refers to the number of employees in an organization.

Relative Advantage: Term used to describe whether an innovation provides an advantage to an organization over an existing technology.

Technology Organization Environment (TOE) Framework: Framework developed by Tornatzy and Fleischer (1990) to explain the process of innovation from the perspective of three organizational contexts: technological, organizational, and environmental.

Top Management Support: The extent to which top management perceives the importance of innovation and is involved in related activities.

Vendor Support: Support necessary for big data adoption – specifically for data availability, reliability, and completeness.

This research was previously published in Optimizing Data and New Methods for Efficient Knowledge Discovery and Information Resources Management; pages 138-171, copyright year 2020 by Information Science Reference (an imprint of IGI Global).

Chapter 90
Exploring Big Data Analytic Approaches to Cancer Blog Text Analysis

Viju Raghupathi

Koppelman School of Business, Brooklyn College of the City University of New York, Brooklyn, USA

Yilu Zhou

Gabelli School of Business, Fordham University, New York, USA

Wullianallur Raghupathi

Gabelli School of Business, Fordham University, New York, USA

ABSTRACT

In this article, the authors explore the potential of a big data analytics approach to unstructured text analytics of cancer blogs. The application is developed using Cloudera platform's Hadoop MapReduce framework. It uses several text analytics algorithms, including word count, word association, clustering, and classification, to identify and analyze the patterns and keywords in cancer blog postings. This article establishes an exploratory approach to involving big data analytics methods in developing text analytics applications for the analysis of cancer blogs. Additional insights are extracted through various means, including the development of categories or keywords contained in the blogs, the development of a taxonomy, and the examination of relationships among the categories. The application has the potential for generalizability and implementation with health content in other blogs and social media. It can provide insight and decision support for cancer management and facilitate efficient and relevant searches for information related to cancer.

DOI: 10.4018/978-1-6684-3662-2.ch090

1. INTRODUCTION

In recent years researchers have begun to realize the value of social media as a source for data that helps us understand health-related phenomena (Chen et al., 2015; Greaves et al., 2013). Numerous past and ongoing studies as well as applications, have applied a range of techniques (including statistical, machine learning, and visualization) to structured and unstructured social media health data to perform sentiment analysis, elicit patterns, and provide decision support. The social media content includes that found in tweets, blogs, web search logs, among others (Katsuki et al., 2015; Mazzocut et al., 2016; Surian et al., 2016). The healthcare domain has seen a tremendous increase in the use of Web 2.0 tools and social media such as blogs, wikis, podcasts, twitter feeds, vlogs (video blogs) and on-line journals that convey health-related information. These and other content-driven applications enable physicians, patients, hospitals, insurance companies, government, and others—key participants in the health care system—to create and disseminate health information via the web (Agarwal et al., 2016; Chan et al., 2013; Chen et al., 2015; Yom-Tov et al., 2014). Patients, for example, need only put health-related terms into Google Search to find useful information related to diagnosis, treatment, and the management of diseases. This development suggests the enormous potential of online media to inform and improve personalized medicine and population health management. Physicians, too, use such tools to conduct research in the context of evidence-based medicine and to address patients' concerns and issues (Miller & Pole, 2010). Hospitals and other providers use these tools as "gateways" to the communities (Hardy, 2012; Kotenko, 2013; White, 2015). As large repositories of unstructured textual data emerge and grow, health entities are examining the potential of text analytics and other methods to evaluate the data and glean patterns and relationships. These patterns and relationships are, in turn, assessed to gain insights for making informed health decisions and improving clinical outcomes (Bian et al., 2012; Konkel, 2013). Spasic et al. (2014) discuss how so-called text mining bridges the gap between free-text and structured representation of cancer information. Text mining uses techniques from natural language processing (NLP), knowledge management, data mining, and machine learning (ML) to process large document collections. These techniques support information retrieval, (which gathers and filters relevant documents), as well as document classification, (which maps documents to appropriate categories based on their content), information extraction (which selects specific facts about pre-specified types of entities and relationships of interest), terminology extraction (which collects domain relevant terms from a corpus of domain-specific documents), named entity recognition (which identifies entities from predefined categories), etc., (Kim, 2009; Lin et al., 2011; Moen et al., 2016; Spasic et al., 2014; Wright et al., 2010; Zhu et al., 2013).

Health data, such as general patient profiles, clinical data, insurance data, and other medical data, are being created for various purposes, including regulatory compliance, public health policy analysis and research, and diagnosis and treatment (Mulins et al., 2006). Data may include both structured data (e.g. patient histories as records in a database) and unstructured data (e.g. audio/video clips, textual information such as in blogs or physician's notes) (Spangler & Kreulen, 2007). Text analytics is typically used to identify patterns and trends in the unstructured data (Popowich, 2005). These patterns can shed light on a wide range of issues such as drug reactions, side effects, treatment outcomes, personalized medical treatments, and efficacy of drugs. One famous example of analytics shedding light on a medical mystery was the discovery of an association between the arthritis drug Vioxx and an increased risk of heart attack/stroke, resulting in the withdrawal of the drug from the market (Rauber, 2004).

With regard to health social media analytics, several papers have examined the potential. Surian et al. (2016), for instance, analyzed 285,417 Twitter posts, also known as tweets, about HPV vaccines. They studied the tweets of some 101,519 users, whose total followers numbered some 4,387,524 individual accounts. The goal of the study was to evaluate the use of community structure and topic modeling methods (methods for discovering the abstract concepts that occur in a corpus of documents), as a process for characterizing the clustering of opinions about human papillomavirus (HPV) vaccines on Twitter. The authors tested Latent Dirichlet Allocation and Dirichlet Multinomial Mixture (DMM) models for inferring topics associated with tweets. This was followed by the application of community agglomeration (Louvain) and the encoding of random walk (Infomap) methods "to detect community structure of the users from their social connections (Surian et al., 2016)." They examined the alignment between community structure and topics using several common clustering alignment measures, and they introduced a statistical measure of alignment based on the concentration of specific topics within a smaller number of communities. They concluded that the use of community detection in concert with topic modeling appears to be a useful way to characterize Twitter communities for the purpose of opinion surveillance in public health applications. Their approach may help identify online communities at risk of being influenced by negative opinions about public health interventions such as HPV vaccines.

Jung et al. (2016) focused on identifying the quality of hospital service automatically using online communities. The authors defined social-media based quality factors for hospitals. In addition, they developed text-mining techniques to detect such factors as professionalism, process, environment, and impression that frequently occur in online health communities. Then, after identifying factors that represent qualitative aspects of hospitals, they applied a sentiment analyses to recognize types of recommendations in messages posted within online health communities. Lardon et al. (2015) examined the potential for post marketing safety surveillance from patient experiences with drugs reported in social media. Kendra et al. (2015) discuss how user content posted on Twitter is subject to bio surveillance: to characterize public perception of health-related topics and as a means of distributing information to the general public. Greaves et al. (2013) examined large amounts of unstructured, free-text information on blogs, social networks, and physician ratings websites that describe the quality of healthcare available. The authors used sentiment analysis techniques to categorize online free-text comments by patients as either positive or negative descriptions of the healthcare they received. From these free-text descriptions, the authors attempted to automate predictions as to whether a patient would recommend a hospital, whether the hospital was clean, and whether they were treated with dignity and to compare those automated predictions to the patient's own quantitative rating of their case (Greaves et al., 2013). The goal was to improve the overall quality of healthcare.

Chan et al. (2013) assessed and explained the online use of alcohol-related Chinese keywords and validated blog searching as an infoveillance method for surveying changes in drinking patterns in Hong Kong. Chen et al. (2015) examined the role of social media in bio surveillance applications. They mined, for instance, for influenza mentions as well as for information dissemination and public sentiment towards such topics as vaccination.

Health forums provide rich, detailed content of the patient experience vis-à-vis various health issues, including temporal and emotional factors that may help us tailor information to fit their needs. Meystre et al. (2008) outline how such extracted information can also be used for decision support and to enrich bio surveillance and biomedical research. Yom-Tov et al. (2014) developed algorithms that alert to possible outbreaks of communicable diseases using Internet data—specifically Twitter and search engine queries. Katsuki et al. (2015) conducted surveillance and analysis of Twitter data to characterize the frequency of non-medical use of prescription medications (NUPM) and identify illegal access to drugs via online pharmacies. Woo et al. (2016) discuss how the logs of queries submitted to search engines could be sources for the detection of emerging influenza epidemics particularly when changes in the volume of search queries are detected (infodemiology). They then describe a methodology for detecting influenza outbreaks using search query data (Woo et al., 2016).

Wang et al. (2015) provide an extensive discussion on how recent studies have demonstrated the utility of social media data sources to address a wide range of public health goals. These include epidemiological surveillance systems for influenza, allergies, tracking health behaviors (such as smoking and exercise), identifying mental health trends, as well as measuring health perceptions and sentiment. In yet another study, results from the authors' experiments suggest that it is possible to accurately predict future patient visits from geotagged mobile search logs (Agarwal et al., 2016). Paparrizos et al. (2016) performed a statistical analysis on the web queries of millions of anonymized searchers. Their specific goal was to mine signals from large-scale Web search logs of symptom queries for pancreatic adenocarcinoma. Their results highlight the promise of using Web search logs as an innovative direction for screening for pancreatic carcinoma. White & Horvitz (2014) analyzed data collected from online search logs to better understand the relationship between patterns in the seeking of online health information and healthcare utilization (HU). For instance, they looked at users' online search and access activities before and after queries that sought medical professionals and facilities. The results provided insight into how users decide whether and when to utilize healthcare resources and what effect health concerns and professional advice have on seeking healthcare facilities and service. The research extracted queries originating in the U.S. via the Bing search engine. Batches of pharmaceuticals are sometimes recalled from the market when a safety issue or a defect is detected in specific production runs of a drug. The study tested the hypothesis that defective production lots can be detected earlier by monitoring queries to Internet search engines. Findings suggested aggregated Internet search engine data can be used to facilitate early warnings of faulty medicines (Yom-Tov, 2017).

Health blogs in particular are rich with information for decision-making. While there are web crawlers and blog analysis software that generate statistics related to blogs (including, say, the number of blogs or Top Ten blogs in a certain category), these tools are relatively primitive and are not useful computationally to aid with the analysis and understanding of the social networks and medical blogs that are evolving around healthcare. Thus, there is a critical need for sophisticated tools to fill this gap. Furthermore, to our knowledge there are not many big data studies or applications in the text analytics of cancer blogs. This study attempts to fill this specific gap while analyzing cancer blogs.

Prior research has applied traditional machine learning techniques to this type of analysis. But considering the volume of data and the fact that it is growing exponentially and in a variety of data types, new and dynamic approaches are needed to analyze these substantial amounts of unstructured text data (Olson, 2010). In this exploratory research, we examine the potential of applying big data analytic techniques, including Hadoop MapReduce, to the analysis of blogs that exist in the cancer domain. Our objective is twofold: to extract from the blogs patterns and insight about cancer diagnosis, treatment, and management; and to apply advanced computation techniques in processing large amounts of unstructured health data. The big data platform Hadoop MapReduce has the potential to address the limitations of prior approaches by distributing the storage and processing of large amounts of data. Scalability, richness of algorithmic application, speed, and robustness are among the potential benefits (Olson, 2010; Raghupathi & Raghupathi, 2014).

The rest of this article is organized as follows: first, we provide background for the research by describing the domain of cancer blogs and by explaining the big data analytics Hadoop MapReduceand its methodology; second, we describe our research objectives and methodology in the text analytics of cancer blogs; third, we discuss our results; fourth, we address the scope and limitations of our study; and finally, we offer conclusions and suggestions for future research.

2. RESEARCH BACKGROUND

2.1. Blogs

Blogs (short for web logs) are web pages that often resemble personal diaries and contain entries or posts, typically in reverse chronological sequence (Kumar et al., 2004). (In other words, an author's most recent blog entry is the first one you read when you visit the site.) Blogs are powerful vehicles for sharing information and voicing opinions on a vast range of issues and causes, including but not at all limited to those that lean toward economics, politics, medicine, society, and the personal (Kaye, 2010), and cover the detail spectrum from complex and technical to trivial. Blogs see various levels of user participation. Some users participate passively by only reading content, while others are more active, posting comments or contributing text (Kaye, 2010) when blog administrators permit it.

As we have described, analyzing health blogs can lead to insights related to diseases and treatments (e.g. alternative medicine, therapy), as well as provide support links. For example, such analysis can reveal the most common issues patients have, the types of diseases that are most commonly discussed and why, the kinds of therapies and treatments discussed most often, and any medical or non-medical information provided. In addition, the information can reveal profiles of and patterns relating to the bloggers themselves—identifying, for instance, which bloggers offer relevant and accurate information and which major factors motivate the postings.

Analyzing the content in blogs (text analytics) requires efficient methods for indexing, codifying, and managing data. However, the analysis and interpretation of health-related blogs is challenging for a number of reasons. First, while blogs enable the formation of social networks of patients and providers, the prolificacy of the health/medical terminology comingled with the subjective vocabulary of the patient can be a challenge to interpret. Second, the blog world is characterized by an absence of rules on the format, method of posting, and structure of the content, which leads to variability in word choice, sentence structure, grammar, and punctuation. Meanwhile, embedded in this free-form text are bits and pieces of important information, which, if aggregated and summarized, could correlate to intelligent responses to integral medical questions (Mack et al., 2004; Spangler & Kreulen, 2007). Third, the content in health blogs incorporates two important psychological facets of the bloggers: their feelings and their mindset in terms of how they are managing their cancer. These meaningful aspects necessitate an element of sentiment analysis. Fourth, the absence of cues that would be present in face-to-face conversations compounds the challenge of interpretation. In a face-to-face exchange, two parties not only send and receive information, but they also interpret information based on body language, facial expressions, vocal cues, and an understanding of each other's circumstances. Fifth, a comment from a blogger cannot be viewed in isolation from its original post and preceding comment. Analyzing a post without considering the thread it relates to means ignoring contextual clues undermining the meaning of the post. Sixth, the amount of available blog content is rapidly expanding, necessitating the creation of more complex and sophisticated techniques for data preparation and analysis (Raghupathi & Raghupathi, 2014).

In the face of such challenges, researchers need a strong framework to analyze the content of health blogs thereby assisting in clinical decision-making and reducing the cost of overall healthcare delivery. Two high-level queries can arise from a text mining of healthcare blogs. How can we make sense of the aggregate healthcare content? And how can one perform a meta-analysis to interpret and generalize healthcare content in terms of patterns of diagnosis, treatment, management, and support? To address these key questions, we adopt a big data analytics approach to processing cancer blog unstructured data.

2.2. Big Data Analytics

By definition, big data in healthcare refers to electronic health data sets so large and complex that they are difficult, if not impossible, to manage with traditional software and/or hardware; nor can they be managed easily with traditional or common data management tools and methods (Raghupathi & Raghupathi, 2014). Big data in healthcare is overwhelming not only because of its volume but also because of the diversity of data types and the speed at which it must be managed (Frost & Sullivan, 2012; Raghupathi & Raghupathi, 2014). The totality of data related to patient healthcare and well-being make up "big data" in the healthcare industry. The scope includes clinical data from CPOE and clinical decision support systems (physician's written notes and prescriptions, medical imaging, laboratory, pharmacy, insurance, and other administrative data); patient data in electronic patient records (EPRs); machine-generated/sensor data, such as from monitoring vital signs; social media posts, including Twitter feeds (tweets) (Bian et al., 2012), blogs (Raghupathi & Raghupathi, 2013), status updates on Facebook and other platforms, and web pages; and less patient-specific information, including emergency care data, news feeds, and articles in medical journals.

For the big data scientist, there is, amongst this vast amount and array of data, opportunity. By discovering associations and understanding patterns and trends within the data, big data analytics has the potential to improve care, save lives and lower costs (Craven & Page, 2016; Dhar, 2014). Thus, big data analytics applications in healthcare take advantage of the explosion in data to extract insights for making better informed decisions (Craven & Page, 2016; Dhar, 2014; jStart, 2012; Knowledgent). As a research category, they are referred to as big data analytics in healthcare (Explorys; IBM, 2013; Intel, 2012; McDonald, 2017). When big data is synthesized and analyzed—and those aforementioned associations, patterns and trends revealed—healthcare providers and other stakeholders in the healthcare delivery system can develop more thorough and insightful diagnoses and treatments, resulting, one would expect, in higher quality care at lower costs and in better outcomes overall (Knowledgent). The potential for big data analytics in healthcare to lead to better outcomes exists across many scenarios, including: by analyzing patient characteristics and the cost and outcomes of care to identify the most clinically and cost effective treatments and offer analysis and tools, thereby influencing provider behavior; applying advanced analytics to patient profiles (e.g. segmentation and predictive modeling) to proactively identify individuals who would benefit from preventative care or lifestyle changes; broad scale disease profiling to identify predictive events and support prevention initiatives; collecting and publishing data on medical procedures, thus assisting patients in determining the care protocols or regimens that offer the best value; identifying, predicting, and minimizing fraud by implementing advanced analytic systems for fraud detection and checking the accuracy and consistency of claims; implementing claim authorizations expeditiously; and creating new revenue streams by aggregating and synthesizing patient clinical records and claims data sets to provide data and services to third parties (such as licensing data to assist pharmaceutical companies in identifying patient candidates for clinical trials). Many payers are developing and deploying mobile apps that help patients manage their care, locate providers, and improve their health. Via analytics, payers are able to monitor adherence to drug and treatment regimens and detect trends that lead to individual and population wellness benefits. (IBM, 2013; Knowledgent; Savage, 2012; Zenger, 2012).

2.3. Conceptual Framework

The conceptual framework for a big data analytics project in healthcare-related social media is similar to that of a traditional health informatics or analytics project. The key difference lies in how processing the data is executed. In an ordinary structured health analytics project with routine amounts of small data the analysis can be performed with a business intelligence tool installed on a stand-alone system, such as a desktop or laptop. Because big data is by definition unwieldy, processing is broken down and executed across multiple nodes. The concept of distributed processing has existed for decades. What is relatively new is its use in analyzing very large data sets as healthcare providers start to tap into their large data repositories to gain insight for making better-informed, health-related decisions. Interestingly, open source platforms such as Hadoop/MapReduce, available on the Cloud, have encouraged the application of big data analytics in healthcare.

While the algorithms and models are similar, the user interfaces of traditional analytics tools and those used for big data are entirely different; traditional health analytics tools have become user friendly and transparent. Big data analytics tools, on the other hand, are extremely complex, programming intensive, and require the application of a variety of skills. They have emerged in an ad hoc fashion mostly as

Figure 1. An applied conceptual architecture of big data analytics Source: Adapted from (Raghupathi & Raghupathi, 2014)

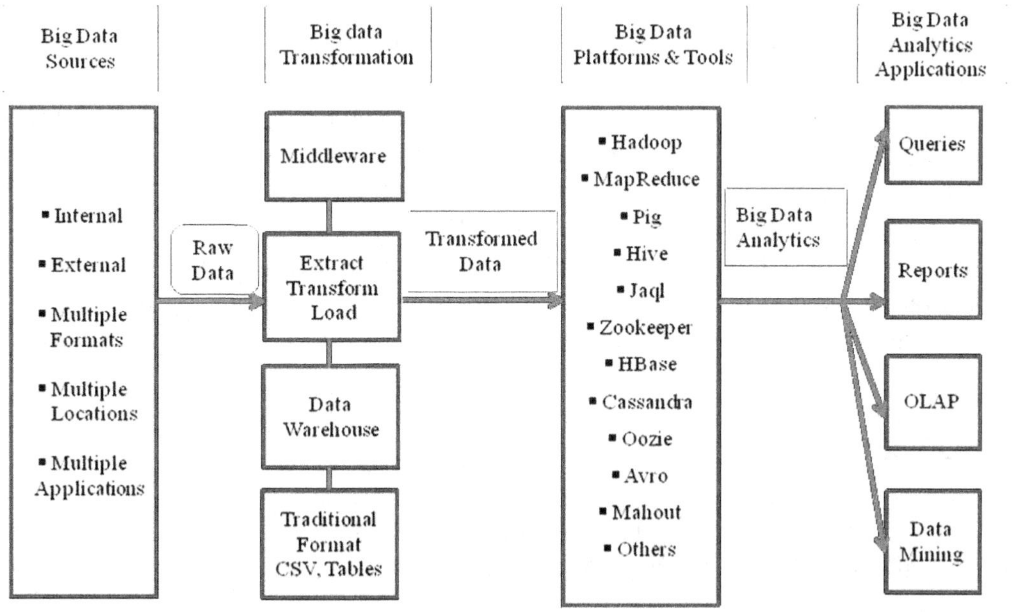

open-source development tools and platforms, and therefore they lack the support and user-friendliness that vendor-driven proprietary tools possess.

As Figure 1 indicates, the complexity begins with the data itself. Big data in healthcare can come from internal sources (e.g. electronic health records, clinical decision support systems, and CPOE, etc.) and external ones (government sources, laboratories, pharmacies, insurance companies & HMOs, etc.). It often appears in multiple formats (flat files, .csv, relational tables, ASCII/text, etc.), resides at multiple locations (geographic as well as in different healthcare providers' sites), and exists in numerous legacy and other applications (transaction processing applications, databases, etc.) (Raghupathi & Raghupathi, 2014). For the purpose of big data analytics, this data has to be pooled. In the second component, the data is in a 'raw' state and must be processed or transformed, at which point several options are available, including data warehouse and service-oriented architecture. The data stays raw, and services are used to call, retrieve, and process the data. Via the steps of extract, transform, and load (ETL), data from these diverse sources is cleansed and readied. Depending on whether the data is structured or unstructured, several data formats can be input to the big data analytics platform. In the next component of the conceptual framework, several decisions are made regarding the data input approach, distributed design, tool selection, and analytics models. The fourth component, on the far right, shows the four typical applications of big data analytics in healthcare. These include queries, reports, OLAP, and data mining. Visualization is an overarching theme across the four applications. Drawing from statistics, machine learning, and visualization, and other fields, a wide variety of techniques and technologies has been developed and adapted to aggregate, manipulate, analyze, and visualize big data in healthcare.

The most significant platform for big data analytics is the open-source distributed data processing platform Hadoop (Apache platform), which was initially developed for such routine functions as aggregating web search indexes. It belongs to the class "NoSQL" technologies—CouchDB and MongoDB are also in this class—that evolved to aggregate data in unique ways. Hadoop has the potential to process extremely large amounts of data mainly by allocating partitioned data sets to numerous servers (nodes), each of which solves different parts of the larger problem and then integrates them for the final result (Borkar et al., 2012; Ohlhorst, 2012; Zikopoulos et al., 2012; Zikopoulos et al., 2013). Hadoop can serve the dual roles of data organizer and analytics tool. It enables enterprises to harness data that, until now, has been difficult to manage and analyze. Specifically, Hadoop makes it possible to process extremely large volumes of data with various structures or no structure at all. (Wang & Krishnan (2014) also confirm that very large data sets with complex structures are difficult to process using traditional methods and tools.) The complex process includes capture, storage, formatting, extraction, curation, integration, analysis, and visualization. Therefore, more robust and scalable platform tools ae needed for managing big data. Cloudera (http://blog.cloudera.com/blog/2014/09/getting-started-with-big-data-architecture/) provides the scalable, flexible, and integrated platform that makes it easy to manage rapidly increasing volumes and varieties of data in the domain. The Cloudera platform can be deployed to manage Apache Hadoop and related projects, manipulate and analyze data, and keep that data secure and private.

3. METHODOLOGY

The objectives of our research project are: (1) to explore the efficacy of the use of Hadoop MapReduce as the framework for analyzing a set of cancer blog postings; (2) to apply a series of algorithms to gain insight into the content; and (3) to start developing a vocabulary and taxonomy of keywords (based on existing medical nomenclature) of cancer.

Some key questions can provide insight into diseases (cancer), treatments (e.g. alternative medicine, therapy), and support links. What are the most common issues patients have (bloggers/responses)? What cancer types (conditions) are most discussed and why? What therapies and treatments are being discussed? What medical and nonmedical information is provided? Which blogs and bloggers provide relevant and accurate information? What are the major motivations for the postings (comments)? Who posts—doctors, nurses, or patients? What are the emerging trends in disease (symptoms), treatment and therapy (e.g. alternative medicine), support systems, and information sources (links, clinical trials) (Raghupathi & Raghupathi, 2014)?

3.1. Data Collection

Data was collected from the website http://www.thecancerblog.com. Most of this data was unstructured, such as responses and comments. Figure 8 shows a sample posting. In order to use the text mining algorithm, we first created two input files: text.dat and dates.dat. Each line in the text.dat file stores the blog text (the blog entry and the comments posted to it), and each line in the dates.dat file stores the corresponding blog creation dates. Initially, all blogs were downloaded directly from the source website and stored in html files. Since the information required by the architecture is mixed with numerous advertisements, hyperlinks, and JavaScripts, extraction programs in Java were then used to extract the blog texts and creation dates. One important point to keep in mind is that because the content is collected from the web, it includes extraneous details. The application enabled semantic searches by the extraction and organization of concepts and relationships.

A co-occurrence matrix could be described as the tracking of an event and given a certain window of time or space, when events seem to occur. Here, "events" are the individual words found in the text, and they track other words that occur within a "window," a position relative to the target word.

3.2. Methods, Analysis and Results

Hadoop MapReduce is a software framework for writing applications that process—in a reliable, fault -tolerant way—vast amounts of data in parallel and on large clusters (# of nodes) of servers. A MapReduce job typically splits the input data set into independent chunks, which are processed by the "map tasks" in a completely parallel manner. The framework sorts the outputs of the maps. These are then input to the "reduce tasks." Typically, both the input and the output of the job are stored in a file-system. The framework takes care of scheduling tasks, monitoring them, and re-executing failed tasks. Usually, the compute nodes and the storage nodes are the same. That is, the MapReduce framework and the Hadoop Distributed File System are running on the same set of nodes. This configuration allows the framework to effectively schedule tasks on the nodes where data is already present, resulting in very high aggregate capacity across the cluster. The MapReduce framework consists of one master JobTracker and one slave TaskTracker per cluster-node. The master is responsible for scheduling the jobs' component tasks on the slaves, monitoring them and re-executing the failed tasks. The slaves execute the tasks as directed, by the master.

At a minimum, applications specify the input/output locations and supply map and reduce functions via implementations of appropriate interfaces and/or abstract classes. These and other job parameters comprise the job configuration. The Hadoop job client then submits the job (jar/executable, etc.) and configuration to the JobTracker, which then assumes the responsibility of distributing the software/ configuration to the slaves, scheduling tasks and monitoring them, and providing status and diagnostic information to the job client. The Cloudera Hadoop MapReduce platform was deployed for the entire project.

In order to extract the key topics discussed in cancer blogs, the 1606 reviews in the cancer blog data set were analyzed by applying the typical clustering algorithm. The purpose was to elicit word groupings, calculate word frequency, and identify word-pair associations. Standard data preparation was conducted first. Python NLTK library was used to eliminate punctuations, numbers, and standard stop words. In order to enhance the quality of the words in clustering, additional stop words such as "feel," "would," "take," and others were incorporated. The Snowball stemming algorithm was used to combine different words with similar meanings into a single word. For instance, "fishing" and "fishes" were stemmed into "fish." Next, with the 1606 text files with stemmed words as the input, K-means clustering, word count, and word co-occurrence algorithms in the Cloudera Hadoop MapReduce platform were applied. The blog post text files were converted into sequence files, and the TF-IDF index was then constructed. The Apache Mahout library was then utilized to perform clustering analysis and output the results from the HDFS to the local machine. Figure 2 shows the top ten keyword clusters, with thirty terms in each cluster. The 333 blog posts in Cluster 1 mention thirty terms, including "prostate cancer," "hormone," "drug" and "risk," indicating the posts were associated with medication and risk. This cluster could be labeled as "prostate cancer." Cluster 2, with 248 postings, is dominated by breast cancer terms, including "breast cancer survivor," "diagnose breast cancer," "pink," (international symbol of breast cancer awareness), and so on. Other clusters are labeled similarly. The third cluster relates to how patients feel generally ("feeling"). The fourth cluster (named "Treatment"), with 200 postings, encompasses treatment and surgery, with terms such as "transplant," "home," and "treatment." Cluster 10, with sixty postings, indicates the discussion is primarily about the Susan G. Komen organization. Therefore, we can label it as "Komen." Meanwhile, Cluster 5 pertains to "chemo" & related effects; Cluster 6 indicates "survivors"; Cluster 7 describes "therapy'; Cluster 8 appears to reflect "HPV"; and Cluster 9 focuses on 'side effect."

The input data for this experiment was the original cancer blog text file, which was uploaded to the HDFS file system. Here we run a word count job to learn how many times a particular word has been used. We approach this task by leveraging the power of Cloudera platform services and then assembling a Java program to count the words in the given data set. We used the Cloudera Hadoop platform to perform word count analysis using built-in Java source code provided by Cloudera. In this experiment, HDFS commands were used to navigate to a folder that contained three different java files: WordCount. java, SumReducer.java, and WordMapper.java. Another command was then used to compile the three Java files into a single JAR file. This JAR file was a MapReduce job, which performed a word count of the words used in all of the text files contained in the folder "Cancer-blog."

Map and reducing data can be based on a variety of criteria. A common example is the Java WordCount class. As the name suggests, WordCount maps (extracts) the words in the input and reduces (summarizes) the results with a count of the number of instances each word is used. WordCount reads text files and counts how often words occur. The input is text files, as is the output, and each line contains a word and the count of how often it occurs, separated by a tab. Each mapper takes a line as input and breaks it into words. It then generates a key/value of pair of the word and 1. Each reducer adds the counts for each word and emits a single key/value with the word and the sum. As an optimization, the reducer is also used as a combiner on the map outputs. This reduces the amount of data sent across the network

Figure 2. Keyword clusters

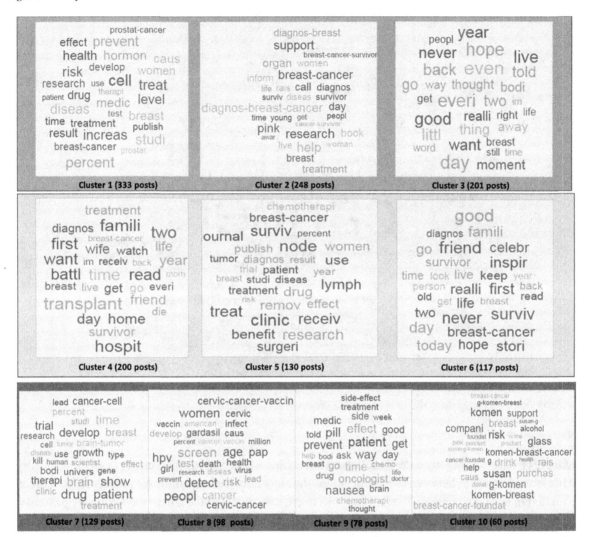

by combining each word into a single record. Figure 3 shows the result of the word count algorithm to cancer blogs. The larger the word, the higher it's frequency. As the word cloud indicates, the top issues are diagnosis and treatment of breast cancer.

This process required Hadoop to go about the usual steps of creating a sequence file and then TF-IDF vectors. TF-IDF stands for term frequency-inverse document frequency and reflects how important a word is to a document or corpus. The application of TF-IDF vectors helps to determine what words in a corpus of documents might be more favorable to use in a query. As the term implies, TF-IDF calculates values for each word in a document through an inverse proportion of the frequency of the word in a particular document to the percentage of documents the word appears in. Words with high TF-IDF numbers imply a strong relationship with the document they appear in, suggesting that if the word were to appear in a query, the document could be of interest to the user. This simple algorithm efficiently categorizes relevant words that can enhance query retrieval.

Figure 3. Word cloud

Once TF-IDF vectors were created, those vector files were used to find similar files for each file in the file store. Distances between the vectors helps the algorithm to determine how closely two documents are related in terms of content. The last step was to create a report of the final-row-similarity job and the distances between document-pairs give you fairly good understanding as to the distance of similarity between the two documents. Each key value in the final output represents an individual input text file. Figure 4 shows the similarity of different blog postings. For example, Key 0 shows the 948th posting is similar to the 433rd, 801th, and 1525th postings—all of which relate to cancer mitigation.

The next analysis applied the word co-occurrence algorithm. Co-occurrence is the frequent occurrence of two terms from a corpus, alongside each other in a certain order. In this context, co-occurrence can be viewed as an indicator of either semantic proximity or an idiomatic expression. In contrast to collocation, co-occurrence assumes interdependency of the two terms. One can use the co-occurrence of words as the primary way of quantifying semantic relations between words. Semantically similar words occur in similar contexts, i.e. they co-occur with the same other words.

For this algorithm, we used Cloudera Hadoop platform to perform word co-occurrence analysis using built-in Java source code provided by Cloudera. Source code for word co-occurrence was compiled to create a .JAR file, which would serve to provide the instructions for our data processing using Hadoop and MapReduce. Before we could produce an executable .JAR file, we needed to compile the source code, which included our mapper and reducer scripts. After compiling the source code, we converted the java file into an executable .JAR file, and uploaded that .JAR file to the Hadoop File System. We then ran

Figure 4. Row similarity

the MapReduce job, which read our unstructured text input file and made a list of all the paired words that were used within the input file. For each word in the input file, the list specified every word-pair, which included that word and listed how many times that word-pair appeared. The top 20 co-concurrent words are displayed in Figure 5. Our purpose here is to identify what combination of binary words adds insight to the analysis. We streamlined the number of co-occurring words because the overall output included more than 20 thousand word pairs. Therefore, via careful pruning combinations, we identified and eliminated such terms as 'one a day,' 'cancer and nation,' 'would and like.' We learned, for instance, that 'breast' and 'cancer' are paired at least 3409 times. This number indicates 'breast cancer' dominates blog discussions. 'Skin cancer' occurs 188 times, 'prostate cancer' occurs 408 times, and 'lung cancer' occurs 304 times.

Using the Cloudera platform with Hadoop and MapReduce, we then performed a classification analysis, employing a naïve-Bayes classification model on the clustered cancer blog data files. We wanted to discern whether there are blogs that belong in clusters other than the ones in which analytics placed them. The output of clustering process then serves as the input to the classification process. This process checks the accuracy of automated clustering analysis while identifying misplaced blog postings. We found some of the cancer blog postings were very closely related to each other, while others were entirely unrelated but had nevertheless been placed in the same cluster.

The purpose of classification analysis is to create and train a predictive model that can read the contents of each document and correctly sort documents into the appropriate cancer blog grouping or cancer blog cluster. With the uploaded clustered cancer blog data, we created a sequence file, a vector file, and a naïve-Bayes classifier. This classifier divided the data into two groups—training and testing—based on the specified proportions. Seventy percent of the data was assigned to the training portion, while 30% was assigned to the testing portion, resulting in a confusion matrix.

Figure 5. Word co-occurrence

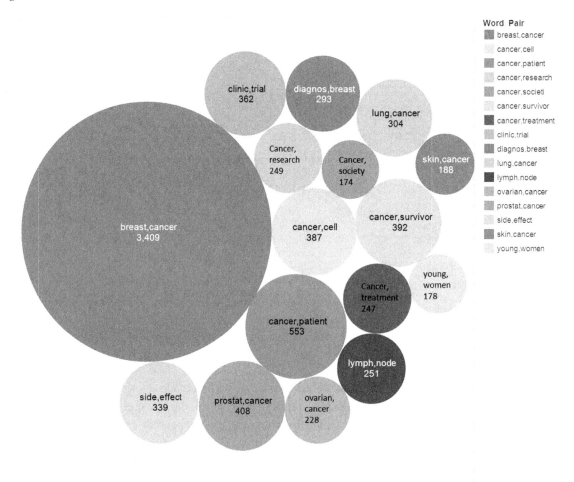

Word Pair and sum of Count. Color shows details about Word Pair. Size shows sum of Count. The marks are labeled by Word Pair and sum of Count.

As shown below in Figures 6 and 7, the model was able to accurately predict the correct cancer blog cluster for each document and produced the model with 99.82% accuracy. Our training portion contained a total of 1,102 documents, 1,100 of which were classified correctly. The high percentage accuracy of our model is very promising and indicates that this model could be used to classify new documents in the future. If documents are currently being classified and sorted manually, this model represents a potentially significant reduction in man-hours and, by extension, large cost reductions.

Figure 8 is a cross section of the blog content. Figure 9 displays the number of blog postings in the study.

Figure 6. Confusion matrix for classification analysis

	A	B	C	D	E	F	G	H	I	J	K	L	M	N	O
1	=========================														
2	Summary														
3	--------------------------------														
4	Correctly Classified Instances	99.82%													
5	Incorrectly Classified Instances	0.18%													
6	Total Classified Instances	:	1102												
7															
8	==														
9	Confusion Matrix														
10	------------------------------------														
11	a	b	c	d	e	f	g	h	i	j		<--Classified as			
12		217	0	0	0	0	0	1	0	0	0	218	a	= Patients-study-risk-prostate	
13		0	9	0	0	0	0	0	0	0	0	9	b	= breast-cancer-survivors	
14		0	0	57	0	0	0	0	0	0	0	57	c	= cervical-cancer-vaccine	
15		0	0	0	89	0	0	0	0	0	0	89	d	= her-his-she-transplant	
16		0	0	0	0	17	0	0	0	0	0	17	e	= her-she-I	
17		0	0	0	0	0	87	0	0	0	0	87	f	= i-my-me	
18		1	0	0	0	0	0	418	0	0	0	419	g	= i-my-you	
19		0	0	0	0	0	0	0	96	0	0	96	h	= patients-researchers-study	
20		0	0	0	0	0	0	0	0	105	0	105	i	= pink-breast-cancer	
21		0	0	0	0	0	0	0	0	0	5	5	j	= wine-redwine-alcohal	
22															
23															
24															
25															

Sheet1 Sheet2 Sheet3

Figure 7. Summary results of classification analysis

=========================

Summary

Correctly Classified Instances	99.82%
Incorrectly Classified Instances	0.18%
Total Classified Instances	: 1102

==:

Confusion Matrix

Cross Sectional View of Input Data

In summary, we applied the big data analytics architecture of Hadoop MapReduce via the Cloudera platform to the analysis of cancer blog content. By applying a number of algorithms, we gained insight into the blog content. The study identifies, for instance, the most discussed topics as well as associations that relate to key phenomena.

Figure 8. Cross sectional view of cancer blog data

I love it when I find research coming straight from the halls of the very hospital where I received my breast cancer treatment. It reminds me that I'm in good hands, that University of Florida researchers are on the cusp of breaking through the mysteries of cancer, that I may one day be the lucky recipient of cutting-edge discoveries, like this.University of Florida researchers report in a paper to be published in the August issue of Stem Cells that bone marrow stem cells attracted to the site of cancerous growths often take on the appearance of the malignant cells surrounding them. While these cells look like cancer, though, they may not act like cancer. They have the same skin, says lead study author Dr. Chris Cogle. But the question is: do they have the same guts?"Our results indicate these cells act as developmental mimics, they come in and look like the surrounding neoplastic tissue, but they aren't actually the seed of cancer," said Cogle who is affiliated with the cancer center I've called home for more than two years."At the worst, these cells could help support cancerous tissue by providing it with growth factors or proteins that help the cancer grow and survive. At the very least, these marrow cells are just being tricked into coming into the cancerous environment and then made to walk and talk like they don't usually do."This phenomenon has been termed developmental mimicry and it could have implications for the integrity of the cell lines scientists use to test new cancer drugs.Up to five percent of cancerous tissue contains marrow-derived cells that look just like surrounding cancer. So when malignant tissue is grown in experiments that test the effects of new drugs, it's possible the results are inaccurate. As a result, drugs may be targeting the marrow cell mimics, not actual cancer cells.Researchers are collaborating with scientists at other institutions as they strive to further understand this issue. Comments. "At the worst, these cells could help support cancerous tissue by providing it with growth factors

854 or proteins that help the cancer grow and survive. At the very least, these marrow cells are just being tricked into coming into the cancerous environment and then made to walk and talk like they don't usually do."This I wrote recently about the hidden amounts of sugar found in the foods we love so dearly. I learned all about this topic during my visit to Tucson's Canyon Ranch -- a world renowned health and healing destination -- and this sweet lesson came right as I'd decided to rid my diet of as much sugar as possible. Learning that one can of soda houses 12 teaspoons of sugar and a typical container of fruit yogurt has eight sealed the refined sugar deal for me. No more, I say. It's just not worth it.Now here comes the lowdown on fat. Some say the fat we eat is the fat we wear. Perhaps. But one thing is for sure -- fat kills. That's Fit blogger Rigel Gregg wrote a May 24 post all about it, documenting five ways wearing fat can kill us -- it strains our heart and raises our insulin, leading to increased risk of heart disease and diabetes, for example. Now I'm here to clue you in on the fat hiding in more of our favorite foods. Here goes.Let's start with chocolate chip cookies. No doubt they contain a lot of sugar. But how about fat? Well, 54 percent of the total calories come from fat. Ouch. Potato chips: 60 percent. One beef hot dog: 82 percent. Mayonnaise: 74 percent. A cheeseburger: 55 percent. Cheddar cheese: 74 percent. A chocolate bar: 99 percent.OK, I've got some new motivation now that I've put these numbers in writing. I'm officially on the hunt for low-fat foods. You should be too.Thanks Canyon Ranch for the worthy wisdom. Comments: Let's start with chocolate chip cookies. No doubt they contain a lot of sugar. But how about fat? Well, 54 percent of the total calories come from fat. Ouch.

855 Potato chips: 60 percent. One beef hot dog: 82 percent. Mayonnaise: 74 percent. A cheeseburger: 55 percent. Cheddar cheese: 74 percent. A chocolate bar: 99 percent.OK, I've got some new motivation now that I've put these Kelly Jo Dowd, mom of 14-year-old golf sensation Dakoda Dowd, died of breast cancer in her Palm Harbor, Fla. home Thursday night. She was 42.Dowd spent years battling the disease that had spread to her bones, liver, and brain. She also spent years waiting to see her young daughter play in an LPGA event. Her wish came true last spring."I'm prouder today than I was yesterday that my daughter has the courage and strength to play with these LPGA professionals," Dowd said after the Ginn Clubs & Resorts LPGA tournament. "And I feel great right now. I feel great. My dream came true out here." Dowd, former Hooters Calendar Cover Girl and the only woman to climb the restaurant's corporate ladder from waitress to general manager, chose to go public with her cancer story to convince women everywhere to be vigilant about self-exams and screening. Dowd had ignored a lump in her breast for several months before her eventual diagnosis."I did something pretty stupid," she said in a 2006. "And the only way that I can let myself feel better about it is if I know that people can learn from our situation." The Dowd family, involved with groups like MakingMemories.org, which grants wishes to people who have been diagnosed with terminal breast cancer, will honor their brave hero at a memorial service on Tuesday at Sylvan Abbey Funeral Home in Clearwater, Fla.Previous Cancer Blog posts about Kelly Jo Dowd are as follows.Hooters: $1 million in honor of calendar girl Kelly Jo DowdYoung teen plays in LPGA for dying momDakoda Dowd phenom golfer walks away due to cancer.Comments. "I'm prouder today than I was yesterday that my daughter has the courage and strength to play with these LPGA professionals," Dowd said after the <EM>Ginn Clubs & Resorts LPGA tournament. "And I feel great right now. I feel great. My dream came true out here." Dowd, former Hooters Calendar Cover Girl and the only woman to climb the restaurant's corporate ladder from waitress to general manager, chose to go public with her cancer story to convince women everywhere to be vigilant about self-exams and screening. Dowd had ignored a lump in her breast for several months before her eventual diagnosis."I did something pretty stupid," she said in a 2006. "And the only way that I can let myself feel better about it is if I know that people can learn from our situation." The Dowd family, involved with groups like <A href="http://makingmemories.org/">MakingMemories.org</A>, which grants wishes to people who have been diagnosed with terminal breast cancer, will honor their brave hero at a memorial service on Tuesday at Sylvan Abbey Funeral Home in Clearwater, Fla.Previous <EM>Cancer Blog posts about Kelly Jo Dowd are as follows.<A href="http://www.thecancerblog.com/2006/08/04/hooters-1-million-in-honor-of-calendar-girl-kelly-jo-dowd">Hooters: $1 million in honor of calendar girl Kelly Jo Dowd</A><A

856 href="http://www.thecancerblog.com/2006/05/01/young-teen-plays-in-lpga-for-dying-mom">Young teen plays in LPGA for dying mom</A><A href="http://www.thecancerblog.com/2006/03/01/dakoda-dowd-phenom-golfer-walks-Cancer Research UK is about to increase its wealth -- once a signed honeymoon photograph of the Prince and Princess of Wales is auctioned. The photograph reportedly came from an unnamed member of the Royal Household and had been purchased by a collector. Taken on the Royal Estate at Balmoral just days after the wedding of Charles and Diana, it's Diana's signature prominently displayed on the photograph -- it reads, Lots of Love, Diana.The

857 auction, organized by a businesswomen whose lost her mother-in-law to breast cancer, will take place on June 9 at a charity ball at the London Marriott Hotel, Grosvenor Square. It is expected to sell for £3,000. Comments: A new and official report shows cancer is the leading cause of death and disability in Australia.The Australian Institute of Health and Welfare reveals that cancer is taking more lives -- about 19 percent -- than cardiovascular disease, currently at 18 percent. Cancer is the now to blame for Australia's burden of disease, according to the report, and the disease doesn't appear to be slowing anytime soon.Burden of disease refers to not only mortality but also takes into account impact of illness and disability. Essentially, this means cancer takes away from healthy life years. The top five leading causes of non-fatal burden of disease in Australia are anxiety and depression, Type-2 diabetes, dementia, adult-onset hearing loss, and asthma. Of the 14 preventable health risks outlined in this same report, tobacco was responsible for the greatest burden. Comments. The top five leading causes of non-fatal burden of disease in Australia are anxiety and depression, Type-2 <A href="http://thediabetesblog.com/">diabetes</A>, dementia, adult-onset hearing loss, and asthma. Of the 14 preventable health risks outlined in this same report, tobacco was responsible for the greatest burden.1. Dear, I was wondering if I could sick some help from you, or at least some suggestions. I would like to supply people with cancer. I am a professional wig maker. I invested in a factory and I have supplied for the past 5 years people in Australia with full custom made wigs for adults and children to cover the part that need to be covered. they still have a normal life and it last for years if well looked after. Lace front wigs are made of real human hair, are light and very comfortable. Unfortunately lace front wigs not that well known yet in Australia.I am specializing in making lace front wigs. It is made by hand and is undetectable. Please see the attached pictures. The scalp can breathe as each hair is carefully hand knotted on a lace. My product has been very successful but selling them to retailers I have noticed they sell it for a very high

858 price. And not every body that would like it can afford it. This is why I would like to be put directly in touch with the person that needs my services. For my products to be accessible and not out of price.Please let me know how I it happened Saturday -- the third annual Yard Sale for the Cure. It took place in thousands of lawns all over Canada, and profits donated from the respective sales will benefit breast cancer charities. And it all started because of one breast cancer survivor's cluttered basement.Rachael Smith, diagnosed with breast cancer in April 2004 and in treatment for the nine months that followed, noticed before cancer that piles of stuff were gathering in the basement of the house she shared with her husband and two young daughters. A sale was in order, she realized, but then cancer arrived and a yard sale fell off her radar. And then she emerged from surgery, chemotherapy, and radiation and realized she had reason to give back to the community that helped her survive.And so Yard Sale for the Cure was born.Smith and a group of close friends worked tirelessly to make the first event a reality -- and a success. A year later, they did it again, and their success multiplied. There were 1,200 registered yard sales in 28 communities, and 100 percent of every dollar donated went directly to one of 10 recipient charities. More than $100,000 was raised, and the event generated $3,200,000 worth of media exposure. I can't wait to hear how this year's event went, once the dust settles and Smith and her volunteers begin to reflect on the fruits of their selfless

4. SCOPE AND LIMITATIONS

This study focuses on a single category of blogs relating to healthcare—cancer blogs. Obviously, a vast number of blogs exist. Indeed, there is a wide array of topics not covered in our analysis, and so the potential for generalizability is limited. Also, the study analyzes the blog content existing at a certain point in time. Given the rapid changes in content and the number of blogs, the health blogosphere will continue to evolve in ways that, naturally, will vary from this snapshot. Finally, the data we analyzed should be characterized as self-reported and subjective. Thus, it can (and should) be scrutinized in terms of accuracy and veracity. Indeed, the quality and validity of blog postings in general is questionable. A more extensive analysis can encompass more websites and a longitudinal study of the content.

Technology is a limitation, especially as it is advancing rapidly. Future research may utilize more sophisticated and advanced platforms and algorithms, such as SPARK, and convolutional neural networks. Also, a big data analytics platform for healthcare social media must support the key functions necessary for processing the data. The criteria for platform evaluation may include availability, continuity, ease of use, scalability, ability to manipulate at different levels of granularity, privacy and security enablement, and quality assurance (Bollier, 2010; IHTT, 2013; Ohlhorst, 2012). In addition, while most platforms currently available are open source, the typical advantages and limitations of open source platforms apply. To succeed, big data analytics in social media needs to be packaged so it is menu-driven, user-friendly, and transparent. Real-time big data analytics is a key requirement in healthcare. The lag between data collection and processing has to be addressed. The dynamic availability of numerous analytics algo-

Figure 9. Number of cancer blogs in study

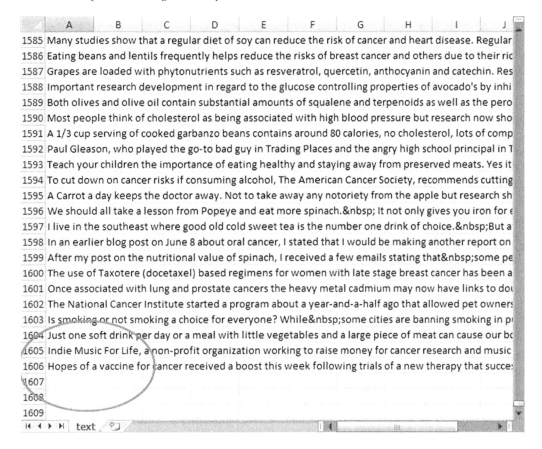

rithms, models and methods in a pull-down type of menu is also necessary for large-scale adoption. The important managerial issues of ownership, governance, and standards have to be considered. And woven through these issues are those of continuous data acquisition and data cleansing. Social media data is rarely standardized, often fragmented, or generated in legacy IT systems with incompatible formats (IHTT, 2013). This great challenge must also be addressed.

5. CONCLUSION

Big data analytics has the potential to transform the way practitioners and researchers gain insight from health social media, especially those in free text, unstructured form. Considering the volume and variety of social media data, and the need for scalability and large-scale processing in real-time, we should in the future see rapid, widespread implementation and use of big data analytics across the healthcare social media content. To that end, the several challenges highlighted above must be addressed. As big data analytics becomes more mainstream, issues such as guaranteeing privacy, safeguarding security, establishing standards and governance, and continually improving the tools and technologies will garner attention. Big data analytics and applications in such healthcare-related social media as blogs are at an early stage, but rapid acceleration is possible with the advancements in models, tools, and technologies.

REFERENCES

Agarwal, V., Zhang, L., Zhu, J., Fang, S., Cheng, T., Hong, C., & Shah, N. H. (2016). Impact of predicting health care utilization via web search behavior: a data-driven analysis. *Journal of medical Internet research*, *18*(9), 1-13.

Bian, J., Topaloglu, U., & F. Yu. (2012). Towards Large-scale Twitter Mining for Drug-related Adverse Events. In *SHB'12*, Maui, Hawaii, October 29.

Zhu, F., Patumcharoenpol, P., Zhang, C., Yang, Y., Chan, J., Meechai, A., ... & Shen, B. (2013). Biomedical text mining and its application in cancer research. *Journal of Biomedical Informatics*, *46*, 200–211. doi:10.1016/j.jbi.2012.10.007 PMID:23159498

Bollier, D. (2010). *The Promise and Peril of Big Data*. The Aspen Institute.

Borkar, V. R., Carey, M. J., & Li, C. (2012). Big Data Platforms: What's next? *XRDS*, *19*(1), 44–49. doi:10.1145/2331042.2331057

Chan, K. L., Ho, S. Y., & Lam, T. H. (2013). Infodemiology of alcohol use in Hong Kong mentioned on blogs: Infoveillance study. *Journal of Medical Internet Research*, *15*(9), 1–17. doi:10.2196/jmir.2180 PMID:23999327

Chen, A. T., Zhu, S.-H., & Conway, M. (2015). What online communities can tell us about electronic cigarettes and hookah use: A study using text mining and visualization techniques? *Journal of Medical Internet Research*, *17*(9), 1–13. doi:10.2196/jmir.4517 PMID:26420469

Craven, M., & Page, C. D. (2016). Big data in healthcare: Opportunities and challenges. *Big Data*, *3*(4), 209–210. doi:10.1089/big.2015.29001.mcr PMID:27441403

Dhar, V. (2014). Big data and predictive analytics in health care. *Big Data*, *2*(3), 113-116.

Explorys. (n.d.). Unlocking the Power of Big Data to Improve Healthcare for Everyone. Retrieved from https://www.explorys.com/docs/data-sheets/explorys-overview.pdf

Frost & Sullivan. (2012). Drowning in Big Data? Reducing Information Technology Complexities and Costs for Healthcare Organizations. Retrieved from http://www.emc.com/collateral/analyst-reports/frost-sullivan-reducing-information-technology-complexities-ar.pdf

Greaves, F., Ramirez-Cano, D., Millett, C., Darzi, A., & Donaldson, L. (2013). Use of sentiment analysis for capturing patient experience from free-text comments posted online. *Journal of Medical Internet Research*, *15*(11), 1–9. doi:10.2196/jmir.2721 PMID:24184993

Hardy, Q. (2012, July 25). McKinsey says social media could add $1.3 trillion to the economy. The New York Times. Retrieved from https://bits.blogs.nytimes.com/2012/07/25/mckinsey-says-social-media-adds-1-3-trillion-to-the-economy

IBM. (2013). Data Driven Healthcare Organizations Use Big Data Analytics for Big Gains. Retrieved from http://www.ibmbigdatahub.com/whitepaper/data-driven-healthcare-organizations-use-big-data-analytics-big-gains

IBM. (2012). How Big Data Analytics Reduced Medicaid Re-admissions. A jStart Case Study. Retrieved from http://www-01.ibm.com/software/ebusiness/jstart/portfolio/uncMedicaidCaseStudy.pdf

Intel. (2012). Leveraging Big Data and Analytics in Healthcare and Life Sciences: Enabling Personalized Medicine for High-Quality Care, Better Outcomes. Retrieved from http://www.intel.com/content/dam/www/public/us/en/documents/white-papers/healthcare-leveraging-big-data-paper.pdf

Jung, Y., Hur, C., Jung, D., & Kim, M. (2015). Identifying key hospital service quality factors in on-line health communities. *Journal of Medical Internet Research*, *17*(4), 1–15. doi:10.2196/jmir.3646 PMID:25855612

Katsuki, T., Mackey, T. K., & Cuomo, R. (2015). Establishing a link between prescription drug abuse and illicit online pharmacies: Analysis of Twitter data. *Journal of Medical Internet Research*, *17*(12), 1–12. doi:10.2196/jmir.5144 PMID:26677966

Kaye, B. K. (2010). Going to the blogs: Toward the development of a uses and measurement scale for blogs. *Atlantic Journal of Communication*, *18*(4), 194–210. doi:10.1080/15456870.2010.505904

Kendra, R. L., Karki, S., Eickholt, J. L., & Gandy, L. (2015). Characterizing the discussion of antibiotics in the Twittersphere: What is the bigger picture? *Journal of Medical Internet Research*, *17*(6), 1–12. doi:10.2196/jmir.4220 PMID:26091775

Kim, S. (2009). Content analysis of cancer blog posts. *Journal of the Medical Library Association: JMLA*, *97*(4), 260–266. doi:10.3163/1536-5050.97.4.009 PMID:19851489

Knowledgent. (n.d.). Big Data and Healthcare Payers. Retrieved from https://knowledgent.com/white-paper/big-data-and-healthcare-payers/

Konkel, F. (2013, January 25). Predictive analytics allows Feds to track outbreaks in real time. FCW. Retrieved from https://fcw.com/articles/2013/01/25/flu-social-media.aspx

Kotenko, J. (2013, April 18). The doctor will see you now: how the Internet and social media are changing healthcare. *Digitaltrends*. Retrieved from http://www.digitaltrends.com/social-media/the-internet-and-healthcare

Kumar, R., Novak, J., Raghavan, P., & Tomkins, A. (2004, December). Structure and evolution of a blogspace. *Communications of the ACM*, *47*(12), 35–39. doi:10.1145/1035134.1035162

Kurashima, T., Tezuka, T., & Tanaka, K. (2005). Blog Map of Experiences: Extracting and geographically mapping visitor experiences from urban blogs. In *Proceedings of the 6th International Conference on Web Information Systems Engineering (WISE)*. 10.1007/11581062_40

Lardon, J., Abdellaoui, R., Bellet, F., Asfari, H., Souvignet, J., Texier, N., ... Bousquet, C. (2015). Adverse drug reaction identification and extraction in social media: A scoping review. *Journal of Medical Internet Research*, *17*(7), 1–16. doi:10.2196/jmir.4304 PMID:26163365

Lin, F. P. Y., Anthony, S., Polasek, T. M., Tsafnat, G., & Doogue, M. P. (2011). BICEPP: An example-based statistical text mining method for predicting the binary characteristics of drugs. *BMC Bioinformatics*, *12*(1), 1–13. doi:10.1186/1471-2105-12-112 PMID:21510898

Mack, R., Cooper, J., Mukherjee, S., Inokuchi, A., Soffer, A., Iyer, B., ... Subramaniam, L. V. (2010). Text Analytics for life sciences using the Unstructured Information Management Architecture. *IBM Systems Journal*, *43*(3), 490–515. doi:10.1147j.433.0490

Mazzocut, M., Truccolo, I., Antonini, M., Rinaldi, F., Omero, P., Ferrarin, E., ... Tasso, C. (2016). Web conversations about complementary and alternative medicines and cancer: Content and sentiment analysis. *Journal of Medical Internet Research*, *18*(6), 1–16. doi:10.2196/jmir.5521 PMID:27311444

McDonald, C. (2017, April 7). "Transforming healthcare through big data. Retrieved from https://www.healthitoutcomes.com/doc/transforming-healthcare-through-big-data-0001

Meystre, S. M., Savova, G. K., Kipper-Schuler, K. C., & Hurdle, J. F. (2008). Extracting information from textual documentations in the electronic health record: a review of recent research. In *IMIA Yearbook of Medical Informatics* (pp. 128–144).

Miller, E. A., & Pole, A. (2010). Diagnosis Blog: Checking up on health blogs in the blogosphere. *American Journal of Public Health*, *100*(8), 1514–1519. doi:10.2105/AJPH.2009.175125 PMID:20558802

Mullins, I. M., Siadaty, M. S., Lyman, J., Scully, K., Garrett, C. T., Miller, W. G., ... Knaus, W. A. (2006). Data mining and clinical data repositories: Insights from a 667,000 patient data set. *Computers in Biology and Medicine*, *36*(12), 1351–1377. doi:10.1016/j.compbiomed.2005.08.003 PMID:16375883

Ohlhorst, F. (2012). *Big Data Analytics: Turning Big Data into Big Money*. John Wiley & Sons. doi:10.1002/9781119205005

Olson, M. (2010). HADOOP: Scalable, flexible, data storage and analysis. *IQT Quarterly*, *1*(3), 14–18.

Papparizos, J., White, R. W., & Horvitz, E. (2016). Screening for pancreatic adenocarcinoma using signals from web search logs: Feasibility study and results. *Journal of Oncology Practice / American Society of Clinical Oncology*, *12*(8), 737–744. doi:10.1200/JOP.2015.010504 PMID:27271506

Popowich, F. (2005). Using text mining and natural language processing for health care claims processing. *SIGKDD Explorations*, *7*(1), 59–66. doi:10.1145/1089815.1089824

Raghupathi, W., & Raghupathi, V. (2013). An Overview of Health Analytics. *Journal of Medical & Health Informatics*, *4*(3).

Raghupathi, W., & Raghupathi, V. (2014). Big data analytics in healthcare: Promise and potential. *Health Information Science and Systems*, *2*(3), 1–10. PMID:25825667

Rauber, C. (2004, October 31). Raising Kaiser's role. Retrieved from https://www.bizjournals.com/sanfrancisco/stories/2004/11/01/story6.html

Savage, N. (2012, October). Digging for Drug Facts. *Communications of the ACM*, *55*(10), 11–13. doi:10.1145/2347736.2347741

Spangler, S., & Kreulen, J. (2007). *Mining the Talk: Unlocking the business value in unstructured information*. IBM Press.

Spasic, I., Livesey, J., Keane, J. A., & Nenadic, G. (2014). Text mining of cancer-related information: Review of current status and future directions. *International Journal of Medical Informatics*, *83*(9), 605–623. doi:10.1016/j.ijmedinf.2014.06.009 PMID:25008281

Surian, D., Nguyen, D. Q., Kennedy, G., Johnson, M., Coiera, E., & Dunn, A. G. (2016). Characterizing Twitter discussions about HPV vaccines using topic modeling and community detection. *Journal of Medical Internet Research*, *18*(8), 1–12. doi:10.2196/jmir.6045 PMID:27573910

Wang, S., Paul, M. J., & Dredze, M. (2015). Social media as a sensor of air quality and public response in China. *Journal of Medical Internet Research*, *17*(3), 1–10. doi:10.2196/jmir.3875 PMID:25831020

Wang, W., & Krishnan, E. (2014). Big data and clinicians: A review on the state of the science. *JMIR Medical Informatics*, *2*(1), 1–11. doi:10.2196/medinform.2913 PMID:25600256

White, J. (2015, October 9). Why hospitals need social media, online presence. Retrieved from http://www.healthcarebusinesstech.com/hospitals-social-media/

White, R. W., & Horvitz, E. (2014). From health search to health care: Explorations of intention and utilization via query logs and user surveys. *Journal of the American Medical Informatics Association*, *21*(1), 49–55. doi:10.1136/amiajnl-2012-001473 PMID:23666794

Woo, H., Cho, Y., Shim, E., Lee, J.-K., Lee, C.-G., & Kim, S. H. (2016). Estimating influenza outbreaks using both search engine query data and social media data in South Korea. *Journal of Medical Internet Research*, *18*(7), 1–11. doi:10.2196/jmir.4955 PMID:27377323

Wright, A., Chen, E. S., & F. L. Maloney. (2010). An automated technique for identifying associations between medications, laboratory results and problems. *Journal of Biomedical Informatics*, *43*, 891.901.

Yom-Tov. E. (2017). Predicting drug recalls from Internet search engine queries. *IEEE Journal of Translational Engineering in Health and Medicine*, *5*.

Yom-Tov, E., Borsa, D., Cox, I. J., & McKendry, R. A. (2014). Detecting disease outbreaks in mass gatherings using Internet data. *Journal of Medical Internet Research*, *16*(6), 1–10. doi:10.2196/jmir.3156 PMID:24943128

Zenger, B. (2012, February). Can Big Data Solve Healthcare's Big Problems? *EquityHealthcare*. Retrieved from https://www.equityhealthcare.com/docs/librariesprovider2/news-item-documents/eh-blog-on-analytics.pdf

Zikopoulos, P. C., deRoos, D., Parasuraman, K., Deutsch, T., Corrigan, D., & Giles, J. (2013). *Harness the Power of Big Data – The IBM Big Data Platform*. McGraw-Hill.

Zikopoulos, P. C., Eaton, C., deRoos, D., Deutsch, T., & Lapis, G. (2012). *Understanding Big Data – Analytics for Enterprise Class Hadoop and Streaming Data*. McGraw-Hill.

This research was previously published in the International Journal of Healthcare Information Systems and Informatics (IJHISI), 14(4); pages 1-20, copyright year 2019 by IGI Publishing (an imprint of IGI Global).

Section 7
Critical Issues and Challenges

Chapter 91
A Survey on Comparison of Performance Analysis on a Cloud–Based Big Data Framework

Krishan Tuli
Chandigarh University, India

Amanpreet Kaur
Chandigarh University, India

Meenakshi Sharma
Galgotias University, India

ABSTRACT

Cloud computing is offering various IT services to many users in the work on the basis of pay-as-you-use model. As the data is increasing day by day, there is a huge requirement for cloud applications that manage such a huge amount of data. Basically, a best solution for analyzing such amounts of data and handles a large dataset. Various companies are providing such framesets for particular applications. A cloud framework is the accruement of different components which is similar to the development tools, various middleware for particular applications and various other database management services that are needed for cloud computing deployment, development and managing the various applications of the cloud. This results in an effective model for scaling such a huge amount of data in dynamically allocated recourses along with solving their complex problems. This article is about the survey on the performance of the big data framework based on a cloud from various endeavors which assists ventures to pick a suitable framework for their work and get a desired outcome.

DOI: 10.4018/978-1-6684-3662-2.ch091

1. INTRODUCTION

1.1 Getting Together with Cloud and Data Analytics: Flawless Alliance

As we all know that, cloud is working & delivering their services on Pay as per use, on demanded and provide scalable services. Data Analysis mainly focuses on the five v's of big data. They are the characteristics of big data.

- First one is the, volume, which means the total amount of data.
- Variety is called the unusual set-up of data or we can say is the different formats of data that can be used in Big Data or data analytics. For example, unstructured videos and pictures, unformatted numbers etcetera.
- Velocity is defined as the speed on which datasets is increasing.
- Furthermore, there is veracity on which the accuracy and trustworthiness of structured or unstructured data and information.
- Value is helpfulness of data.

Huge data over the network can be managed efficiently by Cloud Computing with the help of virtualization technique, consequently, adding the big data availability, accessibility & Scalability (Khan, Shakil, & Alam, 2017; Skourletopoulos, Mavromoustakis, Mastorakis, Batalla, Dobre, Panagiotakis, & Pallis, 2016). Furthermore, Distributed computing also brings high-class numerical trappings for ingenious dispensation and studies of large amount of data over a provision named as Huge Records as a Provision (Khan, Shakil, & Alam, 2017; Zhang, Zhou, Li, & Gao, 2017). Afterward, in cooperation with huge amount of data and cloud unite collected to carry an importance to initiatives by attractive the nimbleness, bounciness, convenience and the comfort of meting out of distributed created large information, and, by dropping its price of possession and application difficulty of large information resolutions (Khan, Shakil, & Alam, 2017). A cloud framework is the best solution for solving this problem & managing the data at sustainable cost. A cloud framework is the accruement of different components which is similar to the development tools, various middleware for particular application & various other database management services that is needed for cloud computing deployment, development & managing the various applications of cloud which results in an effective model for scaling such a huge data at a dynamically allocated recourses along with solving their complex problems.

1.2 Enterprise Based Data Analytics – Distributed

The Social Networking sites and applications that are being used by many people and become their hobby to use such sites, for example: Tweeter, Snapchat, Instagram, WhatsApp Messenger, Facebook & a variety of other online venture application are the enterprise period that broad cast a wide-ranging of data (Exabyte& petabyte data) that is on day to day basis. Such a large amount of data which may be spawning during messages, satellite images, social networking sites, Electronic mail and many more can be structured and unstructured depending on their availability &accessibility and is known to be Big Data. (Skourletopoulos et al., 2017; Math, 2017; Pokorny & Stantic, 2016). As a result, various ventures are in front of a demanding job of tracking and managing such a huge sum of data.

In finding the solution of the problem, Big Data Analytics (BDA) came to its existence, where many big data implementation tools, highly secured techniques, various ways are attain by different organizations to get the correct form of Data which may be structured or unstructured data (Madaan, Sharma, Pahwa, Das, & Sharma, 2017). One among the best tools used by enterprises is Apache Hadoop for off-load key in warehouse data and dispensation purpose. Hadoop is expensive when being multipart through many warehouses from organizations & various business points of view. Various frame works are being implemented by many large enterprises. Analyzing& organizing such a large data sets with the help of BDA is supporting many big IT corporations in precede predictions and improved decision-making process, thus, heighten the growth of their and making them to accomplish the benefits in the various organizations (Dabbèchi, Nabli, & Bouzguenda, 2016). On the other hand, the increased fame and the massive recognition of BDA in the IT companies are getting higher in many issues and challenges (Skourletopoulos et al., 2017). In addition to it, we can say that many companies are opting Big Data Analytics on a cloud-based framework which is a best suite in advancement in technology. The cloud Computing got the problem solution with the cloud based big data analytics which help the user to get their problems solved at a reasonable package. Cloud based Big Data Analytics is a great combination of Hardware, Software & Platform at Pay as per you go basis.

Cloud Computing is very user friendly and anyone can access its services over the internet for speedy provisioning of services, endorse on requirement of accessing the universal cloud resource pool by managing the delivery of data (Skourletopoulos et al., 2017; Vora, Garala, & Raval, 2016; Zhu, 2010).

Figure 1. Architecture of Cloud based Big Data

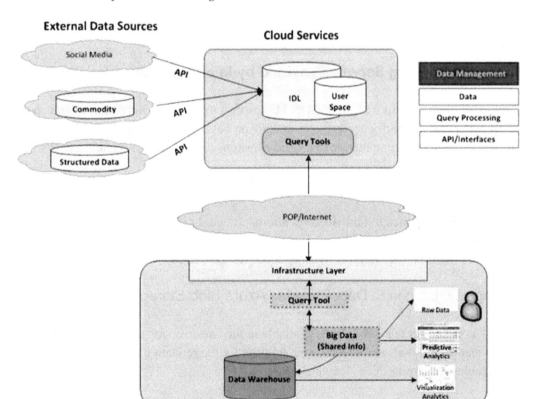

1.3 Large Organization are Offering a Better Solution: Support of Cloud with Data Analytics

As per overall a bridged price of ownership (Skourletopoulos et al., 2017) moreover the other formally discussed benefits of cloud based big data, may lead to many organizations that offer a framework of big data based on cloud framework.

This paper represents survey of comparison of solution frameworks for big data enterprise which is based on cloud & they are mainly focuses on the performance of the framework. Storage and Warehouse of big datasets which is managed by esteemed companies like IBM, Amazon Web Services that provides the platform based on cloud. This paper mainly focuses on the comparison between the various tools of data analytics based on the bases of cloud and shows the various usages of cloud & data analytics. The comparison of data analytics and cloud-based data analytics is done by merging & comparing the data with various large venture companies for example IBM, Microsoft, Google, and Amazon that provides various platforms.

This paper has 5 sections. Section 1& Section 2 shows the big data framework based on cloud which bring out by many companies which was mentioned earlier. In section 3, there is a tabular comparison. Coming to the next section i.e section 4 contains the Literature Review of the paper & in the last section i.e Section 4 is the future work &conclusion.

2. RELATED WORK TO BIG DATA TOOLS BASED ON CLOUD FRAMEWORK

This section has tools that are being used by various cloud-based platforms. They are warehouse, Analytics & Storage of big Data that are used by many esteemed companies.

2.1 A Cloud Computing Service Provided by Microsoft Azure for Storage

A cloud computing service which is provided by Microsoft Azure gives cloud features to much organization for their better working and better decision-making process. It also provides various internet integration tools for the scaling the computation to its grid (Preston, 2016; Nelson, Mccauley, & Wrona, 2006).

2.1.1 Data Analytics Solution is Provided by Azure HDInsight

Azure HDInsight is an application provided by Microsoft and it offered a great accuracy in SLA property particularly a single instance of virtual machine. Many different companies provide SLA on critical Virtual machines (Nelson, Mccauley, & Wrona, 2006; Reagan, 2018).

2.1.2 Storage Solution in Bi Data Provided Azure Blob Storage

Data integrity is the newer feature which is available in the latest version of Azure Blob Storage. It is a very flexible feature and it also provided better solution for the reduction in the bandwidth of network (Nelson, Mccauley, & Wrona, 2006; Reagan, 2018).

2.1.3. Data Warehouse Solution Provided by Azure SQL Data Warehouse

For providing the better big data warehouse solution, Microsoft Azure is the best solution for it. Microsoft Azure is a framework that is particularly used for the parallel processing in association with SQL & also scales the data computing independently (Nelson, Mccauley, & Wrona, 2006; Reagan, 2018).

2.2 A Cloud Computing-Based Service Provided by Amazon Web Services for Data Analytics

Big Data Analysis framework delivers by Amazon Web Services which helps in structuring and deploying Big Data applications in a simple, easy to implement & manage and quick way.

2.2.1 Data Analytics Framework Provided by Amazon ElasticSearch

Amazon ElasticSearch is mainly focused for the big data analytics framework which is used to create clusters and made for the deployment of the data. It also works on the scalability of the data sets (Kumar, Kumar, Divakar, & Gokul, 2017).

2.2.2 A Big Data Storage Framework Provided by Amazon S3

To provide the big data storage and to remove this major problem Amazon S3 was launched. It provides the highly protected and scalable storage pool having a large variety of tools (Dargahi, Dehghantanha, & Conti, 2017; Krishnan & Gonzalez, 2015a).

2.2.3 A Warehouse Framework Designed by Amazon Redshift

Big data Warehouse framework is designed by Amazon Redshift & it's a very effective, well managed &well-known Amazon web services warehouse platform which is provided by Amazon. It is very cost-effective tools which analyses the data sets based on SQL & various other intelligent tools particularly designed for business use (Krishnan & Gonzalez, 2015a).

2.3 A Cloud Computing Service Provided by Google Cloud

GCP bringsa collection of a number of dominant tools for various purposes which in range from data analytics to warehouse then to database and lastly to storage (Krishnan & Gonzalez, 2015b).

2.3.1 A Storage Framework Provided by Google Cloud Storage for Big Data

Google cloud storage is intended especially for object storage which is carried out to perform many tasks & helps the developer, researcher or entrepreneur to perform many tasks ranging from realtime data processing to data analytics for developer & entrepreneur (Krishnan & Gonzalez, 2015b; Yuhuan, 2017).

2.3.2 Data Analytics Warehousing Framework Provided by Google BigQuery

For big data analytics Google Big query provided the best solution which is extremely fast, scalable and very economical. It is helpful in many ways provided the warehousing for various organizations on pay as you use bases (Yuhuan, 2017).

2.4 A Cloud Computing Service Provided by IBM Cloud for Big Data Analytics

This is a very effective tool for many works & it broaden the horizon based on the various services of cloud and other big data services. It has various precise tools which is particularly for precise applications. It is used in many fields ranging from Big data to Networking, monitoring & so on (Serrano, Gallardo, & Hernantes, 2015).

2.4.1 Data AnalyticsFramework Provided by Analytics Engine (IBM Product)

Best solution provided by IBM for Big data analytics is the Analytical engine which provided a lot of benefits & a trouble free data analytics. It has resolved many existing analytical issues which were there in other exiting tools (Serrano, Gallardo, & Hernantes, 2015; Shovic, 2016).

2.4.2 Data Storage Framework Provided by IBM Cloud Object Storage

Data may be structure or unstructured. IBM provided a framework for storing, managing & fetching the contents of data from various sites to provide better solution of self-service portal. It has the better solution for the storing the data & managing the clusters depending on the requirement of the company. Data is fetched through REST which is based on the particular API's (Shovic, 2016; Kalyvas, 2014).

2.4.3 Data Warehouse Framework Which is Provided by IBM Db2 Warehouse

This is the best tools designed by IBM for Database & Data Warehouse. Compatibly of IBM DB2 warehouse best with Narezze and also with the Big Database giant that is Oracle. Mainly it is designed for the hybrid cloud & it gives the best solution which is not provided by various other companies (Shovic, 2016; Kalyvas, 2014).

3. RELATIONSHIP BETWEEN BIG DATA ENTERPRISE BASED ON CLOUD (TABLE 1)

Table 1. Comparison of Big Data Enterprise based on Cloud Framework

S. No	Features & Frame	Amazon Web Service	Microsoft Azure	IBM	Google Cloud Platform
1	**Analytics of Data**	Best tool of Amazon for data analytics is Amazon Elastic Search	A Cloud spark and Hadoop service for Enterprise Azure HDInsight	Combined Apache Spark and Apache Hadoop service IBM Analytics Engine	Build, test and deploy with ease is Google Cloud
	Software Mode	Free	Free	Free	Free
	Type of data	The type of data may be any	Only unstructured datasets	Only unstructured datasets	The type of data may be any
	Applications for Big Data analytics	Ongoing Application	Batch Processing	Solution for many enterprises	Batch processing
	Service Integration	Y	Y	Y	Y
	Deployment Unit	Manual	Manual	Manual	Manual
2	**Storage of Data**	object storage service - Amazon S3	Massively-scalable object storage for unstructured data-azure blob	NVMe Based All-Flash Array with Integrated Infrastructure Virtualization-IBM Cloud Object	Build, test & deploy-Google Cloud
	Type of Data Storage	Dispersed	Dispersed	Dispersed	Dispersed
	Scaling of Data Storage	Programmed	Manual	Manual	Programmed
	Object MetaData	Y	Y	Y	Y
	Deployment locality	Within the Region	Within the Zone	Through Multiple Region	Through Multiple Region
3	Warehouse of data	Cluster Management Guide - Amazon Redshift	Enterprise Data Warehouse - Azure SQL Data Warehouse	formerly IBM dashDB Local - IBM Warehouse	Querying massive datasets - Google BigQuery
	Unit deployment	This is fully clustered deployment	This is fully clustered deployment	This is fully clustered deployment	This is fully clustered deployment
	Compute scaling	Programmed	Manual	Programmed	Programmed
	Deployment locality	Within the region only	Within the region only	Within the region only	Within the region only
	Data formats	CSV, Avro, TSV, ORC	Parquet, ORC, RC	CSV	CSV, AVRO, JSON

4. LITERATURE REVIEW (TABLE 2)

Table 2. Literature Review

Author Name	Year of Publication	Title of paper	Objectives	DOI/Link
Suraj Pandey, Surya Nepal	Dec-18	"Cloud Computing and Scientific Applications — Big Data, Scalable Analytics, and Beyond"	Published paper to be reviewed in Cloud Computing Applications.	10.1016/j.future.2018.04.026
Domenico Talia	Nov-18	"Clouds for Scalable Big Data Analytics"	to get a particular use of cloud in scaling Big Data Analytics.	10.1109/MC.2018.162
Barnabas K. Tannahill, Mo Jamshidi	Jun-18	"System of Systems and Big Data Analytics – Bridging the Gap"	To construct a bridge Data Analytics & Systems.	https://doi.org/10.1018/j.compeleceng.2018.11.018
Iibrahim Abaker Targio Hashem, Ibrar Yaqoob	Feb-18	"Symbioses of Big Data and Cloud Computing: Opportunities & Challenges"	To get the opportunity in Big Data & highlight the main heading.	10.1016/j.is.2018.07.006
OhbyungKwon, Namyeon Lee, Bongsik Shin	Jun-17	"Data quality management, data usage experience and acquisition intention of big data analytics"	Model for Big Data Analytics & their various features.	https://doi.org/10.1017/j.ijinfomgt.2017.02.002
Sharath Chandra Guntuku, Abhishek Thakur	Jan-17	"Big Data Analytics Framework for Peer-to-Peer Botnet Detection Using Random Forests"	Open source tools development in real time detection system.	https://doi.org/10.1017/j.ins.2017.03.066
Srinivas Aluru, Yogesh Simmhan	Jun-16	"A Special Issue of Journal of Parallel and Distributed Computing: Scalable Systems for Big Data Management and Analytics"	To focus on special issues of management in Big data analytics.	10.1016/j.jpdc.2016.04.004
ShaunHipgrave	Dec-13	"Smarter fraud investigations with big data analytics"	Smarter fraud on big data, an investigation.	https://doi.org/10.1016/S1353-4858(13)70135-1
Linquan Zhang; Chuan Wu; Zongpeng Li; Chuanxiong Guo; Minghua Chen; Francis C.M. Lau	Dec-13	"Moving Big Data to the Cloud: An Online Cost-Minimizing Approach"	In this paper, author has proposed 2 algorithms for optimization of data, processing & routing of data.	10.1109/JSAC.2013.131211
Haluk Demirkan, Dursun Delen	Apr-13	"Leveraging the capabilities of service-oriented decision support systems: putting analytics and big data in cloud"	Framework of Decision Support System in cloud computing	https://doi.org/10.1016/j.dss.2012.05.048

5. CONCLUSION

The effort depending upon relative analysis and comparison between the three companies that are dealing in solutions of big data-based cloud. The Big Data is providing mainly the operative processes for various data sets, Collected Data Sets for huge and complex real time development which are mainly carried by of several tools in Big Data research. In other words, we can say that cloud framework is the excellent and best solution for any cloud platform at a sustainable cost. These framesets are used for particularly for managing & deploying the datasets of the users at pay as per use basis.

This survey includes the very deep understanding & knowledge of above mentioned enterprise solution frameworks, the services they provide and the main features, lastly their applications and various cases, with the plan, method of carrying it & relationship among them, in so doing benefiting the society, researchers, IT companies, entrepreneurs& future endeavors.

REFERENCES

Andrade, H., Gedik, B., & Turaga, D. (n.d.). Stream analytics: data pre-processing and transformation. In *Fundamentals of Stream Processing* (pp. 342–387). Academic Press; doi:10.1017/cbo9781139058940.012

Dabbèchi, H., Nabli, A., & Bouzguenda, L. (2016, September). Towards cloud-based data warehouse as a service for big data analytics. In Proceedings of the International Conference on Computational Collective Intelligence (pp. 180-189). Springer. doi:10.1007/978-3-319-45246-3_17

Dargahi, T., Dehghantanha, A., & Conti, M. (2017). Investigating Storage as a Service Cloud Platform: pCloud as a Case Study. In *Contemporary Digital Forensic Investigations of Cloud and Mobile Applications* (pp. 185–204). Syngress; doi:10.1016/b978-0-12-805303-4.00012-5

Darie, C., & Watson, K. (2009). *Beginning ASP. NET E-Commerce in C.* Springer; doi:10.1007/978-1-4302-1073-3_22

Dawelbeit, O., & Mccrindle, R. (2014). A novel cloud based elastic framework for big data preprocessing. In *Proceedings of the 2014 6th Computer Science and Electronic Engineering Conference (CEEC).* Academic Press. doi:10.1109/ceec.2014.6958549

Gonzales, J. U., & Krishnan, S. P. T. (2015). Building your next big thing with Google Cloud Platform. *Aprés, 27.* doi:10.1007/978-1-4842-1004-8

Gulabani, S. (2017). Practical Amazon EC2, SQS, Kinesis, and S3. doi:10.1007/978-1-4842-2841-8

Kalyvas, J. R., & Albertson, D. R. (2015). A big data primer for executives. In *Big data: a business and legal guide.* CRC Press; doi:10.1201/b17406-2

Karpurapu, B. S. H., & Jololian, L. (2017). A framework for social network sentiment analysis using big data analytics. In *Big Data and Visual Analytics* (pp. 203–217). Springer; doi:10.1007/978-3-319-63917-8_12

Khan, S., Shakil, K. A., & Alam, M. (2017). Cloud-Based Big Data Analytics—A Survey of Current Research and Future Directions. In *Advances in Intelligent Systems and Computing Big Data Analytics* (pp. 595–604). Academic Press. doi:10.1007/978-981-10-6620-7_57

Klein, S. (2017). *IoT Solutions in Microsoft's Azure IoT Suite.* Berkeley, CA: Apress; doi:10.1007/978-1-4842-2143-3

Krishnan, S. P. T., & Gonzalez, J. L. U. (2015). Google BigQuery. In *Building Your Next Big Thing with Google Cloud Platform* (pp. 235–253). Apress. doi:10.1007/978-1-4842-1004-8_10

Kumar, V. A., Kumar, V. A., Divakar, H., & Gokul, R. (2017). Cloud enabled media streaming using Amazon Web Services. In *Proceedings of the 2017 IEEE International Conference on Smart Technologies and Management for Computing, Communication, Controls, Energy and Materials (ICSTM).* IEEE Press. 10.1109/ICSTM.2017.8089150

Madaan, A., Sharma, V., Pahwa, P., Das, P., & Sharma, C. (2018). Hadoop: Solution to Unstructured Data Handling. In Big Data Analytics (pp. 47-54). Springer Singapore. doi:10.1007/978-981-10-6620-7_6

Math, R. (2017). Big Data Analytics: Recent and Emerging Application in Services Industry. In *Advances in Intelligent Systems and Computing Big Data Analytics* (pp. 211–219). Springer. doi:10.1007/978-981-10-6620-7_21

Nakhimovsky, A., Myers, T., & Nahkimovsky, A. (2004). Google, Amazon, and Beyond: Creating and Consuming Web Services (pp. 1-2). Apress. doi:10.1007/978-1-4302-0818-1

Nelson, W. A., Mccauley, E., & Wrona, F. J. (2006). Mechanisms for consumer diversity [Reply]. *Nature*, *439*(7072), E2. doi:10.1038/nature04527 PMID:16397458

Nirmala, M. B. (2014). A Survey of Big Data Analytics Systems. In Advances in Data Mining and Database Management Handbook of Research on Cloud Infrastructures for Big Data Analytics (pp. 392–418). Hershey, PA: IGI Global. doi:10.4018/978-1-4666-5864-6.ch016

Pokorny, J., & Stantic, B. (2016). Challenges and Opportunities in Big Data Processing. In Big Data: Concepts, Methodologies, Tools, and Applications (pp. 2074-2097). Hershey, PA: IGI Global. doi:10.4018/978-1-4666-9840-6.ch096

Pradhananga, Y., Karande, S., & Karande, C. (2016). High performance analytics of bigdata with dynamic and optimized hadoop cluster. In *Proceedings of the 2016 International Conference on Advanced Communication Control and Computing Technologies (ICACCCT)*. Academic Press. 10.1109/ICACCCT.2016.7831733

Preston, S. (2016). Microsoft Azure Terminology and Concepts. In *Using Chef with Microsoft Azure* (pp. 29–53). Apress; doi:10.1007/978-1-4842-1476-3_2

Ramesh, B. (2015). Big Data Architecture. In *Studies in Big Data Big Data* (pp. 29–59). Academic Press; doi:10.1007/978-81-322-2494-5_2

Reagan, R. (2018). *Web Applications on Azure*. Berkeley, CA: Apress; doi:10.1007/978-1-4842-2976-7

Serrano, N., Gallardo, G., & Hernantes, J. (2015). Infrastructure as a Service and Cloud Technologies. *IEEE Software*, *32*(2), 30–36. doi:10.1109/MS.2015.43

Shovic, J. C. (2016). Connecting an IOT Device to a Cloud Server-IOTPulse. In *Raspberry Pi IoT Projects* (pp. 147–186). Berkeley, CA: Apress; doi:10.1007/978-1-4842-1377-3_5

Skourletopoulos, G., Mavromoustakis, C. X., Mastorakis, G., Batalla, J. M., Dobre, C., Panagiotakis, S., & Pallis, E. (2016). Big Data and Cloud Computing: A Survey of the State-of-the-Art and Research Challenges. In *Studies in Big Data Advances in Mobile Cloud Computing and Big Data in the 5G Era* (pp. 23–41). Springer. doi:10.1007/978-3-319-45145-9_2

Vora, R., Garala, K., & Raval, P. (2016). An Era of Big Data on Cloud Computing Services as Utility: 360° of Review, Challenges and Unsolved Exploration Problems. In *Proceedings of First International Conference on Information and Communication Technology for Intelligent Systems* (*Vol. 2*, pp. 575–583). Academic Press. 10.1007/978-3-319-30927-9_57

Yuhuan, Q. (2017). Cloud Storage Technology. *Big Data and Cloud Innovation*, *1*(1). doi:10.18063/bdci.v1i1.508

Zhang, P., Zhou, X., Li, W., & Gao, J. (2017). A Survey on Quality Assurance Techniques for Big Data Applications. In *Proceedings of the 2017 IEEE Third International Conference on Big Data Computing Service and Applications (BigDataService)*. IEEE Press. 10.1109/BigDataService.2017.42

Zhu, J. (2010). Cloud Computing Technologies and Applications. In Handbook of Cloud Computing (pp. 21-45). Springer. doi:10.1007/978-1-4419-6524-0_2

This research was previously published in the International Journal of Distributed Artificial Intelligence (IJDAI), 11(2); pages 41-52, copyright year 2019 by IGI Publishing (an imprint of IGI Global).

Chapter 92

Fast Data vs. Big Data With IoT Streaming Analytics and the Future Applications

A. Jayanthiladevi
Jain University, India

Surendararavindhan
Vignan's University, India

Sakthivel
KSR College of Technology, India

ABSTRACT

Big data depicts information volume – petabytes to exabytes in organized, semi-organized, and unstructured information that can possibly be broken down for data. Fast data are facts streaming into applications and computing environments from hundreds of thousands to millions of endpoints. Fast data is totally different from big data. There is no question that we will continue generating large volumes of data, especially with the wide variety of handheld units and internet-connected devices expected to grow exponentially. Data streaming analytics is vital for disruptive applications. Streaming analytics permits the processing of terabytes of data in memory. This chapter explores fast data and big data with IoT streaming analytics.

INTRODUCTION

Data Is Fast Before It Is Big

Enterprises require an innovation stack that not exclusively is equipped for ingesting and examining fast streams of incoming data,, additionally can enhance live surges of fast data with systematic experiences gathered from big information stores – all as fast data enters the channel. Databases used to deal with

DOI: 10.4018/978-1-6684-3662-2.ch092

fast data and big data are for the most part assembled into two camps: online investigative preparing frameworks (OLAP), and online value-based handling frameworks (OLTP). How about we take a gander at the contrasts between these two ways to deal with data management.

IoT (Internet of Things) is an advanced automation and analytics system which exploits networking, sensing, big data, and artificial intelligence technology to deliver complete systems for a product or service. These systems allow greater transparency, control, and performance when applied to any industry or system.IoT systems have applications across industries through their unique flexibility and ability to be suitable in any environment. They enhance data collection, automation, operations, and much more through smart devices and powerful enabling technology (BhagyaRaju et al.,(2017).

IoT has become so vital in our daily life and it is going to create a big impact in the near future. For example, solutions can be provided instantly for the traffic flows, reminding about the vehicle maintenance, reduce energy consumption. Monitoring sensors will diagnose pending maintenance issues, and even prioritize maintenance crew schedules for repair equipment. Data analysis systems will help metropolitan and cosmopolitan cities to function easily in terms of traffic management, waste management, pollution control, law enforcement and other major functions efficiently. Considering it to the next level, linked devices can help the people personally like you get an alert from the refrigerator reminding you to shop some vegetables when the vegetable tray is empty, your home security systems enables you to open the door for some guest with help of connected devices(IoT) explained by Kundhavai et al.,(2016).

Since there is a massive growth in number of devices day by day, the amount of data generated would also be enormous. Here is where Big Data and IoT go hand in hand. Big Data manages the enormous amount of data generated using its technologies. The Internet of Things (IoT) and big data are two vital subjects in commercial, industrial, and many other applications.

The name IoT was framed in approximately a decade ago and refers to the world of machines or devices connected to the Internet, by which a large amount of big data is collected, stored and managed. Big data additionally refers to the analysis of this generated data to produce useful results. The main motivating power behind the IoT and big data has been the collection and analysis of data related to consumer activities in order to find out why and what customers buy

NECESSITY OF IOT AND BIG DATA IMPLEMENTATION

IoT will enable big data, big data needs analytics, and analytics will improve processes for more IoT devices. IoT and big data can be used to improve various functions and operations in diverse sectors. Both have extended their capabilities to wide range of areas. Figure 1 shows the areas of big data produced. Some or the other way, data is produced through connected devices.

The important basis behind why to implement IoT and big data are: Analytical monitoring, More Uptime, Lower reject rates, Higher throughput, Enhanced safety, Efficient use of labor, Enable mass customization, Analyze the activities for real-time marketing, Improved situational alertness, Improved quality, Sensor-driven decision analytics, Process optimization, Optimized resource utilization, Instant control and response in complex independent systems.

The above are some possible reasons to implement IoT and Big data. As the requirements of both the technologies go hand in hand, a proper improved system is needed to overcome the challenges they pose. Many companies strive to meet the challenges and take possible steps to overcome them.

Figure 1.

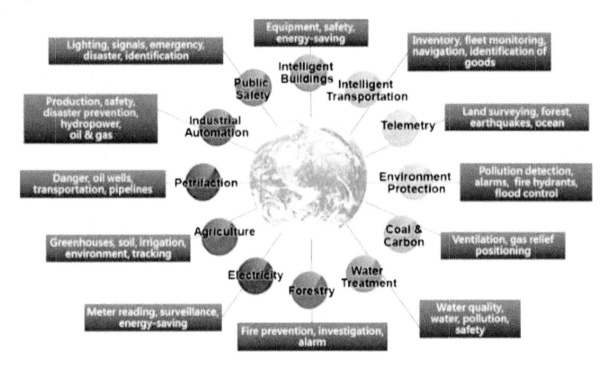

IMPACTS OF IOT ON BIG DATA

IoT is a network consisting of physical devices, which are also implanted with sensors, electronics, and software, thereby allowing these devices to exchange data. This ultimately allows better incorporation between real world physical entities and computer-operated systems. IoT is the next big thing impacting our lives in major ways and number of factors. Technologies like Column-oriented databases, SQL in Hadoop, Hive, Wibidata, PLATFORA, SkyTree, Storage Technologies, Schema-less databases, or NoSQL databases, Streaming Big Data analytics, Big Data Lambda Architecture, Map-reduce, PIG, etc., helps in dealing with the enormous amount of data generated by IoT and other sources.

The main factors that big data is impacted by IoT are:

Big Data Storage

At basis, the key necessities of big data storage are that it can handle very huge amounts of data and continuous balancing to keep up with expansion and that it can provide the input/output operations per second (IOPS) necessary to deliver data to analytics tools. The data is of different form and format and thus, a datacenter for storing such data must be able to handle the load in changeable forms. Obviously IoT has a direct impact on the storage infrastructure of big data. Collection of IoT Big Data is a challenging task because filtering redundant data is mandatorily required. After Collection, the data has to transfer over a network to a data center and maintained. Many companies started to use Platform as a Service (PaaS) to handle their infrastructure based on IT. It helps in developing and running web applications. By this way, Big data can be managed efficiently without the need of expanding their infrastructural facilities to some extent. IoT Big Data Storage is certainly a challenging task as the data grows in a faster rate than expected. Niranjana et al., (2015)

Data Security Issues

The IoT has given new security challenges that cannot be controlled by traditional security methods. Facing IoT security issues require a shift. For instance, how do you deal with a situation when the television and security camera at your home are fitted with unknown Wi-Fi access. Few security problems are:

1. Secure computations in distributed environment
2. Secure data centers
3. Secure transactions
4. Secure filtering of redundant data
5. Scalable and secure data mining and analytics
6. Access control
7. Imposing real time security, etc., (Marc Jonathan Blitz et al., (2013).

A multi-layered security system and proper network system will help avoid attacks and keep them from scattering to other parts of the network. An IoT system should follow rigorous network access control policies and then allowed to connect. Software-defined networking (SDN) technologies should be used for point-to-point and point-tomultipoint encryption in combination with network identity and access policies.

Big Data Analytics

Data analytics is the science of examining raw data with the idea of coming to conclusions about that information. Data analytics is used in many industries to allow them to make better business decisions and in the sciences to verify or disprove existing models or theories. IoT Big data analytics is very much needed to end up in a optimized decision. Big data analytics will help you understand the business value it brings and how different industries are applying it to deal with their sole business necessities. According to the Gartner IT dictionary, Big Data is variety of information assets, high-volume, and high-velocity and, innovative forms of information processing for enhanced approach and decision making. Volume refers to the size of data. Data sources can be social media, sensor and machine-generated data, structured and unstructured networks, and much more (Radha, et al., 2017). Enterprises are flooded with terabytes of big data. Variety refers to the number of forms of data. Big data deals with numbers, 3D data and log files, dates, strings, text, video, audio, click streams. Velocity refers to the speed of data processing. The rate at which data streams in from sources such as mobile devices, click streams, machine-to-machine processes is massive and continuously fast moving. Big data mining and analytics helps to reveal hidden patterns, unidentified correlations, and other business information.

Impact on Day to Day Living

IoT Big Data is slowly redefining our lives. Let us consider a few examples of our lives. At work, the cctv camera in the canteen estimating the time you spend there. The class room sensors can find out how much time you spend in writing on the board. This can be just to measure the productivity of an employee. At home, the home theatre playing the favorite movie of ours as soon as you switch on the television, smart devices could save a lot of power and money by automatically switching off electrical devices when you leave home. A smart wrist band tied to the elder people at home intimates the nearby hospital if they fall sick. The above said is going to happen in a very short time because of the rapid development in IoT and Big Data technologies.

CHALLENGES OF IOT BIG DATA

Major challenges that can fetch momentous rewards when they are solved.

1. Huge data volumes
2. Difficulty in data collection
3. Incompatible standards
4. New security threats
5. No reliability in the data
6. Fundamental shifts in business models
7. Huge amount of data to analyze
8. A rapidly evolving privacy landscape

The above points are some of the challenges that IoT big data faces. The rate in data growth in expanding every second, storage in a big challenge, processing and maintaining is even more tedious. The tools that are developed to manage the both technologies are day by day changing as per the requirements. No doubt, both technologies are going to play a major role in the information technology field.

FAST DATA IN IOT

Fast Data is not a new concept. It has been around before Big Data and IoT came into the picture. Data partitioning, data warehousing and scaling servers were the steps taken to speed up data retrieval prior to IoT and Big Data. The writing on the wall: Big Data volume in no longer the main criteria for gathering quality data. Companies are now vying to build better new platforms to solve data warehousing tasks and in processing analytics.

1. In the modern tech context, Fast Data is about information in real-time or the ability to obtain data insights while it is generated. That is why streaming data is so happening now. Data streams now occur at thousands of times per second, what is now called Fast Data. Brundu, et al.,(2016)
2. The truth is, many companies with big data still don't know what is to be done with it. Most companies use Hadoop for their data storage. Fast Data origins can be linked to Big Data variety, velocity and volume concepts. Fast Data is not just about high frequency data intake. It is about data processing in real-time, arriving at quick action-based results and taking decisions based on these results. All this while dealing with complex analytics. Conclusively, Big Data can only be effective if organizations interpret Big Data findings in real-time.

The Fast/Big Data Channel

Big data systems are centered on a data lake or warehouse, a storage location in which an enterprise stores and analyzes its data. This component is a critical element of a data channel that must capture all information. The big data platform's core requirements are to store historical data that will be sent or shared with other data management products, and also to support frameworks for executing jobs directly against the data in the data lake.Fast data systems include a fast in-memory database component. These Fast data databases have a number of critical requirements, which include the ability to ingest and interact with live data feeds, make decisions on each event in the feeds, and apply real-time analytics to provide visibility into fast streams of incoming data explained by DeFries et al(2010).

Figure 2. Fast Data vs. Big Data

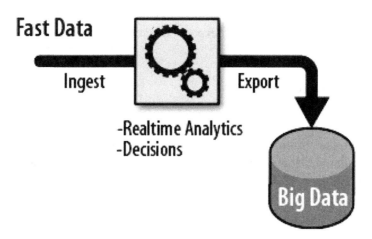

The Fast data/big data channel supports fast incoming streams of live data created in a multitude of new end points. It operationalizes the use of that data in applications, and exports data to a data lake or data warehouse for deep, long-term storage and analytics. The Fast/Big data channel unifies applications, analytics, and application interaction across multiple functions, products, and disciplines.

The Future of Applications

Applications are the most purpose of entry for data streaming into the enterprise. They are the initial assortment purpose for data, and are accountable for interactions – personalized offers, decisions, updates to balances or accounts, changes to the distribution of power in electrical grid. Application interaction has identical characteristics as those delineated for fast data—it ingests events, interacts with data for choices, uses period analytics to reinforce the expertise, and exports the information for storage and additional analysis. The application is both the organization's and the consumer's "interface" to the data. Applications are responsible for interaction. The greatest value from applications and the data they process comes with interactions that are accurately performed in real time. Fast data systems make better, faster real-time applications. The application is each the organization's and therefore the consumer's "interface" to the data. Applications are responsible for interaction. The best worth from applications and therefore the data they method comes with interactions that are accurately performed in real time. Fast data systems build higher, quicker time period applications. Here are the five steps I propose as part of your fast data strategy: Ashton et al.,(2009)

- Identify your fast data opportunity
- Assess and leverage your existing infrastructure
- Understand the (business implications of) alternatives
- Get agreement on success criteria for project
- Prototype, pilot, refine
- Provide Visibility into Fast-Moving Data with Real-Time Analytics
- Real-time analytics analyze streams of incoming data, per-event, at ingestion. Analytic results are used in real-time to guide application interactions.
- Export Processed Data to Long-Term Analytics Systems
- Once Fast Data analytics are completed, the data moves through the channel for storage long-term analytical processing; data ingestion and export flow at the same rate.

DATA PROCESSING TIMELINESS

Picture an online shopping company that wants to recommend its products to a customer. Recommendations are based on the customer's latest purchases. Only, the shopping website can't make these recommendations fast enough. How soon in real-time can the website collect data, summarize and then provide the shopping options – preferably in real-time? Unless they want to lose the customer. This is where Fast Data comes in, adding immediacy to the proceedings. Timeliness and accuracy are two prime Fast Data attributes. Fast Data includes sampled recommendations, sensors that pass on instant trend changes and choices. When it comes to pinpointing loopholes or instances of inefficiency, go for Fast Data. Giusto, et al.,(2010)

DATA ANALYTICS

More focused analytics is now possible, thanks to Fast Data. Analytics enables customization of services or products. It enables better decision-making, leading to better customer service and faster fraud detection, among other things. The question you need to ask is, at what particular time do you go for analytics? The more you are able to analyze in real-time, the more easier it becomes to take action on the basis of analytic results. Eastman et al.,(2010)

STREAMING DATA ANALYTICS

Fast Data makes a critical difference in obtaining results within a limited time span. For example, why would you want information on a customer who has already left the store or website? Fast Data helps organizations make similar make-or-break decisions. Processing streaming data is a vital part of Fast Data. Making automated decisions based on streaming machine data is important for the process. You may call this streaming analytics. At the same time, human intervention in the automated decisions are necessary. That is why the automated dashboards and streaming data sources need to be interactive for that ever important human tweaking and final authorization.

Figure 3.

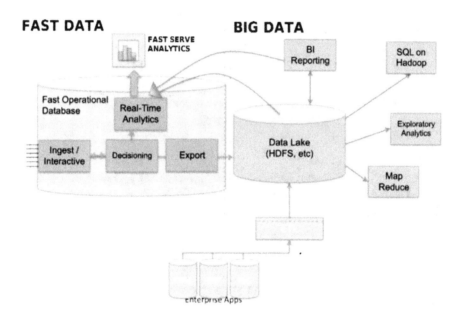

FAST DATA ARCHITECTURE

When we look at Fast Data architecture, it will feature real-time analytics, taking in information, and giving immediate results and resultant decisions. Instant, real-time solutions are possible if you integrate your Big Data system (consisting of a Hadoop database, SQL on Hadoop, MapReduce and related big data components) to the company's applications. This whole set up can then be connected to the Fast Data architecture as displayed in the illustration above.

FAST DATA USAGE

Elements like dashboards can be served quickly, with Fast Data usage. The operations systems can be constantly powered by instant analytics, the entire system thus working at a rapid pace. Building this big data dependent application combined with fast data capability applications can entirely change its efficiency. Architecture plays a key role here.

Figure 4.

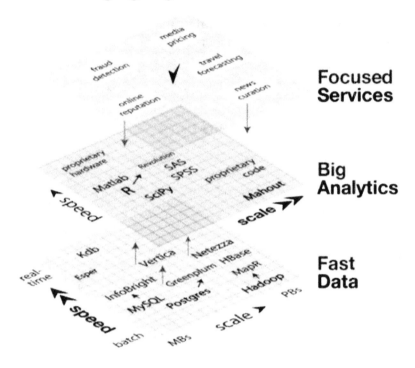

THE EMERGING BIG DATA (FAST DATA) STACK

Finally, Fast Data is Big Data that is constantly moving. Imagine a pipeline through which data is flowing in great speed. Here are the Emerging Big Data (Fast Data) Stack details:

1. The first level concerns focused services. It concerns applying key processes and functions to obtain significant value from streaming data. Fraud detection, travel forecasting and similar services can thus be availed faster.
2. The second layer consists of real-time analytics based on the streaming data. The company's business logic is then put to use to make real-time decisions.
3. In the Fast Data layer, the data is then exported for analytics and long term storage to Hadoop and other data storage options.Speed, real-time and accuracy are key elements of the entire stack.

Streaming is however just a part of the Fast Data solutions. OLTP databases are the in thing for processing streaming data. You can thus have speed and scale using an in-memory database, designed to handle data streaming at great speed. One popular Fast Data database is VoltDB.

The Challenge of Fast Streaming Data

When we talk about fast data, we're not measuring volume in the typical gigabytes, terabytes, and petabytes common to data warehouses. We're measuring volume in terms of time: the number of megabytes per second, gigabytes per hour, or terabytes per day. Fast data means velocity as well as volume -- thousands of events per second, millions of transactions per hour -- which gets to the core of the difference between big data and fast data. The challenge for today's businesses is to capture intelligence from streaming data while it's still live, before it ages and flows into the big data "lake" (Tomlinson et al., 2001).

Streaming Data?

Streaming Data is data that is generated continuously by thousands of data sources, which typically send in the data records simultaneously, and in small sizes (order of Kilobytes). Streaming data includes a wide variety of data such as log files generated by customers using your mobile or web applications, ecommerce purchases, in-game player activity, information from social networks, financial trading floors, or geospatial services, and telemetry from connected devices or instrumentation in data centers. This data needs to be processed sequentially and incrementally on a record-by-record basis or over sliding time windows, and used for a wide variety of analytics including correlations, aggregations, filtering, and sampling. Information derived from such analysis gives companies visibility into many aspects of their business and customer activity such as –service usage (for metering/billing), server activity, website clicks, and geo-location of devices, people, and physical goods –and enables them to respond promptly to emerging situations. For example, businesses can track changes in public sentiment on their brands and products by continuously analyzing social media streams, and respond in a timely fashion as the necessity arises.

Benefits of Streaming Data

Streaming data processing is beneficial in most scenarios where new, dynamic data is generated on a continual basis. It applies to most of the industry segments and big data use cases. Companies generally begin with simple applications such as collecting system logs and rudimentary processing like rolling min-max computations. Then, these applications evolve to more sophisticated near-real-time processing. Initially, applications may process data streams to produce simple reports, and perform simple actions in response, such as emitting alarms when key measures exceed certain thresholds. Eventually, those applications perform more sophisticated forms of data analysis, like applying machine learning algorithms, and extract deeper insights from the data. Over time, complex, stream and event processing algorithms, like decaying time windows to find the most recent popular movies, are applied, further enriching the insights. Kamilaris et al.,(2011).

Challenges in Working With Streaming Data

Streaming data processing requires two layers: a storage layer and a processing layer. The storage layer needs to support record ordering and strong consistency to enable fast, inexpensive and replay able reads and writes of large streams of data. The processing layer is responsible for consuming data from the storage layer, running computations on that data, and then notifying the storage layer to delete data that is no longer needed. You also have to plan for scalability, data durability, and fault tolerance in both the storage and processing layers. As a result, many platforms have emerged that provide the infrastructure needed to build streaming data applications.

Trends in the World of Big and Fast Data Analytics

Big data analytics is moving beyond the realm of intellectual curiosity and is beginning to tangibly affect business operations, offerings, and outlooks. No longer merely hype or a buzzword, big data analytics will soon become a central tenet for every sort of business enterprise. Meanwhile, real-time analytics has become a hot requirement. For example, factories require the use of real-time data such as sensor data to detect abnormalities in plant and machinery.

OPEN ISSUES OF BIG DATA

The analysis of big data is confronted with many challenges but the current research is still in the beginning phase. Considerable research efforts are needed to improve the efficiency of data display, data storage, and data analysis. Although big data is a hot research area in both academia and industry, there are many important problems remain to be solved, which are discussed below

- **Fundamental Problems:** There is compelling need for a rigorous definition of big data, a structural model of big data, formal description of big data, and a theoretical system of data science, etc. At present, many discussions of big data look more like commercial speculation than scientific research. This is because big data is not formally and structurally defined and not strictly verified.
- **Standardization:** An evaluation system of data quality and an evaluation standard of data computing efficiency should be developed. Many solutions of big data applications claim they can improve data processing and analysis capacities in all aspects, but there is still not a unified evaluation standard and benchmark to balance the computing efficiency of big data with rigorous mathematical methods. The performance can only be evaluated by the system is implemented and deployed, which could not horizontally compare advantages and disadvantages of various solutions and compare efficiencies before and after the use of big data. In addition, since data quality is an important basis of data preprocessing, simplification, and screening, it is also an urgent problem to effectively evaluate data quality.
- **Evolution of Big Data Computing Modes:** This includes external storage mode, data flow mode, PRAM mode, and MR mode, etc. The emergence of big data triggers the development of algorithm design, which has transformed from a computing-intensive approach into a data-intensive approach. Data transfer has been a main bottleneck of big data computing. Therefore, many new computing models tailored for big data have emerged and more such models are on the horizon.

TECHNOLOGY DEVELOPMENT

The big data technology is still in its infancy. Many key technical problems, such as cloud computing, grid computing, stream computing, parallel computing, big data architecture, big data model, and software systems supporting big data, etc. should be fully investigated.

- **Format Conversion:** Due to wide and various data sources, heterogeneity is always a characteristic of big data, as well as a key factor which restricts the efficiency of data format conversion. If such format conversion can be made more efficient, the application of big data may create more values.
- **Big Data Transfer:** Big data transfer involves big data generation, acquisition, transmission, storage, and other data transformations in the spatial domain. As discussed, big data transfer usually incurs high costs, which is also the bottleneck for big data computing. However, data transfer is inevitable in big data applications. Improving the transfer efficiency of big data is a key factor to improve big data computing.
- **Real-Time Performance:** The real-time performance of big data is also a core problem in many different application scenarios. Ways to define the life cycle of data, compute the rate of depreciation of data, and build computing models of real-time applications and online applications, will influence the values and analytical and feedback results of big data. As big data research is advanced, new problems on big data processing arise from the traditional simple data analysis, including:
  - Data re-utilization, since big data features big value but low density, with the increase of data scale, more values may be mined from re-utilization of existing data;
  - Data re-organization, datasets in different businesses can be re-organized, with the total re-organized data values larger than the total datasets' value;
  - Data exhaust, unstructured information or data that is a by-product of the online activities of Internet users.

In big data, not only correct data should be utilized, but also the wrong data should be utilized to generate more value. Collecting and analyzing data exhaust can provide valuable insight into the purchasing habits of consumers.

PRACTICAL IMPLICATIONS

- **Big Data Management:** The emergence of big data brings about new challenges to traditional data management. At present, many research efforts are being made on consider big data oriented database and Internet technologies, management of storage models and databases of new hardware, heterogeneous and multistructured data integration, data management of mobile and pervasive computing, data management of SNS, and distributed data management.
- **Searching, Mining, and Analysis of Big Data:** Data processing is always a research hotspot in the big data field, e.g., searching and mining of SNS models, big data searching algorithms, distributed searching, P2P searching, visualized analysis of big data, massive recommendation

systems, social media systems, real-time big data mining, image mining, text mining, semantic mining, multistructured data mining, and machine learning, etc.

- **Integration and Provenance of Big Data:** As discussed, the value acquired from a comprehensive utilization of multiple datasets is higher than the total value of individual datasets. Therefore, the integration of different data sources is a timely problem to be solved. Data integration is to integrate different datasets from different sources, which are confronted with many challenges, such as different data patterns and large amount of redundant data. Data provenance is to describe the process of data generation and evolution over time. In the big data era, data provenance is mainly used to investigate multiple datasets other than a single dataset. Therefore, it is worth of study on how to integrate data provenance information featuring different standards and from different datasets.

- **Big Data Application:** At present, the application of big data is just beginning and we shall explore and more efficiently ways to fully utilize big data. Therefore, big data applications in science, engineering, medicine, medical care, finance, business, law enforcement, education, transportation, retail, and telecommunication, big data applications in small and medium-sized businesses, big data applications in government departments, big data services, and human-computer interaction of big data, etc. are all important research problems.

CHALLENGES AND FUTURE DIRECTIONS OF IOT

The IoT offers several new prospects to the industry and end user in many application fields. The IoT needs theory, technology, architecture, and standards that join the virtual world and the real physical world in a merged outline. Some key challenges are listed in the following subsections.

1. **Architecture Challenge:** IoT covers an extensive variety of technologies. IoT includes a cumulative number of smart interconnected devices and sensors such as cameras, biometric, physical, and chemical sensors. They are often nonintrusive, visible, and hidden. The devices are connected in a wireless or ad hoc manner as the communication may occur at any time and the facilities turn into mobile dependent and more complex. In IoT, data collected from different resources so it will be difficult to integrate these heterogeneous data. The solution is collecting data from various sources and determining the common characteristics between them to explain data and find the associations for support decision-making. The existence of heterogeneous reference architectures in IoT is important. IoT architecture must be reliable and elastic to suit all cases as RFID, Tags, intelligent devices, and smart hardware and software solutions .

2. **Environment Innovation Challenge:** IoT is a complicated network that might be achieved by some sponsors, where services should be openly produced. Therefore, new services or applications should be supported without resulting loads for the market accesses or other operation blocks. So, the cross-domain systems supporting innovation is still deficient.

3. **Technical Challenge:** There are several technical challenges as Heterogeneous architecture in the network technologies and applications. IoT contains different types of networks that are not easy to integrate them. The cost of communication technology should be small and connections must be reliable. Defining the form of suitable security and privacy solution is a complicated process. Activation of automated services stills a challenge.

4. **Hardware Challenge:** Smart devices with enhanced inter-device communication will lead to smart systems with high degrees of intelligence. There are five challenges that face hardware in IoT, cost, electricity and energy, environment related problems, connectivity, and maintenance. IoT connections depend on wireless that somewhat low cost and low size. Hardware devices must be designed to use the smallest amount of power and longtime battery. The outer environment may affect the hardware efficiency as pollution, humidity, and heating. The connection must be reliable and flexible and not depend only on wireless, the Internet or data should be allowed. It is expensive to maintain damages in sensing devices, so maintenance and support should be local.

5. **Privacy and Security Challenge:** Problems of security and privacy in IoT become more obvious than a traditional network. Despite there exist a great number of researchers in security and privacy, there is a continuous demand for security protection and confidential privacy of data. Todays, user's information has an extensive privacy, so privacy protection is a significant issue. There are many issues should be considered in IoT and need new technologies to be solved as the definition of privacy and security, trust mechanism, the privacy of common and user data, and security of services and applications. Security architectures that are designed now may not be suited for IoT systems. Approval of new technologies and services depend on trustfulness of information and protection of data and its privacy.

6. A standard is important to permit easy and equal access and use to all actors. Standard and proposal developments will encourage the development of IoT infrastructures and applications, services and devices. Standardization permits product and services to do the best. The standardization will be difficult because of vast speed in IoT. Protocols and multi-parities can develop standardization. It should be open. In addition, the standard development process should be open to all actors and the resulting standard should be public and free.

7. **Business Challenge:** For advanced application, it is easy to convert business model and application scenario into technical requirements. So the developers do not want to waste time on business aspects. In IoT, there exist many uncertainties in business models and application scenarios. The problem is that there is no solution of business technology algorithm to suit all. The IoT is a prevention to traditional business model. In the first step in business model development in IoT, business requirements must begin with reducing system failure.

8. **Development Strategies:** IoT has been developed in different areas and states in three main plans and chances financing approach. In the states such as the US, the short-term yield to finance drive of the progress of smart energy, smart cities, and RFIDs. Through the social media network, some services, and applications, such as location-based services, augmented reality, and smartphones, are leading to the development of IoT. Although it is not yet obvious which strategy is more effective, all of them can encourage IoT and its applications. However, how to determine the efforts of available resources at a planned level acquires another challenge.

9. **Data Processing Challenges:** Data processing is an essential property in the IoT. By observing the interconnecting devices and objects that exchange different forms of data, the resulting gathered data has an intensive volume. The storage data centers that store this resulting data will need extra spaces, energy and power sources. This data require organization and processing. Semantic data fusion models may be used for extracting meaning from data. Also, artificial intelligence algorithms should be implied to obtain meaning from this redundant data. Data storage and analysis will be a problem during all world will be connected through IoT

Handling out all of the data from the IoT is a practice in Big data that applied three main steps: data ingestion, data storage, and analytics. Thus, enterprises must assimilate new technologies like Hadoop, and MapReduce. It should be able to provide sufficient disk, network, and compute capacity to continue with the inflow of new data, many data processing challenges are listed in the following subsections: a) Heterogeneous Data Processing In IoT applications, the enormous data are gathered from heterogeneous sensors such as cameras, vehicles, drivers, passengers, and medical sensors. It results in heterogeneous sensing data like text, video, and voice. Heterogeneous data processing as fusion, classification gets exclusive challenges and also provides many advantages and new opportunities for system enhancement. An IoT system may include many types of sensors whose data have heterogeneous data structures. For example, IoT system may contain many forms of sensors, such as traffic sensors, hydrological sensors, geological sensors, meteorological sensors, and biomedical sensors. Each category can be separated into different forms of sensors. For example, traffic sensors can include GPS sensors, RFID readers, video-based traffic-flow analysis sensors, traffic loop sensors, road condition sensors, and so on. The sampling data from different sensors may have dissimilar semantics and data structures that critically rises the troubles in data processing .Noisy Data Noisy data is irrelevant data. The term was often used as a replacement for abnormal data, but its meaning has extended to contain data from the unstructured text that cannot be understood by machines. Its meaning has extended to contain any data that cannot be recognized and translated correctly by machines, such as unstructured text. Slightly data that has been collected, stored, or altered in such a manner that it cannot be recognized or used by the program that originally made it can be identified as noisy. Statistical analysis can use the information collected from old data to clear noisy data and simplify data mining .

Anomaly detection is the detection of irregular events or patterns that is not considered as expected events or patterns. Detecting anomalies are significant in a broad range of different fields, such as diagnosing medical problems, bank, insurance fraud, network intrusion, and object imperfections. Algorithms for anomaly detection are employed based on one type of learning formation: supervised, semi-supervised and unsupervised. These techniques vary from training the detection algorithm using completely unstructured data to having a preformed dataset with entries structured normal or abnormal.

In an IoT system, there could be a considerable amount of connected sensors, and these sensors incessantly send sampling data to the data center. The data center needs to save the latest forms of the sampling data. It also needs to save past forms of the data for some period say one week to offer query processing, state monitoring, and data analyzing. The size of data can be visualized to be massive and processing them effectively is a significant challenge.

SUMMARY

Since there is a major impact of IoT on big data we need to quickly improvise the complete structure to manage the daily changing circumstances. There are a few areas of concern and security and privacy and data collection efficiency are probably the most difficult problems we are facing. Security compromise and inefficiencies in data collection mechanisms result in a loss of status, money, time and effort. But there is hope because both the IoT and the big data are at an emerging stage and there will be upgrade.

Fast Data is powering innovation, while using Big Data to obtain key insights and conclusions. Anything real-time, be it security, fraud surveillance, risk analytics, customer choices, etc – Fast Data helps deliver instant, accurate solutions. The Big Data and Fast Data challenge is finally about concurrency.

REFERENCES

Ashton, K. (2009). That Internet of Things Thing. *RFID Journal*. Retrieved from http://www. rfidjournal. com/articles/view

Blitz. (2013). *The Fourth Amendment Future of Public Surveillance: Remote Recording and Other Searches in Public Space*. Academic Press.

Brundu, F. G., Patti, E., Osello, A., Del Giudice, M., Rapetti, N., Krylovskiy, A., ... Acquaviva, A. (2016). IoT Software Infrastructure for Energy Management and Simulation in Smart Cities. *IEEE Transactions on Industrial Informatics*.

DeFries, R. S., Rudel, T., Uriarte, M., & Hansen, M. (2010). Deforestation driven by urban population growth and agricultural trade in the twenty-first century. *Nature Geoscience*, *3*(3), 178–181. doi:10.1038/ngeo756

Eastman, C. M., Eastman, C., Teicholz, P., Sacks, R., & Liston, K. (2011). *BIM handbook: A guide to building information modeling for owners, managers, designers, engineers and contractors*. John Wiley & Sons.

Giusto, D., Iera, A., Morabito, G., & Atzori, L. (Eds.). (2010). *The internet of things: 20th Tyrrhenian workshop on digital communications*. Springer Science & Business Media.

Kamilaris, A., Pitsillides, A., & Trifa, V. (2011). The smart home meets the web of things. *International Journal of Ad Hoc and Ubiquitous Computing*, *7*(3), 145–154. doi:10.1504/IJAHUC.2011.040115

Kundhavai & Sridevi. (2016). IoT and Big Data- The Current and Future Technologies: A Review. *International Journal of Computer Science and Mobile Computing*, *5*(1), 10-14.

Niranjana. (2015). Big data analytics – Tools, techniques and challenges. *International Journal of Advance Research in Science and Engineering*, *4*(3).

Radha, B. S., & Bharathi, T. (2017). A Study On Corporate Valuation On Selected Indian Firms. *Indian Journal of Commerce and Management*, *3*(6).

Raju. (2017, November). A Mutational Approach to Internet of Things. *International Journal for Research in Applied Science and Engineering Technology*, *5*(11).

Tomlinson, R. F. (2001). A geographic information system for regional planning. *The Journal of Geography*, *78*(1), 45–48. doi:10.5026/jgeography.78.45

Chapter 93

Integration of Data Mining and Business Intelligence in Big Data Analytics:
A Research Agenda on Scholarly Publications

Atik Kulakli

iD https://orcid.org/0000-0002-2368-3225

American University of the Middle East, Kuwait

ABSTRACT

The purpose of this chapter is to analyze and explore the research studies for scholarly publication trends and patterns related to the integration of data mining in particular business intelligence in big data analytics domains published in the period of 2010-2019. Research patterns explore in highly prestigious sources that have high impact factors and citations counted in the ISI Web of Science Core Collection database (indexes included SCI-Exp and SSCI). Bibliometric analysis methods applied for this study under the research limitations. Research questions formed based on bibliometric principles concentrating fields such as descriptive of publication, author productivity, country-regions distribution, keyword analysis with contribution among researchers, citation analysis, co-citation patterns searched. Findings showed strong relations and patterns on these important research domains. Besides this chapter would useful for researchers to obtain an overview of publication trends on research domains to be concerned for further studies and shows the potential gaps in those fields.

INTRODUCTION

Data management becomes the center of the decision-making process; Business Intelligence and Analytics (BI&A) has emerged as accessible (Buhl *et al.*, 2013) research area to be studied in academia and industry. With the movement of Big Data (BD) initiatives, these popular fields become more attractive

DOI: 10.4018/978-1-6684-3662-2.ch093

for researchers (Maté *et al.*, 2015). Big data could be defined as the most unstructured and extremely massive data sets to be analyzed to reveal trends, associations, and patterns, related to human interactions (e.g., Social media data). In comparison, data mining is structured data in the databases to generate new information by mining the relations in data patterns. The data warehousing platforms should be established incorporation level with necessary data marts to analyze the large data sets. Moreover, big data analytics (as proper business decision tool); is a complex process of examining large and various data sets to uncover information in unstructured platforms with a variety of data sources and systems to discover hidden patterns, correlations, customer insights, and decisions as well as behaviors.

Data Mining (DM) with Big Data relations studied by Wu *et al.* (2014), it has outlined that Big Data concentrates large-volume, multiple sourced, complex, unstructured and autonomous (various) sources from the entire data platforms. In the research, the HACE theorem studied and proposed the Big Data processing model with mining techniques. While Big Data and traditional Business Intelligence discussed in different platforms, researchers studied the skill set and knowledge requirements for Big Data and Business Intelligence (Debortoli, Müller & vom Brocke, 2014) and conducted latent semantic analysis (LSA). According to findings, business knowledge is a crucial indicator of successful development and execution. Followed by Business Intelligence needs bigger than Big Data competencies, whereas Big Data is much more "human-capital-intensive" than Business Intelligence projects. Sun, Sun & Strang (2018) examined to use of Big Data Analytic services (service-oriented architecture-BASOA) to enhance Business Intelligence. Big Data ontology has three-layer analyses, such as descriptive, predictive, and prescriptive.

Since the number of academic publications has been increased and become very complex to follow, the trends would be a critical point for researchers and audiences. The impact of outcomes has resulted in directing research efforts to be concentrated on the most recent development fields in parallel. Scholars conduct different qualitative and quantitative studies to explore, discover, analyze, and organize the information to provide through wider scientific communities. Therefore, bibliometric methods as a usual proven approach provide systematic, transparent, process-based on the statistical measurement of science, and scientific activities (Aria & Cuccurullo, 2017).

This chapter aims to analyze and explore the research studies on big data, data mining in particular business intelligence, and big data analytics domains published in a recent research period (a decade). The study uses the Web of Science Core Collection database as a primary research platform and analysis the data for the period of 2010 to 2019. In this chapter, the author used a science mapping method with open-source Bibliometrix R-package that conducting bibliometric studies on scholarly high ranked sources. The chapter organized based on the IGI Global's structured template which devoted in seven main sections as Introduction, Background (literature review), Main focus (issues, controversies, problem statement, research methodology, bibliometric study definitions, and data collection strategy), Results and Discussions (analysis, findings, addressing the research questions), Solutions and Recommendations followed by Future research directions (Theoretical implications and research needs, Practical implications, and Limitations and future research), and Conclusion. The study also shows the research patterns and concentration areas in scholarly publications to find out the gap to highlight future research direction needs.

BACKGROUND (LITERATURE REVIEW)

In the information systems literature, data mining, business intelligence studied with different dimensions more than several decades. However, big data and its analytics related to business intelligence studies relatively less, and this study show recent research patterns. Business Intelligence (BI) related topics need the framework to identify the evolution, applications, emerging research areas (Chen, Chiang & Storey, 2012). In the study, the evolution highlighted as Business Intelligence and Analytics, BI&A 1.0 (DBMS-Based structured content), BI&A 2.0 (Web-based unstructured content), and BI&A 3.0 (Mobile and sensor-based content). In the highly cited paper, it was mentioned the emerging Analytics research areas such as "Big Data, Text, Web, Network, and Mobile" (Yu, 2017).

Kranjc *et al.* (2017)'s study provided a real-life platform with distributed computing in Big Data mining. The platform called ClowdFlows (cloud-based web) is to use for the workflow of components of mining, and development, whether batch or real-time processing modes in scientific publications. Similarly, some researches concentrated the forecasting and visualizing the energy consumption behavior with data mining modeling (Singh & Yassine, 2018; Zhu *et al.*, 2018; Kuo, Lin & Lee, 2018). Smart energy capabilities require complicated operational activities and procedures (Chongwatpol, 2016). Proposed Business Intelligent framework augments business analytics along with database management, and business performance approaches to manage the current system in the energy sector plant (Lin & Yang 2019; Liu *et al.*, 2018). An unsupervised data clustering analysis, energy time series data was used to forecast the energy usage with smart meter datasets. Zhu *et al.* (2018) systematically reviewed the scholarly publications on data preprocessing with component analysis. Robust techniques (Shuai *et al.*, 2018) discussed with various characteristics; therefore, Big Data has multi-dimensional, with various perspectives, give opportunities to the community. Wang & Yuan (2014) studied Big Data concerning spatial Data Mining. Geo-spatial data have been found a considerable amount in Big Data, so location-based data (Batran *et al.*, 2018) enormously used by individuals and organizations recently. It has roles and dimensions, such as social, economic, and environmental issues.

Gandomi *et al.* (2016) established a new algorithm of multi-objective genetic programming (MOGP) where addresses the problems by solving sophisticated civil engineering modeling. Big Data is used for model development along with various levels of structural properties. Another study showed that Big Data mining works well in parallel computing and cloud computing platforms (Zhang & Zhang, 2019) where parallel computing use the similar techniques as analytical methods offer, is to divide significant problems into small pieces and then the single processor would be carried out (Tsai *et al.*, 2016). Therefore, those methods used to solve Big Data problems. Parallel computing divides the dataset to work on it simultaneously with the different subsets while cloud-based platform used MapReduce based procedures. In other words, this composes the data on the map, therefore reduces the processes. Margolies *et al.* (2016) contributed to structured reporting and database development with data mining in the health sector. The research showed that breast imaging and diagnosing cancer detection, screening algorithm optimization are key success areas in highly complex datasets. A similar study conducted on Big Data mining on novel cancer cases and reanalyze the profiles of "Gene Expression Omnibus" to explore those "involved for DNS damage repair and genome instability" (Jiang & Liu, 2015).

Moreover, disease diagnosis and treatment have various schemes in classification by different departments and hospitals. These variations create problems such as inexperienced health staff, challenging to identify the symptoms and to apply proper treatment. In that research, the authors proposed a "Disease Diagnosis and Treatment Recommendation System (DDTRS)" to increase the utilization of advanced medical technology for the hospitals (Chen *et al.*, 2018). Similarly, the application and exploration of Big Data Mining studied by Zhang *et al.* (2016) in clinical medicine. The authors reviewed the theories and technologies of Big Data Mining and contributed that it has enormous potential to play a crucial role in the clinical medicine research area. Besides, medical Big Data mining processes have been developed by the support of IoT devices used in the medical services (Song, Jung& Chung, 2019).

Shadroo & Rahmani (2018) revealed the relation among Big Data, Data Mining (Lv *et al.*, 2018), and the Internet of Things (IoT). IoT has emerged in the last decade and can be seen in all devices such as wearable technological products, home appliances, vehicles, smartphones, air conditioning, heaters, natural gas meters, smart cities, and so on. Big Data and Data Mining work well together for efficient operations of IoT to transmit, analyze, and process data. The study was categorized into three clusters of the scholarly publications of 44 records, such as architecture and platform, framework, and application. Authors also outlined the opportunities (such as data aggregation, data analysis; new business models; and global visibility) and challenges (such as volume-variety-velocity-value (Huang *et al.*, 2017); visualization; knowledge extraction; and security-privacy) based on the published results. The furthermore mixed digital method used to combine qualitative and quantitative methods in Data Mining and visualize the data (Qi, Yang, & Wang, 2019) in a multilevel and contextual model for the texts (O'Hallorane *et al.*, 2018). Moreover, it has been contributed that Big Data, Data Mining, and Machine Learning (D'Alconzo *et al.*, 2016) approaches to utilize production, operations, sustainability, and management roles in precision animal agriculture. It helps to growth of complex data from different sources such as sensors, digital images, sound, and visual data used in highly technological platforms and computer systems (Morota *et al.*, 2018).

On the other hand, Xu *et al.* (2014) studied the threat and security issues for the private information of individuals (sensitive information, Xu *et al.*, 2016). It is called privacy-preserving data mining (PPDM), which concentrates data mining algorithms effectively-prepared based on security needs. It was identified four types of users' participated in data mining applications as "data provider, data collector, data miner, and decision-maker."

Mariani *et al.* (2018) outlined the academic developments of Business Intelligence and Big Data in Hospitality and Tourism Research (Li *et al.*, 2019) domains concentrated scholarly publications of 97 journal papers from WoS and Scopus databases. According to findings, although the applied analytical techniques in an upward movement, there is no clear framework of Business Intelligence and Big Data reflected in the literature yet (as of 2017). There is a missing link for the Big Data-driven knowledge development. Besides, more data has become available to use for different business problems to solve. Similarly, another study discovers the scientific publication patterns evolved concerning Business Intelligence and Big Data Analytics. Computer Science and Management Information Systems are dominant fields in the production of research studies. At the same time, "data mining," "social media," and "information systems" are highly common keywords all over the publications, however, "cloud computing," "data warehouse," and "knowledge management" recently evolved topics (Liang & Liu 2018). Unstructured data is available in various sources, and it emerges rapidly. Since the unstructured and complex data become very important for the companies' marketing strategies, Big Data supports the authentic decision-making process (Chow-White & Green, 2013; Liang & Liu 2018) with regarding of social, cultural, marketing campaigns, and consumer behaviors and expectations (Kim, 2014). Also, the cognitive network structure examined to understand the patterns of categorical mapping with Big Data Mining in social media (Sang *et al.*, 2016; Yang *et al.*, 2019) to represent the decision-making structure of consumers (Song *et al.*, 2014).

There is a wide range of studies on Big Data (Mining), Business Intelligence, Data Mining, and Analytics (Azevedo and Santos, 2009) field available in the literature. Big Data acquired in audiology (Mellor, Stone, & Keane, 2018), Privacy preserving big data mining (Zhang *et al*, 2018) for sensitive knowledge leakage, security (Afzali, & Mohammadi, 2017), big data in the food industry (Goti-Elordi *et al,* 2017), multimedia data mining-based smart transportation and telemedicine (Zhu, 2016) manufacturer's prediction of performance (Apgar, 2015), network architecture design with Big Data mining (Njah, Jamoussi & Mahdi, 2019), Agile Business Intelligence as responsive decision model (Chang, 2018), Intelligent SSD for big data mining (Bae *et al*, 2013), Big Data Mining based on high-performance applications (HPC) (Fu *et al*, 2012), "Cloud Computing and Big Data Mining based Intelligent Traffic Control System" (Shengdong, Zhengxian & Yixiang, 2019), "Big Data Mining for Public Distributed Computing" (Jurgelevičius & Sakalauskas, 2018), Stock Market Prediction with Big Data (Das *et al*, 2017), "Data Mining Technology in the Financial Management of Colleges and Universities" (Zhang & Zhang, 2019), Enterprise CRM based on Big Data Mining (Li & Feng, 2018).

MAIN FOCUS OF THE CHAPTER

Issues and Problem Statement

This chapter aims to analyze and explore the research studies on data mining in particular business intelligence and big data analytics domains published in the 2010-2019 period.

The study shows the research patterns and concentration areas in scholarly publications. Research patterns explore in highly prestigious sources that have high impact factors and citations counted in the ISI Web of Science Core Collection (Clarivate Analytics).

This work justifies its interest and importance in the field of Data Mining, Big Data, Business Intelligence, and related Analytics. Therefore, the focus of this study takes into account a variety of perspectives to support developments in the area. First, for authors (academics and researchers in the same fields), it can serve as a publication guideline along with mapping the related content, subject of interest, publication sources which provide detailed information about publishing their papers and in which sources are available to publish the research outcomes give the idea to apply in the publication process. Second, for readers or audiences from different parties, it is beneficial to have an overview of the research outcomes, source types, and subject interest to follow scientific progress to apply their practical sides or for academic fields. Third, for covering a broad community of science or industry experts or any other corporations, this study supports as useful and beneficial directions to show evolution and progress in the research domains. The trends and scientific mapping also aid in outlining the concepts and future research areas to be studied. Therefore the research concentrated those questions for analysis;

Research Concentration and Questions

To understand the patterns of research domains in "integration of big data, data mining in particular business intelligence and analytics"; the design of the research should be framed and structured based on research objective and scope. The study design consists of preparation for the research theme and patterns to explore data of research domains. Therefore, a bibliometric study which enables a researcher to gather all related publication data, and correctly analyze them to answer those questions below;

Q1 How many papers on "data mining, business intelligence, and big data analytics" have been published in 2010 and 2019?

Q2 In which journals/sources were the papers published most frequently, and which keywords used in those publications?

Q3 Who are the most productive authors/co-authors published in those periods?

Q4 What are the most productive institutions and countries?

Q5 What are the results of the citation for those authors and publications?

Although the research conducted in the ISI WoS platform, the consistency of a single data platform assures better citation analysis in highly ranked top publication sources to compare and find out the co-citation, coupling, and collaboration in the research domains. Moreover, for future research directions, the outcome of this study shows the opportunities and challenges to create new publication strategies and form the research ideas. It would also be helpful for journal editors, authors, publishers, readers, and broad audiences too.

Research Methodology

Bibliometric Study

Bibliometric is defined as the use of statistical methods to analyze the bibliometric publications data such as peer-reviewed journal articles, books, conference proceedings, periodicals, reviews, reports, and related documents. It has been widely used to present the relations of research domains with quantitative methods. It maps the patterns of existed knowledge areas in publications related to search criteria to highlight the research gap and direct the potential future studies. Researchers explore the emerging research fields to conduct descriptive analysis then follow with in-depth analysis according to search strategies obtained. After setting the research questions, the data collection stage applied to gather all related data from the database. To prepare data for analysis, filtering, ordering (sorting) should be conducted. Analysis of literature review with specific bibliometric tools further highlights the understandings of the topics in more details (Fahimnia et al., 2015; Kolle, 2016; Kolle et al., 2017; Yu et al., 2018; Oliveria et al., 2017; Kulakli and Valmira, 2020; Kulakli and Shubina 2020).

Data Collection Strategy

In this study, publication data (records) retrieved from the database with below search keyword strategy (Kolle, 2016; Kolle et al. 2017; Fahimnia et al., 2015; Kulakli and Valmira, 2020; Yu et al., 2018; Du et al., 2017, Kulakli and Shubina 2020). There are several search queries run on the database to gather better results. Unrelated documents were extracted, and search criteria filtered. The final search criteria and steps as follows below in Table 1; (in ISI Web of Science Core Collection database).

About Bibliometrix R-package

All 101 records downloaded as plain text and MS Excel spreadsheet file formats. Further, the analysis and data visualization conducted in R Studio (R Package) and MS Excel software. R is open-source

Table 1. Search criteria for the publication records

Search criteria	
TITLE	*("data mining*" OR "business intelligence*")*
TITLE	*("big data*" OR "data analytic*")*
Timespan	*2010 to 2019*
Database	*ISI WoS Core Collection*
Indexes	*SCI-EXPANDED and SSCI*
Search refining criteria	*Language: All*
	Document types: All

Results: 101 publications found (in all document types)

software for programmers and users for specific analysis R Studio is an interface for who does not need or not experienced in programming.

Science mapping is sophisticated and complicated because it is multi-step and requires multiple software tools frequently. The Bibliometrix R-package is a tool for scientific and bibliometric quantitative analysis. Bibliometrix offers various routines for the import of bibliographical data from the science database such as Clarivate Analytics (Web of Science), Scopus, PubMed, and Cochrane; bibliometric analysis. (Aria et al., 2017). In this chapter, all figures, and tables prepared by using R Studio (Bibliometrix package), MS Excel, and MS Word programs.

Research Framework and Flow

Bibliometric studies widely used in library and information science and studies fields. Based on the research domains and objectives of the study, the authors conduct different analyses and tools to present the data set and findings of results. Data analysis and visualization tools such as Payek, BibExcel, Perish, R language, and R Studio (bibliometrix package), VOS viewer commonly use by researchers. The author has designed the research framework based on the literature (see in the Data collection strategy section above) and own experiences. The flow can be seen in Figure 1 below.

RESULTS AND DISCUSSIONS

Publication Profile and Languages (Publication Structure)

Using the above-mentioned search strategy, a total of 101 publications were retrieved from the ISI WoS database related to research domains. The vast majority of the papers written in the English language (99 papers, 98.02%) whereas Chinese and Spanish languages (1 paper with 0.99% each). The descriptive information about the publications was given in Table 2 below. It shows the majority of the publications found in peer-reviewed journal articles with 70 papers (69.31%), editorial material 11 papers (10.89%), reviews nine papers (8.91%), and meeting abstract eight papers (7.92) rest of the publications in total with six papers in total (6%).

Figure 1. Research framework (flow)

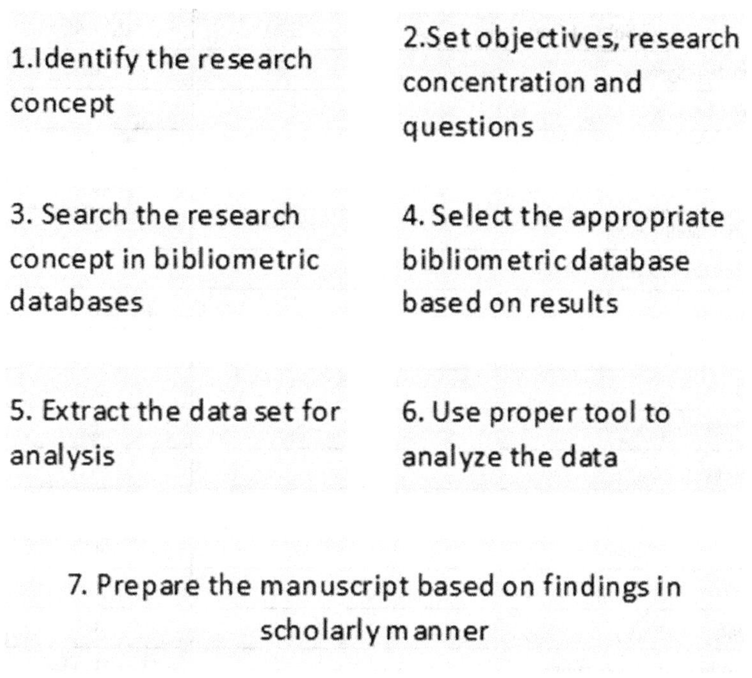

1. Identify the research concept	2. Set objectives, research concentration and questions
3. Search the research concept in bibliometric databases	4. Select the appropriate bibliometric database based on results
5. Extract the data set for analysis	6. Use proper tool to analyze the data

7. Prepare the manuscript based on findings in scholarly manner

Table 2. Distribution of publications by document types (2010-2019)

Document Types	Article	Editorial Material	Review	Meeting Abstract	Early Access	Book Review	Hardware Review	News Item	Proceedings Paper
records	70	11	9	8	2	1	1	1	1
% of 101	69.31%	10.89%	8.91%	7.92%	1.98%	0.99%	0.99%	0.99%	0.99%

Web of Science-Core Collection subject category analysis shows the literature related research domains were categorized under the top 33 major subject areas and detailed the record count with percent of total publication count in Table 3 below;

The top ten WoS subject categories of publication structure have been found as *Computer Science Information Systems, Computer Science Theory Methods, Engineering Electrical Electronics, Telecommunications, Computer Science Artificial Intelligence, Computer Science Software Engineering, Pharmacology Pharmacy, Computer Science Hardware Architecture, Management, and Toxicology.* Therefore, the majority of the subject category records fall into various Computer Science (71) and Engineering (52) fields. Following that, the distribution also shows medical (24), science (13), and management (9) research domains.

Table 3. Top 33 WoS subject areas by publications (2010-2019)

WoS Subject Categories	Record	Percent (%)
Computer Science Information Systems	30	29.70
Computer Science Theory Methods	17	16.83
Engineering Electrical Electronic	14	13.86
Telecommunications	13	12.87
Computer Science Artificial Intelligence	8	7.92
Computer Science Software Engineering	8	7.92
Pharmacology Pharmacy	7	6.93
Computer Science Hardware Architecture	5	4.95
Management	5	4.95
Toxicology	5	4.95
Engineering Multidisciplinary	4	3.96
Genetics Heredity	4	3.96
Operations Research Management Science	4	3.96
Automation Control Systems	3	2.97
Chemistry Multidisciplinary	3	2.97
Computer Science Interdisciplinary Applications	3	2.97
Materials Science Multidisciplinary	3	2.97
Physics Applied	3	2.97
Biotechnology Applied Microbiology	2	1.98
Construction Building Technology	2	1.98
Energy Fuels	2	1.98
Engineering Chemical	2	1.98
Engineering Civil	2	1.98
Engineering Industrial	2	1.98
Environmental Sciences	2	1.98
Environmental Studies	2	1.98
Food Science Technology	2	1.98
Geography Physical	2	1.98
Green Sustainable Science Technology	2	1.98
Medicine General Internal	2	1.98
Multidisciplinary Sciences	2	1.98
Radiology Nuclear Medicine Medical Imaging	2	1.98
Remote Sensing	2	1.98

Distribution of Publication by Years (2010-2019)

Table 4 shows the publications during the search period. At the beginning of the period, the years 2010 and 2011, there was not any publication. The publications started in 2012. The average journal articles were published of this period (2012-2019) was 12.63 records. 2018 and 2019 are the most productive years found with above the average rate, and 2018 is the highest (peak) level with 34 records (33.66%).

Table 4. Publication by years (2010-2019)

Publication by Years	2010	2011	2012	2013	2014	2015	2016	2017	2018	2019
records	0	0	2	2	8	4	15	12	34	24
% of 101	0.00	0.00	1.98	1.98	7.92	3.96	14.85	11.88	33.66	23.76

Figure 2 shows the distribution of the number of publications per year (period of 2012-2019). The linear trend line shows an upward movement and illustrates the increased publication interest in the research domains. The increased number of publications in the period 2016 to 2019 showed that more than the average of total publications per year. In addition to this, 2018 is far more than the average publication records.

Figure 2. The linear trend line of publication count (2010-2019)

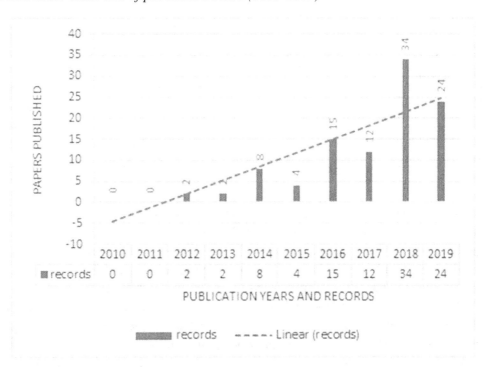

Journal Frequency and Keyword Analysis

Table 5 shows the publication frequency in the most relevant sources. However, there are no significant differences in publication history. The number of journals to some extend the top contributed journals (13 sources) as *Basic Clinical Pharmacology Toxicology, Cluster Comp. the J. of Networks Software Tools and Applications, IEEE Access* with a minimum of 4 papers above published between 2012 and 2019. The majority of the journals in the top publication sources category are *Computer, Engineering, and Information Science* categories. According to the findings, there are 81 single sources, and 101 total publication counts. Table 5 also shows the publication frequency of top sources, 13 journals have categorized as higher the number of publications in the field (more than two articles ranked in the records). Besides, there is 68 source listed as one publication for each in the data set. Although there is no significant number of articles published in one or a few journals, it seems that journals published a similar amount of the papers, respectively.

Table 5. Publication frequency by Journals (2010-2019)

Most Relevant-Top Publication Sources	Records	% of 101
Basic Clinical Pharmacology Toxicology	5	4.95
Cluster Comp. the J. of Networks Software Tools and Applications	4	3.96
IEEE Access	4	3.96
Agro Food Industry Hi-Tech	2	1.98
Applied Sciences Basel	2	1.98
Computer Networks	2	1.98
Concurrency and Computation Practice Experience	2	1.98
Expert Systems with Applications	2	1.98
Information Systems Frontiers	2	1.98
ISPRS International Journal of Geo-Information	2	1.98
KSII Transactions on Internet and Information Systems	2	1.98
Security and Communication Networks	2	1.98
Sustainability	2	1.98

Table 6 highlights the most relevant keywords used in the articles. The first column represents author keywords (DE) which are *"Big Data"*, *"Data Mining"*, *"Big Data Mining"*, and *"Business Intelligence"* are the top keywords. The second column shows the keyword-Plus (ID), which are "Classification", "Prediction," and "Systems" are highly used keywords, among others. Author keyword (DE) analysis shows the frequency of the words in parallel with research titles and those matches.

Figure 3 represents the Word Cloud of Keyword-Plus (ID). The cloud also highlights the weights and distribution of frequency of words yearly basis. Figure 4 shows the word growth of keyword-plus graphics with the same patterns compared to the word cloud. Besides, it represents the distribution of each Keyword-Plus frequency and appearance over the period decade. The *"Classification"*, *"Prediction"*, and *"Analytics"* have higher frequency and appearance.

Table 6. Most relevant keywords (Top 10)

	Author Keywords (DE)	**Articles**	**Keywords-Plus (ID)**	**Articles**
1	Big Data	45	Classification	7
2	Data Mining	25	Prediction	7
3	Big Data Mining	9	Systems	6
4	Business Intelligence	9	Analytics	4
5	Cloud Computing	5	Information	4
6	Big Data Analytics	4	Network	4
7	Deep Learning	4	Algorithm	3
8	Big Data Analysis	3	Algorithms	3
9	Machine Learning	3	Cloud	3
10	Business Analytics	2	Energy	3

Figure 3. Word Cloud of Keywords-Plus

Keyword/Year	2012	2013	2014	2015	2016	2017	2018	2019	
Classification	0	0	1	0	1	0	1	4	7
Prediction	0	0	0	0	4	0	1	2	7
Systems	1	0	0	0	0	1	4	0	6
Analytics	0	0	1	0	1	0	1	1	4
Information	0	0	1	0	0	1	1	1	4
Network	1	0	0	0	2	1	0	0	4
Algorithms	0	0	1	0	1	0	1	0	3
Cloud	0	0	0	0	0	1	1	1	3
Feature-Selection	0	0	0	0	1	0	1	1	3
Knowledge	0	0	1	0	0	0	2	0	3

Moreover, those first two keywords are in an upward movement in the graph. Also, Figure 5 illustrates the mapping of Author Keywords. The map shows the interrelation and the link of published paper's frequency about the author keywords such as "Big Data", "Data mining", and "Big Data Mining" are the highest keywords among all publications.

Figure 4. Word growth of Keywords-Plus

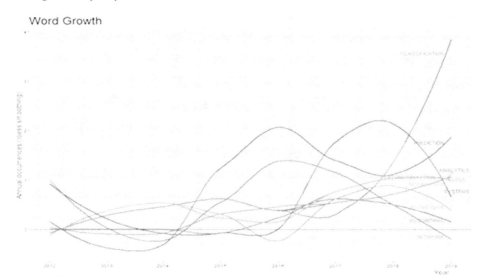

Figure 5. Author's keywords

Most Productive Authors/Co-authors by Publication Count

Table 7 indicates the author and co-author detailed results by documents. Only 15 papers published as single-authored documents, while multi-authored documents stand as 300 documents, and 315 different authors with 348 appearances occur. Documents per author ratio are 0.32, while authors per document are 3.12.

Table 7. Author and co-author descriptive results by documents (2010-2019)

Descriptive results	Records counted
Authors	315
Author Appearances	348
Authors of single-authored documents	15
Authors of multi-authored documents	300
Single-authored documents	15
Documents per Author	0.32
Authors per Document	3.12
Co-Authors per Documents	3.45
Collaboration Index	3.49

Similar findings of publication frequency and the most productive authors can be seen in Figure 6 and their network in Figure 7. Although there is no significant difference among publication records by per author patterns, Wang J comparatively is on the top with four papers in total for the research period, it is followed by Chen J, Liu J, Ren Y, Wang Z, and Zhang X with three papers in total each. Furthermore, the rest of the list concluded Chen BS, Ding W, Hu J, and Jiang C with two papers each.

Figure 6. Most productive authors by publication volume

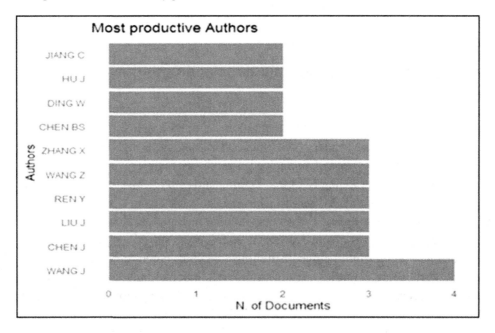

Figure 7. Most productive author's network

Analysis of the Most Productive Institutions and Countries

According to findings, the most productive and active institutions (Organizations Enhanced) on the research domains are Chinese Universities shown in Figure 8 are, Beijing Institute of Technology, Chinese Academy of Sciences, Huazhong University of Science Technology, Tsinghua University, University of Electronic Science Technology of China, Chongqing University, Nanjing University of Science Technology, Nantong University, Southeast University China, Tianjin University, University of Chinese Academy of Sciences CAS, Zhejiang University. In contrast, Harvard University from USA, Nanyang Technological University and Nanyang Technological University National Institute of Education NIE from Singapore, and National Tsing Hua University from Taiwan are as followers stayed on top of the publications list.

Figure 8 illustrates the most productive institutions that contributed to research domains with more than two papers. The leading countries with institutions collaborated research in the field are Chinese institutions with 31 records (27.69%) on top of the list, followed by Singapore with four records (3.96%), and the USA with two papers (1.98%). The contributed institutions with only one paper counted are 194, whereas all institutions counted 210 in total with 233 country-region appearances in a total of 101 publications. In Figure 9, the most productive institutions network could be seen in parallel with Figure 8.

Figure 8. Most productive organizations by publication count

Figure 9. Most productive institutions network

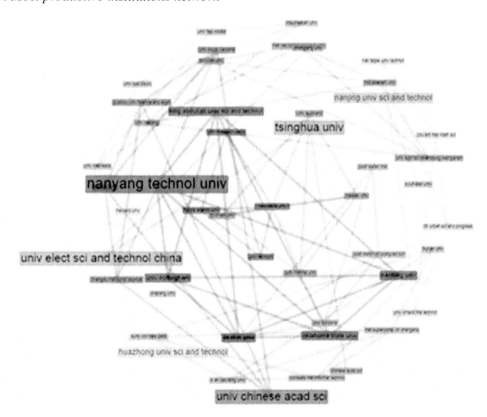

Figure 10 shows the most productive (top 10) countries regions that contributed to the research domain fields. The leading countries are China and the USA, followed by Taiwan, South Korea, Canada, India, Spain, the United Kingdom, Australia, and France. The figure shows two dimensions of collaboration patterns, such as Single Country Publications (SCP) and Multiple Country Publications (MCP).

Figure 10. Most productive Country-Regions by SCP and MCP publication collaboration counts

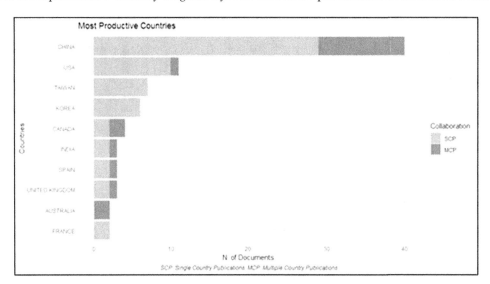

Table 8 identifies the details of publication data with frequency, SCP, MCP, and MCP ratio of top countries. Therefore, China, with 40 articles in total (29 SCP and 11 MCP), is the leading country among the top 10 list. The USA has 11 articles (10 SCP, 1 MCP); Taiwan has seven articles (7 SCP, 0 MCP); South Korea has six articles (6 SCP, 0 MCP); Canada has four articles (2 SCP, 2MCP); India has three articles (2 SCP, 1 MCP); Spain has three articles (2 SCP, 1 MCP); United Kingdom has three articles (2 SCP, 1 MCP); Australia has two articles (0 SCP, 2 MCP); and France has two articles (2 SCP, 0 MCP). SCP and Country article distribution has similar characters in the data set. However, the USA relatively low in MCP with 1 article in comparison with the SCP ratio. It could also be said that authors from the USA prefer publication as a single author compares to China. Similar findings also can be said for Taiwan and South Korea. On the contrary, Australia shows the opposite pattern where multiple country publications were preferred. Figure 11 presents the publication network of most rich countries as parallel with Figure 10 and Table 8.

Citation Analysis of the Research Domains

Citation report for 101 publication results from Web of Science Core Collection between 2010 and 2019 show that the h-index is 14; average citations per item is 29.92; the sum of times cited 3022; without self-citations 3000; citing articles 2891; without self-citations 2874 counted. Figure 12 illustrates the total citation distribution from 2012 to 2019. Although the research period set as last decade (2010 to 2019), publications and citations started the year of 2012. The first two years (2012 to 2014) citation increased as regularly and reached just above 100 counts; then 2014 to 2017 it was sharply increased, citation count reached above 650. The term of 2017 to 2019 showed stability in citation figures as of 650 to 700 counts in the last two years.

Table 8. Corresponding author's countries with frequency and ratios

	Country	Articles	Frequency	SCP	MCP	MCP Ratio
1	China	40	0.4211	29	11	0.2750
2	USA	11	0.1158	10	1	0.0909
3	Taiwan	7	0.0737	7	0	0.0000
4	South Korea	6	0.0632	6	0	0.0000
5	Canada	4	0.0421	2	2	0.5000
6	India	3	0.0316	2	1	0.3333
7	Spain	3	0.0316	2	1	0.3333
8	United Kingdom	3	0.0316	2	1	0.3333
9	Australia	2	0.0211	0	2	1.0000
10	France	2	0.0211	2	0	0.0000

SCP: Single Country Publications
MCP: Multiple Country Publications

Figure 11. Publication network of most productive countries

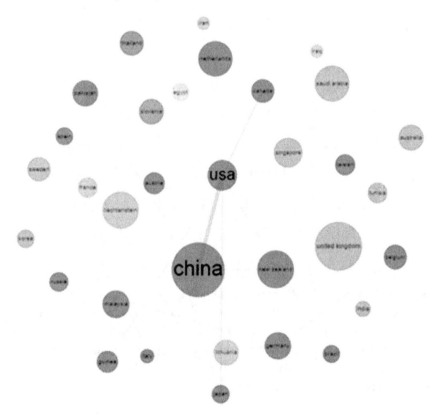

Figure 12. Total citation counts per year (2010-2019)

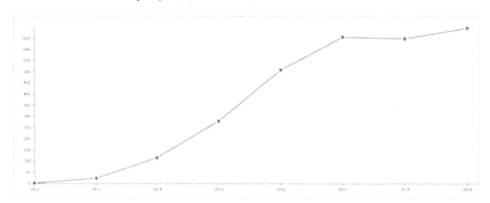

Table 9 demonstrates total citations (Top 10) per country with author and co-author counts are combined. Although the USA has the highest total citations among the top 10 countries, followed by China, Liechtenstein, and Canada. However, Slovenia has a higher average of citations, even with the less total citations figures (35 counted). The data also shows that although China has second higher total citations. However, the average is relatively low. This means they produced more publications, and relatively the citation figures have not shown similar patterns.

Table 9. Total citations per country (Top 10)

	Country	Total Citations	Average Article Citations
1	USA	1510	137.27
2	China	1239	30.98
3	Liechtenstein	47	47.00
4	Canada	43	10.75
5	Taiwan	39	5.57
6	Slovenia	35	35.00
7	South Korea	22	3.67
8	United Kingdom	20	6.67
9	Iran	17	8.50
10	Australia	13	6.50

Table 10 shows the most frequently cited articles during the literature review period. According to the findings, the most cited paper is related to research domains.

Figure 13 and Figure 14 illustrate the network analysis of the "Co-citation network by authors" and "Co-citation network by keywords". The network links for cited authors and related keywords show the connections and collaboration among published studies. The bigger the node size represents the impact and importance, the frequency in the network weights. (In Appendix 1A, 1B, 1C and 1D show the different level of the network sizes with nodes).

Table 10. Top ten articles' citation counts by publication years

	Author	Year	Source	TC	TC per Year
1	Chen H	2012	MIS Q	1421	157.89
2	Wu X	2014	IEEE Trans Knowl Data Eng	985	140.71
3	Xu L	2014	IEEE Access	132	18.86
4	Debortoli S	2014	Bus Inf Syst Eng	47	6.71
5	Kranjc J,	2017	Futur Gener Comp Syst	35	8.75
6	Singh S	2018	Energies	29	9.67
7	Zhu J	2018	Annu Rev Control	28	9.33
8	Gandomi AH	2016	Autom Constr	26	5.20
9	Tsai CF	2016	J Syst Softw	20	4.00
10	Margolies LR	2016	AM J Roentgenol	20	4.00

Figure 13. Co-citation of references network by authors

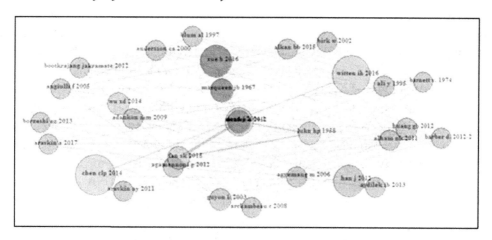

Figure 14. Co-citation of references network by keywords

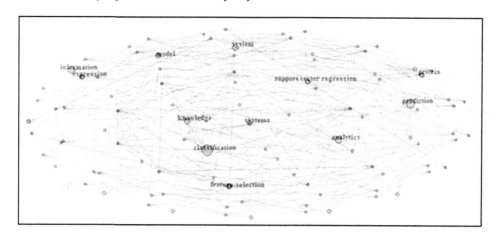

SOLUTIONS AND RECOMMENDATIONS

The aim of this research directed the iterative process of proven bibliometric methods to be conducted from beginning to end of the workflow. Exploring the relations among research domains reveals the publication patterns and answers to research questions formed based on the research strategy. The outcomes of this research have twofold. First, it has presented a descriptive structure of publication data to perform analysis on domains. Secondly, the distribution of institution, region, country, author collaboration, and productivity analyzed in-depth, further citation patterns indicated to show publication impacts and the country-author co-citations networks.

The evolution of the subjects and publication trends showed the concentration areas as "Big Data (in 45 paper)", "Data Mining (in 25 paper)", "Big Data Mining (in 9 paper)", "Business Intelligence/Analytics (in 11 paper)", "Big Data Analytics/Analysis (in 7 papers)" are top author keywords in recent studies of 101 publications. Similarly, "Classification", "Prediction", "Systems", "Analytics", "Algorithms", "Information", and "Network" are top terms in keyword-plus categories for the same publications.

Country-author collaboration is another crucial point of bibliometric study concerns. Most productive institutions and countries are China and the USA (in a total of 50.49%) (See Appendix 2). Followed by Taiwan, South Korea, Canada, India, Spain, the UK, Australia, and France. USA has shown as a leading country for single-authored publications, whereas China is a leading country all over the publications with a combination of single country publications (SCP) and multiple country publications (MCP).

In citation counts, although China is a leading country with publication counts, the USA shows the highest citations (1510 counts), above China (1239 counts). Following countries Liechtenstein, Canada, Taiwan, Slovenia, South Korea, UK, Iran, and Australia on top of the list. Comparing to previous data of publication productivity, Liechtenstein and Slovenia have higher citations than their productivity level. There is an exciting detail that also can be seen in productivity data, like India, Spain, and France appears in the top productive country; however, those do not appear in the top cited publication list. The impact of publication differs from the publication count. The ratio of USA 137.27 average article cited (1510 citations/11 paper=137.27), whereas China 30.98 average article cited (1239 citations/40 paper=30.98) in the period of research.

In light of those data and analysis, the significant developments of the research domains indicate that the impact of research does not depend on the publication quantity, it is more related to quality. Highest cited papers found in "Business Intelligence and analytics (Chen et al., 2012)", "Data mining and big data (Wu et al., 2014)", "Information security in big data: privacy and data mining (Xu et al., 2014)", "Comparison of business intelligence and big data (Debortoli et al., 2014)", "Online workflows in big data mining (Kranjc et al., 2017)", "Big data mining in the energy sector (Singh & Yassine, 2018)", "Review big data with data mining approaches (Zhu et al., 2018)", "Genetic programming for experimental big data mining (Gandomi et al., 2016)", "Big data mining with parallel computing (Tsai et al., 2016)", and "Breast imaging in the era of big data, structured reporting (Margolies et al., 2016)".

This work justifies its interest and importance in the field of Data Mining, Big Data, Business Intelligence, and related Analytics. Therefore, the focus of this study takes into account a variety of perspectives to support developments in the area for authors, readers or audiences from different parties and covering a broad community of science or industry experts or any other corporations.

FUTURE RESEARCH DIRECTIONS

Research domains have been found very popular, and growing interest shows in a parallel upward movement in the trend of publication records. According to results, the majority of the subject category records found in computer science and engineering. Following medical, science, and management subjects are also significant. Further research would be carried out with Big Data dominance to Data Mining, Analytics, and Business Intelligence related issues. More emerging topics such as "Smart Industry (manufacturing and service provision)", "Smart Technology, Smart Cities and Smart Devices", "Industry 4.0", "Cybersecurity", "Internet of Things (IoT)", "Blockchain Technology", "Cloud Computing", "Supply Chain Management", "New (sharing) economy and financial issues" and "Environmental (green) initiatives" should be studied both empirical, conceptual and systematic literature reviews along with in-detailed bibliometric studies too. More business and management case studies should also be conducted in parallel with Big Data emerged in various industries such as airlines, telecommunication, finance (bank, insurance, stock exchange), operations and logistics, tourism, internet services, e-commerce, information systems and services, security, contact centers, health, government and non-profit organizations (NPO).

Theoretical Implications and Research Needs

The originality and value of this chapter would found for researchers to obtain an overview of the publication trends on Big Data, Data Mining, Business Intelligence, and Analytics related areas to be interested in further studies and shows the potential gaps in those fields. The journal audiences in information studies area and the wider community such as academics, professionals, practitioners would also have benefits to extend their knowledge in the research, publication, and teaching purposes as well. The main theoretical contribution of this chapter could be said as systematically reviewed the records to analyze and present the findings of integrating Big Data (Mining), Data Mining, Business Intelligence, and Analytics. Therefore, in-depth literature review in all presented manuscripts showed a keen interest and contributions around the globe. The findings of the bibliometric study reveal several analysis parts as productivity of the publications (author, country, institution, type of publication), most important fields of studies and topics (with keywords, popular areas) supported with citations and co-citations, and mapping the scientific network.

Practical Implications

The purpose of this chapter was to bring together the existing research publications to analyze and represent the relation and gap for further practical research themes. Besides, theoretical concerns of this study more qualitative, quantitative, and inductive research would help to extend the current knowledge level with more practical studies. By introducing new practical ideas for any industry, sector, or country-specific studies would also support the continuation of research efforts. Moreover, it would help to stimulate further industry-specific researches such kind of empirical, conceptual, bibliometric analysis, and case studies. Those research outcomes would also provide comprehensive understandings of information in the specific fields and highlight the opportunities to launch new business projects. The awareness of information could also enlighten the professionals and practitioners' efforts for their successful business operations.

Limitations and Future Research

The paper has some limitations, likewise other scholarly research papers. The findings of the research are limited to the publications covered in the Web of Science Core Collection database (SCI-Exp and SSCI indexes) with the given keywords in the data collection strategy (TITLE and TOPIC search) of the methodology part. The study conducted and analyzed in January and February 2020 for the last decade. Although the publications retrieved from Web of Science Core Collection database, the value of the papers and impact factor of journals is not equivalent when the other papers published in lower impact factors. Besides, the journals ranked in four different quartiles (Q1 to Q4 ranking of ISI), which categorizes the journals within subject categories. The content analysis has not been applied for the study according to data set and structure. However, keyword frequency and analysis conducted and represented the trends in publications by years and highlight the contributions.

Identified research patterns and gaps direct new avenues on the business analytics field and also offer opportunities for researchers to contribute more in-depth researches by theoretical and empirical studies.

CONCLUSION

In this chapter, the author has attempted to explore and analyze the research stream in the literature of published papers related to "integration of big data, data mining in particular business intelligence and analytics", which indexed and ranked in ISI Web of Science Core Collection database between 2010 and 2019. A total of 101 were published on the research domains during the study period (2010-2019), with an average of 15.29 articles per year. However, publications related to the integration of those domains started in 2012. Exponential growth in publication count was observed for the period, in addition to citation patterns show similar growth as well. To understand and discover the research trends, collaboration, and networks around the globe, bibliometric methods were employed. According to the research objectives mentioned earlier, questions were formed, and the data collection stage completed with proper search strategies, the further analysis conducted to explore patterns and relations in more detail.

Publications started in 2012 (in 2010 and 2011, there is no publication). According to results, the study shows that the number of papers published in research topics has increased from 2016 to 2019 than average publication count (15.29 average number of articles per year). From 2012 to 2015 (4 years), 16 papers with 15.85%, on the contrary, between 2016 to 2019 (4 years) 85 paper with 84.15% published. The year in 2018 is the highest publication counted (34 papers with 33.66%).

Research outcome would clearly show that integration of Big Data, Data Mining, Business Intelligence, and related Analytics are popular topics and publication trend also validates the increase. Authors and researchers from different academic fields such as Engineering, Computer Science, Medical studies, and Science in general, as well as Management disciplines, have widely interested in publishing their research outcomes. Presented results also attempted to close the gap between theoretical and practical spheres in domains where Big Data, Data Mining, Business Intelligence, and Analytics plays a significant role. This chapter is relevant for researchers, academics, and practitioners in different disciplines as well as who works and contributes to the field of information studies, engineering, science, medical studies, management-business, and interdisciplinary-multidisciplinary studies.

ACKNOWLEDGMENT

This research received no specific grant from any funding agency in the public, commercial, or not-for-profit sectors.

REFERENCES

Afzali, G. A., & Mohammadi, S. (2017). Privacy preserving big data mining: Association rule hiding using fuzzy logic approach. *IET Information Security*, *12*(1), 15–24. doi:10.1049/iet-ifs.2015.0545

Apgar, D. (2015). The False Promise of Big Data: Can Data Mining Replace Hypothesis-Driven Learning in the Identification of Predictive Performance Metrics? *Systems Research and Behavioral Science*, *32*(1), 28–49. doi:10.1002res.2219

Aria, M., & Cuccurullo, C. (2017). bibliometrix: An R-tool for comprehensive science mapping analysis. *Journal of Informetrics*, *11*(4), 959–975. doi:10.1016/j.joi.2017.08.007

Azevedo, A. I. R. L., & Santos, M. F. (2009). An architecture for an effective usage of data mining in business intelligence systems. *Knowledge Management and Innovation in Advancing Economies: Analyses & Solutions*, 1319-1325.

Bae, D. H., Kim, J. H., Kim, S. W., Oh, H., & Park, C. (2013) Intelligent SSD: a turbo for big data mining. *Proceedings of the 22nd ACM international conference on Information & Knowledge Management*, 1573-1576. 10.1145/2505515.2507847

Batran, M., Mejia, M. G., Kanasugi, H., Sekimoto, Y., & Shibasaki, R. (2018). Inferencing human spatiotemporal mobility in greater Maputo via mobile phone big data mining. *ISPRS International Journal of Geo-Information*, *7*(7), 259. doi:10.3390/ijgi7070259

Buhl, H. U., Röglinger, M., Moser, F., & Heidemann, J. (2013). Big data. *Business & Information Systems Engineering*, *5*(2), 65–69. doi:10.100712599-013-0249-5

Chang, B. J. (2018). Agile Business Intelligence: Combining Big Data and Business Intelligence to Responsive Decision Model. *Journal of Internet Technology*, *19*(6), 1699–1706.

Chen, H., Chiang, R. H., & Storey, V. C. (2012). Business intelligence and analytics: From big data to big impact. *Management Information Systems Quarterly*, *36*(4), 1165–1188. doi:10.2307/41703503

Chen, J., Li, K., Rong, H., Bilal, K., Yang, N., & Li, K. (2018). A disease diagnosis and treatment recommendation system based on big data mining and cloud computing. *Information Sciences*, *435*, 124–149. doi:10.1016/j.ins.2018.01.001

Chongwatpol, J. (2016). Managing big data in coal-fired power plants: A business intelligence framework. *Industrial Management & Data Systems*, *116*(8), 1779–1799. doi:10.1108/IMDS-11-2015-0473

Chow-White, P. A., & Green, S. Jr. (2013). Data Mining Difference in the Age of Big Data: Communication and the social shaping of genome technologies from 1998 to 2007. *International Journal of Communication, 7*, 28.

D'Alconzo, A., Barlet-Ros, P., Fukuda, K., & Choffnes, D. R. (2016). Machine learning, data mining and Big Data frameworks for network monitoring and troubleshooting. *Computer Networks, 107*(1), 1–4. doi:10.1016/j.comnet.2016.06.031

Das, D., Sadiq, A. S., Ahmad, N. B., & Lloret, J. (2017). Stock Market Prediction with Big Data through Hybridization of Data Mining and Optimized Neural Network Techniques. *Multiple-Valued Logic and Soft Computing, 29*(1-2), 157–181.

Debortoli, S., Müller, O., & vom Brocke, J. (2014). Comparing business intelligence and big data skills. *Business & Information Systems Engineering, 6*(5), 289–300. doi:10.100712599-014-0344-2

Du, H. S., Ke, X., Chu, S. K. W., & Chan, L. T. (2017). A bibliometric analysis of emergency management using information systems (2000-2016). *Online Information Review, 41*(4), 454–470. doi:10.1108/OIR-05-2017-0142

Fahimnia, B., Sarkis, J., & Davarzani, H. (2015). Green supply chain management: A review and bibliometric analysis. *International Journal of Production Economics, 162*, 101–114. doi:10.1016/j.ijpe.2015.01.003

Fu, J., Chen, Z., Wang, J., He, M., & Wang, J. (2012). Distributed storage system big data mining based on HPC application-A solar photovoltaic forecasting system practice. International Information Institute (Tokyo) Information.

Gandomi, A. H., Sajedi, S., Kiani, B., & Huang, Q. (2016). Genetic programming for experimental big data mining: A case study on concrete creep formulation. *Automation in Construction, 70*, 89–97. doi:10.1016/j.autcon.2016.06.010

Goti-Elordi, A., de-la-Calle-Vicente, A., Gil-Larrea, M. J., Errasti-Opakua, A., & Uradnicek, J. (2017). Application of a business intelligence tool within the context of big data in a food industry company. *Dyna (Bilbao), 92*(3), 347–353.

Huang, S. C., McIntosh, S., Sobolevsky, S., & Hung, P. C. (2017). Big data analytics and business intelligence in industry. *Information Systems Frontiers, 19*(6), 1229–1232. doi:10.100710796-017-9804-9

Jiang, P., & Liu, X. S. (2015). Big data mining yields novel insights on cancer. *Nature Genetics, 47*(2), 103–104. doi:10.1038/ng.3205 PMID:25627899

Jurgelevičius, A., & Sakalauskas, L. (2018). Big data mining using public distributed computing. *Information Technology and Control, 47*(2), 236–248. doi:10.5755/j01.itc.47.2.19738

Kim, K. Y. (2014). Business Intelligence and Marketing Insights in an Era of Big Data: The Q-sorting Approach. *Transactions on Internet and Information Systems (Seoul), 8*(2).

Kolle, S., Vijayashree, M., & Shankarappa, T. (2017). Highly cited articles in maleria research: A bibliometric analysis. *Collection Building*, *36*(2), 1–12. doi:10.1108/CB-10-2016-0028

Kolle, S. R., & Thyavanahalli, S. H. (2016). Global research on air pollution between 2005 and 2014: A bibliometric study. *Collection Building*, *35*(3), 84–92. doi:10.1108/CB-05-2016-0008

Kranjc, J., Orač, R., Podpečan, V., Lavrač, N., & Robnik-Šikonja, M. (2017). ClowdFlows: Online workflows for distributed big data mining. *Future Generation Computer Systems*, *68*, 38–58. doi:10.1016/j.future.2016.07.018

Kulakli, A., & Osmanaj, V. (2020). Global research on big data in relation with artificial intelligence (A bibliometric study: 2008-2019). *International Journal of Online and Biomedical Engineering*, *16*(2), 31–46. doi:10.3991/ijoe.v16i02.12617

Kulakli, A., & Shubina, I. (2020). A bibliometric study on Mobile Applications for PTSD treatment: The period of 2010-2019. *Proceedings of 6th International Conference on Information Management*, 319-323.

Kuo, C. F. J., Lin, C. H., & Lee, M. H. (2018). Analyze the energy consumption characteristics and affecting factors of Taiwan's convenience stores-using the big data mining approach. *Energy and Building*, *168*, 120–136. doi:10.1016/j.enbuild.2018.03.021

Li, Q., Li, S., Zhang, S., Hu, J., & Hu, J. (2019). A Review of Text Corpus-Based Tourism Big Data Mining. *Applied Sciences (Basel, Switzerland)*, *9*(16), 3300. doi:10.3390/app9163300

Li, X. T., & Feng, F. (2018). Enterprise Customer Relationship Management Based On Big Data Mining. Latin American Applied Research-. *International Journal (Toronto, Ont.)*, *48*(3), 163–168.

Liang, T. P., & Liu, Y. H. (2018). Research landscape of business intelligence and big data analytics: A bibliometric study. *Expert Systems with Applications*, *111*, 2–10. doi:10.1016/j.eswa.2018.05.018

Lin, H. Y., & Yang, S. Y. (2019). A cloud-based energy data mining information agent system based on big data analysis technology. *Microelectronics and Reliability*, *97*, 66–78. doi:10.1016/j.microrel.2019.03.010

Liu, B., Fu, Z., Wang, P., Liu, L., Gao, M., & Liu, J. (2018). Big-data-mining-based improved k-means algorithm for energy use analysis of coal-fired power plant units: A case study. *Entropy (Basel, Switzerland)*, *20*(9), 702. doi:10.3390/e20090702

Lv, S., Kim, H., Zheng, B., & Jin, H. (2018). A review of data mining with big data towards its applications in the electronics industry. *Applied Sciences (Basel, Switzerland)*, *8*(4), 582. doi:10.3390/app8040582

Margolies, L. R., Pandey, G., Horowitz, E. R., & Mendelson, D. S. (2016). Breast imaging in the era of big data: Structured reporting and data mining. *AJR. American Journal of Roentgenology*, *206*(2), 259–264. doi:10.2214/AJR.15.15396 PMID:26587797

Mariani, M., Baggio, R., Fuchs, M., & Höepken, W. (2018). Business intelligence and big data in hospitality and tourism: A systematic literature review. *International Journal of Contemporary Hospitality Management*, *30*(12), 3514–3554. doi:10.1108/IJCHM-07-2017-0461

Maté, A., Llorens, H., de Gregorio, E., Tardío, R., Gil, D., Munoz-Terol, R., & Trujillo, J. (2015). A novel multidimensional approach to integrate big data in business intelligence. *Journal of Database Management*, *26*(2), 14–31. doi:10.4018/JDM.2015040102

Mellor, J. C., Stone, M. A., & Keane, J. (2018). Application of data mining to "big data" acquired in audiology: Principles and potential. *Trends in Hearing*, *22*, 1–10. doi:10.1177/2331216518776817 PMID:29848183

Morota, G., Ventura, R. V., Silva, F. F., Koyama, M., & Fernando, S. C. (2018). Machine learning and data mining advance predictive big data analysis in precision animal agriculture. *Journal of Animal Science*, *96*(4), 1540–1550. doi:10.1093/jasky014 PMID:29385611

Njah, H., Jamoussi, S., & Mahdi, W. (2019). Deep Bayesian network architecture for Big Data mining. *Concurrency and Computation*, *31*(2), e4418. doi:10.1002/cpe.4418

O'Halloran, K. L., Tan, S., Pham, D. S., Bateman, J., & Vande Moere, A. (2018). A digital mixed methods research design: Integrating multimodal analysis with data mining and information visualization for big data analytics. *Journal of Mixed Methods Research*, *12*(1), 11–30. doi:10.1177/1558689816651015

Oliveria, U., Espindola, L., & Marins, F. (2017). Analysis of supply chain risk management research. *Gestão & Produção*, *25*(4).

Qi, E., Yang, X., & Wang, Z. (2019). Data mining and visualization of data-driven news in the era of big data. *Cluster Computing*, *22*(4), 10333–10346. doi:10.100710586-017-1348-8

Sang, J., Gao, Y., Bao, B. K., Snoek, C., & Dai, Q. (2016). Recent advances in social multimedia big data mining and applications. *Multimedia Systems*, *22*(1), 1-3.

Shadroo, S., & Rahmani, A. M. (2018). Systematic survey of big data and data mining in internet of things. *Computer Networks*, *139*, 19–47. doi:10.1016/j.comnet.2018.04.001

Shengdong, M., Zhengxian, X., & Yixiang, T. (2019). Intelligent Traffic Control System Based on Cloud Computing and Big Data Mining. *IEEE Transactions on Industrial Informatics*, *15*(12), 6583–6592. doi:10.1109/TII.2019.2929060

Shuai, H., MingChao, L., QiuBing, R., & ChengZhao, L. (2018). Intelligent determination and data mining for tectonic settings of basalts based on big data methods. *Yanshi Xuebao*, *34*(11), 3207–3216.

Singh, S., & Yassine, A. (2018). Big data mining of energy time series for behavioral analytics and energy consumption forecasting. *Energies*, *11*(2), 452.

Song, C. W., Jung, H., & Chung, K. (2019). Development of a medical big-data mining process using topic modeling. *Cluster Computing*, *22*(1), 1949–1958. doi:10.100710586-017-0942-0

Song, G. Y., Cheon, Y., Lee, K., Park, K. M., & Rim, H. C. (2014). Inter-category Map: Building Cognition Network of General Customers through Big Data Mining. *Transactions on Internet and Information Systems (Seoul)*, *8*(2).

Sun, Z., Sun, L., & Strang, K. (2018). Big data analytics services for enhancing business intelligence. *Journal of Computer Information Systems*, *58*(2), 162–169. doi:10.1080/08874417.2016.1220239

Tsai, C. F., Lin, W. C., & Ke, S. W. (2016). Big data mining with parallel computing: A comparison of distributed and MapReduce methodologies. *Journal of Systems and Software*, *122*, 83–92. doi:10.1016/j.jss.2016.09.007

Wang, S., & Yuan, H. (2014). Spatial data mining: A perspective of big data. *International Journal of Data Warehousing and Mining*, *10*(4), 50–70. doi:10.4018/ijdwm.2014100103

Wu, X., Zhu, X., Wu, G. Q., & Ding, W. (2014). Data mining with big data. *IEEE Transactions on Knowledge and Data Engineering*, *26*(1), 97–107. doi:10.1109/TKDE.2013.109

Xu, L., Jiang, C., Chen, Y., Wang, J., & Ren, Y. (2016). A framework for categorizing and applying privacy-preservation techniques in big data mining. *Computer*, *49*(2), 54–62. doi:10.1109/MC.2016.43

Xu, L., Jiang, C., Wang, J., Yuan, J., & Ren, Y. (2014). Information security in big data: Privacy and data mining. *IEEE Access : Practical Innovations, Open Solutions*, *2*, 1149–1176.

Xu, L., Jiang, C., Wang, J., Yuan, J., & Ren, Y. (2014). Information security in big data: Privacy and data mining. *IEEE Access: Practical Innovations, Open Solutions*, *2*, 1149–1176. doi:10.1109/AC-CESS.2014.2362522

Yang, T., Xie, J., Li, G., Mou, N., Li, Z., Tian, C., & Zhao, J. (2019). Social Media Big Data Mining and Spatio-Temporal Analysis on Public Emotions for Disaster Mitigation. *ISPRS International Journal of Geo-Information*, *8*(1), 29. doi:10.3390/ijgi8010029

Yu, D., Xu, Z., & Wang, W. (2018). Bibliometric analysis of fuzzy theory research in China: A 30-year perspective. *Knowledge-Based Systems*, *141*, 188–199. doi:10.1016/j.knosys.2017.11.018

Yu, W. (2017). Challenges and Reflections of Big Data Mining Based on Mobile Internet Customers. *Agro Food Industry Hi-Tech*, *28*(1), 3221–3224.

Zhang, H., & Zhang, Z. (2019). Research on the Big Data Cloud Computing Based on the Network Data Mining. In Basic & Clinical Pharmacology & Toxicology (Vol. 124, pp. 150-151). Wiley.

Zhang, X., Jang-Jaccard, J., Qi, L., Bhuiyan, M. Z., & Liu, C. (2018). Privacy Issues in Big Data Mining Infrastructure, Platforms, and Applications. *Security and Communication Networks*, *2018*, 1–3. doi:10.1155/2018/6238607

Zhang, Y., Guo, S. L., Han, L. N., & Li, T. L. (2016). Application and exploration of big data mining in clinical medicine. *Chinese Medical Journal*, *129*(6), 731–738. doi:10.4103/0366-6999.178019 PMID:26960378

Zhang, Y. B. (2019). Application of the Data Mining Technology in the Financial Management of Colleges and Universities in the Age of the Big Data. *Basic & Clinical Pharmacology & Toxicology*, *124*(3), 143–143.

Zhu, D. (2016). Big data-based multimedia transcoding method and its application in multimedia data mining-based smart transportation and telemedicine. *Multimedia Tools and Applications*, *75*(24), 17647–17668. doi:10.100711042-016-3466-3

Zhu, J., Ge, Z., Song, Z., & Gao, F. (2018). Review and big data perspectives on robust data mining approaches for industrial process modeling with outliers and missing data. *Annual Reviews in Control*, *46*, 107–133. doi:10.1016/j.arcontrol.2018.09.003

Zhu, L., Li, M., Zhang, Z., Du, X., & Guizani, M. (2018). Big data mining of users' energy consumption patterns in the wireless smart grid. *IEEE Wireless Communications*, *25*(1), 84–89. doi:10.1109/MWC.2018.1700157

ADDITIONAL READING

Chang, B. J. (2018). Agile Business Intelligence: Combining Big Data and Business Intelligence to Responsive Decision Model. *Journal of Internet Technology*, *19*(6), 1699–1706.

Chen, H., Chiang, R. H., & Storey, V. C. (2012). Business intelligence and analytics: From big data to big impact. *Management Information Systems Quarterly*, *36*(4), 1165–1188. doi:10.2307/41703503

Debortoli, S., Müller, O., & vom Brocke, J. (2014). Comparing business intelligence and big data skills. *Business & Information Systems Engineering*, *6*(5), 289–300. doi:10.100712599-014-0344-2

Kulakli, A., & Osmanaj, V. (2020). Global research on big data in relation with artificial intelligence (A bibliometric study: 2008-2019). *International Journal of Online and Biomedical Engineering*, *16*(2), 31–46. doi:10.3991/ijoe.v16i02.12617

Liang, T. P., & Liu, Y. H. (2018). Research landscape of business intelligence and big data analytics: A bibliometric study. *Expert Systems with Applications*, *111*, 2–10. doi:10.1016/j.eswa.2018.05.018

Mariani, M., Baggio, R., Fuchs, M., & Höepken, W. (2018). Business intelligence and big data in hospitality and tourism: A systematic literature review. *International Journal of Contemporary Hospitality Management*, *30*(12), 3514–3554. doi:10.1108/IJCHM-07-2017-0461

Xu, L., Jiang, C., Wang, J., Yuan, J., & Ren, Y. (2014). Information security in big data: Privacy and data mining. *IEEE Access: Practical Innovations, Open Solutions*, *2*, 1149–1176. doi:10.1109/ACCESS.2014.2362522

KEY TERMS AND DEFINITIONS

Bibliometric Analysis: Bibliometric is defined as the use of statistical methods to analyze the bibliometric publications data such as peer-reviewed journal articles, books, conference proceedings, periodicals, reviews, reports, and related documents. It has been widely used to present the relations of research domains with quantitative methods.

Big Data: Is enormous data set (mostly unstructured data) that may be analyzed computationally to reveal patterns, trends, and associations, especially relating to interactions.

Big Data Analytics: Is the often complicated process of examining large and varied data sets, or big data, to uncover information—such as hidden patterns, unknown correlations, market trends, and customer preferences—that can help organizations make informed business decisions.

Business Intelligence: It is a collection of processes, architectures, and technologies that turn raw data into useful knowledge driving productive business behavior. To turn data into actionable knowledge it is a suite of tools and services.

Citation Analysis: Is a way of measuring the relative importance or impact of an author, an article, or a publication by counting the number of times that author, article, or other works have cited publication.

Co-Citation Analysis: Provides a forward-looking assessment on document similarity in contrast to Bibliographic Coupling, which is retrospective. The citations a paper receives in the future depend on the evolution of an academic field; thus, co-citation frequencies can still change.

Data Mining: Is the practice of examining large pre-existing (structured) databases in order to generate new information. The data warehousing platforms should be established incorporation level with necessary data marts to analyze the large data sets.

This research was previously published in Integration Challenges for Analytics, Business Intelligence, and Data Mining; pages 13-43, copyright year 2021 by Engineering Science Reference (an imprint of IGI Global).

APPENDIX 1

A. Co-citation of references level 1 (nod size n=20)
B. Co-citation of references level 2 (nod size n=50)
C. Co-citation of references level 3 (nod size n=100)
D. Co-citation of references level 4 (nod size n=200)

APPENDIX 2

A. Country Collaboration Map

Chapter 94
Mapping the Intellectual Structure of the Big Data Research in the IS Discipline:
A Citation/Co–Citation Analysis

Surabhi Verma

Narsee Monjee Institute of Management Studies, Navi Mumbai, India

ABSTRACT

Big data (BD) is one of the emerging topics in the field of information systems. This article utilized citation and co-citation analysis to explore research articles in the field of BD to examine the scientific development in the area. The research data was retrieved from the WOS database from the period between 2005 and June 2016, which consists of 366 articles. In the citation analysis, this article relies on the degree centrality and betweenness centrality for identifying 38 important papers in BD. In the co-citation analysis, a principal component factor analysis of the co-citation matrix is employed for identifying six major research themes: foundations, BD applications, techniques and technologies, challenges, adoption and impacts and literature review. This literature review is one of the first studies to examine the knowledge structure of BD research in the information systems discipline by using evidence-based analysis methods. Recommendations for future research directions in BD are provided based on the analysis and results of this study.

1. INTRODUCTION

Big data refers to the delivery of real-time insights for decision making by analysing huge amount of structured, semi-structured and unstructured data (Chen and Zhang, 2014). It has five essential characteristics: volume, velocity, variety, veracity and value (Gandomi and Haider, 2015). Since big data can help organizations to continuously improve their strategic agility while reducing the time and complexity of business operations to stay competitive in today's rapidly-changing business environments (Demirkan and Delen, 2013). Therefore, big data has been touted as one of the most promising IT advancements

DOI: 10.4018/978-1-6684-3662-2.ch094

by practitioners and academicians that could fundamentally change firm managers' decision making capabilities (Nudurupati et al., 2016). The rapid development of big data markets has attracted much attention from information technology (IT) practitioners and academicians (Fasso et al., 2015). In recent years, several attempts have been made to summarize existing big data research, map its intellectual structure and predict its future directions. For example, Hashem (2015) reviewed research articles related to MapReduce for understanding the challenges on big data processing with MapReduce. Pospiech and Felden (2012) provide a state-of-the-art for the functional data provisioning of big data. Wienhofen et al. (2015) used a systematic mapping method to understand the characteristics and applications of big data and generated future research questions. Singh et al. (2015), used the analysis maps for understanding the total and growth output, authorship and country level collaboration and contributions, top publication sources, thematic and emerging themes in big data. Akter and Wamba (2016) analysed research progress of big data in the e-commerce field. These reviews provide useful information of current research on big data and facilitate the accumulation of big data knowledge. It indicates that a phase of critical introspection has begun in the big data field. This kind of big data introspection and self-reflection could be viewed as a sign of maturity of big data research. However, the rapid growth of big data research requires periodic review to keep researchers up to date. The existing reviews of big data literature are mainly based on subjective analysis of experienced research scholars in the big data field and the modern bibliometric methodology has not been leveraged to compensate for human subjectivity. Some degree of human subjectivity is indispensable to carry out review of literature (Wang et al., 2016). Yet, reviews of literature purely based on subjective analysis might be constrained by their authors' limited time, energy and cognitive capacity, and their interpretation of the literature is inevitably influenced by their personal perspectives (Raghuram et al., 2010). Therefore, it is possible that several important papers are omitted or misinterpreted to fit with the authors' own research interests (Wang et al., 2016).

Unlike such traditional literature reviews, in this literature review paper citation, co-citation, and main path analyses are used to examine the intellectual structure of big data research. Citation, co-citation, and main path analyses are bibliometric methods that can validate and complement judgements made by human researchers (Pilkington and Meredith, 2009). These bibliometric methods have advantages of being objective and quantifiable (Backhaus et al., 2011). They can also provide an empirically duplicable review of the existing big data research. These bibliometric methods still need to interpret the results of the bibliometric analysis and cannot completely eliminate subjectivity (Koseoglu et al., 2015). But the chances of making human errors can be greatly reduced and a more realistic depiction of a research field can be produced (Backhaus et al., 2011). Thus, objective review and subjective review are complementary to each other and should be used together to improve the quality of big data literature reviews. Therefore, there are two goals for this research study:

- The first goal is to identify the influential papers of big data research in the IS field;
- The second goal is to delineate the themes that constitute the intellectual structure of big data research in the IS discipline and map the relationships among the themes.
- Further, this paper provides recommendations for future research on a variety of issues related to big data based on citation/co-citation analysis.

2. METHODOLOGY

Figure 1 summarizes the steps of this literature review study. This study employed several multiple research methodologies, including citation analysis, co-citation analysis, and social network analysis (SNA). These research methodologies and the rationale for their use are described in the next subsection.

2.1. Citation Analysis

A citation occurs when one paper mentions or refers to another paper known as the source paper (Nerur et al., 2008). As shown in Figure 2A, a citation relationship exists between Paper A and Papers C, D and E. The citation analysis can provide information on the identity of papers which make and receive citations as well as information on the total number citations those papers make or receive (Jeong et al., 2014). The citation analysis can be used to identify source papers, influential papers, and inheritance relationships among related papers (Nerur et al., 2008). It has been extensively used to investigate the intellectual structure of many disciplines of social sciences and natural sciences (Nerur et al., 2008).

2.2. Co-Citation Analysis

Henry Small (1973) introduced the co-citation analysis method to evaluate the semantic similarity of research articles that share citations. Co-citation is an occurrence in which two research papers are cited together by another research paper (Jeong et al., 2014). The strength of co-citation between two articles depends upon the number of time two articles are co-cited (Pilkington and Meredith, 2009). If the co-citation of two research articles are high then the co-citation strength is also high and the two articles are semantically related (Wang et al., 2016). As shown in Figure 2B, Paper A and B are co-cited by Paper C, D, and E. Thus, Paper A and B have a co-citation strength of 3.

Kessler (1963) introduced the concept of bibliographic coupling by using citation analysis to establish a similarity relationship between research articles. This method is similar to co-citation analysis (Wang et al., 2016). In bibliographic coupling method two articles are bibliographic coupled if both articles cite one or more research articles in common (Zhao and Strotmann, 2008). The bibliographic coupling strength of two given research articles is high when the citations these articles share are higher than other articles. Thus, Paper A and B have a In this research paper, co-citation analysis is preferred to bibliographic coupling because the usefulness of bibliographic coupling has been questioned (Wang et al., 2016). Boyack and Klavans (2010) argued that bibliographic coupling only measures a retrospective similarity by only using the past information to establish the similarity relationship between research articles. The coupling strength in bibliographic coupling also cannot change over time (Zhao and Strotmann, 2008). While co-citation is able to overcome this problem by considering incoming citations of two papers' to access their similarity. This measure could change over time (Wang et al., 2016). Also, according to Koseoglu et al. (2015), the co-citation measures reflect the opinion of other researchers and thus is a more reliable indicator of subject similarity. This technique has been used by several researchers to investigate the foundations of several fields in the management discipline. For example, Wang et al. (2016) and Pilkingtom and Meredith (2009) employed citation analysis combined with a network analysis of co-citation analysis to reveal the intellectual structure of cloud computing and operations management field. bibliographic coupling strength of 3.

2.3. Social Network Analysis

The understanding of the flow of communications and exchange of concepts through citations and co-citations is improved by combining these techniques with the social network analysis technique (Wang et al., 2016). Social network analysis techniques enable the measurement, evaluation and visualization of relationships and patterns by combining mathematics, computer science, graph etc. (Polites and Watson, 2009). A social network consists of social actors and relations among these actors (Wasserman and Galaskiewicz, 1994). Social network analysis is an analysis of a network for investigating the relationships like contacts, tie or information exchange between the social actors by using the relational data (Pilkington and Meredith, 2009). The relationships are measured by influence, affinity, cohesion or communication patterns between the actors (Wasserman and Galaskiewicz, 1994).

According to Wang et al. (2016), bibliometric analysis consists of a network of articles, authors or academic journals. Social network analysis is used for analysing a network of research articles for understanding the relationships among articles (actors) by studying the information exchanged among the citation and co-citation (members). This analysis provides insights into the spread of knowledge throughout the academic community (Giannakis, 2012). Therefore, the co-citation and citation analysis are combined with the social network analysis for understanding the intellectual structure of big data research in the information systems discipline by revealing the shape of communications patterns among articles. Researchers have applied social network analysis for understanding the intellectual structure of several fields including cloud computing (Wang et al., 2016), operation management (Pilkington and Meredith, 2009), strategic management (Nerur et al., 2008), supply chain management (Giannakis, 2012), and information systems (Polites and Watson, 2009).

2.4. Data Collection

Big data research resides in an interdisciplinary area that includes technological, managerial, behavioural and social dimensions (Chang et al., 2013). Existing reviews of big data literature mainly focused on papers that study foundations and applications of big data (Akter and Wamba, 2016). Whereas papers that examines other issues related to big data are rarely reviewed (Akter and Wamba, 2016). To analyse the current state of big data research that concerns IS researchers, the data is retrieved from the Web of Science (WOS) database. WOS database is used for the following reasons (Wang et al., 2016):

- It is one of the world's leading and most popular citation database
- This database covers more than 10,000 high impact journals
- It is highly regarded and most popular among researchers.
- It provides a systematic and objective means to trace related information efficiently.

This database is referred by several researchers for co-citation analysis by retrieving the core documents (Acedo et al., 2006; McCain, 1990; Nerur et al., 2007; Small, 1973; White & Griffith, 1981).

The WOS database is searched by using the keywords including big data, big data services, big data analytics, data-as-a-service, analytics-as-a-service, and big data systems. The time span is from 2005 to June 2016. A total of 366 papers about big data are retrieved. The annual distribution of the number of research articles is shown in Figure 3. The analysis indicates that post 2013, research papers on big data increased exponentially. There are clearly two jumps in total number of publications from 2011 to

2012 and from 2014 to 2015, suggesting that big data research entered a new stage in 2012 and 2015, respectively.

Figure 4 depicted the top 15 journal which published most research articles on big data. Information science, knowledge based systems and big data research are the top three journals that have published mostly on big data papers, publishing 19, 16 and 15 research papers respectively. To get an in-depth understanding of the current research on big data, the citation analysis is used for identifying the important articles in the 366 papers and co-citation analysis is used to investigate the research themes of the most important papers.

Figure 1. Research Methodology

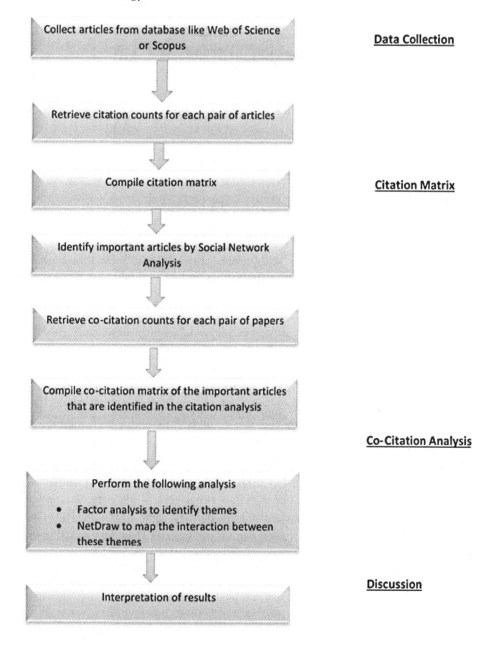

Figure 2. A. Citation Relationship; B. Co-citation Relationship; C. bibliographic coupling

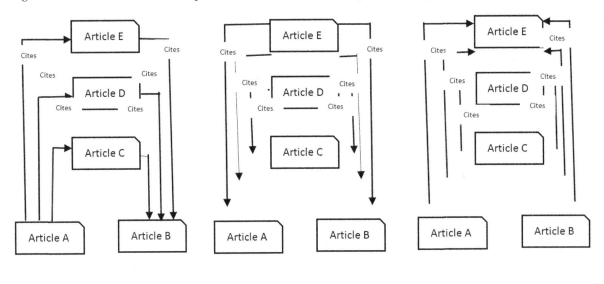

A. Citation Relationship **B. Co-citation Relationship** **C. Bibliographic coupling**

3. RESULTS

3.1. Citation Analysis

Based on the references of the 366 research papers, the citation relationship among the papers is obtained and a 366 X 366 matrix is generated. The citation matrix is then imported into two SNA tools, namely, PAJEK and UCINET for identifying important papers and conducting main path analyses (Wang et al., 2016).

3.1.1. Citation Network

The citation network of the 366 research papers is plotted in Figure 5 and the citation relationship between the papers are sparse, one important metric for the citation network is network density. Network density is the number of connections between nodes in the network (Jeong et al., 2014). If each node in the network is connected to every other node (i.e. the graph is fully connected) then the network density is one (Wang et al., 2016). If there is no connections between any of the nodes in a network then the network density is zero (Wang et al., 2016). Thus, the density of a network range between 0 and 1. According to Abrahamson and Rosenkopf (1997), a density value below 0.5 indicates low density and value above 0.5 indicates high density. For the citation network of big data, the network density is 0.00140729. Further, 271 isolated nodes are removed, the density value is 0.02083102. The low density of network indicates that the connections between papers are scant and big data is still in the early stage and an emerging research field (Figure 6).

Figure 3. Annual distribution of big data paper

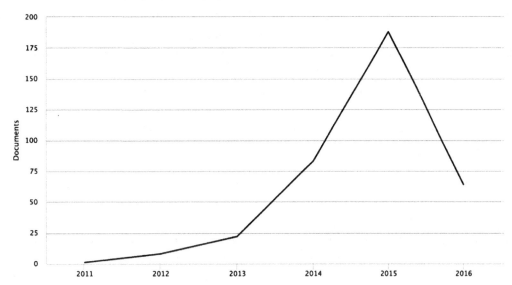

Figure 4. Source distribution of big data papers

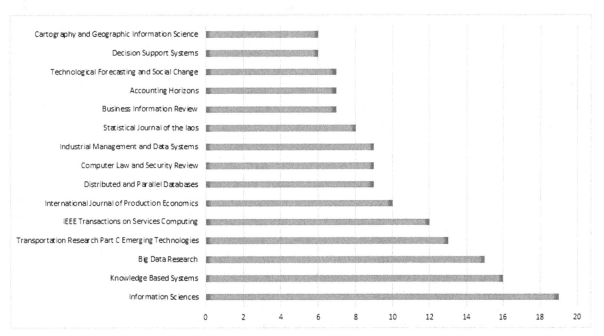

3.1.2. Important Papers

According to Nerur et al. (2008), the importance of a research paper can be determined by its influence in the citation network. The influence of a paper is measured by degree centrality and betweenness centrality (Wang et al., 2016).

- Degree centrality is measured as the number of direct ties that a node has in the network (Freeman, 1979). The more ties the node has, the more active, or more central, the node is. Those on the periphery will be disadvantaged compared with the central nodes because they have fewer ties. For directed networks like citation networks, there are two different types of degree centrality (Wang et al., 2016):

    1. In-degree centrality, measures the number of research papers that cites this focal research paper.
    2. Out-degree centrality, measures the number of research papers that this focal research paper cites.

In this paper in-degree centrality is used to show a research paper's importance because it reflects how the paper is recognized by other researchers.

- Betweenness centrality is concerned with the extent to which one node exists on the shortest path (the geodesic distance) between other nodes (Freeman, 1979). It is the number of times that a given node needs a (different) given node to reach any other node by the shortest path. In a communication network, nodes with high betweenness scores can control the flow of information and thus may be able to take on the role of gatekeeper or broker (Wang et al., 2016). Betweenness values can also indicate which nodes are viewed most often as leading nodes (research papers) (Freeman et al., 1980). Since the citation network is a type of directed graph, we followed White and Borgatti (1994) to compute the betweenness centrality scores of all 366 papers.

Previously several studies only employed citation count or in-degree centrality for identifying important papers (Koseoglu et al., 2015). Wang et al. (2016) argued that combination of in-degree centrality with betweenness centrality could improve the identification of the important papers. Therefore, in this study the in-degree centrality and betweeness centrality are collectively employed for identifying the important research papers in big data literature. As, the big data literature is in its nascent stage (Akter and Wamba, 2016), research papers with in-degree centrality of 1 and above or betweenness centrality greater than 1 and above is considered as an important paper. A total of 38 papers meet this criterion (Table 1). Focusing on the 38 important papers will help in keeping the most valuable information and reduces the complexity of data analysis. The 38 important research papers are categorized based on research type. As Figure 7 depicts, 32, or 84% of the important papers are non-empirical (20 conceptual + 4 literature review + 8 modelling). Thus, suggests that research scholars are still trying to make conceptual sense of big data by elaborating on the basic concepts surrounding this new technology. Only 6, or 15%, important papers report empirical studies, and most of them are case study based. This suggests that researchers are prudent in making efforts to quantitatively investigate big data questions before they can sufficiently understand the concepts related to big data and are able to theoretically define and empirically measure these concepts.

Table 1 depicted that the betweenness centrality of Articles 1, 5, 259, 136, 3, 8, 2, 294, 49 and 231 is relatively high (>100), indicating that these articles are major sources for knowledge for big data studies. Although the betweenness of articles like 43 and 158 is not very high, the in-degree centralities are relatively high (>1). Thus, these articles are vital to the dissemination of knowledge in big data research by bridging between other articles.

Figure 5. Citation Network of 366 big data research papers

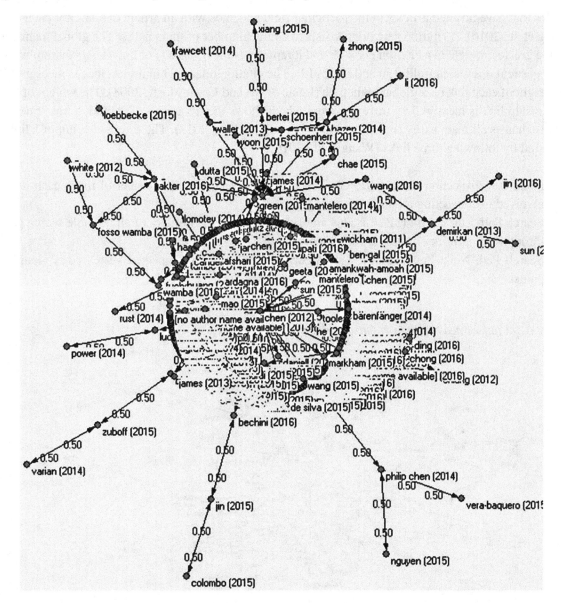

3.1.3. Main Path Analysis

Main path analysis is used by several researchers as a bibliometric tool to conduct literature review (Liang et al., 2015). It enables researchers to make visible structural backbone of a body of literature by constructing the position of each papers (Yin et al., 2006). In the course of development of big data research, new research articles acquire information from previous research articles and add new ideas and information of their own. The citation relationships reveal the dyadic knowledge flow between the citing and cited research articles (Wang et al., 2016). The citation network is a directional network that indicate scientific knowledge flows over a period of time (Koseoglu et al., 2015). It includes several nodes/

articles and links/citation relationships (Pilkington and Meredith, 2009). A main path starts from early articles that have no cited articles in the particular field and ends with an article that has not been cited (Wang et al., 2016). A citation network consists of a large number of main paths. The global main path has the greatest weight in a citation network and it represents the backbone of knowledge dissemination in the particular research field (Liu and Lu, 2012). The citation relationship importance is measured by the weight of each link on a global main path (Lucio-Arias and Leydesdorff, 2008). The weight of each relationship link is measured by traversal count which shows the frequency of a citation link traversed if one exhausts all main paths in a citation network (Liu and Lu, 2012). The traversal count of a link is measured by following three links (Wang et al., 2016):

- Node Pair Projection Count (NPPC): This algorithm accounts the number of times each link is involved in connecting all node pairs;
- Search Path Link Count (SPLC): This algorithm accounts the number of all possible search paths through the network emanating from an origin;
- Search Path Node Pair (SPNP): This algorithm accounts all connected vertex pairs along the paths.

Figure 6. 95 unisolated big data research paper

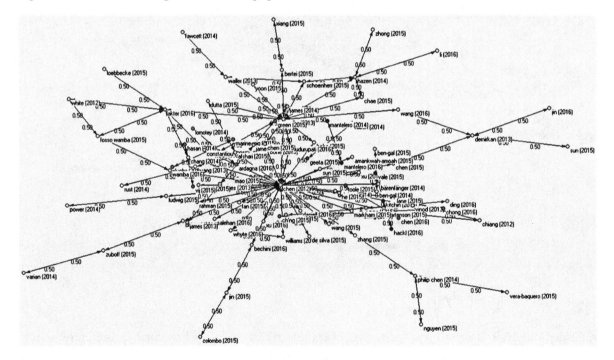

This study followed the guideline recommended by Chuang et al. (2014). In this article the Search Path Link Count (SPLC) algorithm is employed. SPLC algorithm is used to identify the global main path of the citation network of the 366 big data articles. Therefore, this global main path can approximately reveal how big data in the IS discipline has evolved over a period of time.

Figure 7. Research types of the 38 important papers

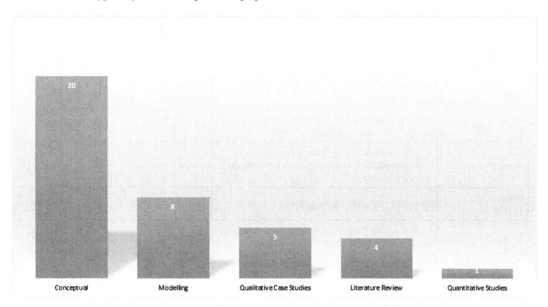

Table 1. Important articles of citation network analysis

No	Author	Title	Research Type	In degree	Betweeness Centrality
1	Chen et al. (2012)	Business intelligence and analytics: From big data to big impact	Conceptual, Literature Review	16	1472.633
5	Waller and Fawcett (2013)	Data science, predictive analytics, and big data: A revolution that will transform supply chain design and management	Conceptual	6.5	661.9
259	Zhang et al. (2015)	Toward effective big data analysis in continuous auditing	Conceptual	1	171
136	Akter and Wamba (2016)	Big data analytics in E-commerce: a systematic review and agenda for future research	Conceptual, Literature Review	3	137.467
3	Demirkan and Delen (2013)	Leveraging the capabilities of service-oriented decision support systems: Putting analytics and big data in cloud	Conceptual	2	118
8	Hazen et al. (2014)	Data quality for data science, predictive analytics, and big data in supply chain management: An introduction to the problem and suggestions for research and applications	Theoretical, Modelling	2.5	117.5
294	Chen et al., (2015)	On the model design of integrated intelligent big data analytics systems	Qualitative, Case study	1	117
2	Chen and Zhang (2014)	Data-intensive applications, challenges, techniques and technologies: A survey on Big Data	Conceptual	1.5	117
231	Bechini et al. (2016)	A MapReduce solution for associative classification of big data	Theoretical, Modelling	1	116
49	Bhimani and Willcocks (2014)	Digitisation, Big Data and the transformation of accounting information	Conceptual	1	116
307	Bertei et al. (2015)	Exploring Qualitative Data: The use of Big Data technology as support in strategic decision-making	Conceptual	1	59

continues on following page

Table 1. Continued

No	Author	Title	Research Type	In degree	Betweeness Centrality
26	Jin et al. (2015)	Significance and Challenges of Big Data Research	Conceptual	1	59
297	Ludwig et al. (2015)	Putting Big Data analytics to work: Feature selection for forecasting electricity prices using the LASSO and random forests	Theoretical, Modelling and simulation	1	59
91	Zuboff (2015)	Big other: Surveillance capitalism and the prospects of an information civilization	Conceptual	1	59
208	Wang et al. (2016)	Big data analytics in logistics and supply chain management: Certain investigations for research and applications	Conceptual	1	51
225	Wamba et al. (2016)	The primer of social media analytics	Conceptual	1	46.7
6	Chang et al. (2014)	Understanding the paradigm shift to computational social science in the presence of big data	Conceptual	1	31.867
42	Constantiou and Kallinikos (2013)	New games, new rules: Big data and the changing context of strategy	Conceptual	1	31.867
178	Lane & Kim (2015)	Big data: Web-crawling and analysing financial news using RapidMiner	Theoretical, Modelling and simulation	1	29
67	Mortenson et al. (2015)	Operational research from Taylorism to Terabytes: A research agenda for the analytics age	Conceptual, Literature Review	1	29
337	Afshari and Peng (2015)	Modeling and quantifying uncertainty in the product design phase for effects of user preference changes	Theoretical, Modelling and simulation	1	18.167
43	Wamba et al., (2015)	How 'big data' can make big impact: Findings from a systematic review and a longitudinal case study	Qualitative, Case study	1.5	11.7
92	Dutta and Bose (2015)	Managing a big data project: The case of Ramco cements limited	Qualitative, Case study	1	6.7
158	Schoenherr and Speier-Pero (2015)	Data science, predictive analytics, and big data in supply chain management: Current state and future potential	Conceptual, Literature Review	1.5	3
103	James (2013)	Out of the box: Information morality - reasonable doubt	Conceptual	1	2
190	James (2014)	Out of the box: Big data needs the information profession - the importance of validation	Conceptual	1	2
112	Ch'ng (2015)	The bottom-up formation and maintenance of a Twitter community analysis of the #FreeJahar Twitter community	Theoretical, Modelling and simulation	1	1
234	Hackl (2016)	Big Data: What can official statistics expect?	Conceptual	1	1
39	Huang and Rust (2013)	IT-Related Service: A Multidisciplinary Perspective	Conceptual	1	1
14	Qian et al. (2015)	Hierarchical attribute reduction algorithms for big data using MapReduce	Theoretical, Modelling and simulation	1	1
9	Chiang et al. (2012)	Business Intelligence and Analytics education, and program development: A unique opportunity for the Information Systems discipline	Conceptual	1	0.5

continues on following page

Table 1. Continued

No	Author	Title	Research Type	In degree	Betweeness Centrality
268	Chen et al. (2015)	How the use of big data analytics affects value creation in supply chain management	Quantitative, Survey	1	0
89	Chae (2015)	Insights from hashtag #supplychain and Twitter analytics: Considering Twitter and Twitter data for supply chain practice and research	Theoretical, Modelling and simulation	1	0
149	Hahn and Packowski (2015)	A perspective on applications of in-memory analytics in supply chain management	Conceptual	1	0
235	Nudurupati (2016)	Contemporary performance measurement and management (PMM) in digital economies	Qualitative, Case study	1	0
44	White (2012)	Digital workplaces: Vision and reality	Conceptual	1	0
140	Whyte et al.(2016)	Managing change in the delivery of complex projects: Configuration management, asset information and 'big data'	Qualitative, Case study	1	0
98	Williams et al.(2014)	Project management maturity in the age of big data	Conceptual	1	0

The global main path contains 13 papers published between 2012 and 2016. As depicted in Figure 8, each research articles on the global main path of big data network is marked by the first author and publication year, and the arrow points to the cited paper in big data. Among the 13 papers, eleven are among the 38 important papers. This finding indicating high consistency between the results of the citation analysis and main path analysis. After analyzing the 13 papers on the global main path, it is contended that big data research evolved through three stages: incubation stage (2005–2011), the exploration stage (2012–2014), and the burgeoning stage (2015–2016). These stages can be confirmed by inspecting Figure 3: there are clearly two jumps in total number of publications from 2011 to 2012 and from 2014 to 2015, suggesting that big data research entered a new stage in 2012 and 2015, respectively.

3.1.3.1. Incubation Stage (2005–2011)

This stage includes 3 articles. During this stage, except in a workshop paper (Foster et al., 2008), the term of big data has not been explicitly defined. But some similar constructs were employed, such as business intelligence and analytics (Cohen et al., 2009), decision support systems (Jacobs, 2009), Analytics-as-a-Service (Panchaksharaiah, 2009), Data-as-a-Service (Agarwal et al., 2010), Information-as-a-Service (Lukashevich et al., 2009) and Data-intensive computing (Kouzes et al., 2009). The commonality of these similar constructs suggests the paradigm shift from traditional database analytics to real-time analytics.

3.1.3.2. Exploration Stage (2012-2014)

This stage includes 113 articles, most of which are focused on ontological issues of big data, including definition, techniques and technology, benefits of big data in different sectors and challenges. In this duration, big data was still a novel notion and research scholars were trying to figure out what big data is, what big data means, what are its characteristics and what can be done with it. Therefore, most articles of big data in this period were conceptual pieces intended to understand big data. For example, Waller and Fawcett (2013) recommended that big data could help the carriers, manufacturers and retailers in forecasting, inventory, transportation and human resources management. Chen and Zhang (2014) propose the concept of big data which includes architecture, big data management strategy, benefits and challenges. Williams and Ferdinand (2014) proposed a business model for developing new insights in project management maturity assessments. Chiang et al. (2012) and Williams et al. (2014) analysed the opportunities and challenges faced by the development of big data. Chen and Zhang (2014) identified big data challenges like data consistency, data integrity, data aggregation, data identification and data confidentiality caused by the quality of big data (i.e. Volume, Velocity, Variety and Veracity). According to Waller and Fawcett (2013), the key challenge in big data and predictive analytics is the identification of relevant factors which may explains the variables of interest.

3.1.3.3. Burgeoning Stage (2015-2016)

During this period, 252 articles on big data were published. Research scholars' attention has switched from pure conceptualization to investigations of specific research questions related to big data. Akter and Wamba (2016) reviewed the literature to explore the aspects, characteristics, types, business value and challenges of big data in e-commerce. Based on resource-based view, Akter and Wamba (2016) argued that big data is a distinctive competence of the high-performance business process to support business needs like determining the optimal price, identification of loyal and profitable customers, determining the lowest possible level of inventory and detecting quality problems. More studies began to examine business and technology related issues of big data, e.g., big data adoption, capacity planning of big data and business impact of big data. For example, Chen et al. (2015) investigated the organizational usage of big data for value creation and antecedents and consequences influencing the organizational level big data usage. Chae et al. (2015) considered supply chain tweets for supply chain management in firms and found that big data could be used for information sharing, communicating with stakeholders, hiring professionals, maintaining logistics and corporate social responsibility, understanding the firms' delivery services, risk and disruption in supply chains, sales performance and environmental standards. Wang et al. (2016) proposed a maturity framework of supply chain analytics based on functional, process-based, collaborative, agile and sustainable capabilities of supply chain analytics. They discussed the usage of methodologies and techniques to collect, disseminate, analyse and use big data driven knowledge in logistic and supply chain management strategy and operations using descriptive, predictive and prescriptive analytics. The research focus on how big data has switched from conceptual development and exploration in the second stage to business and technology related issues in the third stage.

3.2. Co-Citation Analysis

The co-citation analysis method has been used to address the second goal of this paper. The second goal is to identify and illustrate the knowledge groups of big data research in the IS discipline and the relationships between these knowledge groups. The references of the 38 important articles on big data in IS discipline are analysed to determine the commonly co-citation of any two articles. A structural knowledge group is constituted that consists a set of articles which are frequently co-cited. These structural knowledge groups and the relationships among these articles constitute the intellectual structure of a research field (Leydesdorff and Vaughan, 2006).

This paper followed the method of Nerur et al. (2008) to determine the major knowledge groups of big data research in the IS discipline. A Principal Component factor Analysis (PCA) of the co-citation matrix is employed. IBM SPSS21.0 is used in this paper to analyse the correlation matrix of the 38 important big data research papers. PCA is used to identify the citation analysis based on a varimax rotation. The Kaiser–Meyer–Olkin (KMO) measure of sampling adequacy for the co-citation matrix was acceptable at 0.825 and Bartlett's test was significant at the 0.001 level, which indicated that PCA was applicable. Six factors with a minimum eigenvalue of 1 were extracted, which together explained 82.98% of the variance in the correlation matrix. A paper was retained only if its loadings' absolute value is above 0.4 (Nerur et al., 2008). As a result, only 6 factors were kept for further analysis. Table 2 lists the 6 factors identified through PCA.

Figure 8. Main path analysis of big data research

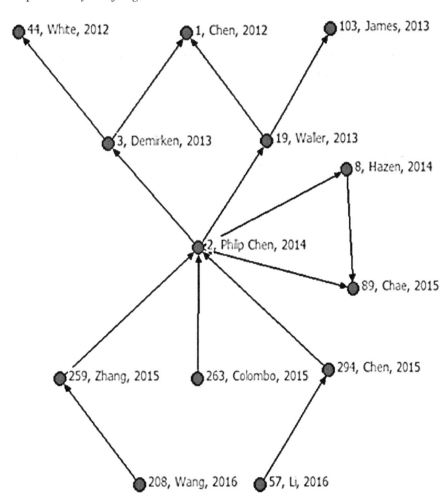

The first factor in Table 2 attempts to define the foundation of big data. It is the most important among the six factors, explaining 38.56% of the total variance. This factor has 11 research papers, and most of these papers are conceptual studies. A careful review of theses research articles reveals six topics, including, definition, characteristics of big data, technologies, benefits and obstacles, applications and research directions. Chen et al. (2012) defined big data as combination of data sets and analytical techniques in applications which is very large (from terabytes and exabytes) and complex (from sensor to social media data) and require advanced and unique data storage, management, analysis and visualized technologies. Several authors acknowledge that big data refers to a computation technique and has five characteristics (volume, velocity, variety, veracity and value). Demirkan and Delen (2013) proposed three service models as the enablers for big data analytics, namely, Data-as-a-Service (DaaS), Information-as-a-Service (IaaS) and Analytics-as-a-Service (AaaS). Service-oriented big data analytics in cloud could reduce the unit service costs due to reduction in unit service costs with increase in number of services developed and provided (scope), increase in operational size (scale) and reduction in unit costs due to increase in number of services through supply and demand chain (speed).

Table 2. Factors extracted for big data research

	Factor 1 Foundations	Factor 2 Techniques and Technologies	Factor 3 Applications	Factor 4 Challenges	Factor 5 Literature Review	Factor 6 Adoption and Impacts
	Chang et al. (2014)	Bechini et al. (2016)	Bertei et al. (2015)	Chiang et al. (2012)	Akter and Wamba (2016)	Chen et al. (2015)
	Chen et al. (2012)	Lane & Kim (2015)	Chae (2015)	Afshari and Peng (2015)	Wamba et al., (2015)	Dutta and Bose (2015)
	Chen et al., (2015)	Ludwig et al. (2015)	Constantiou and Kallinikos (2013)	Hazen et al. (2014)	Mortenson et al. (2015)	Nudurupati (2016)
	Demirkan and Delen (2013)	Wamba et al. (2016)	Wang et al. (2016)	James (2013)	Schoenherr and Speier-Pero (2015)	Whyte et al.(2016)
	James (2014)	Zuboff (2015)	Zhang et al. (2015)	Ch'ng (2015)		
	White (2012)	Hahn and Packowski (2015)	Williams et al. (2014)	Jin et al. (2015)		
	Bhimani and Willcocks (2014)	Qian et al. (2015)				
	Hackl (2016)					
	Huang and Rust (2013)					
	Chen and Zhang (2014)					
	Waller and Fawcett (2013)					
Variance Explained	15.87	5.34	4.83	3.76	2.42	1.96
Percentage of variance explained	38.56	13.08	11.87	9.02	6.63	3.82

The rapid growth in the usage of hand-held digital devices like smartphones and tablets by consumers and suppliers has added technical complexity and led to the beginning of big data era (Bhimani and Willcocks, 2014). The volume, velocity, variety and veracity of big data are leading to problems in delivering business-critical information to giant and small companies (White, 2012). Therefore, firms now need data analysts with skills to validate and interpret big data and manage firm's search applications.

Digital workplace using big data could create macro-economic gains by enabling firms to enhance market share and competitiveness, increase margins on the delivery of products and services, reduce the time of innovations in product and services and to respond quickly to business opportunities and challenges (Bhimani and Willcocks, 2014). The study of big data service is therefore inherently multidisciplinary involving fields like marketing, strategic management, information systems/computer science and operations management/organizational research (Huang and Rust, 2013)

Chen and Zhang (2014) state that the core technologies of big data include data management/storage, advance analytics and visualization techniques and technology. Chen et al. (2012) argue that big data is not a completely new concept; it has intricate relationships with business intelligence and other relevant technologies such as predictive analytics and data warehousing. Many studies compared big data with other analytical, statistical and data mining techniques. For example, Chen et al. (2012) compare big data with business intelligence and analytics from various perspectives such as advanced and unique data storage, management and data handling, analysis, and visualization technologies. Most of these studies agree that big data is derived from previous analytics paradigms and has its own novelties. Big data is leading to a new scientific paradigm called as data intensive scientific discovery or big data problems in several sectors. It also arises with several challenges like difficulties in data capturing, data storage, data analysis and data visualization. According to Chen and Zhang (2014), techniques like cloud computing, quantum computing and biological computing could solve big data problems. A big data systems design requires:

- Good architectures and frameworks that use integration techniques to transfer data into a DBMS data warehouse or operational data store like NoSQL, MapReduce.
- Variety of analytical methods like data mining, statistical analysis, machine learning, distributed programming and visualization for real-time analysis, in-memory analysis and human–computer interaction.
- Huge data storage tools to solve big data problems.
- Coordination between different processing and data units on a cluster is required to improve the scalability, efficiency and fault-tolerance of big data system.

The emergence of new context, data collection technologies and data mining and analytics techniques are changing the discourse of research question, data collection, experimental design, longitudinal empirical research and research methods to study social science phenomenon (Chang et al., 2013). The collection of new contextual information is inexpensive for creating new knowledge in the consumer, business and social insights. Hackl (2016) argued that there is no uniform methodological approach for using big data and a number of challenges involved like development of quality framework, acquisition of skills, costs and privacy. Finding solutions for these challenges and developing standards require substantial effort and time. According to Waller and Fawcett (2013), Logistics predictive analytics is both quantitative and qualitative approach to estimate the past and future trends in the flow and storage of inventory, costs and service levels, adds question related for past events in different conditions (forecasting), optimize a systems operations (optimization), find relationships between variables using deductive mathematical methods for finding conclusions. Waller and Fawcett (2013), recommended to study big data in supply chain management from the perspective of various management theories like transaction cost economics, resource-based view, contingency theory, agency theory and more.

The second factor named as techniques and technology. This factor explains 13.08% of total variance and includes 7 papers. Qian et al. (2015) studied the hierarchical encoded decision table and attribute reduction algorithms using MapReduce and argued that this algorithm could scale and efficiently process big data in cloud computing. They recommended to use the parallelization of other attribute reduction algorithms and extend the rough set models. Bechini et al. (2015) proposed a distributed association rule-based classification scheme for a distributed rule pruning, which is shaped according to the MapReduce programming model. This distributed learning algorithms for associative classifier is suitable to address big datasets problems like accuracy, model complexity and computation time with modest hardware support. Hahn and Packowski (2015) studied the applications of in-memory analytics for decision making in supply chain management by developing and mapping framework to unify multiple taxonomies from top-down and bottom-up perspectives. They recommended for investigation of in-memory analytics architecture, methodological contribution, benefits and impact of processes, organizational structure and operational performance for the implementation and adoption of in-memory analytics. Zuboff (2015) identified and theorized the institutionalizing logic of accumulation which produces hyper-scale assemblages of subjective and objective data about individuals, their behaviours and habits for the purpose of controlling, knowing and modifying behaviour for producing new varieties of monetization (architecture for data capture and analysis), commodification and control. According to Ludwig et al. (2015) big data requires appropriate algorithms for predicting the relevant causal relationships between exploratory variables and the predicted variables for more accurate behavioural patterns and long-term trends. Inclusion of external variables and re-estimation procedure for algorithms are necessary to increases the prediction quality. The time series analysis and statistical learning techniques has been used for improving forecasting accuracy like electricity price, weather condition and more.

Lane and Kim (2015) used RapidMiner as analytical tool to analyse real-world social media big data as an empirical test and found that social media big data does not provide valuable insights to predict the future of stock market. Techniques like web-crawling, social media analysis, probabilistic topic models are used for analysing big data from social media (Lane and Kim, 2015). Wamba et al., (2016) studied the diffusion and adoption of social media platforms where people share information and opinions like Twitter, Facebook and Pinterest and mobile devices generates tremendous business values like improved operational efficiency, improved revenue and more (Agarwal et al., 2011). Chen et al. (2012) defined social media analytics as an informatics tools and framework to collect, monitor, analyse to uncover the individual's thought and feeling by analysing structured and unstructured online data for extracting useful patterns and intelligence. It includes sentiment/opinion mining to analyse opinions, sentiment, attitude, evaluation, emotions and judgements of individuals or groups towards products, services, firms etc (Liu, 2012). Trend analysis is used to uncover industry current trends like product demands, service quality and consumer insights (White, 2015).

The third factor is labelled as Application which focuses on the applications of big data in various sectors and explain 11.87% of the total variance and having seven research papers. Constantiou and Kallinikos (2015) stated that big data is important for wider developments of contemporary patterns detection associated with the information related to product and consumer. The authors recommended research focused on data and information for understanding the relationships between firms and their business environment. Bertei et al. (2015) argued that not all the data in big data is meaningful and qualitative data need more exploration. Based on the contingency theory, Bertei et al. (2015) recommended to decode and use the tacit unstructured data collectively to improve the strategic decision-making process. They also recommended to maintain balance between the objectivity and subjectivity information component at the strategic level. According to Lin et al. (2014), strategic information in not only limited in database formats but can also be located in sources like e-mails, social media, internal firms' documents etc.

Williams et al. (2014) recommended that adoption of data analytical approaches from big data could enable the creation of holistic and adaptive maturity models that could provide rapid insights based on the flow of information within a firm. Big data have potential to develop approaches to project maturity model assessment to overcome the limitations of existing qualitative and quantitative approaches (Williams et al., 2014). The authors recommended to employ techniques like social network analysis and text analysis in project maturity model. Zhang et al. (2015) studied the application of big data in continuous auditing systems. They identified five gaps of big data based on the features of big data namely: data consistency, data integrity, data aggregation, data identification and data confidentiality. According to Zhang et al. (2015), the quality of big data (i.e. Volume, Velocity, Variety and Veracity) led to the creation of these challenges.

Chae et al. (2015) argued that supply chain tweets could be used by supply chain firms for information sharing, communicating with stakeholders, hiring professionals, maintaining logistics and corporate social responsibility, understanding the firms' delivery services, risk and disruption in supply chains, sales performance and environmental standards. Wang et al. (2016) proposed a maturity framework of supply chain analytics based on functional, process-based, collaborative, agile and sustainable capabilities of supply chain analytics. According to Wang et al. (2016), there is need to focus on the scope of analytics and the criticality of the task to the firm's activities, the industry types (service or manufacturing industry), organizational goals and objectives, market and technological capabilities and competencies of the firm (Gunasekaran et al., 2015). The usage of big data methodologies and techniques in firms are heavily depended on the robust data collection and data cleansing, technological infrastructure (computational systems) and human resources (data analysts). Waller and Fawcett (2013) proposed several opportunities to revolutionize supply chain management dynamics by changing business model design and real-time decision making, using data science, predictive analytics and big data.

The fourth factor explains 9.02% of total variance and named as challenges of big data. It includes six research articles. According to Chiang et al. (2012), the challenge with big data is to develop the capability to understand and interpret the derived meaning from burgeoning volume of data. They recommended for development of analytical and interpretive skills in students, management and IT professionals. Afshari and Peng (2015) proposed an agent based model to quantify the internal (dependencies between components) and external (user preferences) uncertainties in product life cycle design process. They stated that big data could be applied for identifying product changes during its life cycle for evaluating the most affected product components under uncertainty.

Hazen et al. (2014) argued that big data quality is a challenge and it requires interdisciplinary collaboration for data collection, storage, processing and retrieval. They examined the data quality problem through the lenses of knowledge based view, systems theory and organizational information processing view. They measured the data quality by two dimensions, namely, intrinsic and contextual. Intrinsic refers to attributes which are objective and native to the data. Intrinsic data quality is described by four dimensions: accuracy; timeliness; consistency; and completeness (Blake and Mangiameli, 2011; Haug and Arlbjørn, 2011). Contextual refers to attributes which are dependent on the context in which data are observed and used. It includes relevancy, value-added, believability, accessibility, quantity (Wang and Strong, 1996), and reputation of the data (Lee et al., 2004).

According to James (2013) increasing usage of information could change reasonableness because increased use of information could increase signal and noise and finally led to produce falsehoods. The essential skill in information poverty requires husbandry and information excess requires interpretation (James, 2013). Jin et al. (2015) argued that the characteristics of big data cause challenge in harnessing the potential of big data. These challenges includes the data complexity associated with the complicated data types, patterns and inter-relationships and makes its representation, perception, understanding and computation challenging and results in sharp increases in the computational complexity. The volume, velocity and variety of big data increases the computational and system complexity.

The fifth factor is titled as Literature Review. This factor explains 6.63% of total variance and includes four research papers. All of these four research papers review the big data literature. Schoenherr and Speier-Pero (2015) reviewed the use of big data and predictive analytics in supply chain management and understand the motivation, perceived benefits and barriers of big data. They also discussed about the skills required by data scientists for harnessing big data. Akter and Wamba (2016) reviewed the literature to explore the aspects, characteristics, types, business value and challenges of big data in e-commerce. Based on resource-based view, Akter and Wamba (2016) argued that big data is a distinctive competence of the high-performance business process to support business needs like determining the optimal price, identification of loyal and profitable customers, determining the lowest possible level of inventory and detecting quality problems. Through literature Akter and Wamba (2016) found six mechanisms to enhance business value of e-commerce, including personalization, dynamic pricing, customer service, supply chain visibility, security and fraud detection and predictive analytics. The challenges of big data environment include unclear direction to reach targets by aligning with the existing organizational culture and capabilities (Chen et al., 2016), big data trustworthy and understandable to managers, data security and privacy, finding right information of each customer from the large amount of data, method to insert big data in marketing, production and operations management using sophisticated database management tools. Other challenges include technical, analytical and governance skills to handle big data. Availability of good quality data, easy accessibility and usage of these data are major drivers of big data in firms. Wamba et al. (2015) proposed an interpretive framework for analysing the definitional perspective and the applications of big data by systematically reviewing the big data research articles and through in-depth analysis of the longitudinal case study.

The sixth factor explains 3.82% of total variance and is termed as Adoption and Impacts. This category includes four research articles which focuses on questions about big data adoption and business impacts. Chen et al. (2015) studied the organizational usage of big data for value creation and antecedents and consequences influencing the organizational level big data usage by employing technology-organization-environment (TOE) framework. They found that organizational big data usage like information processing capability generates organizational value creation like asset productivity and business growth. They also argued that the environmental dynamism moderates the big data usage influence on asset productivity and business growth, i.e. in dynamic environment big data usage influence business growth more. Firms are reluctant to make commitments based on lack of knowledge about how to effectively process and uncertainty of the payoff. Technological factors like expected benefits and compatibility are important to link to big data usage. Big data championship by top management is important for bridging the organizational (i.e. organizational readiness) and environmental factors (i.e. competitive pressure) into actionable usage of big data (Chen et al., 2015). Dutta and Bose (2015) investigated the big data implementation and developed a framework for understanding the holistic roadmap for conceptualizing, planning and implementation of big data in firms. They argued that big data project requires clear understanding of the business problem, planned project map, cross-functional project team, adoption of innovation visualization techniques, top management involvement and data-driven culture for decision making. According to Whyte (2016), the firms perceives a greater need for integrity in asset information and control processes through configuration management. Due to this reason ensuring integrity in operations is important in regulated and safety critical industries. But the complexity of organizations, large distributed supply-chains and time pressure has increased the challenges of projects delivering the asset information (Whyte, 2016). Nudurupati et al. (2016) proposed a robust performance measurement and management models to overcome the challenges associated with performance measurement and management in digital era includes the constant change in the external environment and availability of varieties and volume of data. They recommended firms to refocus on their measurement efforts to incorporate evaluation of their performance with different stakeholders, to understand how technological developments creates competitive advantages through strategy and deploy it to relevant positivistic and behavioural measures.

NetDraw is applied in this study to depict the relationships among the 6 factors and to identify their network structure (Wang et al., 2016). NetDraw is a Windows program for visualizing social network data (Wang et al., 2016). In Figure 9, the size of a node representing a paper is proportionate to the paper's co-citation count. Articles which are co-cited with several other articles will tend to be centrally located while those articles which are co-cited with fewer other articles lie toward the outskirts of the diagram (Wang et al., 2016). As depicted in Figure 9, Foundations is the central and largest group and research articles in this group interacts more strongly among themselves than with research articles in the other groups, indicating that most of the efforts have been dedicated to the basic propositions of big data research and the research articles in Foundations lay the foundation for the studies in other knowledge groups. Group 2(Techniques and Technologies), Group 3 (Applications), Group 4 (Challenges), Group 5(Literature review) and Group 6 (Adoption and Impacts) are peripherally located. These groups interact primarily with Factor 1 and sparsely interacted with each other. This suggests that studies in these five groups have been independently conducted and few articles have integrated multiple perspectives which need to cite articles from other group simultaneously.

4. DISCUSSION

In this section, future directions in big data research based on the co-citation analysis findings is discussed. Given the increased knowledge of big data and rapid growth of big data research, the author(s) predict that conceptual papers that only focus on conceptualizations of big data will greatly decrease and more attention will be paid to substantive and empirical issues, including applications, challenges, techniques and technology, literature review, and adoption and impacts.

Figure 9. Relationship among the 6 knowledge groups of big data research in the IS discipline

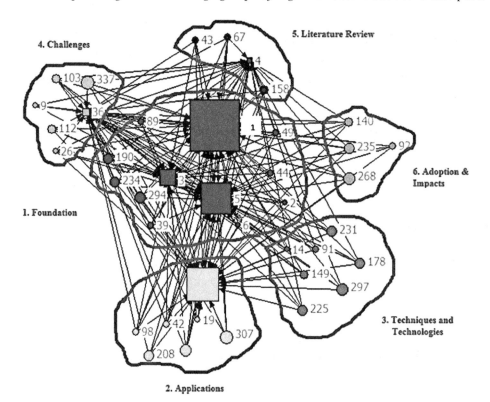

4.1. Big Data Application

Big data is an emerging technology that has been successfully applied in various business processes. There is tremendous potential for applying big data across sectors and increasing number of industries have already started to successfully use it in real-world environment. According to Gandomi and Haider (2015), big data is likely to be among the most exciting and fastest-growing technology in the next generation of business analytics. Based on various industry areas that are included in the reviewed literature, applications of big data is sub-categorized into

1. **Healthcare:** In healthcare, big data have potential to gain insight from clinical and other data repositories that could be used for decision making for patients (Berg and Black, 2014).
2. **Accounting and Finance:** In financial sector, big data can lead to better forecasts of estimates, going concern, fraud, and reduction of other internal and external risk by increasing the effectiveness and credibility of decision making (Fitzpatrick et al., 2015). Big Data has a potential to reduce the costs of their audits, affect the quality of auditors' judgments and enhance profitability in the case of external auditors and cost effectiveness as far as internal auditors are concerned (Brown-Liburd et al. (2015); Warren et al. (2015); Griffin and Wright (2015))

3. **Supply Chain, Manufacturing and Production:** The main benefits of big data in manufacturing and supply chain includes shortened order to delivery cycle times, greater integration across the supply chain, optimization of inventory and asset productivity and improve interaction with customers and suppliers (Dubey et al., 2015).

4. **Customer Relationship Management (CRM):** Big data can change the way firms manage their customer relationships by offering new tools for identifying sales opportunities and analysing customers' responses to product by combining firms' internal data with unstructured data from (Wang et al., 2015). It also improves CRM by analysing customer touch points for predicting needs and directing product development, better decision making, benchmarking (Spiess et al., 2014).

5. **Marketing and Sales Management:** Big data can improve the sales and marketing strategy of a firm by giving valuable insights on customers buying behaviours, needs and market trends (Dubey and Gunasekaran, 2015). It also enables firms with targeted dynamic advertisements, improves life-cycle management, new markets identification, sales funnel leakage and more (Li et al., 2015).

6. **Social Administration and Governance:** Big data could help government to derive valuable insights from data of social communication, industrial sensors, video, email and websites (Halaweh, 2015). These insights could help them to serve their citizens and to overcome national challenges like healthcare, epidemics, job creation, natural disasters and terrorism (Chang et al., 2014).

7. **Transportation and Tourism Management:** Then main application of big data for transportation includes asset maintenance, to inform transport users' decisions, road traffic managements, reduce environmental effects and security and planning to public transport services (Shi and Abdel-Aty, 2015)

8. **Smart Cities:** The main benefits of big data in smart city components includes smart healthcare, smart energy, smart transportation, smart safety, smart education and smart governance (Nuaimi et al., 2015).

9. **Education and Research:** Through big data educational institute could harness cross disciplinary data and intelligence to improve their content and delivery and curricula by integrating and linking the traditional data with new sources of data. It also provides a good learning environment to educational institute by making better use of latest research practices and outcomes to improve teaching practices. It could also be used in data intensive scientific fields like meteorology, astronomy, bioinformatics (Krumholz, 2014), social computing (Freelon, 2014) and computational biology (Ireton, 2009).

4.2. Big Data Challenges

While the potential benefits of big data are significant and real, there remains many challenges that must be addressed to fully realise its potential value. The literature is this category is mainly classified into four sub-categories, namely, data policy, skills, big data quality and other challenges.

1. **Data Policy:**
    ◦ **Individual Privacy:** Privacy of big data is a huge concern and is mainly related to the violation and invasion of individual and business privacy by the big data users (Matzner, 2014). The main challenge with big data is to prevent the breaching of personal location privacy, people's identity and their movement patterns (Van der Sloot, 2015). Study of big data pri-

vacy and protection issues, and especially those that examine big data in relation to privacy protection and human rights policies and data protection laws are included in this review.

- ◦ **Information Security:** Data security concerns revolve around vulnerabilities and protection of data from unauthorised access and manipulation (Lafuente, 2015). Big data systems are subject to a number of security problems including data security protection, personal privacy protection, intellectual property protection, financial information protection and commercial secrets (Chen and Zhang, 2014). Other fundamental big data security issues includes integrity, confidentiality, authorization, non-repudiation, authentication and anonymity, which could be overcome by building special security mechanisms in the big data systems (Hashem, 2015).

- ◦ **Ethical Use of Big Data:** Creating, aggregating and selling big data can change relationships and business models and could force the firm to rethink their information governance strategies including issues concerning ethics (Booch, 2014).The crucial ethical issues of big data includes the negative externality of surveillance and destructive demands. Selling big data increases the risk of secondary misuses of the information which could eventually impact the users, value destruction and diminished rights for stakeholders (Martin, 2015).

2. **Skills:** The skills needed for using big data includes data scientists, big data architecture, information strategists and data governance professionals (Miller, 2014). Firms also need working groups to address data policy issues like security, privacy and ethical use of big data (Tambe, 2014). Industry, government and academia can work collaboratively to close the knowledge and skills gaps for leveraging big data.

3. **Big Data Quality:** Big data quality includes data inconsistency, incompleteness, timeliness and scalability of data (Kouzes, 2009). It also includes efficient access and analysis of semi-structured and unstructured data (Cumbley and Church, 2013). A good quality of big data is noise free and well-constructed (Gonzalez Bailon, 2013).

4.3. Big Data Techniques and Technologies

The explosion of data accelerates the advancement in technologies for data acquisition, data and information extraction processing, modelling and analysis (Gandomi and Haider, 2015). Different technologies and techniques are needed for analysing and exploiting big data intensive applications. According to current technologies and techniques of big data, we divided this category into four sub-categories, namely:

1. **Big Data Storage:** Big data's nature has changed the way of capturing and storing data which includes data storage device, architecture and data access mechanism. A good data storage platform can improve the performance of data-intensive computing like data replication, migration, distribution and access parallelism, performance, reliability and scalability (Labrinidis and Jagadish, 2012).

2. **Architecture and Models:** Big data is such a large datasets that separate systems for different workloads is very expensive and requires a lot of time to load data into multiple systems (Zhang et al., 2015). Therefore, big data systems need different parallel and distributed processing architectures and models to handle heterogeneous workloads on a single infrastructure that is flexible enough to handle different workloads like customer retention, risk assessment, brand management and more (Chen et al., 2012).

3. **Optimization Methods/Algorithms:** Optimization techniques and algorithms are needed for big data to solve various machine learning and data mining problems (Zhou, 2015). This section includes articles on randomized approximation algorithms, convex, stochastic algorithms and more.

4. **Advance Analytics:** Advance analytics are techniques used for analysing and acquiring intelligence from big data (Gandomi and Haider, 2015). Applications of big data is so humongous and complex that it need a range of different advance analytics techniques synchronised in different big data platform (Demirkan and Delen, 2013) for unlocking the value from big data. The advance analytics techniques include machine learning, statistical analysis, data mining, distributed programming, in-memory analysis, text, audio and video analytics, social media analytics, predictive analytics and visualization (Gandomi and Haider, 2015).

The nature of big data models, optimization algorithms and advance analytics could be different from other IT models and thus require separate investigation. Therefore, following two managerial questions requires focus:

*   How to design on solution for handling big data problems?
*   Which technique or technology is most suited in a particular business case?

4.4. Literature Review

According to Webster and Watson (2002), literature review on a regular basis plays a critical role in evaluating the progress of a research area, facilitating further knowledge creation, disseminating accumulated knowledge among researchers and theory building in the research field. Several researchers from various scientific disciplines have been agreed that reviewing relevant literature is required for understanding the boundary, constructs, context, relationships and competing theories of a phenomenon before a research study can be carried out to build theory (Van de Ven, 2007). However, existing review of literature of big data research are limited (Akter and Wamba, 2015). Therefore, it is recommended that future literature reviews should address issues like theory building and improved methodological rigor.

The uniqueness of big data warrants indigenous theories and these theories should emerge from extensive literature reviews. In this literature review it was found that, big data can be built from several perspectives, but there is no single indigenous theory which has been developed especially for big data. For example, the changing relationships among users in a big data enables value chain challenge applicability of the value chain theory. The vastness of big data extends the boundary of the departments and firms and its focus of IS management. Earlier firms pay more attention to their own strategies and the enabling and supporting roles of IT (Piccoli and Ives, 2005). But firms should consider business cocreation mechanisms form the perspective of big data enabled value chain is required for the planning of big data deployment. Another area where big data theory could be built is to explain and predict how big data influences firms' IT strategies and creates strategic benefits (Chen et al., 2012).

Second, the existing literature reviews are mainly based on subjective analysis and there is a lack of literature review using rigorous methodology exists. Therefore, qualitative methods like bibliometric analysis and meta-analysis should be applied to conduct literature reviews on big data studies in a more objective manner. This literature review paper is one of the first attempts to quantitatively review big data research in the information systems discipline by using citation and co-citation analysis. Through literature review it is recommended that more literature reviews based on bibliometric methods is required in the field of big data. The finding of these reviews should provide accurate pictures of the field and facilitate building indigenous theories of big data.

Although this literature review paper is not intended for theory building, it could provide an accurate understanding of big data field that sets the foundation for building big data theories later. The findings of this research reveal definitions, features, applications, challenges, core technologies, techniques, adoption and impacts of big data. These findings could help other big data researchers to identify what is lacking and where an indigenous theory is most required. In future literature reviews of big data should be focused on meta-analysis on selecting an interesting perspective of big data and identifying important constructs and their relationships in previous studies to synthesize theories unique to big data.

4.5. Adoption and Impacts

Theories like diffusion of innovation, institutional theory, TOE framework, dynamic capability, transaction costs and information process view have been employed by researchers for understanding the individual, technological, organizational and environmental factors influencing the adoption intention of big data and the determinants of big data adoption vary across different countries and different industries (Chen et al., 2015). Just adopting big data is not enough and big data must be appropriately assimilated into the adopting organization's business processes to realize the potential benefits after its adoption by firms (Chen et al., 2015). To realize more business value of big data, it is imperative to advance the research focus from adoption to assimilation of big data and to understand the conditions that enable and inhibits the assimilation of big data.

Few studies have examined the strategic impacts of big data, but the in-depth understanding in this area is lacking (Wamba et al., 2015). Given that big data represents a paradigm shift in IT strategy management (Chen et al., 2012), several traditional IT strategy management issues in the context of big data will appear as new research questions and require rigorous academic investigations. These questions include:

- Does big data has the potential to be a source of competitive advantage?
- What is the dynamics of big data enabled value chain?
- What are the causal mechanisms of IT business value co-creation in the big data enables value chain?
- Whether and how does big data enable and support business model innovation?
- Does big data enhance business-IT alignment and organizational agility and how?

Big data has great impacts on IT functions (Chen and Zhang, 2014). For example, operation and maintenance of big data provided by external service providers and the job for IT professionals will switch to the governing of relationships and contracts with service providers (Dutta and Bose, 2015). Unfortunately, the new collaboration of IT and other departments in the big data context, have not been investigated. Therefore, following questions require more focus:

- How to redesign IT functions in terms of function reform, service process, organization mode, basic tasks and performance indicator?
- Which IT capabilities are needed in realizing the business value of big data?
- What mechanism should be used by business manager to govern the relationships with big data service providers: contract, relationship or both?

- How do the subscribing firm and big data vendor maintain effective cooperative relationship in the post-adoption stage?

5. CONCLUSION

Big data has greatly influenced several industries and attracted attention of several IS scholars. To understand the current literature of big data, this study conduct citation and co-citation analyses based on 366 research papers from 2005 to June 2016. In the citation analysis, in-degree and betweeness centrality are used to identify the important research papers on big data in IS discipline. Main path analysis is also employed to make the structural backbone of the network consisted of these big data research papers. In the co-citation analysis, a matrix is formed by retrieving co-citations counts for each pair of the research papers which is identified form in the citation analysis. Principal component factor analysis is conducted on this matrix to reveal the knowledge groups of big data research. This literature review makes several contributions to the IS literature:

- First, this literature review find that big data is still in infancy and the relationships between big data researches lack clarity and cusality. The research topics of big data are scattered without a core paper group which is consistent with the results of Wamba et al., (2015) and Pospiech and Felden (2012)
- Second, this paper identifies 38 important research papers based on citation analysis. Most of these important research papers are about the conceptualization and applications of big data. Therefore, big data research in IS is heavily dependent on publications in reference disciplines.
- Third, the main path analysis depicts that big data research has evolved through three stages, i.e., incubation, exploration and burgeoning. Research papers in the incubation stage doesn't explicitly define the term and characteristics of big data and used some similar constructs. Papers in the exploration stage mostly focus on the definition and characteristics, technical features, opportunities and challenges of the development of big data. Research papers in burgeoning stage start to address specific research topics. This finding extends past literature reviews on big data (Pospiech and Felden, 2012; Singh et al., 2015; Abaker et al., 2016) from a cross-sectional perspective to an evolutionary perspective that can provide insights for future studies.
- Fourth, this paper is different from previous reviews on big data which employ a preset subjective framework to structure the related research themes, like the works of Wamba et al. (2015) and Akter and Wamba (2015). This study adopts a factor analysis of the co-citation matrix of 38 important papers and identify six major knowledge groups of big data research. Foundations is the largest knowledge group and the other five (applications, techniques and technology, challenges, adoption and impacts and literature review) interact primarily with Foundations and very less with each other.
- Also, this paper provides future research directions based on review of the big data literature. In summary, this paper is probably the first literature review that integrates citation analysis and co-citation analysis to systematically review the big data literature. The findings of this paper will help IS researchers gain an in-depth understanding of the current status of the big data research field, and the recommendations for future research directions of this paper will assist researchers to decide what topics are important when they explore into this promising but unchartered territory of big data.

6. FURTHER RESEARCH QUESTIONS AND DIRECTIONS

One of the greatest challenges in big data research is to bridge the gap between big data service providers, practitioners, and academicians. This literature survey depicts that approximately a half (47%) of all big data research concentrates on foundations and techniques and technologies of big data. As the technology matures, more attention should be paid to less developed research areas, such as business and technological challenges while implementing big data, different applications to leverage the big data for various value chain and factors affecting its adoption. Moreover, there is need to provide useful guideline principles for service providers and practitioners for the process of big data system design, development, deployment, implementation and evaluation. Furthermore, through this review, it is clear that future research effort is needed in this area.

However, despite the numerous opportunities for big data, it seems that there is still a long way for big data to go before its extensive global application is achieved. There are many issues and challenges prevailing that need to be overcome for expedite widespread implementation of big data. Following are few research questions that remain unanswered:

- What big data theories and models on big data design, deployment, implementation and evaluation have been developed by service providers and practitioners?
- Does the big data concepts, methods, theories, framework, models, techniques and tools that are applied in practice are thoroughly developed?
- Does the big data research meet the needs of business managers and practitioners?

More specifically, the following are few areas of big data research that merit future attention:

- Strategic, tactical and operational consideration (such as system design and type of database and computing installed) and work/job design factors (such as employee data analytics skill level and training). The educational requirements, training and curricular implications of big data technologies also deserve attention.
- The cost benefit analysis of big data systems is also required. This includes the costs associated with designing, developing, implementing, maintaining, controlling and updating the big data systems.
- The formulation of detailed economic and technical decision rules to guide business managers and practitioners to choose the appropriate big data system for adoption and implementation.
- The impact of big data systems on firms in various industrial situations and creation of business models for the big data adoption.
- The impact of business or technical issues, whether real or perceived, on the acceptance and adoption of big data at the user level.
- The critical success factors and barriers of big data adoption.

Many firms are investigating heavily in big data technology research and development. But the support from their governments also play an important role in promoting big data adoption (Fasso et al., 2015). It would be interesting to examine whether the countries that have not formulated policies and standards to promote individual or organizational adoption of big data are being left behind technologically. It is also important to understand the strategic use of big data technology and the regulations and policies for the access of big data.

Furthermore, it is also important for business management and social science researchers to understand the impact of big data for competing globally. The number of organizations making the initiatives of big data adoption and adding uses for the technology in marketing, sales, customer relationship management, logistics and more has increased. Therefore, it is important for information technology researchers to ensure that future research directions are managerially useful. The researchers should focus on studies that involve the design, deployment, implementation and adoption of big data systems. It is hoped that this literature review paper will provide a better understanding of the current status of big data research and some viable research directions for future academic work to the readers.

REFERENCES

Abrahamson, E., & Rosenkopf, L. (1997). Social network effects on the extent of innovation diffusion: A computer simulation. *Organization Science*, *8*(3), 289–309. doi:10.1287/orsc.8.3.289

Afshari, H., & Peng, Q. (2015). Modeling and quantifying uncertainty in the product design phase for effects of user preference changes. *Industrial Management & Data Systems*, *115*(9), 1637–1665. doi:10.1108/IMDS-04-2015-0163

Agrawal, D., Das, S., & Abbadi, A. (2010) Big Data and Cloud Computing. In *Proceedings of the VLDB*, Singapore, September 13-17 (pp. 1647-1648). ACM.

Akter, S., & Wamba, S. F. (2016). Big data analytics in E-commerce: A systematic review and agenda for future research. *Electronic Markets*, *26*(2), 173–194. doi:10.100712525-016-0219-0

Al Nuaimi, E., Al Neyadi, H., Mohamed, N., & Al-Jaroodi, J. (2015). Applications of big data to smart cities. *Journal of Internet Services and Applications*, *6*(1), 1–15. doi:10.118613174-015-0041-5

Backhaus, K., Lügger, K., & Koch, M. (2011). The structure and evolution of business-to-business marketing: A citation and co-citation analysis. *Industrial Marketing Management*, *40*(6), 940–951. doi:10.1016/j.indmarman.2011.06.024

Bechini, A., Marcelloni, F., & Segatori, A. (2016). A MapReduce solution for associative classification of big data. *Information Sciences*, *332*, 33–55. doi:10.1016/j.ins.2015.10.041

Bertei, M., Marchi, L., & Buoncristiani, D. (2015). Exploring Qualitative Data: the use of Big Data technology as support in strategic decision-making.

Bhimani, A., & Willcocks, L. (2014). Digitisation, 'Big Data' and the transformation of accounting information. *Accounting and Business Research*, *44*(4), 469–490. doi:10.1080/00014788.2014.910051

Blake, R., & Mangiameli, P. (2011). The effects and interactions of data quality and problem complexity on classification. *Journal of Data and Information Quality*, *2*(2), 8. doi:10.1145/1891879.1891881

Booch, G. (2014). The human and ethical aspects of big data. *IEEE Software*, *31*(1), 20–22. doi:10.1109/MS.2014.16

Boyack, K. W., & Klavans, R. (2010). Co-citation analysis, bibliographic coupling, and direct citation: Which citation approach represents the research front most accurately? *Journal of the American Society for Information Science and Technology, 61*(12), 2389–2404. doi:10.1002/asi.21419

Brown-Liburd, H., & Vasarhelyi, M. A. (2015). Big Data and Audit Evidence. *Journal of Emerging Technologies in Accounting, 12*(1), 1–16. doi:10.2308/jeta-10468

Ch'ng, E. (2015). The bottom-up formation and maintenance of a twitter community: Analysis of the# FreeJahar Twitter community. *Industrial Management & Data Systems, 115*(4), 612–624. doi:10.1108/IMDS-11-2014-0332

Chae, B. K. (2015). Insights from hashtag# supply chain and Twitter analytics: Considering Twitter and Twitter data for supply chain practice and research. *International Journal of Production Economics, 165*, 247–259. doi:10.1016/j.ijpe.2014.12.037

Chang, R. M., Kauffman, R. J., & Kwon, Y. (2014). Understanding the paradigm shift to computational social science in the presence of big data. *Decision Support Systems, 63*, 67–80. doi:10.1016/j.dss.2013.08.008

Chen, C. P., & Zhang, C. Y. (2014). Data-intensive applications, challenges, techniques and technologies: A survey on Big Data. *Information Sciences, 275*, 314–347. doi:10.1016/j.ins.2014.01.015

Chen, D. Q., Preston, D. S., & Swink, M. (2015). How the Use of Big Data Analytics Affects Value Creation in Supply Chain Management. *Journal of Management Information Systems, 32*(4), 4–39. doi:10.1080/07421222.2015.1138364

Chen, H., Chiang, R. H., & Storey, V. C. (2012). Business Intelligence and Analytics: From Big Data to Big Impact. *Management Information Systems Quarterly, 36*(4), 1165–1188.

Chen, K., Li, X., & Wang, H. (2015). On the model design of integrated intelligent big data analytics systems. *Industrial Management & Data Systems, 115*(9), 1666–1682. doi:10.1108/IMDS-03-2015-0086

Chiang, R. H., Goes, P., & Stohr, E. A. (2012). Business intelligence and analytics education, and program development: A unique opportunity for the information systems discipline. *ACM Transactions on Management Information Systems, 3*(3), 12. doi:10.1145/2361256.2361257

Chuang, T. C., Liu, J. S., Lu, L. Y., & Lee, Y. (2014). The main paths of medical tourism: From transplantation to beautification. *Tourism Management, 45*, 49–58. doi:10.1016/j.tourman.2014.03.016

Cohen, J., Dolan, B., Dunlap, M., Hellerstein, J. M., & Welton, C. (2009). MAD skills: New analysis practices for big data. *Proceedings of the VLDB Endowment International Conference on Very Large Data Bases, 2*(2), 1481–1492. doi:10.14778/1687553.1687576

Constantiou, I. D., & Kallinikos, J. (2015). New games, new rules: Big data and the changing context of strategy. *Journal of Information Technology, 30*(1), 44–57. doi:10.1057/jit.2014.17

Cumbley, R., & Church, P. (2013). Is "Big Data" creepy? *Computer Law & Security Review, 29*(5), 601–609. doi:10.1016/j.clsr.2013.07.007

Demirkan, H., & Delen, D. (2013). Leveraging the capabilities of service-oriented decision support systems: Putting analytics and big data in cloud. *Decision Support Systems, 55*(1), 412–421. doi:10.1016/j.dss.2012.05.048

Dubey, R., & Gunasekaran, A. (2015). Education and training for successful career in Big Data and Business Analytics. *Industrial and Commercial Training, 47*(4), 174–181. doi:10.1108/ICT-08-2014-0059

Dubey, R., Gunasekaran, A., Childe, S. J., Wamba, S. F., & Papadopoulos, T. (2015). The impact of big data on world-class sustainable manufacturing. *International Journal of Advanced Manufacturing Technology*.

Dutta, D., & Bose, I. (2015). Managing a big data project: The case of ramco cements limited. *International Journal of Production Economics, 165*, 293–306. doi:10.1016/j.ijpe.2014.12.032

Fitzpatrick, B. D., Nguyen, Q. Q. A., & Cayan, Z. (2015). An upgrade to competitive corporate analysis: creation of a" personal finance platform" to strengthen Porter's five competitive forces model in utilizing. *Journal of Business & Economics Research (Online), 13*(1), 54.

Freeman, L. C. (1978). Centrality in social networks conceptual clarification. *Social Networks, 1*(3), 215–239. doi:10.1016/0378-8733(78)90021-7

Gandomi, A., & Haider, M. (2015). Beyond the hype: Big data concepts, methods, and analytics. *International Journal of Information Management, 35*(2), 137–144. doi:10.1016/j.ijinfomgt.2014.10.007

Giannakis, M. (2012). The intellectual structure of the supply chain management discipline: A citation and social network analysis. *Journal of Enterprise Information Management, 25*(2), 136–169. doi:10.1108/17410391211204392

Griffin, P. A., & Wright, A. M. (2015). Commentaries on Big Data's importance for accounting and auditing. *Accounting Horizons, 29*(2), 377–379. doi:10.2308/acch-51066

Hackl, P. (2016). Big Data: What can official statistics expect? *Statistical Journal of the IAOS, 32*(1), 43–52. doi:10.3233/SJI-160965

Hahn, G. J., & Packowski, J. (2015). A perspective on applications of in-memory analytics in supply chain management. *Decision Support Systems, 76*, 45–52. doi:10.1016/j.dss.2015.01.003

Halaweh, M., & Massry, A. E. (2015). Conceptual Model for Successful Implementation of Big Data in Organizations. *Journal of International Technology and Information Management, 24*(2), 2.

Hashem, I. A. T., Yaqoob, I., Anuar, N. B., Mokhtar, S., Gani, A., & Khan, S. U. (2015). The rise of "big data" on cloud computing: Review and open research issues. *Information Systems, 47*, 98–115. doi:10.1016/j.is.2014.07.006

Haug, A., & Stentoft Arlbjørn, J. (2011). Barriers to master data quality. *Journal of Enterprise Information Management, 24*(3), 288–303. doi:10.1108/17410391111122862

Hazen, B. T., Boone, C. A., Ezell, J. D., & Jones-Farmer, L. A. (2014). Data quality for data science, predictive analytics, and big data in supply chain management: An introduction to the problem and suggestions for research and applications. *International Journal of Production Economics, 154*, 72–80. doi:10.1016/j.ijpe.2014.04.018

Huang, M. H., & Rust, R. T. (2013). IT-related service a multidisciplinary perspective. *Journal of Service Research, 16*(3), 251–258. doi:10.1177/1094670513481853

Ireton, R. (2009). *Computational systems biology.* Humana. doi:10.1007/978-1-59745-243-4

Jacobs, A. (2009). The pathologies of big data. *Communications of the ACM, 52*(8), 36–44. doi:10.1145/1536616.1536632

Jagadish, H. V., Gehrke, J., Labrinidis, A., Papakonstantinou, Y., Patel, J. M., Ramakrishnan, R., & Shahabi, C. (2014). Big data and its technical challenges. *Communications of the ACM, 57*(7), 86–94. doi:10.1145/2611567

James, R. (2013). Out of the box Information morality–reasonable doubt. *Business Information Review, 30*(1), 35–39. doi:10.1177/0266382113484202

James, R. (2014). Out of the box Big data needs the information profession–the importance of validation. *Business Information Review, 31*(2), 118–121. doi:10.1177/0266382114542552

Jeong, Y. K., Song, M., & Ding, Y. (2014). Content-based author co-citation analysis. *Journal of Informetrics, 8*(1), 197–211. doi:10.1016/j.joi.2013.12.001

Jin, X., Wah, B. W., Cheng, X., & Wang, Y. (2015). Significance and challenges of big data research. *Big Data Research, 2*(2), 59–64. doi:10.1016/j.bdr.2015.01.006

Kessler, M. M. (1963). Bibliographic coupling between scientific papers. *American Documentation, 14*(1), 10–25. doi:10.1002/asi.5090140103

Koseoglu, M. A., Akdeve, E., Gedik, İ., & Bertsch, A. (2015). A bibliometric analysis of strategic management articles in healthcare management literature: Past, present, and future. *International Journal of Healthcare Management, 8*(1), 27–33. doi:10.1179/2047971914Y.0000000089

Kouzes, R. T., & Gordon, A. (2009). The changing paradigm of data-intensive computing. *Computer, 42*(1), 26–34. doi:10.1109/MC.2009.26

Krumholz, H. M. (2014). Big data and new knowledge in medicine: The thinking, training, and tools needed for a learning health system. *Health Affairs, 33*(7), 1163–1170. doi:10.1377/hlthaff.2014.0053 PMID:25006142

Lafuente, G. (2015). The big data security challenge. *Network Security, 2015*(1), 12–14. doi:10.1016/S1353-4858(15)70009-7

Lane, J., & Kim, H. J. (2015). Big data: Web-crawling and analysing financial news using RapidMiner. *International Journal of Business Information Systems, 19*(1), 41–57. doi:10.1504/IJBIS.2015.069064

Lee, Y. W., Pipino, L., Strong, D. M., & Wang, R. Y. (2004). Process-embedded data integrity. [JDM]. *Journal of Database Management, 15*(1), 87–103. doi:10.4018/jdm.2004010104

Leydesdorff, L., & Vaughan, L. (2006). Co-occurrence matrices and their applications in information science: Extending ACA to the web environment. *Journal of the American Society for Information Science and Technology, 57*(12), 1616–1628. doi:10.1002/asi.20335

Liang, H., Wang, J. J., Xue, Y., & Cui, X. (2016). IT outsourcing research from 1992 to 2013: A literature review based on main path analysis. *Information & Management, 53*(2), 227–251. doi:10.1016/j.im.2015.10.001

Liu, J. S., & Lu, L. Y. (2012). An integrated approach for main path analysis: Development of the Hirsch index as an example. *Journal of the American Society for Information Science and Technology, 63*(3), 528–542. doi:10.1002/asi.21692

Lucio-Arias, D., & Leydesdorff, L. (2008). Main-path analysis and path-dependent transitions in Hist-Cite™-based historiograms. *Journal of the American Society for Information Science and Technology, 59*(12), 1948–1962. doi:10.1002/asi.20903

Ludwig, N., Feuerriegel, S., & Neumann, D. (2015). Putting Big Data analytics to work: Feature selection for forecasting electricity prices using the LASSO and random forests. *Journal of Decision Systems, 24*(1), 19–36. doi:10.1080/12460125.2015.994290

Lukashevich, H., Nowak, S., & Dunker, P. (2009, June). Using one-class SVM outliers detection for verification of collaboratively tagged image training sets. In *Proceedings of the 2009 IEEE International Conference on Multimedia and Expo* (pp. 682-685). IEEE. 10.1109/ICME.2009.5202588

Martin, K. E. (2015). (Forthcoming). Ethical issues in the Big Data industry. *MIS Quarterly Executive*.

Matzner, T. (2014). Why privacy is not enough privacy in the context of "ubiquitous computing" and "big data". *Journal of Information. Communication and Ethics in Society, 12*(2), 93–106. doi:10.1108/JICES-08-2013-0030

Miller, S. (2014). Collaborative Approaches Needed to Close the Big Data Skills Gap. *Journal of Organization Design, 3*(1), 26–30. doi:10.7146/jod.9823

Mortenson, M. J., Doherty, N. F., & Robinson, S. (2015). Operational research from Taylorism to Terabytes: A research agenda for the analytics age. *European Journal of Operational Research, 241*(3), 583–595. doi:10.1016/j.ejor.2014.08.029

Nerur, S. P., Rasheed, A. A., & Natarajan, V. (2008). The intellectual structure of the strategic management field: An author co-citation analysis. *Strategic Management Journal, 29*(3), 319–336. doi:10.1002mj.659

Nudurupati, S. S., Tebboune, S., & Hardman, J. (2016). Contemporary performance measurement and management (PMM) in digital economies. *Production Planning and Control, 27*(3), 226–235. doi:10.1080/09537287.2015.1092611

Panchaksharaiah, U. (2009) How to Address Big Data. *Communications of the ACM, 52,* 12.

Piccoli, G., & Ives, B. (2005). Review: IT-dependent strategic initiatives and sustained competitive advantage: a review and synthesis of the literature. *Management Information Systems Quarterly, 29*(4), 747–776.

Pilkington, A., & Meredith, J. (2009). The evolution of the intellectual structure of operations management—1980–2006: A citation/co-citation analysis. *Journal of Operations Management, 27*(3), 185–202. doi:10.1016/j.jom.2008.08.001

Polites, G. L., & Watson, R. T. (2009). Using social network analysis to analyze relationships among IS journals. *Journal of the Association for Information Systems*, *10*(8), 2.

Pospiech, M., & Felden, C. (2012). Big data–a state-of-the-art.

Qian, J., Lv, P., Yue, X., Liu, C., & Jing, Z. (2015). Hierarchical attribute reduction algorithms for big data using MapReduce. *Knowledge-Based Systems*, *73*, 18–31. doi:10.1016/j.knosys.2014.09.001

Raghuram, S., Tuertscher, P., & Garud, R. (2010). Research note-mapping the field of virtual work: A cocitation analysis. *Information Systems Research*, *21*(4), 983–999. doi:10.1287/isre.1080.0227

Schoenherr, T., & Speier-Pero, C. (2015). Data science, predictive analytics, and big data in supply chain management: Current state and future potential. *Journal of Business Logistics*, *36*(1), 120–132. doi:10.1111/jbl.12082

Shi, Q., & Abdel-Aty, M. (2015). Big Data applications in real-time traffic operation and safety monitoring and improvement on urban expressways. *Transportation Research Part C, Emerging Technologies*, *58*, 380–394. doi:10.1016/j.trc.2015.02.022

Singh, V. K., Banshal, S. K., Singhal, K., & Uddin, A. (2015). Scientometric mapping of research on 'Big Data'. *Scientometrics*, *105*(2), 727–741. doi:10.100711192-015-1729-9

Small, H. (1973). Co-citation in the scientific literature: A new measure of the relationship between two documents. *Journal of the American Society for Information Science*, *24*(4), 265–269. doi:10.1002/asi.4630240406

Spiess, J., T'Joens, Y., Dragnea, R., Spencer, P., & Philippart, L. (2014). Using big data to improve customer experience and business performance. *Bell Labs Technical Journal*, *18*(4), 3–17. doi:10.1002/bltj.21642

Tambe, P. (2014). Big data investment, skills, and firm value. *Management Science*, *60*(6), 1452–1469. doi:10.1287/mnsc.2014.1899

Van de Ven, A. H. (2007). *Engaged scholarship: A guide for organizational and social research*. Oxford University Press on Demand.

Van der Sloot, B. (2015). How to assess privacy violations in the age of Big Data? Analysing the three different tests developed by the ECtHR and adding for a fourth one. *Information & Communications Technology Law*, *24*(1), 74–103. doi:10.1080/13600834.2015.1009714

Waller, M. A., & Fawcett, S. E. (2013). Data science, predictive analytics, and big data: A revolution that will transform supply chain design and management. *Journal of Business Logistics*, *34*(2), 77–84. doi:10.1111/jbl.12010

Wamba, S. F., Akter, S., Edwards, A., Chopin, G., & Gnanzou, D. (2015). How 'big data' can make big impact: Findings from a systematic review and a longitudinal case study. *International Journal of Production Economics*, *165*, 234–246. doi:10.1016/j.ijpe.2014.12.031

Wamba, S. F., Akter, S., Kang, H., Bhattacharya, M., & Upal, M. (2016). The Primer of Social Media Analytics. *Journal of Organizational and End User Computing*, *28*(2), 1–12. doi:10.4018/JOEUC.2016040101

Wang, G., Gunasekaran, A., Ngai, E. W., & Papadopoulos, T. (2016). Big data analytics in logistics and supply chain management: Certain investigations for research and applications. *International Journal of Production Economics*, *176*, 98–110. doi:10.1016/j.ijpe.2016.03.014

Wang, N., Liang, H., Jia, Y., Ge, S., Xue, Y., & Wang, Z. (2016). Cloud computing research in the IS discipline: A citation/co-citation analysis. *Decision Support Systems*, *86*, 35–47. doi:10.1016/j.dss.2016.03.006

Wang, R. Y., & Strong, D. M. (1996). Beyond accuracy: What data quality means to data consumers. *Journal of Management Information Systems*, *12*(4), 5–33. doi:10.1080/07421222.1996.11518099

Warren, J. D. Jr, Moffitt, K. C., & Byrnes, P. (2015). How Big Data will change accounting. *Accounting Horizons*, *29*(2), 397–407. doi:10.2308/acch-51069

Wasserman, S., & Galaskiewicz, J. (Eds.). (1994). *Advances in social network analysis: Research in the social and behavioral sciences* (Vol. 171). Sage Publications.

Webster, J., & Watson, R. T. (2002). Analyzing the past to prepare for the future: Writing a literature review. *Management Information Systems Quarterly*.

White, D. R., & Borgatti, S. P. (1994). Betweenness centrality measures for directed graphs. *Social Networks*, *16*(4), 335–346. doi:10.1016/0378-8733(94)90015-9

White, M. (2012). Digital workplaces Vision and reality. *Business Information Review*, *29*(4), 205–214. doi:10.1177/0266382112470412

Whyte, J., Stasis, A., & Lindkvist, C. (2016). Managing change in the delivery of complex projects: Configuration management, asset information and 'big data'. *International Journal of Project Management*, *34*(2), 339–351. doi:10.1016/j.ijproman.2015.02.006

Wienhofen, L., Mathisen, B. M., & Roman, D. (2015). Empirical Big Data Research: A Systematic Literature Mapping. arXiv:1509.03045

Williams, N. P., Ferdinand, N., & Croft, R. (2014). Project management maturity in the age of big data. *International Journal of Managing Projects in Business*, *7*(2), 311–317. doi:10.1108/IJMPB-01-2014-0001

Yin, L. C., Kretschmer, H., Hanneman, R. A., & Liu, Z. Y. (2006). The evolution of a citation network topology. *Scientometrics*, 92-102.

Zhang, J., Yang, X., & Appelbaum, D. (2015). Toward effective Big Data analysis in continuous auditing. *Accounting Horizons*, *29*(2), 469–476. doi:10.2308/acch-51070

Zhao, D., & Strotmann, A. (2008). Evolution of research activities and intellectual influences in information science 1996–2005: Introducing author bibliographic-coupling analysis. *Journal of the American Society for Information Science and Technology*, *59*(13), 2070–2086. doi:10.1002/asi.20910

Zuboff, S. (2015). Big other: Surveillance capitalism and the prospects of an information civilization. *Journal of Information Technology*, *30*(1), 75–89. doi:10.1057/jit.2015.5

This research was previously published in Information Resources Management Journal (IRMJ), 31(1); pages 21-52, copyright year 2018 by IGI Publishing (an imprint of IGI Global).

Chapter 95

Big Data Analytics in Undergraduate Advertising Curricula:
A Global Survey of Higher Education Institutions

Kenneth C. C. Yang

Department of Communication, The University of Texas at El Paso, El Paso, USA

Yowei Kang

Department of Oceanic Cultural Creative Design Industries, National Taiwan Ocean University, Keelung, Taiwan

ABSTRACT

The rapid ascent of data-driven advertising practices has allowed advertising professionals to develop highly-targeted and personalized advertising campaigns. The success of data-driven advertising relies on if future professionals are proficient with basics of Big Data analytics. However, past research of undergraduate advertising curricula around the world has shown that higher education institutions tend to fall behind in offering the most up-to-dated training for advertising students. Findings have shown that undergraduate advertising programs have slowly taken advantage of the potential of the data analytics tools and techniques. This trend is observed among higher education institutions around the world. Practical, research, and pedagogical implications are discussed.

INTRODUCTION

Agency's abilities to manage audience's data effectively to identify and target the key market segment is critical to the success of advertising campaigns (Aitken, 2017). However, many advertising professionals are often found to be lacking in maximizing the capability of audience data (cited in Aitken, 2017). According to a 2017 survey by *AdAge* and Neustar, only 23% of its respondents indicate that they are

DOI: 10.4018/978-1-6684-3662-2.ch095

presently making the best use of their data management platform (cited in Aitken, 2017). In a recent 2018 CES panel, organized by Deloitte Consulting, to discuss the future of advertising, several panelists have mentioned the importance of delivering relevant advertising to consumers after taking advantage of massive amount of data from consumers' connected devices (Deloitte Development LLC, 2018). New connected technologies (through Internet-of-Things, Over-the-Top, or Artificial Intelligence) have enabled a large amount of consumer data collection (Andrew & Brynjolfsson, 2012; Deloitte Development LLC, 2018). Organizations now are able to increase their performance by using their information flow to its full capacity (Andrew & Brynjolfsson, 2012). As a result, clients would expect more accountability of advertising agencies to deliver more effective advertising campaigns in the future.

The rapid ascent of data-driven advertising has also led some industry pundits to claim it will be "the next frontier" (Rothental, 2017). Data is "[a]dvertising's North Star" (Salesforce, 2018). The advertising industry has displayed "a big crush" on Big Data (Marshall, 2013) that has produced a dedicated topic session ("Big Data") in *AdWeek.com* as well as several professional conferences on related topics such as Big Data, data-driven marketing and advertising, or data analytics (Kaye, 2014; Yang & Kang, 2016). Ranging from brand preference to previous contact and online transaction information, CRM data is employed by 94% of the advertisers to track campaign effectiveness (Columbus, 2018). According to *Digital Advertising 2020* Report by Salesforce Research (2018), 47% of advertisers in North America plan to increase their use of 3rd party data to help them create personalized advertising messages to better target their market segments. The same survey of 900 global advertising leaders also reports that 91% of them have adopted or plan to adopt data management platforms (Salesforce Research, 2018).

Although the advertising industry has been catching up with Big Data analytics in various facets of their professional practices, global higher education institutions in charge of training future talents seem less responsive to challenges and opportunities of Big Data. According to Yang and Kang's (2016) survey of global advertising programs, only a few U.S. universities have incorporated Big Data courses into their advertising curricula in 2015. It is apparent that both international and national advertising programs are slow to react to the challenges and opportunities in the age of increasingly data-driven advertising practices. However, accreditation agencies such as AACSB International (n.d.) have included skills related to big data analytics as an essential area in General Business and Management Knowledge area. ACBSP, another accreditation agency of business programs, also widely discusses the impacts of big data analytics in its annual conference (Pearson, 2014). Furthermore, according to a report by Internet Advertising Bureau (IAB), 50 top-level business executives and thought leaders conclude that predictive analytics and market segmentation tools are ranked as most commonly used information technologies (Kaye, 2015; Winterberry Group, 2015). This is concurred by many industry experts who noticed the lack of talents produced by higher education institutions to meet the demand of Big Data specialists, in spite that the market is expected to reach USD$58.9 billion in 2020 (ITBusinessEdge, 2012; Orihuela, & Bass, 2015; Patrizio, 2015; Yang & Kang, 2016; Zhu, 2017). Advertising educators such as the renowned integrated marketing communications guru, Don Schultz (2014) once pointed out that many advertising and marketing educators are not familiar with these technological advancements, which results in their inabilities to develop more up-to-dated curricula to better prepare their students. Given the growing importance of Big Data for the advertising industry, the objectives of this study intend to provide an up-to-dated assessment of undergraduate advertising curricula among higher education institutions around the world. When compared with a similar curriculum assessment project (Yang & Kang, 2016), this study aims to demonstrate the integration of Big Data analytics courses into undergraduate advertising curricula among global higher education institutions.

LITERATURE REVIEW

Advertising in the Age of Big Data

Technological advancements in computing and data storage capacities have created a massive amount of data (Hu, Wen, Chua, & Li, 2014). The term, Big Data, also known as "Data Intensive Technologies" (Demchenko et al., 2014, p. 104) often refers to "the collection, storage and analysis of data that is very large in size" (Cloud Standards Customer Council, 2013, p. 20). Big Data has enhanced the business value of technological convergence trends in social and mobile media (Ballve, 2014; Cloud Standards Customer Council, 2013; Demchenko, Laat, & Membrey, 2014; Hoelzel, 2014). Big Data has been claimed to be "disruptive" and "a catalyst" for the transformation of many enterprises (Accenture, 2014, p. 2). Big Data, a concept first proposed in 2001 by Doug Laney, 2001), inherently implies "bigger and bigger data sets over time" (Mahrt & Scharkow, 2012, p. 22). According to Doug Laney (2001), three properties characterizes what Big Data are: extremely high volume and amount of data, a wide range of varieties in terms of their types and sources, and a faster rate of data flow speed (i.e., velocity) (Cloud Standards Customer Council, 2013; Esteves & Cuto, 2013). These characteristics are likely to demand new forms of data processing capabilities to transform strategic decision-making processes in the advertising industry (Esteves & Cuto, 2013; Smith, 2014). Some emerging data-driven advertising practices include audience clustering, brand sentiment analysis, predictive marketing, and location-based advertising campaigns (Aquino, 2012; Smith, 2014; Yang & Kang, 2016).

From the advertising practitioners' perspectives, the concept of Big Data has often been defined as "datalization, digitalization, interpretation, and commercialization" (Chen & Zhou, 2017). Big Data can help advertisers make better decisions in strategizing their campaigns and personalizing advertising messages by means of new technologies (Brunell, 2016; Fulgoni, 2013; Fulgoni & Lipsman, 2014; Hendrick, 2014; Glass & Callahan, 2014). Big Data can also help advertising professionals "to decide on the basis of evidence rather than intuition" (McAfee & Brynjolfsson, 2012, p. 63). The relevance of Big Data to the advertising industry goes beyond its technical attributes discussed above. The disruptive and transformational nature of Big Data (Strong, 2013) has transformed many advertising agencies like WPP to become a data company, instead of an advertising agency (Marshall, 2013). A survey by Rocket Fuel (2013) has showed that 92% of the marketers said Big Data has met or exceeded their goals to plan their marketing activities. Hazan and Banfi (2013) conclude that "'Big data' offers companies unlimited possibilities to improve their marketing efficiency…"

Because advertising professionals require data and business intelligence to make strategically-sound decisions, Big Data analytics has been observed as one of the main catalysts to generate a large amount of data to facilitate the planning of advertising campaigns (Glass & Callahan, 2014; Hendrick, 2014; Nesamoney, 2015; Yang & Kang, 2016). Big Data will enable advertisers to make data-driven decisions to plan a successful advertising campaign. Advertising agency's capability to collect and analyze consumer behavioral data will allow advertising professionals to "decide on the basis of evidence rather than intuition" (McAfee & Brynjolfsson, 2012, p. 63). Because Big Data have enhanced advertising agency's abilities to conduct real-time analysis to better understand consumer behaviors, to produce more personalized and targeted advertising campaigns, and to develop hyper-localized advertising messages (Philip, 2014; Yang & Kang, 2016). Researchers and practitioners have noted agency's capabilities in generating better targeted and more effective advertising campaigns (Ball, 2014; Cunningham, 2010; Glass & Callahan, 2014; Hallahan et al., 2007; Yang & Kang, 2016).

In conclusion, the impacts of Big Data on the advertising industry are not only on the extent that consumer data will be collected, but also on how consumer data will be analyzed and interpreted to generate consumer insights to help the advertising planning process (Marshall, 2013). Nichols (2013) observes how analytics help advertisers to attribute, optimize, and allocate to make the most effective campaign decisions. Big Data analytics have enabled advertising professionals to better predict an array of consumer behaviors and create more effective advertising campaigns (Yang & Kang, 2016). However, the growing dependence on Big Data analytics for business decision-making has led to a talent gap as to whether existing advertising curricula are able to train future advertising professionals to meet these skill requirements (Yang & Kang, 2016). In an IBM survey, 71% of chief marketing officers admit that their companies are not well-prepared for the advent of Big Data in the next few years (cited in Smith, 2014). Therefore, in order to prepare students with the most current professional knowledge and skills, higher educational institutions around the world need to revamp their curricula. Yang and Kang (2016) has observed that some universities have begun the curricular revision processes. For example, many business schools in the U.S. are pondering over the integration of Big Data into existing business courses to better understand consumer behaviors (Chaturvedi, 2015; Yang & Kang, 2016). Columbia Business School has similarly revamped its Decision Models core courses to include Big Data in the business ecosystem (Autheres, 2013; Columbia Business School, 2013; Yang & Kang, 2016). The Department of Advertising at the University of Texas-Austin has shown its innovativeness in its program. In upper level courses such as, *Advertising 337M (Media Studies)*, contents related to Big Data and analytics tools have been incorporated into the course (Yang & Kang, 2016).

Revamping Advertising Curricula to Meet Big Data Talent Shortage

Curriculum theorists (Lau, 2001) argue that "[c]urriculum is a vital part of education" (p.31) and its development will be affected by social changes, social context, and various stakeholders. The process of developing a curriculum involves the identification of specific goals and students' learning outcomes and the assessment of the curriculum for future revisions (Knight, 2010). What students need to learn, how they will be assessed, and what future revisions are needed to increase students' competitiveness will be affected by social changes and agency's perspectives. Similarly, advertising curricula require continuous revisions to better address the needs of industry stakeholders and the challenges of new technologies.

Integrating new technologies into advertising and marketing curricula has been a topic of great pedagogical importance among educators, researchers, and practitioners (see Schlee & Harich, 2013 for review). For example, Tuten and Marks (2012) surveyed marketing educators and found that around 35% of them employed Facebook into their teaching to some extent. Their main adoption reasons are content delivery, communication (with students), and student engagement (Tuten & Marks, 2012, cited in Schlee & Harich, 2013). In terms of the implementation of Big Data analytics by organizations, scholars have often employed the theory of planned action or the technology acceptance model to understand their decisions (Esteves & Curto, 2013; Fan, Lau, & Zhou, 2015; Venkatesh, 2006; Vogel, Zhou, & Hu, 2015). For example, Esteves and Curto (2013) report that perceived risk and value factors can influence businesses' adoption of Big Data. Among these studies, the inclusion of Big Data is often considered as a rational decision for many business organizations (Esteves & Curto, 2013). In Table 1, business organizations will assess both benefits and risks before adopting Big Data (Esteves & Curto, 2013, p. 38) (Refer to Table 1). Some of the benefits are also applicable to advertising agencies in terms of enhanc-

Table 1. Benefit and risk perceptions related to Big Data adoption among business organizations

Benefits	Risks
• Creating transparency by making data accessible to relevant stakeholders in a time manner. • Improve operational efficiency (cost, revenue and risk) • Use data and experiments to expose variability and raise performance • Segmentation populations to customize the way your systems treat people • Use automated algorithms to replace and support human decision making • Innovate with new business models, products, and services • Sector-specific business value creation	• Data quality • Talent scarcity (lack of data scientists) • Privacy and security concerns • Big data integration capabilities • Decision-making • Organizational maturity level

Source: Esteves & Curto, 2013, p. 38

ing performance, operational efficiency, and creating value chain. Similarly, undergraduate advertising programs also need to be responsive to the demands from the advertising industry.

In contrast with the eager embrace of Big Data by many business organizations, higher education institutions are relatively slow to adopt (Mortimer & Sathre, 2007). A few exceptions will be among university business programs that are the most proactive to address the challenges and opportunities of Big Data (Authers, 2013; Columbia Business School, 2013; Gupta, Goul, & Dinter, 2015). With the growing importance of Big Data, the year of 2016 is claimed to mark the adoption of Big Data by higher education institutions when data-driven performance indicators are used to assess student graduation rate (such as in George State University) and funding decision (Burns, 2016). Burns (2016) also notes that many university job postings have begun to use titles such as "predictive analytics."

The process of curriculum revisions in higher education institutions are often influenced by external, organizational, and internal influences (Stark & Lattuca, 1997). External pressure includes those from alumni, government, society, and accreditation organizations (Stark & Lattuca, 1997). These outside stakeholders are likely to hold diverse perspectives in terms of the economic, technological, social, and educational impacts that Big Data may have on higher educational institutions (Daniel, 2014). As Daniel (2014) points out Big Data will demand educators to ponder over what students' learning needs will be, what pedagogy will be developed, and how to better assess students' learning outcomes.

Interacting with many outside influences, organizational influences include the disciplinary boundaries among various units inside a higher education institution (Innes, 2004). Internal influencers may include change agents, faculty members, and campus community (Oliver & Hyun, 2011) that will help the revamping process of college curricula. In his interview about recent changes in marketing curricula in University of Western Ontario, Dr. Dawar describes the integration of Big Data into its business curriculum after considering both current business practices (i.e., external influences) and change agents among the faculty members (i.e., internal influences) (Yang & Kang, 2016). In their study of how business intelligence/Big Data courses are integrated into undergraduate, M.S. graduate, and M.B.A. programs, Gupta et al. (2015) explain the importance of involving both the faculty and industry experts in their multi-year curriculum development project.

The revamping of advertising curricula to include Big Data analytics courses will no doubt involve perspectives from advertising agencies. Past curricular revamping efforts have survey advertising agencies to better understand their needs. For example, Robbs (1996) used a quantitative survey of 290 top advertising agencies to identify essential skills and course contents for entry-level creative strategies. From the returned survey of 134 agencies, conceptual, strategic thinking, and writing abilities are considered to be significant for entry-level creative applicants (Robbs, 1996). Similarly, Otnes, Spooner, and Treise (1993) also studied what essential skills would be expected among entry-level creative professionals in large advertising agencies and confirmed the skills mentioned in Robbs (1996). Otnes et al. (1993) pointed out that the ability to develop portfolio is lacking in current advertising curriculum. With the increasing diversities of the American society, multi-cultural issues are integrated into advertising curriculum (Rose & Robbs, 2001). However, sometimes, new advertising practices may not be well-received among educators even within similar disciplines (Pasadeos, 2000). For example, Pasadeos' (2000) survey of advertising and public relations faculty members found that the popular integrated marketing communications approach is perceived more favorably by advertising instructors, but less so by their counterparts teaching public relations. It is likely that the integration of Big Data into advertising curricula is likely to face similar obstacles of faculty resistance.

Research Questions

This study intends to describe the current state of undergraduate advertising curricula among higher education institutions to address the challenges and opportunities of Big Data analytics and data-driven advertising practices. The study aims to provide discussions about and answers to the following research questions pertinent to undergraduate advertising education among higher education institutions around the world:

Research Question 1: How have undergraduate advertising programs responded to the challenges and opportunities of data-driven advertising practices through their curriculum revamp?

Research Question 2: In what way has Big Data analytics courses been integrated into existing undergraduate advertising curricula among higher education institutions around the world?

RESEARCH METHOD

Sampling and Sampling Characteristics

To better understand how undergraduate advertising programs around the world have responded to the opportunities and challenges of data-driven advertising practices by integrating Big Data analytics courses into training their students, this study collected curricular information from undergraduate advertising programs around the world.

The researchers use the list of undergraduate advertising programs complied in *FindtheBest* site (http://colleges.findthebest.com/d/o/Advertising) that was discontinued in 2018. A total of 161 programs is identified in the list, ranging from the prestigious global University of Florida (95% smart rating on the basis of admission selectivity, academic excellence, expert opinion, and financial affordability), The University of Texas at Austin (94% smart rating), to a less known local university, Miami Ad School (at San Francisco) (24% smart rating) (Yang & Kang, 2016). In spite of its discontinuation, we manage to Google each university.

Similar to Yang and Kang (2016), *BachelorStudies.com* (http://www.bachelorstudies.com/Bachelor/Advertising/Europe/) is used to locate eleven "Bachelor Programs Advertising in Europe 2018." In the

Greater China Region (which include Taiwan, Hong-Kong, SAR, Macao, SAR, and Republic of Singapore), ten undergraduate advertising programs are included in the sample after conducting Google searches.

Procedure to Collect Curricular Data

After downloading and analyzing curricula information from 182 undergraduate advertising programs of the U.S., Europe, and Asia (the Greater China Region), the researchers focus on course keywords such as "Big Data", "Data-Driven Advertising", "Data-Driven Marketing", "Consumer Analytics", "Predictive Analytics", "Metrics", and "Data Mining." In Yang and Kang (2016) study, only very few advertising programs across all three geographical regions have course titles including the above keywords in their curricula at time of their study in 2015 (Refer to Table 2).

Table 2. Analysis of big data-related courses in undergraduate advertising curricula of different geographical areas (2015)

Course Title (Description) Containing the Following Keywords	U.S. Programs (N=116)	European Programs (N=10)	Asian Programs in the Greater China Region (N=10)
"Big Data"	0	0	0
"Data-Driven Marketing or Advertising"	0	0	0
"Consumer Analytics"	0	0	0
"Predictive Analytics"	0	0	0
"Analytics"	1	0	0
"Metrics"	1	0	0

Source: Yang and Kang (2016)

FINDINGS AND DISCUSSIONS

This study replicates Yang and Kang (2016) study, and examines curricula data collected in 2018 to examine whether undergraduate advertising programs around the world have responded to the challenges and opportunities of Big Data. This study has found that, increasingly, undergraduate advertising programs have integrated Big Data analytics courses into their curricula. Eight courses related to the keywords are found in the curricula of 161 higher education institutions in the United States. Only related course is found in the eleven European advertising programs, while six courses are found among ten undergraduate advertising programs in the Greater China Region (Refer to Table 3).

Data-Driven Advertising Practices and Impacts on the Advertising Education

The first research question asks, "How have college advertising programs responded to the challenges and opportunities of data-driven advertising practices through their curriculum revamp?" In spite of the buzz about how Big Data will impact the advertising industry, comments from advertising professionals seem to suggest the essential skills for advertising professionals depend on whether they are able to

Table 3. Analysis of big data-related courses in undergraduate advertising curricula of different geographical areas (2018)

Course Title (Description) Containing the Following Keywords	U.S. Programs (N=116)	European Programs (N=11)	Asian Programs in the Greater China Region (N=10)
"Big Data"	0	1	0
"Data-Driven Marketing or Advertising"	1	0	0
"Consumer Analytics"	0	0	0
"Predictive Analytics"	0	0	0
"Analytics"	6	0	3
"Metrics"	1	0	0
"Data Mining"	0	0	3

Source: The authors (2018)

analyze and integrate these data-based insights (Pollack, 2014). Mr. Tham Khai Meng, worldwide chief creative officer and chairman of Ogilvy, commented on what essential skills are needed to train advertising professionals in the age of Big Data: "At its heart, data are insights best used as an inspiration to reach and identify an audience" and "Human beings are not a collection of algorithms," (Pollack, 2014, para. 4). Consumer insights help create memorable campaigns such as Dove's *Real Beauty* campaign, or Johnny Walker' *Keep Walking* (Pollack, 2014).

Technology always plays a central role in shaping the advertising education. On the basis of a preliminary literature review of *Journal of Advertising Education* have found that technology often affects what will be taught in the advertising curricula (Barnes, 1996; Martin, 2001). Barnes' (1996) article describes the influence of then nascent World Wide Web on how national advertising curricula need to be revamped. Martin (2001) examines other computer-mediated technologies on media planning courses. Emerging social media, Web 2.0, and Web 3.0 has similarly motivated advertising educators to revamp advertising curricula as seen in several Journal of Advertising Education (JAE) articles. (Caravella, Ekachai, Jaeger, & Zahay, 2009; Kalamas, Mitchell, & Lester, 2009; Scovotti & Jones, 2011). While Caravella et al. (2009) study the opportunities and challenges proposed by Web 2.0, Scovott and Jones (2011) examine the impacts of Web 3.0 on the existing advertising curricula. Considering the close relationship between advertising practices and technological advances, advertising educators should be similarly responsive when dealing with these changes to better train future advertising professionals (Robbs, 2010). However, the present lukewarm responses may be contributed to what Don Schultz (2014) has observed, the highly technical nature of Big Data analytics courses (no matter whether they are data mining or predictive analytics) may have prevented many advertising educators (trained in the social scientific disciplines) from embracing these new practices.

The second research question asks, "In what way has Big Data analytics courses been integrated into existing advertising curricula among higher education institutions around the world?" Yang and Kang (2016) found that, when compared with other departments in the communication discipline, a relatively sluggish response among global undergraduate advertising programs is necessary to better address the challenges and opportunities of Big Data analytics.

For example, the diploma program in Creative Advertising and Branding at IED Barcelona offers its Big Data & Communication course (4 credits). IED is the only school in the European sample that offers Big Data analytics courses. In the Greater China Region (including countries like Taiwan, Hong-Kong, Macao, and Singapore), a total of six Big Data analytics courses are found in the undergraduate advertising curricula. For example, Data Mining course is offered at the advertising department (Ming-Chuan University, Taiwan). In Hong-Kong Baptist University, *Web Survey and Data Mining* is offered as part of its Public Relations and Advertising curriculum, while City University of Hong-Kong offers *Media and Data Analytics* in its Integrated Strategic Communication Program. Similarly, Nanyang Technological University in Singapore offers *Data Mining and Social Media Mining* courses. Also included in its advertising curriculum are courses such as *Foundation of Information Analytics, Information Analytics Tools, Techniques, and Technologies.*

When compared with the eager integration of Big Data analytics courses into advertising curricula among 10 higher education institutions in the Greater China Region, most undergraduate advertising programs show lukewarm responses to the challenges and opportunities of Big Data analytics courses. Among 161 advertising curricula reviewed, only eight related courses are found. While top advertising programs such as University of Texas at Austin, Michigan State University, Temple University, schools offering certificates, technical degrees are more likely to offer Big Data analytics courses. It is likely that these less known schools feel a strong need to take advantages of the opportunities. For example, the advertising curriculum at Ferris State University offers its Data Analytic Certificate. Johnson & Wales University at Denver offers its *Data –Driven Marketing* and *Market Analytics* courses.

CONCLUSION

As the founder of the renowned advertising department, at the University of Illinois, Charles H. Sandage envisions, "A university should be concerned with training future leaders." The abilities to collect, analyze, visualize, and interpret data to generate insights are found to be essential to the success of future advertising professionals (Yang & Kang, 2016). Big Data analytics involve data collection, analysis, and visualization skills (Daniel, 2014) that correspond to the increasingly data-driven advertising and marketing practices. Accountability as demanded by the advertising industry to justify a return on investment has also increased with the presence of multi-platform advertising channels, ranging from digital TV, social media, websites, and mobile devices (Price, 2014; Yang & Kang, 2016). To excel in this competitive environment, future advertising professionals need to be proficient in integrating insights from these analytics tools into planning more effective campaigns (Yang & Kang, 2016).

Curricula in a higher education institution can be regarded as an educational project that constitutes its identities through three main domains: action, knowledge, and self (Barnett, Parry, & Coate, 2010). Higher education institutions are expected to meet demands of various stakeholders in society (Daniel, 2014); particularly, in the context of advertising curricula, those from advertising agencies and advertisers. Recent advances in media technologies have greatly impacted media education and curricula around the world (Berkeley, 2009), leading to a more complex and competitive environment for higher education institutions (Daniel, 2014). For example, Berkeley (2009) uses a case study approach to record the curricular changes at RMIT University to explore the effects of technological advances on media education to create a more student-centered learning environment. Revamping advertising, communication, and media curricula are likely not only to create educational contents more in line with the industry demands, but also to enable students to become independent learners in a fast-changing environment (Berkeley, 2009; Lester, 2012; Yang & Kang, 2016). To respond to challenges from social media, advertising educators have revamped their current courses by assimilating emerging media platforms into students' campaign projects (Lester, 2012). Other incentives include the teaching of data visualization courses in journalism programs (e.g., the University of Nebraska-Lincoln, University of California at Berkeley, University of Missouri, and The University of Maryland) (Yang & Kang, 2016; Wordsman, 2014).

Research Limitations and Future Directions

This study has the following limitations that need to be cautioned when interpreting the findings. First, curricular data are collected from the websites of universities, colleges, departments, and programs from higher education institutions. It is likely that the curricular data might not be as up-to-dated, depending on how different institutions utilize their websites to publicize their curricular information.

Secondly, our analyses rely on course titles and descriptions posted on the program websites. Syllabi of the courses are often not available to examine detailed course contents and topics. It is likely that instructors may have included Big Data analytics topics in curricula that do not carry the data analytics titles.

Thirdly, this study analyzes curricular data, but do conduct quantitative surveys on advertising/marketing professionals and educators to learn about their perspectives in the revamping process (Otnes et al., 1997; Robbs, 1996; Salesforce Research, 2018).

Therefore, there are several potential research directions that can be derived from this study to further explore curricular revamping initiatives among national and international advertising programs. First, a more thorough analysis of employment ads in advertising, marketing, and marketing communication areas will ensure the identification of essential skill requirements for entry-level, mid-career, and senior positions to allow higher education institutions to revamp their curricula to prepare students at various stages of their careers (Yang & Kang, 2016). Secondly, quantitative, qualitative, or multi-method study should also be conducted to examine instructors' perceptions of, attitudes toward, and possible resistance to these opportunities and challenges brought up by Big Data analytics and an array of analytic tools available to them (Yang & Kang, 2016). Thirdly, how will advertising instructors respond to the challenges of innovative pedagogical needs as well their adjustment of emerging performance measurement and metrics should be further examined (Daniel, 2014). Lastly, the perspectives of students in the educational process should be studied in a more systematic way to understand their ever-changing learning needs once the revamping of existing advertising program is undertaken (Yang & Kang, 2016).

REFERENCES

AACSB International. (n.d.). Standard 9: Curriculum content is appropriate to general expectations for the degree program type and learning goals. Retrieved June 26, 2015 from http://www.aacsb.edu/en/accreditation/standards/2013-business/learning-and-teaching/standard9/

Accenture. (2014). *Big success with big data*. Retrieved from https://www.accenture.com/us-en/_acnmedia/Accenture/Conversion-Assets/DotCom/Documents/Global/PDF/Industries_14/Accenture-Big-Data-POV.pdf

Aitken, R. J. (October 24, 2017). How to transform your traditional sell-side ad organization. *AdAge,* Retrieved April 15, 2018 from http://adage.com/article/deloitte-digital/transform-traditional-sell-side-ad-organization/310978/

Aquino, J. (2012, January). 5 hot marketing trends: Customer strategists must step up their engagement efforts as mobile's mercury rises. *CRM Magazine, 16*, 20.

Authers, J. (2013, December 8). The changing face of the MBA curriculum. *FT.Com,* Retrieved March 1, 2015 from http://www.ft.com/cms/s/2/b52b57d8-5d07-11e3-81bd-00144feabdc0.html#axzz3RGW3FcND

Ballve, M. (2014, October 22). Mobile, social, and big data: The convergence of the internet's three defining trends. *Business Insider,* Retrieved June 26, 2015 from http://www.businessinsider.com/mobile-and-social-drive-big-data-industry-2014-2019

Barlow, M., & Safari Tech Books Online. Real-time big data analytics emerging architecture. Retrieved January 4, 2015 from http://proquest.safaribooksonline.com/?uiCode=yaleu&xmlId=9781449364670

Barnes, B. E. (1996). Introducing introductory advertising student to the World Wide Web. *Journal of Advertising Education, 1*(1), 5–12.

Barnett, R., Parry, G., & Coate, K. (2010, August 25). Conceptualising curriculum change. Teaching in Higher Education, *6*(4), 435-449.

Berkeley, L. (2009). Media education and new technology: A case study of major curriculum change within a university media degree. *Journal of Media Practice, 10*(2-3), 185–197. doi:10.1386/jmpr.10.2-3.185_1

Bessis, N., & Dobre, C. (Eds.). (2014). *Big data and internet of things: A roadmap for smart environments.* Springer; doi:10.1007/978-3-319-05029-4

Bruell, A. (2016, May 2). The ad agency of the future is coming. Are you ready? *AdAge.* Retrieved April 16, 2018 from http://adage.com/article/print-edition/agency-future/303798/

Burns, B. (2016, January 29). Big data's coming of age in higher education. *Forbes.com.* Retrieved April 18, 2018 from https://www.forbes.com/sites/schoolboard/2016/2001/2029/big-datas-coming-of-age-in-higher-education/#2013feb2079a2041c2041

Caravella, M., Ekachai, D., Jaeger, C., & Zahay, D. (2009, Spring). Web 2.0 opportunities and challenges for advertising educators. *Journal of Advertising Education, 13*(1), 58–63. doi:10.1177/109804820901300109

Chaturvedi, A. (2015, February 5). Big data embedded into marketing curriculum at B-schools: Niraj dawar, ivey business school. *The Economic Times of India.* Retrieved January 10, 2015 from http://articles.economictimes.indiatimes.com/2015-02-03/news/58751790_1_big-data-customers-tilt

Chen, H., & Zhou, L. (2017, June 28). The myth of big data: Chinese advertising practitioners' perspective. *International Journal of Advertising.* doi:10.1080/02650487.2017.1340865

Church, A. H., & Dutta, S. (2013). The promise of big data for OD: Old wine in new bottles or the next generation of data driven methods for change? *OD Practitioner, 45*(4), 23–31.

Cloud Standards Customer Council. (2013, June). *Convergence of social, mobile and cloud: 7 steps to ensure success*. Retrieved March 1, 2015 from http://www.cloud-council.org/Convergence_of_Cloud_Social_Mobile_Final.pdf

Columbia Business School. (2013, August 28). Press release, Columbia Business School unveils redesigned core curriculum for first-year MBA students. Retrieved January 10, 2015 from http://www8.gsb.columbia.edu/newsroom/newsn/2450/columbia-business-school-unveils-redesigned-core-curriculum-for-first-year-mba-students

Columbus, L. (2018, January 18). Analytics are defining the future of digital advertising. *Forbes.com*, Retrieved April 15, 2018 from https://www.forbes.com/sites/louiscolumbus/2018/2001/2018/analytics-are-defining-the-future-of-digital-advertising/#2011d2860fde2786f

Daniel, B. (2014). Big data and analytics in higher education: Opportunities and challenges. *British Journal of Educational Technology*, 1–17. doi:10.1111/bjet.12230

Daugherty, T., & Reece, B. B. (2002). The adoption of persuasive internet communication in advertising and public relations curricula. *Journal of Interactive Advertising*, *3*(1), 46–55. doi:10.1080/15252019.2002.10722067

Deloitte Development LLC. (2018). User friendly podcast at CES: The future of advertising. In CES (Producer). Las Vegas, CES. Retrieved April 15, 2018 from https://www2.deloitte.com/content/dam/Deloitte/us/Documents/technology-media-telecommunications/us-tmt-user-friendly-podcast-at-ces-the-future-of-advertising.pdf

Demchenko, Y., Laat, C. D., & Membrey, P. (2014). Defining architecture components of the big data ecosystem. In 2014 International Conference on Collaboration Technologies and Systems (CTS) (pp. 104-112). IEEE.

Esteves, J., & Curto, J. (2013). A risk and benefits behavioral model to assess intention to adopt big data. *Journal of Intelligence Studies in Business*, *3*(3), 37–46.

Fan, S., Lau, R. Y. K., & Zhao, J. L. (2015, March). Demystifying big data analytics for business intelligence through the lens of marketing mix. *Big Data Research*, *2*(1), 28–31. doi:10.1016/j.bdr.2015.02.006

Fulgoni, G. (2013, December). Big data: Friend or foe of digital advertising? Five ways marketers should use digital big data to their advantage. *Journal of Advertising Research*, *53*(4), 372–376. doi:10.2501/JAR-53-4-372-376

Gartner. (2012, October 22). Gartner says Big Data creates big jobs: 4.4 million IT jobs globally to support Big Data by 2015. Retrieved January 15, 2015 from http://www.gartner.com/newsroom/id/2207915

Glass, R., & Callahan, S. (2014). *The big data-driven business: How to use big data to win customers, beat competitors, and boost profits*. Hoboken, NJ: Wiley.

Gupta, B., Goul, M., & Dinter, B. (2015). Business intelligence and big data in higher education: Status of a multi-year model curriculum development effort for business school undergraduates, MS graduates, and MBAs. *Communications of the Association for Information Systems, 36*, 449-476. Retrieved April 418, 2018 from https://www.researchgate.net/publication/274709810_Communications_of_the_Association_for_Information_Systems

Hazan, E., & Banfi, F. (2013, August). *Leveraging big data to optimize digital Marketing*. McKinsey & Company. Retrieved January 13, 2015 from http://www.mckinsey.com/client_service/marketing_and_sales/latest_thinking/leveraging_big_data_to_optimize_digital_marketing

Hendrick, D. (2014, December 11). 6 ways big data will shape online marketing in 2015. *Forbes.com*. Retrieved June 26, 2015 from http://www.forbes.com/sites/drewhendricks/2014/2012/2011/2016-ways-big-data-will-shape-online-marketing-in-2015/

Hoelzel, M. (2014). The social media advertising report: Growth forecasts, market trends, and the rise of mobile. *Business Insider.* Retrieved January 5, 2015 from http://www.businessinsider.com/social-media-advertising-spending-growth-2014-2019

Hu, H., Wen, Y. G., Chua, T. S., & Li, X. L. (2014). Toward scalable systems for big data analytics: A technology tutorial. *IEEE Translations and Content Mining, 2*, 652–687.

Ignatius, A. (2012, October). "Big Data for Skeptics." *Harvard Business Review*, Retrieved January 5, 2015 from https://hbr.org/2012/10/big-data-for-skeptics

Innes, R. (2004). *Reconstructing undergraduate education: Using learning science to design effective courses*. Mahwah, NJ: Lawrence Erlbaum Associates.

ITBusinessEdge. (n.d.). Big Data is creating big jobs: 4.4 million by 2015. Retrieved January 5, 2015 from http://www.itbusinessedge.com/slideshows/big-data-is-creating-big-jobs-4.4-million-by-2015.html

Jeffery, M. (2010). *Data-driven marketing the 15 metrics everyone in marketing should know*. John Wiley & Sons.

Kalamas, M., Mitchell, T., & Lester, D. (2009, Spring). Modeling social media use: Bridging the gap in higher education. *Journal of Advertising Education, 13*(1), 44–57. doi:10.1177/109804820901300108

Kaye, K. (2014, August 20). Get a hands on education at Ad Age Data Conference 2014: Two days of practical and entertaining insights in New York this October. *AdAge.com*. Retrieved January 3, 2015 from http://adage.com/article/datadriven-marketing/hands-education-ad-age-data-conference-2014/294635/

Kaye, K. (2015, January 20). IAB survey: Marketers using a hodge-podge of data-tech tools trade group's study showed marketers use upwards of 12 systems. *AdAge.com*. Retrieved from http://adage.com/article/datadriven-marketing/iab-surveys-marketing-execs-data-tech/296653/

Knight, P. T. (2010, August). Complexity and curriculum: A process approach to curriculum-making. *Teaching in Higher Education, 6*(3), 369–381. doi:10.1080/13562510120061223

Kudyba, S., & Davenport, T. H. (2014). *Big data, mining, and analytics: Components of strategic decision making. Boca Rotan*. CRC Press. doi:10.1201/b16666

Laney, D. (2001). 3d data management: Controlling data volume, velocity and variety. *Gartner*. Retrieved January 4, 2015 from http://blogs.gartner.com/doug-laney/files/2012/01/ad949-3D-Data- Management-Controlling-Data-Volume-Velocity-and-Variety.pdf

Lau, D. C.-M. (2001). Analysing the curriculum development process: Three models. *Pedagogy, Culture & Society*, *9*(1), 29–44. doi:10.1080/14681360100200107

Lester, D. H. (2012, January). Social media: Changing advertising education. *Online Journal of Communication and Media Technologies*, *2*(1), 116–125.

Mahrt, M., & Scharkow, M. (2012). The value of big data in digital media research. *Journal of Broadcasting & Electronic Media*, *57*(1), 20–33. doi:10.1080/08838151.2012.761700

Maimon, O. Z., & Rokach, L. (2005). *Data mining and knowledge discovery handbook*. New York: Springer. doi:10.1007/b107408

Marshall, J. (2013, September 25). The advertising industry has a big crush on Big Data. *DigiDay*, Retrieved March 1, 2015 from http://digiday.com/platforms/dstillery-advertising-data-crush/

Martin, D. G. (2002, Spring). In search of the golden mean: Impact of computer mediated technologies on the media planning course. *Journal of Advertising Education*, *6*(1), 25–35. doi:10.1177/109804820200600106

McAfee, A., & Brynjolfsson, E. (2012, October). Big data: The management revolution. *Harvard Business Review*, *90*(10), 59–68. PMID:23074865

Mortimer, K. P., & Sathre, C. O. (2007). The art and politics of academic governance: Relations among boards, presidents, and faculty. Westport, CT: Praeger Publishers.

Nesamoney, D. (2015). *Personalized digital advertising: How data and technology are transforming how we market*. Old Tappan, NJ: Pearson Education, Inc.

NetworkWorld Asia. (2013, March/April). Big data - big hype or big worry?

Nichols, W. (2013). Advertising analytics 2.0. *Harvard Business Review*, *91*(3), 61–68.

Nunan, D., & Domenico, M. D. (2013). Market research and the ethics of big data. *International Journal of Market Research*, *55*(3), 2–13.

Oliver, S. L., & Hyun, E. (2011). Comprehensive curriculum reform in higher education: Collaborative engagement of faculty and administrators. *Journal of Case Studies in Education*, *2*, 1–20.

Orihuela, R., & Bass, D. (2015, June 4). Help wanted: Black belts in data. *Bloomberg Businessweek*, Retrieved June 26, 2015 from http://www.bloomberg.com/news/articles/2015-2006-2004/help-wanted-black-belts-in-data

Otnes, C., Spooner, E., & Treise, D. M. (1993). Advertising curriculum ideas from 'new creatives.'. *Journalism Educator*, *48*(3), 9–17.

Pasadeos, Y. (2000). Conflicting attitudes toward an integrated curriculum. *Journalism and Mass Communication Educator*, *55*(1), 73–78.

Patrizio, A. (2015, March 23). 4 ways to beat the big data talent shortage. *Network World.* Retrieved June 26, 2015 from http://www.networkworld.com/article/2897617/big-data-business-intelligence/2897614-ways-to-beat-the-big-data-talent-shortage.html

Pearson, P. G. (2014, June 27-30). Putting the learner at the center: Just saying 'digital' is not enough. *Paper presented at the ACBSP 2014 Annual Conference: Teaching Excellence and Teaching Excellence Global Business Education Concurrent Sessions*, Chicago, IL.

Philip, N. (March 14, 2014). *The impact of big data on the digital advertising industry.* Mountain View, CA: Qubole Data Service. Retrieved January 3, 2015 from http://www.qubole.com/blog/big-data/big-data-advertising-case-study/

Pollack, C. (2014, September 29). It's not big data, it's the big idea, stupid. *AdAge,* Retrieved January 2, 105 from http://adage.com/article/advertising-week-2014/big-data-big-idea-stupid/295199/

Price, C. (2014, September 2). Attracting the right audience with big data insights. *The Telegraph,* Retrieved January 2, 2015 from http://www.telegraph.co.uk/sponsored/technology/4g-mobile/engaging-customers/11070094/attract-right-audience-big-data.html

PWC. (2015, February). Data driven: What students need to succeed in a rapidly changing business world. Retrieved June 26, 2015 from http://www.Pwc.Com/us/en/faculty-resource/assets/pwc-data-driven-paper-feb2015.Pdf

Richards, J. I. (2000). Interactive advertising concentration. *Journal of Interactive Advertising, 1*(1), 15–22. doi:10.1080/15252019.2000.10722041

Robbs, B. (1996). The advertising curriculum and the needs of creative students. *Journalism and Mass Communication Educator, 50*(4), 25–34.

Robbs, B. (2010). Preparing young creatives for an interactive world: How possible is it? *Journal of Advertising Education, 14*(2), 7–14. doi:10.1177/109804821001400205

Rosenthal, V. (2017, August 14). Why data-driven advertising will be the next frontier. *Forbes.* Retrieved April 15, 2018 from https://www.forbes.com/sites/vivianrosenthal/2017/2008/2014/why-data-driven-advertising-will-be-the-next-frontier-2012/#e2016ea2018af2217e2013

Sagirouglu, S., & Sinanc, D. (2013). Big data: A review. *Paper presented at the 2013 International Conference on Collaborative Technologies and Systems*, San Diego, CA, May 20-24.

Salesforce Research. (2018). *Digital advertising 2020: Insights into a new era of advertising and media buying.* Salesforce Research.

Salesforce Research. (2018). *The 4th annual state of marketing.* Retrieved April 26, 2018 from https://c2011.sfdcstatic.com/content/dam/web/en_us/www/assets/pdf/datasheets/salesforce-research-fourth-annual-state-of-marketing.pdf

Schlee, R. P., & Harich, K. R. (2013, Fall). Teaching students how to integrate and assess social networking tools in marketing communications. *Marketing Education Review, 23*(3), 209–223. doi:10.2753/MER1052-8008230301

Schultz, D. E. (2014, May). Why Big Data is so difficult. Marketing News, American Marketing Association. Retrieved January 2, 2015 from https://www.ama.org/publications/MarketingNews/Pages/why-big-data-so-difficult.aspx

Scovotti, C., & Jones, S. K. (2011, Spring). From Web 2.0 to Web 3.0: Implications for advertising courses. *Journal of Advertising Education, 15*(1), 6–15. doi:10.1177/109804821101500102

Smith, C. (2014, March 20). Reinventing social media: Deep learning, predictive marketing, and image recognition will change everything. *Business Insider.* Retrieved April 16, 2018 from http://www.businessinsider.com/social-medias-big-data-future-2014-2013

Stark, J. S., & Lattuca, L. R. (1997). *Shaping the college curriculum: Academic plans in action.* Needham Heights, MA: Allyn and Bacon.

Strong, C. (2013). When marketing meet big data. *Marketing Leaders*, 32-35.

Vogel, D., Zhou, H., & Hu, D. (2015, March). Special issue on computation, business, and health science. *Big Data Research, 2*(1), 1. doi:10.1016/j.bdr.2015.03.002

Wordsman, E. (2014, December 14). Journalism schools add courses in sports, emerging technology. *American Journalism Review.* Retrieved January 4, 2015 from http://ajr.org/2014/12/18/journalism-schools-add-courses-sports-emerging-technology/

Yang, K. C. C., & Kang, Y. W. (2016). Integrating Big Data analytics into advertising curriculum: Opportunities and challenges. In Smith, Brent & Porath, Amiram (Eds.), Global Perspectives on Contemporary Marketing Education (pp. 131-152). Hershey, PA: IGI-Global Publisher.

Young, M. (2013). Overcoming the crisis in curriculum theory: A knowledge-based approach. *Journal of Curriculum Studies, 45*(2), 101-118. doi:10.1080/00220272.00222013.00764505

Zhu, L. (2017, November 21). Surge in demand for big data talent. *China Daily.* Retrieved April 15, 2018 from http://www.chinadaily.com.cn/business/tech/2017-2011/2021/content_34808794.htm

This research was previously published in the International Journal of Technology and Educational Marketing (IJTEM), 8(1); pages 34-47, copyright year 2018 by IGI Publishing (an imprint of IGI Global).

Chapter 96
How Big Data Transforms Manufacturing Industry:
A Review Paper

Victor I. C. Chang

https://orcid.org/0000-0002-8012-5852

Xi'an Jiaotong-Liverpool University, Suzhou, China

Wanxuan Lin

Xi'an Jiaotong-Liverpool University, Suzhou, China

ABSTRACT

This article describes an overview of what Big Data is and explains how it transforms the manufacturing industry. First, this article defines what Big Data means for the manufacturing industry. It explains four advantages about Big Data analytics and their benefits to manufacturing. Then, it describes about what ethical issues of Big Data are. Next, it discusses more deeply about the ethical issues of Big Data in manufacturing with both individual and organizational perspectives. Finally, this article sums up with some principles to show the ethical governance of the interests of Big Data stakeholders.

INTRODUCTION

This paper discusses the role of Big Data in the manufacturing industry. It attempts to provide a holistic review of the literature and offers discussion around the underlying gaps. The manuscript further discusses the ethical issues within the context.

DOI: 10.4018/978-1-6684-3662-2.ch096

BIG DATA

Big Data is a term that describes the large volume of structured and unstructured data with the potential to be mined for information. It figures a new technology paradigm for data that are created at massive volume and high velocity, and comes from various sources (Lee, 2017). Herschel and Miori introduces Big Data is to capture, store, share, evaluate, and act upon information that generated and distributed by humans and equipment using networks and computer-based technologies (Herschel & Miori, 2017). Gartner also defined Big Data as a high volume, high velocity and high variety information property that requires new handle mode to enhance decision-making ability, insight discovery, and process optimization (Gandomi & Haider, 2015).

Big Data is defined by IBM data scientists in terms of four dimensions: volume, variety, velocity, and veracity (Yin & Kaynak, 2015). Volume means the amount of data is huge, which is from TB level up to PB level. Variety means data comes from different kinds of formats, such as video, image, location, weblog and so on. Velocity means the speed of data processing is very fast and this is essentially different from traditional data mining. Veracity means the quality and trustworthiness of the data. The importance of Big Data depends on the support for decision-making. The size of the data does not determine whether it helps to make decisions, but the authenticity and quality of the data are the basis for making successful decisions.

In a word, the ability to acquire valuable information rapidly from various data can be classified as Big Data technology. Using Big Data becomes a critical factor in improving core competitiveness, and decision-making is transforming business-driven into data-driven in all walks of life (Carillo, 2017).

Nowadays, data has infiltrated every industry and business function. It is generated always and transmitted by every digital process and social media exchange, such as GPS positioning, purchase transaction records and posts on social platform. How to manage and further use data and information to support the decision-making of organizations has become an urgent need and even become the core competitiveness of enterprises (Dobbs et al., 2011).

The emergence of Big Data keeps changing people's existing habits and life patterns and gradually changing the production patterns of manufacturing enterprises. The demand for today is no longer in short supply situation like 30 years ago but the era that manufactures rack their brains for marketing. In China, since the reform and opening-up, the Internet has played an important role on the rapid development of science and technology (Xu, He, & Li, 2014). As the same time, both logistics technology and information and communication technology have provided a great support for the development of the Internet. Therefore, the increasing amount of data has brought great challenges to manufacturing industry while also offering golden opportunities for business and transformation.

BIG DATA IN MANUFACTURING INDUSTRY

Manufacturing is one of the main areas of Big Data applications and it can be described as a 5M system consisting of materials, machines, methods, measurements and modeling (Lee et al., 2013). Big Data provides a transparent infrastructure for manufacturing that addresses such uncertainties as inconsistent component performance and availability (Inukollu, 2014). One of the Big Data applications in manufacturing is predictive manufacturing and its conceptual framework starts with data collection, where it is possible to obtain different types of sensory data such as stress, vibration, acoustics, voltage, current, and controller data (Inukollu, 2014). These sensory data combine with historical data to form the Big Data for manufacturing.

Big Data analytics plays a catalytic role in realizing the idea of digital manufacturing and also forms the basis of modern mass customization, which means meeting the needs of a personalized customer market (Mourtzis, Viachou, & Milas, 2016). In addition, Big Data analytics will have an important influence on R & D, manufacture, customer service, maintenance, recycling and remanufacturing, promoting the implementation of cleaner production and the development of sustainable production and consumption effectively (Zhang et al., 2016; Daneshkhah et al., 2017).

As shown in Figure 1, the process of using Big Data for manufacturing can be in a sequential way. It starts with the exploratory study on how Big Data's influences on manufacturing. Benefits in manufacturing should be highlighted. When Big Data and manufacturing are connected together, manufacturing begins to be influenced by Big Data and data analytics. There is no doubt that Big Data and analytics technology can bring great convenience to manufacturing. They not only improve the production efficiency and the quality of products, but also make the products serve consumers more accurately. Meanwhile, the application of Big Data also comes with ethical issues like privacy and safety and these issues should arouse people's wide concerns. In terms of the manufacturing sector, there are also ethical issues posed by Big Data. Therefore, it is necessary to propose the ethical governance to deal with these issues.

Figure 1. The process of using big data for manufacturing

In manufacturing, the whole lifecycle of the product will generate a mass of structured and unstructured data from the process of market planning, design, production, sales, maintenance and so on, which will form the Big Data of manufacturing industry (Shao, Shin, & Jain, 2014). Generally, product lifecycle consists of three phases: beginning of life, middle of life, and end of life (Zhang et al., 2016). The first phase involves design and making; the second involves use, service and maintenance; and the last phase includes remanufacturing, recycling, reuse and disposing (Zhang et al., 2016), as shown in Figure 2.

Figure 2. Three stages of product lifecycle

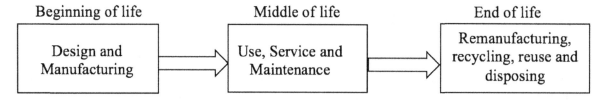

The leaders in manufacturing companies are increasingly interested in effectively using lifecycle Big Data to benefit their companies (Zhang et al., 2017; Chang, 2017). Given the volume and complexity of production activities that affects the decision of manufacturing companies, manufacturers need more effective ways to diagnose and correct problems in the decision-making process (Auschitzky, Hamemer, & Rajagopaul, 2014). Manufacturing enterprises can use Big Data and advanced analytics to make an in-depth analysis of historical lifecycle data, to discover patterns and relationships for each step, and then to optimize the process of product lifecycle management (Zhang et al., 2017).

To understand how Big Data can be used by the manufacturing industry, there are two ways that Big Data can help traditional manufacturing industry transform into a new generation of smart factories.

The first way is to adopt and implement intelligent production. After analyzing and transmitting data, manufacturing enterprises can monitor the production data in real time. This production mode, which is terminal control through the data, simplifies the production process and improves the production efficiency. The second way is to achieve mass customization. Due to the huge change in consumption patterns, the original seller's market has become the current buyer's market. This kind of consumption pattern requires manufacturers to take personalization as the main manufacturing paradigm. Through the integration of a large number of buyers' information, sellers can tailor their production strategies to improve the sales speed.

Data measurements collected by devices, physical environments and processes will lead to the increase of data production. These raw data can be transmitted by the technologies such as the Cyber Physical Systems (CPS) and Internet of Things (IoT), both of which offer new and emerging paradigms (O'Donovan et al., 2015; Hosseinian-Far et al., 2018). While the recent developments have offered the increased usability and affordability of sensors, data collection systems, and computer networks, an increasing number of factories have to adopted high-tech approaches to survive in today's environment (Lee, Bagheri, & Kao, 2015). To the current manufacturing, Big Data and advanced analytics are critical competitive weapons for manufacturers and enterprises.

HOW BIG DATA ANALYTICS ARE BENEFICIAL TO MANUFACTURING

Data has become an important factor of production for various purposes (Nedelcu, 2013). However, raw data could not produce any useful information until it is transformed into a high value strategic asset by data analytics (Lee, 2017). Several benefits are contributed using Big Data analytics (Hosseinian-Far et al., 2017), such as reducing the costs (Campbell et al., 2015), making better decisions, and providing more satisfactory products and services (Davenport, 2014).

In a recent survey, McKinsey & Company introduces the significance of Big Data for manufacturing. The report said that the exploitation of Big Data in manufacturing can reduce product development and assembly costs up to 50% and may result in a reduction of working capital by 7% (Dobbs et al., 2011).

Compared with the traditional manufacturing industry, the biggest breakthrough of Big Data technology is to test product defects, enhance quality, and improve supply planning. In addition, the benefits of big data include predicting manufacturing output, simulating new manufacturing processes, and prompting energy efficiency (Nedelcu, 2013).

Manufacturing can generate massive amounts of data from thousands of sources at every step in the chain. With Big Data and data analytics, a growing number of traditional manufacturing industries are constantly upgrading their industries. There are a lot of obvious value that Big Data analytics can be beneficial to the manufacturing, as shown in Table 1 (Msrcosmos.com, 2018).

Table 1. Benefits of big data analytics for manufacturers

Reduced process flaws	Save time and money
Reduced production and packaging costs	Inventory costs savings
Improved quality and safety	Improved workforce efficiency
Better collaboration	Regulatory compliance
Have real-time shop-floor data	Increased process performance
Better forecasting	Avoid / remove unplanned down-time

The first major benefit is the cost reduction. Big Data can help change the way the process has been designed. It can help save the cost of production and operation. Data analysis can also reduce transportation, packaging, and storage costs, so the cost of inventory has been greatly reduced. Manufacturing firms use Big Data analytics to achieve more accurate demand forecasting, more efficient transmission path with visualization and real-time tracking, and more optimal distribution network management (House, 2014).

The second major benefit is security and quality improvement. While there are a lot of manufacturing enterprises use computer sensors to filter out products of the poor quality through assembly lines in the manufacturing process (Lee, Kao, & Yang, 2014). With the right software analytics, factories can use the data generated by such sensors to improve product performance instead of simply discarding these poor products. For example, some car manufacturers use large amounts of data to produce simulation models through software analysis prior to production. Thus, before these products enter the market, the risk is reduced, and the quality is also improved by these models.

The third major benefit is the improvement in work efficiency. Management and employee productivity can be improved using Big Data. Manufacturing companies use data analytics to avoid mistakes in the production line and use this information to assess where employees work well and where they do not perform well enough (Rüßmann et al., 2015). The speed of the production floor can be increased by the same set of Big Data software and data information, especially in heavy-duty factories. Using Big Data analytics also helps managers identify whether products are good or not.

The fourth major benefit is a better cooperation. Improving the ability of information processing within the group is one of the great benefits of IT-based data collection and data analysis. Data and information, machine operations, engineering, management, and quality control combined with the workflow, so that teams can play a better job in the work. The fast feedback mechanism in a data-driven environment, so that each employee can timely adjust the work behavior according to the situation.

Big Data has already transformed manufacturing in a good way but on the edge of technology development and corporate earnings, there are some ethical problems waiting to be explored.

ETHICAL ISSUES OF BIG DATA

Nowadays, Big Data and data analytics has brought huge benefits to individuals, organizations, and society. The changing technology provides detection of fraud and abuse (Lopez-Rojas & Axelsson, 2016), personalized service (Rust & Huang, 2014), efficient use of resources (Sun et al., 2016) and prevention of failure or accident (Huang et al., 2017). People start to consider what questions are raised about the ethics of Big Data and data analytics. From 2001 to 2016, Big Data usage has increased along with the instances of actual and perceived ethical violations (White & Ariyachandra, 2016). Many industries affected by data and ethics including manufacturing, retail, education, and healthcare.

Within these industries, there are four major ethical themes found in literature and each of the challenges is being illustrated below (White & Ariyachandra, 2016).

- **Privacy:** Sharing of personal information without permission
- **Security:** Protection of data from outside threats
- **Ownership:** The rightful ownership of the data used for analytics
- **Evidence-Based Decision Making:** The use of data to make decisions about a population based solely on quantitative information

Sensors are widespread in various electronic products such as smart health equipment and smart car emergency services. Privacy has attracted public's attention since these sensors collect a mass of data on users' position and moving route, physical conditions, and buying preferences (Lee, 2017). Data security is a serious challenge that it is not only related to the safety of personal information but also involves an enterprise's reputation and financial risk. Speak of ownership, although users believe that they are the owner of their data, the fact is that their data are used without knowing. As data can be gathered from a variety of platforms and they are hard to track the source, most people even do not know how to use their data (White & Ariyachandra, 2016). Often individuals do not have the ownership of the data but just have a stop in the transmission of Big Data (White & Ariyachandra, 2016). Evidence based on decision making is a kind of predictive analysis. It may arouse controversy on individuals and society, keeping prejudices, which are no longer new (Tene & Polonetsky, 2013). For instance, classifying individuals into the group based on race, gender, wealth, and social position could lead to discrimination as a kind of ethical issues to the society (Zuboff, 2015). Individuals or groups will be offered or restricted by special services or treatments because of this profiling (Newell & Marabelli, 2015).

In addition, there are still a number of potential ethical concerns bringing impacts on individuals, organizations, and society. One of the ethics is the use of algorithms which enables Big Data analytics to support human decisions. This algorithm analyzes data that are collected and combined from a variety of sources and designs to forecast individual's favor and behavior based on their past and current behavior, which is called algorithmic decision-making (Newell & Marabelli, 2015). The purpose of this algorithm is to identify the relationships within large quantities of data sets but sometimes may ignore the essence of things (Mayer-Schonberger & Cukier, 2013).

Another ethical issue is individuals have less awareness of what happens to their data after they provided them consciously or unconsciously (Asadi Someh et al., 2016). Due to the high speed and various approach to data transmission, ethical problems could happen in each segment of the information value chain when initial data begins to move and flow. Thus, the initial consumers who generated the data at the original place will face potential risks and dangers because the initial intention and the using purpose of the final data might have a great difference (Asadi Someh et al., 2016).

Laws and regulations guide the people and the society to define what can be done and what cannot be done with enforcement. However, the definition of ethics is more like a moral guidance for behaviors and principles of truth. Big Data usage has significantly increased in the past decade and ethical guidelines are still in the development. Researchers and experts have studied ethics in information systems and information technology for a long time but the discussion in Big Data ethics is still in the infancy (White & Ariyachandra, 2016).

Therefore, identifying and exploring ethical implications of Big Data technology is significant and urgent for people who produce the data and those who use the data. Next, this review will further explore the ethical issues of Big Data in the manufacturing industry.

ETHICAL ISSUES OF BIG DATA IN THE CONTEXT OF MANUFACTURING

Every coin has two sides. While Big Data has brought profits to the manufacturing industry, it has also generated some ethical problems when people collect data and use data. This review will discuss them from individuals and organizations these two perspectives.

INDIVIDUALS

For individuals, privacy can be one of the ethical issues. The development of Big Data in the manufacturing industry is more about making products into a data terminal. There are many products have sensors like smartphone and smart band which will generate data when customers use them. By collecting these data, they can be re-analyzed and used. Some customers might consider they are safe if they do not tell their personal information like name, address and credit card, they are safe (Eastin et al., 2016). However, since data can be used again and again, information fragments can be intersected, recombined, and correlated. When all these data put together, manufacturers can find a large amount of valuable information. As a result, data become the most asset, but it also comes along with two ethical questions for customers.

1. Do Customers Have the Right to Ask for Their Own Information to Be Deleted?

In fact, the possibility of this is low unless they refuse to use these products. Once their data are recorded by the sensors or uploaded to the website, these data will be stored permanently. Now everything people have done is stored in the form of data, so it is easy to get their privacy if master their data. So, if the manufacturers want to get our privacy, they just need to have our data. For example, the sensors record our location. Of course, just having our data alone is not necessarily a source of our privacy, and they have to be able to deal with it quickly. Data can be processed rapidly by cloud computing that allows large-scale and complex computing and parallel processing (Hashem et al., 2015). Other methods such as dimensional reduction and sampling can also be used to speed up the computation time of data analytics (Tsal et al., 2015). The wide variety of data types opens up the door to our privacy and glimpses our privacy through different forms of data. The value of data is a fundamental incentive for malicious people to steal privacy (Inukollu, Arsi, & Rao Ravuri, 2014). Precisely because of its immense value, some manufacturing industries are continually tapping into the data the treasure they need, driven by profit. Thus, although customers are Big Data producers, they even do not have the right to choose what kind of data can be saved and what kind of data can be deleted.

2.   Can Customers Protect Their Privacy?

Data is known as the Big Data era of oil, which holds great value. Due to the essential modalities of Big Data manipulation, data may impact privacy after they are reused, repurposed, recombined, or reanalyzed (Collmann & Mateo, 2016). Once industrialized oil was consumed, it disappeared, or in another form - energy - existed. The data in the era of Big Data, after being used for the first time, is still presented to us in its original appearance. It not only has not disappeared, but also can continue to be used, and does not generate waste to form pollution. This means that once our privacy is leaked out, it seems like the ink on a white cloth can never be eliminated.

In the Big Data era, there are three main types of Big Data stakeholders: Big Data collectors, Big Data utilizers, and Big Data generators (Zwitter, 2014). In manufacturing, products like mobile devices are Big Data collectors that they decide and govern the collection, storage and expiration of data (Chen & Liu, 2015). Manufactures are Big Data utilizers that they mainly use the data collected and stored by Big Data collectors to define the purpose of the data usage (Zwitter, 2014). Each of us can be considered as a "Big Data generator" who consciously and unconsciously produces data every moment of the day. Once the data customers produced is captured and stored by Big Data collectors, it will be continually mined and used by Big Data utilizers, making it hard to hold onto privacy. Customers do not know exactly what purpose the data they produced was queried and exploited, and how many times it was queried and exploited.

Therefore, since data can be used repeatedly, and other people may be involved in the process, it is not easy to keep privacy. Although some information about users can be processed anonymously, the Big Data utilizers have to inform people how they use and where they use with our permission. Nowadays many users feel that their privacy has been compromised and as Big Data becomes more prevalent, the situation will be even worse. The traceability of data dictates that Big Data collectors and Big Data utilizers are in a state of flux, or Big Data producers simply do not know who their information is captured, saved and used. In this way, customers certainly cannot hold the privacy.

ORGANIZATIONS

For organizations, security and labor force can be related to the ethical issues. In many factories, the manufacturing process relies on the computer or relies on the Internet. During the product design, product making and the final service throughout the process can rely on the Internet, which requires Big Data analytics technology and manufacturing technology generated. As a result, in all stages of the product is based on the data. In manufacturing industries, data are getting from manufacture devices, factory equipment, and network devices. By monitoring and analyzing the data, manufacturing companies can improve the productivity and make a huge profit. There is a great deal of benefits for data, so manufacturers all want to get as much as data and ensure that their own data are safe and in good quality. Besides, due to the high technology, many manufacturing factories have used advanced machines to reduce the labor cost and improve the productivity. Thus, data security and quality and labor force are two ethical issues that need manufacturing industries to raise concerns.

1. How to Ensure the Safety and Quality of Enterprise Data?

The term of security is defined as the protection of data to ensure that others without the permission do not access the data (Jahankhani et al., 2014). Before data analysis, manufacturing industries acquire the data from their products and production process, they need platforms to locate and store these data. However, these platforms are vulnerable to hacking, especially there are thousands of users involved and some services need to lower security restrictions for optimum functioning. Many manufacturing factories are in different areas and their processors are not under the jurisdiction of the company. Besides, other service providers are also likely to steal data while the user company does not realize their data is being re-analyzed. The lack of suitable solutions to protect the data is a violation of ethics.

Data quality is one of the challenges that enterprises will face in Big Data (Cai & Zhu, 2015). Data quality means the suitability of data using with a specific purpose (Lee, 2017). As data quality is one of the keys in decision-making, if the manufacturing company uses the erroneous data, it is likely to make wrong decision and cause ethical problems. When the manufacturer makes an inference about individuals based on poor data, even not understand the algorithms, it may result in intricate ethical issues (Wigan & Clarke, 2013). In addition, if the data quality is low, manufacturers will give up using the data and turn it over to other parties (Lee, 2017).

2. Where Is the Labor Replaced by Machines to Be?

Another ethical issue can happen when increasing manufacturing industries are replacing labor with machines, where the laid-off workers go. The development of the science and technology is to help manufacturing industries increase efficiency and provide consumers better products. However, higher efficiency means more advanced machines, which reduce labor greatly. The combination of smart machines and Big Data leads to task automation which could substitute a large proportion of employees soon (The Harbus, 2018). Researchers from Oxford University also estimate that nearly half of all jobs in the United States will be replaced due to the computerization in the next 20 years (Frey and Osborne, 2017). The potential ethical issue is how manufacturing companies deal with these surplus labors. It is important for them to think of this issue and take effective measures to solve this problem.

FURTHER DISCUSSION: ETHICAL GOVERNANCE OF THE INTERESTS OF BIG DATA STAKEHOLDERS

As discussed in previous sections, in manufacturing industry, products are Big Data collectors, manufactures are Big Data utilizers and each of us is a Big Data generator. In order to coordinate the conflicts of interests between Big Data stakeholders, it is necessary to carry out the corresponding ethical governance in order to achieve the orderly data sharing, and then to achieve the smooth development of the era of Big Data. Therefore, the corresponding ethical principles need to be formulated for Big Data stakeholders.

Relative to Big Data collectors and Big Data utilizers, they should follow the following principles:

- **Principle One:** Announcement. When collecting, storing, mining, forecasting, and using data, it is important to inform Big Data producers of the goals and uses, what the great value will be, and what negative effects it will have. People also consider what major precautions would be taken by Big Data gatherers and Big Data producers if there would be a significant negative impact. If the use of data harms Big Data producers, then what compensation would be taken must be announced to Big Data producers. In this way, data sharing can be achieved in a harmonious and orderly manner among Big Data stakeholders.
- **Principle Two:** Confidentiality. In the process of data collection, storage, mining, prediction and utilization, it is necessary to achieve confidentiality. In particular, when it comes to the privacy of Big Data generators, it is necessary to take measures to deal with anonymity and ensure that Big Data producers will not get hurt unnecessarily because their own data was illegally stolen in the process of sharing. This is an important ethical principle that will ensure that the rights and interests of Big Data generators are not harmed.
- **Principle Three:** Self-discipline. Self-discipline is a basic ethical principle that Big Data collectors and Big Data utilizers must work hard to develop. They must develop good ethical discipline in data collection, storage, mining, forecasting and utilization to ensure compliance with minimum codes of ethics and guidelines. Of course, this is a long-term process that cannot be achieved in a day or two. However, good ethical self-discipline should be developed anyway.
- **Principle Four:** Responsibility. This requires Big Data collectors and Big Data utilizers to take responsibility. The strength of any technological force will lead to system rebound, leading to ecological imbalance (Herring and Roy, 2007). The fundamental reason for this is that some manufacturers did not assume the corresponding responsibility when using the technology. This requires that manufacturing enterprises must be brave enough to take on their responsibilities while struggling with data values, especially when negative consequences arise. Otherwise, the conflicts of interest between Big Data stakeholders will be difficult to be resolved satisfactorily.

In addition, as a consumer, he or she should also follow the following principles to avoid ethical issues:

- **Principle One:** Change idea. In the era of Big Data, as Big Data can "read the past, understand the current and predict the future", essentially everyone could be transparent in the process. This requires that every consumer must change their idea and actively protect the data they produce instead of being indifferent to the data they produce as the atomic age did. If they ignore the importance of their data, they will have possibilities of human crises that threaten privacy, confidentiality, transparency, identity, and freedom of choice. Therefore, Big Data generators must always pay attention to the data they produce and measure what negative effects these data will have rather than take for granted that the data will not have any impact on their future.
- **Principle Two:** Self-protection. As Big Data producers are in a passive position, this requires them to raise their awareness of self-protection and actively pick up the corresponding legal and moral weapons to protect their legitimate rights and interests so that they will not be violated. When their legitimate rights and interests are violated, they should dare to pick up the corresponding legal moral weapons to fight against them and actively seek corresponding spiritual and ma-

terial compensation. In short, consumers as the Big Data generators should actively adapt to the needs of the development of the Big Data era and become more proactive and active.

- **Principle Three:** Focus on the data. As data are mainly produced by Big Data generators, this requires that they should pay more attention to the data they produce. They cannot allow the data to be used for illegal purposes and negatively affect society as a whole. It is important to point out that Big Data producers should pay close attention to data rights.

CONCLUSION

This paper reviews the benefits of Big Data and discusses ethical issues of Big Data in manufacturing to illustrate how Big Data can transform manufacturing industry as follows. First, the meaning of Big Data and their ethical implications have been presented. Second, this paper turns to the analytical perspectives and the benefits of Big Data for the manufacturing industry. Third, this paper discusses about how Big Data combines with manufacturing and the impact it has made, with the equal emphasis for both benefits and ethical concerns. Around benefits by Big Data, four advantages of Big Data analytics were provided with explanations in each of them. For the ethical concerns, this paper analyzes the ethical implications of manufacturing from the perspective of individuals and organizations and explain them separately. Finally, this paper gives a further discussion about the ethical governance of the interests of Big Data stakeholders.

REFERENCES

Asadi Someh, I., Breidbach, C., Davern, M., & Shanks, G. (2016). Ethical implications of Big Data analytics. In *Twenty-Fourth European Conference on Information Systems (ECIS)*.

Auschitzky, E., Hammer, M., & Rajagopaul, A. (2014). *How big data can improve manufacturing*. McKinsey & Company.

Cai, L., & Zhu, Y. (2015). The Challenges of Data Quality and Data Quality Assessment in the Big Data Era. *Data Science Journal*, *14*, 2. doi:10.5334/dsj-2015-002

Campbell, J., Chang, V., & Hosseinian-Far, A. (2015). Philosophising Data: A Critical Reflection on the 'Hidden'Issues. In Big Data: Concepts, Methodologies, Tools, and Applications (pp. 302–313). Hershey, PA: IGI Global.

Carillo, K. (2017). Let's stop trying to be "sexy" – preparing managers for the (big) data-driven business era. *Business Process Management Journal*, *23*(3), 598–622. doi:10.1108/BPMJ-09-2016-0188

Chang, V. (2017). Presenting cloud business performance for manufacturing organizations. *Information Systems Frontiers*, 1–17.

Chen, X., & Liu, C. (2015). Big Data Ethics in Education: Connecting Practices and Ethical Awareness. *Journal of Educational Technology Development and Exchange*, *8*(2). doi:10.18785/jetde.0802.05

Collmann, J., & Matei, S. (2016). *Ethical reasoning in Big Data*. Switzerland: Springer. doi:10.1007/978-3-319-28422-4

Daneshkhah, A., Hosseinian-Far, A., & Chatrabgoun, O. (2017). Sustainable Maintenance Strategy Under Uncertainty in the Lifetime Distribution of Deteriorating Assets. In A. Hosseinian-Far, M. Ramachandran, & D. Sarwar (Eds.), *Strategic Engineering for Cloud Computing and Big Data Analytics* (pp. 29–50). Cham, Switzerland: Springer. doi:10.1007/978-3-319-52491-7_2

Davenport, T. (2014). *Big data at work: dispelling the myths, uncovering the opportunities*. Boston, MA: Harvard Business Review Press. doi:10.15358/9783800648153

Dobbs, R., Manyika, J., Roxburgh, C., & Lund, S. (2011). *Big Data: The next frontier for innovation, competition, and productivity*. McKinsey Global Institute.

Eastin, M., Brinson, N., Doorey, A., & Wilcox, G. (2016). Living in a Big Data world: Predicting mobile commerce activity through privacy concerns. *Computers in Human Behavior*, *58*, 214–220. doi:10.1016/j.chb.2015.12.050

Frey, C., & Osborne, M. (2017). The future of employment: How susceptible are jobs to computerisation? *Technological Forecasting and Social Change*, *114*, 254–280. doi:10.1016/j.techfore.2016.08.019

Gandomi, A., & Haider, M. (2015). Beyond the hype: Big Data concepts, methods, and analytics. *International Journal of Information Management*, *35*(2), 137–144. doi:10.1016/j.ijinfomgt.2014.10.007

Hashem, I., Yaqoob, I., Anuar, N., Mokhtar, S., Gani, A., & Ullah Khan, S. (2015). The rise of "Big Data" on cloud computing: Review and open research issues. *Information Systems*, *47*, 98–115. doi:10.1016/j.is.2014.07.006

Herring, H., & Roy, R. (2007). Technological innovation, energy efficient design and the rebound effect. *Technovation*, *27*(4), 194–203. doi:10.1016/j.technovation.2006.11.004

Herschel, R., & Miori, V. (2017). Ethics & Big Data. *Technology in Society*, *49*, 31–36. doi:10.1016/j.techsoc.2017.03.003

Hosseinian-Far, A., Ramachandran, M., & Sarwar, D. (2017) Strategic Engineering for Cloud Computing and Big Data Analytics. Cham, Switzerland: Springer. doi:10.1007/978-3-319-52491-7

Hosseinian-Far, A., Ramachandran, M., & Slack, C. L. (2018). Emerging Trends in Cloud Computing, Big Data, Fog Computing, IoT and Smart Living. In M. Dastbaz, H. Arabnia, & B. Akhgar (Eds.), *Technology for Smart Futures* (pp. 29–40). Cham: Springer. doi:10.1007/978-3-319-60137-3_2

House, J. (2014). Big data analytics = Key to successful 2015. *Supply Chain Strategy*.

Huang, L., Wu, C., Wang, B., & Ouyang, Q. (2017). A new paradigm for accident investigation and analysis in the era of Big Data. *Process Safety Progress*.

Inukollu, V., Arsi, S., & Rao Ravuri, S. (2014). Security Issues Associated with Big Data in Cloud Computing. *International Journal of Network Security & Its Applications*, *6*(3), 45–56. doi:10.5121/ijnsa.2014.6304

Jahankhani, H., Al-Nemrat, A., & Hosseinian-Far, A. (2014). Cybercrime classification and characteristics. In B. Akhgar, A. Staniforth, & F. Bosco (Eds.), *Cyber Crime and Cyber Terrorism Investigator's Handbook* (pp. 149–164). ScienceDirect. doi:10.1016/B978-0-12-800743-3.00012-8

Lee, I. (2017). Big data: Dimensions, evolutions, impacts, and challenges. *Business Horizons*, *60*(3), 293–303. doi:10.1016/j.bushor.2017.01.004

Lee, J., Bagheri, B., & Kao, H. (2015). A Cyber-Physical Systems architecture for Industry 4.0-based manufacturing systems. *Manufacturing Letters*, *3*, 18–23. doi:10.1016/j.mfglet.2014.12.001

Lee, J., Kao, H., & Yang, S. (2014). Service Innovation and Smart Analytics for Industry 4.0 and Big Data Environment. *Procedia CIRP*, *16*, 3–8. doi:10.1016/j.procir.2014.02.001

Lee, J., Lapira, E., Bagheri, B., & Kao, H. (2013). Recent advances and trends in predictive manufacturing systems in big data environment. *Manufacturing Letters*, *1*(1), 38–41. doi:10.1016/j.mfglet.2013.09.005

Lopez-Rojas, E., & Axelsson, S. (2016). A review of computer simulation for fraud detection research in financial datasets. In *Future Technologies Conference (FTC)* (pp. 932-935). 10.1109/FTC.2016.7821715

Mayer-Schonberger, V., & Cukier, K. (2013). *Big Data: A Revolution That Will Transform How We Live, Work, and Think*. New York: Houghton Mifflin Harcourt Publishing Company.

Mourtzis, D., Vlachou, E., & Milas, N. (2016). Industrial Big Data as a Result of IoT Adoption in Manufacturing. *Procedia CIRP*, *55*, 290–295. doi:10.1016/j.procir.2016.07.038

Msrcosmos.com. (2018). Benefits of Big Data Analytics for Manufacturers. Retrieved from https://www.msrcosmos.com/wp-content/uploads/2017/08/Benefits-of-manufacturing.jpg

Nedelcu, B. (2013). About big data and its challenges and benefits in manufacturing. *Database Systems Journal*, *4*(3), 10–19.

Newell, S., & Marabelli, M. (2015). *Strategic Opportunities (and Challenges) of Algorithmic Decision-Making: A Call for Action on the Long-Term Societal Effects of 'Datification.'* SSRN Electronic Journal.

O'Donovan, P., Leahy, K., Bruton, K., & O'Sullivan, D. (2015). Big data in manufacturing: A systematic mapping study. *Journal of Big Data*, *2*(1).

Rüßmann, M., Lorenz, M., Gerbert, P., Waldner, M., Justus, J., Engel, P., & Harnisch, M. (2015). *Industry 4.0: The Future of Productivity and Growth in Manufacturing Industries*. Boston Consulting Group.

Rust, R., & Huang, M. (2014). The Service Revolution and the Transformation of Marketing Science. *Marketing Science*, *33*(2), 206–221. doi:10.1287/mksc.2013.0836

Shao, G., Shin, S., & Jain, S. (2014). Data analytics using simulation for smart manufacturing. In *Proceedings of the 2014 Winter Simulation Conference* (pp. 2192-2203). 10.1109/WSC.2014.7020063

Sun, Y., Song, H., Jara, A., & Bie, R. (2016). Internet of Things and Big Data Analytics for Smart and Connected Communities. *IEEE Access*, *4*, 766–773. doi:10.1109/ACCESS.2016.2529723

Tene, O., & Polonetsky, J. (2013). Big data for all: Privacy and user control in the age of analytics. *Northwestern Journal of Technology and Intellectual Property*, *11*(5), 253.

The Harbus. (2018). Big data + smart machines = unemployment? - The Harbus. Retrieved from http://www.harbus.org/2014/big-data-smart-machines-unemployment/

Tsai, C., Lai, C., Chao, H., & Vasilakos, A. (2015). Big Data analytics: A survey. *Journal of Big Data*, *2*(1), 21. doi:10.118640537-015-0030-3 PMID:26191487

White, G., & Ariyachandra, T. (2016). Big Data and ethics: examining the grey areas of big data analytics. *Issues in Information Systems*, 17.

Wigan, M., & Clarke, R. (2013). Big Data's Big Unintended Consequences. *Computer*, *46*(6), 46–53. doi:10.1109/MC.2013.195

Xu, L., He, W., & Li, S. (2014). Internet of Things in Industries: A Survey. *IEEE Transactions on Industrial Informatics*, *10*(4), 2233–2243. doi:10.1109/TII.2014.2300753

Yin, S., & Kaynak, O. (2015). Big Data for Modern Industry: Challenges and Trends [Point of View]. *Proceedings of the IEEE*, *103*(2), 143–146. doi:10.1109/JPROC.2015.2388958

Zhang, Y., Ren, S., Liu, Y., & Si, S. (2016). A Big Data analytics architecture for cleaner manufacturing and maintenance processes of complex products. *Journal of Cleaner Production*, *142*, 626–641. doi:10.1016/j.jclepro.2016.07.123

Zuboff, S. (2015). Big other: Surveillance capitalism and the prospects of an information civilization. *Journal of Information Technology*, *30*(1), 75–89. doi:10.1057/jit.2015.5

Zwitter, A. (2014). Big Data ethics. *Big Data & Society*, *1*(2), 2053951714559253. doi:10.1177/2053951714559253

This research was previously published in the International Journal of Strategic Engineering (IJoSE), 2(1); pages 39-51, copyright year 2019 by IGI Publishing (an imprint of IGI Global).

APPENDIX

Table 2. Major ethical themes in literature

Theme	Ethical Challenges	Example
Privacy	Sharing of personal information without permission – de- identifying information	Data used to determine Ebola outbreak in 2015 Facebook study in 2012 to test user's emotions without their consent
Security	Protection of data from outside threats	Hospital data ransomed in 2016 due to lax security
Ownership	The rightful ownership of the data used for analytics	Research in illegal behaviors where the courts want the data to build a case against a person
Evidence Based Decision Making	The use of data to make decisions about a population based solely on quantitative information	States make decisions about welfare guidelines using income as the sole factor

Index

G

H

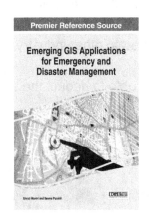
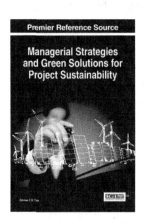

IGI Global
PUBLISHER of TIMELY KNOWLEDGE
www.igi-global.com

Publisher of Peer-Reviewed, Timely, and
Innovative Academic Research Since 1988

IGI Global's Transformative Open Access (OA) Model:
How to Turn Your University Library's Database Acquisitions Into a Source of OA Funding

Well in advance of Plan S, IGI Global unveiled their OA Fee Waiver (Read & Publish) Initiative. Under this initiative, librarians who invest in IGI Global's InfoSci-Books and/or InfoSci-Journals databases will be able to subsidize their patrons' OA article processing charges (APCs) when their work is submitted and accepted (after the peer review process) into an IGI Global journal.

How Does it Work?

Step 1: **Library Invests in the InfoSci-Databases:** A library perpetually purchases or subscribes to the InfoSci-Books, InfoSci-Journals, or discipline/subject databases.

Step 2: **IGI Global Matches the Library Investment with OA Subsidies Fund:** IGI Global provides a fund to go towards subsidizing the OA APCs for the library's patrons.

Step 3: **Patron of the Library is Accepted into IGI Global Journal (After Peer Review):** When a patron's paper is accepted into an IGI Global journal, they option to have their paper published under a traditional publishing model or as OA.

Step 4: **IGI Global Will Deduct APC Cost from OA Subsidies Fund:** If the author decides to publish under OA, the OA APC fee will be deducted from the OA subsidies fund.

Step 5: **Author's Work Becomes Freely Available:** The patron's work will be freely available under CC BY copyright license, enabling them to share it freely with the academic community.

Note: This fund will be offered on an annual basis and will renew as the subscription is renewed for each year thereafter. IGI Global will manage the fund and award the APC waivers unless the librarian has a preference as to how the funds should be managed.

Hear From the Experts on This Initiative:

"I'm very happy to have been able to make one of my recent research contributions *freely available* along with having access to the *valuable resources* found within IGI Global's InfoSci-Journals database."

– **Prof. Stuart Palmer,**
Deakin University, Australia

"Receiving the support from IGI Global's OA Fee Waiver Initiative *encourages me to continue my research work without any hesitation*."

– **Prof. Wenlong Liu,** College of Economics and Management at Nanjing University of Aeronautics & Astronautics, China

Printed in the United States
by Baker & Taylor Publisher Services